Street by Street

BUCKINGHAI

GW00672188

Enlarged areas AYLESBURY, HIGH WYCOMBE, MILTON KEYNES

Plus Amersham, Beaconsfield, Berkhamsted, Bicester, Brackley, Buckingham, Henley-on-Thames, Leighton Buzzard, Maidenhead, Marlow, Slough, Thame, Uxbridge, Windsor

3rd edition January 2009
© Automobile Association Developments Limited 2009

Original edition printed May 2001

Enabled by **OS Ordnance Survey** This product includes map data licensed from Ordnance Survey® with the permission of the Controller of Her Majesty's Stationery Office. © Crown copyright 2009. All rights reserved. Licence number 100021153.

The copyright in all PAF is owned by Royal Mail Group plc.

RoadPilot® Information on fixed speed camera locations provided by RoadPilot © 2008 RoadPilot® Driving Technology.

Published by AA Publishing (a trading name of Automobile Association Developments Limited, whose registered office is Fanum House, Basing View, Basingstoke, Hampshire RG21 4EA. Registered number 1878835).

Produced by the Mapping Services Department of The Automobile Association. (A03811)

A CIP Catalogue record for this book is available from the British Library.

Printed by Oriental Press in Dubai

Key to map symbols	ii
Key to map pages	1
Map pages - 1:10,000	2–7
Map pages - 1:17,500	8–125
Map pages - 1:25,000	126–191
Index – towns & villages	192–193
Index – streets	194–220
Index – featured places	221–226
Acknowledgements	226

ii Map Symbols

Junction 9   Motorway & junction

Services   Motorway service area

Primary road single/dual carriageway

Services   Primary road service area

A road single/dual carriageway

B road single/dual carriageway

Other road single/dual carriageway

Minor/private road, access may be restricted

←   One-way street

Pedestrian area

Track or footpath

Road under construction

Road tunnel

30   Speed camera site (fixed location) with speed limit in mph

V   Speed camera site (fixed location) with variable speed limit

40   Section of road with two or more fixed camera sites; speed limit in mph or variable

50→ ←50   Average speed (SPECS™) camera system with speed limit in mph

P   P+   Parking, Park & Ride

Bus/coach station

Railway & main railway station

Railway & minor railway station

Underground station

Light railway & station

Preserved private railway

LC   Level crossing

Tramway

Ferry route

Airport runway

County, administrative boundary

---

156   Page continuation 1:25,000

93   Page continuation 1:17,500

7   Page continuation to enlarged scale 1:10,000

River/canal, lake

Aqueduct, lock, weir

465 ▲ Winter Hill   Peak (with height in metres)

Beach

Woodland

Park

Cemetery

Built-up area

Industrial/business building

Leisure building

Retail building

Other building

City wall

A&E   Hospital with 24-hour A&E department

PO   Post Office

Public library

ℹ   Tourist Information Centre

ℹ   Seasonal Tourist Information Centre

Petrol station, 24 hour
Major suppliers only

†   Church/chapel

Public toilets, with facilities for the less able

PH   Public house
AA recommended

Restaurant
AA inspected

Madeira Hotel   Hotel
AA inspected

Theatre or performing arts centre

Cinema

Golf course

Camping
AA inspected

Caravan site
AA inspected

Camping & caravan site
AA inspected

Theme park

Abbey, cathedral or priory

Castle

Historic house or building

Wakehurst Place (NT)   National Trust property

Museum or art gallery

Roman antiquity

Ancient site, battlefield or monument

Industrial interest

Garden

Garden Centre
Garden Centre Association Member

Garden Centre
Wyevale Garden Centre

Arboretum

Farm or animal centre

Zoological or wildlife collection

Bird collection

Nature reserve

Aquarium

Visitor or heritage centre

Country park

Cave

Windmill

Distillery, brewery or vineyard

Other place of interest

IKEA   IKEA store

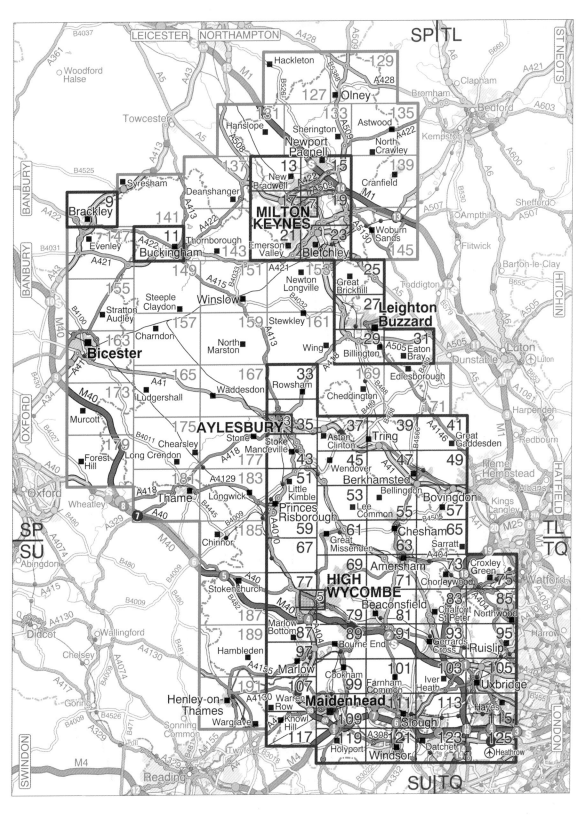

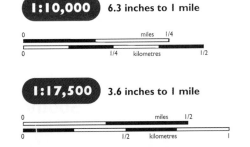

1:10,000 6.3 inches to 1 mile

miles 1/4

0 1/4 kilometres 1/2

1:17,500 3.6 inches to 1 mile

miles 1/2

0 1/2 kilometres 1

2.5 inches to 1 mile **1:25,000**

miles 1/2

0 1/2 kilometres 1

National Grid references are shown on the map frame of each page.
Red figures denote the 100 km square and the blue figures the 1km square.

Example, page 19 : Willen Lake **488 240**

The reference can also be written using the National Grid two-letter prefix
shown on this page, where 4 and 2 are replaced by SP to give SP**8840**

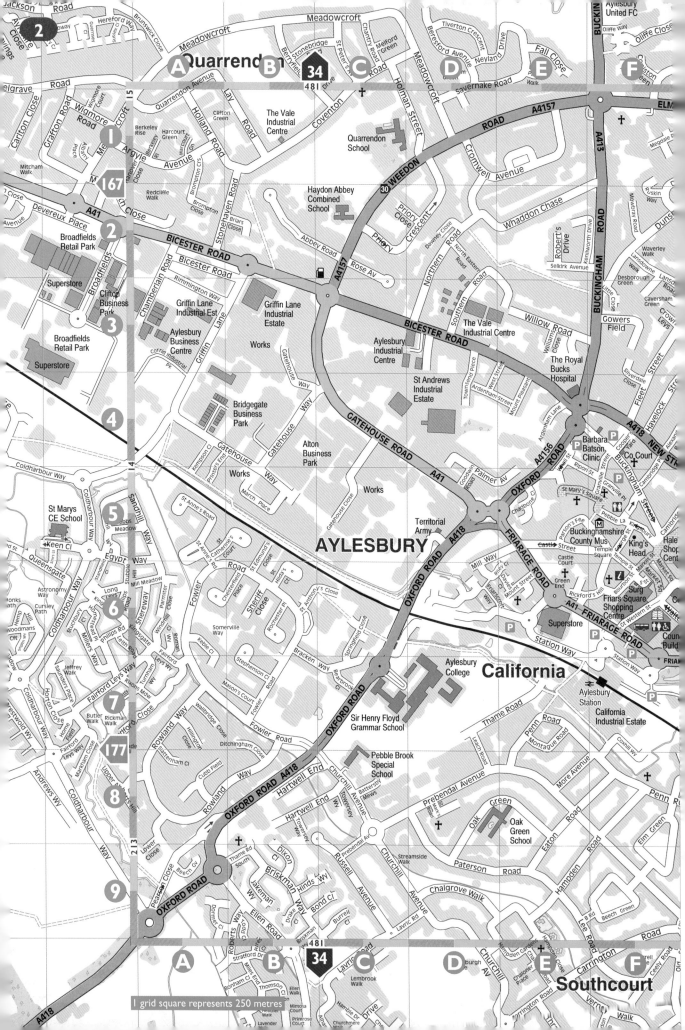

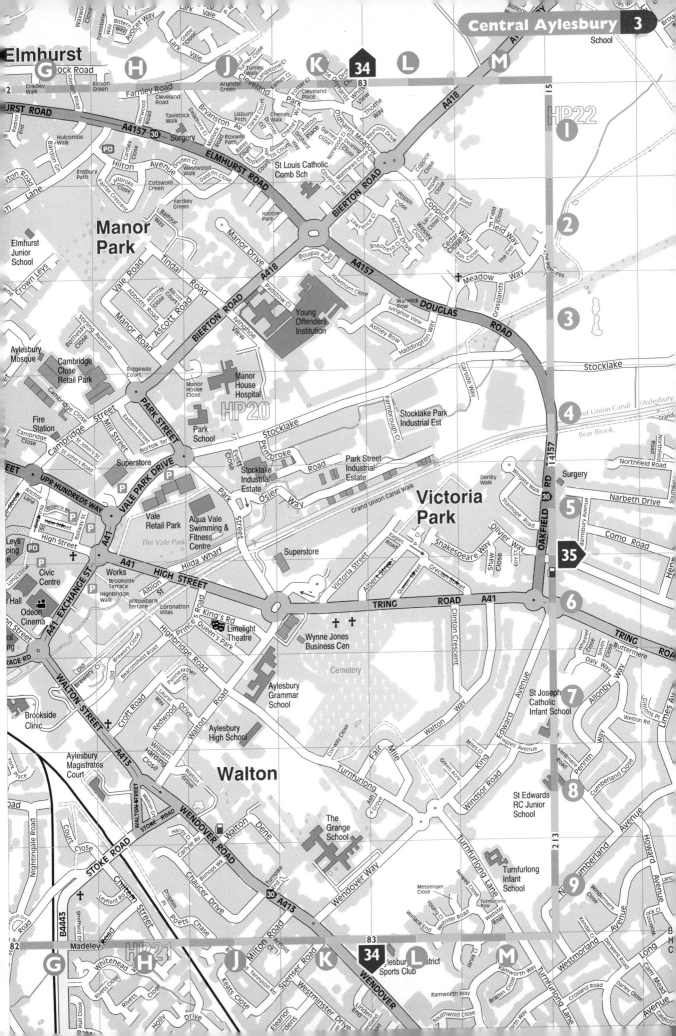

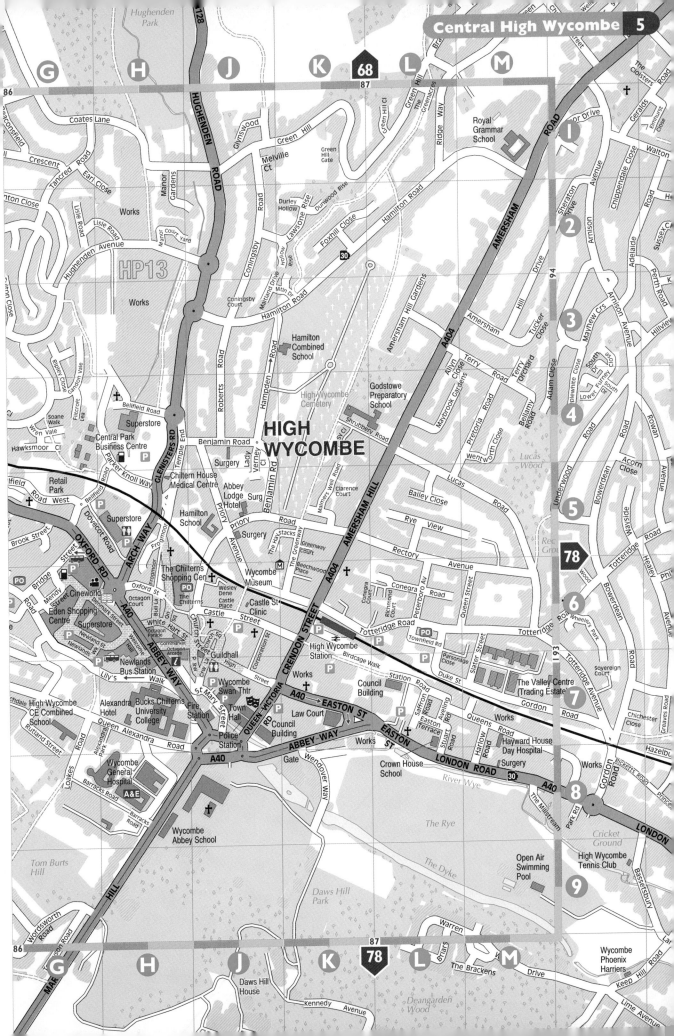

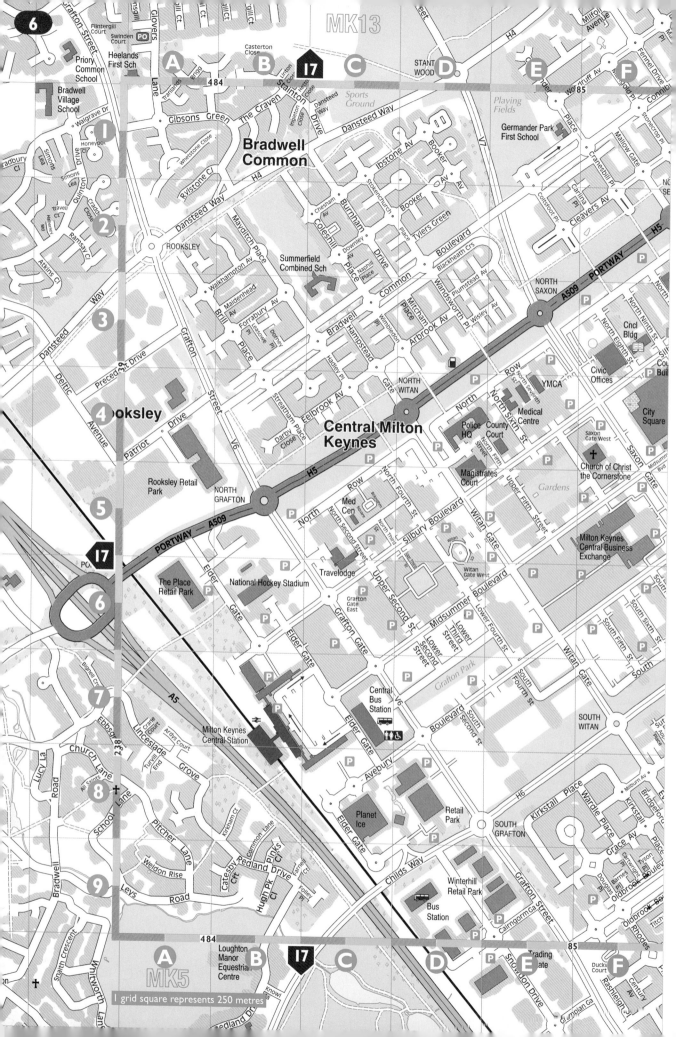

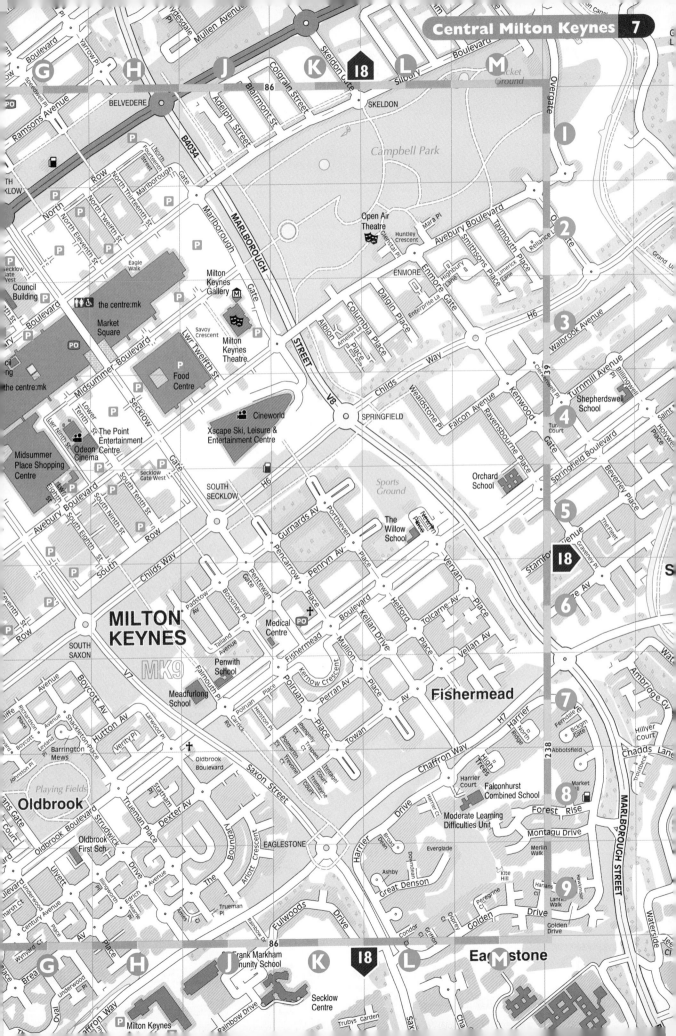

G   H   J   K   L   M

I

2

3

4

I40

5

6

7

237

8

60   61   62

Coldharbour Farm

Hoppersford Farm

The Avenue

Farrer Close

Chapel Lane

Chestnut Cn

Mill Road

Whitfield

Works

Dropshort Farm

A43

A43

Northamptonshire County
Buckinghamshire County

Turweston Airfield

Ash Furlong Lane

Westw

Turweston

Oatleys Hall

Westbury Circular Ride

Main Street

Chapel La

South Bank

Westbury Circular Ride

Oatleys Farm

Westbury Circular Ride

A43

A422

The Motorsport Centre

60   I47   61   62

G   H   J   K   L   M

Grovehill Farm

Westbury Circu

dlesden Road

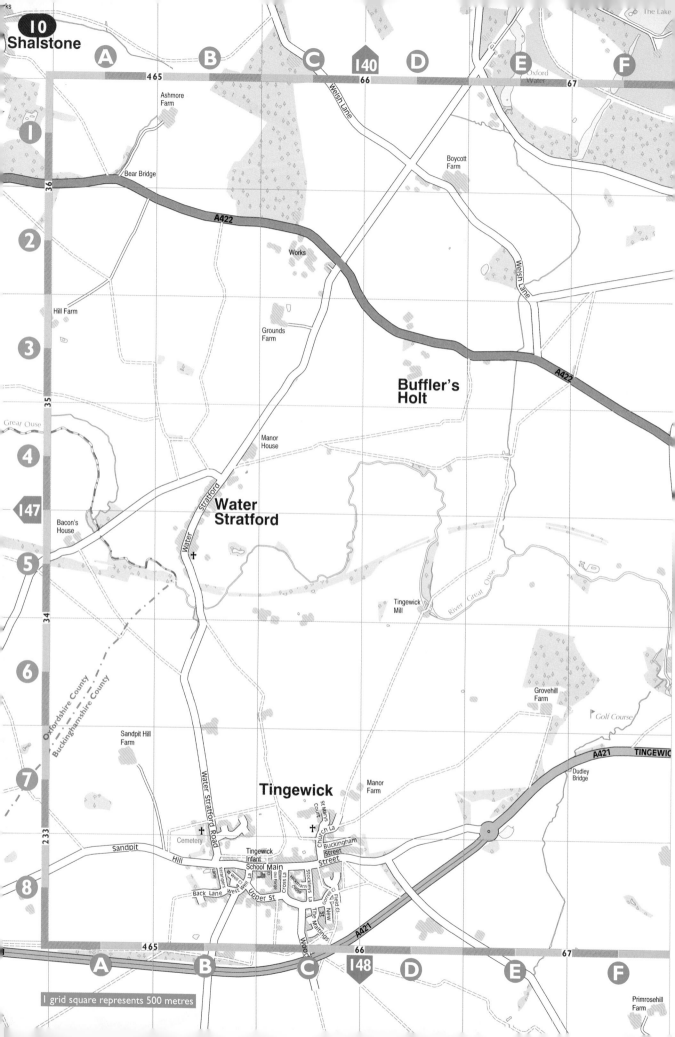

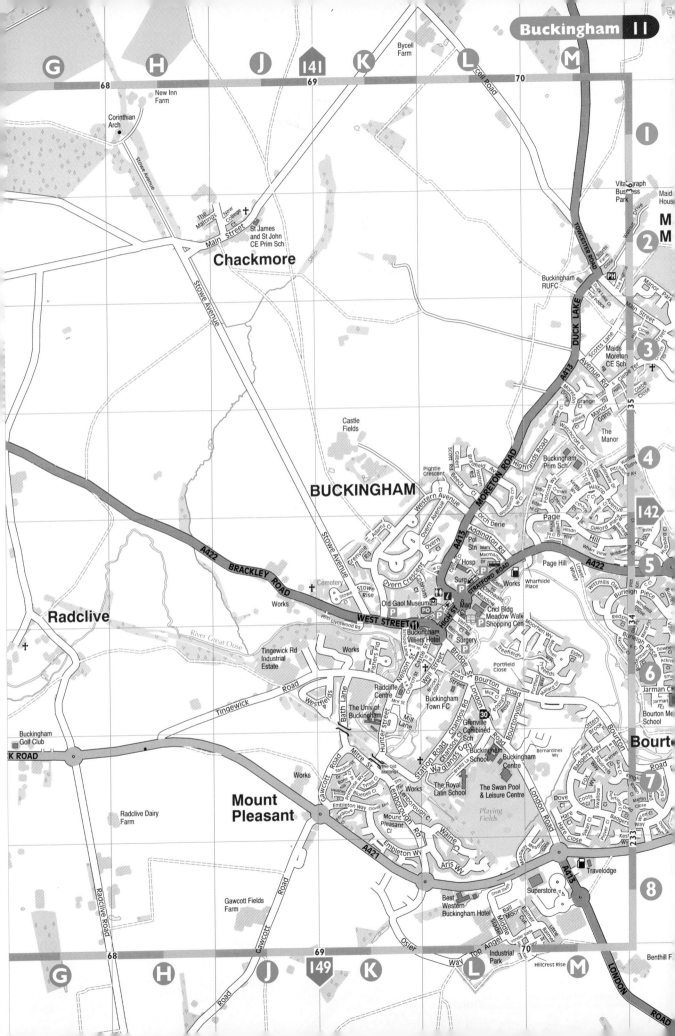

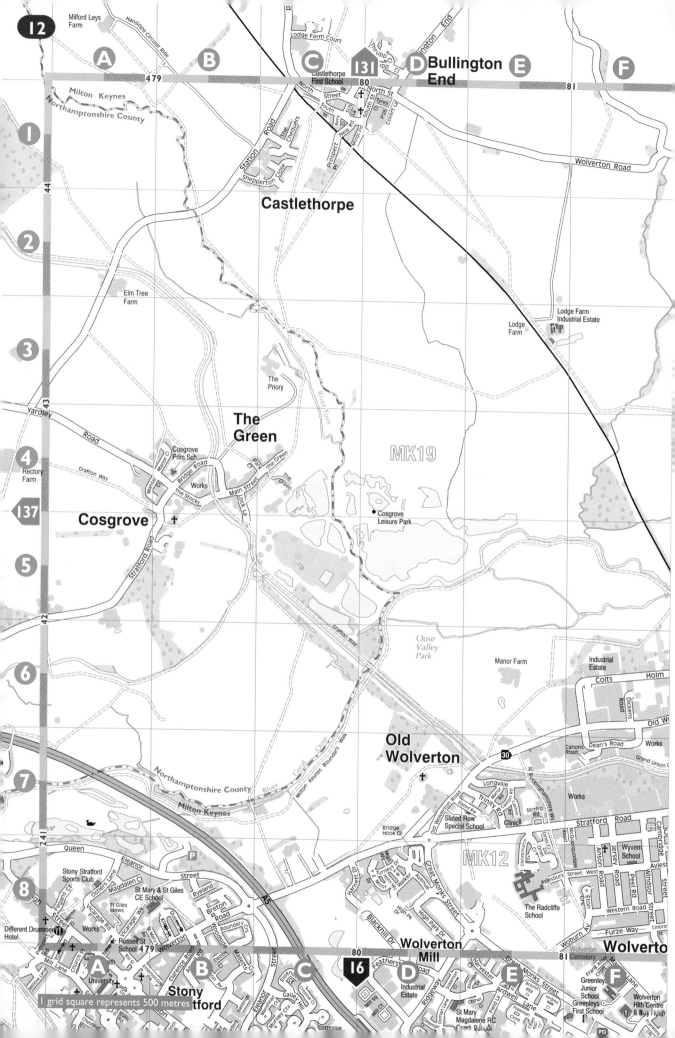

G   H   J   132   K   L   M

82   83   84

Little Linfo

1

2

3

4

14

5

6

7

8

Pineham Farm

Field House

ke's Farm

Hill Farm

Mill Road

Hanslope Circular Ride

Hanslope Circular Ride

Hanslope Circular Ride

Haversham

High Street

Granary Ct

Haversham First School

Wolverton Road

Chalmers Av

Rowan Dr

Keppel Avenue

Brookfield Road

Manor Drive

Beech Tree Close

The Crescent

Haversham Manor

Haversham Road

River Great Ouse

P

Linford

Linford Lakes RSPB Reserve

Grand Union Canal Walk

Grand Union Canal

Stantonbury Park Farm

Midshires Way

Sandy Cl

Church

43

44

42

New Bradwell

Newport Road

Marlborough Street

Cem

Spencer

Melton

Ashfield

Kents Rd

Westhill

Stantonb

Works

Wolverton Road

Grafton St

Wolverton Rd

Bridgeturn Avenue

verton Road

Newport Road

New Bradwell Mosque

Guest Gdns

Peters Wy

Mason

Lincoln

Spencer

Kersey

Stowe

Cawardon

Wood End First School

Stonebridge

Superstore

Radcliffe Street

Works

Church St

Creed

St Georges Wy

McConnell Drive

Caledonian Rd

Newport Rd

Grafton Street

St Anne St

Wood St

Wallace St

Bounty St

St James St

Edward St

St Mary St

North Street

Thompson St

Spencer St

Church St

Permayne

High St

Bradwell

Harwood

Bridgeway

Chipperfield Rd

Pepper Hill First School

Midshires Way

Grand Union Canal Walk

Howitt Drive

Sheerling Ga

Minstrel Ct

Woodstock Ct

Harrowden

Crispin

The Ct

Temple

Fowler

Goring

Tyrill

Burnet

Jennings

Wood End

Buckingham St

PO

Stantonbury Health Centre

Stantonbury Campus Leisure Centre

Stantonbury Campus

Sta Stadium

Soskin Drive

New Bradwell Combined School

Works

Fingle Dr

Twizel Cl

Nightingale Crs

Aqueduct

Mill La

Windmill

Bradville

Bradwell Road

White

Ashwood

Kingsfold

Hume Cl

Stanton Middle School

Naseby Court

Barry Avenue

Saxon Street

Purbeck

Cleveland

Soskin Drive

Bu Sch

Blue Bridge

Bushfield School

Culbertson Lane

Mortons

Fork

High Park Dr

vn br dr ct

Grand Union Canal Walk

Wheelers Lane

Esther Cl

Chime Cl

Parker

Amos

Stanton Crescent

Edwards Cft

Althorpe

Tarry Court

Mercers Drive

Vauxhall

Donnington

Blundells Road

Fairfax

Wolverton Sports Club

Marina Drive

Stacey Avenue

Victoria Street

Green Lane

Milton Keynes Museum of Industry & Rural Life

Gardiner Ct

Vienna Gr

Haitonchesters

Mathiesen Rd

Randoph Cl

Sunbury

PO

Meads Cl

Brad've Crs

Abbey Way

Bridle Cl

Shipton

Blundells Road

Breckland

East St

Saxon Street

Linfor

Enfield Chase

G   H   J   17   K   L   M

82   83   84

n

Gloucester Rd

Southern Way

Miller Way

Spoonle Wd

Lullington Dr

Constantine Wy

Midshires Way

Bancroft

Chesterton

Radcliffe

Arrians

Greatchesters

Stonegate

Withington

Wallingford

Bishopstone

A422

High Pk

W Dales

Scardale

Lotheresdale

Grizedale

Arncliffe Drive

Lundholme

Cricklebeck

MK13

Bancroft

Bancroft Park

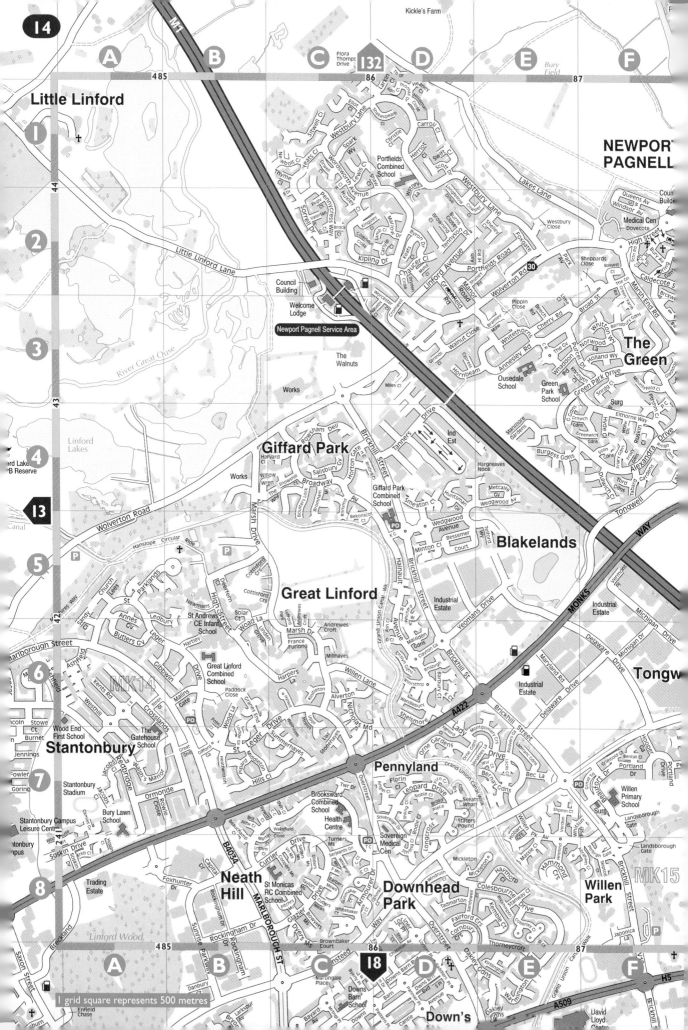

G H J I33 K L M

88 89 90

I

2

3

43

4

I38

5

42

6

7

241

8

Sherington Road

Woad Farm

B526

Works

North square

Ousebank Street

Mill St

Cemetery

Clinic PO

Swan Revived Hotel

Tickford Abbey

St JOHN ST

River Side

Works

TICKFORD STREET

Priory Street

Milton Carlton Dr

Keynes

Chicheley St

Tickford End

Cedars Combined School

Works

Severn Dr

Trent Dr

Dove Cl

Lagonda Close

St Margaret

Highfield Wy

Leary Crs

Avon Cl

Works

Thames Dr

Stour Cl

Mdwy Cl

B526

Nene Close

Tickford Park Prim Sch

Thurne Close

Downs Fld

Welland Drive

Middleton Swimming Pool

Cem

Vantage Court

North Crawley Road

Ind Est

Jenna Wy

Tickford Lodge Farm

Willen Road

Marsh End

Road

LONDON ROAD

Penny Park Road

Hopton Cv

Plover Cl

Howard Wy

Cromwell Business Centre

A509

A422

Caldecote Lane

Newport Stables

Caldecote

River Ouzel or River Loxat

Willen Road

LONDON ROAD

Tickford Farm

Tickford Park

Newport Road

Industrial Estate

Wellfield Dr

Dobben Ct

Aldrich Dr

Ketton

Carteton Cl

Soumfield

Tongwell Street

Aldrich Dr

A509

Thursby

Bates Cl

Christian Ct

Milton Road

Linford Lane

Corbett Close

The Hooke

Aldrich Dr

Pineham

Willen

Tongwell Street

River Ouzel

V11

M1

Junction 14

Hermitage Farm

Works

P+

88 89 90

G RTWAY H J I9 K L M

A5130

Industrial Estate

Northfield Drive

Northfield

London

M1

Broughton Farm

Emerald Gate

Broughton

Hill Farm

Chicheley

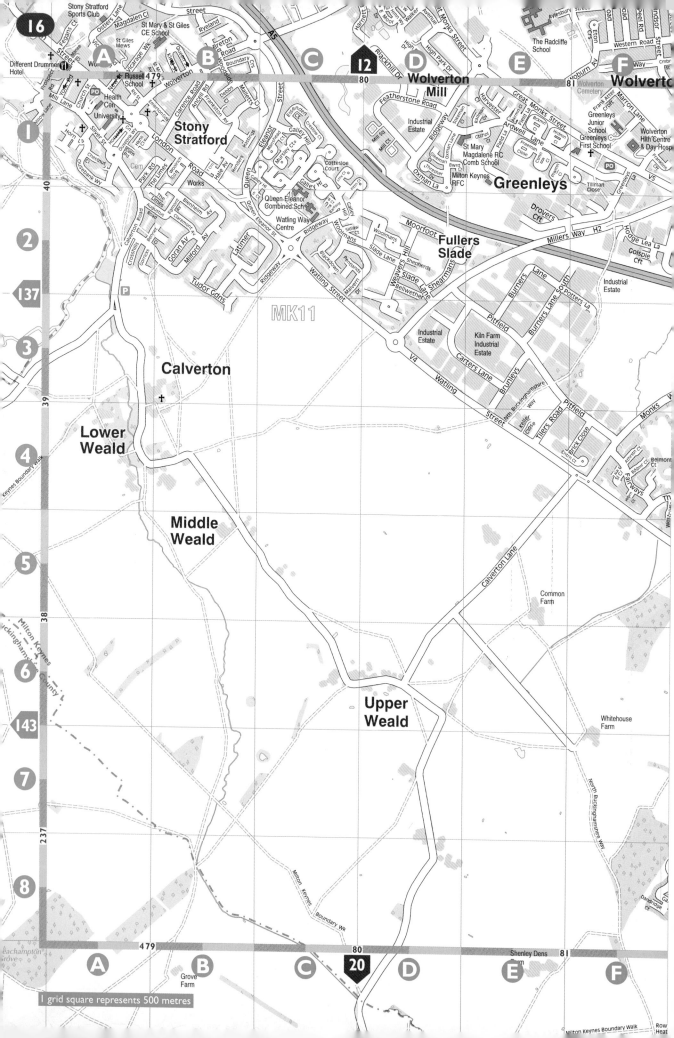

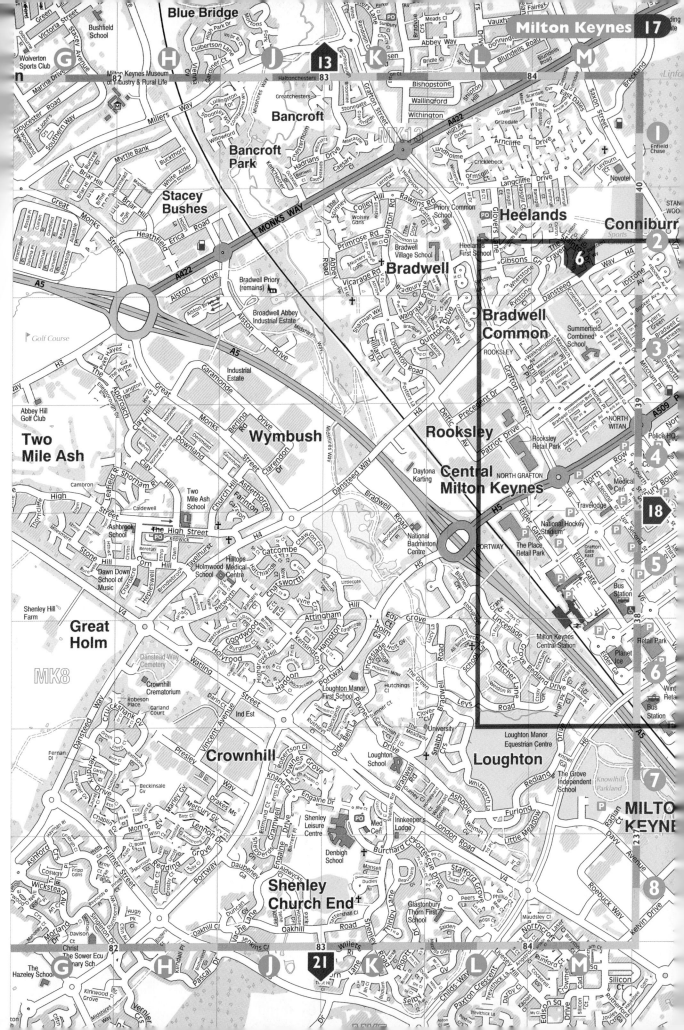

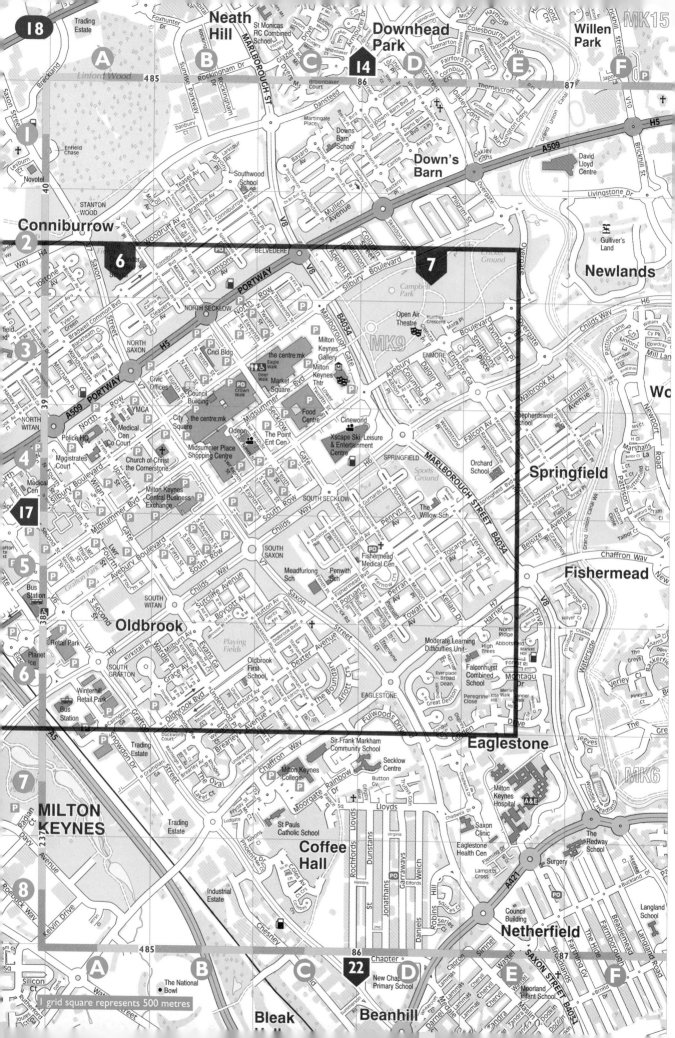

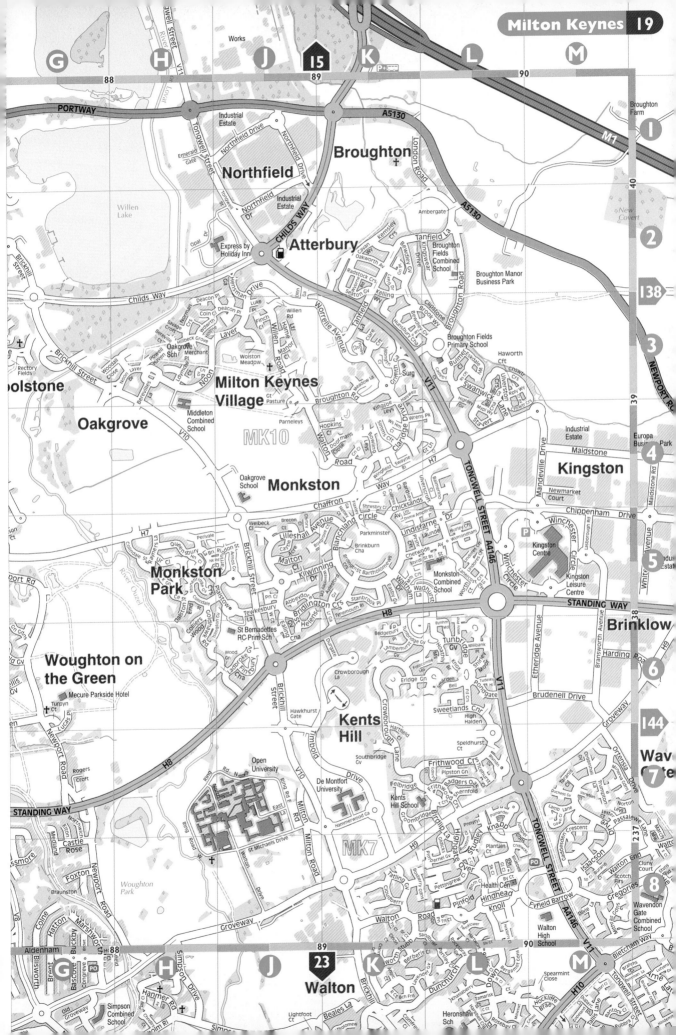

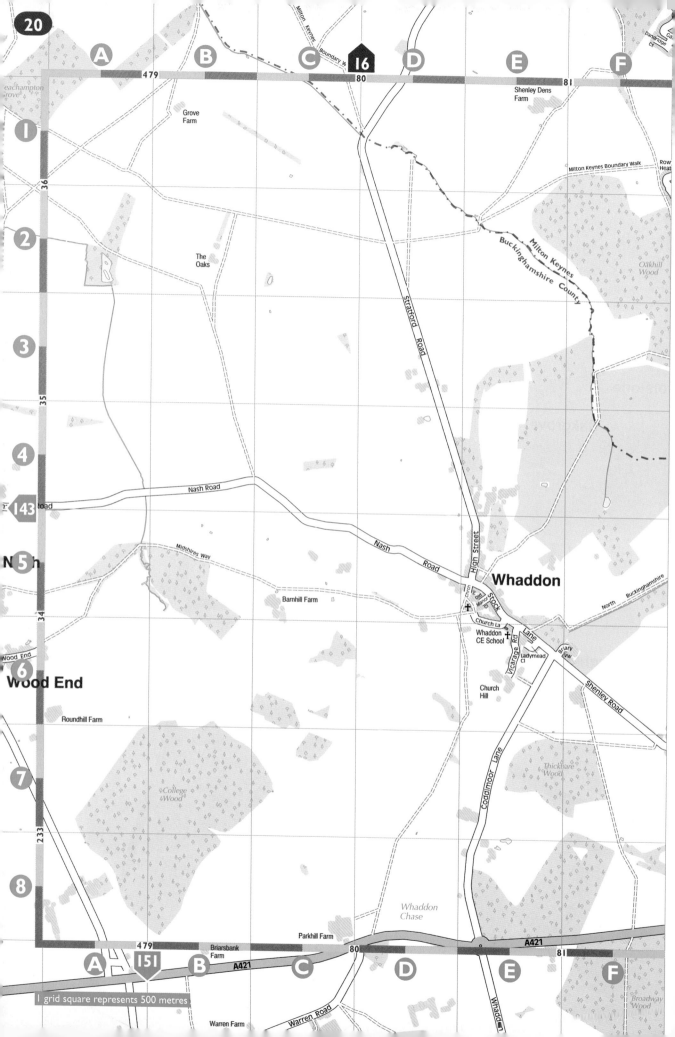

A 479 B C **16** 80 D E 81 F

Shenley Dens Farm

1

36

Grove Farm

Milton Keynes Boundary Walk

Row Heat

2

The Oaks

Milton Keynes

Buckinghamshire County

Oakhill Wood

35

3

Stratford Road

4

Nash Road

143 road

5

Midshires Way

Nash Road

High Street

Whaddon

North Buckinghamshire

34

Barnhill Farm

Church Hill

Manor

Stock

Church La

Whaddon CE School

Vicarage Rd

Lane

Briary Vw

N **5** h

Wood End

6

Wood End

Roundhill Farm

Ladymead Cl

Church Hill

Shenley Road

7

College Wood

Coddimoor Lane

Thickbare Wood

233

8

Whaddon Chase

A421

Parkhill Farm

A 479 B A421 C 80 D E 81 F

151

Briarsbank Farm

Warren Road

Whaddon

Broadway Wood

Warren Farm

1 grid square represents 500 metres

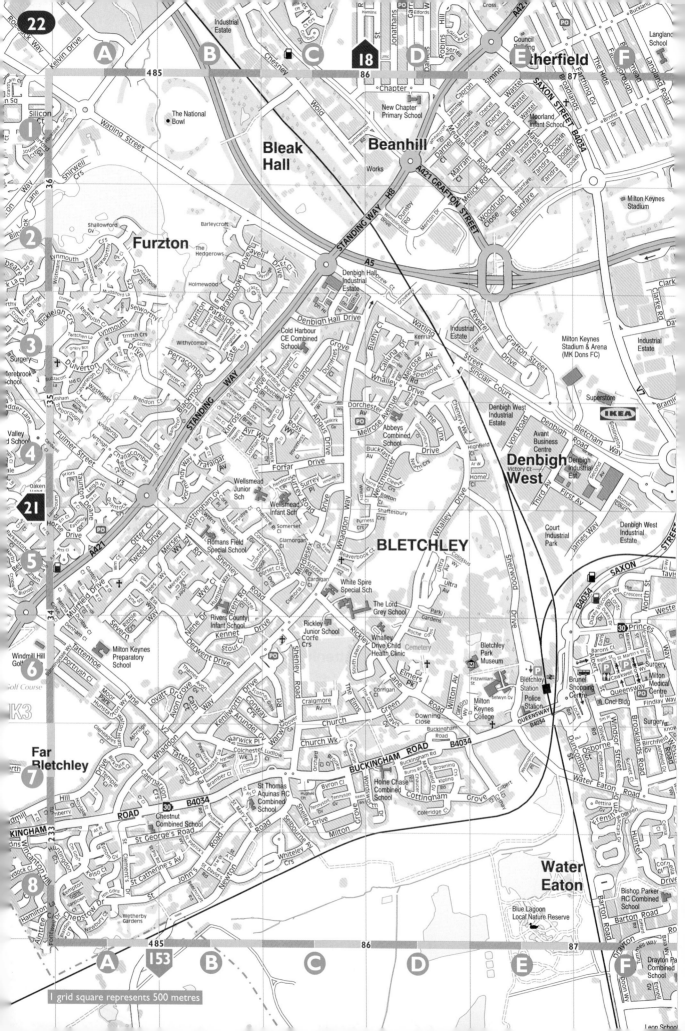

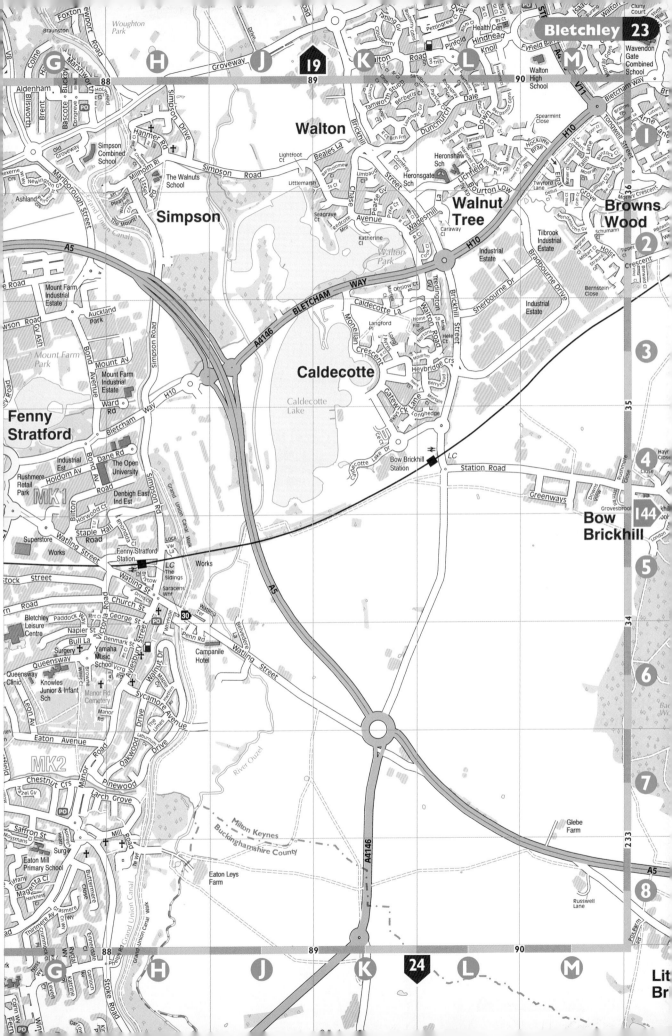

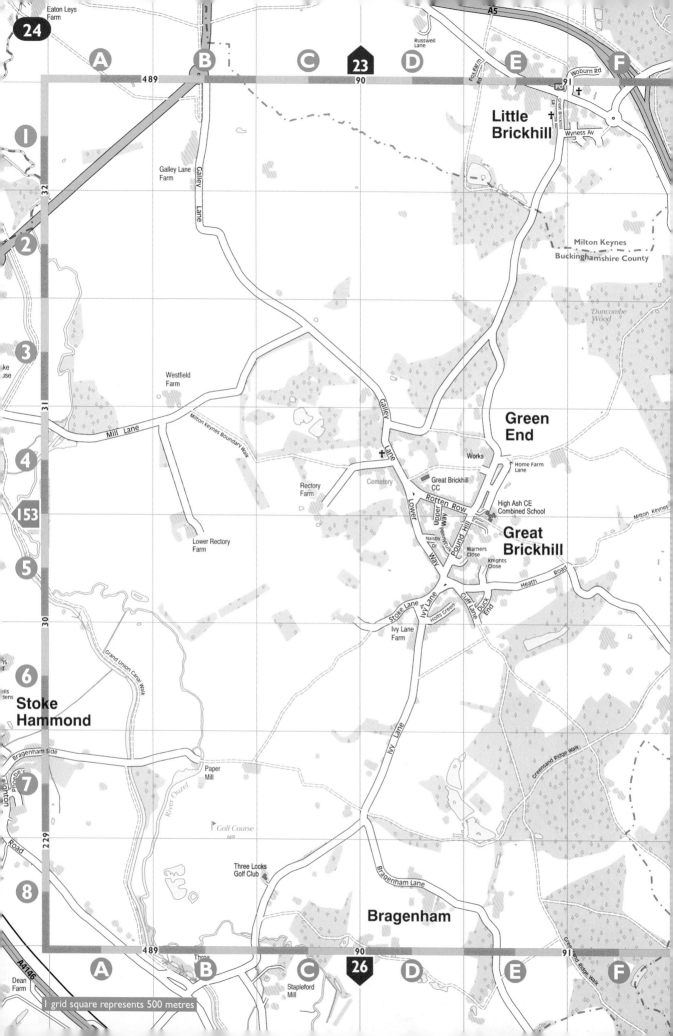

Eaton Leys
Farm

A5

Woburn Rd

POl

†

Little
Brickhill

I

Russwell
Lane

Fox Farm Rd

Galley Lane
Farm

Galley
Lane

Wyness Av

Great Brickhill

2

32

Milton Keynes
Buckinghamshire County

Duncombe
Wood

3

31

Westfield
Farm

Galley
Lane

Green
End

Mill   Lane

Milton keynes Boundary Walk

†

Works

Home Farm
Lane

Milton Keynes

4

Rectory
Farm

Cemetery

Great Brickhill
CC

High Ash CE
Combined School

153

Rotten Row

Lower
Way

Upper Way

Pennycuik

Great
Brickhill

Lower Rectory
Farm

Naisby
Dr

Pound Hill

Warners
Close

5

30

Knights
Close

Heath   Road

Stoke Lane

Ivy Lane

Holts Green

Cliff Lane

Duck
End

Grand Union Canal Walk

Ivy Lane
Farm

6

Stoke
Hammond

Bragenham Side

Ivy   Lane

Greensand Ridge Walk

Paper
Mill

River Ouzel

7

229

Leighton

Road

Golf Course

A4146

8

Three Locks
Golf Club

Bragenham Lane

Bragenham

Greensand Ridge Walk

Dean
Farm

Three

Stapleford
Mill

I grid square represents 500 metres

G H J K L M

Leighton
Greens

92 93 94

I 44

32

Sheeplane

Job's
Farm

Utcoate
Grange

Lowe's
Wood

Greensand Ridge Walk

Milton Keynes Boundary Walk

Buttermilk
Wood

Apesfield
Farm

Park
Farm

Boundary Walk

Rammamere
Farm

Buckinghamshire County
Bedfordshire County

Kings Wood

Kings Wood
National Nature
Reserve

Rammamere
Heath

King's
Wood

Bushycommon
Wood

Works

Sheeplane

Woburn Rd

Works

Woburn Road

Works

Works

A5

Brickhill Road

Stockgrove
Country Park

**Fox
Corner**

30

Reach Gn
Bakers Wd
Close

Woburn Road

Grange Gdns

Overend

Overendgreen
Farm

Green Lane

92 St Leonards
Heath &
Reach VA S

93

94

27

**Heath and
Reach**

Thomas St

Works

Reach Lane

Works

Sheepcote
Crs

PO

The Deli

Thrift Road

Birds Hill

Emu

St Sylvester St

Pinkle Hill

Gig Lane

Kingsway
Farm

G H J K L M

2
3
4
5
6
7
8

31
30
2 29

F

A4146
Dean Farm
Golf Club
Bragenham Lane
Bragenham
24
489
90
91
28

I

Three Locks

Stapleford Mill

River Ouzel

Bragenham Lane

2

Rislip Farm

Grand Union Canal

153

Grand Union Canal Walk

Greenland Rdg Walk

The Heath

3 oulbury

Chelmscote Manor

Broad Oak

Cross Bucks Way

Greenland Rdg Wk

Dukes Park

Chapel Hl

Cross Bucks Way

A4146

Grand Union Canal

Old Linslade

Linslade Road

Cem

27

IGH ROAD

Manor Farm Cl

4

Leighton Road

Old

Greenland Ridge Walk

B4032

LEIGHTON ROAD

Dollar Farm

Buckinghamshire County
Bedfordshire County

Stoke Road

PH Grand Union

Globe Lane

5

Liscombe Park

Valley Farm

Chestnut Rise

26

Mileush

Soulbury Road

Chestnut Hill

Alwins Field

Hill

Rowley

Knaves

Furrows

Uppr Cmb

Uncombe Slade

Rothsc

Golden Riddy

6

Home Farm

Cleveland Drive

Malvern

Bideford Green

Bideford Green

Knaves Slade

Corbet Ride

St Marys Way

Hawthorne Close

Beech Grove

Lime

The Padd

30

161

Derwent Road

Fyne

Lovne

Lochy Dr

Southcott Lower Sch

Mowbray Dr

Works

Rosebery Av

Stoke Road

Harcourt

7

Greenleas Lower School

Lomond Dr

Maree

Lochy Drive

Linslade

Hanover Ct

Linslade Lower School

Grasmere Wy

Springfield Rd

Leven Cl

Carlton

Pentewan Gardens

Swan

Conston Road

Kendal

Rock Lane

Rock Cl

Durrell Cl

Levens Rd

Rock Lane

225

Eribol Cl

Melfort Dr

Melfort Dr

Blakedown Rd

Ullswater

Grasmere Way

New Road

PO

Church Road

8

Rocklane Farm

Himley Green

Ascot Dr

Chelsea Green

Southcourt Av

Bunkers Lane

Southcott Village

Village Court

Grange Close

Leighton Buzzard Station

Woodside Wy

Orchard Cl

Strathenson Close

Wing Road

Victoria Rd

Waterloo Road

Wingates

Memo Park

Finch Crts

Mentmore Gdns

Tiddenfoot Leisure Ce

Linslade Middle

489
90
91

A
B
C
28
D
E
F

Golf Course

Dunstable

Tils**G**orth

Warren Knoll

Stanbridge Road

Bury Rise

Dunstable Rd

Blackhill

PH

Dickens La

Manor Farm

Bury Farm

A5

Watling Street

Icknield Way Path

Chalk Hill

A505

Sewell Lane

Sewell Lane

Sewell

French's

Barley Brow

Cheyne

Palma

Suncote Cl

Suncote Av

Works

Dunstable FC

Brewers Hill Middle School

Caddilan

Cusworth Wy

Bryony Wy

Orchard Cl

Aldens Cl

Greenfield Cl

Hillcroft

Scawsby Cl

Bre

Hill

Aldbanks

Beecroft Lower School

PO

Weatherfield School

Saxon

Norman

Bunhill

Drovers

Spinney Ct

Beecro

Weatherby

Icknield Way Path

Coxfield

Knolls View

Works

Castle Hill Road

Chapel Lane

wick

Brownlow Rd

Castle Cl

Totternhoe Quarry Nature Reserve

Castle Hill Road

Park Avenue

Lancotbury

Totternhoe

Church Gn

Furlong Lane

Totternhoe FC

Dunstable Town CC

Dunstable Road

Badgers Gate

Badgers Cl

Lancot Lower School

Lancot Drive

Totternhoe Road

Oakwell

Harvey Rd

Marina Dr

Gardner's Cl

Coombe Dr

Beacon Avenue

Tring Road

The Avenue

Leighton Road

Totternhoe Lower School

The Ride

Church Road

Ellesmere Cl

Brightwell Av

Well Head Road

Church End

Bray School

Bray La

Gurney Ct

Eaton Pk

Eaton Bray

B489

Icknield Way

Medley Close

Bower Lane

Yew Tree

Dunstable Road

171

Well Head

Manton Rd

Bottom Dr

Springfield Rd

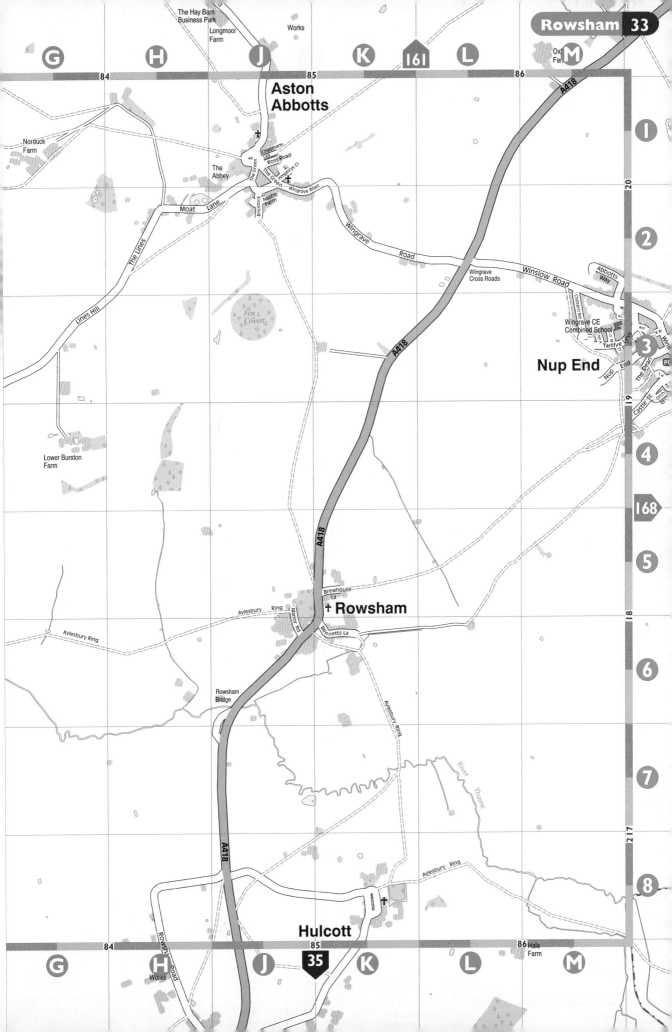

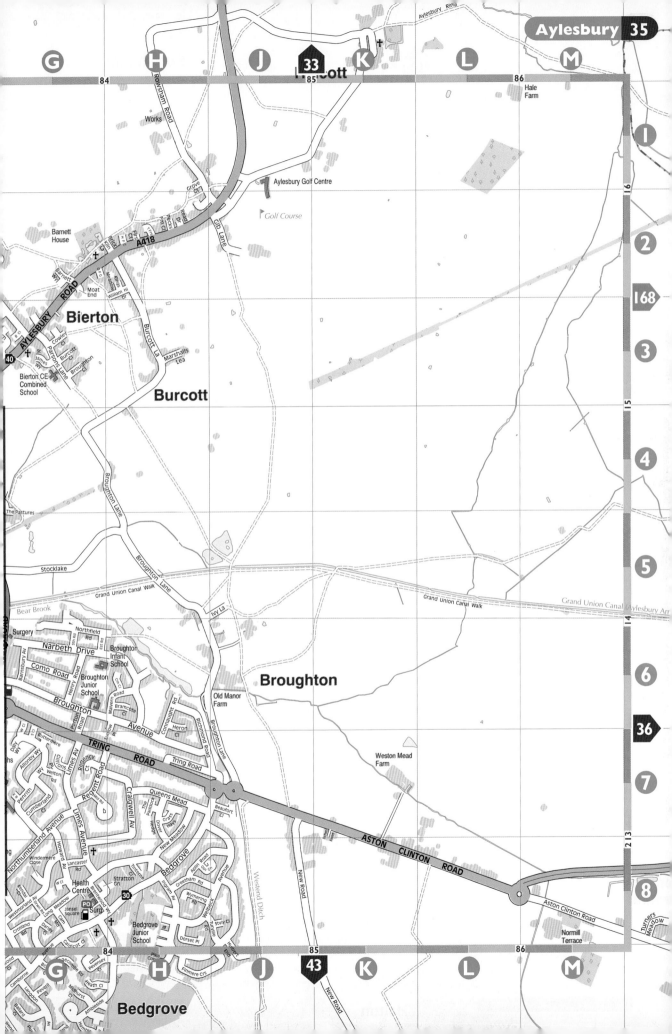

G H J K L M

84 33 85 86

I
16
2
168
3
15
4
5
14
6
36
7
213
8

Aylesbury Ring

✝

Hale Farm

Works

Rowsham Road

Aylesbury Golf Centre

Golf Course

Grove Ct

Pecks Cl

Pearl Ct

Club Lane

Barnett House

✝

A418

Flr Ct H F F

Barnett Wy

AYLESBURY ROAD

King William Rd

King Meadow

Moat End

Cowley

Burcott Cl

Parsons Lane

Broughton Rd

Burcott La

Marshalls Lea

Bierton

✝

40

St James'

✝

Bierton CE Combined School

Burcott

Broughton Lane

The Pastures

Stocklake

Grand Union Canal Walk

Grand Union Canal Walk

Grand Union Canal (Aylesbury Arm)

Bear Brook

Surgery

Northfield Rd

Narbeth Drive

Como Road

Broughton Infant School

Ivy La

Broughton Junior School

Bramcote Cl

Broughton

Old Manor Farm

Broughton

RING ROAD

Avenue

Connaught Rd

Heron Cl

Richmond Road

Broughton Lane

36

Weston Mead Farm

TRING ROAD

Tring Road

Regent Road

Queens Mead

Beaufort Cl

Craigwell Av

Penrith

Cumberland Cl

Limes Av

Regency Ct

The Poplars

Dovey Cl

New Meadow

Northumberland Avenue

Limes Avenue

Bedgrove

✝

Lancaster Way

Stratton Grn

Aston Roxd

Ingram Av

New Road

Westend Ditch

ASTON CLINTON ROAD

Aston Clinton Road

Health Centre

30

PO Surg.

Jansel Square

✝

Bedgrove Junior School

Greetham Rd

Wymering Rd

Welbeck Av

Dorset Pl

Turnvile Cl

Normill Terrace

Turners Meadow

8

Bedgrove

G H J K L M

170

Beacon Road

Iving Common

Hall Farm

Ri

96 97 98

Ickneild Way

Down Farm

Clipper Down

Duncombe Farm

Alderton Drive

14

I

2

Barley End

Ickneild Way

Stocks

Ickneild Way

Sallow Copse

3

Ashridge Golf Clu

13

Stocks Golf & Country Club

Stocks

Pitstone Common

Bridgewater Monument

Ashridge Estate Visitor Centre

Ashridge Estate (NT)

Old Park Lodge

4

Golf Course

Stocks Road

40

Aldbury

Aldbury Primary School

PH

Ickneild Way

Aldbury Common

5

Church Farm

PO

Station Road

Stocks Road

Trooper Road

Toms

Beechwood Drive

Stoney Croft

PH

Malting Lane

Tom's Hill Road

12

B4506

Woo Cotts

6

Berkha Common

Newground Road

B4506

Co Far

7

Ickneild Way

H

2 11

8

Grand Union Canal Walk

Northchurch Common

ow ast

A4251

96 Norcott Hall Farm 97 **47** K L B4506 Hill Farm M 98

G H J K L M

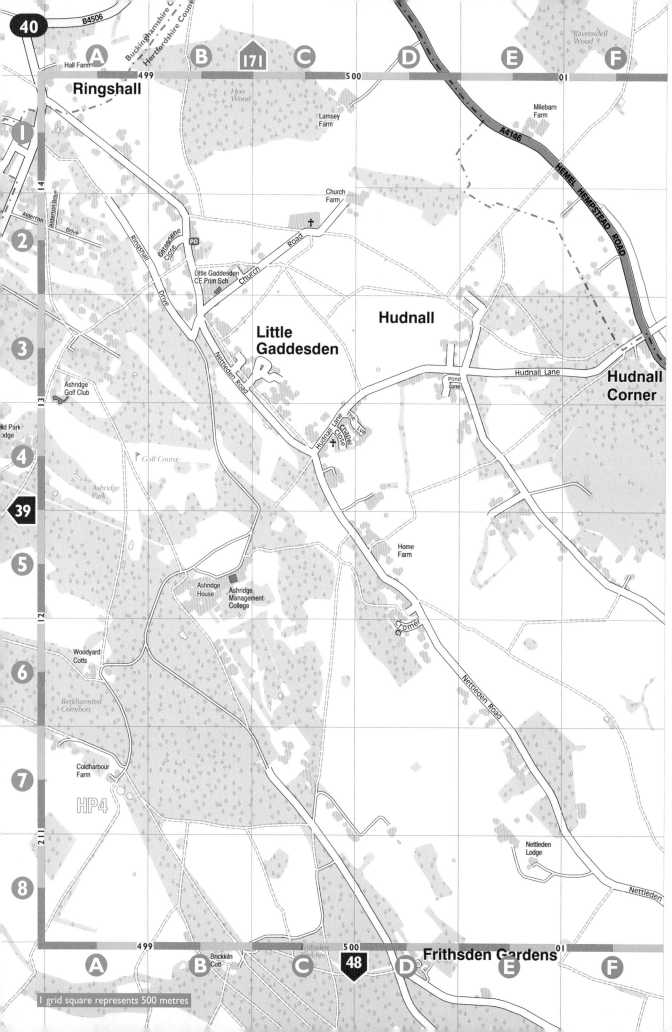

40

A B **171** C D E F

B4506

Buckinghamshire Co.
Hertfordshire Coun.

Hall Farm

499 500 01

Ringshall

Hoo Wood

Lamsey Farm

Ravensdell Wood

Milebarn Farm

A4146

HEMEL HEMPSTEAD ROAD

1

14

Church Farm

Alderton Drive

Alderton Drive

Gateadene Close

Ringshall Drive

PO

Church Road

2

Little Gaddesden CE Prim Sch

Church

Hudnall

3

Little Gaddesden

Nettleden Road

Hudnall Lane

Pond Lane

Hudnall Corner

Ashridge Golf Club

13

The Lye

Chapel Close

Hudnall Lane

4

Golf Course

Ashridge Park

ld Park dge

39

Home Farm

5

Ashridge House

Ashridge Management College

12

Cromer Cl

Nettleden Road

Woodyard Cotts

6

Berkhamsted Common

Coldharbour Farm

7

HP4

Nettleden Lodge

2 11

8

Nettleden

499 500 01

A B C **48** D E F

Brickkiln Cott

Frithsden Beeches

Frithsden Gardens

1 grid square represents 500 metres

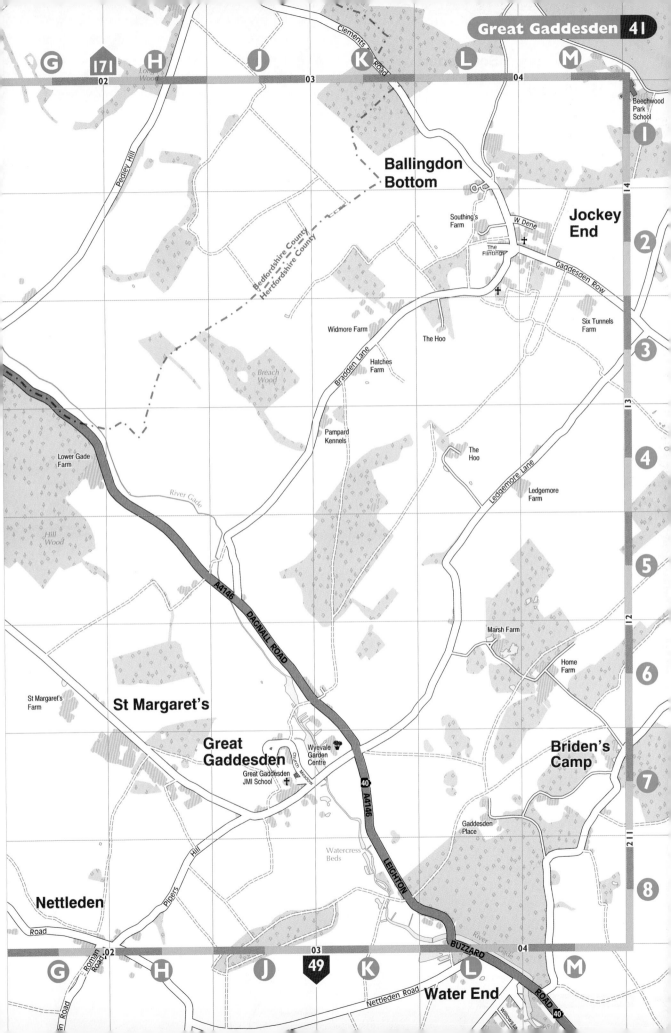

G **171** H J K L M
02 03 04

I

Beechwood
Park
School

**Ballingdon
Bottom**

Southing's
Farm

W Dene

**Jockey
End**

2

The Flintings

Gaddesden Row

Widmore Farm

The Hoo

Six Tunnels
Farm

3

Bradden Lane

Hatches
Farm

Breach
Wood

Pampard
Kennels

The
Hoo

4

Ledgemore Lane

Ledgemore
Farm

Lower Gade
Farm

River Gade

5

A4146

Hill
Wood

DAGNALL ROAD

Marsh Farm

6

Home
Farm

St Margaret's
Farm

St Margaret's

**Briden's
Camp**

7

**Great
Gaddesden**

Church Meadow

Wyevale
Garden
Centre

Great Gaddesden
JMI School

40

A4146

Gaddesden
Place

Watercress
Beds

Pipers Hill

Nettleden

LEIGHTON

8

Road

Roman Road

BUZZARD

River Gade

ROAD

49

Nettleden Road

Water End

40

Willows La

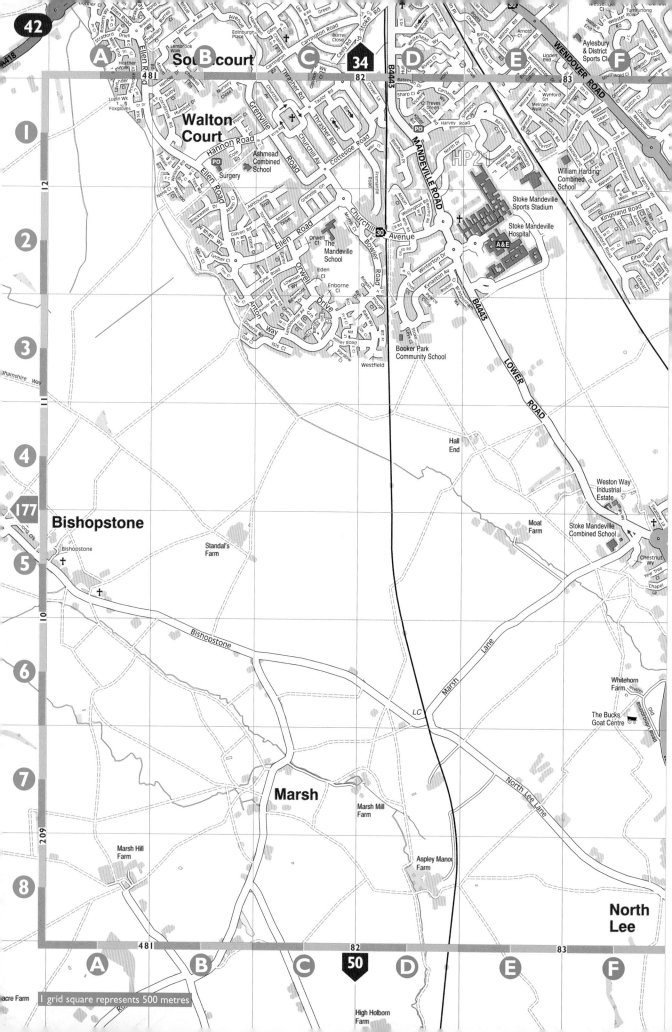

Bedgrove

Weston Turville

Stoke Mandeville

World's End

Nash Lee

Bye Green

Weston Turville Golf & Squash Club

Golf Course

Rectory Farm

Aylesbury RFC

Weston Turville CE School

Innkeeper's Lodge

Stoke Mandeville Station

Meadow Park

Triangle Business Park

Wyevale Garden Centre

Weston Turville Reservoir

Chiltern Brewery

Health Centre

Bedgrove Junior School

WENDOVER ROAD

STATION ROAD

A413 WENDOVER ROAD

WENDOVER ROAD B4009

A4010

RISBOROUGH ROAD

LEE ROAD B4009

Nash Lee Lane

AYLESBURY RD

Main Street

Brook

New Road

Marroway

The Pony Field

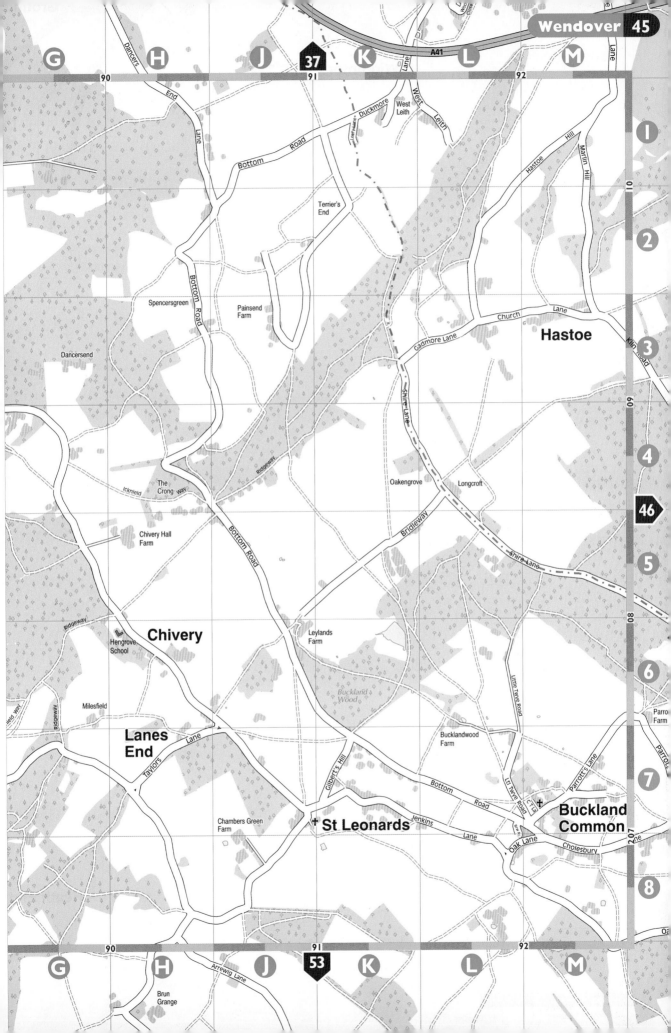

G H J K L M

37

I
2
3
4
46
5
6
7
8

A41

West Leith

Duckmore

West Leith

Hastoe Hill

Martin Hill

Kiln Road

Dancers End Lane

Bottom Road

Terrier's End

Spencersgreen

Painsend Farm

Bottom Road

Dancersend

Church Lane

Gadmore Lane

Hastoe

Shire Lane

Oakengrove

Longcroft

Ridgeway

Icknield Way

The Crong

Chivery Hall Farm

Bridleway

Shire Lane

Ridgeway

Leylands Farm

Buckland Wood

Little Twye Road

Parrott's Farm

Parrott's Lane

Chivery

Hengrove School

Milesfield

Lanes End

Taylors Lane

Lane

Gilbert's Hill

Bucklandwood Farm

Parrott's Lane

Buckland Common

Ask Way

Ridgeway

Chambers Green Farm

† **St Leonards**

Jenkins Lane

Bottom Road

Ltl Twye Road

Oak Lane

Cholesbury

Arrewig Lane

Brun Grange

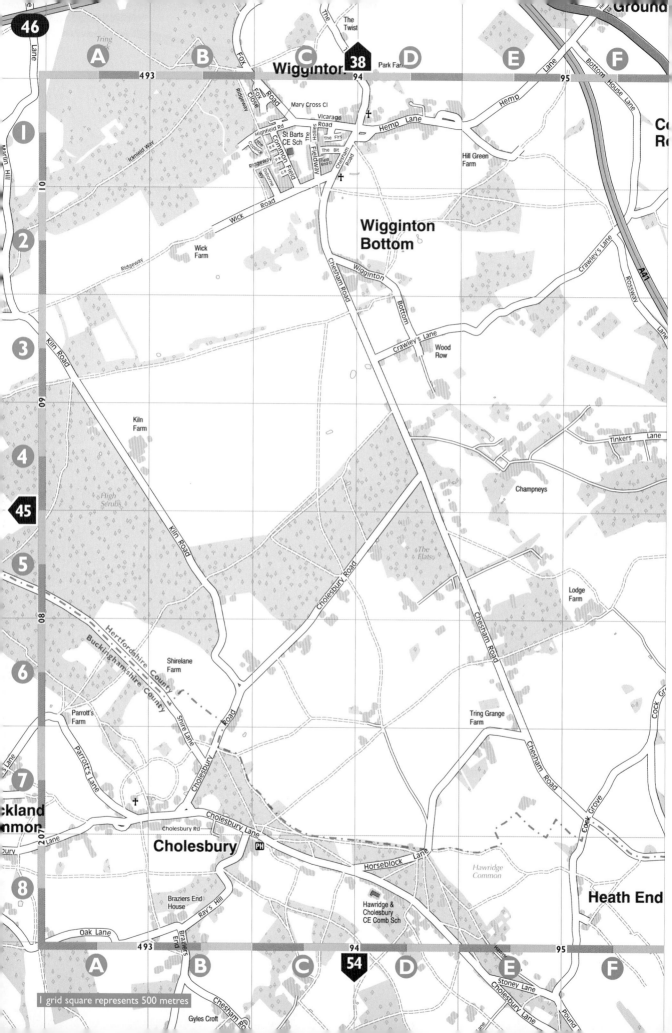

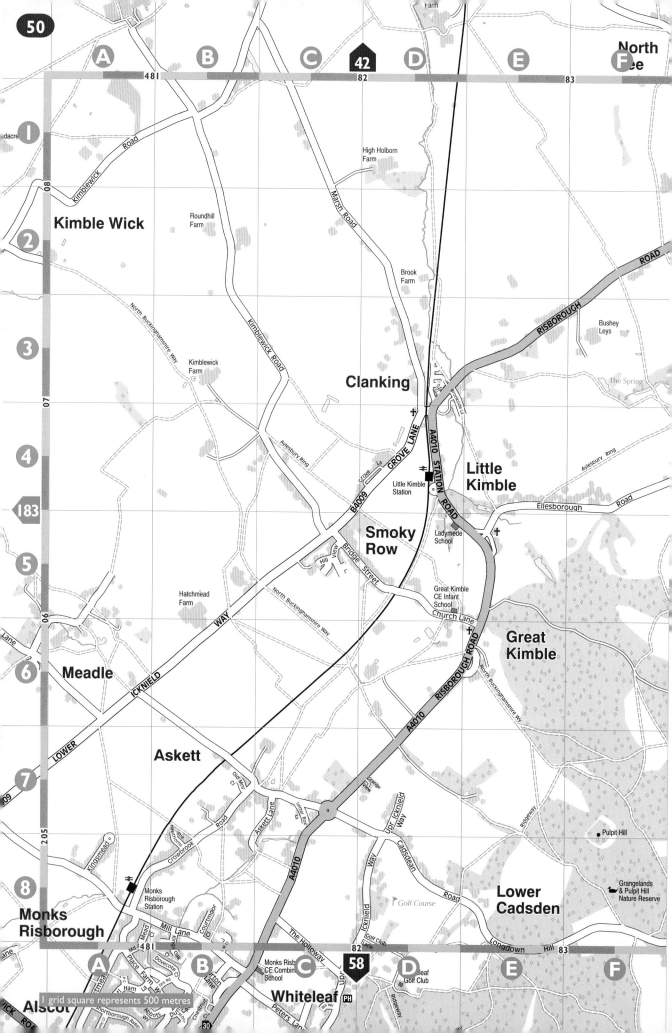

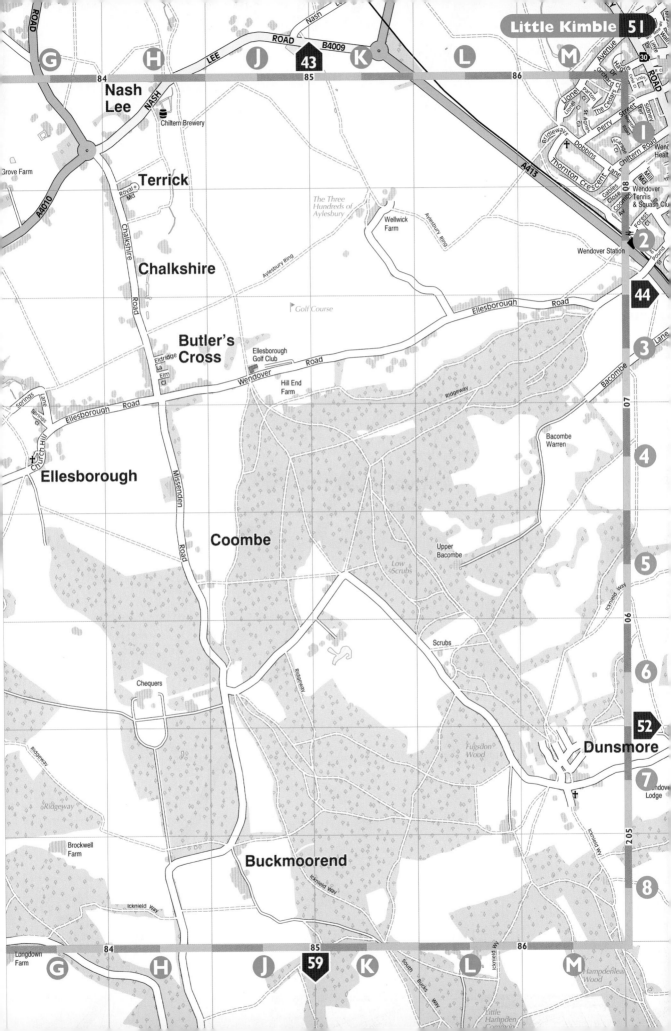

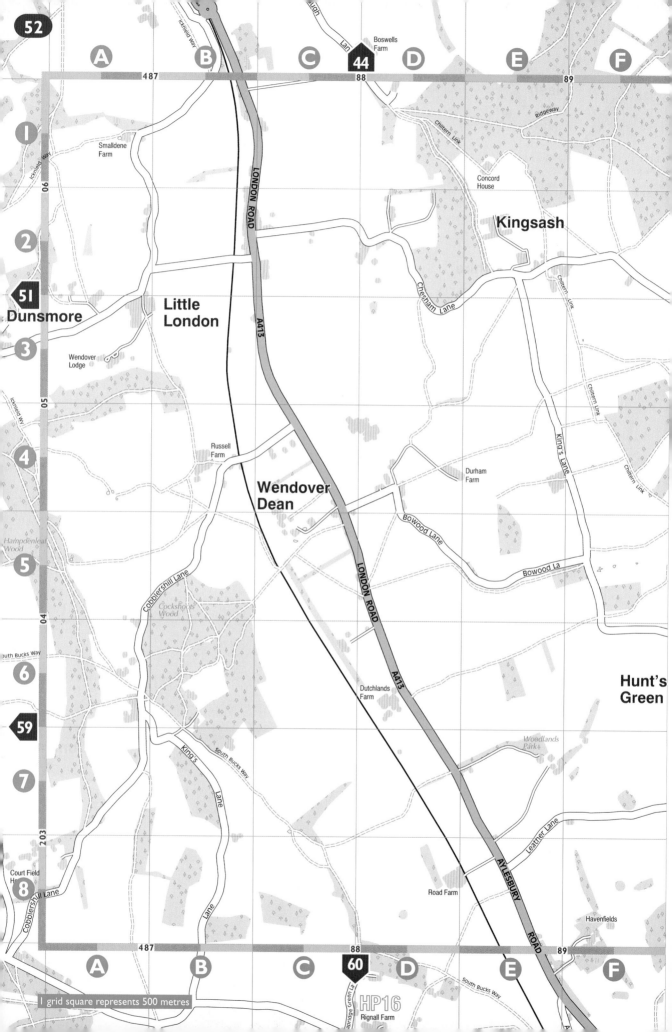

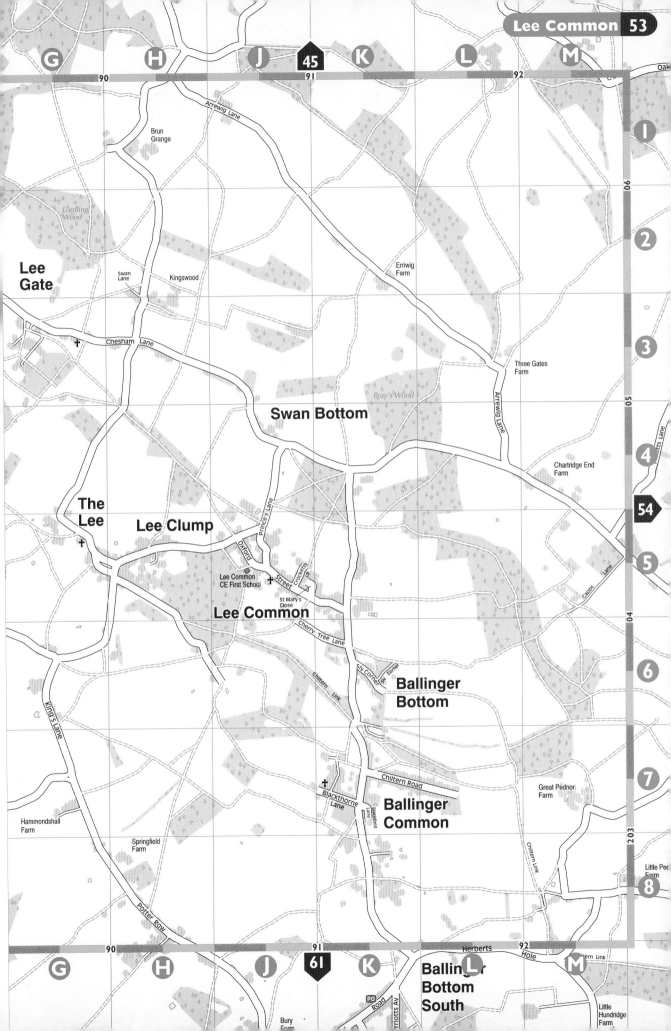

G H J **45** K L M

90 91 92 Oak

1

Brun
Grange

2

Arrewig Lane

Lördling
Wood

Erriwig
Farm

**Lee
Gate**

Swan
Lane Kingswood

3

Chesham Lane

Three Gates
Farm

Swan Bottom

Bray's Wood

Arrewig Lane

Chartridge End
Farm

4

54

**The
Lee** **Lee Clump**

Prince's Lane

Lee Common
CE First School

Oxford

Street Crockerts

St Mary's
Close

Lee Common

Capps Lane

5

Cherry Tree Lane

6

Chiltern Link

Sly Corner St Corner

**Ballinger
Bottom**

7

King's Lane

Chiltern Road

Great Pednor
Farm

Blackthorne
Lane Blackfield Lane

**Ballinger
Common**

Chiltern Link

Hammondshall
Farm

Springfield
Farm

Little Ped
Farm

8

Potter Row

90 91 **61** 92 Herberts
Hole

G H J K L M

PO Road **Ballin** r
**Bottom
South**

Bury
Form rriotts Av Little
Hundridge
Farm

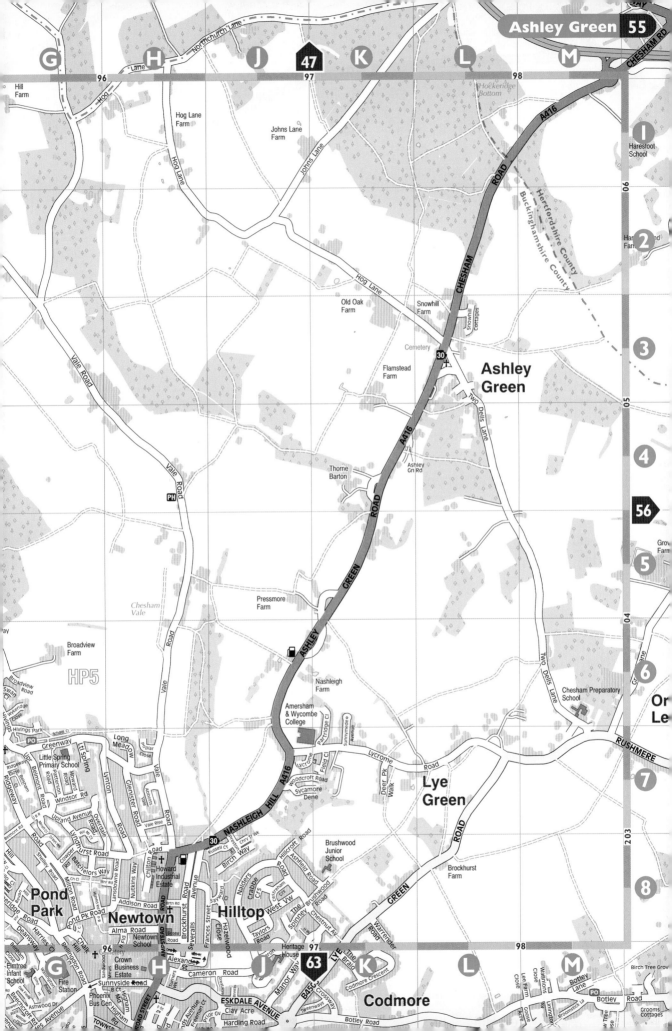

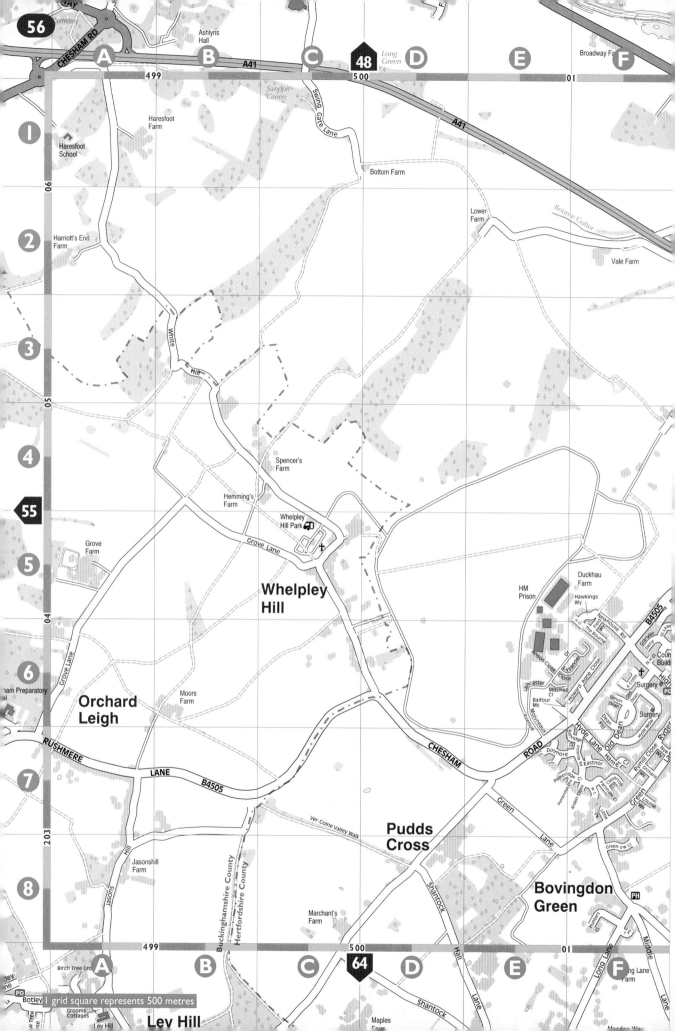

A **B** A41 **C** 48 Long Green **D** **E** Broadway Fa **F**

499 500 01

CHESHAM RD

06

I
Haresfoot Farm
Haresfoot School
Ashlyns Hall
Sandpit Green
Swing Gate Lane
Bottom Farm

2
Harriott's End Farm
Lower Farm
Vale Farm
Bourne Gutter

White Hill

05

3

4
Spencer's Farm
Hemming's Farm

55
Whelpley Hill Park
Grove Lane

5
Grove Farm
Whelpley Hill
HM Prison
Duckhau Farm
Hawkings WY
Newhouse Rd
B4505

04

6
ham Preparatory
Moors Farm
Orchard Leigh
Anson Close
Lancaster
Mitchell Cl
Balfour Ms
Molyneaux Avenue
Surgery
Surgery

RUSHMERE LANE B4505

7
Jasonshill Farm
Jason's Hill
Ver-Colne Valley Walk
CHESHAM ROAD
Green Lane
Pudds Cross

203

8
Buckinghamshire County
Hertfordshire County
Marchant's Farm
Shantock Hall
Bovingdon Green
PH

499 500 01

A **B** **C** 64 **D** **E** **F**

Birch Tree Gro
Botley
PO
grid square represents 500 metres
Grooms Cottages
Ley Hill
Lev Hill
Maples
shantock Lane
Long Lane
ing Lane
Farm

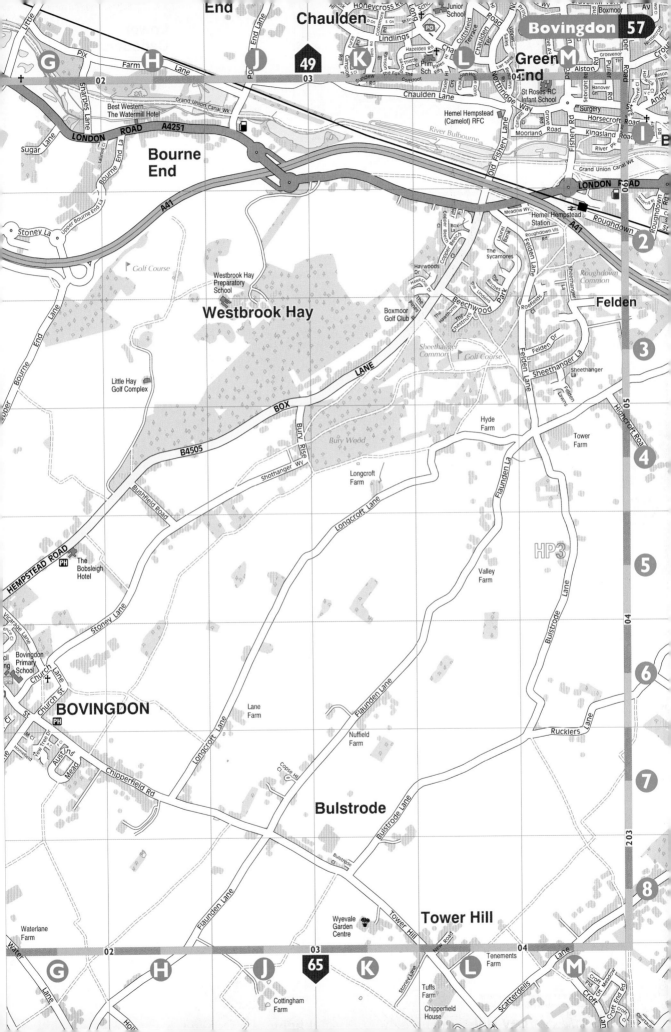

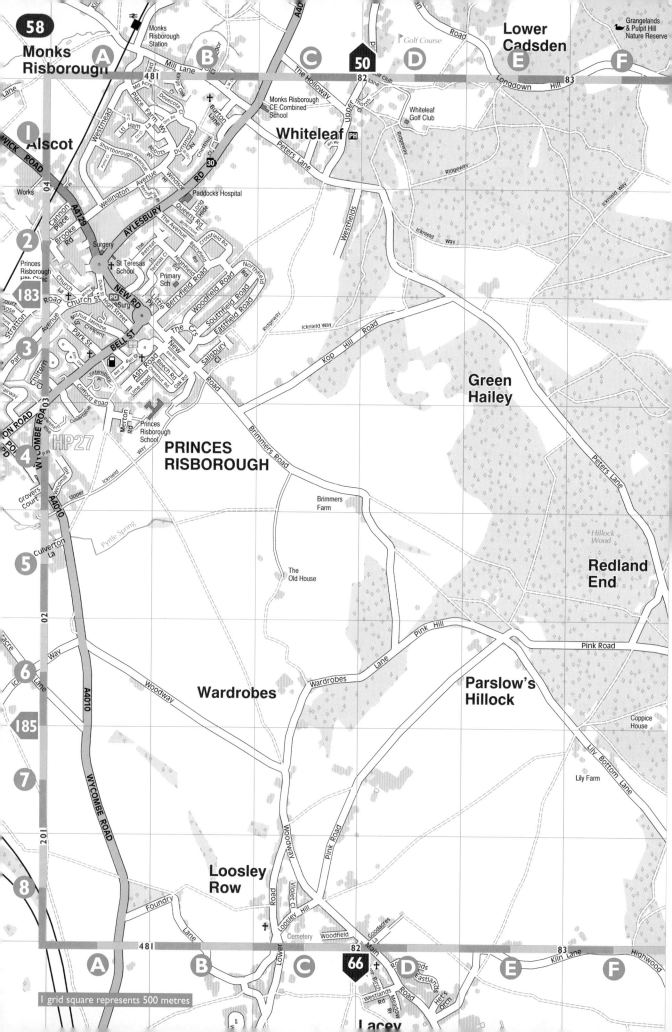

G H J 51 K L M

Icknield Way

Icknield Way

84 85 86

Longdown Farm

Dirtywood Farm

Solinger Farm

Hampden Bottom Farm

South Bucks Way

Little Hampden Common

Hampdenleaf Wood

PH

South Bucks Way

Little Hampden

52

Court Field House

Cobblershill Lane

Honor End Lane

Honor End Farm

Ledge Wood

60

Sprinters Leisure Centre

Ferns Farm

PH **Great Hampden**

Monkton Wood

Hampden Common

Hampden Road

Honour En

Hanglings Lane

Monkton Farm

Grubbi... Lane

Moses Plat Lane

Cornerways Cher...

Coleheath B...

Spring Coppice Lane

Bryants Bottom Ro...

Bottom

84 85 67 86

G H J K L M

I
2
3
4
5
6
7
8

04
03
02
01

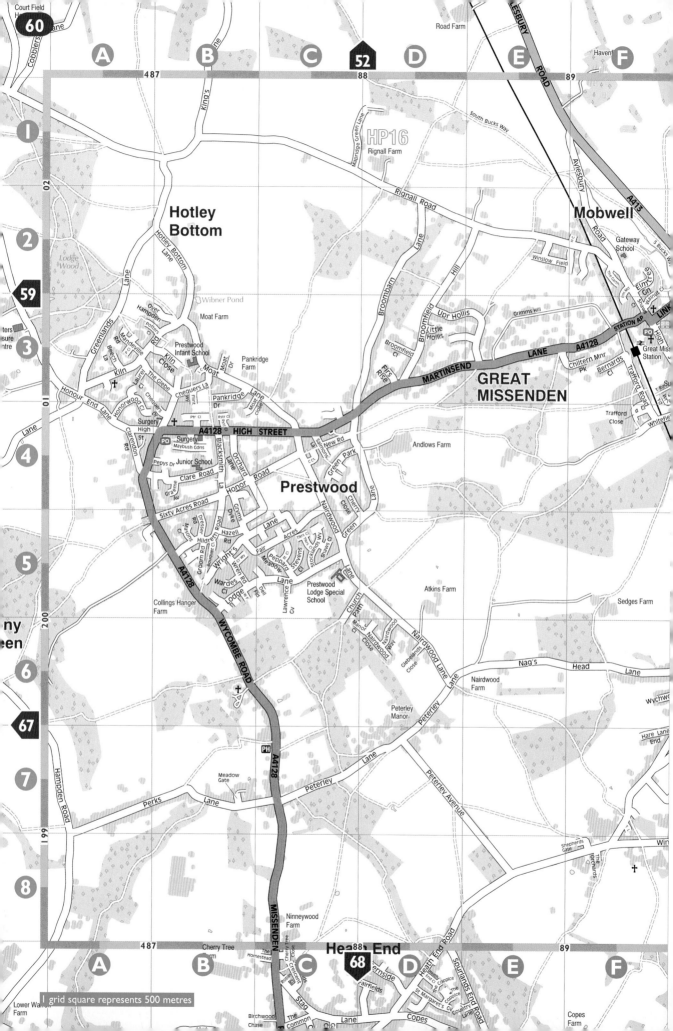

G   H   J   **53**   K   L   M

90   91   92   02

I

Ballinger Bottom South

Herberts Hole

Chiltern Link

Little Hundridge Farm

Bury Farm

PO Road

Marriotts Av

Ballinger Meadow La

Sibley's Rise

King's Lane

Loppetts Lane

South Heath

Wood Lane

Little Wood Corner

Little Hundridge Lane

Blind

2

Hill House

Frith Hill

Frith-hill

Middlegrove Farm

Cudsden's Farm

Cudsdens Court

Mill La

B485   CHESHAM   ROAD

B485

Browns Rd

Hyde Heath Road

Hyde House

3

The Roald Dahl Museum & Story Centre

Great Missenden CE Combined School

Church St Future School

Church La

Hyde Lane

Hyde Farm

4

62

Warren Water

Abbey Park

Rook Wood

Misbourne School

London Road

River Misbourne

A413

Rook Wd

S Bucks Way

RK WY

Bank's Pond

01

200

5

Nag's Head Lane

Windsor La

Sylvia Close

Reyners Green

Pines Cl

London Rd

The Chiltern Hospital

Deepmill Farm

Hyde Lane

Mantle's Farm

6

S Bucks Way

Nag's Head Lane

Road

New

Hare Lane

Pinewood

Peasmead

Wyckwood

Rise

Longfield

Larch Wood

Windsor Lane

Grange Farm

Deep   Mill   Lane

A413

Chalk Lane

7

Little Kingshill

dsor   Lane

St Christopher Close

South Bucks Way

Little Missenden CE Infant School

Taylors Lane

199

Little Kingshill Combined School

Little Boys Heath

Affrick's Farm

Haleacre Wood

South Bucks Way

Beamond Wood

Littl Miss

8

90   91   **69**   92

G   H   J   K   L   M

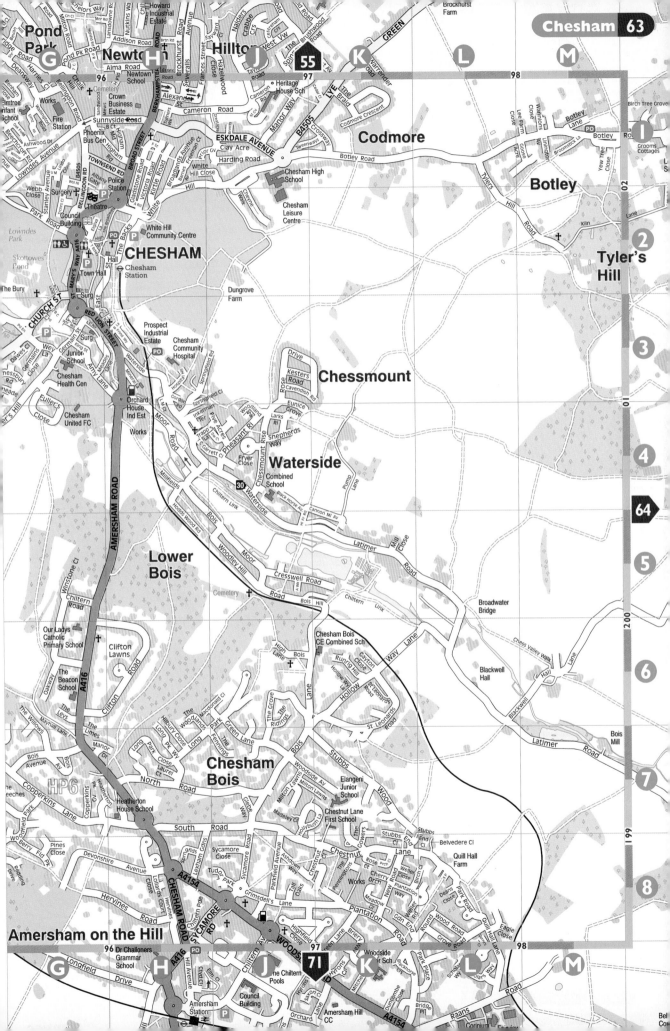

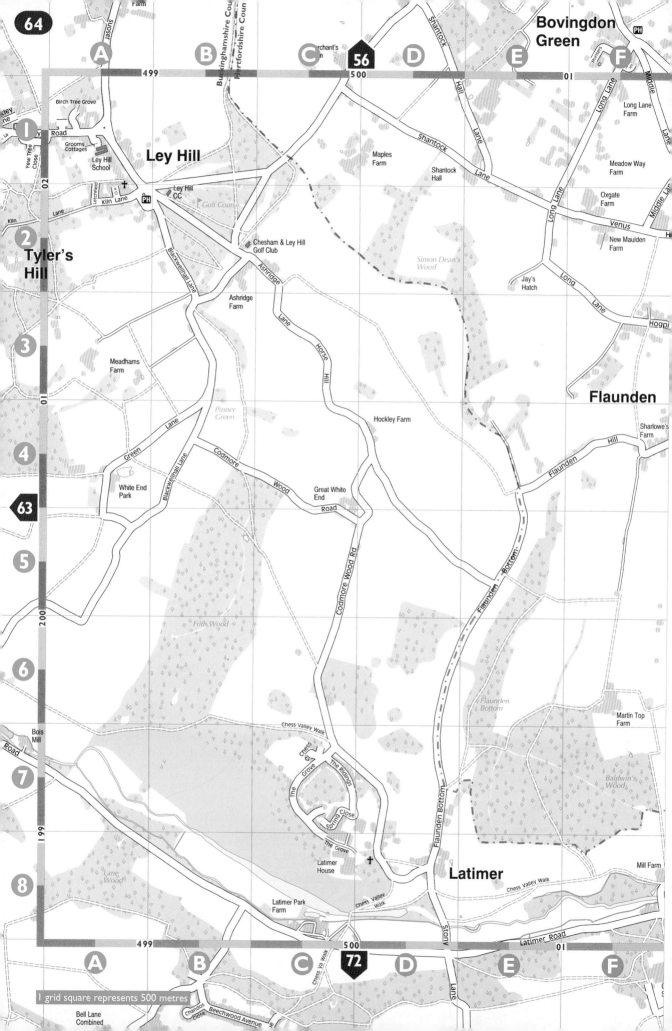

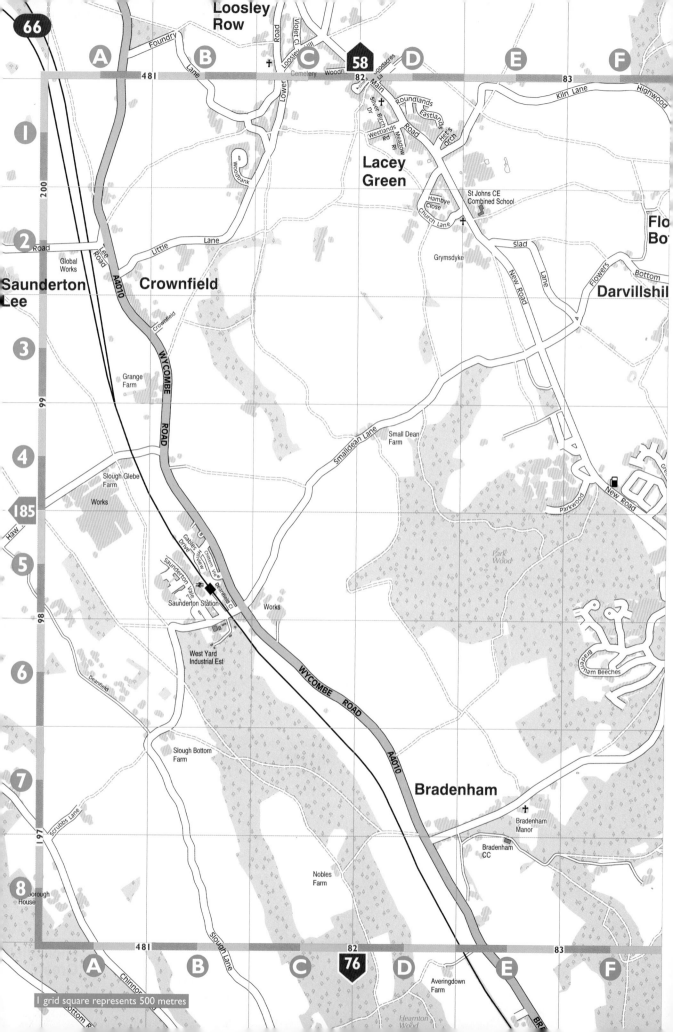

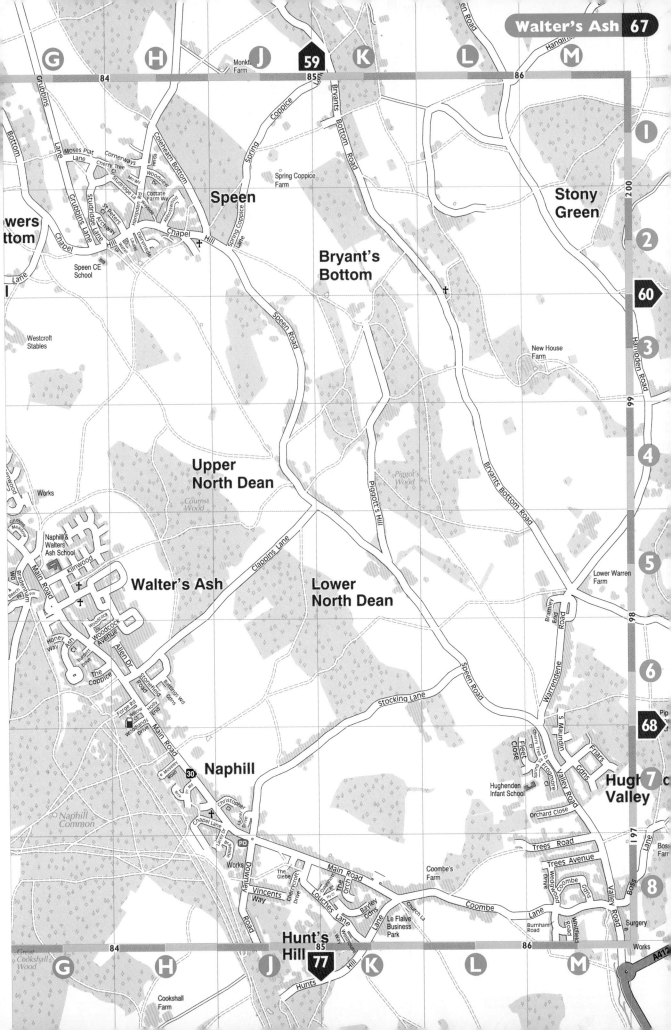

G　H　J　59　K　L　M

1

84　85　86

Monkton Farm

Grubbins Lane

Moses Plat Lane
Cornerways
Cherry Tree Cl
Studridge Lane
Woodview Dr
Colehearth Bottom

Spring Coppice

Bryants Bottom Road

Speen

Stony Green

2

St Peters
Archway
Grubbins Lane
Chapel Hill
Chapel Lane
Spring Coppice Lane

Speen CE School

Bryant's Bottom

60

3

Westcroft Stables

Speen Road

Hampden Road

99

New House Farm

Upper North Dean

Piggot's Wood

4

Works

Cournse Wood

5

Naphill & Walters Ash School

Klinwood

Clappins Lane

Piggott's Hill

Lower Warren Farm

98

Walter's Ash

Lower North Dean

Bramley End Road

6

Woodcock Avenue
Allen Dr
Stonefield Rd
Holly Hedge
Barlings Wd

Speen Road

Warrendene Road

The Coppice

Stocking Lane

68

Forge Rd
Willow
Woodlands Drive
Main Road

Fleet Close
Cherry Tree
S Maundin Gdns
Frogmore
Valley Road
Friars

7

Moseley Road

Naphill

30

Hughenden Infant School

Orchard Close

Hughd Valley

Christopher Cl
Laurel Drive
Chapel Lane

Naphill Common

Trees Road

97

Boss Lane

Vincents Way
Downley Road
The Glebe
Cherrycroft Drive
Louches Lane

Main Road

Trees Avenue
Wedgwood Drive
Coombe Gdns

8

Coombe's Farm

Bayley Gdns
Wellhouse Way
Church La
Le Flaive Business Park

Coombe Lane

Burnham Road
Whitfield Road
Valley Road

Surgery

Hunt's Hill

84　85　77　86

G　H　J　K　L　M

Works

A4128

Great Cookshall Wood

Cookshall Farm

Hunts Hill

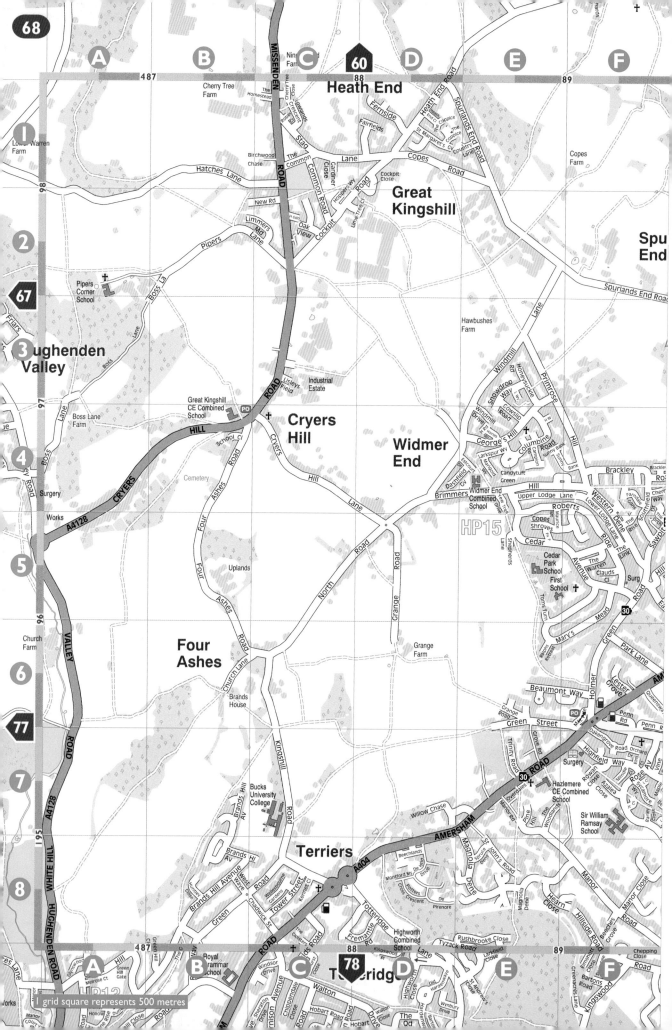

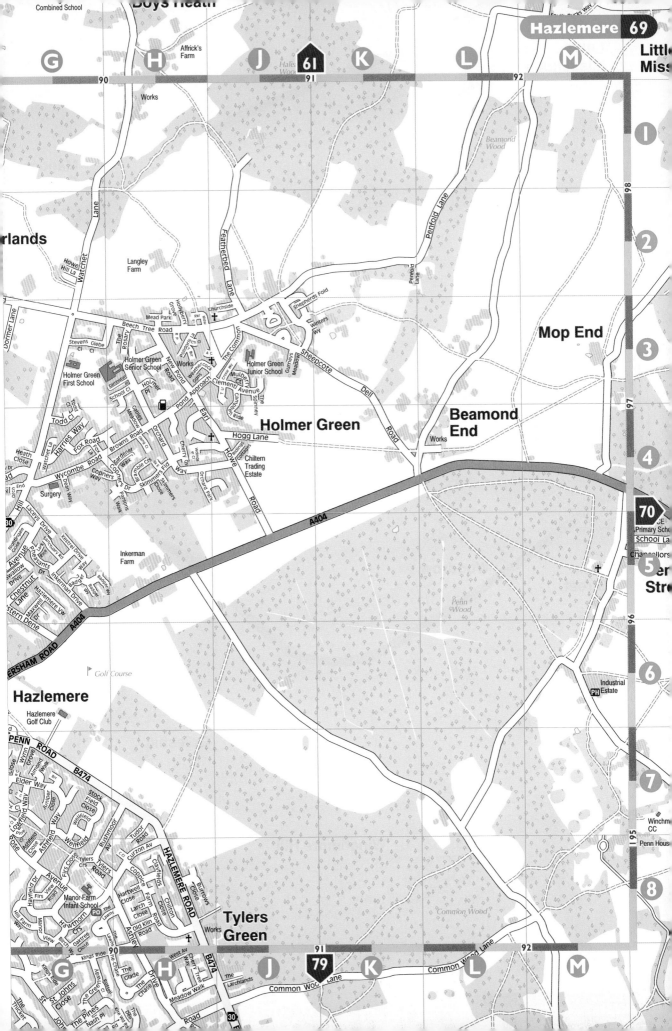

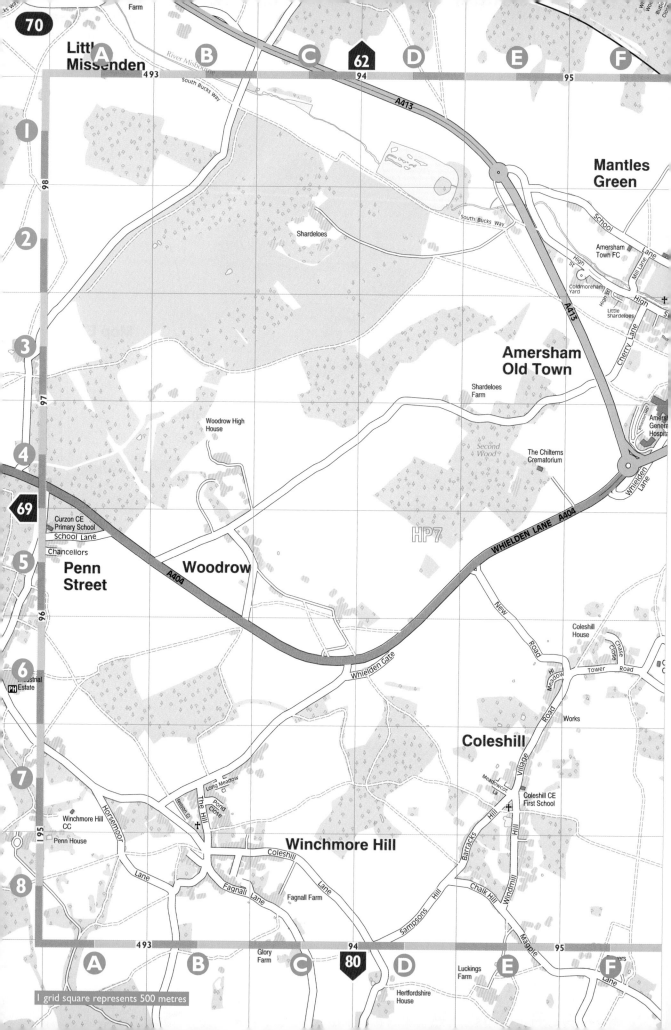

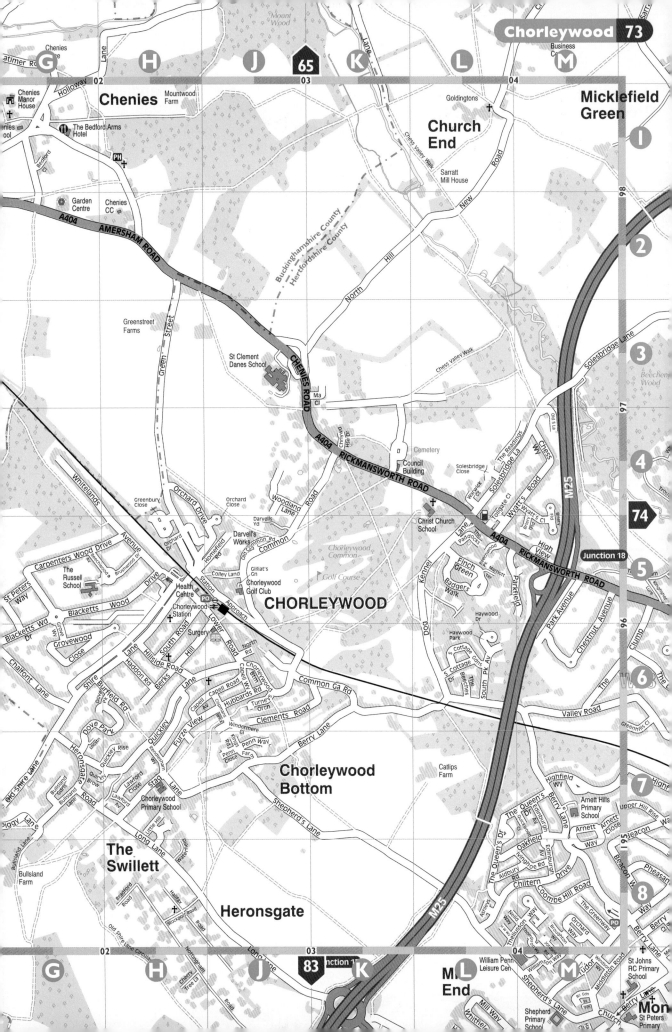

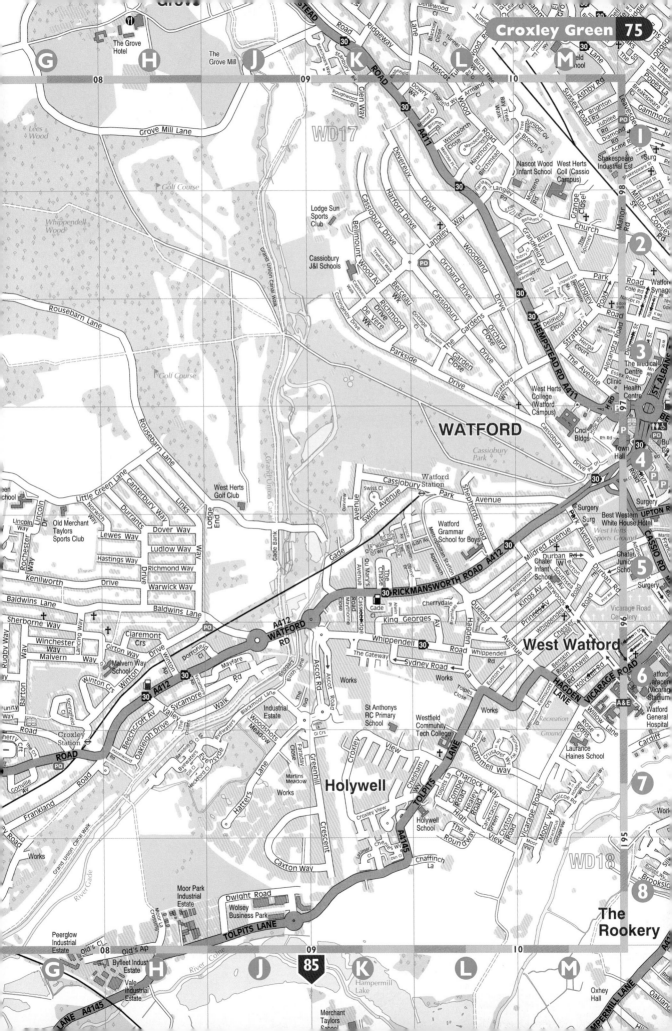

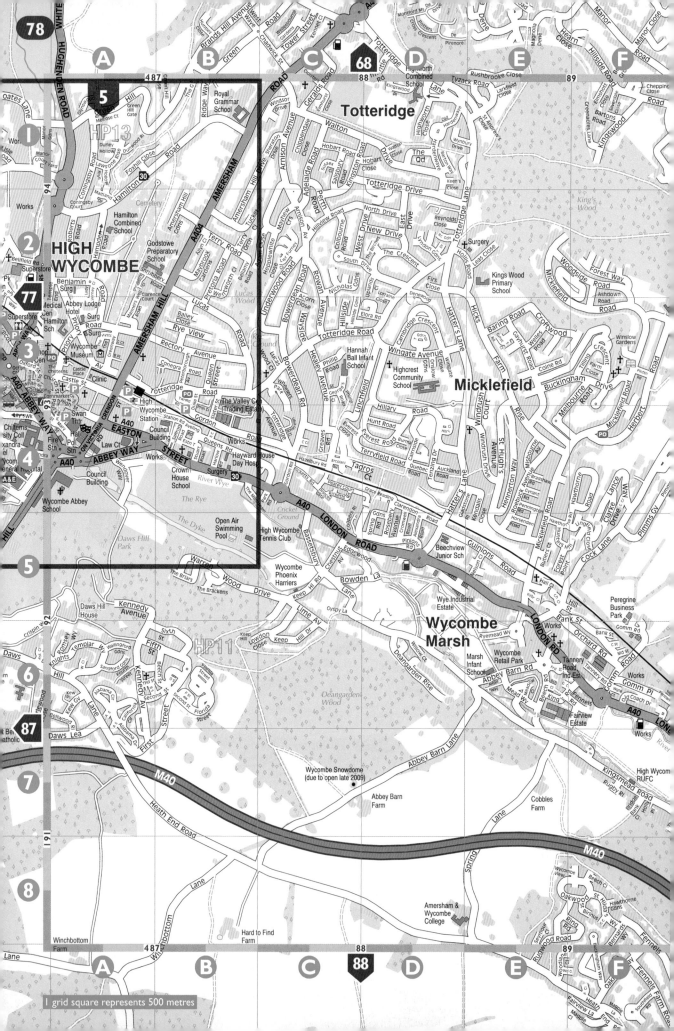

G H J **71** K L M

I

CHALFONT
ST GILES

Three
Households

Butlers
Cross

82

Seer Green

Jordans

Wilton Park

Layte
Green

Seer Green Station

Beaconsfield Golf Club

Seer Green
CE Combined
School

G H J **91** K L M

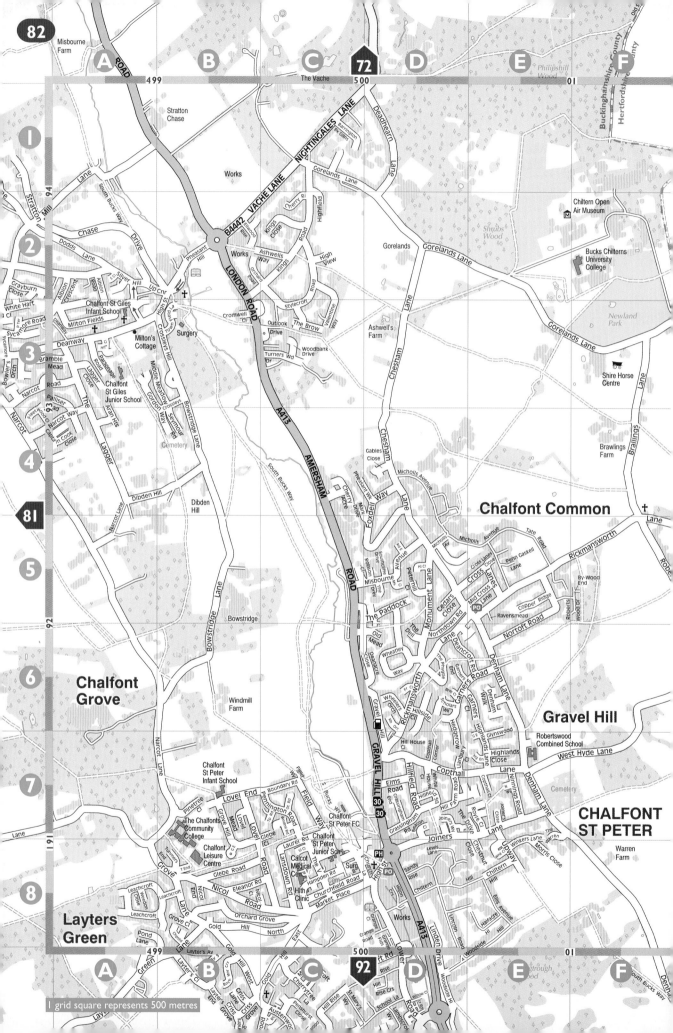

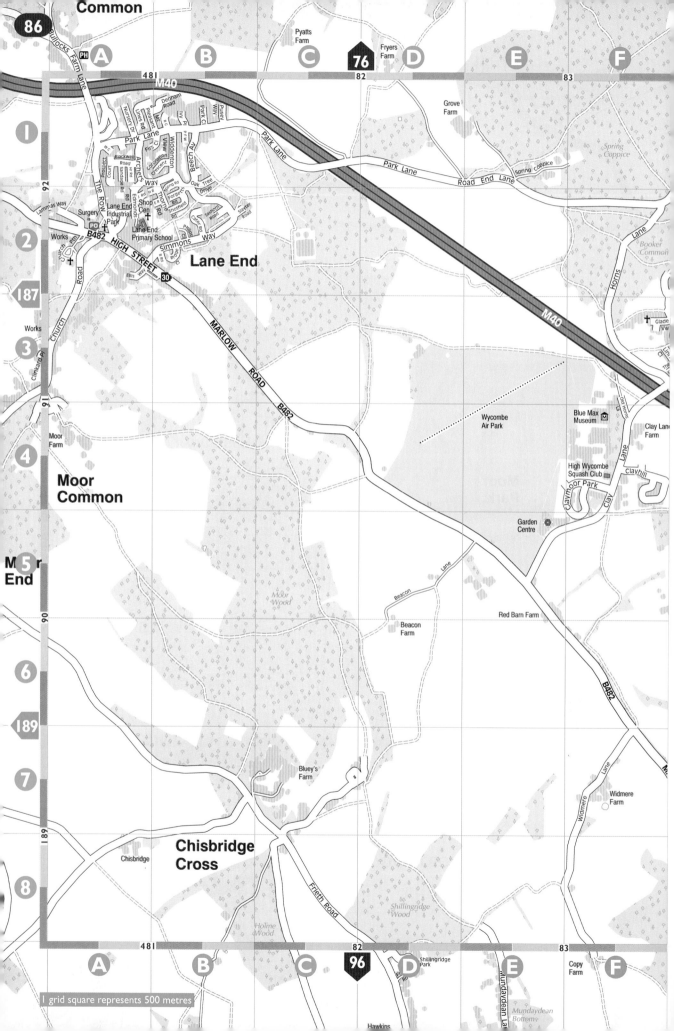

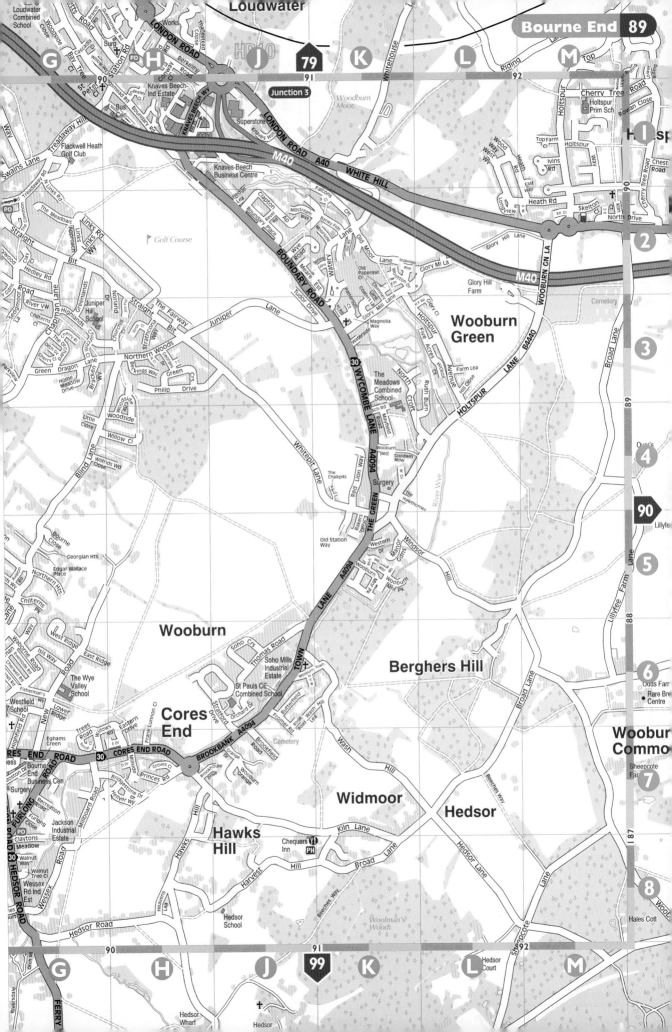

Wilton Park

Layter
Green

G | **H** | **J** | 81 | **K** | **L** | **M**
97

Minerva Way

96

Gorell
Rd
Nowell Road
Dume CT's
Baldwin
Berwick
Close

Minerva
Way

Works

Porkiln
Lane

Stone Dean
Farm

Stampwell
Farm

Mumfords
Lane

I

90

2

Siblet's
Wood

LONDON 50 ROAD A40

Hyde
Farm

Mumfords
Farm

The Manor
House

3

OXFORD ROAD A40

89

Chiltern
Hundreds

4

M40

92

Hillmott's Farm

Common
Lane

Beaconsfield
Lane

Slade Farm

Hedgerley Lane

Moat
Farm

5

88

Wapseys
Lane

**Hedgerley
Green**

6

Village
Lane

PH

Church Wood
RSPB Reserve

✝

Pennlands
Farm

Andrew
Hill
La

Hedgerley

Kiln
Lane

7

87

COLLINSWOOD

Coppice Way

Stevenson Road

**Hedgerley
Hill**

Hedgerley
Park

8

Old Nursery
Court

Gregory Rd

Gilbert Rd

Hill

Jones Way

Elkins
Road

Cottage Park
Road

Hedgerley

Longfield

97

G | **H** | **J** | 101 | **K** | **L** | **M**
96

ROAD
Egypt
Lane

Parish Lane

Collum Green Road

Tara

Cemetery

Timberwood

Wood End
Close

Colley Hill
Lane

98

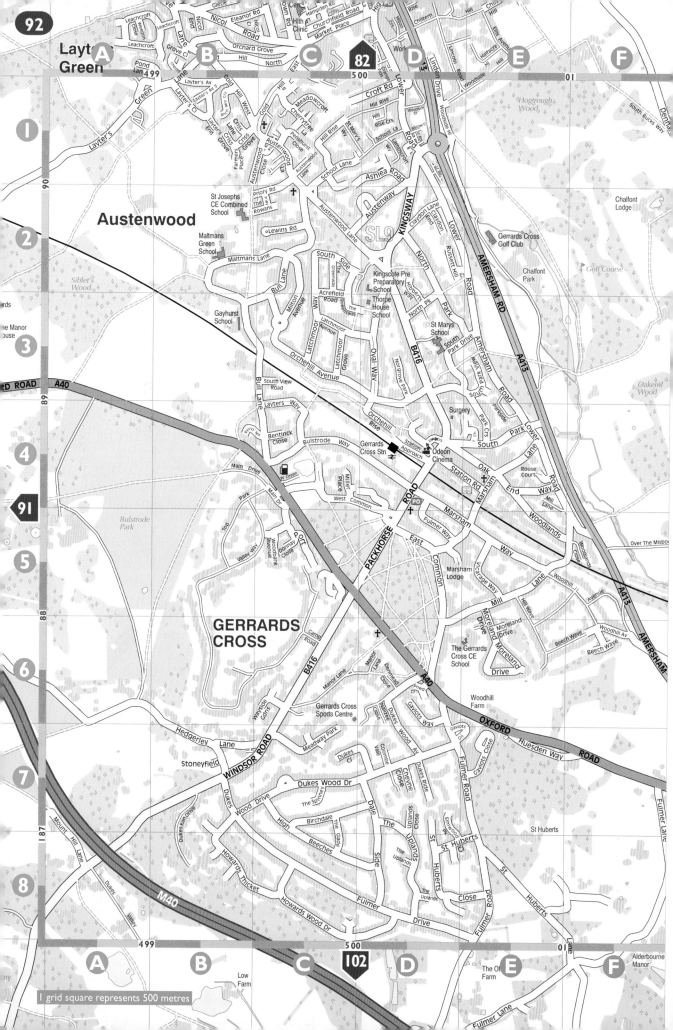

G H J **83** K L M

02 03 04

Colney
Farm

I

Mopes
Farm

Hillingdon

South Bucks Way

Old Shire Lane Circular Walk

Old Uxbridge Road

Grand Union Canal

2

90

Grand Union

A412

River Colne

3

89

Coldharbour
Farm

Marish Lane

The Marish

Hallings Lane

Hangar Road

Tilehouse Lane

Denham
Aerodrome

NORTH

88

4

Mirrie Lane

Isle of Wight
Farm

Over The Misbourne Road

Slade Oak Lane

ORBITAL

Woodhurst Drive

Denham Green Lane

Bosch Broadwater
Park Business
Estate

94

5

Golf Course

Denham
Golf Club

Tilehouse Lane

Tilehouse
Combined
School

St Francis
Road

**Denham
Green**

ROAD

Link Way

Moorfield Road

Savay
Farm

Savay Lane

UB

Doggetts
Fm Rd

Denham Golf
Course Station

Upper Road

Middle Road

Lower Road

Side Road

Penn Drive

Ashcroft Drive

Nightingale Way

Bowyer Cr

Pollard Avenue

Tilehouse

Way

Savay Close

PO

Denham
Station

6

Works

Higher Denham

Old Rectory Lane

Tilehouse Lane

Martin Baker
Sports Ground

South Bucks Way

87

7

**Tatling
End**

ROAD

Old Amersham Rd

Misbourne
Meadows

Broken Gate Lane

Moor House
Farm

Bakers Wood

DENHAM AVENUE A412

PH
Village Road

PH

Council
Building

Denham

Neal Cl

Capswood
Business
Centre

OXFORD ROAD

Beta
Works

Skylark Road

Baker's Wood

Ford End

Ashmead Lane

Cheapside Lane

Neal Cl

Pirstone Way

A40 OXFORD ROAD

Hollybush Lane

Mount Lane

A40

Southlands Rd

Denham
Village
Infant School

South Bucks Way

8

M25

Hollybush
Farm

Denham
Mount

Blacksmith's Lane

PO

Denham Mill

OXFORD ROAD

Lindsey Road

Old Priory Close

Wenlack Cl

02 03 **103** 04

G H J K L M

Field Road

Froggy

A B C **86** D E F

481 82 83

I

88

2

Holywick

Woodend House

Holme Wood

Shillingridge Wood

Shillingridge Park

Erleth Rd

Hawkins Farm

Copy Farm

Mundaydean Bottom

Mundaydean Lane

Frieth Road

3

87

Heath Wood

Woodend Farm

Homefield Wood

Lower Woodend

Marlow Common

Common

Marlow

Boving Green

4

189

5

86

Bockmer House

Bockmer Lane

Bockmer End

Davenport Wood

Hook's Farm

Spin

6

A4155

Widefield Wood

Rassler Wood

A4155

7

185

Kings Barn Farm

West Close

North Close

South Cl

Buckingham Gate

Crest Rd

Danesfield School

Golf Course

Home Copse

8

Bockmer Lane

School Lane

Thames Reach

Danesfield

Harleyford Golf Club

A4155

481

Dan Ho Hotel

82 **106** D Buckinghamshire County E Harleyfor **83** Manor

Windsor and Maidenhead

Thames Path

F

River Thames

1 grid square represents 500 metres

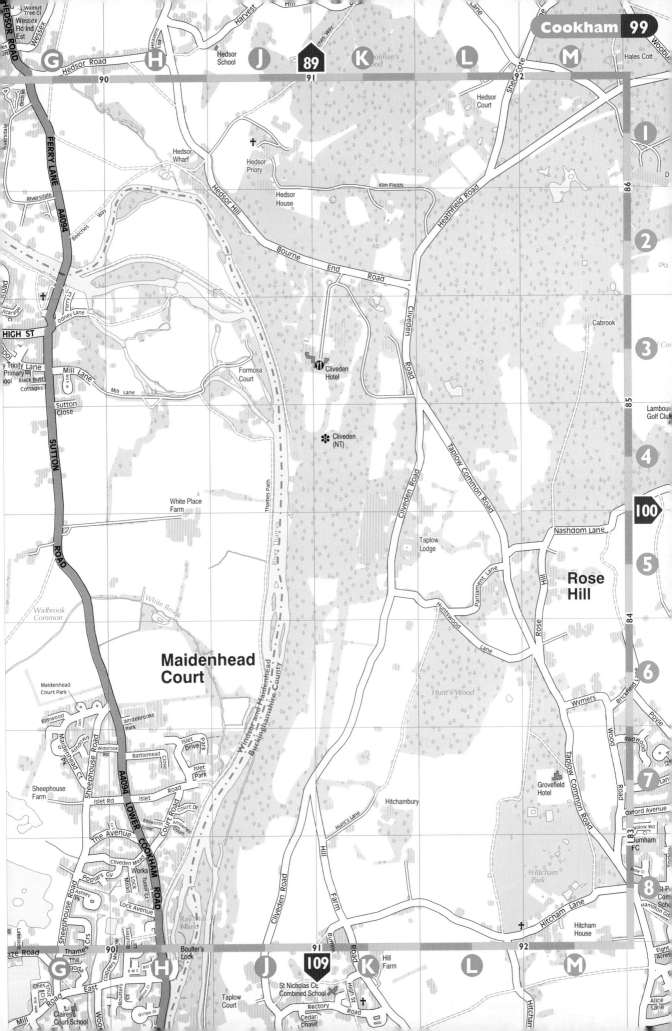

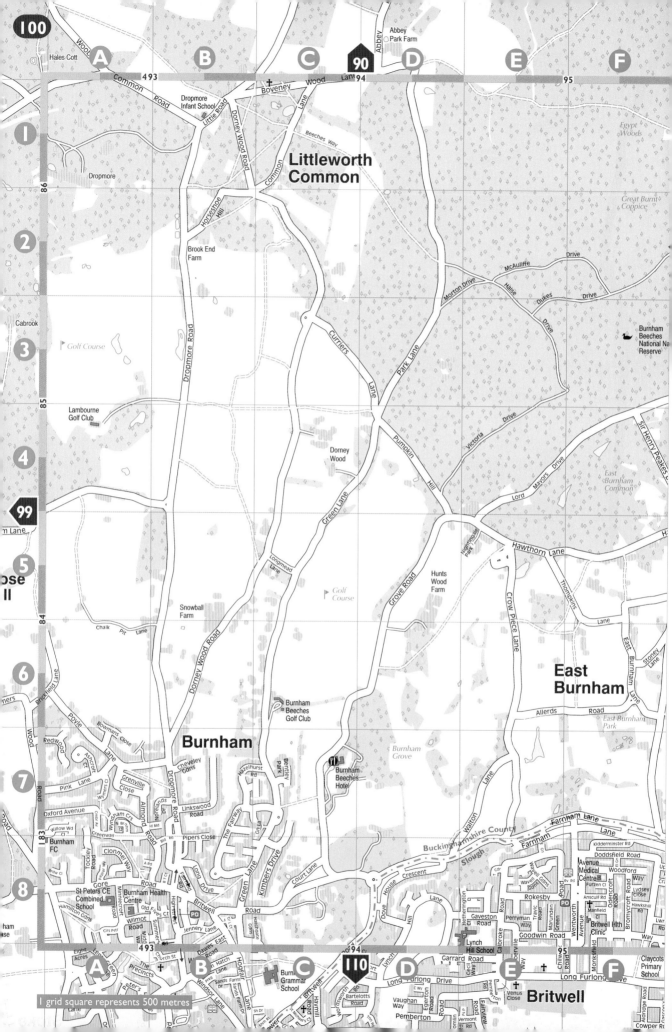

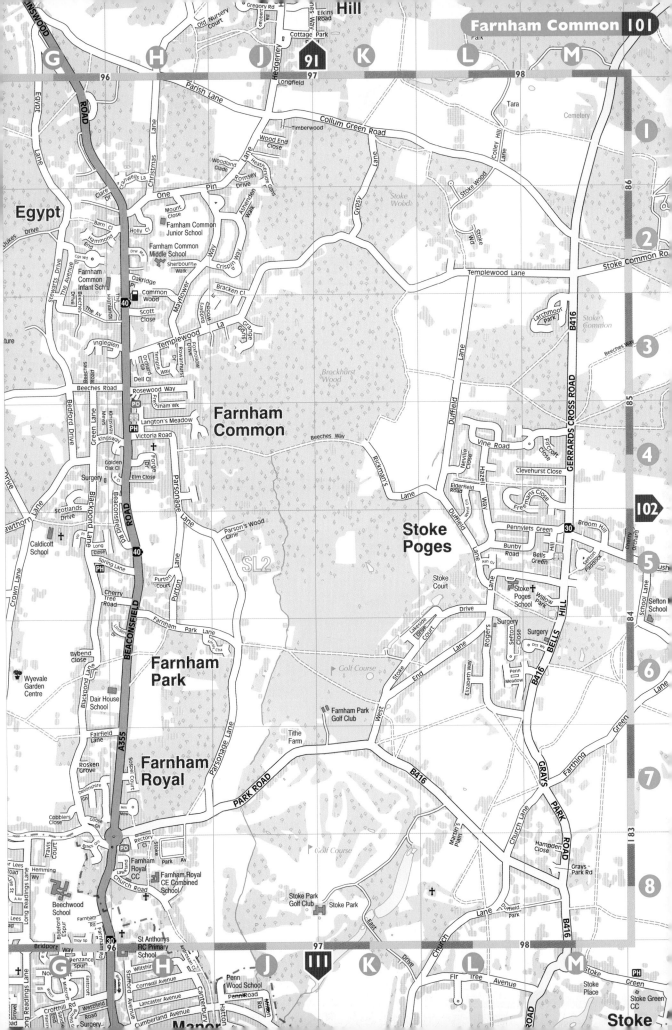

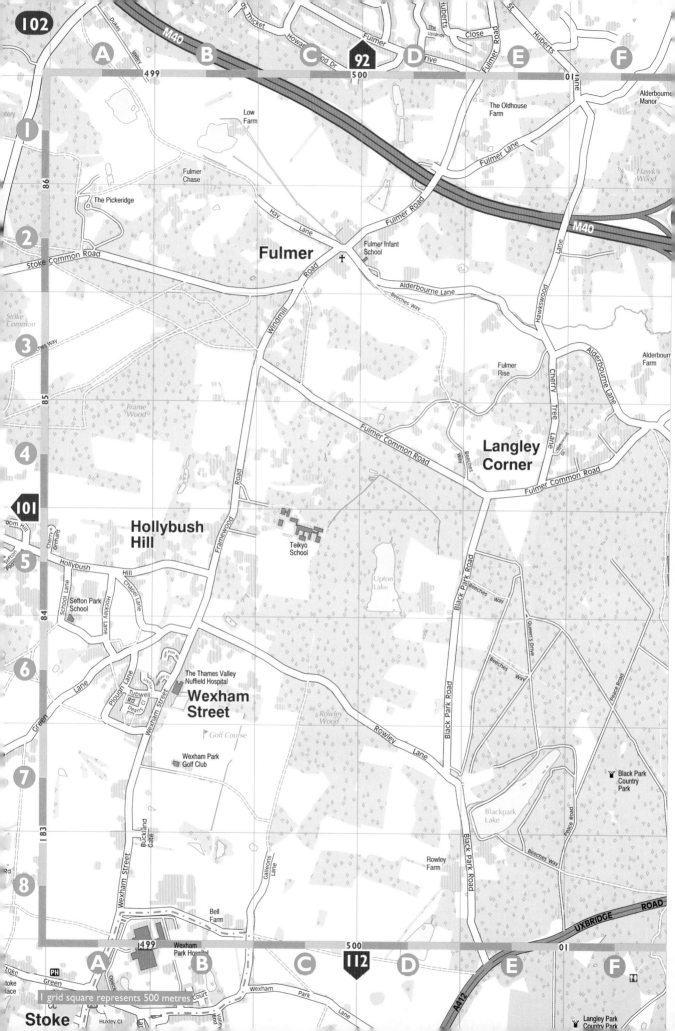

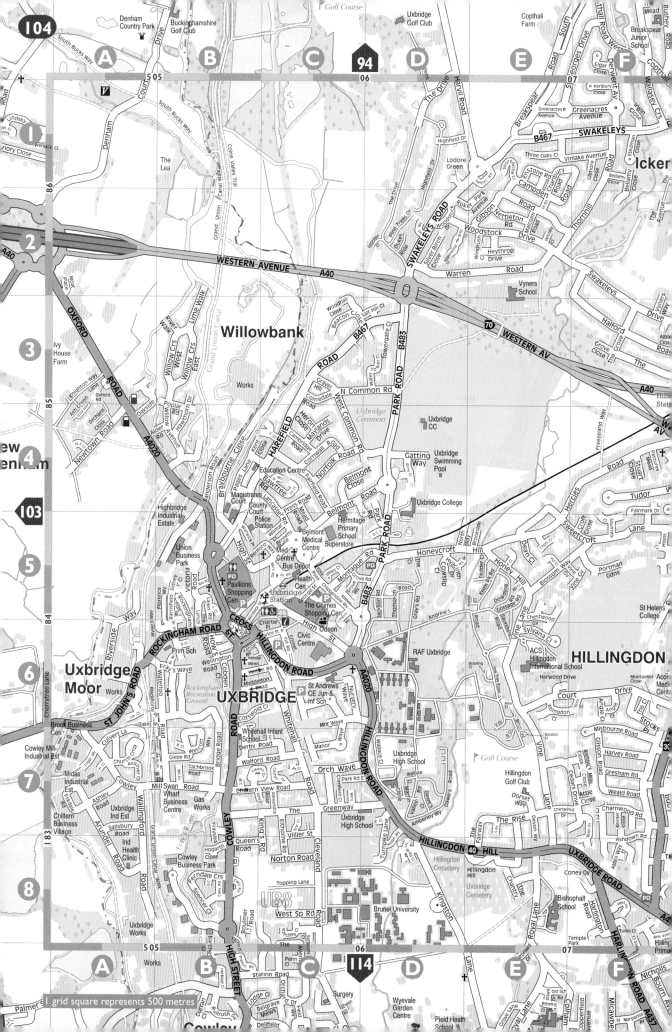

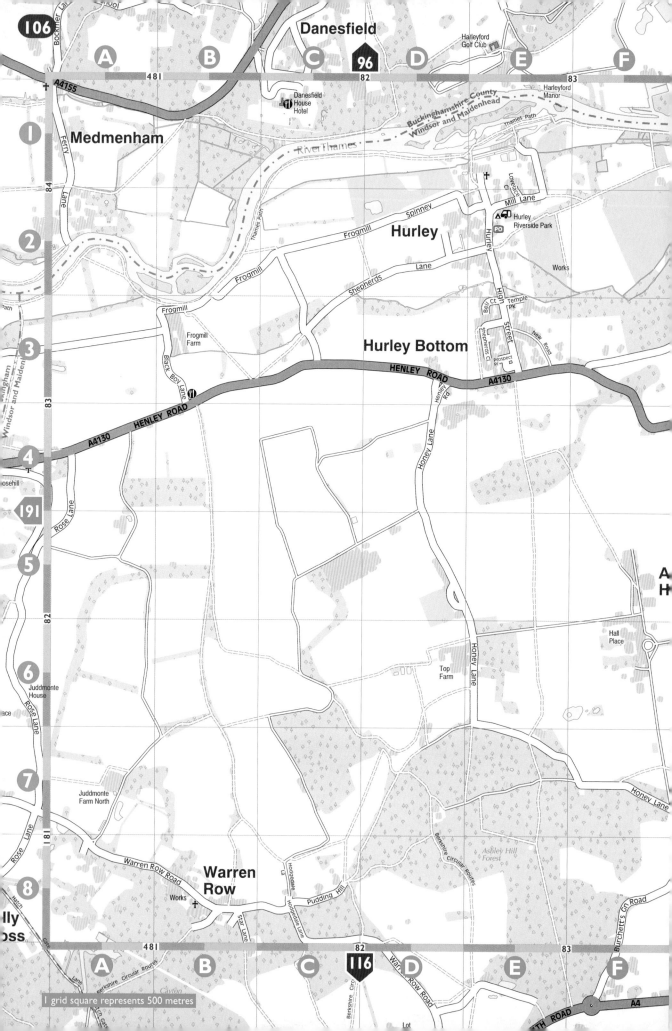

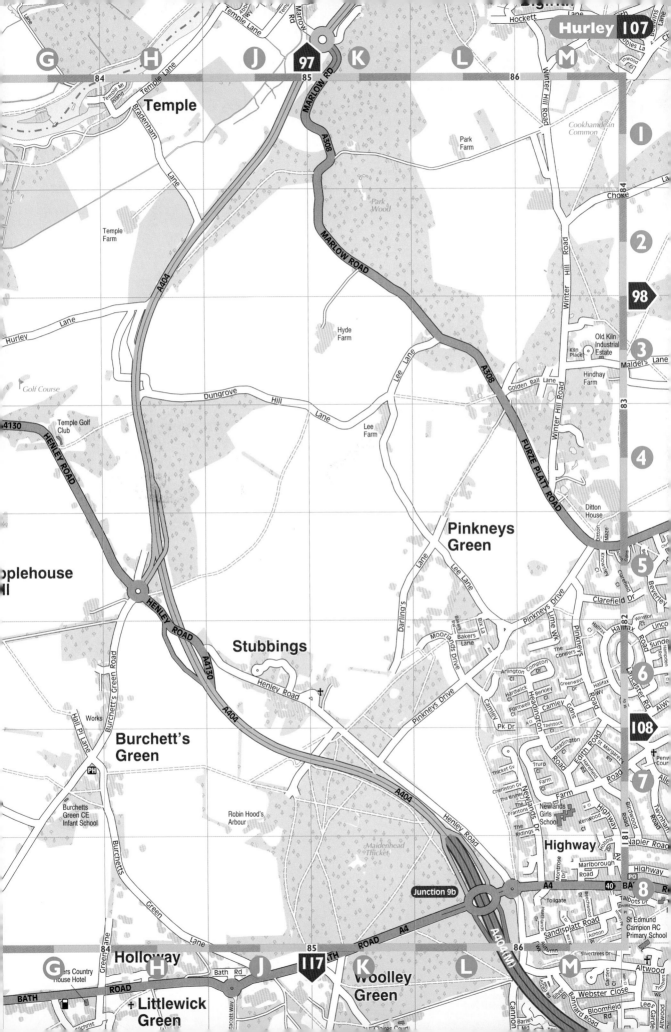

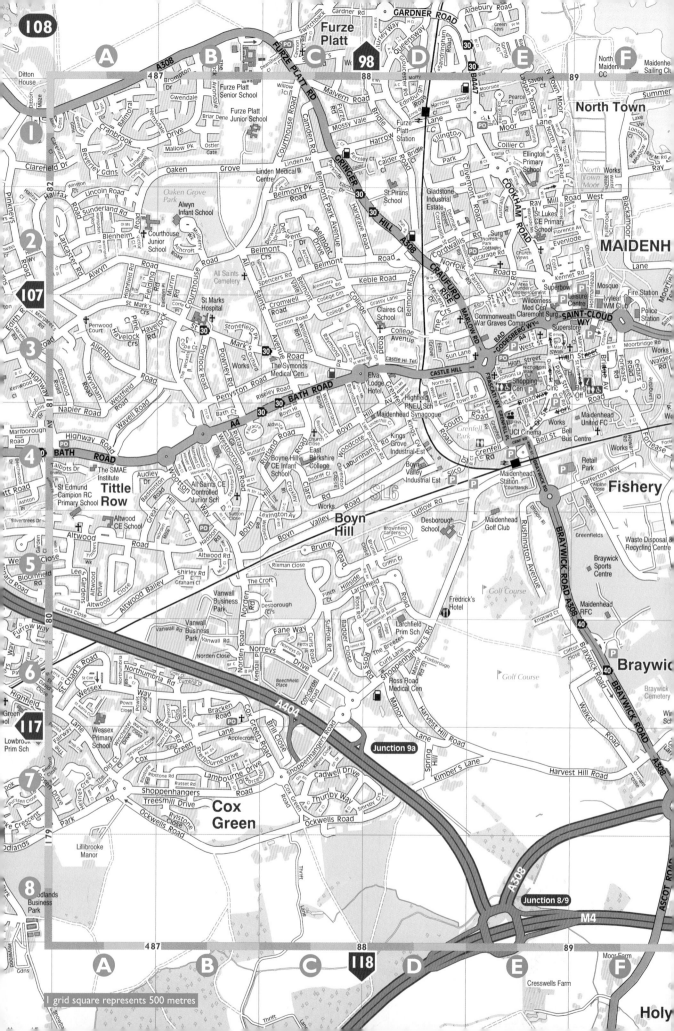

Map Labels

Grid references (top): G · H · J · 99 / 91 · K · L · M · 92

Grid references (right, top to bottom): I · 82 · 2 · Lent Rise · 3 · 18 · B3026 · 4 · LA · 110 · 5 · 80 · 6 · 7 · 178 · 8

Grid references (bottom): G · H · 90 · J · 119 / 91 · K · L · M · 92

Place names
- Taplow
- Lent
- Lent Rise
- Bray
- Dorney Reach

Roads and features
- Ray Mill Road (A4094)
- Woodhurst Rd
- Boulter's Lock
- Ray Mill Island
- Mill Lane
- Berry Hill
- Boundary Road
- Hitcham Road
- Hitcham Lane
- Poplar Farm
- Milner Road
- Burlington Road
- Harkness Road
- Eastfield Road
- Maypole Road
- Fairview Road
- Coulson Way
- Oldfield Rd Industrial Estate
- Oldfield Rd
- Bridge Road A4
- Thames Riviera Hotel
- Maidenhead Rowing Club
- Ellington Court
- Silchester Manor School
- Approach Road
- Bath Road A4
- Institute Road
- Taplow Works
- Taplow Station
- Station Road
- Taplow Health Centre
- Superstore
- Chauntry Road
- Astor Primary School
- Cannock Cl
- Chiltern
- Cotswold
- River Thames
- Bray Road B3028
- Avenue Road
- Glebe Rd
- Church Rd
- Fishery Road
- Amerden Ponds
- Ye Meads
- West Town Farm
- Barge Farm
- Jubilee River (Maidenhead, Windsor & Eton Flood Alleviation Scheme)
- Thames Path
- Amerden House
- Amerden Lane
- Old Marsh Lane
- Marsh Lane
- Glebe Close
- Green Lane
- Vicarage Walk
- Vicarage Drive
- Church Lane
- Ferry Road
- The Causeway
- High Street
- Hanover Mead
- Braybank
- Beaufort Place
- River Gardens
- Old Mill Lane
- Monkey Island Lane
- Dorney County Combined School
- Harcourt Close
- Harcourt Road
- Oak Stubbs Lane
- Meadow Way
- M4
- Monkey Island Hotel
- Monkey Island
- Dorney Reach Road
- Ashfo
- Dorney Court
- Court Lane
- Hibbert Road
- The Binghams
- Upper Bray Road
- Bray Road B3028
- Windsor Road A308
- Canon Hill Way
- Priors Way
- Priors Way Industrial Estate
- Bray Court
- Court Close
- Eskdale
- Springfield Park
- Byland Drive
- Cemetery
- Windsor Road A308
- Bray Marina
- Queen's Eyot
- Works
- Monkey Island Lane
- Broadwater
- Tithe Barn Drive

Schools and notable buildings
- St Nicholas CE Combined School
- Taplow Court
- Taplow House Hotel
- Stockwells
- Claires Court School
- Ray Park Road
- Ray Lodge Mews

G H J **103** K L M

02 03 04

A412

Wood Lane Close

Billet Lane

The Close

Lower Mead

Swallowdale

Moorwards

Hardings Row

Coopers Row

White Lodge

Bangors Road So

Works

I

Palmer's Mool

Norwood Lane

Martindale

Beeches Way

V

IVER LANE

82

2

St Johns

Wood Lane

Swallow Street

Love Green Lane

SLO

Iver Ldg

Coppins Lane

Coppins

Huntsmoor Park

Ford Lane

B470

Colne valley Way

Beeches Way

Heath Lodge

Love Lane

Barnfield Road

Evreham Road

Iver Village Junior School

Cecil Rd

Swan

Iver

Old Orch

Colne Brook

3

81

Shreding Green

Honeysuckle Close

Hollybush Lane

B470 LANGLEY PARK ROAD

Stonecroft Av

Widecroft Rd

B470

HIGH ST

Surgery

Drive

High St

B470

Works

Thorney Lane North

M25

Reed Cl

Iver Village Infant School

Blythe Cl

Old Orch

Barnes Way

30

Marina Way

Victoria Cts

Beeches Way

4

PARK ROAD

Iverdale Cl

Langley Park Road

Lossie Dr

Mansion Lane

Leacroft Road

Leas

Reed Cl

Dutton Dr

Ward Close

Way

Colne Orch

Homsdale Lane

Court Lane

114

80

Parsonage Farm

Iver Golf & Leisure Centre

Hollow Hill Lane

Trading Estate

Ridge

Way

Works

5

Golf Course

Grand Union Canal Walk

Grand Union Canal

Works

Colne valley Way

6

Industrial Estate

Iver Station

Thorney Lane South

Bathurst Walk

Bathurst Close

PO

Golf Course

Thorney Pa Golf Club

T

Mead Wk

Mead Cl

Tilbury Wk

Maplin Av

Maplin PK

Southwood

Market Lane

St James Walk

Syke Cluan

Wellesley Avenue

Somerset Way

Thorney Ml Rd

Colne Valley Way

179

M25

7

Meadfield Road

Ember Road

Parlaunt Park Combined School

Ash

Radclot

Syke Ings

Richings Park Sports Club

Richings

Way

St Leonards Walk

Thorney House

Richings Park

Richings Pl

North PK

Kennett

Hinksey Cl

Windrush Av

Burroway Road

Sharney Av

Seacourt Road

Parlaunt Road

North Park Parlaunt Road

Main Dr

Walnut Grov

St Leonards Walk

Old Slade Lane

The Poyntins

The Richings

8

Tamar Way

Longwood Way

Hurricane Wy

Blunden Dr

Deverills Wy

Gresholm Wy

Stornaway Rd

Heron Dr

Richings Park Golf Club

Junction 15/4b

G H **123** J K L M

02 03 04

Sutton

Golf Course

Colne Valley Way

Buckinghamshire County

M4

Old Slade La

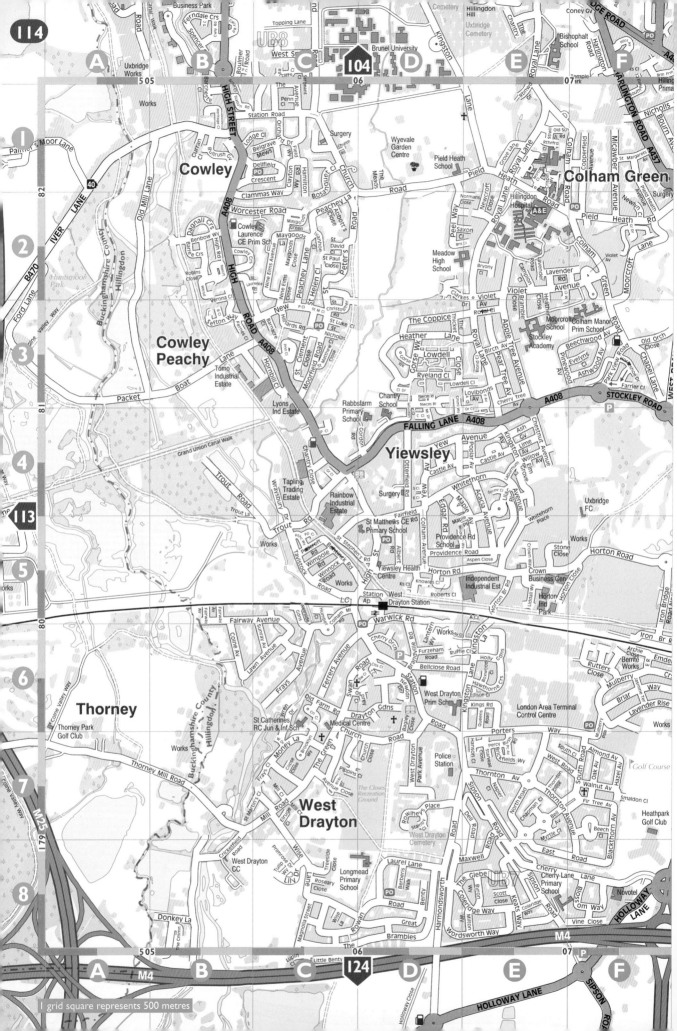

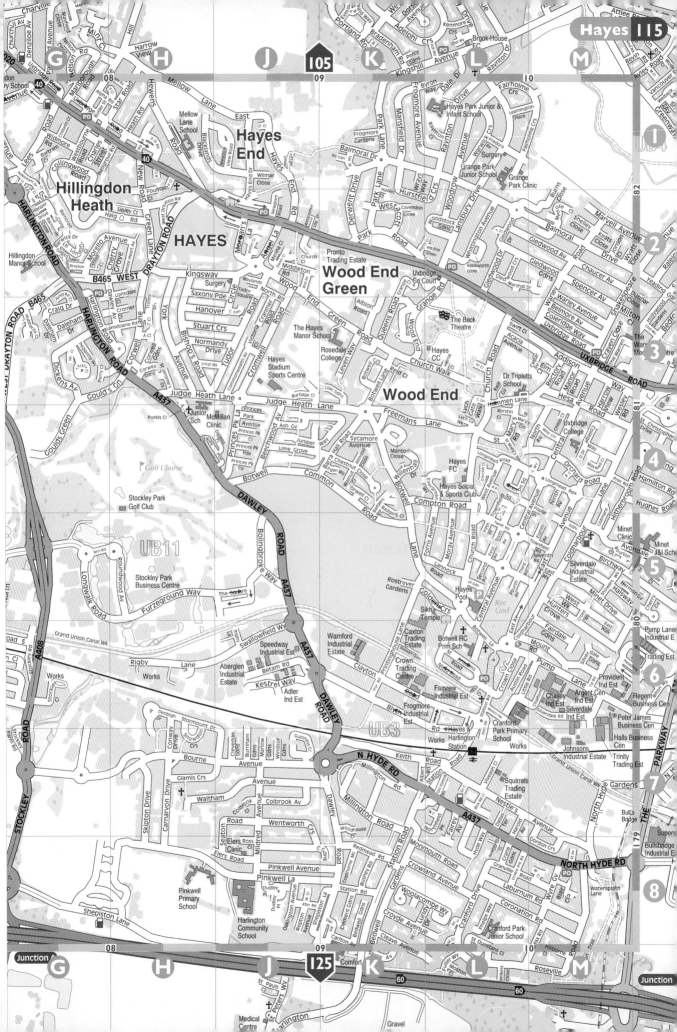

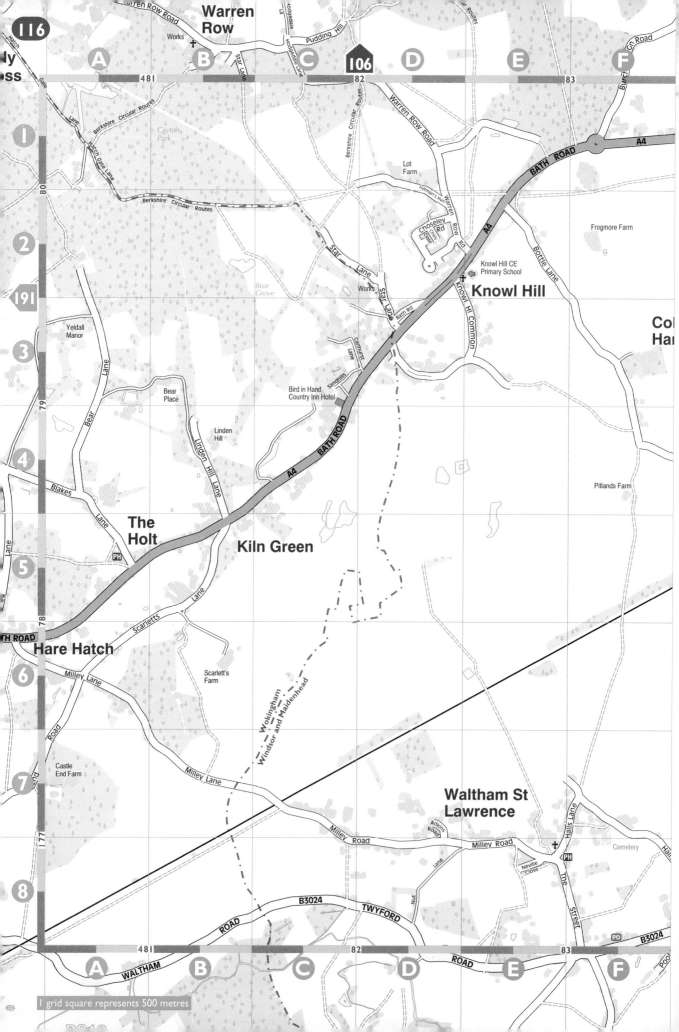

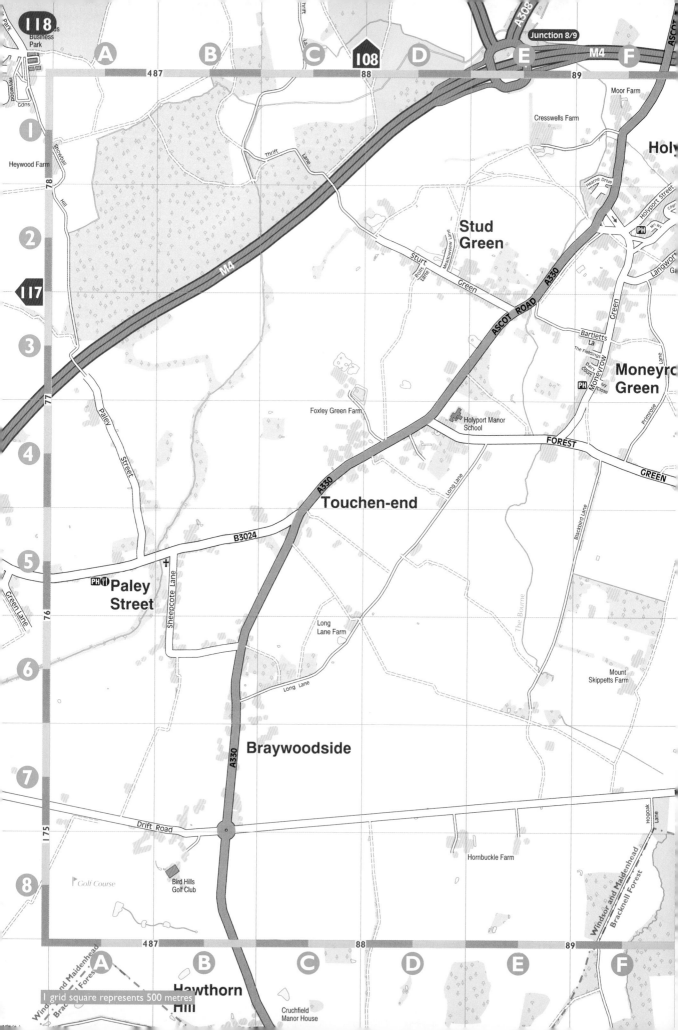

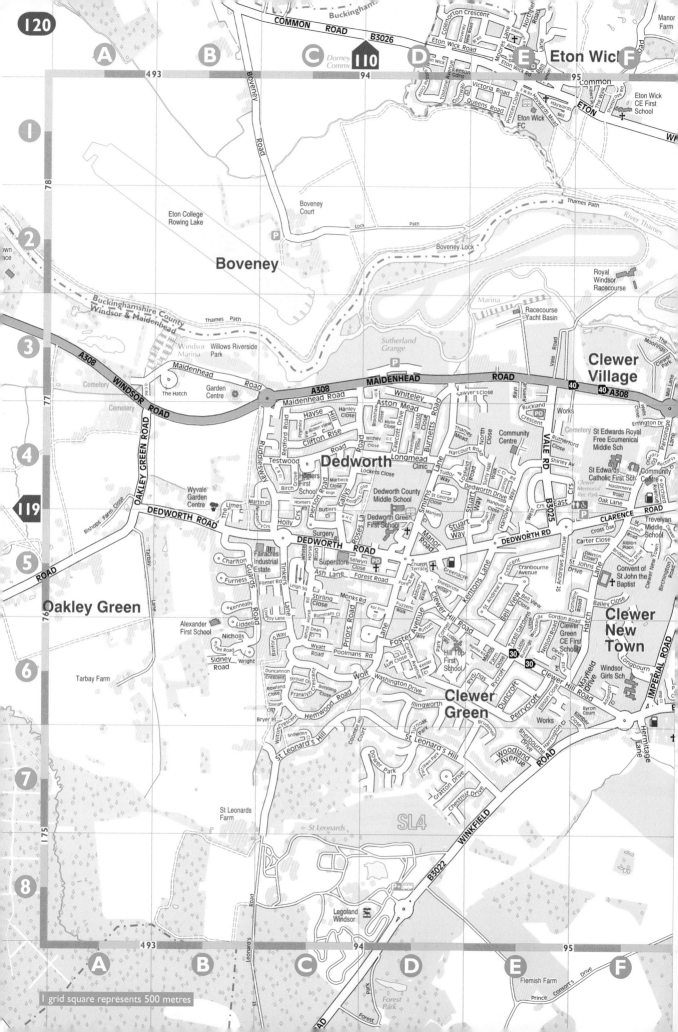

Junction 1

Sutton

Golf Course

Richings Park
Golf Club

113

Buckinghamshire County

M4

Slough

Old Slade La

Colne Valley Way

Slough Hillingdon

Lakeside Industrial Estate

LONDON ROAD

Quality Hotel

PO

Pepys Cl

Brands Road

Springfield Road

A4 COLNBROOK BY-PASS

Colne Valley Way

Lakeside Industrial Estate

Lakeside Road

Brands Hill

Mildridge Farm

Horton Road

High Street

Vicarage Wy

Mill St

Works

Coln Industrial Estate

Colnbrook

Slough Windsor and Maidenhead

Colne Brook

Colnbrook CE Primary School

Bridge Park

PO Albany

Fawsley Cl

Laurel Coleridge Crs

Aintree

Dawley Ride

Winchester

Raymond Cl

The Hawthorns

The Pippins Sch

Coln Industrial Est

Galleymead Road

Poyle

Bath Rd

Rodney Way

Daventry Cl

Bath Road

Colnbrook Sports Club

Junction 14

Poyle Road

Millbrook

Mathisen Wy

Meadowbrook Cl

124

Coln dale

Arkwright Rd

Britannia Industrial Est

Willow Road

David Road

Polygon Business Centre

Junction 14

McKay Trading Est

Prescott Rd

Blackthorne Road

Blackthorne Crs

Augustine

Stanwell Road

Foundry La

Mill Lane

Cherry Wy

Colne Bank

Horton Trading Estate

Manor Farm

Stanwell Road

Poyle Rd

Viscount Industrial Est

Trident Industrial Estate

Newlands

Calder Wy

Horton Rd

River Colne

Junction 14

A3113 AIRPORT

Works

Leylands La

Horton

Flintlock

Spout Lane

Horton Rd

Coppermill Road

Windsor and Maidenhead Surrey County

Wraysbury Reservoir

Wraysbury River

M25

Silverbeck Wy Vine

Leylands La

Meadow View

PO

Sheffield

Horton Rd

Horton

Benen Stock Rd

Works

Farm La

Russet Cl

Hithermoor Rd

Stanwell Moor

Colne Valley Way

Hithermoor Rd

124

A Donkey Lane B 505 C 114 D E M4 07 F

M4

1

78

HOLLOWAY LANE

SIPSON ROAD

Russell Gdns

Sipson

Slough
2 Hilling River Colne Saxon Way Moor Lane Harmonds-worth A3044 PO High St Cambridge Cl Priory Wy Harmondsworth Lane Heathrow Primary School Vineries Cl Hollycroft Close Chamber Business Park Vincent Cl A408 SIPSON

Accommodation Lane Moorland Road School Summ Hatch Candover Close Wilton Cl Hollycroft Gardens Sipson Cl Bomer Close Ashby Way

77

3 Tarmac Way Speedbird Wy Speedbird Wy COLNBROOK BY-PASS A4 LANE Skyport Dr Zealand Av Pinglestone Close Airport Gate Business Centre Junction 4a Blunts Avenue

STANWELL MOOR ROAD A3044 Baysfarm Ct Bath Road PO BATH ROAD Newbury Rd Newbury Rd 50 West Ramp Coach Park West Ramp

4 Heathrow Cl Thistle Hotel BATH ROAD P Newbury Rd P Fire & Ambulance Station

123 Works Longford Northern Perimeter Rd (West) Northolt Rd Northolt Rd Northern Perimeter Rd (West) P

5 A3044 Western Perimeter Road

76

STANWELL Western Perimeter Road

TW6

Heathrow Terminal 5 Station Terminal 5

D'Albiac House

Airbus Coach Station

6 River Colne Bedfont Court P Arrivals Bus & Coach S Terminal 3 Departures P

Burrows Hill Cl

AIRF Works Spout Lane North

7 WAY Spout Lane MOOR

175

8 Horton Road Southern Perimeter Road Seaforth Rd Sandringham Rd Riverside Shoreham Road (West) Shoreham Road (East) Heathrow World Cargo Centre

Stanwell
Stanwell Place

Stanwell
oor A 505 B C D PO Southern Perimeter Road E 07 F

1 grid square represents 500 metres PARK RD Gibson Stanwell Gdns High St Callis Farm Court Farm Industrial Estate Bedfont Road Sealand Road

B378

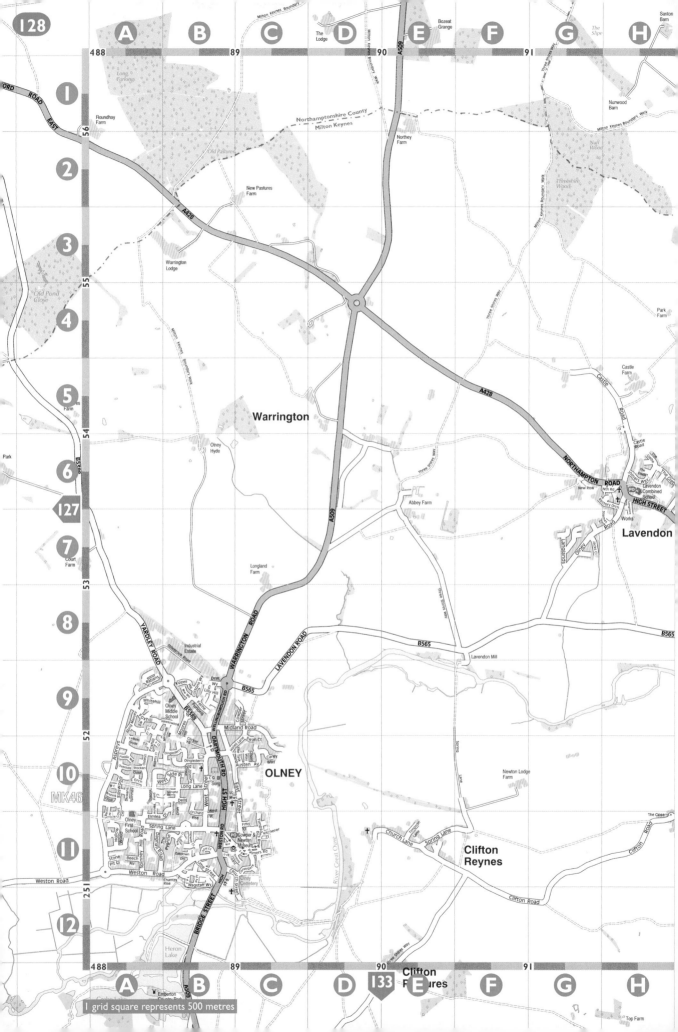

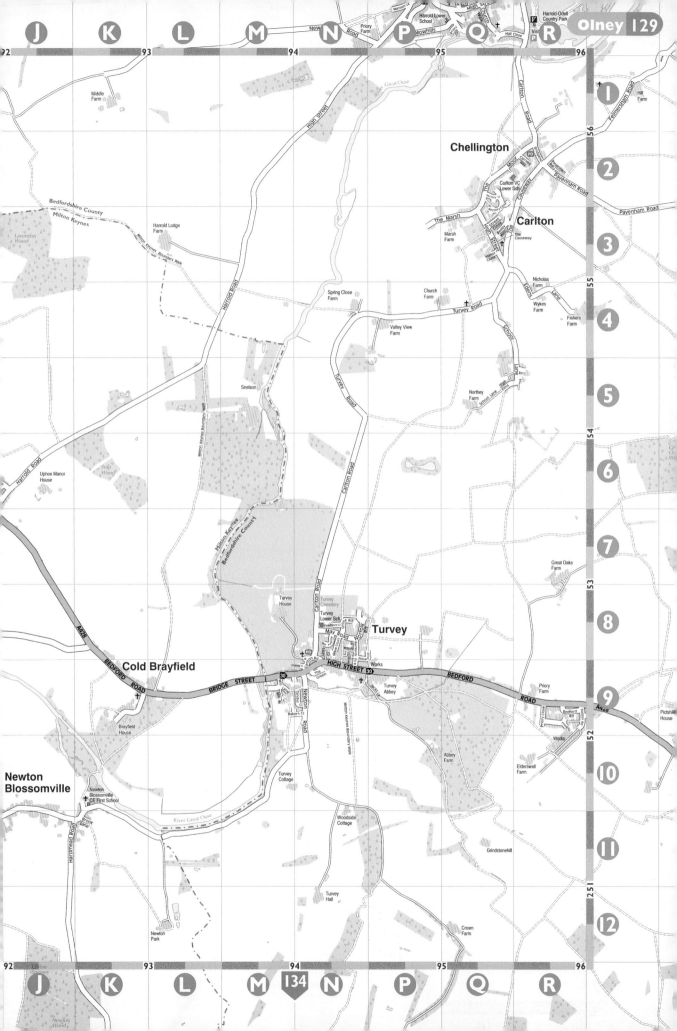

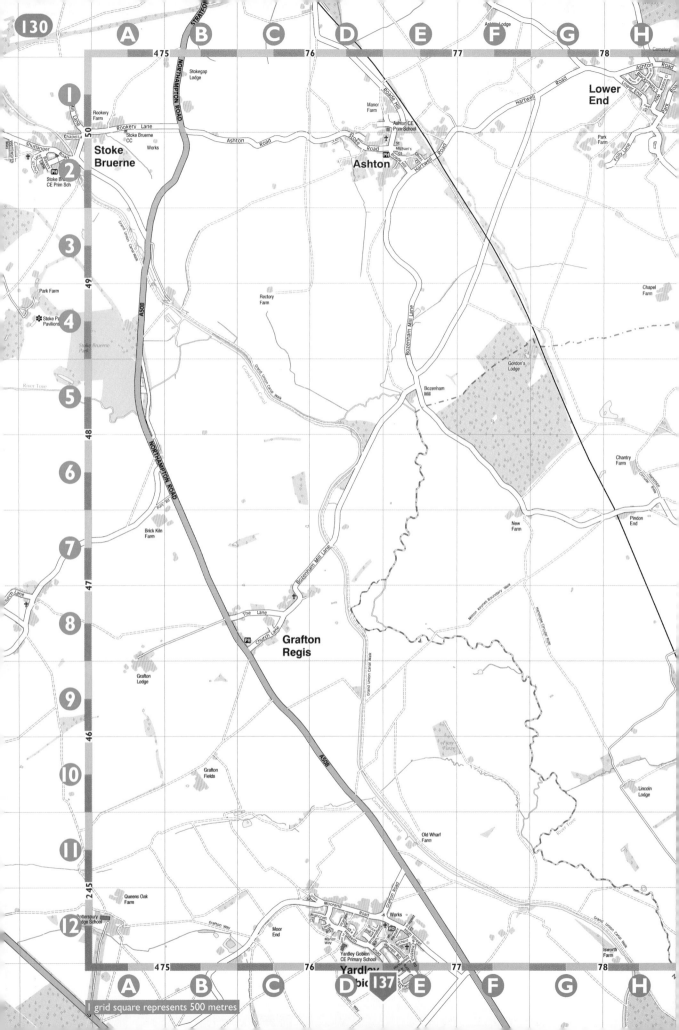

A B C D E F G H

475 76 77 78

50 49 48 47 46 45

Stoke Bruerne

Rookery Farm
Rookery Lane
Stokegap Lodge
Stoke Bruerne CC
Works
Chapel La
Shutlanger Road
Stoke Bruerne CE Prim Sch
PH

NORTHAMPTON ROAD
STRATFORD

A508

Mill Lane

Park Farm

Stoke Bruerne Pavilions
Stoke Bruerne Park

River Tove

Grand Union Canal Walk
Grand Union Canal

Church Lane

Brick Kiln Farm
Pury Rd

Ashton

Manor Farm
Ashton CE Prim School
St Michael's
Rooke Hill
Stoke Road
Ashton Road
PH
Hartwell Road

Rectory Farm

Bozenham Mill Lane
Bozenham Mill

Gordon's Lodge

New Farm

Pindon End

Lower End

Ashton Road
Lower End
Park Farm
Colly Lane

Chapel Farm

Chantry Farm

Milton Keynes Boundary Walk

Hanslope Circular Ride

River Tove

Lincoln Lodge

Grafton Regis

The Lane
Church Lane
PH

Grafton Lodge

Grafton Fields

Grand Union Canal Walk

Old Wharf Farm

Queens Oak Farm

Pottersbury Lodge School

Moorend Road
Grafton Road
Works
Moor End
Grafton Way

Manor Way
Yardley Gobion
Yardley Gobion CE Primary School

Isworth Farm

Grand Union Canal Walk

475 76 77 78

A B C D E F G H

1 grid square represents 500 metres

I 2 3 4 5 6 7 8 9 10 11 12

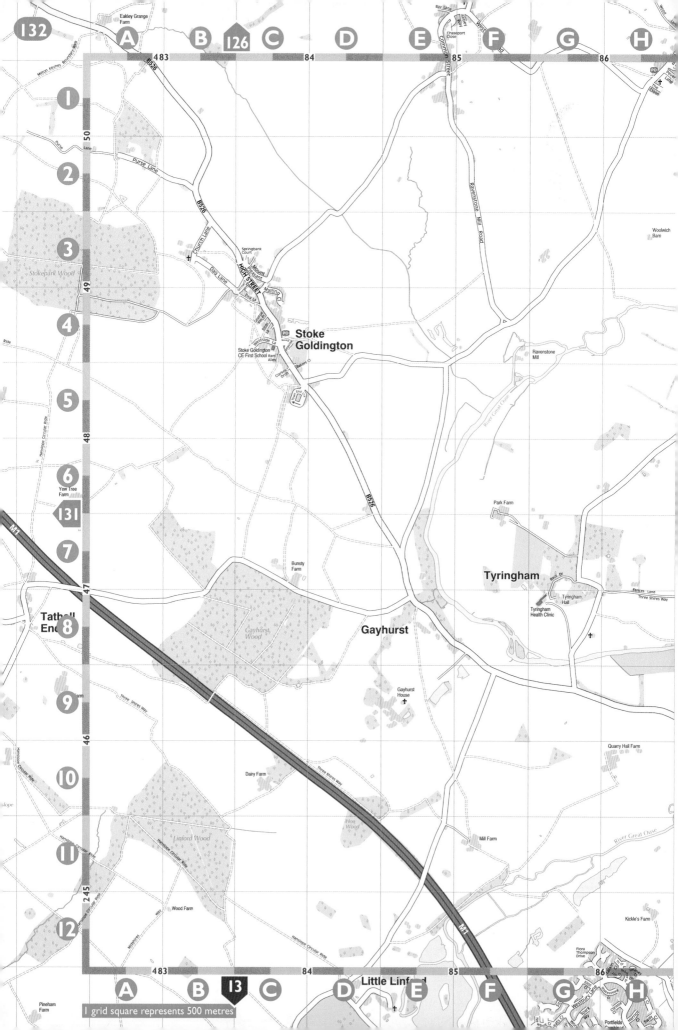

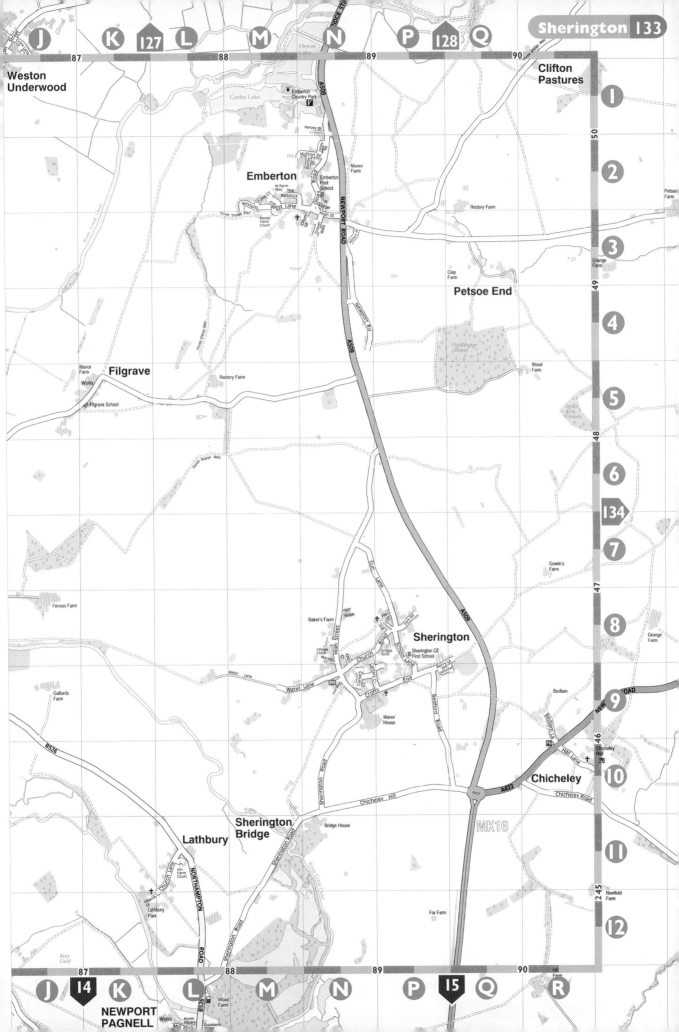

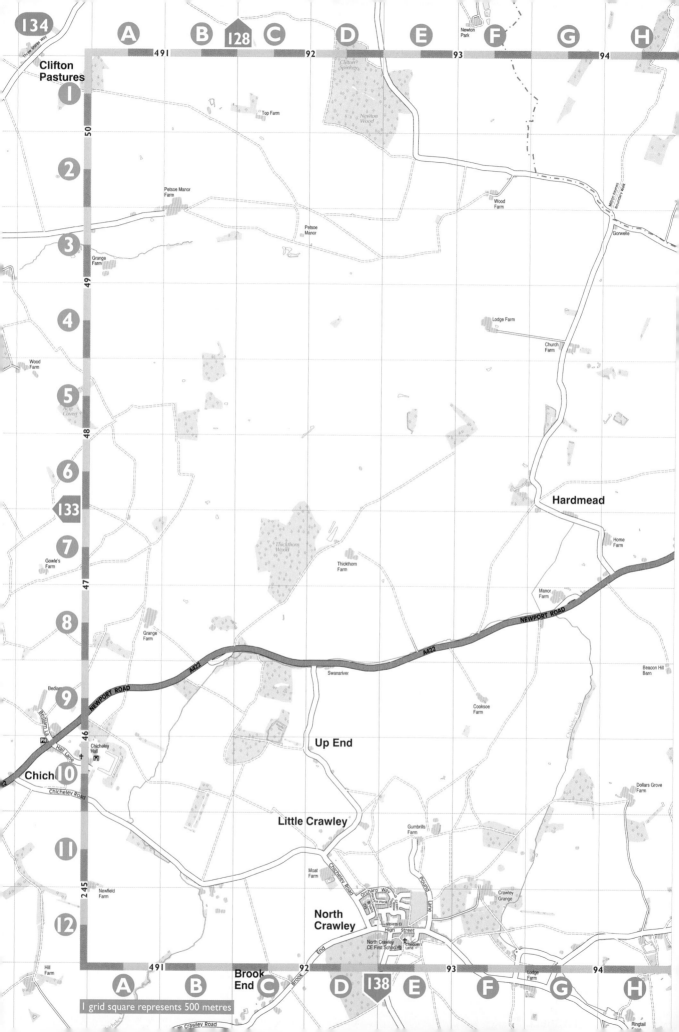

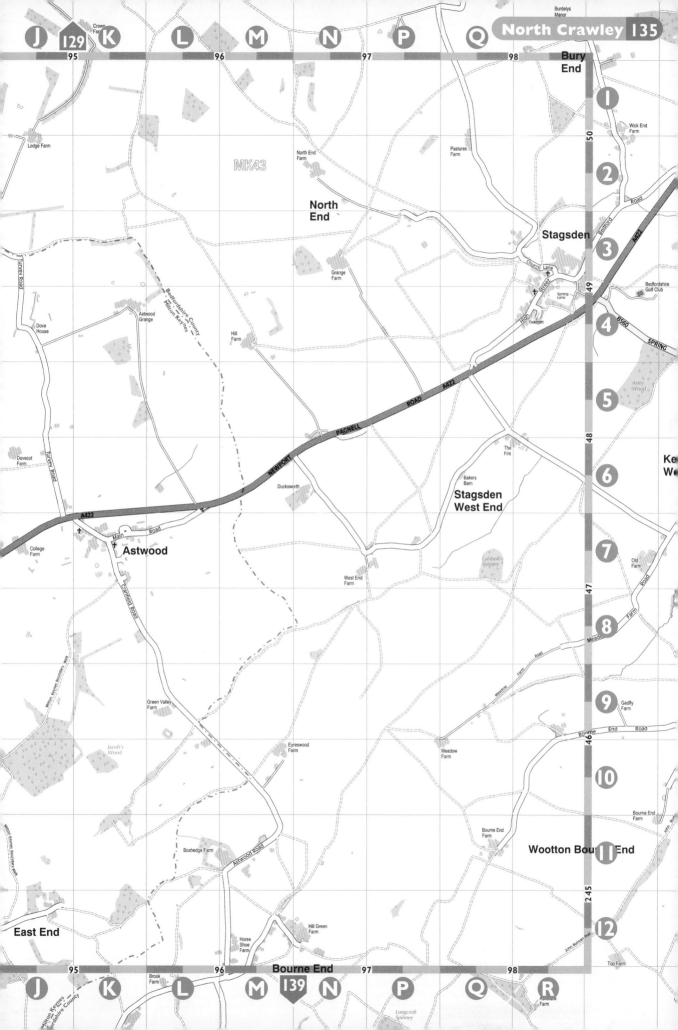

136

A B C D E F G H

471 72 73 74

44

Potter
Lodge

Bradlem
Pond

King's
Copse

Waterslade
Copse

1

2

Grafton Way

Bear's
Copse

Whittlewood
Forest

Lady
Copse

Old Tun
Copse

Say's
Copse

Kennels   Drive

Wakefield
Farm

3

43

Buckingham Thick
Copse

Northamptonshire County

Buckinghamshire County

Main Drive

Wakefield
Lodge

4

Linshire
Copse

Home
Farm

Briary
Wood

Wakefield
Lawn

Redmoor
Copse

Birch
Copse

5

42

Manor
House

Briary Wood
Farm

Heathencote Drive

East Ashills
Copse

Lovel
Wood

6

Boundary
Farm

Briary
Wood

141

7

41

Keyes
Farm

Forest
Farm

8

Lillingstone
Lovell

Bradley Fields
Farm

Wicken
Wood

Hurst
Farm

Church   Brookside

9

40

Leckhampstead
Wood

Lillingstone Dayrell

10

A413

Hill Farm

Lillingstone House

Northamptonshire County

Buckinghamshire County

Cross

11

239

Leckhampstead Road

12

Park
Copse

Stockholt Farm

471 72 73 74

A B C 142 D E F G H

Lodge
Farm

Akeley Wood
Junior School

1 grid square represents 500 metres

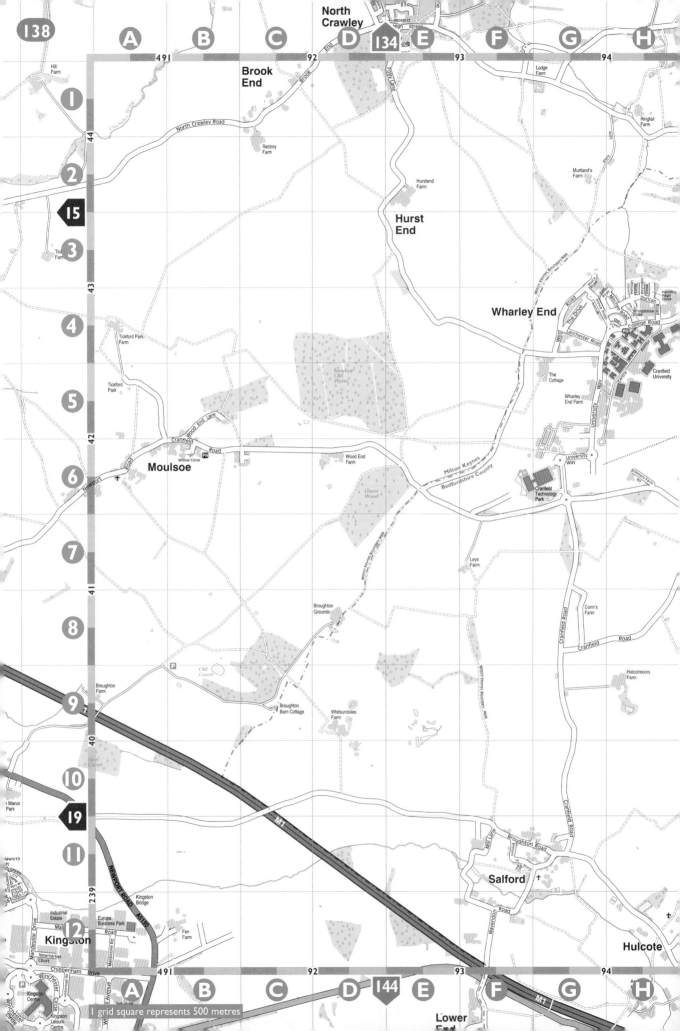

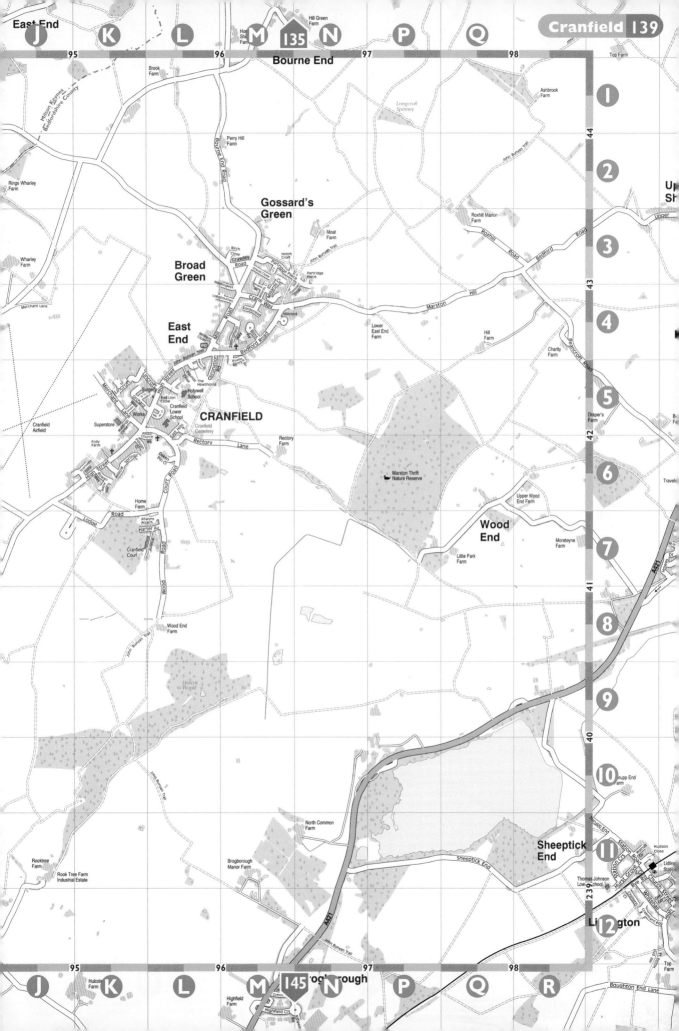

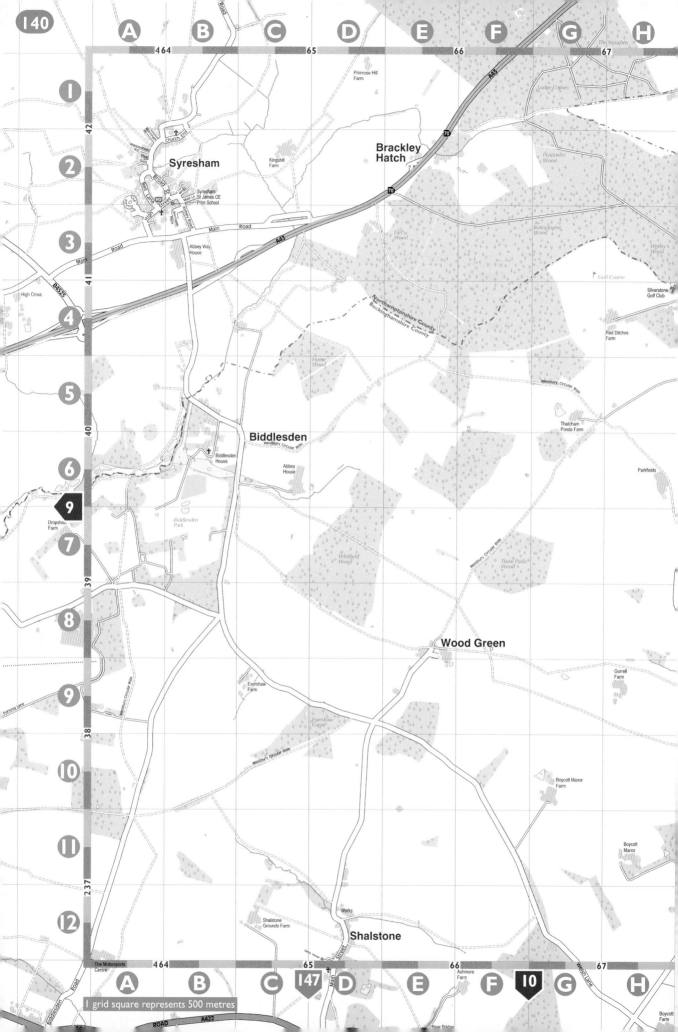

J K L M N P Q

68 69 70 71

I
2
136
3
4
5
6
7
8
9
10
142
11
12

42
41
40
39
38
237

Coldthorn

Hall Hotel

Whittlebury Park Golf
& Country Club

f Course

Chapel
Copse

Linslow
Copse

Birch
Copse

Northamptonshire County
Buckinghamshire County

Becketts
Corner

Loxel
Wood

Boundary
Farm

Shrine's
Wood

Hatch-
hill Wood

Hatch-hill
Farm

Stowe
Corner

Keyes
Farm

**Lillings
Lovell**

Point
Copse

Sawpits
Wood

Heine
Wood

Blackpit
Farm

Stowe
Woods

Lillingstone **hyrell**

Woodlands
Farm

Tile House
Farm

Bycell   Road

Lillingstone House

Tilehouse
Wood

Charmandean
School

Tile House
Farm

Whitehouse

Akeley
Wood
Farm

Dadford

Stockholt Farm

Bourbon
Tower

Bycell Road

Cedars
Close

St James & St Joh
CE Primary Schoo

Ak

Home
Farm

Akeley Wood
School

Akeley Wood
School

Stowe School

Stowe
House

Stowe Landscape
Gardens

Palladian
Bridge

Stowe Castle
Farm

Stowe Castle
Business Park

142

ampstead Road

Stowe
Park

The Lake

Oxford
Water

Bycell
Farm

Bycell Road

New Inn
Farm

Corinthian
Arch

11

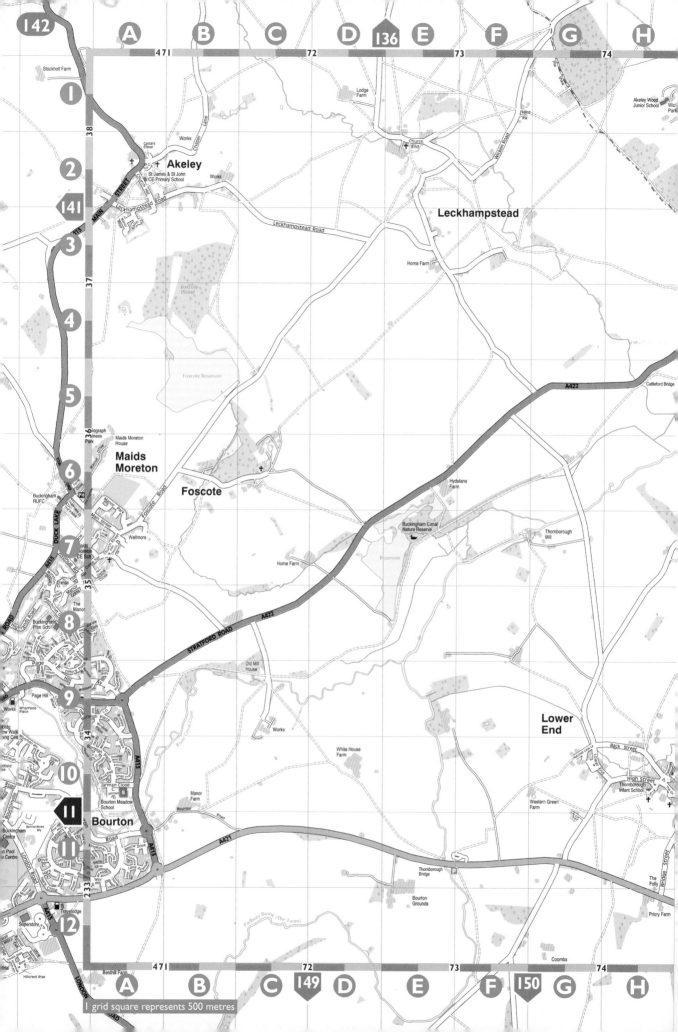

A 471 B 72 C D 136 E F G 73 H 74

1

Stockolt Farm

38

2 Akeley

141

3 37

4

5

36

Maids
Moreton

Foscote

6

Buckingham
RUFC

DUCK LAKE

7 35

8

Page
Hill

9

Page Hill

34

10

11 Bourton

11

233

Lower
End

12

Travelodge

Superstore

A 471 B 72 C 149 D E F G 73 150 H 74

Leckhampstead

Lodge
Farm

Church
End

Leckhampstead Road

Home Farm

A422

Cattleford Bridge

Akeley Wood
Junior School

Hydelane
Farm

Buckingham Canal
Nature Reserve

Thornborough
Mill

Reservoir

Home Farm

A422

STRATFORD ROAD

Old Mill
House

Works

White House
Farm

Manor
Farm

A421

Thornborough
Bridge

Bourton
Grounds

Back Street

High Street
Thornborough
Infant School

Western Green
Farm

The
Folly

Priory Farm

Coombs

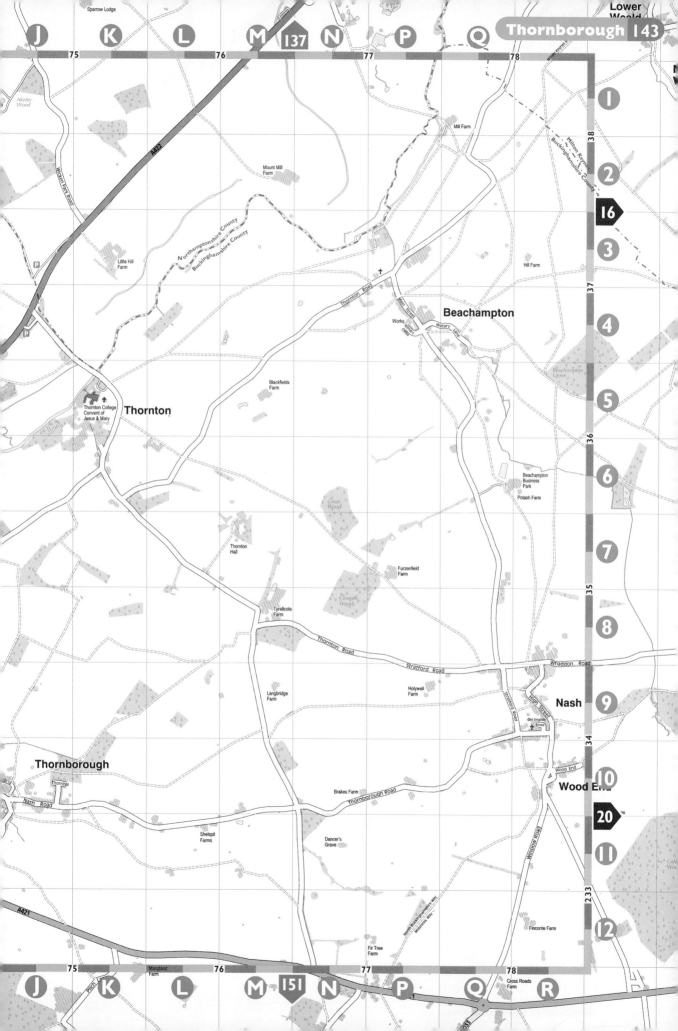

J K L M 139 N P Q

95 96 97 98

Brogborough

Boughton End Lane

1

38

Boughton
End 2

Boulevard Road

Highfield
Farm

New
Crescent

Highfield Crs

Flying
Farm 3

Hulcote
Farm

Salford Road

Bedford Road

Junction 13

Salford Station Road

Ridgmont
Station LC

A507 37

4

Hayfield
Farm

A507

M1

Beckerings
Park

Station Road

Bedford Road

A5012

Woburn
Experimental
Farm

Lydas Hill

High Street

5

36

Ridgmont

Church
End

Husborne
Crawley

School Lane

Crow Lane

Husborne Crawley
Lower School

Church Street

Segenhoe
Manor

Ridgmont
Lower School

6

Aspley Guise
Lower School

Guise
Court

Crawley
Park

San Remo Rd

Ridgmont Road

Eversholt Road

Horsepool Lane

A5012

Sandy Lane
Plantation

Cobb Lane

7

35

Sandy Lane

Crawleyheath
Farm

Hay
Wood

Berry End

8

Birchmoor
Farm

The
Evergreens

Woburn
Safari Park

9

34

Birchmoor
Green

CRAWLEY ROAD

TURNPIKE ROAD

10

New
Water E

Bedford Street

Drapers

Surgery

Eleanor
Close

Froxfield

Whitnoe
Orchard Pond

Woburn
Park

11

33

Woburn

High Street

The
Bell Hotel

Works

Park Street

Park
Farm

Horse
Pond

Charcoal
Pond

Water
Farm

Eversholt

Woburn Lower School
Woburn Heritage Centre

Market
Pl

The Inn at
Woburn Hotel

Bloomsbury
Close

London End
Street

George Street

Greensand Ridge Walk

Basin
Pond

Shoulders of
Mutton Pond

Duncombe's
Breeches
Pond

12

95 96 97 98

Greensand Ridge Walk

Woburn
Abbey

Eversholt
Lower

Linden
Lake

J K L M N P Q R

London Road

Speedwell
Farm

New
Pond

Abbot's
Oak

Lower Hopgarden
Pond

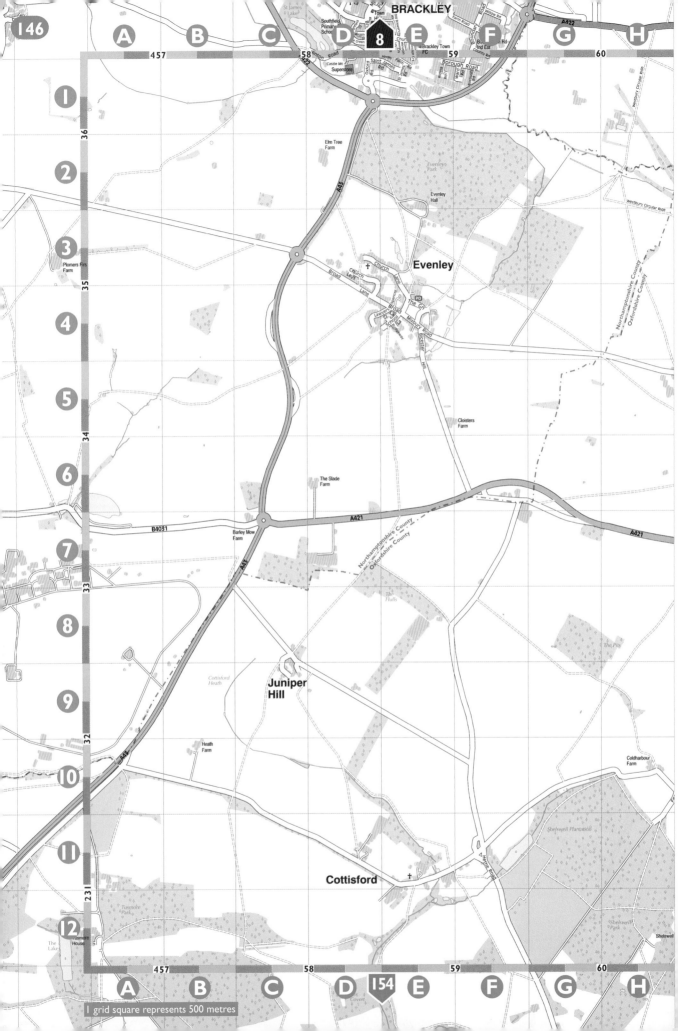

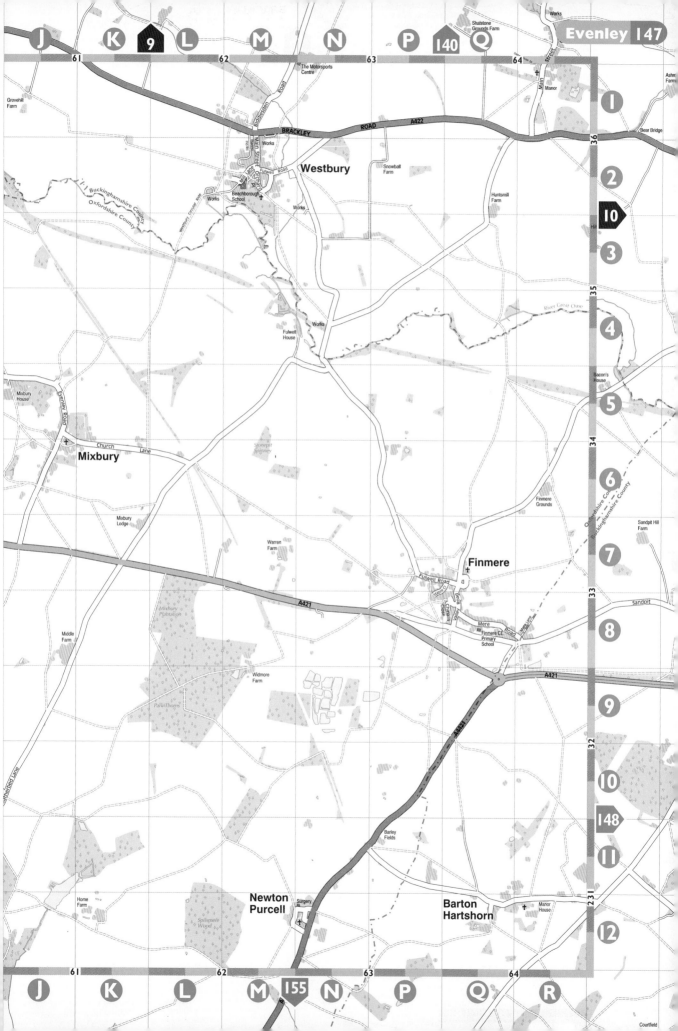

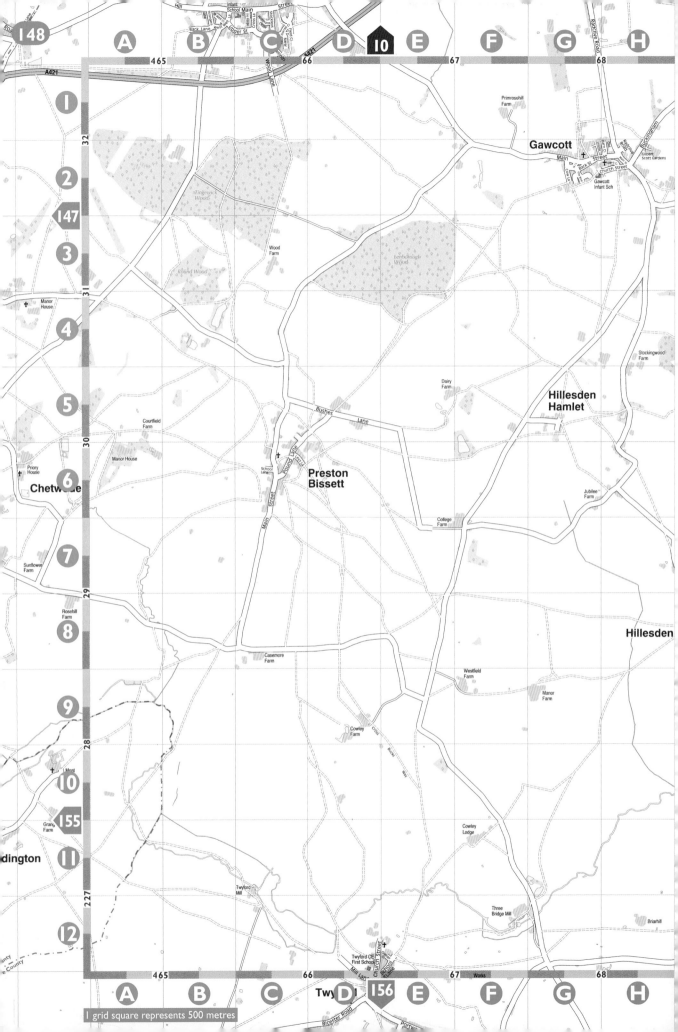

A   B   C   D   10   E   F   G   H

A421
465
Wood Lane
66
67
68

I

32

Primroshill Farm

Gawcott

2

147

Main Street
Back St
Church Street
Gawcott Infant Sch
Gilbert Scott Gardens
Buckingham

3

Tingewick Woods

31

Wood Farm

Manor House

Benborough Wood

Stockingwood Farm

4

Roland Wood

Dairy Farm

Hillesden Hamlet

5

Courtfield Farm

Bushes Lane

30

Manor House

School Lane
Pound Lane

Priory House

6

Preston Bissett

Jubilee Farm

Chetwode

Main Street

College Farm

7

Sunflower Farm

29

Hillesden

Rosehill Farm

8

Casemore Farm

Westfield Farm

Manor Farm

9

Cowley Farm

Cross Way

Bucks Way

28

Moat

10

155

Cowley Lodge

Grange Farm

ddington

11

227

Twyford Mill

Three Bridge Mill

Briarhill

12

Works

County County

465
66
67
68

A   B   C   D   156   E   F   G   H

Twy   Bicester Road   Portway

Church Street
School Lane
Mill Lane
Twyford CE First School

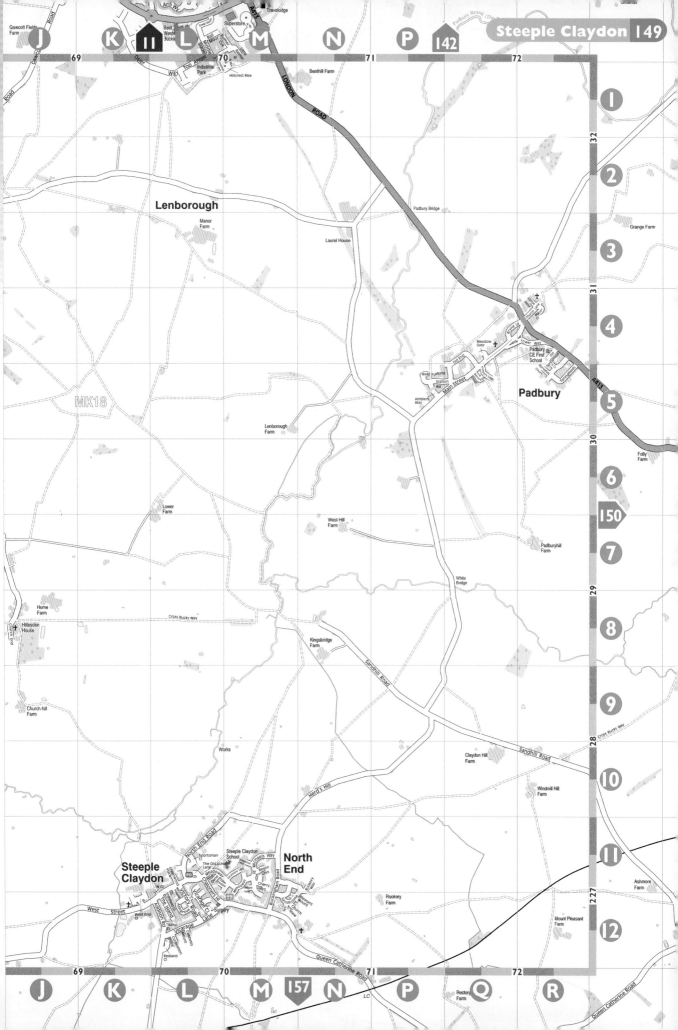

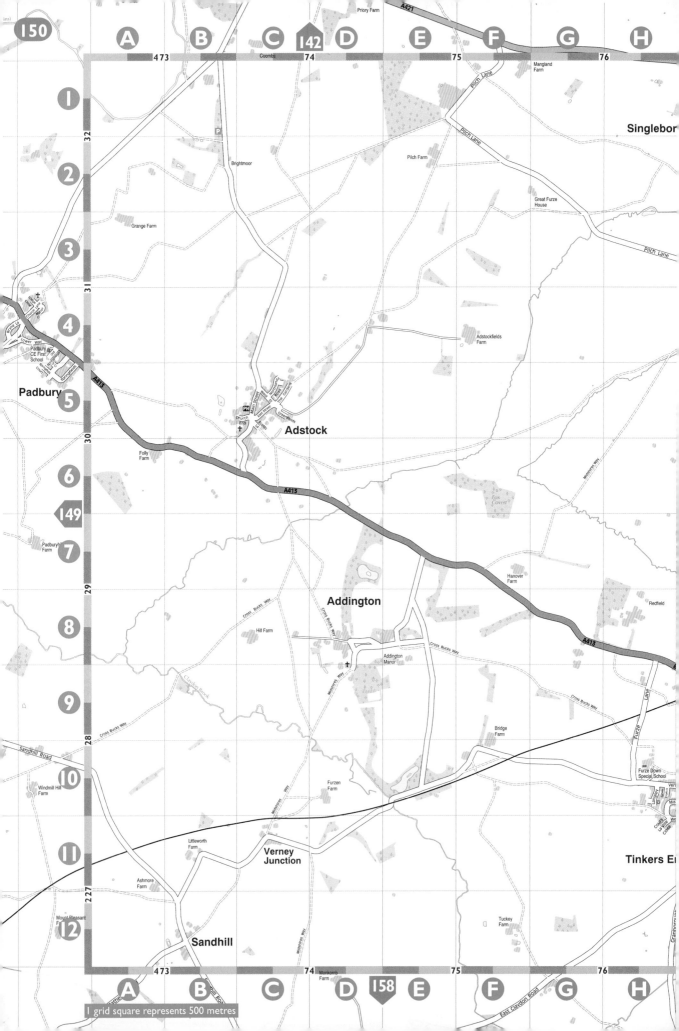

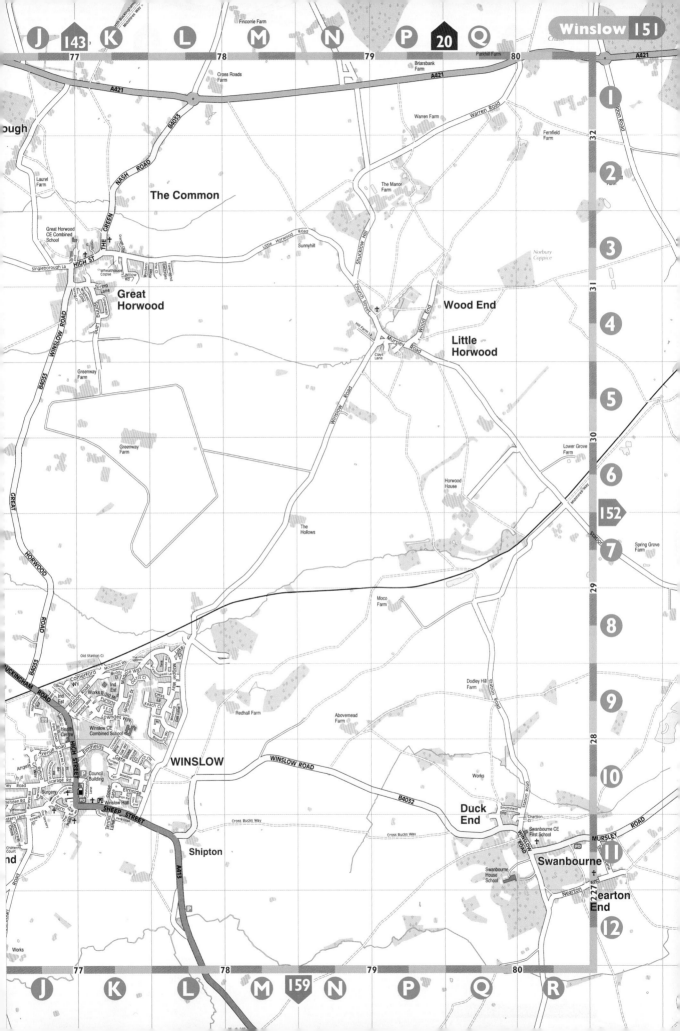

A **20** B C D A421 E F **21** G H

A421 481 82 83 84

1

32

Fernfield
Farm

2

Stearthill
Farm

Chase
Farm

Woodpond

Bletchley Leys
Farm

The
Leys

Manor
Farm

PH

Lower
End

3

Norbury
Coppice

31

Crabtree
Farm

Lower Salden
Farm

Salden
Wood

Orchard
Cl
Yew Tree
Cl
Newton Longville
CE Combined S

4

Springfield
Farm

5

30

Lower Grove
Farm

Cowpasture
Farm

MK17

6

Salden

151

7

Station Road

Spring Grove
Farm

Whaddon Road

Lwr End Yd

29

8

Mursley

Mursley CE
School

St Mary's
Close

The Beechams

Cooks   Lane

Lodge
Industrial
Centre

Carrington
Hall Rd

Newmans
courtyard

Drayton Parslow
Village School

**Drayton
Parslow**

Main

North Close

New Road

9

28

Church   Lane

High Street

Mursley
Cemetery

Harbury
House

Richmond
Lodge

Merrymead

10

Station Road

Smithfield
Rd

Charlton
Cl

Swanbourne CE
First School

SWANBOURNE   ROAD

Shorndown Equine
Clinic

B4032

Stewkley   Lane

B4032

The
Grange

11

WINSLOW
ROAD

MURSLEY   ROAD

27

Nearton End

Swanbourne

Nearton
End

Station Lane

12

Cross Bucks Way

Lower
Dean Farm

**Stewkley
De**

Dean   Road

Cross Banks

A 481 B C D **160** E 82 F 83 G 84 H

Water Eaton

Newton Longville

Stoke Hammond

Hollingdon

Soulbu

North End

Stewkley

A   B   C   D   E   F   G   H

4 65   66   67   68

1

2

3

4

5

6

7

8

9

10

11

12

30

29

28

27

26

2 25

Tusmore House

The Lake

Lime Kiln Hovel

Stoke Bushes

Lone Barn

Coneygre Farm

Fox Covert

Willaston Farm

Hethe Road

Hardwick

Tangley Farm

Hardwick Road

Hethe

Main Street

The Green

The Laurels

Friing Prim

Rectory Farm

Shelswell Park

Shelsw

Bainton Road

Hethe Brede

St Peter's

School La

The Street

Stoke Lyne

Stratton Audley Road

B4100

Stoke Little Wood

ts House

Glebe Farm

Kelly Farm

Waterloo Farm

Bainton

Watergate Farm

Cotmore Farm

Cotmore House

Stratton Aud

A4421

B4100

Fringford Lodge

Dymock's Farm

Bicester Cree

A4421

Bainton Rd

Manor House

ROW

Bucknell

Bicester Road

B4100

Caversfield House

Caversfield

Old School

Springfield Road

Fairhaven Rd

Elderfield

Woodcote Rd

Brashfield House

Thompson Rd

Bales

Gdns

Baynes End

Benmove

Barnfield Close

Huntingdon Lane

Manns Rd

Turnpike Rd

A4421

Bicester Airfield

A   B   C   D   E   F   G   H

4 65   66   67   68

Crowmarsh Farm

Hawkwell Farm

Lord's

Bucknell Road

1 grid square represents 500 metres

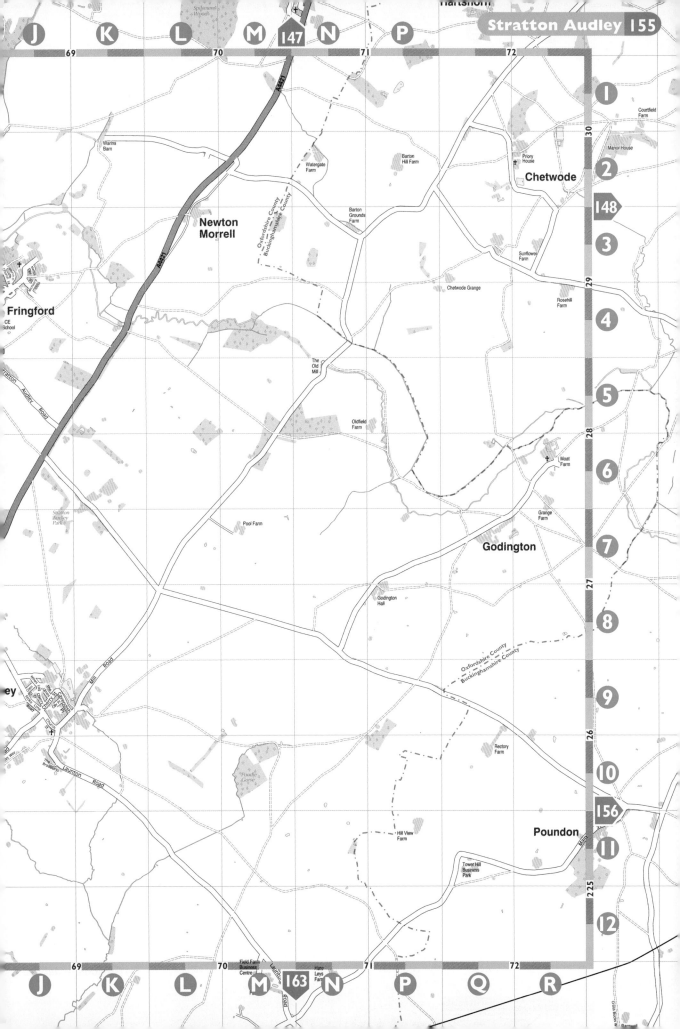

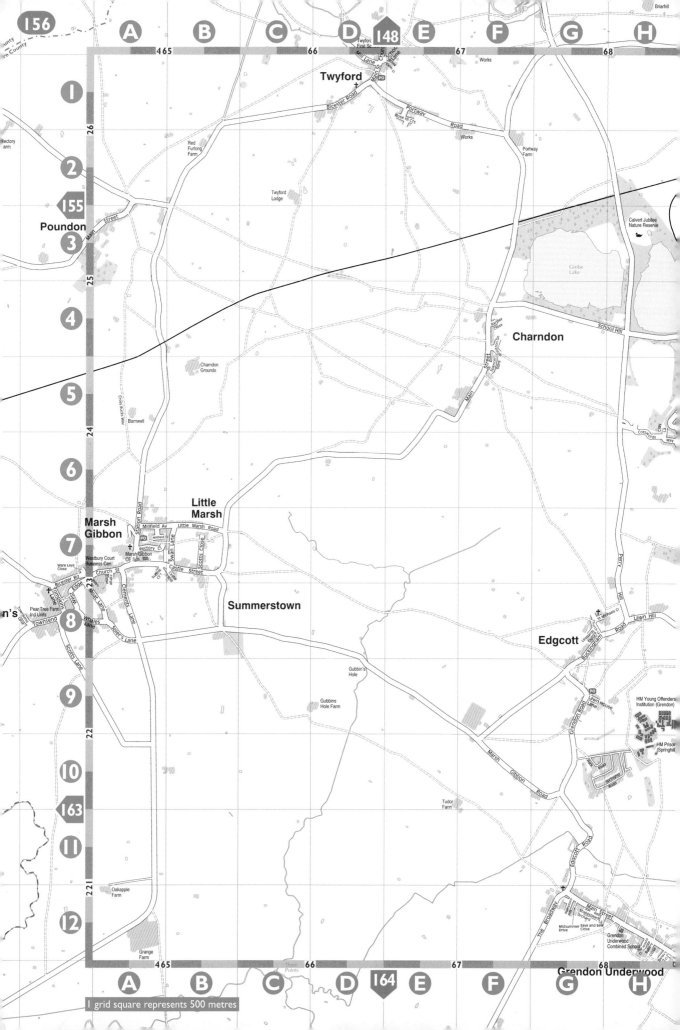

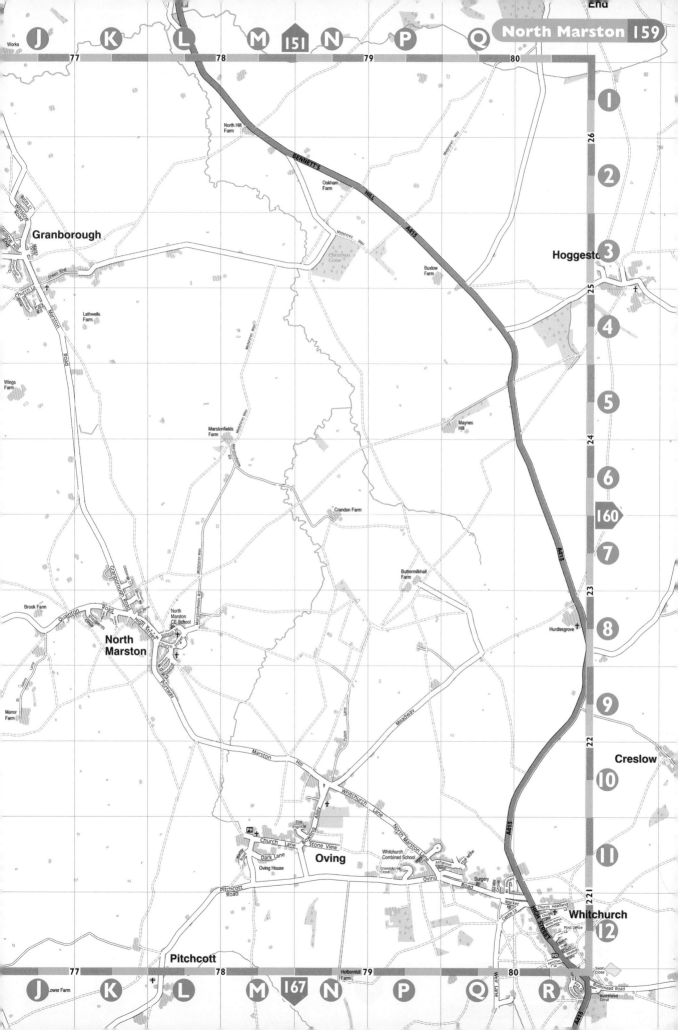

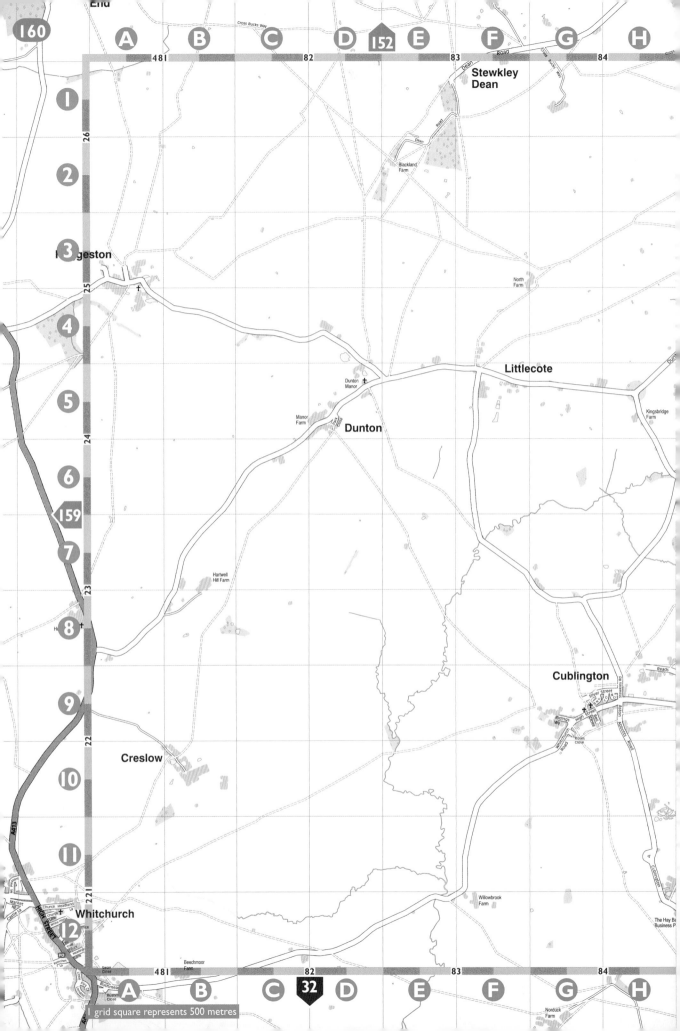

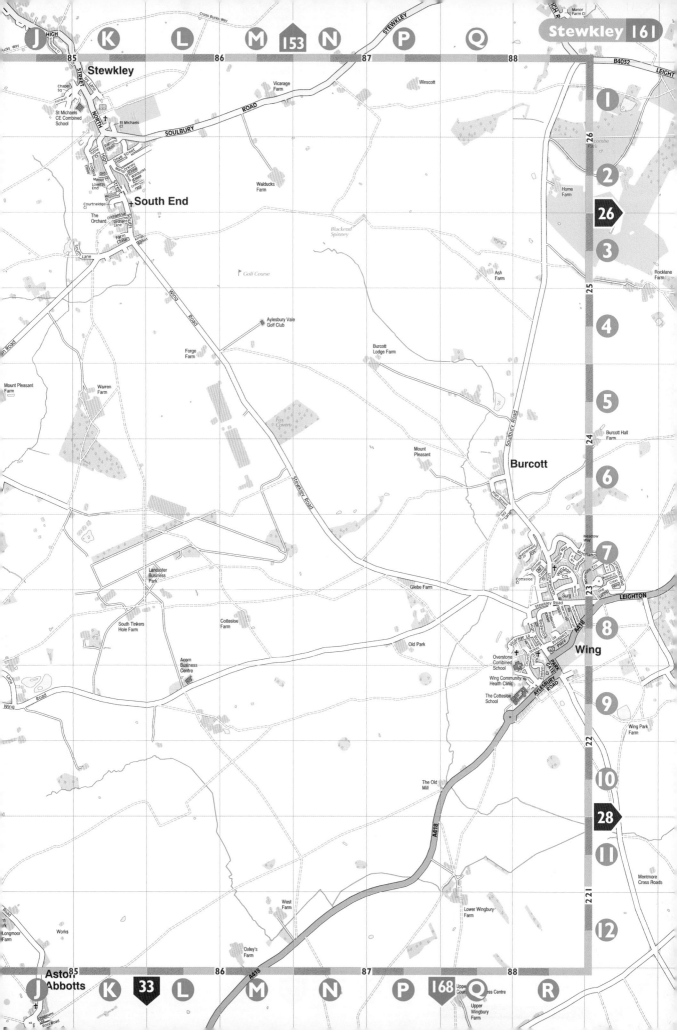

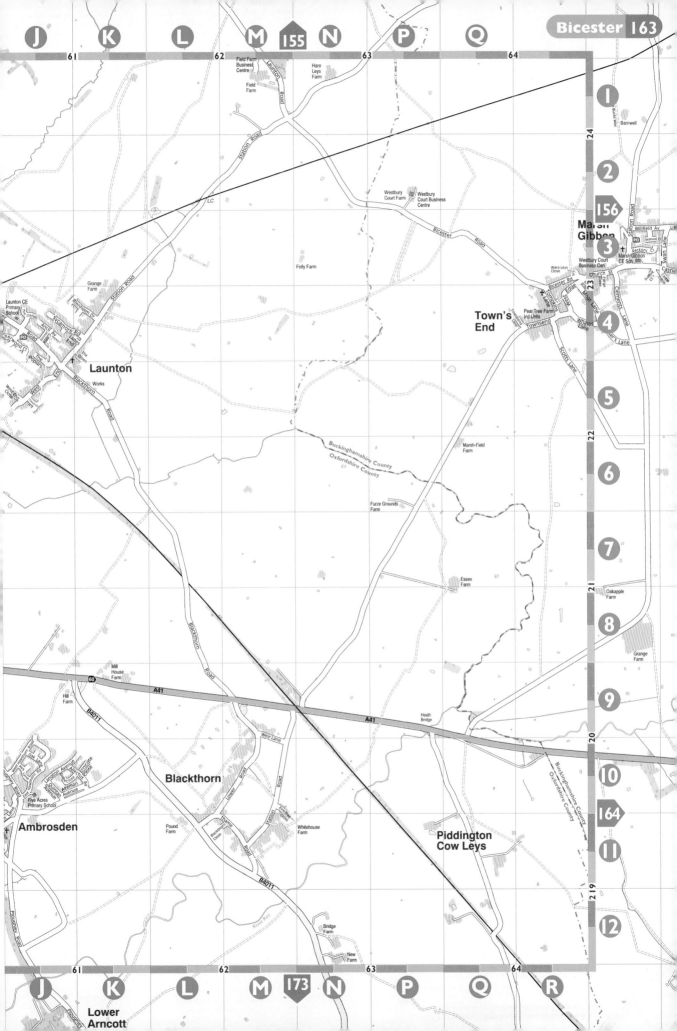

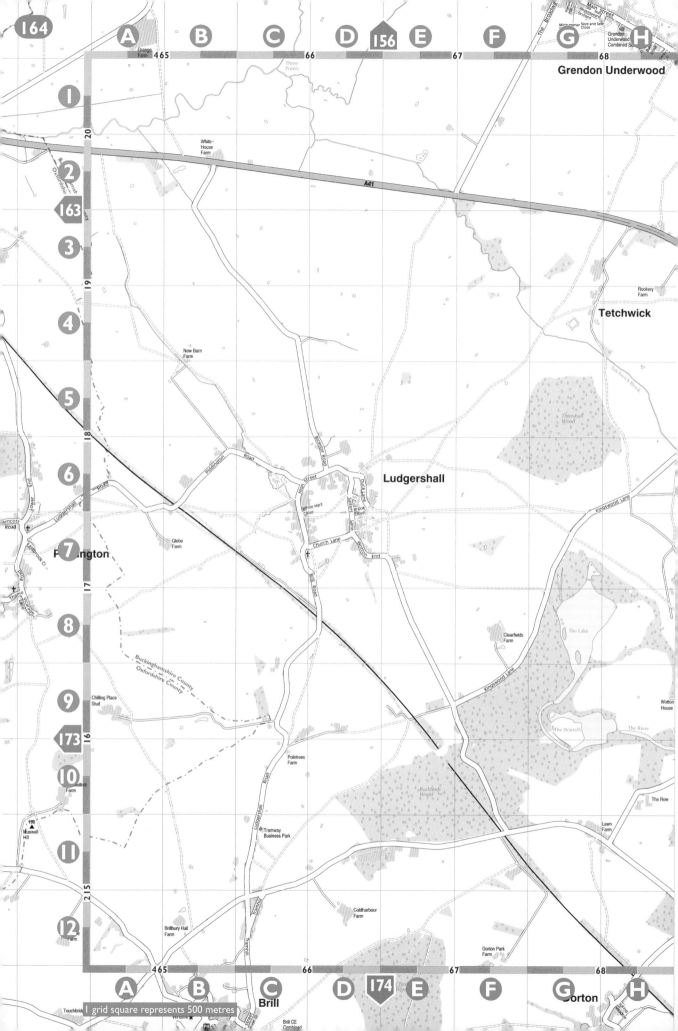

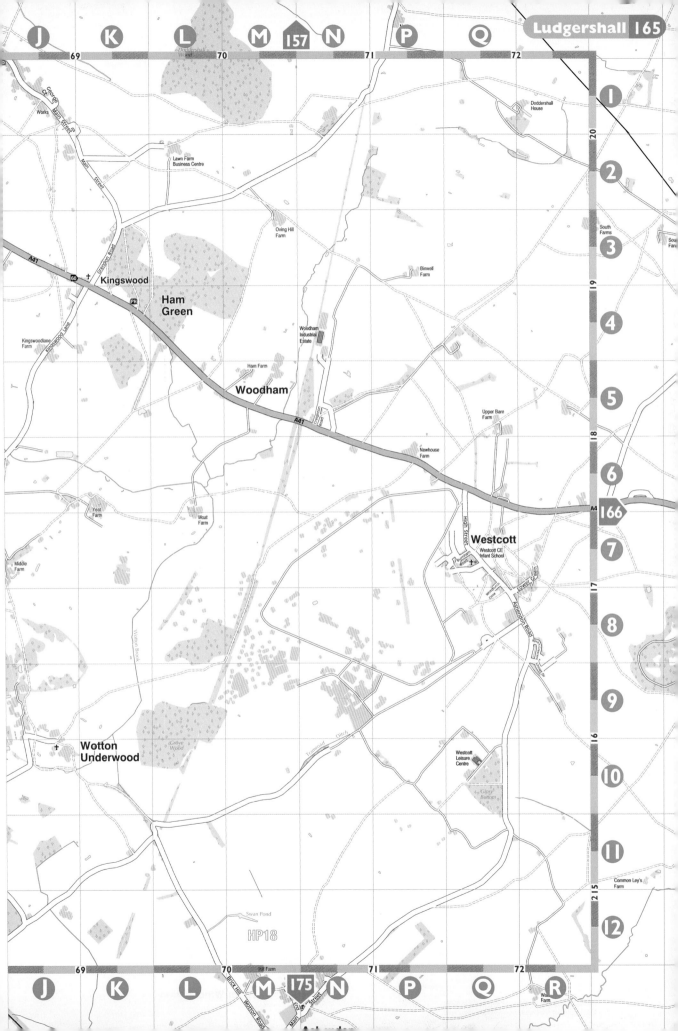

J K L M **157** N P Q

69 70 71 72

Doddershall Wood

I 20

Works

George Cl

Main Street

Lawn Farm Business Centre **2**

Main Street

Doddershall House

Oving Hill Farm

3 South Farms Sou Far

A41

60 Croydon Road

† **Kingswood** 19

PH

Ham Green

Binwell Farm

4

Kingswoodlane Farm

Kingswood Lane

Woodham Industrial Estate

5

Ham Farm

Woodham

A41 Cranston Road

Upper Barn Farm 18

6

Newhouse Farm

A4 **166**

Yeat Farm

Moat Farm

High Street

Pitchman Road

Westcott

Westcott CE Infant School †

7

Middle Farm

Wotton Brook

Windmills Close

Lower Green Lane 17

Apsterton Road

8

Queen Cl

9

Tramwood Ditch

Wotton Underwood †

Gallows Wood

16

Westcott Leisure Centre

10

Gipsy Bottom

11

Common Ley's Farm

2 15

Swan Pond

12

HP18

69 70 71 72

J K L M **175** N P Q R

Hill Farm

Brick Hill

Wotton Road

Main Street

Elm Farm

Wall Farm

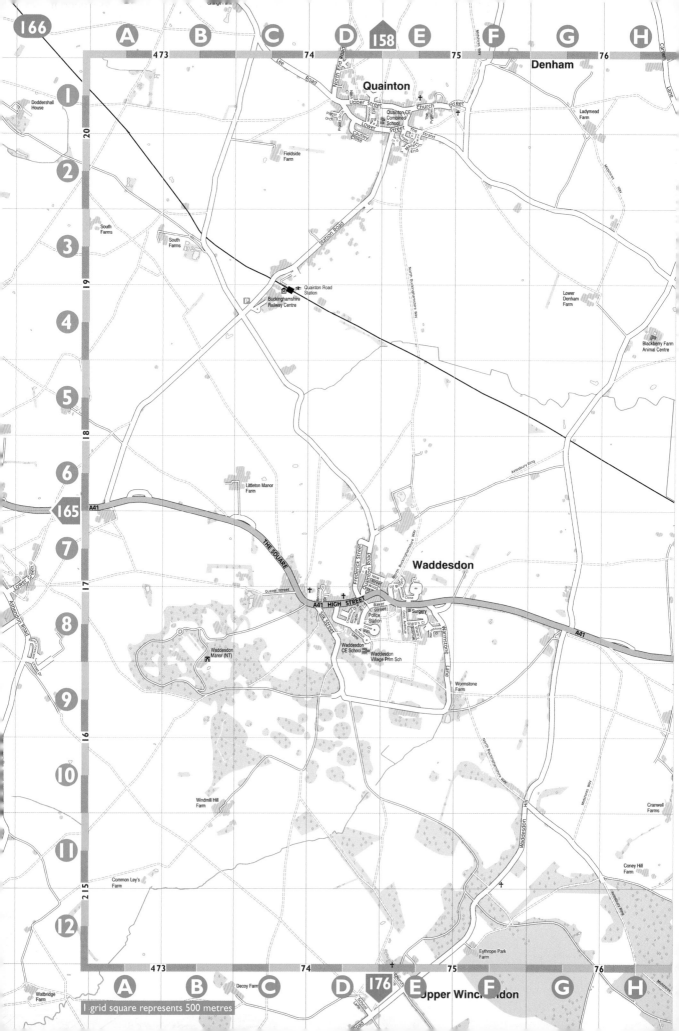

A   B   C   D   E   F   G   H

473   74   75   76

Denham

1

Doddershall
House

2

20

South
Farms

3

19

South
Farms

Fieldside
Farm

Quainton

Upper Street
Quainton CE
Combined
School
Lower
Street
Cautley
Close
The Strand
Church
Street
Pigeon
Orch

Ladymead
Farm

4

Station Road

North Buckinghamshire Way

Lower
Denham
Farm

Blackberry Farm
Animal Centre

5

18

Quainton Road
Station
Buckinghamshire
Railway Centre

6

165

A41

Littleton Manor
Farm

Aylesbury Ring

7

17

THE SQUARE

Frederick Street
Quainton Road
New Street

Waddesdon

Queen Street

8

16

Silk Street

A41 HIGH STREET
Baker
Street
Police
Station
Surgery
Sharp's Cl
Goss Avenue

Warmstone
Lane

Waddesdon
Manor (NT)

Waddesdon
CE School
Waddesdon
Village Prim Sch

Wormstone
Farm

9

Windmill Hill
Farm

Waddesdon Hill

North Buckinghamshire Way

Cranwell
Farms

10

11

Common Ley's
Farm

Coney Hill
Farm

Aylesbury Ring

215

12

Eythrope Park
Farm

Watbridge
Farm

A   B   C   D   E   F   G   H

473   74   75   76

Upper Winchendon

1 grid square represents 500 metres

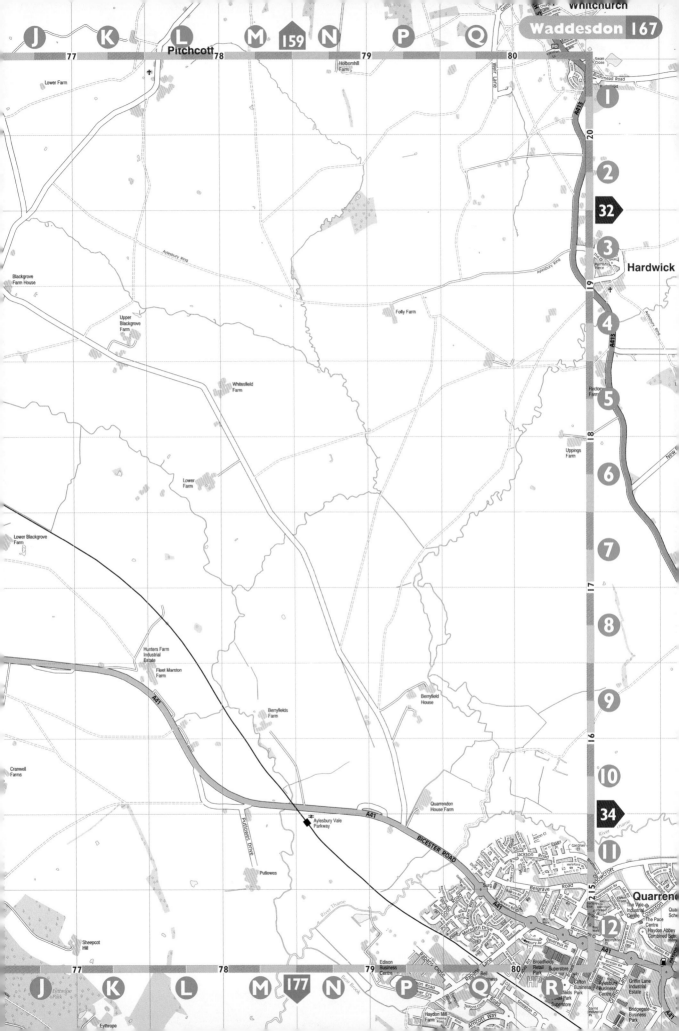

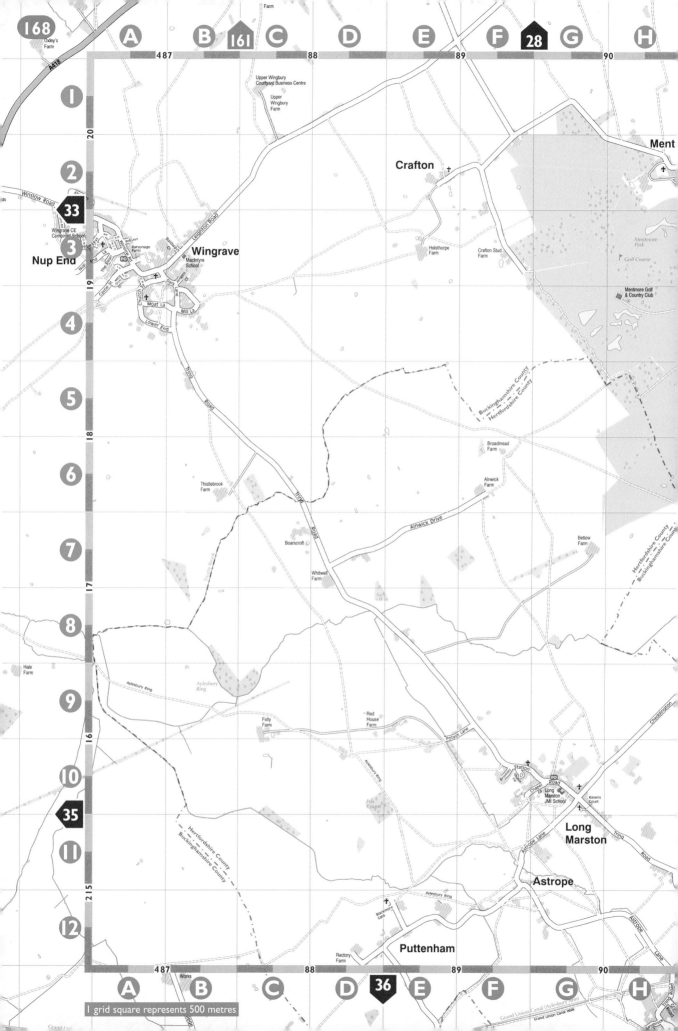

A 495 B C 96 D **30** E 97 F G 98 H

1

Whistle Brook
Station Lane

Hall Farm

Church Lane

Northall

20

2

South End

Knolls View
The Pightle
Two Bridges Link
The Peppiatts
The Sears
Beacon View

A4146

Edlesborough

Moor End

Cantilupe Cl
Rose Ct
Wallace
The Nurse
Eaton Bray Lower School
Church Street
Saffron Rd
Gurney Ct
Church La

Broomstick Industrial Est
Surgery
High Street
The Green

Bellows Mill

Dunstable Road

Medley Close
Bower Lane
Eaton Pk
Sickett's Lane

3

Butler's Manor

Church Crom
Edlesborough School

Chiltern Avenue

30

19

4

Ivinghoe Aston

Grove Farm

Swan Close

Two Ridges Link

Coombe Bottom

St Leonard's Way

LEIGHTON ROAD

ICKNIELD

5

18

169

Crabtree Cottage

Coombe Hole

Travellers Rest

Tring Road

RAF Edlesborough

B489

MAIN ROAD

6

7

17

8

Ford End Farm

Town Farm

Hill Fort
Two Ridges Link
Ridgeway

Icknield Way

Fairview Farm

STATION RO
B489
HIGH STREET
CHURCH ROAD

9

Brook School
Ladymead
Yewtree Close

Ivinghoe

B489

Ward's Coombe

16

Pitstone Green

Surgery
Ridgeway View

10

Pitstone Green Windmill (NT)

Icknield Way

Ward's Hurst Farm

Ringshall Coppice

15

tstone

11

Meadow Lane

itstone

Church E

12

ICKNIELD WAY
Buckinghamshire
Herbert County

Ridgeway

Down Farm

Clipper Down

Ivinghoe Common

Beacon Road

Duncombe Farm

A 495 B C 96 D **39** E 97 F G 98 H

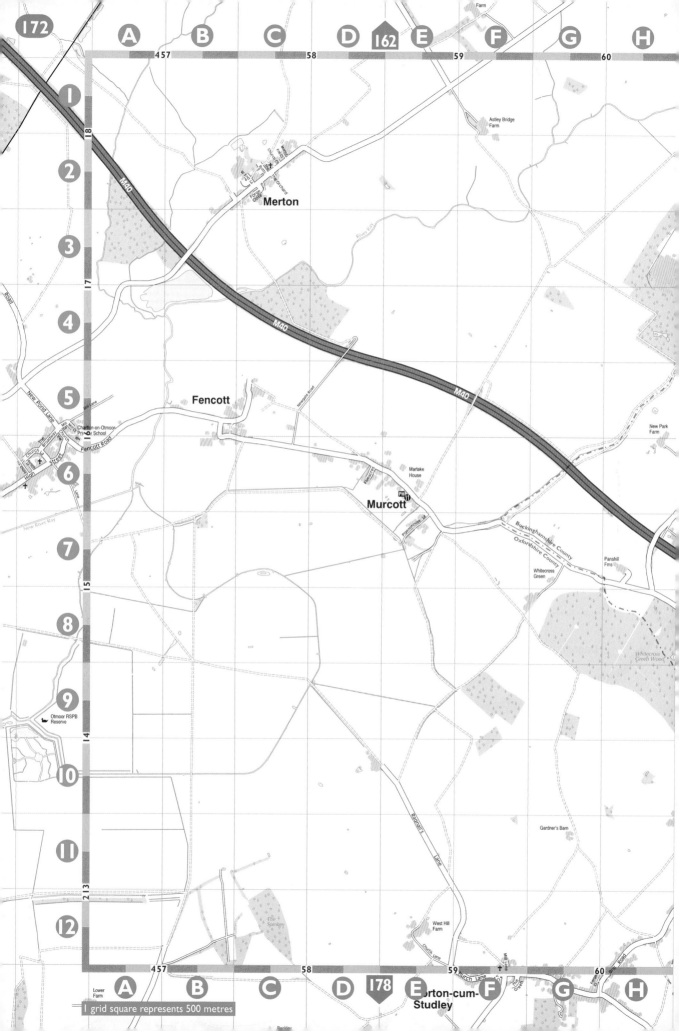

A 457 B C 58 D 162 E 59 F G 60 H

1

18

2

3

17

4

M40

5

Fencott

Merton

River Ray

Astley Bridge Farm

M40

M40

6

Charlton-on-Otmoor Priory School

Fencott Road

High Street

New River Ray

Murcott

PH

Marlake House

New Park Farm

Newgate Road

Byways

Pinsothouse La

Buckinghamshire County

Oxfordshire County

7

15

Whitecross Green

Panshill Fms

8

Whitecross Green Wood

9

Otmoor RSPB Reserve

14

10

11

2 13

12

The Spinney

West Hill Farm

Gardner's Barn

Rectory La

Church Lane

Mill Lane

A 457 B C 58 D 178 E Otton-cum-F The Green G 60 H

Lower Farm

Studley

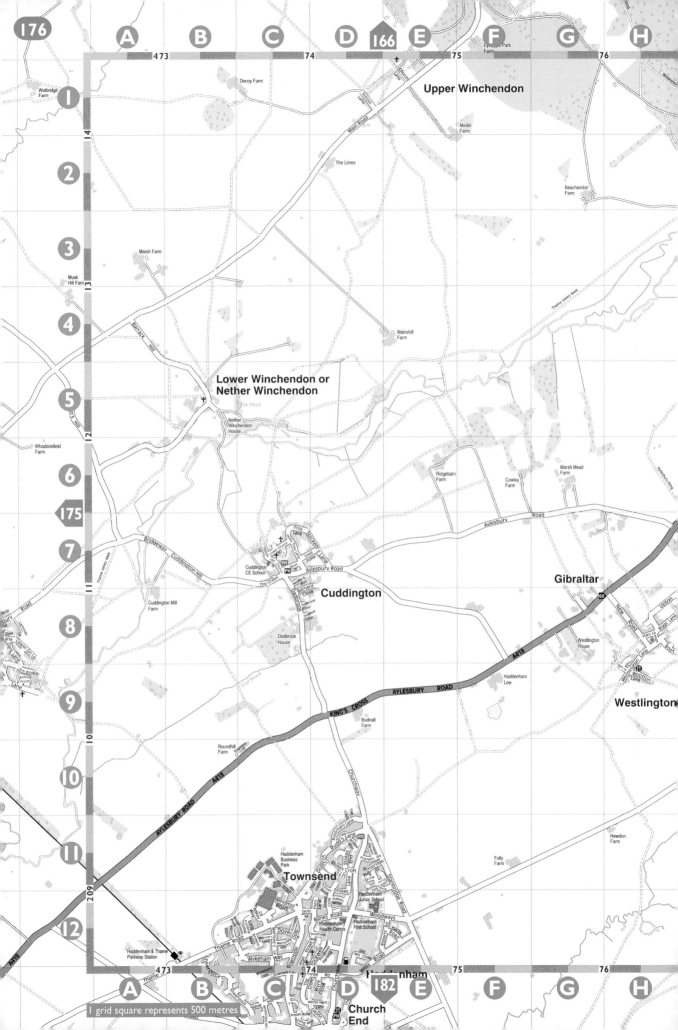

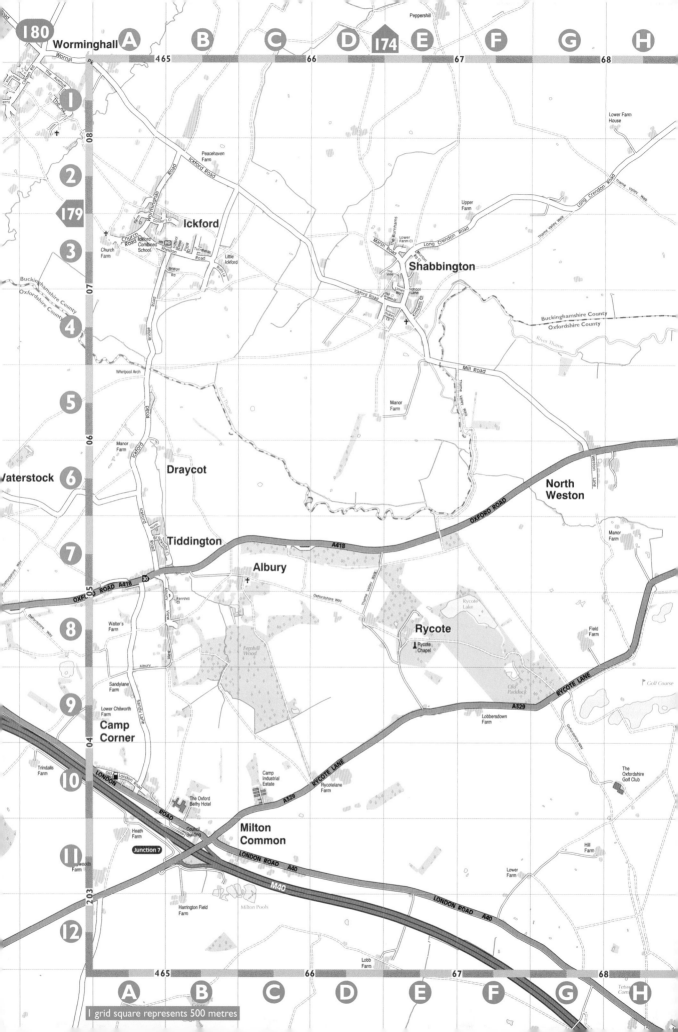

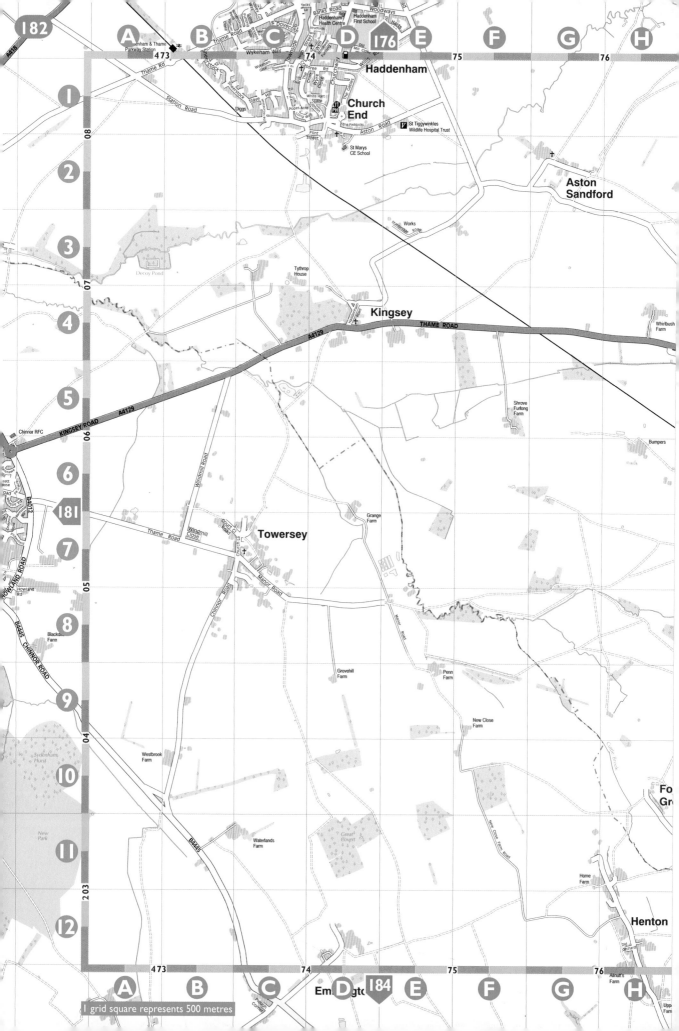

A B C D 176 E F G H

Haddenham

08

Haddenham & Thame
Parkway Station
473

Thame Road

Wykeham Way

74

75

76

Banks Road
Woodways

Dovecote

Haddenham
Health Centre

Haddenham
First School

Church
End

Station Road

Diggs

White Hart

Popes Acre

Flint
Street

Aston Road

St Tiggywinkles
Wildlife Hospital Trust

St Marys
CE School

Aston
Sandford

1

2

07

3

Decoy Pond

Tythrop
House

Works

4

Kingsey

A4129

THAME ROAD

Whirlbush
Farm

5

06

Chinnor RFC

KINGSEY ROAD   A4129

Shrove
Furlong
Farm

Bumpers

6

B4012

181

Windmill Road

Thame Road

Windmill
Close

Court Close

Grange
Farm

Towersey

7

05

HOWLAND ROAD

Howland
Rd

Chinnor Road

Manor Road

Manor Road

8

B4445 CHINNOR ROAD

Blackditch
Farm

Grovehill
Farm

Penn
Farm

9

04

New Close
Farm

Westbrook
Farm

10

Sydenham
Hurst

11

New
Park

B4445

Waterlands
Farm

Great
Covert

New Close Farm Road

12

Henton

Home
Farm

203

473

74

75

76

A B C D 184 E F G H

Em   gt   Henton

Alnutt's
Farm

1 grid square represents 500 metres

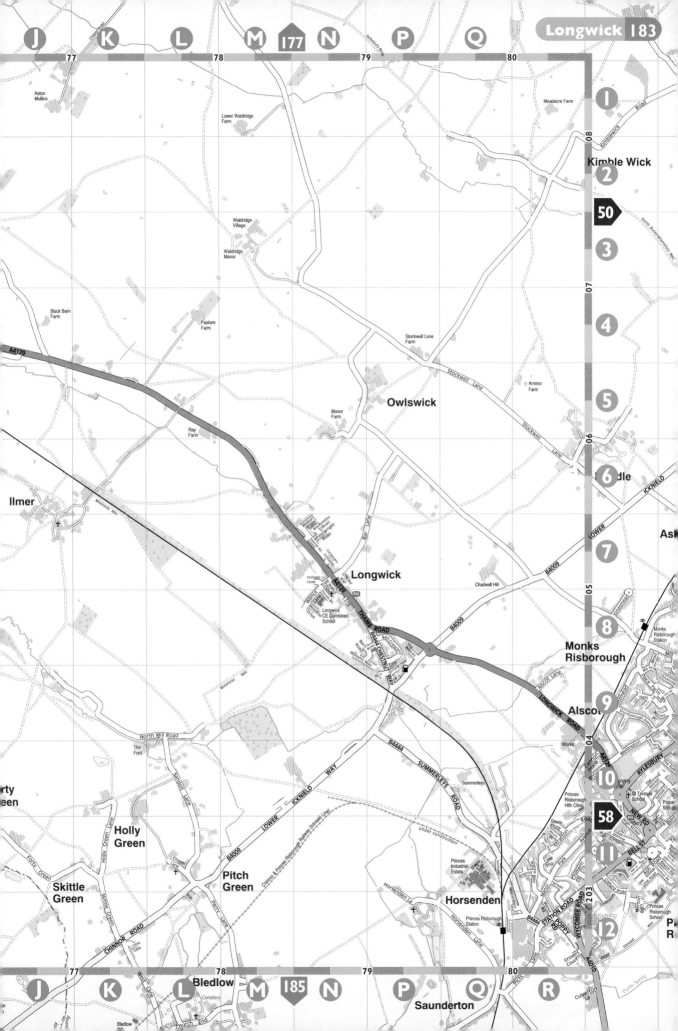

J K L M **177** N P Q

77 78 79 80

I

2 Kimble Wick

50

3

4

5

6 dle

7 As

8 Monks Risborough

9 Alscot

10

58

11

12

Aston Mullins

Lower Waldridge Farm

Meadacre Farm

Waldridge Village

Waldridge Manor

Black Barn Farm

Pasture Farm

Stockwell Lane Farm

Armour Farm

Owlswick

Stockwell Lane

Stockwell Lane

A4129

Ray Farm

Midshires Way

Manor Farm

Ear Lane

ICKNIELD

LOWER

B4009

Ilmer

Longwick

Chadwell Hill

THAME ROAD

Orchard Close

Longwick CE Combined School

B4009

CHESTNUT WAY

Williams Way

Bell Crescent

Alscot Lane

LONGWICK ROAD

Monks Risborough Station

Works

ASTON

Cannon Place

Princes Risborough Hlth Clinic

North Mill Road

The Ford

B4444

SUMMERLEYS ROAD

Summerleys

under construction

WELLINGTON AVENUE

AYLESBURY

St Teresas School

Princes Risborough School

Holly Green

LOWER ICKNIELD WAY

Chinnor & Princes Risborough Railway (Icknield Line)

Chapel Lane

B4009

NEW RD

BELL ST

Skittle Green

Holly Green Lane

Skittle Green

Pitch Green

Perry Lane

Princes Industrial Estate

Horsenden La

Horsenden

Horsenden Station

Princes Risborough Station

STATION ROAD

POPPY RD

WYCOMBE ROAD

A4010

CHINNOR ROAD

West Lane

Little Gibb

77 78 79 80

J K L **Bledlow** M **185** N P Q R

Cemetery

Saunderton

Church End

Bledlow

Henton

473   74   75   76

Allnutt's Farm

Manor Farm

Emmington

1

Sydenham

The Slades

PH

2

LOWER ICKNIELD WAY

Holliers Close

Garden Centre

Malyns Close

CHINNOR

3

Kingston Ste

Manor Farm

Mill Lane Primary School

St Andrews CE Primary School

STATION ROAD

LOWER ROAD

Surgery

4

Oakley Lane

Church Road

Mill Farm Court

OAKLEY ROAD

B4009

30

Oakley

CROWELL RD

Chinnor Station

Chinnor & Princes Risborough Railway (Icknield)

5

CHINNOR ROAD

200

6

B4009

Crowell

Manor Farm

Chinnor Hill

Brook Street

Kingston Blount

HIGH STREET

Kingston House

Swan's Way

7

Aston Rowant CE Primary School

School Lane

Phoebe's Park

Aston Rowant CC

B4009

Park Lane

Crowellhill Wood

8

Aston Rowant

Church Lane

The Green

ROAD

Aston Park Stud

Woodway Farm

CHINNOR

Crowellhill Farm

Crowell Hill

PH

9

LONDON ROAD

M40

Swan's Way

Kingston Grove

Kingston Wood

High Wood

10

B4009

Junction 6

Grove Wood

Gurdon's Farm

M40

11

Aston Wood

ASTON HILL

A40

Hill Farm

BUTTERY ROAD

Hallbottom Farm

Mallard's Court

12

Aston Rowant National Nature Reserve

Kiln Farm

OXFORD ROAD

A40 M40

Red Lion Drive

Stokenchurch Health Centre

Best Western Kings Hotel

Stockfield Place

Independent Business

CR Bates

473   M40   74   75   76

Junction 5

1 grid square represents 500 metres

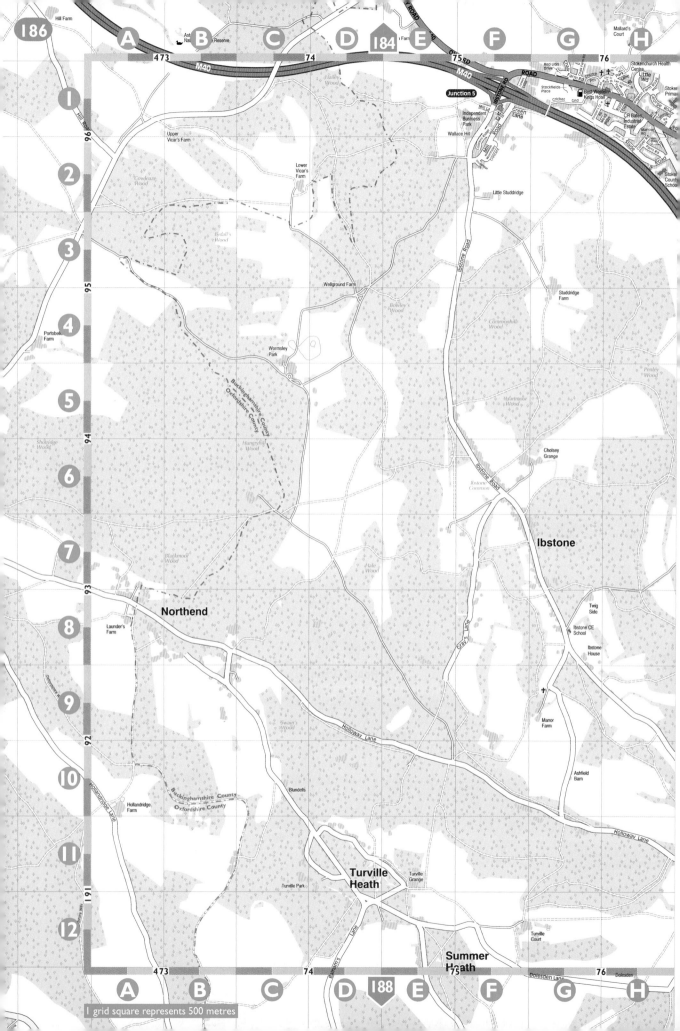

A   B   C   D   184   E   F   G   H

473   74   75 RD   76

M40

Hill Farm

Ast Nat Reserve

Junction 5

Mill La

Independent Business Park

Wallace Hill

Upper Vicar's Farm

Lower Vicar's Farm

Halley Wood

Little Studdridge

1
2
3
4
5
6
7
8
9
10
11
12

96

95

94

93

92

91

Cowkeaze Wood

Bydall's Wood

Wellground Farm

Bowley's Wood

Wormsley Park

Buckinghamshire County
Oxfordshire County

Hungryhill Wood

Shotridge Wood

Portobello Farm

Blackmoor Wood

Northend

Launder's Farm

Studdridge Farm

Commonhill Wood

Penley Wood

Mortimoor Wood

Cholsey Grange

Ibstone Common

Ibstone Road

Gray's Lane

Ibstone

Twig Side

Ibstone CE School

Ibstone House

Manor Farm

Hale Wood

Swain's Wood

Holloway Lane

Ashfield Barn

Greenfield W.

Hollandridge Lane

Hollandridge Farm

Buckinghamshire County
Oxfordshire County

Blundells

Turville Park

Turville Heath

Turville Grange

Holloway Lane

Turville Court

Summer Heath

Dolesden Lane

Dolesden

Banham S

Barton S Lane

Red Lion Drive

Stockfields Place

Best Western Kings Hotel

CR Bates Industrial Estate

Stokenchurch Health Centre

Little Wd

Stoker Primar

George Road

Stoker County Schoo

Marrow Rd

Parts Rd

Green Lane

Mill Road

Mallard's Court

A   B   C   D   188   E   F   G   H

473   74   75   76

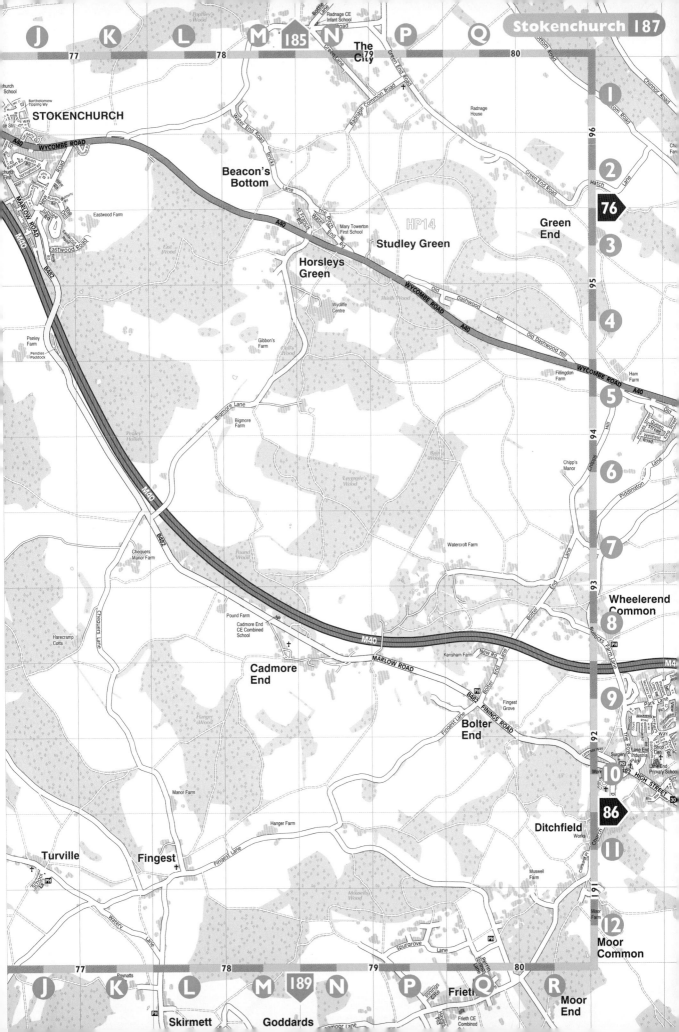

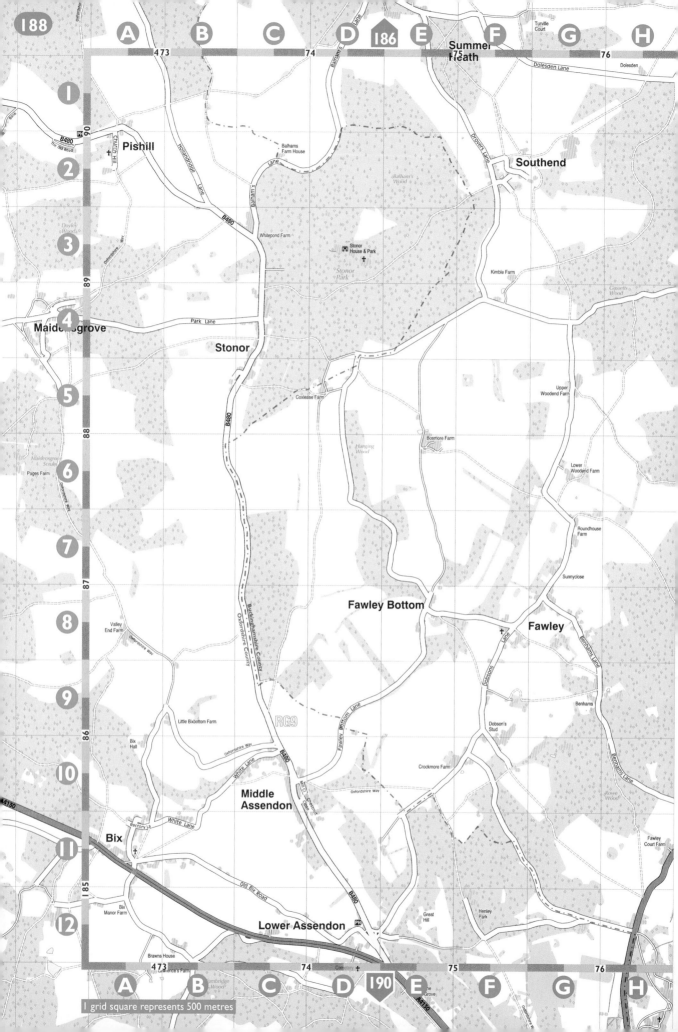

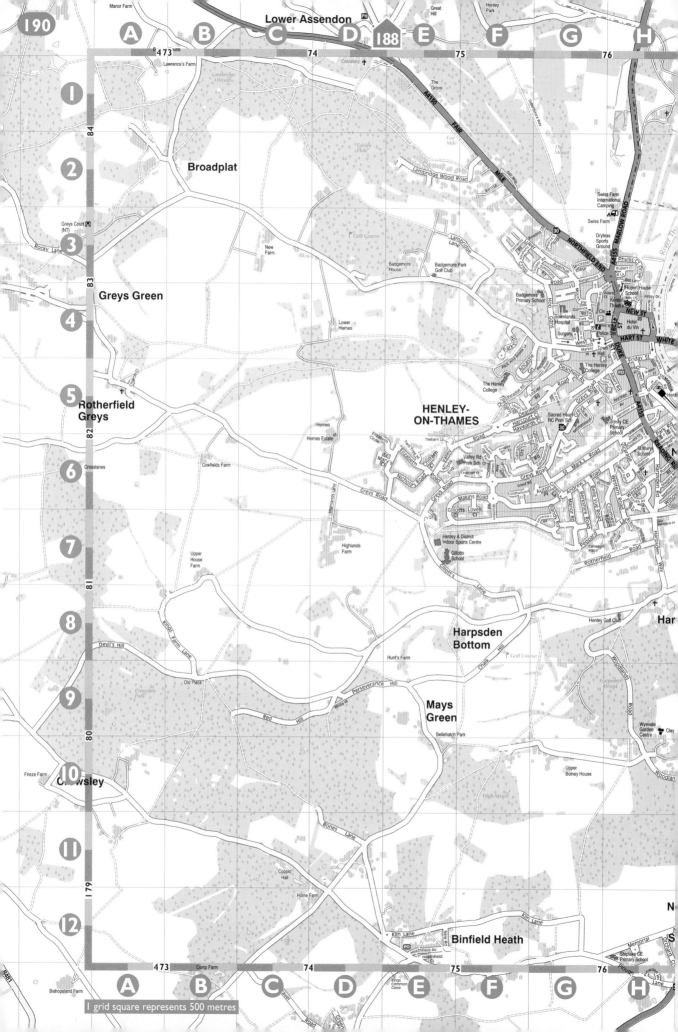

Addington 150 D8
Adstock 150 C5
Akeley 142 B2
Albury 180 C7
Aldbury 39 H4
Alscot 183 R9
Altmore 117 K2
Ambrosden 163 J11
Amersham 71 J2
Amersham Common 71 J2
Amersham Old Town 70 E3
Amersham on the Hill 63 C8
Applehouse Hill 106 F5
Ashendon 175 N1
Asheridge 54 C5
Ashley Green 55 L3
Ashton 130 D2
Askett 50 E7
Aspley Guise 144 H4
Aspley Heath 144 D6
Aston 191 M1
Aston Abbotts 33 J1
Aston Clinton 36 B5
Aston Sandford 182 C4
Astrope 168 G11
Astwood 135 K7
Atterbury 19 J2
Austenwood 92 A2
Aylesbury 2 B5
Bainton 154 D7
Baker's Wood 93 K7
Ballingdon Bottom 41 K1
Ballinger Bottom 53 K6
Ballinger Bottom South 61 L1
Ballinger Common 53 K7
Bancroft 17 J1
Bancroft Park 17 J1
Barley End 39 H2
Barton Hartshorn 147 Q12
Batchworth 84 E2
Batchworth Heath 84 F4
Beachampton 143 Q4
Beacon Hill 79 J3
Beacon's Bottom 187 L2
Beaconsfield 90 B1
Beamond End 69 L4
Beanhill 22 D1
Beckley 178 A3
Bedgrove 43 H1
Beecroft 31 M2
Bellingdon 54 D3
Belsize 65 K3
Bennett End 185 L11
Berghers Hill 89 K6
Berkhamsted 47 M6
Bicester 162 D5
Biddlesden 140 C6
Bierton 35 G3
Bigfrith 97 M8
Billington 29 M4
Billington Park 29 L1
Binfield Heath 190 E12
Birchmoor Green 145 J10
Bisham 97 K7
Bishopstone 42 A1
Bix 188 A11
Blackthorn 163 L10
Blakelands 14 E5
Bleak Hall 22 C1
Bledlow 185 L1
Bledlow Ridge 185 P10
Bletchley 22 D5
Blue Bridge 13 H8
Boarstall 173 N9
Bockmer End 96 B5
Bolter End 187 Q9
Booker 87 C2
Botley 63 M2
Botolph Claydon 158 C4
Boughton End 145 R2
Bourne End 57 H1
Bourne End 88 E6
Bourne End 139 M1
Bourton 142 A11
Boveney 120 B2
Bovingdon 57 C6
Bovingdon Green 56 E8
Bovingdon Green 96 F3
Bow Brickhill 23 M5
Boyn Hill 108 C5
Brackley 8 E8
Bradenham 66 D7
Bradville 13 J7
Bradwell 17 K2
Bradwell Common 6 B1
Bragenham 24 D8
Brands Hill 123 G3
Bray 109 J7
Bray Wick 108 F6
Braywoodside 118 D3
Briden's Camp 41 M7
Brill 174 C1
Brinklow 19 M6
Britwell 110 E1
Broad Green 139 L3
Broadplat 190 B2
Brogborough 145 N1
Brook End 138 C1
Broughton 19 K1
Broughton 35 J6
Browns Wood 23 M2
Bryant's Bottom 67 K2
Buckingham 11 J4
Buckland 36 E4
Buckland Common 45 M7
Bucklandwharf 36 F6
Buckmoorend 51 G8
Buffler's Holt 10 D3
Bulbourne 38 A2
Bullington End 131 M12
Bulstrode 57 K7
Burcott 107 H7
Burcott 35 H3
Burcott 191 Q6
Burnham 100 B7
Burroughs Grove 87 L7
Butler's Cross 51 H3
Butlers Cross 81 L4
Bye Green 43 M3
Cadmore End 187 M9
Caldecote 15 G5
Caldecotte 23 J3
California 2 D7
Calvert 157 J4
Calverton 16 B3
Camp Corner 180 A9
Carlton 129 R3
Castlethorpe 12 C2
Caversfield 154 C11
Central Milton Keynes 6 C2
Chackmore 11 J2
Chalfont Common 82 C4
Chalfont Grove 82 A6

Chalfont St Giles 81 L2
Chalfont St Peter 82 F7
Chalkshire 51 H2
Chalvey 111 H6
Chandler's Cross 74 E1
Charndon 156 F4
Chartridge 54 B7
Chaulden 49 J8
Chearsley 175 P8
Cheddington 169 L8
Chellington 129 Q2
Chenies 73 H1
Frith-hill 61 J3
Chesham 63 H2
Chesham Bois 63 H7
Chessmount 63 K3
Chetwode 155 R2
Chicheley 133 R10
Chilton 174 H6
Chinnor 184 G3
Chisbridge Cross 86 B8
Chivery 45 H6
Cholesbury 46 B8
Chorleywood 73 J5
Chorleywood Bottom 73 J7
Chorleywood West 72 F6
Church End 31 K8
Church End 73 L1
Church End 145 K5
Church End 169 R12
Church End 182 D1
Cippenham 110 C5
The City 185 N12
Clanking 50 C3
Clewer Green 120 D6
Clewer New Town 120 F5
Clewer Village 120 F3
Clifton Pastures 133 R1
Clifton Reynes 128 F11
Clipstone 27 M5
Codmore 63 K1
Coffee Hall 18 C8
Cold Brayfield 129 K9
Cold Harbour 116 F3
Coleshill 70 E7
Colham Green 114 E1
Colnbrook 123 H4
Colstrope 189 M5
The Common 151 L2
Commonwood 65 M5
Conniburrow 17 M2
Cookham 98 F2
Cookham Dean 98 A3
Cookham Rise 98 E4
Coombe 51 J5
Cores End 89 H6
Cosgrove 12 A5
Cottisford 146 D11
Counters End 49 M7
Court Garden 97 J5
Cowley 114 B1
Cowley Peachy 114 B3
Cow Roast 46 F1
Cox Green 108 B7
Crafton 168 F2
Cranfield 139 L5
Cranford 125 M3
Crazies Hill 191 P8
Creslow 160 A10
Cressex 87 J2
Cross End 144 C3
Crowell 184 E6
Crowell Hill 184 G9
Crownfield 66 A2
Crownhill 17 H7
Croxley Green 74 F6
Cryers Hill 68 C4
Cublington 160 G9
Cuddington 176 D8
Dadford 141 J9
Dagnall 171 K8
Danesfield 96 C8
Darvillshill 66 F2
Datchet 122 A4
Datchet Common 122 B5
Deanshanger 137 L10
Dedworth 120 C4
Denbigh West 22 E4
Denham 93 M8
Denham 166 G1
Denham Green 93 K5
Dinton 177 J7
Ditchfield 187 R11
Dorney 110 A7
Dorney Reach 109 L7
Dorton 174 G1
Downhead Park 14 D8
Downley 77 J3
Down's Barn 18 D1
Draycot 180 B6
Drayton Beauchamp 37 H5
Drayton Parslow 152 H8
Duck End 151 Q10
Dudswell 47 J2
Dunsmore 51 M7
Dunton 160 D5
Eaglestone 18 E7
Easington 174 H9
East Burnham 100 E6
Eastbury 85 L4
East Claydon 158 C2
East End 32 D5
East End 139 L4
Eaton Bray 31 G8
Eaton Green 30 D7
Edgcott 156 G8
Edlesborough 170 E2
Egypt 101 G2
Ellesborough 51 G4
Elmhurst 34 C4
Emberton 133 M2
Emerson Valley 21 K5
Emmington 184 D1
Eton 121 H2
Eton Wick 110 E8
Evenley 146 E2
Far Bletchley 21 M7
Farnham Common 101 J4
Farnham Park 101 H6
Farnham Royal 101 L4
Fawley 188 F8
Fawley Bottom 188 D8
Felden 57 M3
Fencott 172 C9
Fenny Stratford 23 G4
Fern 88 C5
Fields End 49 J6
Fifield 119 J4
Filgrave 133 K5
Fingest 187 K11
Finmere 147 Q7
Fishermead 7 L7
Fishery 108 F4
Flackwell Heath 88 F3

Flaunden 64 F3
Flowers Bottom 66 F2
Ford 177 L11
Forest Hill 178 E10
Forty Green 79 M6
Forty Green 182 H10
Foscote 142 B6
Four Ashes 68 B3
Fox Corner 25 J8
Frieth 189 Q1
Fringford 155 J4
Frith-hill 61 J3
Frithsden 48 F2
Frithsden Gardens 48 D1
Froxfield 145 P11
Fullers Slade 16 D2
Fulmer 102 C2
Furze Platt 98 C8
Furzton 22 A2
Gadebridge 49 L5
Gawcott 148 G2
Gayhurst 132 B8
George Green 112 D2
Gerrards Cross 92 B6
Gibraltar 176 G7
Giffard Park 14 B4
Godalming 189 N1
Godington 155 Q7
Gossard's Green 139 M2
Grafton Regis 130 C8
Granborough 159 J3
Gravel Hill 82 E6
Great Brickhill 24 E5
Great Gaddesden 41 H7
Greatgap 169 Q8
Great Hampden 59 J6
Great Hivings 54 F7
Great Holm 17 G6
Great Horwood 151 K4
Great Kimble 50 E6
Great Kingshill 68 D2
Great Linford 14 C5
Great Missenden 60 E3
Greatmoor 157 M9
Green End 24 E4
Green End 49 L8
Green End 187 R3
Green Hailey 58 E3
Greenlands 189 K10
Greenleys 16 E1
The Green 12 B4
The Green 14 F3
The Green 171 N6
Grendon Underwood 164 G1
Greys Green 190 A4
Grove 29 G4
Gubblecote 169 J12
Hackleton 126 B3
Haddenham 182 D1
Haddington Hill 44 D3
Halton 44 C1
Hambleden 189 N9
Ham Green 165 L4
Hanslope 131 M7
Hardmead 134 C6
Hardwick 32 A3
Hardwick 154 C2
Harefield 94 B1
Harefield Grove 84 C7
Harlington 125 H2
Harmondsworth 124 B2
Harpsden 190 B8
Harpsden Bottom 190 B8
Hartwell 131 K1
Hastoe 45 M3
Hatton 125 K7
Haversham 13 J3
Hawks Hill 89 H8
Hayes 115 H2
Hayes End 115 J1
Hazlemere 69 G6
Heath and Reach 27 J1
Heath End 46 F8
Heath End 68 C1
Hedgerley 91 J7
Hedgerley Green 91 L6
Hedgerley Hill 91 K8
Hedsor 89 L7
Heelands 17 L2
Hempton Wainhill 185 K3
Henley-on-Thames 190 E5
Henton 182 H12
Heronsgate 73 J8
Hethe 154 F2
Higher Denham 93 H6
Highfield 162 C3
Highway 107 M8
High Wycombe 5 J4
Hill End 84 A6
Hillesden 148 H8
Hillesden Hamlet 148 G5
Hillingdon 104 F6
Hillingdon Heath 115 G2
Hilltop 55 J8
Hoggeston 159 R3
Hogpits Bottom 65 G3
Hollington 153 P11
Holloway 17 J4
Hollybush Hill 102 A5
Holly Cross 191 R8
Holly Green 183 K11
Holmer Green 69 J4
Holtspur 90 A1
The Holt 116 A5
Holyport 118 F1
Holywell 75 K7
Holywell 171 R7
Honeywick 30 F6
Horn Hill 83 G4
Horsenden 183 Q12
Horsleys Green 187 N3
Horton 122 F6
Horton 126 D5
Horton 169 M3
Horton-cum-Studley 178 E1
Horton Wharf 169 P2
Hotley Bottom 60 B2
Hudnall 40 D3
Hudnall Corner 40 F5
Hughenden Valley 67 M7
Hulcote 138 H12
Hulcott 33 J8
Hungate End 131 J8
Hunt's Green 52 F6
Hunt's Hill 77 J1
Hurley 106 D2
Hurley Bottom 106 C3
Hurst End 138 E3
Husborne Crawley 145 L5
Hyde Heath 62 B5
Ibstone 186 G1
Ickenham 104 F1
Ickford 180 B3

Ilmer 183 J6
Iver 113 L3
Iver Heath 103 L6
Ivinghoe 170 A9
Ivinghoe Aston 170 B5
Jockey End 41 M2
Jordans 81 L7
Juniper Hill 146 A6
Kents Hill 19 K6
Kiln Green 116 B5
Kimble Wick 50 E2
Kingsash 52 E2
King's End 162 C4
Kingsey 182 G2
Kingsmead 20 F5
Kingston 19 M4
Kingston Blount 184 B7
Kingswood 165 K3
Knotty Green 80 C5
Knowl Hill 116 E2
Lacey Green 66 D1
Lake End 110 A6
Lane End 86 D2
Lanes End 45 H7
Langford Village 162 F5
Langley 112 E7
Langley Corner 102 E4
Lathbury 133 L11
Latimer 64 D8
Launton 163 K5
Lavendon 128 H7
Layters Green 82 A3
Leckhampstead 142 E3
Ledburn 28 D5
Lee Clump 53 H5
Lee Common 53 J5
Leedon 27 K6
Lee Gate 53 G2
The Lee 53 G4
Leighton Buzzard 27 J6
Lenborough 149 L2
Lent 109 M1
Lent Rise 109 M2
Ley Hill 64 A1
Lillingstone Dayrell 141 R6
Lillingstone Lovell 136 A8
Linslade 26 D7
Little Billington 29 K5
Little Boys Heath 61 H8
Little Brickhill 24 F1
Little Chalfont 72 A3
Littlecote 160 F5
Little Crawley 134 C11
Littlefield Green 117 L8
Little Gaddesden 40 C3
Little Hampden 59 M2
Little Heath 48 F5
Little Horwood 151 Q4
Little Kimble 50 E4
Little Kingshill 61 G7
Little Linford 13 M1
Little London 52 B3
Little London 174 A5
Little Marlow 88 B5
Little Marsh 156 B6
Little Missenden 62 A8
Little Tring 37 K4
Littlewick Green 117 H1
Little Wood Corner 61 L2
Littleworth Common 100 C1
Long Crendon 182 A1
Longford 124 A4
Long Marston 168 G13
Long Street 131 L6
Longwick 183 N7
Loosley Row 58 B8
Loudwater 74 C4
Loudwater 79 J8
Loughton 17 L7
Love Green 113 J2
Lower Arncott 173 K1
Lower Assendon 188 C12
Lower Bois 63 H5
Lower Cadsden 50 E8
Lower End 30 F5
Lower End 130 G1
Lower End 142 G9
Lower End 144 E1
Lower End 187 J11
Lower Hartwell 177 N4
Lower North Dean 67 J5
Lower Pollicott 175 M4
Lower Shiplake 191 J11
Lower Wainhill 185 J3
Lower Weald 16 A4
Lower Winchendon or Nether Winchendon 176 B5
Lower Woodend 96 D3
Ludgershall 164 E6
Lye Green 55 L7
Maidenhead 108 F2
Maidenhead Court 99 H6
Maids Moreton 142 A6
Manor Park 3 H2
Manor Park 111 H1
Mantles Green 70 F1
Maple Cross 83 J4
Marlow 97 H3
Marlow Bottom 88 C7
Marsh 42 C7
Marsh Gibbon 163 R3
Marsworth 169 N12
Mays Green 190 E9
Meadle 50 A6
Medmenham 106 A1
Mentmore 168 H2
Merton 172 C2
Mickfield 78 D3
Micklefield 73 M1
Middle Assendon 188 C10
Middle Claydon 157 R2
Middle Green 112 D4
Middle Weald 16 B5
Mill End 83 L1
Mill End 189 N11
Milton Common 180 C11
Milton Keynes 7 H1
Milton Keynes Village 19 J3
Mixbury 147 K6
Mobwell 60 F3
Moneyhill 84 A1
Moneyrow Green 118 F3
Monks Risborough 183 R8
Monkston 19 H5
Monkston Park 19 H5
Moor Common 86 A4
Moor End 170 F1
Moor End 189 N1
Moor Park 85 H4
Mop End 69 M3
Moreton 181 L8
Moulsoe 138 A6
Mount Pleasant 11 J7

Mount Pleasant 84 A8
Murcott 172 D6
Mursley 152 C8
Naphill 67 H7
Nash 143 R9
Nash Lee 51 H1
Nearton End 152 A12
Neath Hill 14 E8
Netherfield 18 E8
Nettleden 41 G8
New Bradwell 13 J6
New Cross 190 H12
New Denham 103 M4
New Ground 38 F8
Newlands 18 F2
New Mill 38 A4
Newport Pagnell 14 F1
Newton Blossomville 129 J10
Newton Longville 153 J3
Newton Morrell 153 L3
Newton Purcell 147 M12
Newtown 55 H8
Newtown 190 H6
Newyears Green 94 F6
Northall 170 B1
Northchurch 47 J4
North Crawley 134 D12
North End 135 N2
North End 149 M11
North End 153 J12
Northend 186 A3
Northfield 19 J1
North Hillingdon 105 G5
North Lee 42 F8
North Marston 159 K8
North Town 108 F1
North Weston 180 G6
Northwood 85 H8
Northwood Hills 95 J1
Nup End 33 M3
Oakgrove 19 G4
Oakley 174 C1
Oakley 184 E5
Oakley Green 119 M5
Oldbrook 7 G8
Old Farm Park 144 B5
Old Linslade 26 D4
Old Stratford 137 P7
Old Wolverton 12 D7
Olney 128 C10
Orchard Leigh 56 H6
Oving 175 N11
Owlswick 183 P5
Oxley Park 21 H3
Padbury 149 R5
Paley Street 118 A5
Parmoor 189 P5
Parslow's Hillock 58 E6
Passenham 137 L12
Pednor Bottom 54 B8
Pednormead End 62 E3
Penn 79 K3
Penn Bottom 79 L2
Penn Street 70 A5
Pennyland 14 D7
Petsoe End 133 Q4
Pheasants 189 P4
Pheasant's Hill 189 M7
Piddington 76 B5
Piddington 126 A5
Piddington 173 M3
Piddington Cow Leys 163 P11
Pineham 15 H7
Pinfoldpond 144 H12
Pinkneys Green 107 L5
Pishill 189 A2
Pitchcott 159 L12
Pitstone 169 Q11
Pitstone Green 169 Q10
Pitch Green 183 M11
Pond Park 55 G8
Potten End 48 F4
Potterspury 137 M4
Pouchen End 49 J8
Poundon 155 R11
Poyle 123 K4
Preston Bissett 148 D6
Prestwood 60 C4
Princes Risborough 58 B4
Pudds Cross 56 F7
Puttenham 168 E12
Puxley 137 L7
Quainton 166 D1
Quarrendon 34 A4
Radclive 11 G5
Radnage 185 N9
Ravenstone 127 K12
Redland End 58 F5
Remenham 191 J4
Remenham Hill 191 L3
Richings Park 113 K3
Rickmansworth 74 C7
Ridgmont 145 Q5
Ringshall 40 A1
Rockwell End 189 Q5
The Rookery 75 M8
Rooksley 17 K4
Rose Hill 99 M5
Rout's Green 185 N9
Rowsham 33 K5
Ruislip 95 K5
Ruislip Common 95 H3
Ruislip Gardens 95 K1
Ruislip Manor 95 M4
Rushmere 27 G2
Rycote 180 E8
St Leonards 45 K7
St Margaret's 41 H6
Salcey Green 131 M3
Salden 152 D6
Salford 138 F11
Salt Hill 111 G5
Sandhill 150 B12
Sandhills 178 A10
Sands 77 G7
Sarratt 65 M6
Sarratt Bottom 65 L4
Saunderton 185 P1
Saunderton Lee 185 R6
Sedrup 177 G6
Seer Green 80 E5
Sewell 31 L4
Shabbington 180 E3
Shalstone 140 D12
Sheeplane 25 L3
Sheepridge 88 E3
Sheeptick End 139 R11
Shenley Brook End 21 K3
Shenley Church End 17 J8
Shenley Lodge 21 K4
Shenley Park 21 G4
Shenley Wood 21 H5
Sherington 133 P8

Sherington Bridge ...133 M11	Stokenchurch ...187 J1	Touchen-end ...118 C4	Warners End ...49 K6	Willen Park ...14 F8
Shiplake ...190 H12	Stoke Poges ...101 K5	Towerage ...76 D6	Warren Row ...106 B8	Willowbank ...104 B3
Shipton ...151 L11	Stone ...177 M5	Tower Hill ...57 L8	Warrington ...128 C5	Wilstone ...37 J1
Shipton Lee ...158 A11	Stonebridge ...13 G7	Towersey ...182 C7	Water Eaton ...22 E8	Wilstone Green ...37 J2
Shootersway ...47 K6	Stoney Ware ...97 J6	Town End ...185 M9	Water End ...49 L1	Wilton Park ...81 G8
Shreding Green ...113 G3	Stonor ...188 B4	Town's End ...163 Q4	Watermead ...34 E2	Winchmore Hill ...70 C8
Simpson ...23 H2	Stony Green ...67 M2	Townsend ...176 C11	Waterside ...63 J4	Windsor ...121 K4
Singleborough ...150 H1	Stony Stratford ...16 B1	Travellers Rest ...170 F6	Water Stratford ...10 B4	Wing ...38 A5
Sipson ...124 E1	Stratton Audley ...154 H9	Tring ...38 A7	Watford ...75 L4	Wingrave ...168 D3
Skirmett ...189 L1	Stubbings ...107 J6	Tringford ...37 K2	Wavendon ...144 A4	Winslow ...151 L10
Skittle Green ...183 J11	Stud Green ...118 D2	Tring Wharf ...38 A3	Wavendon Gate ...144 A3	Woburn ...144 H11
Slapton ...29 L8	Studham ...71 Q9	Turvey ...129 P8	Weedon ...32 C5	Woburn Sands ...144 D6
Smoky Row ...153 R11	Studley Green ...187 P3	Turville ...187 J11	Well End ...88 E5	Wolverton ...12 F8
Soulbury ...50 D5	Summer Heath ...186 E12	Turville Heath ...186 D11	Wendover ...44 B6	Wolverton Mill ...16 D1
Southcourt ...34 B8	Summerstown ...156 B8	Turweston ...9 H6	Wendover Dean ...52 C4	Wooburn ...89 H6
South End ...161 K2	Sunnymeads ...122 D7	Two Mile Ash ...17 G4	Westbrook Hay ...57 H3	Wooburn Common ...89 M7
Southend ...188 F2	Sutton ...123 H1	Twyford ...156 D1	Westbury ...147 N2	Wooburn Green ...89 L3
South Field ...121 G1	Swan Bottom ...53 J4	Tylers Green ...69 J8	Westcott ...165 Q5	Woodcock Hill ...84 D4
South Harefield ...94 C3	Swanbourne ...151 R11	Tyler's Hill ...63 M2	Westcroft ...21 H4	Wood End ...115 K3
South Heath ...61 K2	The Swillett ...73 H8	Tyringham ...132 F7	West Drayton ...114 C7	Wood End ...139 Q7
Speen ...67 J2	Sydenham ...184 A2	Up End ...134 D10	Westlington ...176 H9	Wood End ...143 R10
Spinfield ...96 F5	Syresham ...140 B2	Upper Arncott ...173 K2	Weston Turville ...43 M4	Wood End ...151 Q4
Spital ...121 G7	Taplow ...109 K1	Upper Dunsley ...38 B7	Weston Underwood ...133 J11	Wood End Green ...115 K2
Sprig's Alley ...184 H8	Tathall End ...131 R8	Upper North Dean ...67 H4	West Ruislip ...95 H7	Woodfield ...162 D2
Springfield ...18 E4	Tatling End ...93 G7	Upper Pollicott ...175 M2	West Watford ...75 M6	Wood Green ...140 E8
Spurlands End ...68 F2	Tattenhoe ...21 K6	Upper Weald ...16 D6	West Wycombe ...76 F4	Woodham ...165 M5
Stacey Bushes ...17 H2	Temple ...107 H1	Upper Winchendon ...176 E1	Wexham Street ...102 B6	Woodlands ...190 H4
Stagsden ...135 R3	Terrick ...51 H1	Upton ...111 M7	Whaddon ...20 E5	Woodlands Park ...117 L4
Stagsden West End ...135 Q6	Terriers ...68 C8	Upton Lea ...111 M3	Wharley End ...138 F4	Woodrow ...78 E5
Stanbridge ...30 D1	Tetchwick ...164 C4	Uxbridge ...104 A6	Wheelerend Common ...76 A8	Woolley Green ...117 K1
Stanbridgeford ...30 E3	Tetworth ...181 P5	Uxbridge Moor ...104 A6	Whelpley Hill ...56 C5	Woolstone ...18 F5
Stantonbury ...13 M7	Thame ...181 H1	Venus Hill ...65 Q2	Whipsnade ...171 P6	Wootton Bourne End ...135 R11
Stanton St John ...178 B6	Thornborough ...143 J10	Verney Junction ...150 C11	Whitchurch ...159 R12	World's End ...43 L7
Startop's End ...37 L1	Thorney ...114 A6	Victoria Park ...3 L5	Whiteleaf ...58 C1	Worminghall ...179 R8
Steeple Claydon ...149 K11	Thornton ...143 K5	Waddesdon ...166 E7	White Waltham ...117 K7	Wotton Underwood ...165 K10
Stewkley ...161 K1	Three Households ...81 L3	Walnut Tree ...23 L2	Whitfield ...9 K3	Woughton on the Green ...19 G6
Stewkley Dean ...160 F1	Tickford End ...15 J2	Walter's Ash ...67 H5	Wicken ...137 J11	Wycombe Marsh ...78 D6
Stoke Bruerne ...130 A2	Tiddington ...180 B7	Waltham St Lawrence ...116 D7	Widmer End ...68 D4	Wymbush ...17 J4
Stoke Goldington ...132 C4	Tingewick ...10 C7	Walton ...3 H1	Widmoor ...89 K7	Yardley Gobion ...137 M1
Stoke Green ...111 M1	Tinkers End ...150 H11	Walton ...23 J1	Wigginton ...38 C5	Yiewsley ...114 D4
Stoke Hammond ...153 R6	Tittle Row ...108 A4	Walton Court ...42 B1	Wigginton Bottom ...46 D2	
Stoke Lyne ...154 A5	Tongwell ...14 F6	Wardrobes ...58 B6	Willen ...15 G7	
Stoke Mandeville ...43 G5	Totteridge ...78 C1			
	Totternhoe ...31 J7			

USING THE STREET INDEX

Street names are listed alphabetically. Each street name is followed by its postal town or area locality, the Postcode District, the page number, and the reference to the square in which the name is found.

Standard index entries are shown as follows:

Abbey Barn La *FLKWH/TG* HP10 ..**78** D7

Street names and selected addresses not shown on the map due to scale restrictions are shown in the index with an asterisk:

Abbey Sq *RBEDW* MK43 * **75** G1

GENERAL ABBREVIATIONS

ACC	ACCESS	CTYD	COURTYARD	HLS	HILLS	MWY	MOTORWAY	SE	SOUTH EAST
ALY	ALLEY	CUTT	CUTTINGS	HO	HOUSE	N	NORTH	SER	SERVICE AREA
AP	APPROACH	CV	COVE	HOL	HOLLOW	NE	NORTH EAST	SH	SHORE
AR	ARCADE	CYN	CANYON	HOSP	HOSPITAL	NW	NORTH WEST	SHOP	SHOPPING
ASS	ASSOCIATION	DEPT	DEPARTMENT	HRB	HARBOUR	O/P	OVERPASS	SKWY	SKYWAY
AV	AVENUE	DL	DALE	HTH	HEATH	OFF	OFFICE	SMT	SUMMIT
BCH	BEACH	DM	DAM	HTS	HEIGHTS	ORCH	ORCHARD	SOC	SOCIETY
BLDS	BUILDINGS	DR	DRIVE	HVN	HAVEN	OV	OVAL	SP	SPUR
BND	BEND	DRO	DROVE	HWY	HIGHWAY	PAL	PALACE	SPR	SPRING
BNK	BANK	DRY	DRIVEWAY	IMP	IMPERIAL	PAS	PASSAGE	SQ	SQUARE
BR	BRIDGE	DWGS	DWELLINGS	IN	INLET	PAV	PAVILION	ST	STREET
BRK	BROOK	E	EAST	IND EST	INDUSTRIAL ESTATE	PDE	PARADE	STN	STATION
BTM	BOTTOM	EMB	EMBANKMENT	INF	INFIRMARY	PH	PUBLIC HOUSE	STR	STREAM
BUS	BUSINESS	EMBY	EMBASSY	INFO	INFORMATION	PK	PARK	STRD	STRAND
BVD	BOULEVARD	ESP	ESPLANADE	INT	INTERCHANGE	PKWY	PARKWAY	SW	SOUTH WEST
BY	BYPASS	EST	ESTATE	IS	ISLAND	PL	PLACE	TDG	TRADING
CATH	CATHEDRAL	EX	EXCHANGE	JCT	JUNCTION	PLN	PLAIN	TER	TERRACE
CEM	CEMETERY	EXPY	EXPRESSWAY	JTY	JETTY	PLNS	PLAINS	THWY	THROUGHWAY
CEN	CENTRE	EXT	EXTENSION	KG	KING	PLZ	PLAZA	TNL	TUNNEL
CFT	CROFT	F/O	FLYOVER	KNL	KNOLL	POL	POLICE STATION	TOLL	TOLLWAY
CH	CHURCH	FC	FOOTBALL CLUB	L	LAKE	PR	PRINCE	TPK	TURNPIKE
CHA	CHASE	FK	FORK	LA	LANE	PREC	PRECINCT	TR	TRACK
CHYD	CHURCHYARD	FLD	FIELD	LDG	LODGE	PREP	PREPARATORY	TRL	TRAIL
CIR	CIRCLE	FLDS	FIELDS	LGT	LIGHT	PRIM	PRIMARY	TWR	TOWER
CIRC	CIRCUS	FLS	FALLS	LK	LOCK	PROM	PROMENADE	U/P	UNDERPASS
CL	CLOSE	FM	FARM	LKS	LAKES	PRS	PRINCESS	UNI	UNIVERSITY
CLFS	CLIFFS	FT	FORT	LNDG	LANDING	PRT	PORT	UPR	UPPER
CMP	CAMP	FTS	FLATS	LTL	LITTLE	PT	POINT	V	VALE
CNR	CORNER	FWY	FREEWAY	LWR	LOWER	PTH	PATH	VA	VALLEY
CO	COUNTY	FY	FERRY	MAG	MAGISTRATE	PZ	PIAZZA	VIAD	VIADUCT
COLL	COLLEGE	GA	GATE	MAN	MANSIONS	QD	QUADRANT	VIL	VILLA
COM	COMMON	GAL	GALLERY	MD	MEAD	QU	QUEEN	VIS	VISTA
COMM	COMMISSION	GDN	GARDEN	MDW	MEADOWS	QY	QUAY	VLG	VILLAGE
CON	CONVENT	GDNS	GARDENS	MEM	MEMORIAL	R	RIVER	VLS	VILLAS
COT	COTTAGE	GLD	GLADE	MI	MILL	RBT	ROUNDABOUT	VW	VIEW
COTS	COTTAGES	GLN	GLEN	MKT	MARKET	RD	ROAD	W	WEST
CP	CAPE	GN	GREEN	MKTS	MARKETS	RDG	RIDGE	WD	WOOD
CPS	COPSE	GND	GROUND	ML	MALL	REP	REPUBLIC	WHF	WHARF
CR	CREEK	GRA	GRANGE	MNR	MANOR	RES	RESERVOIR	WK	WALK
CREM	CREMATORIUM	GRG	GARAGE	MS	MEWS	RFC	RUGBY FOOTBALL CLUB	WKS	WALKS
CRS	CRESCENT	GT	GREAT	MSN	MISSION	RI	RISE	WLS	WELLS
CSWY	CAUSEWAY	GTWY	GATEWAY	MT	MOUNT	RP	RAMP	WY	WAY
CT	COURT	GV	GROVE	MTN	MOUNTAIN	RW	ROW	YD	YARD
CTRL	CENTRAL	HGR	HIGHER	MTS	MOUNTAINS	S	SOUTH	YHA	YOUTH HOSTEL
CTS	COURTS	HL	HILL	MUS	MUSEUM	SCH	SCHOOL		

POSTCODE TOWNS AND AREA ABBREVIATIONS

AMS	Amersham	CNH/GTH/TMA	Crownhill/Great Holm/Two Mile Ash	HEN	Henley-on-Thames	OLN	Olney	STKPK	Stockley Park
AMSS	Amersham south	CSHM	Chesham	HEST	Heston	OXHEY	Oxhey	STSTR	Stoney Stratford
AYL	Aylesbury	CSTG	Chalfont St Giles	HGDN/ICK	Hillingdon/Ickenham	PIN	Pinner	STWL/WRAY	Stanwell/Wraysbury
AYLS	Aylesbury south	DBGH	Denbigh	HHNE	Hemel Hempstead northeast	PRRI	Princes Risborough	THAME	Thame
AYLW	Aylesbury west	DEN/HRF	Denham/Harefield	HHS/BOV	Hemel Hempstead south/Bovingdon	RAYLNE/WEN	Princes Risborough north & east/Wendover	TOW	Towcester
BDWL	Bradwell	DTCH/LGLY	Datchet/Langley	HHW	Hemel Hempstead west	RAYLW	Rural Aylesbury west	TRING	Tring
BEAC	Beaconsfield	DUN/HR/TOD	Dunstable/Houghton Regis/Toddington	HSLWW	Hounslow west	RBEDW	Rural Bedford west	UX/CGN	Uxbridge/Colham Green
BERK	Berkhamsted	DUN/WHIP	Dunstable/Whipsnade	HTHAIR	Heathrow Airport	RBICN	Rural Bicester north	WAR/TWY	Wargrave/Twyford
BIC	Bicester	EAG/OLD/WTN	Eaglestone/Oldbrook/Woughton	HWYN	High Wycombe north	RBICS/W	Rural Bicester south & west	WAT	Watford
BNEND	Bourne End	EBED/NFELT	East Bedfont/North Feltham	HWYW	High Wycombe west	RKW/CH/CXG	Rickmansworth/Chorleywood/Croxley Green	WATN	Watford north
BNFD	Binfield	EMV/FZ	Emerson Valley/Furzton	HYS/HAR	Hayes/Harlington	RMKN	Rural Milton Keynes north	WATW	Watford west
BOZ/IR/WOL	Bozeat/Irchester/Wollaston	FLKWH/TG	Flackwell Heath/Tylers Green	IVER	Iver	RMKS/WB	Rural Milton Keynes south/Woburn	WDR/YW	West Drayton/Yiewsley
BRACKY	Brackley	GTLIN	Great Linford	KGLGY	Kings Langley	RNHPTN	Rural Northampton	WDSR	Windsor
BTCHLY	Bletchley	GTMIS/PWD	Great Missenden/Prestwood	KID	Kidlington	RSLP	Ruislip	WEAT	Water Eaton
BUCK/WIN	Buckingham/Winslow	HADM	Haddenham	LBUZ	Leighton Buzzard	SHEN	Shenley	WHLY	Wheatley
CAV/SC	Caversham/Sonning Common	HAZ/HG	Hazlemere/Holmer Green	MDHD	Maidenhead	SKCH	Stokenchurch	WLLN	Willen
CFSP/GDCR	Chalfont St Peter/Gerrards Cross	HEAD	Headington	MKV	Milton Keynes village	SL	Slough	WOLV	Wolverton
CHNR	Chinnor			MLW	Marlow	SLN	Slough north	WTLGN	Watlington
CMK	Central Milton Keynes			NPAG	Newport Pagnell	STAD	Stadhampton	WTR/OFPK	Walnut Tree/Old Farm Park
				NTHLT	Northolt	STALW/RED	St Albans west/Redbourn	WYM	Wycombe Marsh
				NTHWD	Northwood			YEAD	Yeading
				NWDGN	Norwood Green				

A

Abbey Barn La
  FLKWH/TG HP10 ... 78 D7
Abbey Barn Rd WYM HP11 ... 78 E6
Abbey CI SL SL1 ... 110 D4
Abbeydore Gv MKV MK10 ... 19 J5
Abbey Park La SL SL1 ... 90 D8
Abbey Rd AYLW HP19 ... 2 B2
  BDWL MK13 ... 17 K2
  BNEND SL8 ... 88 E5
  BRACKY NN13 ... 140 B3
  EAG/OLD/WTN MK6 ... 23 H1
Abbey Sq RBEDW MK43 * ... 129 N9
The Abbey BNEND SL8 * ... 88 E6
Abbey Wk GTMIS/PWD HP16 *... 61 G3
  LBUZ LU7 ... 27 H2
Abbey Wy BDWL MK13 ... 13 K8
  MLW SL7 ... 97 J8
  OLN MK46 ... 127 L12
  WYM HP11 ... 5 H6
Abbot Rdg RAYLW HP18 ... 181 L1
Abbotsbury EMV/FZ MK4 ... 21 H4
Abbots CI BDWL MK13 * ... 13 L8
Abbot's Wk WDSR SL4 ... 120 D5
Abbots Wy HWYW HP12 ... 87 J3
  PRRI HP27 ... 58 A1
Abbotswood PRRI HP27 ... 67 G2
Abbotts CI AYL HP20 ... 3 H3
Abbott's CI UX/CGN UB8 ... 114 C2
Abbotts Rd AYL HP20 ... 3 H3
Abbotts V CSHM HP5 ... 55 H7
Abbotts Wy
  RAYLNE/WEN HP22 ... 33 M2
  SL SL1 ... 110 C5
Abell Gdns MDHD SL6 ... 107 M5
Abercorn Gv RSLP HA4 ... 95 J3
Abercromby Av HWYW HP12 ... 4 C4
Aberdeen Av SL SL1 ... 110 F4
Aberdeen CI BTCHLY MK3 ... 22 C4
Abingdon CI HGDN/ICK UB10 ... 104 C6
  THAME OX9 ... 181 N5
Abney Court La BNEND SL8 ... 88 F3
Abraham CI WLLN MK15 ... 14 F1
Abrahams Rd HEN RG9 ... 190 F3
Abstacle HI TRING HP23 ... 37 L7
Acacia Av HYS/HAR UB3 ... 115 L3
  RSLP HA4 ... 95 M7
  STWL/WRAY TW19 ... 122 D7
  WDR/YW UB7 ... 114 E4
Acacia CI BRACKY NN13 ... 8 E5
  CSHM HP5 ... 62 F1
  LBUZ LU7 ... 27 L8
Acacia Gv BERK HP4 ... 48 A2
Acacia Ms WDR/YW UB7 ... 124 C2
Acacia Wk BIC OX26 ... 162 D1
Accommodation La
  WDR/YW UB7 ... 124 B2
Ackerman CI BUCK/WIN MK18 ...142 A10
Acme Rd WATN WD24 ... 75 M1
Acorn CI BIC OX26 ... 162 D1
  DTCH/LGLY SL3 ... 123 G1
  HWYN HP13 ... 78 C3
Acorn Gdns HWYW HP12 ... 87 K2
Acorn Gv HYS/HAR UB3 ... 125 L3
  RSLP HA4 ... 105 L2
Acorn Wk CMK MK9 * ... 7 G3
Acrefield Rd CFSP/GDCR SL9 ... 92 C3
Acres End AMSS HP7 ... 71 K2
The Acres HWYN HP13 ... 4 D2
The Acre MLW SL7 ... 97 L4
Acre Wy NTHWD HA6 ... 85 J5
Adam CI SL SL1 ... 110 F5
  HWYN HP13 ... 5 M4
Adam Ct HEN RG9 ... 190 C4
Adams CI BDWL MK13 ... 17 G5
Adams Bottom LBUZ LU7 ... 27 H5
Adams CI HGDN/ICK UB10 * ... 11 K5
Adams Wy TRING HP23 ... 38 A5
Adastral Av LBUZ LU7 ... 29 L7
Addington CI WDSR SL4 ... 120 F6
Addington Rd
  BUCK/WIN MK18 ... 11 L5
  NTHWD HA6 ... 85 M8
Addison CI IVER SLO ... 113 K4
  NTHWD HA6 ... 85 M8
Addison Ct MDHD SL6 ... 109 G1
Addison Rd BUCK/WIN MK18 ...149 L12
  CSHM HP5 ... 55 H8
Addison Wy HYS/HAR UB3 ... 115 M3
  NTHWD HA6 ... 85 L8
Adelaide CI SL SL1 ... 110 F6
Adelaide Rd HWYN HP13 ... 78 C2
  WDSR SL4 ... 121 L4
Adelaide Sq WDSR SL4 ... 121 J5
Adelphi Crs YEAD UB4 ... 105 K8
Adelphi Gdns SL SL1 ... 111 K6
Adelphi St CMK MK9 ... 7 J1
Adelphi Wy YEAD UB4 ... 105 L8
Adhara Rd NTHWD HA6 ... 85 M5
Adkins CI AYLW HP19 ... 167 Q11
Adkins Rd WAR/TWY RG10 ... 116 D7
Admiralty CI WDR/YW UB7 ... 114 D6
Admiral Wy BERK HP4 ... 47 L4
Adrian CI DEN/HRF UB9 ... 84 C8
Adrians Wk SL SL1 ... 111 L5
Adstock Rd CFSP/GDCR SL9 * ... 82 C8
Adwell Sq HEN RG9 ... 190 D4
Agars PI DTCH/LGLY SL3 ... 121 M2
Aidan CI AYLS HP21 ... 42 F2
Aidans CI DUN/WHIP LU6 ... 31 M5
Ailward Rd AYLW HP19 ... 167 Q12
Ailwyns Acre RBEDW MK43 ...139 K7
Ainsdale CI BTCHLY MK3 ... 22 B3
Aintree CI BTCHLY MK3 ... 152 H1
  DTCH/LGLY SL3 ... 123 K4
  UX/CGN UB8 ... 115 G1
Airport Rd STWL/WRAY TW19 ...123 M7
Aiston PI AYL HP20 ... 3 K1
Ajax Av SL SL1 ... 111 G4
Akeman Av RBICS/W OX25 ... 163 J10
Akeman St TRING HP23 ... 37 M7
Akerlea CI EAG/OLD/WTN MK6 ... 18 F8
Akerman CI WOLV MK12 ... 16 E1
Akister CI BUCK/WIN MK18 ... 11 M6
Alabama Cir WYM HP11 ... 78 A6
Alabama Dr WYM HP11 ... 78 A6
Alan Wy DTCH/LGLY SL3 ... 112 C3
Alaska St WYM HP11 ... 78 A6
Albany CI HGDN/ICK UB10 ... 104 F3
Albany Ga CSHM HP5 ... 63 G1
Albany Pk DTCH/LGLY SL3 ... 112 A3
Albany Rd AYLW HP19 ... 167 R12
Albany Rd LBUZ LU7 ... 29 K4
  WDSR SL4 ... 121 J5
Albany Ter TRING HP23 * ... 38 A4
Albert Br WDSR SL4 ... 122 A4
Albert PI WDSR SL4 ... 120 F1
Albert Rd CSHM HP5 ... 63 H2
  HEN RG9 ... 190 H5
  HYS/HAR UB3 ... 115 K7
  WDR/YW UB7 ... 114 D5

WDSR SL4 ... 121 K7
Albert St AYL HP20 ... 3 K6
  MDHD SL6 ... 108 D3
  SL SL1 ... 111 K7
  TRING HP23 ... 37 M3
  WDSR SL4 ... 121 G4
  WEAT MK2 ... 22 F6
Albion CI SLN SL2 ... 111 M5
Albion Rd CSTG HP8 ... 82 A3
Albion PI CMK MK9 ... 7 K3
Albion Rd CSTG HP8 ... 82 K3
  HWYW HP12 ... 87 H1
  HYS/HAR UB3 ... 115 K3
  LBUZ LU7 ... 169 Q9
Albion St AYL HP20 ... 3 H6
Albury Ct CNH/GTH/TMA MK8 ... 17 J6
Albury Vw THAME OX9 ... 180 A9
Alchester Ter BIC OX26 ... 162 F5
Aldborough Sp SL SL1 ... 111 K3
Aldbourne Rd SL SL1 ... 110 A2
Aldbury Gdns TRING HP23 * ... 38 A4
Aldbury Rd RKW/CH/CXG WD3 ... 73 L8
Aldbury Rd MDHD SL6 ... 98 D8
Aldene Rd RMKN MK19 ... 131 M7
Aldenham EAG/OLD/WTN MK6 ... 23 G1
Aldenham Dr UX/CGN UB8 ... 115 G1
Alden Vw WDSR SL4 ... 120 C4
Alderbourne La
  DTCH/LGLY SL3 ... 102 D2
  IVER SLO ... 102 F3
Alderbury Rd DTCH/LGLY SL3 ...112 E6
Alderbury Rd West
  DTCH/LGLY SL3 ... 112 E6
Aldergate Rd BIC OX26 ... 162 B5
Aldergill BDWL MK13 ... 17 M1
Alderley Ct BERK HP4 ... 48 A1
Aldermead WOLV MK12 ... 17 G2
Alderney PI SHEN MK5 ... 21 J2
Alder Rd DEN/HRF UB9 ... 104 A4
  IVER SLO ... 103 H7
  RAYLNE/WEN HP22 ... 43 H2
Alderson CI AYLW HP19 * ... 167 R12
The Alders DEN/HRF UB9 * ... 104 B4
Alderton Dr BERK HP4 ... 39 M2
Aldin Av North SL SL1 ... 111 M6
Aldin Av South SL SL1 ... 111 M6
Aldrich Dr WLLN MK15 ... 15 G7
Aldridge Rd SL SL1 ... 110 F1
Aldwick Dr MDHD SL6 ... 108 C4
Aldwycks CI SHEN MK5 ... 17 J8
Alexander Rd AYL HP20 ... 2 F7
Alexander St CSHM HP5 ... 63 H1
Alexandra Dr NPAG MK16 ... 14 F4
Alexandra Ms WAT WD17 ... 75 M3
Alexandra Pk HWYN HP13 ... 78 D5
Alexandra Rd HWYN HP13 ... 78 D5
  KGLGY WD4 ... 65 M1
  MDHD SL6 ... 108 C2
  RKW/CH/CXG WD3 ... 65 M7
  SL SL1 ... 111 J7
  UX/CGN UB8 ... 104 C7
  WAT WD17 ... 75 M3
  WDSR SL4 ... 121 J5
Alford Rd HWYW HP12 ... 87 H3
Alham Rd AYLS HP21 ... 34 A8
Alice CI HAZ/HG HP15 ... 69 H3
Alice La SL SL1 ... 110 A1
Alladale PI WOLV MK12 ... 17 J8
Allanson Rd MLW SL7 ... 97 L3
Allectus Av RBICS/W OX25 ... 163 J10
Allen CI MLW SL7 ... 108 A3
Allen Dr SKCH HP14 ... 67 H6
Allens Ga BRACKY NN13 ... 8 C7
Allerds SL SL1 ... 100 A5
Allerford CI EMV/FZ MK4 ... 21 M2
Alleyns La MDHD SL6 ... 98 C2
Allington Ga EMV/FZ MK4 ... 21 H5
Allison Ct WLLN MK15 ... 18 F5
Allkins Ct WDSR SL4 ... 121 J5
Allonby Dr RSLP HA4 ... 95 G6
Allonby Wy AYLS HP21 ... 35 G7
All Saints Av MDHD SL6 ... 108 B2
All Saints La
  RKW/CH/CXG WD3 ... 74 F7
All Saints Vw SHEN MK5 ... 17 L6
Allyn CI HWYN HP13 ... 5 L4
Alma Rd BERK HP4 ... 47 K4
  CSHM HP5 ... 55 H8
  WDSR SL4 ... 121 H5
Alma St SL SL1 ... 111 L7
Almond CI BIC OX26 ... 162 B3
  LBUZ LU7 ... 27 K6
  SLN SL2 ... 100 A7
Almond Tree Dr
  RAYLNE/WEN HP22 ... 43 H2
Almond Wk HAZ/HG HP15 ... 69 H4
Almond Wy PRRI HP27 ... 183 R12
Almons Wy SLN SL2 ... 112 A2
Alnwick Dr TRING HP23 ... 168 E7
Alpha Est HYS/HAR UB3 * ... 115 K4
Alpha Rd HGDN/ICK UB10 ... 115 G1
Alpha St North SL SL1 ... 111 M6
Alpha St South SL SL1 ... 111 L7
Alpine CI MDHD SL6 ... 108 F4
Alpine Cft SHEN MK5 ... 21 K2
Alscot La PRRI HP27 ... 183 R9
Alston CI BDWL MK13 ... 17 H3
Alstonefield EMV/FZ MK4 ... 21 L3
Alston Gdns MDHD SL6 ... 108 D3
Alston Rd HHW HP1 ... 49 M8
Altair Wy NTHWD HA6 ... 85 L5
Althorpe Crs BDWL MK13 ... 13 K8
Altmore MDHD SL6 ... 117 K2
Altona Rd FLKWH/TG HP10 ... 79 H7
Altona Wy SL SL1 ... 111 G3
Alton Ga EMV/FZ MK4 ... 21 J4
Altwood Bailey MDHD SL6 ... 108 A5
Altwood CI MDHD SL6 ... 108 A5
  SL SL1 ... 110 D2
Altwood Dr MDHD SL6 ... 108 A5
Altwood Rd MDHD SL6 ... 117 M1
Alverton GTLIN MK14 ... 14 C6
Alvista Av MDHD SL6 ... 110 A3
Alvric Wy WOLV MK12 ... 16 E2
Alwin CI AYLS HP21 ... 42 B2
Alwin PI HHW HP1 ... 48 B8
Alwins Fld LBUZ LU7 ... 26 C5
Alwyn Rd MDHD SL6 ... 108 A2
Alyngton BERK HP4 ... 48 A3
Alyson Ct SL SL1 ... 110 F2
Amanda Ct DTCH/LGLY SL3 ...112 D5
Ambergate MKV MK10 ... 19 K2
Amberleigh Gdns
  RKW/CH/CXG WD3 ... 65 L7
Amberley Ct MDHD SL6 ... 99 H7
Amberley PI WDSR SL4 ... 121 J4

Amberley Rd RNHPTN NN7 ... 130 H1
  SLN SL2 ... 110 D2
Amberley Wk HGDN/ICK UB10 ... 104 D3
Amblers Wy BUCK/WIN MK18 ...149 P5
Ambleside AYLS HP21 ... 43 G7
Ambridge Gv
  EAG/OLD/WTN MK6 ... 18 E5
Ambrose Ct WLLN MK15 ... 18 F4
Amelias La CMK MK9 ... 7 K3
Amerden CI MDHD SL6 ... 109 J3
Amerden La MDHD SL6 ... 109 J3
Amerden Wy SL SL1 ... 110 F6
Amersham HI HWYW HP13 ... 5 K5
Amersham Hill Dr HWYW HP13 ... 5 K5
Amersham Hill Gdns
  HWYN HP13 ... 5 L3
Amersham PI AMSS HP7 ... 72 B2
Amersham Rd
  AMS HP6 ... 72 D2
  AMSS HP7 ... 71 C8
  BEAC HP9 ... 80 F5
  CFSP/GDCR SL9 ... 82 C4
  CSTG HP8 ... 72 A1
  HAZ/HG HP15 ... 68 D8
  HWYN HP13 ... 5 M2
  RKW/CH/CXG WD3 ... 73 G2
Amersham Wy AMS HP6 ... 72 D2
Ames CI EAG/OLD/WTN MK6 ... 7 H9
Amos CI BDWL MK13 ... 13 K8
Ampleforth MKV MK10 ... 19 K5
Amy La CSHM HP5 ... 63 G3
Ancastle Gn HEN RG9 ... 190 F5
Ancell Rd STSTR MK11 ... 16 B1
Anchor La AYL HP20 ... 3 G5
Ancil Av BIC OX26 ... 163 J4
Ancona Gdns SHEN MK5 ... 21 J3
Andermans WDSR SL4 * ... 120 C4
Andersen Ga EMV/FZ MK4 ... 21 G1
Anderson CI DEN/HRF UB9 ... 83 M8
  SKCH HP14 ... 187 J2
Anding CI OLN MK46 ... 128 A10
Andover CI BIC OX26 ... 162 F2
  UX/CGN UB8 ... 104 A7
Andrewes CI GTLIN MK14 ... 14 C8
Andrew Hill La SLN SL2 ... 91 H7
Andrews Wy AYLW HP19 ... 177 R3
  MLW SL7 ... 87 H4
Anershall RAYLNE/WEN HP22 ...168 A3
Angel CI WLLN MK15 ... 14 D7
Angelica CI WDR/YW UB7 ... 114 E3
Angelica Ct WTR/OFPK MK7 ... 23 K1
Angel La HYS/HAR UB3 ... 115 J2
Angels CI BUCK/WIN MK18 ... 151 J10
Angle CI HGDN/ICK UB10 ... 104 F6
Anglefield Rd BERK HP4 ... 47 M6
Anglesey Ct
  CNH/GTH/TMA MK8 ... 17 J6
Angood Ct PRRI HP27 ... 183 R11
Angora Ct SHEN MK5 ... 21 K3
Angus Dr BTCHLY MK3 ... 22 C4
Angus Rd AYLW HP19 ... 167 R11
Annandale Gv HGDN/ICK UB10 ... 105 H1
Anne CI MDHD SL6 ... 98 D8
Annes Gv GTLIN MK14 ... 14 E3
Annesley Rd NPAG MK16 ... 14 E3
Anniversary Av BIC OX26 ... 162 D8
Anns CI AYLS HP21 ... 42 F2
  TRING HP23 ... 37 K7
Anscuff Rd SLN SL2 ... 100 F8
Anslow Gdns IVER SLO ... 103 J7
Anslow PI SL SL1 ... 110 B2
Anson CI AYLS HP21 ... 42 D2
  HHS/BOV HP3 ... 56 E6
Anson Rd WOLV MK12 ... 12 F8
Anson Wk NTHWD HA6 ... 85 H4
Anson Wy BIC OX26 ... 162 E3
Anstey Brook
  RAYLNE/WEN HP22 ... 43 M3
Anstey CI RAYLW HP18 ... 166 E8
Anthony CI HWYN HP13 ... 4 E2
Anthony Wy SL SL1 ... 110 C4
Anthus Ms NTHWD HA6 ... 85 J7
Anton Wy AYLS HP21 ... 42 B3
Anvil CI HHS/BOV HP3 ... 57 F7
Anxey Wy NTHWD HA6 ... 63 J8
Aplin Rd AYLS HP21 ... 35 H8
Apollo Av NTHWD HA6 ... 85 J7
Appenine Wy LBUZ LU7 ... 27 G1
Appleacres RMKS/WB MK17 ...153 Q6
Appleby CI UX/CGN UB8 ... 115 G1
Appleby Heath WEAT MK2 ... 23 G7
Apple Cots HHS/BOV HP3 ... 56 F6
Applecroft BERK HP4 ... 47 K4
  MDHD SL6 ... 108 B7
  RMKS/WB MK17 ... 153 Q2
Applefield AMSS HP7 ... 72 B2
Appleton CI AMSS HP7 ... 72 A3
Appleton Ms EMV/FZ MK4 ... 21 L3
Apple Tree Av WDR/YW UB7 ... 114 E3
Apple Tree CI LBUZ LU7 ... 26 E7
Appletree Dell
  RKW/CH/CXG WD3 * ... 74 F7
Appletree La DTCH/LGLY SL3 ... 112 B7
Appletree Wk CSHM HP5 ... 63 J5
Applewick La HWYW HP12 ... 77 H6
Applewood CI HGDN/ICK UB10 ... 104 D2
Appleyard PI
  EAG/OLD/WTN MK6 * ... 6 F7
Approach Rd MDHD SL6 ... 109 K3
The Approach BIC OX26 ... 162 C3
  CNH/GTH/TMA MK8 ... 17 G3
Aquarius Wy NTHWD HA6 ... 85 M5
Aquila Rd LBUZ LU7 ... 27 L6
Aran Hts CSTG HP8 ... 82 A3
Arborfield CI SL SL1 ... 111 K7
Arbour Vw AMSS HP7 ... 72 A2
Arbroath CI BTCHLY MK3 ... 22 B3
Arbroath Gn OXHEY WD19 ... 85 M3
Arbrook Av BDWL MK13 ... 6 D8
The Arcade BEAC HP9 ... 80 D8
  MDHD SL6 * ... 108 D3
Archdale WYM HP11 ... 4 F7
Archer Dr AYL HP20 ... 3 L2
Archers Wy SKCH HP14 ... 86 A1
Archers Wls BTCHLY MK3 ... 22 E4
The Arches WDSR SL4 * ... 121 H4
Archford Cft EMV/FZ MK4 ... 21 M3
Archie CI WDR/YW UB7 ... 114 D5
Archive Rd RAYLNE/WEN HP22 ... 36 C5
Archive Rd RAYLNE/WEN HP22 ... 36 C5
Archway PRRI HP27 ... 67 G2
Arch Wy WYM HP11 ... 5 H6
Arden CI HHS/BOV HP3 ... 56 F7
Ardenham La AYLW HP19 ... 2 D4
Ardenham St AYLW HP19 ... 2 D4
Ardley CI DUN/WHIP LU6 ... 171 H1
Ardrossan CI SLN SL2 ... 110 A2
Ardross Av NTHWD HA6 ... 85 K5
Ardwell La WOLV MK12 ... 16 E1
Ardys Ct SHEN MK5 ... 6 A7

The Arena STKPK UB11 * ... 115 H5
Argyle Av AYLW HP19 ... 167 R12
Argyle Ct WATW WD18 * ... 75 L5
Argyll Av SL SL1 ... 110 F4
Aries Ct LBUZ LU7 ... 27 K6
Arizona St WYM HP11 ... 78 A6
Arklay CI UX/CGN UB8 * ... 114 E1
Arkley Ct MDHD SL6 ... 119 G1
Arkwright Rd BIC OX26 ... 162 F3
  DTCH/LGLY SL3 ... 123 K5
Arlington CI MDHD SL6 ... 107 L6
Arlington Ct EMV/FZ MK4 ... 22 B3
  HYS/HAR UB3 ... 125 J1
Arlington Dr RSLP HA4 ... 95 J3
Arlott Crs EAG/OLD/WTN MK6 ... 7 J9
Armadale Rd
  EBED/NFELT TW14 ... 125 M8
Armand CI WAT WD17 ... 75 J1
Armitage CI RKW/CH/CXG WD3 ... 74 C5
Armourer Dr GTLIN MK14 ... 14 C8
Armstrong CI
  CNH/GTH/TMA MK8 ... 17 H8
  RSLP HA4 ... 95 M5
Arncliffe Dr BDWL MK13 ... 17 L1
Arncott Rd RBICS/W OX25 ... 173 Q3
Arncott CI AYLW HP19 ... 177 R2
Arncott Wood Rd
  RBICS/W OX25 ... 173 L4
Arne La WTR/OFPK MK7 ... 144 A5
Arnett CI RKW/CH/CXG WD3 ... 73 M7
Arnett Wy RKW/CH/CXG WD3 ... 73 M7
Arnison Av HWYN HP13 ... 78 C3
Arnold CI RAYLNE/WEN HP22 ... 43 H3
Arnold CI AYLS HP21 ... 34 E8
Arnold Wy THAME OX9 ... 181 M7
Arnos Gv MKV MK10 ... 19 J5
Arnott's Yd RAYLNE/WEN HP22 ...175 L12
  TRING HP23 ... 53 H1
Arrow PI WEAT MK2 ... 153 Q2
Arthur Rd SL SL1 ... 111 J6
  WDSR SL4 ... 121 H4
Artichoke Dell
  RKW/CH/CXG WD3 * ... 73 K5
Arundel CI MDHD SL6 ... 107 M6
Arundel Ct DTCH/LGLY SL3 ... 112 C8
Arundel Gn AYL ... 34 E3
Arundel Gv HWYW HP12 ... 87 C1
Arundel Rd HWYW HP12 ... 87 C1
  UX/CGN UB8 ... 104 A7
Ascot Ct RKW/CH/CXG WD3 * ... 75 K5
Ascot Dr LBUZ LU7 ... 26 E8
Ascot PI BTCHLY MK3 ... 22 B3
Ascot Rd MDHD SL6 ... 118 E3
  WATW WD18 ... 75 K6
Ascott Ct AYL HP20 ... 3 H3
  PIN HA5 * ... 95 M3
Ascott Rd AYL HP20 ... 3 H3
Ashbourne Sq NTHWD HA6 ... 85 K6
Ashbourne End AYLS HP21 ... 42 B2
Ashbourne Gv MDHD SL6 ... 108 B7
Ashburnham CI OXHEY WD19 * ... 85 M3
Ashburn Ham CI EMV/FZ MK4 ... 21 M3
Ashburnham CI OXHEY WD19 ... 85 M3
Ashburnham Crs LBUZ LU7 ... 26 F8
Ashburnham Dr OXHEY WD19 ... 85 M3
Ashburton Rd RSLP HA4 ... 95 M8
Ashbury Dr HGDN/ICK UB10 ... 95 G3
Ashby EAG/OLD/WTN MK6 ... 7 L9
Ashby Ct BERK HP4 ... 47 J3
  BIC OX26 ... 162 B4
  WATN WD24 ... 75 M1
Ashby Wy WDR/YW UB7 ... 124 F3
Ash CI AYL HP20 ... 3 L2
  DEN/HRF UB9 ... 84 C8
  DTCH/LGLY SL3 ... 113 F7
  SKCH HP14 ... 67 G6
Ashcroft CI SL SL1 ... 100 A7
Ashcroft Dr DEN/HRF UB9 ... 93 L5
Ashcroft Rd MDHD SL6 ... 108 B2
Ashdene BIC OX26 ... 162 B5
Ashdown CI MDHD SL6 ... 99 G7
Ashdown CI GTLIN MK14 ... 14 D6
Ashdown Rd HGDN/ICK UB10 ... 104 F8
  HWYN HP13 ... 78 D2
Ashdown Wy AMS HP6 ... 63 J8
Ashenden Wk SLN SL2 ... 101 J2
Ashendon Rd RAYLW HP18 ... 165 Q8
Asheridge CI CSHM HP5 ... 54 E7
Ashfield GTLIN MK14 ... 13 M6
Ashfield CI HAZ/HG HP15 ... 69 G8
Ashfield Gv WEAT MK2 ... 22 F7
Ashfield Ri RAYLW HP18 ... 179 Q1
Ashfield Rd CSHM HP5 ... 55 J8
Ashfield Vly HAZ/HG HP15 ... 69 G8
Ashford CI AYLS HP21 ... 42 F1
Ashford Crs
  CNH/GTH/TMA MK8 ... 17 G8
Ashford La WDSR SL4 ... 110 A6
Ashford Rd IVER SLO ... 103 J7
Ash Furlong La BRACKY NN13 ... 9 L3
Ash Gra LBUZ LU7 ... 29 J1
Ash Gn DEN/HRF UB9 ... 104 A4
  AYLS HP21 ... 3 K8
Ashgrove BUCK/WIN MK18 ...149 L12
Ash Gv DEN/HRF UB9 ... 84 C8
  HYS/HAR UB3 ... 115 J4
  LBUZ LU7 ... 27 H6
  SLN SL2 ... 101 J2
  WDR/YW UB7 ... 114 E4
Ashgrove Gdns
  RAYLNE/WEN HP22 ... 159 P11
Ash Hill Rd NPAG MK16 ... 14 D2
Ash La CSTG HP8 ... 82 A3
  RBICS/W OX25 ... 163 J10
  UX/CGN UB8 ... 105 H1
Ashlea OLN MK46 ... 128 A11
Ashlea Rd CFSP/GDCR SL9 ... 92 D1
Ashley CI LBUZ LU7 ... 169 M6
Ashley Dr FLKWH/TG HP10 ... 69 H8
Ashley Green Rd CSHM HP5 ... 55 J8
Ashley Hill PI WAR/TWY RG10 ... 191 M7
Ashley Pk MDHD SL6 ... 99 J8
Ashley Rd UX/CGN UB8 ... 104 A7
Ashleys RKW/CH/CXG WD3 ... 73 L8
Ashlong CI LBUZ LU7 ... 27 H6
Ashlyns Ct BERK HP4 ... 48 A1
Ashlyns Rd BERK HP4 ... 47 L5
Ash Md HWYW HP12 ... 87 H2
Ashmead Gn DEN/HRF UB9 ... 93 M8
Ashmead Pl AMSS HP7 ... 72 B2
Ashotts La CSHM HP5 ... 54 A4
Ashpole Furlong SHEN MK5 ... 21 H3
Ashridge CHNR OX39 ... 184 D4
Ashridge CI LBUZ LU7 ... 26 C2
Ashridge La CSHM HP5 ... 64 C3
Ashridge Ri BERK HP4 ... 47 L5
Ash Rd HWYW HP12 ... 87 H2
  HHS/BOV HP3 ... 56 F7
  PRRI HP27 ... 58 A3
  TRING HP23 ... 37 L6

Ashton PI MDHD SL6 ... 107 M8
Ashton Rd RNHPTN NN7 ... 130 H1
  TOW NN12 ... 130 B2
Ashtree Wy HHW HP1 ... 49 M8
Ashurst CI NTHWD HA6 ... 85 K7
Ash V RKW/CH/CXG WD3 ... 83 J5
Ashwells FLKWH/TG HP10 ... 79 G2
Ashwells Manor Dr
  FLKWH/TG HP10 ... 79 G2
Ashwell St LBUZ LU7 ... 27 H6
Ashwells Wy CSTG HP8 ... 82 B2
Ashwin CI BRACKY NN13 ... 8 D5
Ashwood BDWL MK13 ... 13 K7
Ashwood Av UX/CGN UB8 ... 114 F3
Ashwood Dr CSHM HP5 ... 63 G1
Ashwood Gdns HYS/HAR UB3 ... 115 G8
Askett La PRRI HP27 ... 50 C7
Askew Rd NTHWD HA6 ... 85 G4
Aspen CI AYL HP20 ... 3 L2
  BIC OX26 ... 162 D1
  SLN SL2 ... 111 G3
  WDR/YW UB7 ... 114 E5
Aspen Gv PIN HA5 ... 95 L2
Aspens PI HHW HP1 ... 57 L2
Asplands CI RMKS/WB MK17 ...144 E6
Aspley HI RMKS/WB MK17 ... 144 E6
Aspley La RMKS/WB MK17 ... 144 G9
Aspreys OLN MK46 ... 128 A10
Assheton Rd BEAC HP9 ... 80 C6
Astlethorpe
  CNH/GTH/TMA MK8 ... 17 J4
Astley Rd THAME OX9 ... 181 Q5
  RAYLNE/WEN HP22 ... 32 D5
Aston Clinton Rd
  RAYLNE/WEN HP22 ... 35 K8
Aston CI AYLW HP19 ... 167 R11
  SHEN MK5 ... 21 L1
Aston Ferry La HEN RG9 ... 191 M1
Aston Gdns WTLGN OX49 ... 184 A7
Aston HI WTLGN OX49 ... 184 C11
Aston La HEN RG9 ... 191 M3
Aston Md WDSR SL4 ... 120 D4
Aston Pk WTLGN OX49 ... 184 A8
Aston Rd HADM HP17 ... 182 D1
Aston Rowant Rd
  WTLGN OX49 ... 184 A8
Astons Dr NTHWD HA6 ... 85 H3
Astor CI MDHD SL6 ... 109 G4
Astronomy Wy AYLW HP19 ... 177 R2
Astrope La TRING HP23 ... 168 F11
Astwood Rd RBEDW MK43 ...135 M11
Athena PI NTHWD HA6 ... 85 L8
Atherstone Ct
  CNH/GTH/TMA MK8 ... 16 F4
Athlone CI MDHD SL6 ... 108 D1
Athol Wy HGDN/ICK UB10 ... 104 F8
Atkins CI BDWL MK13 ... 17 L3
Atria Rd NTHWD HA6 ... 85 M5
Atterbrook BDWL MK13 ... 17 K2
Atterbury Av LBUZ LU7 ... 27 H6
Attingham HI
  CNH/GTH/TMA MK8 ... 17 J6
Attle CI HGDN/ICK UB10 ... 104 F7
Attlee Rd YEAD UB4 ... 105 M8
Atwell CI CNH/GTH/TMA MK8 ... 17 H8
Aubreys Rd HHW HP1 ... 49 K8
Auckland CI BIC OX26 ... 162 G3
Auckland Pk DBGH MK1 ... 23 G3
Auckland Rd HWYN HP13 ... 78 D4
Auden Ct NPAG MK16 ... 14 D1
Audley Dr MDHD SL6 ... 108 A4
Audley Md BDWL MK13 ... 17 K3
August End DTCH/LGLY SL3 ... 112 D3
Augustine CI DTCH/LGLY SL3 ... 123 K6
Augustus Rd STSTR MK11 ... 16 A2
Auriol Dr HGDN/ICK UB10 ... 105 G4
Austen Av OLN MK46 ... 128 C10
Austen PI AYLW HP19 ... 167 Q12
Austenway CFSP/GDCR SL9 ... 92 D2
Austenwood CI
  CFSP/GDCR SL9 ... 92 B1
  WYM HP11 ... 87 M7
Austenwood La
  CFSP/GDCR SL9 ... 92 C1
Austin Rd HYS/HAR UB3 ... 115 L6
Austinsgate MDHD SL6 ... 107 L6
Austins Md HHS/BOV HP3 ... 57 G7
Austin Wy DTCH/LGLY SL3 ... 122 E2
Australia Av MDHD SL6 ... 108 C2
Australia Rd SL SL1 ... 112 A6
Austwick La EMV/FZ MK4 ... 21 L4
Auton PI HEN RG9 ... 190 G6
Autumn CI AYLW HP19 ... 167 R11
  SL SL1 ... 110 E3
Autumn Wk MDHD SL6 ... 107 M8
  WAR/TWY RG10 ... 191 N12
Avalon Rd BNEND SL8 ... 89 G5
Avebury SL SL1 ... 110 F5
Avebury Bvd CMK MK9 ... 6 E5
Aveling Rd HWYN HP13 ... 5 L2
Avenue Bernard
  BRACKY NN13 ... 8 D6
Avenue CI WDR/YW UB7 ... 114 C7
Avenue Dr DTCH/LGLY SL3 ... 112 E2
Avenue Gdns HEST TW5 * ... 125 M3
Avenue Rd BUCK/WIN MK18 ... 151 J10
  BUCK/WIN MK18 ... 11 M3
  MDHD SL6 ... 109 G5
The Avenue AMSS HP7 ... 71 H1
  BNEND SL8 ... 88 E6
  BRACKY NN13 ... 9 J2
  CHNR OX39 ... 184 G4
  DTCH/LGLY SL3 ... 122 A4
  DUN/WHIP LU6 ... 31 M7
  HEST TW5 ... 125 M4
  HGDN/ICK UB10 ... 104 F1
  HHW HP1 ... 49 K6
  MDHD SL6 ... 99 G8
  NTHWD HA6 ... 85 H6
  PRRI HP27 ... 58 B2
  RAYLW HP18 ... 179 R9
  SLN SL2 ... 101 G2
  STWL/WRAY TW19 ... 122 C6
  UX/CGN UB8 ... 114 C1
  WAT WD17 ... 75 M3
  WDSR SL4 ... 122 A8
Averil Ct MDHD SL6 ... 110 B3
Avery Av HWYN HP13 ... 77 J4
Avery CI LBUZ LU7 ... 29 K1
Avington CNH/GTH/TMA MK8 ... 17 J8
Avior Dr NTHWD HA6 ... 85 L5
Avocet Wy AYLW HP19 ... 34 D3
  BIC OX26 ... 162 G6
Avon CI NPAG MK16 ... 15 C3
  SL SL1 ... 110 D4
Avon Crs BIC OX26 ... 162 G4
Avondale MDHD SL6 ... 108 F1
Avondale Dr HYS/HAR UB3 ... 115 M5
Avon Gv BTCHLY MK3 ... 22 B6
Avon PI AYLS HP21 ... 42 C2
Awberry Rd WATW WD18 * ... 7 F1

Aylesbury Crs SL SL1 111 J3
Aylesbury End BEAC HP9 90 D1
Aylesbury Ring
RAYLNE/WEN HP22 51 L2
RAYLW HP18 166 F6
Aylesbury Rd LBUZ LU7 161 R9
PRRI HP27 58 A2
RAYLNE/WEN HP22 35 G3
THAME OX9 181 N4
TRING HP23 37 K7
Aylesbury St WEAT MK2 23 H6
WOLV MK12 12 F8
Aylesbury St West WOLV MK12 12 E8
Aylesford Gv MKV MK10 19 K5
Aylesvater AYLW HP19 34 D2
Aylesworth Av SLN SL2 101 G8
Aylsham Dr HGDN/ICK UB10 95 H8
Aylward Gdns CSHM HP5 62 F1
Aynho Ct CNH/GTH/TMA MK8 17 J6
Ayres Cl AYLS HP21 34 A8
Ayrshire Cl AYLW HP19 167 R11
Ayrton Cl CNH/GTH/TMA MK8 17 G8
Ayr Wy BTCHLY MK3 22 B4
Aysgarth Pk MDHD SL6 119 G1
Azalea Cl HAZ/HG HP15 68 F7
Azalea Wy DTCH/LGLY SL3 112 D3

B

Babington Cl MKV MK10 19 K3
Babington Rd
RAYLNE/WEN HP22 44 C4
Babylon Gv EMV/FZ MK4 21 J5
Baccara Gv WEAT MK2 22 F7
Bachelors Acre WDSR SL4 121 J4
Back Dr NPAG MK16 132 G7
Back La BUCK/WIN MK18 10 B8
GTMIS/PWD HP16 61 G3
Backleys WTR/OFPK MK7 23 K4
Backsideans WAR/TWY RG10 191 N12
The Backs CSHM HP5 63 H2
Back St BUCK/WIN MK18 148 G2
BUCK/WIN MK18 142 H10
RAYLNE/WEN HP22 44 A6
SKCH HP14 186 G1
The Back BERK HP4 49 G3
Bacombe La
RAYLNE/WEN HP22 51 M3
Bacon Hl OLN MK46 128 A11
Baconsmead DEN/HRF UB9 93 M8
Bader Gdns SL SL1 110 F6
Badgebury Ri MLW SL7 87 H7
Badgemore Ct
CNH/GTH/TMA MK8 16 F4
Badgemore La HEN RG9 190 G3
Badger Cl MDHD SL6 108 C6
WHLY OX33 178 D10
Badgers Brook LBUZ LU7 27 H5
Badgers Cl HYS/HAR UB3 115 K4
Badgers Ga DUN/WHIP LU6 31 M6
Badgers Meadow
RAYLNE/WEN HP22 44 B5
Badgers Oak WTR/OFPK MK7 19 L7
Badgers Ri HADM HP17 177 M5
Badgers Wk HEN RG9 191 K11
RKW/CH/CXG WD3 73 L5
Badgers Wy BUCK/WIN MK18 11 M7
MLW SL7 87 H7
Badgers Wd SLN SL2 101 H3
Badger Wy HAZ/HG HP15 69 G5
Bad Godesberg Wy MDHD SL6 108 E3
Badminton Rd MDHD SL6 108 A4
Badminton Vw
CNH/GTH/TMA MK8 17 J5
Badrick Rd AYLW HP19 167 Q12
Bagley Cl WDR/YW UB7 114 D6
Bailey Cl HWYN HP13 5 L5
MDHD SL6 108 E3
WDSR SL4 120 F5
Baily Ct SHEN MK5 21 K1
Bainton Cl BIC OX26 162 G4
Bainton Rd RBICN OX27 154 A10
Baird Cl SL SL1 111 G6
Baker Cl RBICN OX27 154 E11
Bakers Cl NPAG MK16 132 C5
RBEDW MK43 129 M9
Bakers La MDHD SL6 107 L6
Bakers Orch FLKWH/TG HP10 89 K5
Baker's Piece CHNR OX39 184 C6
Baker's Rd UX/CGN UB8 104 C5
Bakers Rw MDHD SL6 107 L5
Baker St LBUZ LU7 27 H7
RAYLW HP18 166 D8
WYM HP11 4 F5
Bakers Wk RAYLNE/WEN HP22 43 L4
Bakers Wd DEN/HRF UB9 93 J7
Bakers Wood Cl LBUZ LU7 25 H8
Bakery Cl RAYLW HP18 156 H12
RBEDW MK43 139 L4
Bala Wy WEAT MK2 22 F8
Balcary Gdns BERK HP4 47 K7
Baldways Cl
RAYLNE/WEN HP22 168 A3
Baldwin Pl MDHD SL6 108 B3
Baldwin Rd BEAC HP9 91 G1
SL SL1 100 B8
Baldwins La
RKW/CH/CXG WD3 74 F5
Baldwin's Shore WDSR SL4 121 J2
Balfe Ms WTR/OFPK MK7 144 A6
Balfour Ms HHS/BOV HP3 56 E6
Balfour Pl MLW SL7 97 H2
Balfour Wy AYL HP20 3 H2
Balham's La HEN RG9 188 C2
Ballard Cl AYLS HP21 43 G1
Ballard Gn WDSR SL4 120 D3
Ballards Rw
RAYLNE/WEN HP22 * 36 C4
Ballinger Ct BERK HP4 47 M7
Ballinger Rd GTMIS/PWD HP16 61 K1
Balliol Rd BIC OX26 162 E3
BRACKY NN13 8 C6
Ball Moor BUCK/WIN MK18 11 L8
Balmer Br BUCK/WIN MK18 149 M1
Balmer Cut BUCK/WIN MK18 11 L8
Balmerino Cl MKV MK10 19 L4
Balmoral MDHD SL6 108 A1
Balmoral Cl SL SL1 110 D3
Balmoral Dr BRACKY NN13 8 D7
YEAD UB4 115 K1
Balmoral Gdns WDSR SL4 121 J6
Balsam Cl WTR/OFPK MK7 19 L8
Bamfords La RBEDW MK43 129 N8
Bamfords Yd RBEDW MK43 129 N9
Bampton Cl EMV/FZ MK4 22 B4
Banburies Cl BTCHLY MK3 22 D4
Banbury Av SL SL1 110 E2
Banbury Rd BIC OX26 162 D2
BRACKY NN13 8 C7
Banbury St WATW WD18 75 M6
Bandet Wy THAME OX9 181 Q8
Bandon Cl HGDN/ICK UB10 104 E7
Bangors Cl IVER SL0 113 L3
Bangors Pk IVER SL0 * 113 K1
Bangors Rd North IVER SL0 103 J6
Bangors Rd South IVER SL0 113 K1
Bank Gn CSHM HP5 54 B2
Bank Mi BERK HP4 48 D6
Bankmill Br BERK HP4 48 E7
Bank Mill La BERK HP4 48 D7
Bank Rd FLKWH/TG HP10 79 J2
Bankside RAYLNE/WEN HP22 44 A5
Bankside Av NTHLT UB5 105 M7
Bankside Cl DEN/HRF UB9 83 M6
Bankside Down
RKW/CH/CXG WD3 * 74 C7
Banks Rd HADM HP17 176 D12
Banks Sp SL SL1 111 G6
The Banks RNHPTN NN7 126 B3
Bank St HWYN HP13 78 E5
Bannard Rd MDHD SL6 117 M1
Bannerman Dr BRACKY NN13 8 C7
Bannister Cl DTCH/LGLY SL3 112 D6
Bannister Rd THAME OX9 181 R7
Bantock Cl WTR/OFPK MK7 23 M1
Barberry Pl BIC OX26 162 D2
Barberry Rd HHW HP1 49 M7
Barbers Ms GTLIN MK14 14 C8
Barbers Wk TRING HP23 37 L7
Barbers Wood Cl HWYW HP12 87 G2
Barbury Ct GTLIN MK14 14 D6
Barchester Cl UX/CGN UB8 104 B8
Barchester Rd DTCH/LGLY SL3 112 E6
Barclay Cl RBICN OX27 156 F4
WATW WD18 75 M7
Barden Cl DEN/HRF UB9 84 B8
Bardney Cl MDHD SL6 108 C7
Bardolphs Cl PRRI HP27 58 B2
Bardon Gn AYL HP20 3 G1
Bardsey Ct MKV MK10 19 K4
Bardwell Ter BIC OX26 162 D4
Barford STSTR MK11 16 C2
Bargeman Rd MDHD SL6 108 D6
Bargrove Av HHW HP1 49 M8
Baring Rd BEAC HP9 80 B7
HWYN HP13 78 E3
Barker Cl NTHWD HA6 85 L7
Barkestone Cl EMV/FZ MK4 21 M5
Barkham Cl LBUZ LU7 169 L7
Barkus Wy SKCH HP14 187 J1
Bar La PRRI HP27 183 N7
Barlee Crs UX/CGN UB8 114 B2
Barley Brow DUN/WHIP LU6 31 M3
Barley Cl HAZ/HG HP15 68 F7
RAYLNE/WEN HP22 43 L4
Barleycorn Cl LBUZ LU7 27 L7
Barley Crs AYLS HP21 42 C3
Barleycroft EMV/FZ MK4 22 B2
Barley Flds FLKWH/TG HP10 89 K2
Barley Md MDHD SL6 117 L1
Barley Wy MLW SL7 97 J5
Barlow Rd RAYLNE/WEN HP22 44 B5
Barnabas Rd LBUZ LU7 26 E8
Barnacre Cl UX/CGN UB8 114 C3
Barnard Crs AYLS HP21 42 E1
Barnards Hl MLW SL7 97 I4
Barn Cl MDHD SL6 98 E8
SLN SL2 101 G2
Barn Ct HWYW HP12 77 H7
Barncroft RBEDW MK43 129 N8
Barncroft Cl UX/CGN UB8 115 G2
Barncroft Rd BERK HP4 47 L7
Barn Dr MDHD SL6 117 M2
Barnes Av CSHM HP5 63 H1
Barnes Pl EAG/OLD/WTN MK6 6 F9
Barnes Wy IVER SL0 113 L4
Barnet Cl SHEN MK5 21 G1
Barnett Wy
RAYLNE/WEN HP22 35 G2
Barnfield IVER SL0 113 K3
SL SL1 110 C5
Barnfield Cl MDHD SL6 98 E5
RBICN OX27 154 E12
Barnfield Dr
EAG/OLD/WTN MK6 22 F1
Barnhill Cl MLW SL7 97 J2
Barnhill Gdns MLW SL7 97 J2
Barnhill Rd MLW SL7 97 J2
Barn La HEN RG9 190 F2
Barn Lea RKW/CH/CXG WD3 83 M1
Barn Rd PRRI HP27 183 N8
Barnsbury Av AYL HP20 35 G6
Barnsbury Gdns NPAG MK16 14 F3
Barnsdale Dr EMV/FZ MK4 21 J4
Barnsfield Pl UX/CGN UB8 104 B5
Barnwood Cl RSLP HA4 95 J8
Barons Cl WEAT MK2 22 F6
Baronsmead HEN RG9 190 G3
Baronsmead Rd HWYW HP12 4 D8
Barrack Hl RAYLW HP18 176 A4
Barrack La WDSR SL4 121 J4
Barracks Hl AMSS HP7 70 E8
Barracks Rd WYM HP11 5 G8
The Barracks
BUCK/WIN MK18 * 148 G2
Barra Hall Rd HYS/HAR UB3 115 K4
Barrards Wy BEAC HP9 81 H6
Barratt Pl WYM HP11 * 5 L7
Barrett Pl SHEN MK5 17 J8
Barrie Av DUN/WHIP LU6 31 M3
Barrie Cl AYLW HP19 167 Q12
Barrington Dr DEN/HRF UB9 83 M7
Barrington Ms
EAG/OLD/WTN MK6 7 G7
Barrington Park Gdns
CSTG HP8 82 C1
Barr's Rd MDHD SL6 110 A3
Barry Av BDWL MK13 13 M7
BIC OX26 162 C2
WDSR SL4 121 G3
Barry Cl HWYW HP12 87 H3
Bartelotts Rd SLN SL2 110 C1
Bartholomew Cl
WTR/OFPK MK7 23 K1
Bartholomew Tipping Wy
SKCH HP14 187 J1
Bartlett Ct BRACKY NN13 8 C7
Bartlett Pl BUCK/WIN MK18 11 M5
Bartletts La MDHD SL6 118 F3
Barton Rd DTCH/LGLY SL3 112 E6
WEAT MK2 22 F8
Bartons Rd FLKWH/TG HP10 78 F1
Barton Wy HWYN HP13 78 D1
RKW/CH/CXG WD3 75 G6
Bartram Cl UX/CGN UB8 115 G1
Bartsia Rd BIC OX26 162 D2
Barwick Dr UX/CGN UB8 115 G2
Bascote EAG/OLD/WTN MK6 23 G1
Base Cl AYL HP20 * 3 K1
Basford Wy WDSR SL4 120 C6
Basildon Cl WATW WD18 75 H7
Basildon Ct
CNH/GTH/TMA MK8 17 J6
LBUZ LU7 * 27 G6
Basing Rd RKW/CH/CXG WD3 83 L1
Baskerfield Gv
EAG/OLD/WTN MK6 18 F6
Baskerville La HEN RG9 191 K11
Basmore La HEN RG9 191 L10
Basset Rd SKCH HP14 86 B2
Bassetsbury La WYM HP11 78 C5
Bassett Av BIC OX26 162 E3
Bassett Ct NPAG MK16 14 F2
Bassett Rd LBUZ LU7 27 G7
UX/CGN UB8 104 B5
Bass Md MDHD SL6 98 E5
Batchelor Cl AYL HP20 * 3 K1
Batchelors Wy AMSS HP7 71 J2
CSHM HP5 55 G8
Batchworth Hl
RKW/CH/CXG WD3 * 84 D2
Batchworth La NTHWD HA6 85 H5
Bateman Dr AYLS HP21 42 D1
Bateman Rd
RKW/CH/CXG WD3 74 F7
Bates Cl BUCK/WIN MK18 159 J2
DTCH/LGLY SL3 112 D3
WLLN MK15 15 G7
Bates Ct AYL HP20 3 J1
Bates Gdns RMKS/WB MK17 152 G8
Bates La RAYLNE/WEN HP22 43 L4
Bath Ct MDHD SL6 108 B4
Bath La BUCK/WIN MK18 11 K6
Bath Rd DTCH/LGLY SL3 123 K4
HSLWW TW4 125 M4
HTHAIR TW6 125 K4
HYS/HAR UB3 125 G4
MDHD SL6 108 C3
SL SL1 110 C4
WAR/TWY RG10 116 C4
WDR/YW UB7 124 A4
Bathurst Cl WDR/YW UB7 113 L6
Bathurst Wk DTCH/LGLY SL3 113 K6
Battersby Ms AYLS HP21 2 C8
Batt Furlong AYLS HP21 42 D3
Batting Cl SKCH HP14 185 Q10
Battings Wood Gdns
SKCH HP14 67 H6
Battle Cl BIC OX26 162 F3
OLN MK46 133 N2
Battlemead Cl MDHD SL6 99 H7
The Baulk LBUZ LU7 169 L7
Bawtree Rd UX/CGN UB8 104 C4
Baxter Cl CNH/GTH/TMA MK8 17 H7
HGDN/ICK UB10 105 G8
SL SL1 111 K7
Bayard Av GTLIN MK14 18 C1
Bayard Brow BRACKY NN13 8 D6
Bayhurst Dr NTHWD HA6 85 L6
Bay La OLN MK46 127 K12
Bayley Crs SL SL1 109 M2
Bayley Gdns SKCH HP14 67 K8
Baylis Pde SL SL1 111 K3
Baylis Rd SL SL1 111 J4
Bayne Hl BEAC HP9 81 J7
Bayne Hill Cl BEAC HP9 81 J7
Baynham Md WTR/OFPK MK7 19 L6
Baysfarm Ct WDR/YW UB7 124 B4
Bay Tree Cl RMKS/WB MK17 153 J2
WYM HP11 79 G8
Bay Tree Ct SL SL1 100 B8
Bay Tree Wk WAT WD17 75 L1
Beacham Rd HWYW HP12 87 H4
Beacon Av DUN/WHIP LU6 31 M7
Beacon Cl CFSP/GDCR SL9 82 D7
HADM HP17 177 M5
UX/CGN UB8 104 C3
Beacon Ct DTCH/LGLY SL3 123 H3
EMV/FZ MK4 22 A4
Beacon La MLW SL7 86 D5
Beacon Rd BERK HP4 170 G12
Beaconsfield Av HWYN HP13 4 F1
Beaconsfield Common La
SLN SL2 91 H6
Beaconsfield Pl NPAG MK16 14 F2
Beaconsfield Rd AYLS HP21 3 H7
RAYLNE/WEN HP22 36 D5
SLN SL2 101 H6
TRING HP23 37 K7
Beacon Vw DUN/WHIP LU6 170 C2
HADM HP17 * 51 G3
LBUZ LU7 30 E1
Beacon Wy RKW/CH/CXG WD3 73 M8
TRING HP23 38 B5
Beadlemead
EAG/OLD/WTN MK6 18 F8
Beales La WTR/OFPK MK7 23 K1
Bealings End BEAC HP9 80 C5
Beamish Wy BUCK/WIN MK18 151 L9
Beancroft Rd RBEDW MK43 139 R4
Beanfare EAG/OLD/WTN MK6 22 E2
Bearbrook Cl AYLS HP21 2 C7
Bear La WAR/TWY RG10 116 A4
Bearswood End BEAC HP9 80 D6
Beatrice Cl PIN HA5 95 M3
Beauchamp Cl GTLIN MK14 14 B7
Beauchamp Gdns
RKW/CH/CXG WD3 83 M1
Beaudesert LBUZ LU7 27 H7
Beaufort Cl AYLS HP21 35 J7
BIC OX26 162 F3
Beaufort Dr WLLN MK15 14 F7
Beaufort Gdns MLW SL7 97 K4
Beaufort Pl MDHD SL6 109 J6
Beaufort Rd RSLP HA4 * 95 J8
Beaulieu Cl DTCH/LGLY SL3 122 A4
Beaumaris Gv SHEN MK5 17 K8
Beaumont Cl MDHD SL6 117 M3
Beaumont Crs BRACKY NN13 8 D7
Beaumont Ri MLW SL7 97 K4
Beaumont Rd SLN SL2 111 J2
WDSR SL4 * 121 H5
Beaumont Wy HAZ/HG HP15 68 E6
Beaverbook Ct BTCHLY MK3 22 C5
Beaver Cl BUCK/WIN MK18 11 M7
Beckdale Cl BIC OX26 162 A3
Beckets Sq BERK HP4 * 47 M4
Beckett Cha DTCH/LGLY SL3 122 E1
Beckings Wy FLKWH/TG HP10 89 H3
Beckinsale Gv
CNH/GTH/TMA MK8 17 H7
Beckley Ct HEAD OX3 178 A4
Beckton Ri MKV MK10 19 H5
Beckwell Rd SL SL1 111 H6
Bec La WLLN MK15 14 E7
Bedder Rd HWYW HP12 87 H3
Beddoes Cft SHEN MK5 21 H2
Bedfont Ct STWL/WRAY TW19 123 M6
Bedfont Court Est
STWL/WRAY TW19 * 124 A7
Bedford Av AMS HP6 72 B2
SL SL1 110 F3
Bedford Cl MDHD SL6 117 M3
RKW/CH/CXG WD3 73 G1
Bedford Dr SLN SL2 101 G3
Bedford Rd NPAG MK16 133 P9
NTHWD HA6 85 J4
OLN MK46 129 K9
RBEDW MK43 139 M4
RMKS/WB MK17 145 K5
RSLP HA4 105 L2
Bedford Rd East RNHPTN NN7 127 Q1
Bedford St BERK HP4 48 C6
LBUZ LU7 27 H7
RMKS/WB MK17 145 J11
WEAT MK2 22 F6
WOLV MK12 13 G8
Bedgebury Pl WTR/OFPK MK7 19 K6
Bedgrove AYLS HP21 35 H8
Bedlam La NPAG MK16 133 R9
Bedwell Gdns HYS/HAR UB3 115 K8
Bedwins La MDHD SL6 98 A4
Beeby Wy RBEDW MK43 129 Q3
The Beechams
RMKS/WB MK17 152 C8
Beech Av OLN MK46 128 A11
SKCH HP14 86 B1
Beech Cl BUCK/WIN MK18 11 L4
FLKWH/TG HP10 78 F8
MDHD SL6 108 A2
RAYLNE/WEN HP22 35 G3
RNHPTN NN7 126 B3
SKCH HP14 187 J3
WDR/YW UB7 114 F7
WYM HP11 78 E6
Beech Ct MLW SL7 * 97 K4
PRRI HP27 * 58 B3
Beechcroft BERK HP4 48 B7
Beechcroft Av
RKW/CH/CXG WD3 75 H7
Beechcroft Rd BTCHLY MK3 22 B8
CSHM HP5 62 F1
Beech Dr BERK HP4 48 B7
BRACKY NN13 8 D5
Beechen Wd
RKW/CH/CXG WD3 83 J4
Beeches Dr SLN SL2 101 G2
Beeches Gv FLKWH/TG HP10 68 F8
Beeches Pk BEAC HP9 80 C8
Beeches Rd SLN SL2 101 G3
The Beeches AMS HP6 62 F7
RAYLNE/WEN HP22 44 B5
RKW/CH/CXG WD3 73 L6
RMKN MK19 137 M11
TRING HP23 * 38 B6
Beeches Wy BNEND SL8 99 G2
FLKWH/TG HP10 89 K8
SL SL1 100 C1
SLN SL2 101 J4
Beech Fern WTR/OFPK MK7 23 K1
Beechfield Pl MDHD SL6 108 B6
Beech Gn AYLS HP21 2 F9
Beech Gv AMSS HP7 71 H2
AYLW HP19 2 A9
LBUZ LU7 26 F7
TRING HP23 38 B6
Beech Hill Ct BERK HP4 48 C5
Beech House Dr TOW NN12 137 M3
Beechingstoke MLW SL7 97 L3
Beechlands HAZ/HG HP15 68 D8
Beech La BEAC HP9 81 K7
GTMIS/PWD HP16 60 A3
Beech Leys BUCK/WIN MK18 149 M11
Beech Pk SKCH HP14 67 G5
TRING HP23 * 46 E5
Beech Rd AYLS HP21 2 E9
CHNR OX39 184 F4
DTCH/LGLY SL3 112 D6
NPAG MK16 14 E3
PRRI HP27 58 B3
THAME OX9 181 L6
WYM HP11 78 E6
Beech St WYM HP11 78 B6
Beechtree Av MLW SL7 97 J1
Beech Tree Cl RMKN MK19 13 G4
Beech Tree Ct
RAYLNE/WEN HP22 159 R12
Beech Tree Rd HAZ/HG HP15 69 H3
Beech Trees Rd HWYW HP12 87 H3
Beech Waye CFSP/GDCR SL9 92 E6
Beechwood Av AMS HP6 72 B1
HYS/HAR UB3 115 J4
RSLP HA4 95 L8
UX/CGN UB8 114 E3
Beechwood Cl AMS HP6 72 B2
Beechwood Dr MDHD SL6 107 M8
MLW SL7 97 G6
TRING HP23 39 J5
Beechwood Gdns SL SL1 111 K6
Beechwood La
RAYLNE/WEN HP22 44 C5
Beechwood Pk HHS/BOV HP3 57 L3
RKW/CH/CXG WD3 73 L5
Beechwood Pl HWYN HP13 5 K6
Beechwood Rd BEAC HP9 80 B8
HWYW HP12 77 G4
SLN SL2 111 J2
Beechwood Wy
RAYLNE/WEN HP22 36 D5
Beehive Cl HGDN/ICK UB10 104 E5
Beel Cl AMSS HP7 72 B2
Beethoven Cl WTR/OFPK MK7 144 B6
Beeward Cl WOLV MK12 16 D1
Beggars Bush La WATW WD18 75 J6
Beggars La TRING HP23 38 E6
Bekonscot Ct GTLIN MK14 14 C5
Belfast Av SL SL1 111 H3
Belfry Av DEN/HRF UB9 83 M8
Belfry La RKW/CH/CXG WD3 84 B1
Belgrave Ms UX/CGN UB8 114 C1
Belgrave Pde SL SL1 * 111 K4
Belgrave Rd AYLW HP19 167 R11
SL SL1 111 K4
Bellamy Cl HGDN/ICK UB10 104 F1
WAT WD17 75 M2
Bellamy Ms EMV/FZ MK4 21 H3
Bellamy Rd HWYN HP13 5 M4
Bell Av WDR/YW UB7 114 E7
Bell Cl LBUZ LU7 160 G9
PRRI HP27 58 A3
RMKS/WB MK17 152 G9
SLN SL2 112 A2
THAME OX9 181 N5
Bellclose Rd WDR/YW UB7 114 D6
Bell Ct MDHD SL6 106 E3
Bell Crs PRRI HP27 183 P8
Belle Vue HADM HP17 177 M5
Belle Vue Pl SL SL1 * 111 L7
Belle Vue Rd HEN RG9 190 G6
Belle Vue Ter DEN/HRF UB9 * 83 M7
Bellfield Rd HWYN HP13 5 G3
Bellfield Rd West HWYN HP13 4 F5
Bell Gn HHS/BOV HP3 * 57 G6
Bellingdon Rd CSHM HP5 63 G2
Bellini Cl WTR/OFPK MK7 144 A5
Bellis Gv EAG/OLD/WTN MK6 18 F6
Bell La AMSS HP7 72 A2
BERK HP4 47 K5
BIC OX26 162 D4
BRACKY NN13 140 A2
HEN RG9 190 H3
PRRI HP27 58 A3
THAME OX9 181 N5
WDSR SL4 110 E8
Bell Leys RAYLNE/WEN HP22 168 A3
Bellmount Wood Av
WAT WD17 75 K2
Bellows Mill La DUN/WHIP LU6 170 H2
Bellridge Pl BEAC HP9 80 A4
Bells Hl SLN SL2 101 M6
Bells Hill Gn SLN SL2 101 M5
Bells La DTCH/LGLY SL3 123 G6
Bells Meadow WLLN MK15 * 14 E7
Bell St HEN RG9 190 G4
MDHD SL6 108 E4
PRRI HP27 58 A3
Bellswood La IVER SL0 113 G2
Bell Vw WDSR SL4 120 E6
Bell View Cl WDSR SL4 120 E5
Bell Wk BUCK/WIN MK18 151 J10
RAYLNE/WEN HP22 168 A3
Bellway RMKS/WB MK17 144 C4
Bellwether STSTR MK11 16 D2
Bellwood Ri WYM HP11 87 M2
Belmers Rd TRING HP23 46 C1
Belmont SLN SL2 110 F2
Belmont Cl UX/CGN UB8 104 C4
Belmont Ct
CNH/GTH/TMA MK8 16 F4
Belmont Crs MDHD SL6 108 B2
Belmont Dr MDHD SL6 108 C2
Belmont Ms THAME OX9 181 N6
Belmont Park Av MDHD SL6 108 C1
Belmont Park Rd MDHD SL6 108 C2
Belmont Rd CSHM HP5 55 G7
MDHD SL6 108 C2
UX/CGN UB8 104 C5
Belmont V MDHD SL6 108 C2
Belmore Av YEAD UB4 115 M3
Belsham Cl CSHM HP5 55 G7
Belsize RKW/CH/CXG WD3 * 65 J4
Belsize Av EAG/OLD/WTN MK6 18 E5
Belton Rd BERK HP4 47 M5
Belvedere GTLIN MK14 7 H1
Belvedere Cl AMS HP6 63 L8
Belvedere La RMKS/WB MK17 23 J5
Belvoir Av EMV/FZ MK4 21 M5
Bembridge Gdns RSLP HA4 95 J8
Benacre Cft EMV/FZ MK4 21 K6
Benbow Ct SHEN MK5 17 K7
Benbow Moorings
UX/CGN UB8 * 114 B2
Benbow Wy UX/CGN UB8 114 B2
Benchleys Rd HHW HP1 49 L8
Bench Manor Crs
CFSP/GDCR SL9 92 B1
Bencombe Rd MLW SL7 97 J1
Benham Cl CSHM HP5 55 G8
Benhams La HEN RG9 188 G8
Benjamin Rd HWYN HP13 5 J4
Benmore Ri EMV/FZ MK4 21 H4
Bennet Cl STSTR MK11 16 A2
Bennetsfield Rd STKPK UB11 115 G5
Bennett Cl NTHWD HA6 85 L7
STSTR MK11 16 B2
Bennett End Rd SKCH HP14 185 M11
Bennetts CSHM HP5 63 J1
Bennetts Cl BUCK/WIN MK18 149 Q5
SL SL1 110 F5
Bennett's Hl BUCK/WIN MK18 159 M2
Bennetts La
RAYLNE/WEN HP22 33 K6
Bennetts Yd UX/CGN UB8 104 C5
Benning Cl WDSR SL4 120 C6
Benningfield Gdns BERK HP4 48 D4
Bens Cl RMKN MK19 12 C1
Benskin Rd WATW WD18 75 M6
Benson Cl BIC OX26 162 G3
SLN SL2 111 M5
UX/CGN UB8 114 D2
Bentall Cl WLLN MK15 14 F7
Bentinck Cl CFSP/GDCR SL9 92 C4
Bentinck Rd WDR/YW UB7 114 C5
Bentley Pk SL SL1 100 C7
Bentley Rd SL SL1 110 E5
Benton Dr CHNR OX39 184 F3
Benwell Cl BDWL MK13 17 J1
Benwells CHNR OX39 184 F4
Berberis Cl WTR/OFPK MK7 23 K1
Berberis Wk WDR/YW UB7 114 D8
Berceau Wk WAT WD17 75 K2
Bercham CNH/GTH/TMA MK8 17 H4
Beresford Av AYLW HP19 34 B3
SLN SL2 112 B4
Beresford Cl EMV/FZ MK4 21 L3
Beresford Rd
RKW/CH/CXG WD3 83 L1
Beretun CNH/GTH/TMA MK8 17 H5
Bereville Ct MKV MK10 19 H3
Berevilles La MKV MK10 19 H3
Bergamot Gdns
WTR/OFPK MK7 23 L1
Bergman Cl EMV/FZ MK4 21 G4
Berkeley Av CSHM HP5 54 E8
HSLWW TW4 125 M4
Berkeley Cl CSHM HP5 62 F1
RSLP HA4 105 L1
Berkeley Ct
RKW/CH/CXG WD3 * 75 J6
Berkeley Ms MLW SL7 * 97 L4
Berkeley Ri AYLW HP19 2 A1
Berkeley Rd FLKWH/TG HP10 79 H8
HGDN/ICK UB10 105 H5
THAME OX9 181 P5
Berkhampstead Rd CSHM HP5 63 H1
Berkhamsted Rd HHW HP1 49 J5
Berkley Cl LBUZ LU7 169 Q11
MDHD SL6 107 M6
Berkley Rd BEAC HP9 80 C4
Berks Hl RKW/CH/CXG WD3 73 H6
Berkshire Av SL SL1 111 G3
Berkshire Circular Routes
WAR/TWY RG10 116 A1
Berkshire Gn SHEN MK5 21 J3
Berkshire Rd HEN RG9 190 G6
Berling Rd CNH/GTH/TMA MK8 17 J4
Bernard Cl RAYLW HP18 176 C8
Bernardines Wy
BUCK/WIN MK18 11 M7
Bernards Cl GTMIS/PWD HP16 60 F3
Bernard's Cl RAYLW HP18 175 Q8
Bernards Wy FLKWH/TG HP10 88 F1
Bernay Gdns WLLN MK15 14 E7
Berndene Ri PRRI HP27 58 A1
Berners Cl SL SL1 110 D4
Bernewode Cl RAYLW HP18 175 K11
Bernstein Cl WTR/OFPK MK7 23 M2
Bernwood Rd BIC OX26 162 D4
Berries Rd MDHD SL6 98 F3
Berrington Gv EMV/FZ MK4 21 H4
Berry Cl RKW/CH/CXG WD3 74 A8
RNHPTN NN7 126 B3
Berry End RMKS/WB MK17 145 R8

Berryfield *LBUZ* LU7 ... 169 L7
Berry Fld *SLN* SL2 ... 112 B3
Berry Field Pk *AMS* HP6 ... 63 G8
Berryfield Rd *AYLW* HP19 ... 34 A3
  PRRI HP27 ... 58 B2
Berry HI *MDHD* SL6 ... 109 J3
Berry La *RKW/CH/CXG* WD3 ... 73 J7
  RMKS/WB MK17 ... 144 H4
Berrystead *WTR/OFPK* MK7 ... 23 L3
  RMKS/WB MK17 ... 152 H2
Bertram CI *BDWL* MK13 ... 13 L6
Berwald CI *WTR/OFPK* MK7 ... 144 H4
Berwick Av *SL* SL1 ... 111 G4
Berwick CI *BEAC* HP9 ... 91 G1
  MLW SL7 ... 97 H3
Berwick Dr *BTCHLY* MK3 ... 22 C4
Berwick La *MLW* SL7 ... 97 J3
Berwick Rd *MLW* SL7 ... 97 H3
Bessemer CI *BIC* OX26 ... 162 E4
  DTCH/LGLY SL3 ... 122 E1
Bessemer Ct *GTLIN* MK14 ... 14 C4
Bessemer Crs *AYLW* HP19 ... 177 P1
Bessingby Rd *RSLP* HA4 ... 95 M8
Bestobell Rd *SL* SL1 ... 111 H8
Betam Rd *HYS/HAR* UB3 ... 115 J6
Betjeman CI *WDR/YW* UB7 * ... 114 C5
Betony Wy *BIC* OX26 ... 162 D2
Bettina Gv *WEAT* MK2 ... 22 F7
Bettles CI *LBUZ* LU7 ... 108 B7
Betty's CI *RMKS/WB* MK17 ... 152 H2
Betty's La *TRING* HP23 ... 37 M6
Bevan HI *CSHM* HP5 ... 55 G8
Bevelwood Gdns *HWYW* HP12 * ... 4 A3
Beverley Gdns *BIC* OX26 ... 162 F2
  MDHD SL6 ... 108 A1
Beverley PI
  EAG/OLD/WTN MK6 ... 18 E4
Bevin HI *LBUZ* UB4 ... 105 M4
Bewcastle Rw *EMV/FZ* MK4 ... 21 H6
Bewdley Dr *LBUZ* LU7 ... 26 D7
Bewdley Gv *MKV* MK10 ... 19 K2
Bexley St *WDSR* SL4 ... 121 G4
Bicester HI *BRACKY* NN13 ... 146 E4
Bicester Rd *AYLW* HP19 ... 2 A2
  BIC OX26 ... 162 H4
  BUCK/WIN MK18 ... 156 D1
  RAYLW HP18 ... 179 N1
  RBICN OX27 ... 163 P3
  RBICN OX27 ... 154 H10
Bickleigh Crs *EMV/FZ* MK4 ... 21 M3
Biddles CI *SL* SL1 ... 110 D5
Biddlesden Rd *BRACKY* NN13 ... 147 M1
Bideford Gn *LBUZ* LU7 ... 26 D6
Bideford Sp *SLN* SL2 ... 101 G8
Bierton Rd *AYL* HP20 ... 3 J3
Bigfrith La *MDHD* SL6 ... 97 M8
Biggs La *HADM* HP17 ... 176 H8
Bigmore La *SKCH* HP14 ... 187 L5
Bignell Cft *SHEN* MK5 ... 17 L5
Bigmore Ga *MKV* MK10 ... 19 L4
Biko CI *UX/CGN* UB8 ... 114 B3
Bilbrook La *EMV/FZ* MK4 ... 21 M2
Billet La *BERK* HP4 ... 47 M4
  DTCH/LGLY SL3 ... 113 G3
Billings CI *SKCH* HP14 ... 187 J1
Billington Ct *LBUZ* LU7 * ... 27 J8
Billington La *LBUZ* LU7 ... 29 J7
Billingwell PI
  EAG/OLD/WTN MK6 ... 18 E3
Billwell *RAYLW* HP18 ... 175 K12
Bilton Rd *DBGH* MK1 ... 23 G5
Bingham CI *EMV/FZ* MK4 ... 21 M5
  HHW HP1 ... 49 G5
Bingham Rd *SL* SL1 ... 109 M2
The Binghams *MDHD* SL6 ... 109 G7
Birch CI *AMS* HP6 ... 63 K8
  IVER SLO ... 103 J7
  RBEDW MK43 ... 139 M3
Birch Crs *AYLS* HP21 ... 42 C1
Birch Crs *HGDN/ICK* UB10 ... 104 E6
Birchdale *CFSP/GDCR* SL9 ... 92 C7
Birch Dr *RKW/CH/CXG* WD3 ... 83 J5
Birchen Lee *EMV/FZ* MK4 ... 21 M4
Birches Ri *HWYW* HP12 ... 4 C3
The Birches *HHS/BOV* HP3 ... 57 H4
  HWYN HP13 ... 78 D2
Birchfield Gv *WEAT* MK2 ... 22 F7
Birch Gdns *AMSS* HP7 ... 71 K2
Birch Gn *HHW* HP1 ... 49 L6
Birch Gv *SLN* SL2 ... 111 G2
  WDSR SL4 ... 120 C4
Birchington Rd *WDSR* SL4 ... 120 F5
Birch La *HHS/BOV* HP3 ... 65 G4
Birchmead *WAT* WD17 ... 75 L1
Birch Rd *BERK* HP4 ... 47 J3
  RBICS OX25 ... 162 H10
Birch St *WYM* HP11 ... 78 A6
Birch Tree Gv *CSHM* HP5 ... 64 A1
Birch Wy *CSHM* HP5 ... 55 J8
  HAZ/HG HP15 ... 69 G8
Birchway *HYS/HAR* UB3 ... 115 M5
Birchwood Cha *HAZ/HG* HP15 ... 68 B1
Birchwood CI *HWYW* HP12 ... 77 G8
Birdcage Wk *WYM* HP11 ... 5 K7
Birdlip La *WTR/OFPK* MK7 ... 19 L7
Bird's HI *LBUZ* LU7 ... 27 H1
Birds La *NPAG* MK16 ... 132 C4
Birdwood Rd *MDHD* SL6 ... 108 A3
Birfield Rd *FLKWH/TG* HP10 ... 79 H8
Birinus CI *HWYW* HP12 ... 87 H1
Birkdale CI *BTCHLY* MK3 ... 22 A4
Birkett Wy *CSTG* HP8 ... 72 C4
Birley Rd *SL* SL1 ... 111 J3
Bisham CI *MLW* SL7 ... 97 K8
Bisham Rd *MLW* SL7 ... 97 J7
Bishop CI *LBUZ* LU7 ... 27 L8
Bishop Ct *MDHD* SL6 ... 108 C4
Bishops Av *NTHWD* HA6 ... 85 M4
Bishops CI *BRACKY* NN13 ... 8 D5
Bishop's CI *HGDN/ICK* UB10 ... 104 C7
Bishops Farm CI *WDSR* SL4 ... 120 A5
Bishops Flat
  RAYLNE/WEN HP22 ... 36 F2
Bishops Meadow
  RAYLNE/WEN HP22 ... 34 F3
Bishops Orch *SLN* SL2 ... 101 G2
Bishops Rd *SL* SL1 ... 111 M6
Bishop's Rd *HYS/HAR* UB3 ... 115 H3
Bishopstone *BDWL* MK13 ... 17 G1
  HADM HP17 ... 177 M7
Bishopstone Rd *HADM* HP17 ... 177 N6
Bishops Wk *AYLS* HP21 ... 3 J1
  FLKWH/TG HP10 ... 89 K5
  RMKS/WB MK17 ... 144 F7
Biskra *WAT* WD17 ... 75 M2
Bisley CI *BIC* OX26 ... 162 F3
Bissley Dr *MDHD* SL6 ... 117 M3
Bittenham CI *HADM* HP17 ... 177 N6
Bittern Wy *AYLW* HP19 ... 34 D1
The Bit *AMSS* HP7 * ... 70 E7

  TRING HP23 ... 46 C1
Bix La *MDHD* SL6 ... 107 L5
Black Acre CI *AMSS* HP7 ... 71 K2
Blackamoor La *MDHD* SL6 ... 108 F2
Blackberry Ct *WTR/OFPK* MK7 ... 19 L8
Blackbird CI *BRACKY* NN13 ... 8 D5
Blackbird La *MDHD* SL6 ... 118 F5
Black Boy La *MDHD* SL6 ... 106 B3
Black Butt Cots *MDHD* SL6 ... 99 G3
Blackdown *STSTR* MK11 ... 16 C2
Blacketts Wood Dr
  RKW/CH/CXG WD3 ... 73 G5
Blackfield La
  GTMIS/PWD HP16 ... 53 K7
Blackham Ct
  EAG/OLD/WTN MK6 ... 18 B7
Blackheath Crs *BDWL* MK13 ... 6 C2
Blackhill Dr *WOLV* MK12 ... 12 D8
Black Horse Av *CSHM* HP5 ... 63 J4
Blackhorse Crs *AMS* HP6 ... 71 K1
Blackhorse PI *UX/CGN* UB8 ... 104 B8
Blackmoor Ga *EMV/FZ* MK4 ... 21 H1
Blackmoor La *WATW* WD18 ... 75 J6
Blackmore CI *THAME* OX9 ... 181 P7
Blackmore Ga
  RAYLNE/WEN HP22 ... 36 F6
  TRING HP23 ... 168 D12
Black Park Rd *DTCH/LGLY* SL3 ... 102 D7
Blackpond La *SL* SL1 ... 101 G6
Blackpool Gdns *YEAD* UB4 ... 115 K1
Black Rod CI *HYS/HAR* UB3 ... 115 L7
Blacksmith La
  GTMIS/PWD HP16 ... 60 B8
Blacksmith Rw *DTCH/LGLY* SL3 ... 112 F8
Blacksmith's La *DEN/HRF* UB9 ... 93 J8
Blacksmith's Wy *RNHPTN* NN7 ... 130 H1
Blackthorn Av *WDR/YW* UB7 ... 114 F8
Blackthorn CI *RBICS* OX25 ... 163 L11
Blackthorn Dell
  DTCH/LGLY SL3 ... 112 B7
Blackthorne Crs
  DTCH/LGLY SL3 ... 123 K5
Blackthorne La
  GTMIS/PWD HP16 ... 53 K7
Blackthorne Rd
  DTCH/LGLY SL3 ... 123 K6
Blackthorn Gv
  RMKS/WB MK17 ... 144 D6
Blackthorn Rd *BIC* OX26 ... 163 J15
Blackwater Dr *AYLS* HP21 ... 42 B2
Blackwell End *TOW* NN12 ... 137 K3
Blackwellhall La *CSHM* HP5 ... 64 B4
Blackwell Hall La *CSHM* HP5 ... 63 L6
Blackwell PI *SHEN* MK5 ... 21 K2
Blackwell Rd *SKCH* HP14 ... 86 A1
Blaine CI *TRING* HP23 ... 37 M4
Blair CI *HYS/HAR* UB3 ... 115 M8
Blairmont St *CMK* MK9 ... 18 C2
Blair Rd *SL* SL1 ... 111 K5
Blakedown Rd *LBUZ* LU7 ... 26 D8
Blakeney Ct *EMV/FZ* MK4 ... 21 M4
  SL SL1 ... 108 E1
Blake Rd *BIC* OX26 ... 162 D2
Blakes La *WAR/TWY* RG10 ... 116 A4
Blakes Rd *WAR/TWY* RG10 ... 191 N12
Blake Wy *THAME* OX9 ... 181 P5
Blanchard Dr *WATW* WD18 ... 75 J4
Blanchland Cir *MKV* MK10 ... 19 K5
Blandford CI *DTCH/LGLY* SL3 ... 112 C7
Blandford Rd North
  DTCH/LGLY SL3 ... 112 C7
Blandford Rd South
  DTCH/LGLY SL3 ... 112 C7
Blandy Rd *HEN* RG9 ... 190 G6
Blansby Cha *EMV/FZ* MK4 ... 21 M3
Blatherwick Ct *SHEN* MK5 ... 17 J7
Blaydon CI *BTCHLY* MK3 ... 22 A8
Bleasdale *BDWL* MK13 * ... 17 M1
Bledlow Ridge Rd *PRRI* HP27 ... 185 M1
Bledlow Rd *PRRI* HP27 ... 185 P2
Blegberry Gdns *BERK* HP4 ... 47 K7
Blencowe CI *RBICN* OX27 ... 154 E12
Blencowe Dr *BRACKY* NN13 ... 8 B3
Blenheim Crs *RSLP* HA4 ... 95 J8
Blenheim Cft *BRACKY* NN13 ... 8 E8
Blenheim CI *BIC* OX26 ... 163 J4
  BIC OX26 ... 162 B3
Blenheim Pde
  HGDN/ICK UB10 * ... 115 C1
Blenheim PI *AYLS* HP21 ... 42 D1
  BRACKY NN13 ... 140 B3
Blenheim Rd *DTCH/LGLY* SL3 ... 112 C8
  HWYW HP12 ... 87 J2
  MDHD SL6 ... 108 A2
Bletcham Wy *DBGH* MK1 ... 22 H4
  WTR/OFPK MK7 ... 23 J3
Bletchmore CI *HYS/HAR* UB3 ... 125 J1
Blinco La *DTCH/LGLY* SL3 ... 113 D3
Blind La *BNEND* SL8 ... 88 F6
  GTMIS/PWD HP16 ... 62 A2
Bliss Av *WDR/YW* UB7 ... 114 C1
Bliss Ct *WTR/OFPK* MK7 ... 23 M7
Blissworth *EAG/OLD/WTN* MK6 ... 23 G1
Blondell CI *WDR/YW* UB7 ... 124 C2
Bloomfield Rd *MDHD* SL6 ... 117 M1
Bloomsbury CI
  RMKS/WB MK17 ... 145 J12
Blossom Wy *HGDN/ICK* UB10 ... 104 E5
  WDR/YW UB7 ... 114 F8
Blucher St *CSHM* HP5 ... 63 G6
Bluebell CI *BUCK/WIN* MK18 ... 11 K7
  HHW HP1 * ... 49 K8
Bluebell Cft *WTR/OFPK* MK7 ... 19 L8
Blumfield Crs *SL* SL1 ... 110 C1
Blundells Rd *BDWL* MK13 ... 13 L8
Blunden Dr *DTCH/LGLY* SL3 ... 113 G8
Blunts Av *WDR/YW* UB7 ... 124 D8
Blyth Ct *EMV/FZ* MK4 ... 21 K6
Blythe CI *HYS/HAR* UB3 ... 115 J1
  IVER SLO ... 113 L3
  NPAG MK16 ... 15 G2
Blythe PI *BIC* OX26 ... 162 A3
Blyth Rd *HYS/HAR* UB3 ... 115 K6
Blyton CI *BEAC* HP9 ... 91 G3
Boadicea CI *SL* SL1 ... 110 D5
Boarlands CI *SL* SL1 ... 110 E4
Bobmore La *MLW* SL7 ... 97 K5
Bockmer La *MLW* SL7 ... 96 A8
Boddington Rd
  RAYLNE/WEN HP22 ... 44 B6
Boddington Wy *BRACKY* NN13 ... 8 A10
Bodenham CI *BUCK/WIN* MK18 ... 142 A10
Bodiam CI *AYLS* HP21 ... 43 D1
  SHEN MK5 ... 21 K1
Bodle CI *WLLN* MK15 ... 14 D7
Bodmin Av *SLN* SL2 ... 110 F2

Bodnant Ct *EMV/FZ* MK4 ... 21 J4
Bodwell CI *HHW* HP1 ... 49 M6
Bois Av *AMS* HP6 ... 63 G7
Bois HI *CSHM* HP5 ... 63 J5
Bois La *AMS* HP6 ... 63 J5
Bois Mi *CSHM* HP5 * ... 63 M7
Bois Moor Rd *CSHM* HP5 ... 63 K6
Bolan Ct *CNH/GTH/TMA* MK8 ... 17 H8
Bolingbroke Wy *HYS/HAR* UB3 ... 115 J2
Bolney La *HEN* RG9 ... 191 K10
Bolney Rd *HEN* RG9 ... 191 J10
Bolter End La *SKCH* HP14 ... 187 Q8
Bolton Av *WDSR* SL4 ... 121 H5
Bolton CI *BTCHLY* MK3 ... 22 A5
Bolton Crs *WDSR* SL4 ... 121 H6
Bolton Rd *WDSR* SL4 ... 121 H6
Boltons CI *BRACKY* NN13 ... 8 D5
Bolton's La *HYS/HAR* UB3 ... 125 H3
Boltwood Gv *SHEN* MK5 ... 21 H1
Bomer CI *WDR/YW* UB7 ... 124 F3
Bond Av *DBGH* MK1 ... 23 G4
Bond CI *WDR/YW* UB7 ... 114 E3
Bondfield Av *YEAD* UB4 ... 105 M8
Bone HI *BUCK/WIN* MK18 ... 11 K7
Bones La *HEN* RG9 ... 190 D11
Bonham Carter Rd
  RAYLNE/WEN HP22 ... 44 C3
Bonham CI *AYLS* HP21 ... 34 C3
Bonham Ct *RAYLNE/WEN* HP22 ... 36 C5
Boniface Rd *HGDN/ICK* UB10 ... 105 G1
Bonnards Rd *RMKS/WB* MK17 ... 153 J2
Bonnersfield *RAYLW* HP18 ... 175 K11
Booker CI *BDWL* MK13 ... 6 D2
Bookerhill Rd *HWYW* HP12 ... 87 H1
Booker La *HWYW* HP12 ... 4 A6
Booker PI *HWYW* HP12 ... 87 G3
Booth PI *DUN/WHIP* LU6 ... 30 F8
Boot La *HADM* HP17 ... 176 H8
Borderside *SL* SL1 ... 111 M3
Borodin Ct *WTR/OFPK* MK7 ... 144 A5
Borough Rd *BRACKY* NN13 ... 146 E1
Bosanquet CI *UX/CGN* UB8 ... 114 C2
Bossard Ct *LBUZ* LU7 ... 27 H7
Boss Av *LBUZ* LU7 ... 29 H1
Bossiney PI
  EAG/OLD/WTN MK6 ... 7 J6
Bossington La *LBUZ* LU7 ... 26 F7
Boss La *HAZ/HG* HP15 ... 68 A3
Bostock La *BUCK/WIN* MK18 * ... 11 K6
Boston Dr *BNEND* SL8 ... 89 G7
Boston Gv *RSLP* HA4 ... 95 H5
  SL SL1 ... 111 H3
Boston Rd *BIC* OX26 ... 162 F2
  HEN RG9 ... 190 H6
Boswell CI *BUCK/WIN* MK18 ... 11 H4
Boswell La *RMKN* MK19 ... 137 M10
Boswick La *BERK* HP4 ... 47 J2
Bosworth CI *BTCHLY* MK3 ... 22 B4
Botham Dr *SL* SL1 ... 111 K7
The Bothy *WAR/TWY* RG10 ... 191 N12
Botley La *CSHM* HP5 ... 63 M1
Botley Rd *CSHM* HP5 ... 63 K1
Bottesford CI *EMV/FZ* MK4 ... 22 A5
Bottle La *MDHD* SL6 ... 107 K8
Bottle Square La *SKCH* HP14 ... 185 N12
Bottom Dr *DUN/WHIP* LU6 ... 171 L1
Bottom House Farm La
  CSTG HP8 ... 81 J1
Bottom House La *TRING* HP23 ... 38 F1
Bottom La *BEAC* HP9 ... 81 H6
Bottom Orch *RAYLW* HP18 ... 175 R9
Bottom Rd *SKCH* HP14 ... 185 P11
  TRING HP23 ... 45 J7
Bottrells La *CSTG* HP8 ... 81 L2
Botwell Common Rd
  HYS/HAR UB3 ... 115 J4
Botwell Crs *HYS/HAR* UB3 ... 115 K3
Botwell La *HYS/HAR* UB3 ... 115 L6
Botyl Rd *BUCK/WIN* MK18 ... 158 B4
Boughton Wy *AMS* HP6 ... 72 B2
Boulevard *WATW* WD18 * ... 75 K7
The Boulevard *WATW* WD18 ... 75 J6
Boulmer Rd *UX/CGN* UB8 ... 104 B8
Boulters CI *SL* SL1 ... 110 F6
Boulters Ct *MDHD* SL6 ... 109 H1
Boulters Gdns *MDHD* SL6 ... 109 H1
Boulters La *MDHD* SL6 ... 109 H1
Boulters Lock *GTLIN* MK14 ... 14 C5
Boundary Crs *STSTR* MK11 ... 16 A4
Boundary PI *FLKWH/TG* HP10 ... 89 J2
Boundary Rd *BRACKY* NN13 ... 8 C7
  CFSP/GDCR SL9 ... 82 C7
  FLKWH/TG HP10 ... 89 H1
  MDHD SL6 ... 109 L2
The Boundary
  EAG/OLD/WTN MK6 ... 7 J9
Bounty St *BDWL* MK13 ... 17 F3
Bouquet CI *GTMIS/PWD* HP16 ... 60 B5
Bourbon St *AYL* HP20 ... 2 F6
Bourn Av *UX/CGN* UB8 ... 114 F1
Bourne Av *HYS/HAR* UB3 ... 115 H7
  WDSR SL4 ... 120 D6
Bourne CI *BIC* OX26 ... 162 C5
  BNEND SL8 ... 89 G7
Bourne End La *HHW* HP1 ... 57 H1
Bourne End Rd *BNEND* SL8 ... 89 G4
  NTHWD HA6 ... 85 K4
  RBEDW MK43 ... 129 K2
Bournemead Av *NTHLT* UB5 ... 105 M7
Bournemead CI *NTHLT* UB5 ... 105 M7
Bourne Rd *BERK* HP4 ... 47 L1
The Bourne *HHS/BOV* HP3 ... 56 F6
Bourton CI *HYS/HAR* UB3 ... 115 M5
Bourton Low *WTR/OFPK* MK7 ... 23 L1
Bourton Rd *BUCK/WIN* MK18 ... 11 L6
Bourtonville
  BUCK/WIN MK18 ... 11 L7
Bouverie Wy *DTCH/LGLY* SL3 ... 122 D1
Boveney CI *SL* SL1 ... 110 F6
Boveney New Rd *WDSR* SL4 ... 110 B8
Boveney Rd *WDSR* SL4 ... 110 B8
Boveney CI *SL* SL1 ... 110 F6
Boveney Wood La *SL* SL1 ... 100 C1
Bovingdon Hts *MLW* SL7 ... 97 G4
Bow Brickhill Rd
  RMKS/WB MK17 ... 144 C7
Bowden La *WYM* HP11 ... 5 G6
Bowen CI *WTR/OFPK* MK7 ... 23 M2
Bower CI *DUN/WHIP* LU6 ... 170 G1
Bowerdean Rd *HWYN* HP13 ... 5 C3
Bower La *DUN/WHIP* LU6 ... 170 G1
Bower's La *SKCH* HP14 ... 185 N11
Bowes CI *NPAG* MK16 ... 14 F2
Bowes Lyon CI *WDSR* SL4 ... 120 F6
Bowland Dr *EMV/FZ* MK4 ... 21 L5
Bowler Lea *HWYN* HP13 ... 77 J4
Bowler Rd *AYLS* HP21 ... 42 D2
Bowler's Orch *CSTG* HP8 ... 81 M3

Bowling Aly
  RAYLNE/WEN HP22 ... 159 N11
Bowling CI *HGDN/ICK* UB10 ... 104 E6
Bowling Ct *HEN* RG9 ... 190 F3
Bowling Green Rd
  RBEDW MK43 ... 139 M5
Bowling Leys *MKV* MK10 ... 19 K4
Bowmans CI *SL* SL1 ... 100 A6
Bowmont Dr *AYLS* HP21 ... 42 C3
Bowood Ct
  CNH/GTH/TMA MK8 ... 17 J5
Bowood La
  RAYLNE/WEN HP22 ... 52 D5
Bowstridge La *CSTG* HP8 ... 82 B6
Bowyer Crs *DEN/HRF* UB9 ... 93 L5
Bowyer Dr *SL* SL1 ... 110 D2
Bowyers Ms *GTLIN* MK14 ... 14 C3
Boxberry Gdns
  WTR/OFPK MK7 ... 19 K8
Boxer Rd *PRRI* HP27 ... 183 P8
Boxgrove St *MKV* MK10 ... 19 J5
Box La *HHS/BOV* HP3 ... 57 J4
Box Tree CI *CSHM* HP5 * ... 63 J4
Boxwell Rd *BERK* HP4 ... 48 A4
Boxwood CI *WDR/YW* UB7 ... 114 E6
Boyce Crs *WTR/OFPK* MK7 ... 144 A5
Boycott Av
  EAG/OLD/WTN MK6 ... 7 G7
Boyle CI *HGDN/ICK* UB10 ... 104 E7
Boyndon Rd *MDHD* SL6 ... 108 C4
Boyn HI Av *MDHD* SL6 ... 108 C4
Boyn Hill CI *MDHD* SL6 ... 108 C4
Boyn Valley Rd *MDHD* SL6 ... 108 C5
Bozenham Mill La *TOW* NN12 ... 130 C7
Bracken CI *SLN* SL2 ... 101 J2
Brackenforde *DTCH/LGLY* SL3 ... 112 B6
Bracken HI *HP4* ... 48 B5
Bracken Rd *MDHD* SL6 ... 108 B6
Brackenwood *SKCH* HP14 ... 67 H1
Brackley Dr *HAZ/HG* HP15 ... 68 C3
Brackley Corse
  BRACKY NN13 * ... 8 A5
Brackley La
  BRACKY NN13 ... 8 D7
Brackley Lodge Ms
  BRACKY NN13 ... 8 D7
Brackley Rd *BRACKY* NN13 ... 147 M1
  BUCK/WIN MK18 ... 11 J5
  HAZ/HG HP15 ... 68 C3
Bradbery *RKW/CH/CXG* WD3 ... 83 J5
Bradbourne Dr
  WTR/OFPK MK7 ... 23 M2
Bradbury Rd *BDWL* MK13 ... 17 K2
The Bradburys *RBICN* OX27 ... 155 J10
Bradcutts La *MDHD* SL6 ... 98 C3
Braddenham Wk *AYLS* HP21 ... 42 D2
Bradden La *HHNE* HP2 ... 41 K3
Braddons Furlong
  RAYLW HP18 ... 175 K12
Braden CI *AYLS* HP21 ... 34 F8
Bradenham Beeches
  SKCH HP14 ... 66 F6
Bradenham La *MLW* SL7 ... 107 H1
Bradenham Rd *SKCH* HP14 ... 76 E1
  YEAD UB4 ... 105 K8
Bradenham Wd *SKCH* HP14 ... 67 G5
Bradfield Av *BUCK/WIN* MK18 ... 11 L4
Bradford Rd
  RKW/CH/CXG WD3 ... 73 H8
  SL SL1 ... 110 F3
Bradley CI *RAYLW* HP18 ... 179 G3
Bradley Gv *EMV/FZ* MK4 ... 21 H3
Bradley Rd *SL* SL1 ... 111 J4
Bradshaw Dr *WDSR* SL4 ... 120 D4
Bradshaw Rd *WDSR* SL4 ... 78 E4
Bradvue Crs *BDWL* MK13 ... 13 K8
Bradwell Common Bvd
  BDWL MK13 ... 6 C3
Bradwell Rd *BDWL* MK13 ... 13 K7
  CNH/GTH/TMA MK8 ... 17 K4
  RAYLNE/WEN HP22 ... 35 H2
Brae HI *RAYLW* HP18 ... 174 F7
Brae Hill CI *RAYLW* HP18 ... 174 F7
Braemar Gdns *SL* SL1 ... 110 F6
Braeside *SKCH* HP14 ... 67 J8
Brafield Rd *RNHPTN* NN7 ... 126 D4
Bragenham La *LBUZ* LU7 ... 24 D8
Bragman's La
  RKW/CH/CXG WD3 ... 65 J4
Brahms CI *WTR/OFPK* MK7 ... 23 M1
The Braid *CSHM* HP5 ... 63 K1
Brakynbery *BERK* HP4 ... 47 K3
Brallings La *CFSP/GDCR* SL9 ... 82 F4
Bramber CI *SL* SL1 ... 110 F5
Bramber Ct *SL* SL1 ... 110 F5
Bramble Av *GTLIN* MK14 ... 14 C5
Bramble CI *CFSP/GDCR* SL9 ... 82 D6
  LBUZ LU7 ... 27 K8
  UX/CGN UB8 ... 114 E2
Bramble Crs *HAZ/HG* HP15 ... 69 H4
Bramble Dr *MDHD* SL6 ... 117 M2
Bramble La *AMSS* HP7 ... 71 K4
Bramble Md *CSTG* HP8 ... 81 M3
Brambles Farm Dr
  HGDN/ICK UB10 ... 104 D7
Brambleside *HWYN* HP13 ... 79 G6
The Brambles *WDR/YW* UB7 ... 124 C3
Brambling *AYLW* HP19 ... 34 D3
The Bramblings *BIC* OX26 ... 162 F5
Bramcote CI *AYL* HP20 ... 35 H6
Bramham Ct *NTHWD* HA6 * ... 85 K5
Bramleas *WATW* WD18 ... 75 L6
Bramley Cha *WATW* WD18 ... 75 L6
Bramley CI *HYS/HAR* UB3 ... 115 M4
  MDHD SL6 ... 117 M2
  PIN HA5 ... 95 L2
Bramley End *SKCH* HP14 ... 67 M6
Bramley Mdw *AYLS* HP21 ... 14 E3
Bramley Rd *DBGH* MK1 ... 22 H4
Brammas CI *SL* SL1 ... 110 E5
Brampton Cha *HEN* RG9 ... 191 N10
Brampton Ct *MDHD* SL6 ... 109 G2
Brampton Ms *MLW* SL7 * ... 97 J5
Brampton Rd *HGDN/ICK* UB10 ... 105 G1
  OXHEY WD19 ... 85 M3
Bramshaw Wy *OXHEY* WD19 ... 85 M3
Branch Rd *FLKWH/TG* HP10 ... 79 G8
Brandon Rd *HWYW* HP12 ... 87 H3
Brands Hill Av *HWYN* HP13 ... 5 G8
Brands Rd *DTCH/LGLY* SL3 ... 123 G2
Brandville Rd *WDR/YW* UB7 ... 114 D6
Bransgill Ct *BDWL* MK13 ... 13 J8
Bransworth Av *MKV* MK10 ... 19 M6
Brantham CI *WTR/OFPK* MK7 ... 23 K3
Brantwood CI *HWYN* HP13 ... 21 H5
Braséwood Dr *BRACKY* NN13 * ... 8 C5

Braunston *EAG/OLD/WTN* MK6 ... 19 G8
Braybank *HHS/BOV* HP3 ... 109 J6
Braybourne CI *UX/CGN* UB8 ... 104 B4
Braybrooke Dr *EMV/FZ* MK4 ... 22 B7
Bray Ct *MDHD* SL6 ... 109 H7
Bray CI *BDWL* MK13 ... 109 H8
Brayfield Rd *MDHD* SL6 ... 109 G6
Bray Rd *MDHD* SL6 ... 109 G6
Brays CI *AMS* HP6 ... 62 B6
Brays Green La *AMS* HP6 ... 62 B6
Brays Meadow *AMS* HP6 ... 62 B6
Brayton Ct *SHEN* MK5 ... 17 M8
Braywick Rd *MDHD* SL6 ... 108 E4
Braziers End *CSHM* HP5 ... 54 B2
Breachwell PI *LBUZ* LU7 ... 169 M5
Breadcroft La *MDHD* SL6 ... 117 K2
Breadmarch Rd *RSLP* HA4 ... 95 C5
Breadmort La *MDHD* SL6 ... 117 L3
Breamore CI *MLW* SL7 ... 97 H6
Breamore
  CNH/GTH/TMA MK8 ... 17 J6
Brearley Av
  EAG/OLD/WTN MK6 ... 18 B7
Brearley CI *UX/CGN* UB8 ... 104 D4
Breckland *GTLIN* MK14 ... 17 H1
Brecon Ct *MKV* MK10 ... 19 J5
Brecon Wy *HWYN* HP13 ... 4 D3
Bredward CI *SL* SL1 ... 100 A8
The Breezes *MDHD* SL6 ... 108 D6
Bremen Gv *SHEN* MK5 ... 21 K2
Brenchwood CI *HWYN* HP13 ... 77 H4
Brendon CI *HYS/HAR* UB3 ... 125 H3
Brendon Ct *EMV/FZ* MK4 ... 22 A3
Brent *EAG/OLD/WTN* MK6 ... 23 G1
Brent Rd *BNEND* SL8 ... 88 F6
Brentwood Wy *AYLS* HP21 ... 35 G8
Bretby Cha *EMV/FZ* MK4 ... 21 J4
Breton *STSTR* MK11 ... 12 B8
Brett CI *THAME* OX9 ... 181 Q6
Brewery Ct *BUCK/WIN* MK18 * ... 11 L6
Brewhouse La
  RAYLNE/WEN HP22 ... 33 K5
Brewin CI *BRACKY* NN13 ... 8 C5
Brewster CI *SHEN* MK5 ... 21 H1
Briarcliff *HHW* HP1 ... 49 K6
Briar CI *BERK* HP4 ... 48 F3
  BRACKY NN13 ... 8 E5
  MDHD SL6 ... 110 A3
Briar Dene *MDHD* SL6 ... 108 B1
Briar Gln *MDHD* SL6 ... 98 B4
Briar HI *WOLV* MK12 ... 17 G1
Briars CI *AYLW* HP19 ... 3 H1
The Briars *DTCH/LGLY* SL3 ... 122 E1
  HAZ/HG HP15 ... 69 H3
  RKW/CH/CXG WD3 ... 65 M7
Briarswood *HAZ/HG* HP15 ... 69 G7
Briarswood CI *SKCH* HP14 ... 186 H1
Briar Wy *BERK* HP4 ... 48 B7
  SKCH HP14 ... 111 G2
  WDR/YW UB7 ... 114 F7
Briarwood Dr *NTHWD* HA6 ... 95 M1
Briary Vw *RMKS/WB* MK17 ... 20 C6
Brices Meadow *SHEN* MK5 ... 21 K3
Brick CI *STSTR* MK11 ... 16 F4
Brickett La *RSLP* HA4 ... 95 H4
Brickfield La *HYS/HAR* UB3 ... 125 J2
  SL SL1 ... 99 M6
Brickfields Wy *WDR/YW* UB7 ... 114 E7
Brick HI *RAYLW* HP18 ... 175 L1
Brickhill Manor Ct
  RMKS/WB MK17 * ... 144 A12
Brickhill St *LBUZ* LU7 ... 25 H7
Brickhill St *GTLIN* MK14 ... 14 C4
  WLLN MK15 ... 19 G3
Brickhill Wy *BUCK/WIN* MK18 ... 157 J5
Brick Kiln La
  RAYLNE/WEN HP22 ... 35 H2
Bricks La *SKCH* HP14 ... 187 M2
Brickwall La *RSLP* HA4 ... 95 K7
Bridestow *RAYLNE/WEN* HP22 ... 33 J2
Bridgens Wy *HADM* HP17 ... 176 C12
Bridge Av *MDHD* SL6 ... 98 D9
Bridge Bank CI *WYM* HP11 ... 78 F7
Bridge CI *SL* SL1 ... 110 E4
Bridgeford Ct
  EAG/OLD/WTN MK6 ... 6 F8
Bridge Hook CI *WOLV* MK12 ... 12 D7
Bridgeman Dr *WDSR* SL4 ... 120 F5
Bridge PI *AMS* HP6 ... 71 K1
Bridge Rd *MDHD* SL6 ... 109 G3
  RAYLW HP18 ... 180 A4
  RMKN MK19 ... 12 B4
  UX/CGN UB8 ... 104 B7
Bridgestone Dr *BNEND* SL8 ... 89 G7
Bridge St *BDWL* MK13 ... 13 J7
  BERK HP4 ... 48 C6
  BRACKY NN13 ... 8 D8
  BUCK/WIN MK18 ... 11 L5
  DTCH/LGLY SL3 ... 123 J3
  HADM HP17 ... 50 C5
  LBUZ LU7 ... 27 G7
  MDHD SL6 ... 108 F3
  OLN MK46 ... 128 B12
  RBEDW MK43 ... 129 J9
  WYM HP11 ... 5 G6
Bridgeturn Av *WOLV* MK12 ... 13 G6
Bridge Wk *RMKN* MK19 ... 137 M10
Bridgewater Ct *BRACKY* NN13 ... 8 D8
Bridgewater Ct *BRACKY* NN13 ... 8 C8
  DTCH/LGLY SL3 ... 112 F8
Bridgewater Crs
  BRACKY NN13 ... 8 E6
Bridgewater HI *BERK* HP4 ... 48 L3
Bridgewater Ri *BRACKY* NN13 ... 8 E6
Bridgewater St *BERK* HP4 ... 48 A4
  BRACKY NN13 ... 8 E6
Bridgewater Ter *WDSR* SL4 ... 121 J4
Bridgeway *BDWL* MK13 ... 13 J5
Bridge Wy *HGDN/ICK* UB10 ... 105 G3
Bridgeway *AYLW* HP19 ... 34 A7
Bridgewater Dr *EMV/FZ* MK4 ... 21 H5
Bridgwater Rd *RSLP* HA4 ... 95 H2
Bridle CI *BDWL* MK13 ... 108 D1
  MDHD SL6 ... 108 D1
Bridle Ga *WYM* HP11 ... 5 K6
Bridle La *RKW/CH/CXG* WD3 ... 74 B4
Bridle Rd *MDHD* SL6 ... 108 D1
Bridle Wy *BERK* HP4 ... 47 M4
Bridle Wy *RAYLNE/WEN* HP22 ... 45 L4
Bridleways *RAYLNE/WEN* HP22 ... 51 J3
Bridlington Crs *MKV* MK10 ... 19 J5
Bridlington Sp *SLN* SL2 ... 111 G7
Bridport Wy *SLN* SL2 ... 111 G4

Brierley Cl *DUN/WHIP* LU6....171 R1
Briery Fld *RKW/CH/CXG* WD3....73 M4
Briery Wy *AMS* HP6....63 K8
Brighton *HGDN/ICK* UB10....105 G3
Brighton Rd *WATN* WD24....75 M1
Brighton Sp *SLN* SL1....111 G1
Brightwell Cl *AYLW* HP19....31 K1
Brightwell Rd *WATW* WD18....75 M6
Brill Cl *MDHD* SL6....108 C6
  MLW SL7....97 H4
Brill Pl *BDWL* MK13....6 A3
Brill Rd *RAYLW* HP18....174 H4
  RAYLW HP18....6 D7
  WHLY OX33....178 H1
Brimmers Hl *HAZ/HG* HP15....68 D4
Brimmers Rd *PRRI* HP27....58 B4
Brimmers Wy *AYLW* HP19....177 Q1
Brimstone Wy *BERK* HP4....47 L4
Brindlebrook
  CNH/GTH/TMA MK8....17 H5
Brindles La *BEAC* HP9....79 M6
Brindley Av *HWYN* HP13....4 B3
Brinkburn Cha *MKV* MK19....19 K5
Briskman Wy *AYLS* HP21....2 B9
Bristle Hl *BUCK/WIN* HP18....11 K6
Bristol Rd *OX26*....162 F3
Bristol Wy *SL1* SL1....111 K5
Bristow Cl *WEAT* MK2....23 H5
Britannia Rd *CSHM* HP5....55 H5
Britannia St *AYL* HP20....3 C5
Britannia Wk *AYL* HP20....3 F3
Britten Gv *WTR/OFPK* MK7....144 A5
Brittons La *RMKS/WB* MK17....138 F11
Britwell Dr *BERK* HP4....48 D4
Britwell Rd *SL* SL1....100 B8
Brixham Crs *RSLP* HA4....95 M4
Broadacre Cl *HGDN/ICK* UB10....105 G1
Broad Arrow Cl *GTLIN* MK14....14 B7
Broad Dean
  EAG/OLD/WTN MK6....7 L8
Broadlands *AYLW* HP19....177 R1
Broadlands
  EAG/OLD/WTN MK6....18 E8
Broadlands Av *CSHM* HP5....63 H1
Broad La *BRACKY* NN13....146 D3
  FLKWH HP10....89 H8
Broad Leys *PRRI* HP27....183 R11
Broadmark Rd *SLN* SL2....112 A4
Broadmoor Rd
  WAR/TWY RG10....117 G8
Broad Oak Cl *SLN* SL2....111 H1
Broad Oak Ct *SLN* SL2....111 H1
Broad Piece *WLLN* MK15....14 C7
Broad Platts *DTCH/LGLY* SL3....112 C7
Broad St *BRACKY* NN13....140 A2
  CSHM HP5....63 H1
  WEAT MK2....16 F3
Broadview Rd *CSHM* HP5....55 G6
The Broadwalk *NTHWD* HA6....95 H1
Broadwater *BERK* HP4....48 B5
  EAG/OLD/WTN MK6....23 G1
Broadwater Gdns
  DEN/HRF UB9....94 A3
Broadwater La *DEN/HRF* UB9....94 A3
Broadwater Pk
  DEN/HRF UB9....93 M5
  MDHD SL6....119 K1
Broadwaters Av *THAME* OX9 *....181 M7
Broadway *DEN/HRF* UB9 *....93 M6
  MDHD SL6....108 C4
Broadway Av *GTLIN* MK14....14 C4
Broadway Ms *AMSS* HP7....71 G3
Broadway Pde *WDR/YW* UB7 *....114 D6
The Broadway *AMSS* HP7....71 G3
  RAYLW HP18....156 G12
Broadwell Ct *BIC* OX26....162 C6
Broadwood Av *RSLP* HA4....95 K5
Brocas St *WDSR* SL4....121 J3
Brocas Ter *WDSR* SL4....121 H3
Brocas Wy *LBUZ* LU7....169 M3
Brockhampton *WLLN* MK15....14 E8
Brock La *MDHD* SL6....108 C3
Brocks Wy *HEN* RG9....191 K11
Brockton Ct *MDHD* SL6....108 C4
Brockwell *NPAC* MK16....14 C2
Broken Furlong *WDSR* SL4....121 H1
Broken Gate La *DEN/HRF* UB9....93 H7
Bromet Cl *WAT* WD17....75 L1
Bromham Mi *GTLIN* MK14....14 C4
Bromley *TRING* HP23....168 F10
Bromley Crs *RSLP* HA4....105 L1
Bromley La *AMS* HP6....62 A5
Brompton Cl *AYLW* HP19....2 F1
Brompton Crs *AYLW* HP19....2 F1
Brompton Dr *MDHD* SL6....108 B1
Bromycroft Rd *SLN* SL2....100 F8
Bronte Cl *AYLW* HP19....167 Q12
Brookbank *FLKWH/TG* HP10....89 H7
Brook Cl *RAYLNE/WEN* HP22....36 C5
  RAYLW HP18....164 D6
  RSLP HA4....95 K6
Brook Ct *RNHPTN* NN7....126 C4
Brook Crs *SL* SL1....110 D3
Brookdene Cl *MDHD* SL6....98 D6
Brookdene Dr *NTHWD* HA6....85 L7
Brook Dr *RSLP* HA4....95 K5
Brooke Cl *BTCHLY* MK3....22 C7
Brooke Furmston Pl
  MLW SL7....97 K3
Brook End *NPAC* MK16....138 C1
  RAYLNE/WEN HP22....43 L3
Brooke Rd *PRRI* HP27....58 A2
Brook Farm Cl
  BUCK/WIN HP18....156 E8
Brookfield Cl *TRING* HP23....38 A6
Brookfield La *BUCK/WIN* MK18....11 L7
Brookfield Pk
  DUN/WHIP LU6 *....31 H6
Brookfield Rd *FLKWH/TG* HP10....89 H7
  HEN RG9....13 G4
  RMKS/WB MK17....153 J3
Brookhouse Dr *BNEND* SL8....89 H7
Brooklands Av *LBUZ* LU7....27 J8
Brooklands Dr *LBUZ* LU7....27 J8
Brooklands *WEAT* MK2....22 F6
Brook La *BERK* HP4....48 A5
  RBEDW MK43....129 K11
  THAME OX9....181 M6
Brooklyn Wy *WDR/YW* UB7....114 D6
Brook Pth *SL* SL1....110 E4
Brook Rd *BIC* OX26....162 B3
Brooks Cl *BUCK/WIN* MK18....11 L6
Brookside *BUCK/WIN* MK18....136 E6
  DTCH/LGLY SL3....123 H3
  FLKWH/TG HP10 *....79 H4
  HGDN/ICK UB10....104 E5
  RAYLNE/WEN HP22....179 Q1
  RAYLW HP18....179 Q1
  TRING HP23....38 A4
  WOLV MK12....17 G2
Brookside Av
  STWL/WRAY TW19....122 C6

Brookside Cl *RMKN* MK19....137 Q8
  THAME OX9....180 A7
Brookside La *HADM* HP17....50 D3
Brookside Ter *AYLS* HP21....3 H6
Brookside Wk *LBUZ* LU7....27 K7
Brook St *CHNR* OX39....184 C6
  DUN/WHIP LU6 *....170 C2
  LBUZ LU7....27 G2
  RAYLNE/WEN HP22....36 C5
  TRING HP23....38 A6
  WDSR SL4....121 J5
  WYM HP11....5 G3
Brookway *RMKN* MK19....137 L10
Broombarn La
  GTMIS/PWD HP16....60 D3
Broom Cl *HAZ/HG* HP15 *....68 F7
Broomfield *WOLV* MK12....17 G2
Broomfield Cl
  GTMIS/PWD HP16....60 D3
Broomfield Ga *SLN* SL2....111 G1
Broomfield Hl
  GTMIS/PWD HP16....60 D3
Broom Gv *WAT* WD17....75 M1
Broom Hl *HHW* HP1....49 K8
  MDHD SL6....98 D4
  SLN SL2....101 H5
Broomhills Rd *LBUZ* LU7....27 H5
Broomlee *BDWL* MK13....17 K1
Broomstick La *CSHM* HP5....63 M1
Brotheridge Ct *AYLS* HP21....34 A8
Brough Cl *SHEN* MK5....21 K1
Broughton Av *AYL* HP20....35 G6
Broughton Cl
  RAYLNE/WEN HP22....35 G3
Broughton La
  RAYLNE/WEN HP22....35 H4
Broughton Rd *MKV* MK19....19 J4
Broughton Ter *AYL* HP20 *....35 G6
Broughton Wy
  RKW/CH/CXG WD3....73 M8
Brownbaker Ct *GTLIN* MK14....14 C8
Browne Willis Cl *WEAT* MK2....23 C6
Brownfield Gdns *MDHD* SL6....108 D5
Browngraves Rd
  HYS/HAR UB3....125 H3
Browning Cl *NPAC* MK16....14 D2
Browning Crs *BTCHLY* MK3....22 D7
Browning Dr *OX26*....162 B2
Brownlow Dr *DUN/WHIP* LU6....170 G3
Brownlow La *LBUZ* LU7....169 L7
Brownlow Ri *DUN/WHIP* LU6....31 H6
Brownlow Rd *BERK* HP4....48 B5
Brownset Dr *EMV/FZ* MK4....21 G5
Brownsfield Rd *TOW* NN12....130 D12
Browns Hedge *LBUZ* LU7....169 P11
Brownslea *LBUZ* LU7....169 P11
Brown's Ri *TRING* HP23....45 L7
Browns Rd *GTMIS/PWD* HP16....61 M3
  HAZ/HG HP15....69 M3
Browns Spring *BERK* HP4....47 H3
Browns Wy *RMKS/WB* MK17....144 H5
Brownswood Dr *TOW* NN12....137 L3
The Brow *CSTG* HP8....82 C3
Broxbourne Cl *GTLIN* MK14....14 C4
Bruce Cl *SL* SL1....110 D5
Bruckner Gdns
  WTR/OFPK MK7....144 A5
Brudenell Cl *WDSR* SL4....120 E6
Brudenell Dr *MKV* MK19....19 M6
  RAYLNE/WEN HP22....43 G5
Brunel Cl *MDHD* SL6....108 D5
Brunel Wy *SL* SL1....111 L5
Brunswick Cl *AYLW* HP19....167 R11
Brushford Cl *EMV/FZ* MK4....22 A3
Brushmakers Ct *CSHM* HP5....63 H1
Brushwood Dr
  RKW/CH/CXG WD3....73 H5
Brushwood Rd *CSHM* HP5....55 J8
Bryans Crs *NPAC* MK16....134 D12
Bryanston Av *AYL* HP20....3 J1
Bryant Av *SLN* SL2....111 J2
Bryants Acre
  RAYLNE/WEN HP22....44 A5
Bryants Bottom Rd
  GTMIS/PWD HP16....67 L4
Bryer Rd *WDSR* SL4....120 C5
The Bryher *MDHD* SL6....107 L7
Bryne La *BUCK/WIN* MK18....149 Q4
Bryony Cl *UX/CGN* UB8....114 A1
Bryony Pl *GTLIN* MK14....18 B1
Bryony Rd *BIC* OX26....162 D1
Buccleuch Rd *DTCH/LGLY* SL3....121 K1
Buchan Cl *UX/CGN* UB8....104 B8
Buchan Rd *BIC* OX26....162 B3
Buckby *EAG/OLD/WTN* MK6....23 G1
Buckfast Av *BTCHLY* MK3....22 D4
Buckingham Av East *SL* SL1....111 H3
Buckingham Av *HWYN* HP13 *....78 F8
Buckingham Crs *OX26*....162 E3
Buckingham Dr *HWYN* HP13....78 E3
Buckingham Gdns *SL* SL1....111 L6
Buckingham Ga
  GTMIS/PWD HP16....67 L4
  SL SL7....96 C7
Buckingham Gv
  HGDN/ICK UB10....104 F7
Buckingham Pde
  CFSP/GDCR SL9 *....82 D8
Buckingham Pl *HWYN* HP13 *....34 C3
Buckingham Rd *AYLW* HP20....34 C3
  AYLW HP19....2 F3
  BIC OX26....162 D3
  BRACKY NN13....8 E7
  BTCHLY MK3....21 M8
  BUCK/WIN MK18....148 A2
  RAYLW HP18....156 G9
  RMKN MK19....137 N11
  TRING HP23....37 K7
Buckingham Sq *CMK* MK9....2 F4
Buckingham St *AYL* HP20....2 F5
  BUCK/WIN MK18....10 C8
  WOLV MK12....13 G8
Buckingham Wy
  FLKWH/TG HP10....78 F8
Buckland Av *DTCH/LGLY* SL3....112 A7
Buckland Crs *WDSR* SL4....120 A7
Buckland Dr
  EAG/OLD/WTN MK6....18 E8
  RAYLW HP18....164 A8
Buckland Rd
  RAYLNE/WEN HP22....36 F5
Buckleberry Cl *MDHD* SL6....119 H2
Buckley Ct *STSTR* MK11....16 C2
Buckman Cl *WOLV* MK12....16 E1
Buckmaster Rd *HWYW* HP12....87 H3

Bucknell Rd *RBICN* OX27....162 A1
Buckthorn *WOLV* MK12....17 H1
Buckwood La *DUN/WHIP* LU6....171 R7
Budge Rd *TOW* NN12....137 N1
Buffins *MDHD* SL6....99 K8
Bulbourne Ct *BERK* HP4....47 L4
  HHW HP1....49 M8
Bulbourne Rd *TRING* HP23....38 A3
Bulkeley Av *WDSR* SL4....121 G6
Bullace Cl *HWYN* HP13....49 L6
Bullbaiters La *AMS* HP6....62 A5
Bullbeggars La *BERK* HP4....48 F6
Bullfinch Gdns *AYLW* HP19....34 E3
Bullington End Rd
  RMKN MK19....131 M12
Bull La *CFSP/GDCR* SL9....92 C2
  WEAT MK2....23 K3
  WYM HP11....5 H6
Bullocks Farm La *SKCH* HP14....187 H4
Bullrush Gv *UX/CGN* UB8....114 B1
Bull's Br *NWDGN* UB2....115 M7
Bullsland Gdns
  RKW/CH/CXG WD3....73 G7
Bullsland La
  RKW/CH/CXG WD3....73 G7
Bulls La *RAYLW* HP18....180 B3
Bulmer Cl *MKV* MK19....19 L3
Bulstrode Cl *KGLCY* WD4....57 M7
Bulstrode Wy *CFSP/GDCR* SL9....92 C4
Bunby Rd *SLN* SL2....101 L5
Bunces Cl *WDSR* SL4....121 G1
Bungalow Cl *HEAD* OX3....178 B4
Bunkers La *LBUZ* LU7....26 E8
Bunsen Pl *SHEN* MK5....21 M2
Bunstrux *TRING* HP23....37 L6
The Buntings *BIC* OX26....162 F5
Bunyan La *TRING* HP23....38 A5
Bunyan Rd *BIC* OX26....162 C1
Burano *RKW/CH/CXG* WD3....73 M8
Burbage Cl *HYS/HAR* UB3....115 J3
Burchard Crs *SHEN* MK5....17 K3
Burchetts Green La *MDHD* SL6....107 H8
Burchett's Green Rd
  MDHD SL6....116 F1
Burcot Gdns *MDHD* SL6....98 D2
Burcott Cl *RAYLNE/WEN* HP22....35 G3
Burcott La *RAYLNE/WEN* HP22....35 H3
Burdeleys La *SHEN* MK5....21 K2
Burdett Dr *SKCH* HP14....67 G6
Burdock Ct *NPAC* MK16....14 C2
Bure Pl *BIC* OX26....162 D4
Burewelle *CNH/GTH/TMA* MK8....17 H1
Burfield Rd *RKW/CH/CXG* WD3....73 G6
Burford Cl *HGDN/ICK* UB10....104 D2
  MLW SL7....97 H1
Burford Gdns *SL* SL1....110 B2
Burgage Pl *THAME* OX9....181 M6
Burgess Gdns *NPAC* MK16....14 E4
Burgess La *HADM* HP17....177 L11
Burgess Wood Rd *BEAC* HP9....80 A8
Burgess Wood Rd South
  BEAC HP9....90 A1
Burgett Rd *SL* SL1....111 C7
Burghley Ct
  CNH/GTH/TMA MK8....17 J6
Burholme *EMV/FZ* MK4....21 M3
Burke Rd *RAYLNE/WEN* HP22....44 A5
Burkes Cl *BEAC* HP9....90 A2
Burkes Ct *BEAC* HP9....80 C8
Burkes Crs *BEAC* HP9....80 C8
Burleigh Ms
  BUCK/WIN MK18....11 M5
Burleigh Wy *STSTR* MK11....16 E3
Burleys Rd *BUCK/WIN* MK18....151 J10
Burlington Av *SL* SL1....111 K6
Burlington Cl *SL* SL1....111 K6
Burlington Rd *SL* SL1....110 A2
Burma Rd *HWYN* HP13....78 D3
Burners La *STSTR* MK11....16 E2
Burners La South *STSTR* MK11....16 E2
Burness Cl *UX/CGN* UB8....104 C3
Burnet *GTLIN* MK14....13 M7
Burnetts Rd *WDSR* SL4....120 C5
Burnham Av *BTCHLY* MK3....22 D4
  HGDN/ICK UB10....105 H2
Burnham Gdns *HYS/HAR* UB3....115 J1
Burnham La *SL* SL1....110 C2
Burnham Pl *BRACKY* NN13....140 A1
Burnham Rd *BEAC* HP9....90 D5
  RAYLW HP18....165 G2
  SKCH HP14....67 M8
Burnhams Fld
  RAYLNE/WEN HP22....35 K8
The Burnhams
  RAYLNE/WEN HP22....36 B5
  RAYLW HP18....180 E3
Burnmoor Cl *WEAT* MK2....153 M2
Burns Cl *NPAC* MK16....175 K11
  RAYLW HP18....164 A8
  YEAD UB4....115 M2
Burns Crs *BIC* OX26....162 B3
Burns Rd *BTCHLY* MK3....22 D7
Burnt Oak *MDHD* SL6....98 D3
Burrell Cl *AYLS* HP21....2 C9
The Burren *AMS* HP6 *....63 K8
Burroughs Crs *BNEND* SL8....88 F7
Burroway Rd *DTCH/LGLY* SL3....113 G7
Burrows Cl *FLKWH/TG* HP10....89 H8
  RMKS/WB MK17....144 E5
Burrows Hill Cl
  STWL/WRAY TW19....124 A7
Burton Av *WATW* WD18....75 M5
Burton La *PRRI* HP27....58 B1
Burtons La *CSTG* HP8....72 B3
Burton's Wy *CSTG* HP8....72 B3
Burton Wy *WDSR* SL4....120 D6
Burtree Cl *WOLV* MK12....17 G1
Burt's La *RAYLW* HP18....175 L12
Burwell Hl *BRACKY* NN13....8 E6
Burwell Hill La *BRACKY* NN13....8 E6
Bury Av *NPAC* MK16....14 C2
  RSLP HA4....95 K5
  YEAD UB4....115 K7
Bury Farm Cl *DTCH/LGLY* SL3....123 K3
Bury La *CSHM* HP5....63 G2
  RKW/CH/CXG WD3....84 C1
Bury Mdw *RKW/CH/CXG* WD3....84 C1
Bury Ri *HHS/BOV* HP3....57 J4
  LBUZ LU7....31 G1
Bury St *NPAC* MK16....14 F2
  RSLP HA4....95 J3
The Bury *CSHM* HP5....63 G3
Busby Rd *BUCK/WIN* MK18....142 A9

Buscot Pl *CNH/GTH/TMA* MK8....17 J6
Bushell Cl *LBUZ* LU7....29 L1
Bushel Whf *TRING* HP23....37 M4
Bushes La *BUCK/WIN* MK18....148 D5
Bushey Bartrams *SHEN* MK5....21 K3
Bushey
  HGDN/ICK UB10....94 B7
  HWYW HP12....4 B7
Bushey Rd *BUCK/WIN* MK18....94 F8
  HYS/HAR UB3....115 K3
Bushfield Rd *HHS/BOV* HP3....57 H4
Bushmead Cl
  RAYLNE/WEN HP22....32 A1
Bushmead Rd
  RAYLNE/WEN HP22....32 A1
The Bush *HADM* HP17....182 C1
Bushy Cl *BTCHLY* MK3....22 D3
Buslins La *CSHM* HP5....54 D7
Butcher La *EMV/FZ* MK4....21 J4
Butchers La *MDHD* SL6....117 H5
Bute Brae *BTCHLY* MK3....22 B4
Butlers Cl *HWYN* HP13....78 E5
Butlers Court Rd *BEAC* HP9....90 F4
Butlers Gv *GTLIN* MK14....14 A6
Butler St *HGDN/ICK* UB10....115 C1
Butler Wk *AYLW* HP19....177 R3
Butterbur Gdns *BIC* OX26....162 D1
Butterfield Cl *FLKWH/TG* HP10....89 J6
Butterfield La
  RAYLNE/WEN HP22....18 F4
Butterly Rd *SKCH* HP14....184 E11
Butter Market *THAME* OX9....181 M6
Buttermere *AYL* HP20....35 G7
Buttermere Cl *WEAT* MK2....23 C8
Buttermere Cl *SL* SL1....110 B2
Butterton
  RKW/CH/CXG WD3....83 J5
Buttlehide *RKW/CH/CXG* WD3....83 J5
Button Cl *EAG/OLD/WTN* MK6....18 C7
Butts End *HHW* HP1....49 H6
Buttsmead *NTHWD* HA6....85 H7
The Butts *PRRI* HP27 *....58 A3
  RBICS/WY OX25....172 C2
Buzzacott La *EMV/FZ* MK4....21 M3
Byebend Cl *SLN* SL2....101 H4
Bycell Rd *BUCK/WIN* MK18....141 N10
Bye Gn *RAYLNE/WEN* HP22....43 K3
Byerly Rd *LBUZ* LU7....18 C1
Byewaters *WATW* WD18....75 H7
The Byway
  RKW/CH/CXG WD3....84 D2
Byford Ptn *LBUZ* LU7....29 L1
Byford Wy *BUCK/WIN* MK18....151 J10
  LBUZ LU7....29 L1
Byland Cl *BDWL* MK13....119 G1
Byrd Crs *WTR/OFPK* MK7....144 A4
The Byres *HADM* HP17 *....176 C12
Byron Cl *BTCHLY* MK3....22 C7
  MLW SL7....97 L3
Byron Ct *WDSR* SL4....120 F6
Byron Dr *NPAC* MK16....14 D2
Byron Pde *HGDN/ICK* UB10 *....115 C1
Byron Rd *AYLS* HP21....34 E8
Byron Wy *BIC* OX26....162 B3
Byward Cl *GTLIN* MK14....14 B7
Byways *BERK* HP4....48 D5
  SL SL1....109 M2
Bywell Ct *EMV/FZ* MK4....21 L3
By-Wood End *CFSP/GDCR* SL9....82 F5

C

Cadeby Ct *MKV* MK10....19 L3
Cadman Sq *SHEN* MK5....21 M1
Cadogan Cl *MDHD* SL6....118 F2
Cadsdean Rd *PRRI* HP27....50 D8
Cadwell Dr *MDHD* SL6....108 C7
Caernarvon Crs *BTCHLY* MK3....22 A7
Caesars Cl *BDWL* MK13....17 L3
Caesars Ga *BRACKY* NN13....8 F8
Cages Wood Dr *SLN* SL2....101 H3
Cain's La *EBED/NFELT* TW14....125 J3
Cairngorm Ga
  EAG/OLD/WTN MK6....6 F1
Cairnside *HWYN* HP13....78 D3
Caithness Ct *BTCHLY* MK3....22 B4
Calamus Ct *WTR/OFPK* MK7....19 L8
Calbroke Rd *SLN* SL2....100 F1
Caldecote La *WTR/OFPK* MK7....23 K1
Caldecote Sq *NPAC* MK16....14 F2
Caldecotte Lake Dr
  WTR/OFPK MK7....23 K1
Calder Cl *MDHD* SL6....108 A7
Calder Ct *DTCH/LGLY* SL3....122 E1
  MDHD SL6....108 C1
Calder Gdns *LBUZ* LU7....26 C7
Calder V *BTCHLY* MK3....22 B5
Calder Wy *DTCH/LGLY* SL3....123 K6
Caldewell *CNH/GTH/TMA* MK8....17 H4
Caldicot Cl *AYLS* HP21....35 G8
Caledon Rd *BEAC* HP9....80 D7
Caledonian Rd *BDWL* MK13....13 M7
Caledon Rd *BEAC* HP9....80 D7
Calewen *CNH/GTH/TMA* MK8....17 G4
California Cir *WYM* HP11....78 A5
Callingham Pl *BEAC* HP9....80 D4
Calluna Dr *BTCHLY* MK3....22 A5
Calshot Rd *HTHAIR* TW6....125 G5
Calshot Rd *HTHAIR* TW6....124 F5
Calumet *BEAC* HP9....80 C7
Calverleigh Crs *EMV/FZ* MK4....22 A3
Calverley Crs *HWYN* HP13....77 L4
Calverton La *RMKN* MK19....16 E3
Calverton Rd *STSTR* MK11....16 A2
Calves Cl *SHEN* MK5....21 K3
Camber Cl *BTCHLY* MK3....22 A7
Camberton Rd *LBUZ* LU7....28 F1
Camborne Av *AYLS* HP21....43 G5
Camborne Av *HTHAIR* TW6....124 F5
Camborne Crs *HTHAIR* TW6....124 F5
Cambridge Av *SL* SL1....100 A3
  WDR/YW UB7....124 C2
Cambridge Pl *AYLW* HP20....2 F3
Cambridge Rd *BEAC* HP9....80 D4
  UX/CGN UB8....104 C3
Cambridge Sq *AYL* HP20....2 F3
  WEAT MK2....23 K3
Cambridge Ter *BERK* HP4....48 C6
Cambron *EAG/OLD/WTN* MK6....22 F1
Cam Cd *BTCHLY* MK3....22 M1
Camden Pl *BNEND* SL8....88 F7
Camden Rd *MDHD* SL6....108 C1

Cameron Rd *CSHM* HP5....63 H1
Camlet Gv *GTLIN* MK14....14 A7
Camley Gdns *MDHD* SL6....107 H6
Camley Park Dr *MDHD* SL6....107 L6
Camm Av *WDSR* SL4....120 D6
Camomile Ct *AMKT* MK7....23 L1
Camomile Wy *WDR/YW* UB7....114 D3
Campania Cl *MKV* MK15....19 K4
Campbell Cl *BIC* OX26....162 D4
  BUCK/WIN MK18....142 A10
  HWYN HP13....4 F5
  RSLP HA4....95 M5
Campbell Ride *HAZ/HG* HP15....69 J3
Campden Rd *HGDN/ICK* UB10....104 E1
Camperdown *MDHD* SL6....109 G1
Campion Cl *AYL* HP20....35 H6
  DEN/HRF UB9....103 M1
  UX/CGN UB8....114 E2
Campion Pl *BIC* OX26....162 C1
Campion Rd *HAZ/HG* HP15....68 E4
  HHW HP1....49 K8
Campions Ct *BERK* HP4....47 M7
Camp Rd *CFSP/GDCR* SL9....92 C6
Canada Rd *SL* SL1....112 A6
Canal Est *DTCH/LGLY* SL3 *....112 F6
Canal La *RMKN* MK19....137 M10
Canalside *BERK* HP4....47 L4
  RMKN MK19....137 R7
Canal Wy *DEN/HRF* UB9....103 M6
Canal Whf *DTCH/LGLY* SL3....112 F6
Canberra Rd *HTHAIR* TW6....124 F6
Candleford Ct *BRACKY* NN13....8 C6
Candlemas La *BEAC* HP9....80 D8
Candlemas Md *BEAC* HP9....80 D8
Candlewicks *WTR/OFPK* MK7....19 L8
Candover Cl *WDR/YW* UB7....124 C3
Candy La *SHEN* MK5....21 L2
Candytuft Gn *HAZ/HG* HP15....68 E4
Cane End *PRRI* HP27....183 R11
Canfield Ct *AYLS* HP21....42 E1
Cangels Cl *HHW* HP1....57 M1
Canhurst La *WAR/TWY* RG10....116 C3
Cannock Cl *MDHD* SL6....109 G4
Cannon Ct *AYL* HP20....34 D3
Cannon Court Rd *MDHD* SL6....98 C6
Cannondown Rd *MDHD* SL6....98 D5
Cannon Ga *SLN* SL2....112 B4
Cannon Hill Cl *MDHD* SL6....109 H8
Cannon La *AMD* MDHD SL6....117 L3
Cannon Mill Av *CSHM* HP5....63 J4
Cannon Pl *PRRI* HP27....58 A2
Cannon Rd Hi *RAYLW* HP18....175 R5
Cannons Orch
  RAYLNE/WEN HP22....166 E2
Cannon Gn Dr *MDHD* SL6....109 H4
Cannon Hill Wy *MDHD* SL6....109 G8
Canons Cl *RAYLW* HP18....180 D8
Canons Rd *WOLV* MK12....12 F7
The Canons *AMKT* MK16....15 H3
Canopus Wy *NTHWD* HA6....85 M4
Cantell Cl *BUCK/WIN* MK18....11 L5
Canterbury Av *SLN* SL2....111 H1
Canterbury Cl *AMSS* HP7....71 K2
  NTHWD HA6....85 L6
  PRRI HP27....58 A1
Canterbury Wy
  RKW/CH/CXG WD3....75 H4
Cantilupe Cl *DUN/WHIP* LU6....30 E8
Cantle Av *GTLIN* MK14....18 D1
Cantley Cl *AYL* HP20....3 H1
Cape Farewell
  WAR/TWY RG10 *....191 L12
Capel Cl *BUCK/WIN* MK18....142 A11
Capel Dr *GTLIN* MK14....18 D1
Capella Rd *NTHWD* HA6....85 L5
Capell Av *RKW/CH/CXG* WD3....73 H6
Capell Rd *RKW/CH/CXG* WD3....73 J6
Capelvere Wk *WAT* WD17....75 K2
Capital Dr *GTLIN* MK14....14 B8
Capps La *CSHM* HP5....53 M5
Capron *EAG/OLD/WTN* MK6....22 F1
Capshill Av *LBUZ* LU7....27 K7
Captain Cook Cl *CSTG* HP8....81 M4
Captain's Cl *CSHM* HP5....54 F6
Captain's Ct *RNHPTN* NN7....126 C5
Captains Wk *BERK* HP4....48 C7
Caractacus Cottage Vw
  WATW WD18....75 M8
Caractacus Gn *WATW* WD18....75 M8
Caravan La *RKW/CH/CXG* WD3....74 D8
Caraway Cl *WTR/OFPK* MK7....23 L1
Cardigan Cl *BTCHLY* MK3....22 C5
  SL SL1....110 E4
Cardinals Wk *MDHD* SL6....110 B3
Cardwell Cl *EMV/FZ* MK4....21 M4
Carew Rd *NTHWD* HA6....85 K6
Carey Cl *AYLS* HP21....42 C2
  WDSR SL4....121 G6
Carey Rd *RNHPTN* NN7....126 A3
Careys Cft *BERK* HP4....47 L3
Carey Wy *OLN* MK46....128 C10
Carfax Rd *HYS/HAR* UB3....125 M1
Carhampton Cl *EMV/FZ* MK4....22 A3
Carina Dr *LBUZ* LU7....27 G8
Carisbrooke Av *AYLS* HP21....42 D1
Carina Cl *AYLW* HP19....167 R12
Carina Gv *LBUZ* LU7....27 H3
Carisbrooke Wy *EMV/FZ* MK4....21 H5
Careggili Pl *HEN* RG9....190 C1
Careton Ga *WLLN* MK15....13 H7
Carisbrooke Ct
  BUCK/WIN MK18 *....11 L4
  SL SL1....111 L4
Carlina Pl *GTLIN* MK14....6 E1
Carlisle Rd *SL* SL1....111 J4
Carlton Av *HYS/HAR* UB3....115 K8
Carlton Cl *AYLW* HP19....167 R12
  NPAC MK16....14 C1
Carlton Gv *LBUZ* LU7....27 H3
Carlton Rd *RBEDW* MK43....129 N8
  SLN SL2....112 A4
Carlyle Av *SL* SL1....3 H9
Carlyle Cl *NPAC* MK16....14 C2
Carman Ct *TRING* HP23....37 L2
Carmarthen Rd *SL* SL1....111 K4
Carmichael Ct *RAYLW* HP18....165 H7
Carnarvon Dr *HYS/HAR* UB3....115 H1
Carnation Cl *AYLW* HP21....27 H5
Carnation Wy *AYLS* HP21....42 D1
The Carne *STSTR* MK11....16 D5
Carnot Cl *EMV/FZ* MK4....21 M7
Carnoustie Cl *BTCHLY* MK3....21 M7
Carnweather Ct *EMV/FZ* MK4....21 M4
Caroline Cl *WDR/YW* UB7....114 C6
Caroline Ct *MLW* SL7....97 J3
Caroline Pl *HYS/HAR* UB3....125 K3
Caroline Creek *WLLN* MK15....14 D8
Carpenter Ct *GTLIN* MK14....14 C8
Carpenters Wood Dr
  RKW/CH/CXG WD3....73 G5
Carpenters Yd *TRING* HP23....38 A8
Carr Cl *AYLW* HP19....167 R12

Carrick Rd EAG/OLD/WTN MK6 .... 7 J7
Carriers Cl RMKN MK19 .... 131 M8
Carriers Wy RBEDW MK43 .... 129 K2
Carrington Av FLKWH/TG HP10 .... 88 F2
Carrington Crs
  RAYLNE/WEN HP22 .... 43 M7
Carrington Hall Rd
  RMKS MK17 .... 152 H8
Carrington Pl HAZ/HG HP15 .... 69 H3
  TRING HP23 .... 38 A5
Carrington Rd AYLS HP21 .... 34 C8
  HWYW HP12 .... 4 B8
  NPAG MK16 .... 14 F2
  SL SL1 .... 111 K4
Carrington Wy
  GTMIS/PWD HP16 .... 60 B5
Carroll Cl NPAG MK16 .... 14 D1
Carron Cl LBUZ LU7 .... 26 C7
Carron Ct WEAT MK2 .... 153 P2
Carrs Dr HWYW HP12 .... 77 H6
Carteret Cl WLLN MK15 .... 15 H6
Carters Cl NPAG MK16 .... 133 N8
Carters La RAYLNE/WEN HP22 .... 158 H12
  RAYLW HP18 .... 175 J11
  STSTR MK11 .... 16 D3
Carters Meadow
  BUCK/WIN MK18 .... 159 K10
Carters Ride
  RAYLNE/WEN HP22 .... 43 G4
Cartmel Cl BTCHLY MK3 .... 21 M8
Cartwright Crs BRACKY NN13 .... 8 C7
Cartwright Pl
  EAG/OLD/WTN MK6 .... 6 F9
Carver Hill Rd WYM MK11 .... 4 H1
Carvers Ms GTLIN MK14 * 14 C8
Cascadia Dr WYM MK11 .... 79 C8
Cashmere Cl SHEN MK5 .... 21 K2
Cassiobridge Rd WATW WD18 .... 75 K5
Cassiobridge Ter
  RKW/CH/CXG WD3 * 75 J6
Cassiobury Dr WAT WD17 .... 75 K5
Cassiobury Park Av
  WATW WD18 .... 75 K4
Cassio Pl WATW WD18 .... 75 K4
Cassio Whf WATW WD18 * 75 J6
Casterton Cl BDWL MK13 .... 17 M2
Castier Ct EMV/FZ MK4 .... 21 H6
Castle Av RVS/LGLY SL3 .... 121 M2
  WDR/YW UB7 .... 114 D4
Castle Cl DUN/WHIP LU6 .... 31 H6
  LBUZ LU7 .... 169 Q11
  LBUZ LU7 .... 161 R7
  RBICN OX27 .... 156 B7
  RBICN OX27 .... 154 E12
Castle Ct AYL HP20 .... 2 E5
  MDHD SL6 .... 108 C3
Castle Dr OLN MK46 .... 128 C3
Castlefields
  RAYLNE/WEN HP22 .... 43 H3
Castle Gate Wy BERK HP4 .... 48 B4
Castle HI BERK HP4 .... 48 B4
  MDHD SL6 .... 108 D3
  WDSR SL4 .... 121 J4
Castle Hill Av BERK HP4 .... 48 B5
Castle Hill Cl BERK HP4 .... 48 A5
Castle Hill Ct BERK HP4 .... 48 B4
Castle Hill Rd DUN/WHIP LU6 .... 31 G5
Castle Hill Ter MDHD SL6 .... 108 D3
Castle La RAYLNE/WEN HP22 .... 159 H12
Castle Meadow Cl NPAG MK16 .... 15 G2
Castle Ms BERK HP4 * 48 C6
  MDHD SL6 .... 108 C3
Castle Mt BRACKY NN13 .... 146 D1
Castle Park Rd
  RAYLNE/WEN HP22 .... 43 M8
Castle Pl HWYN HP13 .... 5 J6
Castle Rd OLN MK46 .... 128 C5
Castle Rose
  EAG/OLD/WTN MK6 .... 19 C8
Castlesteads BDWL MK13 .... 17 J1
Castle St AYL HP20 .... 2 E5
  BERK HP4 .... 48 B6
  BUCK/WIN MK18 .... 11 K6
  HWYN HP13 .... 5 J6
  RAYLNE/WEN HP22 .... 168 A4
  RBICN OX27 .... 156 B7
  SL SL1 .... 111 L7
Castlethorpe Rd RMKN MK19 .... 131 L10
Castle View Gdns HWYW HP12 .... 4 B5
Castleview Rd DTCH/LGLY SL3 .... 112 B8
Catalina Rd HTHAIR TW6 .... 125 C6
Catchpole Cl WOLV MK12 .... 16 E1
Cater Rd SKCH HP14 .... 86 B2
Catesby Cft SHEN MK5 .... 6 C7
Cathay Cl BTCHLY MK3 .... 22 E7
Catherines Cl WDR/YW UB7 * 114 C6
Catherine Ct
  BUCK/WIN MK18 .... 11 M4
Catkin Cl HWYW HP12 .... 87 C3
Cattleford Br RMKN MK19 .... 142 H5
Cattle Market BIC OX26 .... 162 E4
Causeway BIC OX26 .... 162 C5
The Causeway MDHD SL6 .... 109 H6
  MLW SL7 .... 97 M4
  RBEDW MK43 .... 129 G3
Cautley Cl RAYLNE/WEN HP22 .... 166 D1
Cavalier Ct BERK HP4 .... 48 B6
Cavalier Gdns HYS/HAR UB3 .... 115 J3
Cavalier Rd THAME OX9 .... 181 P5
Cavalry Crs WDSR SL4 .... 121 P6
Cavandish Wk THAME OX9 .... 181 Q5
Cava Wy MKV MK10 .... 19 L3
Cavendish Cl AMS HP6 .... 72 A2
  MDHD SL6 .... 109 M3
  RAYLNE/WEN HP22 .... 44 A5
  YEAD UB4 .... 115 K2
Cavendish Ct
  RKW/CH/CXG WD3 * 75 J3
  SHEN MK5 .... 17 K6
Cavendish Pl RBICN OX27 .... 155 J9
Cavendish Rd CSHM HP5 .... 63 J3
Cavendish Wy AYLW HP19 .... 177 Q2
Cavenham CNH/GTH/TMA MK8 .... 17 J4
Caversham Gn AYL HP20 .... 2 F3
Cawardon GTLIN MK14 .... 13 M7
Cawcott Dr WDSR SL4 .... 120 D4
Cawdor Ri EMV/FZ MK4 .... 21 H4
Cawkwell Wy WEAT MK2 .... 22 F6
Caxton Dr UX/CGN UB8 .... 104 B7
Caxton Rd WOLV MK12 .... 16 E1
Cayman Wy WATW WD18 .... 75 J3
Cecil Rd IVER SL0 .... 113 K3
Cecils Yd BUCK/WIN MK18 .... 11 L5
Cecil Wy SLN SL2 .... 110 C4
Cecily Ct SHEN MK5 .... 21 K1
Cedar Av HAZ/HG HP15 .... 68 E5
  HYS/HAR UB3 .... 115 M3
  WDR/YW UB7 .... 114 C3
Cedar Cha MDHD SL6 .... 109 J1
Cedar Cl AYL HP20 .... 3 L2

BRACKY NN13 .... 8 E4
CSHM HP5 .... 63 K1
IVER SL0 .... 103 H6
Cedar Crs THAME OX9 .... 181 L6
Cedar Dr BIC OX26 .... 162 E3
  CSHM HP5 .... 62 F1
  MDHD SL6 .... 98 C4
  MLW SL7 .... 87 H7
Cedar Gv AMSS HP7 .... 71 J2
  CSHM HP5 .... 54 C2
Cedar Lodge Dr WOLV MK12 .... 13 G7
Cedar Rdg AMS HP6 .... 62 B5
Cedar Rd BERK HP4 .... 48 C7
Cedars Av RKW/CH/CXG WD3 .... 84 B1
Cedars Cl BUCK/WIN MK18 .... 142 A2
  CFSP/GDCR SL9 .... 82 D5
Cedars Dr HGDN/ICK UB10 .... 104 F7
Cedars Rd MDHD SL6 .... 108 F3
The Cedars BERK HP4 * 48 D6
  RAYLNE/WEN HP22 .... 51 M1
  SLN SL2 .... 100 E8
Cedars Wy LBUZ LU7 .... 26 F8
  NPAG MK16 .... 14 F2
Cedar Ter WYM MK11 .... 4 E5
Cedar Wy BERK HP4 .... 48 C7
  DTCH/LGLY SL3 .... 112 D8
Ceely Rd AYLS HP21 .... 34 C8
Celandine Cl BIC OX26 .... 162 B2
Celandine Ct WTR/OFPK MK7 .... 19 K8
Celina Cl WEAT MK2 .... 22 F7
Cell Farm Av WDSR SL4 .... 122 A8
Cemetery Rd BIC OX26 .... 162 D5
Centauri Cl LBUZ LU7 .... 27 K6
Centenary Crs PRRI HP27 .... 183 N7
Central Av DUN/WHIP LU6 .... 171 M6
  HYS/HAR UB3 .... 115 L6
  RBEDW MK43 .... 138 H5
Central Dr SL SL1 .... 110 E4
Central Wy NTHWD HA6 .... 85 K7
Centre Pde PRRI HP27 .... 58 B1
Centre Rd WDSR SL4 .... 120 B3
Centurion St STSTR MK11 .... 16 E4
Century Av
  EAG/OLD/WTN MK6 .... 7 G9
Century Cha WAR/TWY RG10 * 116 E1
Century Ct WATW WD18 * 75 H8
Century Point HWYW HP12 .... 87 H2
Cervantes Ct NTHWD HA6 .... 85 L7
Cestreham Crs CSHM HP5 .... 55 J8
Cetus Crs LBUZ LU7 .... 27 K6
Chacombe Pl BEAC HP9 .... 80 B5
Chadbone Cl AYL HP20 .... 2 E5
Chaddesley La EAG/OLD/WTN MK6 .... 18 F1
Chadwick Dr
  EAG/OLD/WTN MK6 .... 18 D7
Chadwick St HWYN HP13 .... 68 B8
Chaffinch Av HP19 .... 34 E3
Chaffinch La WATW WD18 .... 75 L8
Chaffron Wy BIC OX26 .... 162 B5
  BRACKY NN13 .... 8 D5
  EAG/OLD/WTN MK6 .... 7 L8
  EMV/FZ MK4 .... 21 J5
  MKV MK10 .... 19 M8
Chairborough Rd HWYW HP12 .... 4 A9
Chalcot Pl CNH/GTH/TMA MK8 .... 17 J4
Chalcraft Cl CNH OX39 .... 190 F6
Chalet Cl BERK HP4 .... 47 L6
Chalfont Av AMS HP6 .... 72 C2
Chalfont Cl BDWL MK13 .... 17 M2
Chalfont La RKW/CH/CXG WD3 .... 83 H7
  RKW/CH/CXG WD3 .... 73 G6
Chalfont Rd BEAC HP9 .... 81 J5
Chalfont Station Rd
  AMSS HP7 .... 72 B3
Chalfont Wy HWYN HP11 .... 87 J3
Chalford Cl AYLW HP19 .... 177 Q2
Chalgrove End
  RAYLNE/WEN HP22 .... 43 G4
Chalgrove Rd THAME OX9 .... 181 P5
Chalgrove Wk AYLS HP21 .... 2 D3
Chalkdell Dr SHEN MK5 .... 21 J1
Chalk Farm Rd SKCH HP14 .... 184 G12
Chalk HI AMSS HP7 .... 70 E7
  CSHM HP5 .... 55 G8
  HEN RG9 .... 190 F9
Chalklands BNEND SL8 .... 88 F6
Chalk La AMSS HP7 .... 61 M7
Chalkpit La MLW SL7 .... 97 G3
Chalk Pit La SL SL1 .... 100 A6
The Chalkpits FLKWH/TG HP10 .... 89 K4
Chalkshire Rd HADM HP17 .... 51 H2
Challacombe EMV/FZ MK4 .... 22 H4
Challener Rd HWYW HP12 .... 87 H3
Challow Cft MDHD SL6 .... 108 C1
Chalmers Av RMKN MK19 .... 13 G4
Chaloner Ct LBUZ LU7 .... 29 J7
Chaloner Pl AYLS HP21 .... 34 C8
Chaloner Rd AYLS HP21 .... 34 C8
Chaloners HI BUCK/WIN MK18 .... 11 L11
Chalvey Gv SL SL1 .... 111 G7
Chalvey Pk SL SL1 .... 111 K6
Chalvey Rd BIC OX26 .... 162 C5
Chalvey Rd East SL SL1 .... 111 K6
Chalvey Rd West SL SL1 .... 111 J6
Chalwell Rdg SHEN MK5 .... 21 L2
Chamberlain La PIN HA5 .... 95 M3
Chamberlain Rd AYLW HP19 .... 2 A3
Chamberlains Gdns LBUZ LU7 .... 27 H5
Champflower EMV/FZ MK4 .... 22 A5
Champion Ct BRACKY NN13 .... 8 D6
Champney Ct DTCH/LGLY SL3 .... 122 F6
Chancellors AMSS HP7 .... 70 A5
Chancery Cl BDWL MK13 .... 13 K8
Chandlers Ct
  EAG/OLD/WTN MK6 .... 23 H1
  BUCK/WIN MK18 .... 11 L7
Chandos Av AMS HP6 .... 72 B1
  BUCK/WIN MK18 .... 11 L7
Chandos Rd BUCK/WIN MK18 .... 11 L7
Channer Dr FLKWH/TG HP10 .... 89 H3
Channory Cl EMV/FZ MK4 .... 21 K5
Chantry Cl RMKS/WB MK17 .... 144 D5
  WDR/YW UB7 .... 114 C3
  WDSR SL4 .... 120 F7
Chantry Ri OLN MK46 .... 128 B11
Chantry Rd AYLW HP19 .... 34 B3
The Chantry AYL HP20 .... 2 E5
  UX/CGN UB8 .... 104 C8
Chapel Cl BERK HP4 .... 40 C4
  MDHD SL6 .... 108 C6
Chapel Cft KGLGY WD4 * 85 M2
Chapel Crofts BERK HP4 .... 47 K6
Chapel Dr RAYLNE/WEN HP22 .... 36 D5
Chapel End CFSP/GDCR SL9 * 92 C1
  RNHPTN NN7 .... 126 A4
Chapel End La TRING HP23 .... 37 H2
Chapel Flds TRING HP23 .... 37 H2

Chapel HI LBUZ LU7 .... 153 R11
  PRRI HP27 .... 67 G2
Chapel La BRACKY NN13 .... 9 G7
  BUCK/WIN MK18 .... 142 B2
  DUN/WHIP LU6 .... 31 G6
  HWYW HP12 .... 77 H9
  PRRI HP27 .... 183 L11
  RAYLNE/WEN HP22 .... 42 F5
  RAYLW HP18 .... 175 J7
  RMKS/WB MK17 .... 152 G9
  SKCH HP14 .... 185 P9
  SLN SL2 .... 102 H3
  TRING HP23 .... 168 G10
  UX/CGN UB8 .... 114 F3
Chapel Rd FLKWH/TG HP10 .... 88 F7
  HADM HP17 .... 177 K12
Chapel Rw DEN/HRF UB9 .... 84 B8
Chapels Cl SL SL1 .... 110 D5
Chapel Sq BERK HP4 .... 48 B6
  BIC OX26 .... 162 D5
  HWYN HP13 .... 77 J3
  MLW SL7 .... 97 J4
  RMKS/WB MK17 .... 144 E6
  SL SL1 .... 111 L6
  TRING HP23 .... 37 L2
Chaplin Gv CNH/GTH/TMA MK8 .... 17 G7
Chapman Av GTLIN MK14 .... 18 D1
Chapman Cl AYLS HP21 .... 34 D1
Chapman La BNEND SL8 .... 88 B3
Chapmans Crs CSHM HP5 .... 54 F8
Chapmans Dr RMKN MK19 .... 137 G7
Chapmans Lea
  RAYLNE/WEN HP22 .... 33 J1
Chappel Meadow TRING HP23 .... 38 A4
Chapter EAG/OLD/WTN MK6 .... 22 D1
Chapter HGDN/ICK UB10 .... 104 E5
Chapter Ms WEAT MK2 .... 121 J3
Charbray Crs SHEN MK5 .... 21 J5
Charbridge La BIC OX26 .... 162 H4
Charbridge Wy BIC OX26 .... 162 G4
Chardacre CNH/GTH/TMA MK8 .... 17 H5
Chardins Cl HHW HP1 .... 49 J1
Chariotts Pl WDSR SL4 * 121 J4
Charity Whf LBUZ LU7 * 26 F8
Charlbury Rd HGDN/ICK UB10 .... 104 B2
Charles Cl AYLS HP21 .... 43 C2
Charles Dr THAME OX9 .... 181 P5
Charles Gdns SLN SL2 .... 111 M3
Charles St BERK HP4 .... 48 A6
  HGDN/ICK UB10 .... 115 G1
  TRING HP23 .... 37 M7
  WDSR SL4 .... 121 H4
Charles Wy NPAG MK16 .... 14 F2
Charlock Cl NPAG MK16 .... 14 C2
Charlock Wy WATW WD18 .... 75 L7
Charlotte Av SLN SL2 .... 111 L4
Charlton WDSR SL4 .... 120 B5
Charlton Cl HGDN/ICK UB10 .... 95 G5
  RMKS/WB MK17 .... 151 R11
  SL SL1 .... 111 G6
Charmfield Rd AYLS HP21 .... 42 F5
Charnwood Cl HWYN HP13 .... 78 E5
Charnwood Rd
  HGDN/ICK UB10 .... 104 F7
Charsley Cl AMS HP6 .... 72 A1
Charter Cl SL SL1 .... 111 L7
Charterhouse Cl BRACKY NN13 .... 8 D7
Charter Pl UX/CGN UB8 .... 104 C6
Charter Rd SL SL1 .... 110 C4
Chartley Ct SHEN MK5 .... 17 K6
Chartmoor Rd LBUZ LU7 .... 29 H1
Chartridge Grange Dr
  CSHM HP5 .... 54 C6
Chartridge La CSHM HP5 .... 54 C7
Chartwell Rd NPAG MK16 .... 15 H3
Charville La HGDN/ICK UB10 .... 105 H8
  YEAD UB4 .... 105 H8
Charville La West
  HGDN/ICK UB10 .... 105 G8
Chasden Rd HHW HP1 .... 49 L4
Chase Av WTR/OFPK MK7 .... 23 K1
Chase Cl AMSS HP7 .... 72 A1
Chase Park Av RNHPTN NN7 .... 127 M6
Chaseport Cl OLN MK46 .... 127 K12
Chaseside Cl LBUZ LU7 .... 169 M7
The Chase CSHM HP5 .... 55 G8
  FLKWH/TG HP10 .... 79 G1
  HGDN/ICK UB10 .... 104 A3
  MDHD SL6 .... 98 D4
  MLW SL7 .... 97 M3
  RMKS/WB MK17 .... 153 J3
  WATW WD18 .... 75 J3
Chaucer Av YEAD UB4 .... 115 M2
Chaucer Cl BERK HP4 .... 47 L5
  BIC OX26 .... 162 A2
  NPAG MK16 .... 14 D2
  WDSR SL4 .... 121 J4
Chaucer Dr AYLS HP21 .... 3 H9
Chaucer Rd BTCHLY MK3 .... 22 D7
Chaucer Wy SL SL1 .... 111 L5
Chaulden House Gdns
  HHW HP1 .... 57 L1
Chaulden La HHW HP1 .... 57 L1
Chaulden Ter HHW HP1 .... 49 L8
Chauntry Cl MDHD SL6 .... 109 H4
Chauntry Ms MDHD SL6 .... 109 G4
Chauntry Rd MDHD SL6 .... 109 G4
Chawton Crs
  CNH/GTH/TMA MK8 .... 17 J5
Cheapside La DEN/HRF UB9 .... 93 L8
Chearsley Rd RAYLW HP18 .... 175 M11
Cheddington La TRING HP23 .... 168 H9
Cheddington Rd LBUZ LU7 .... 169 N9
Chelsea Gn LBUZ LU7 .... 26 D9
Chelsea Rd AYLW HP19 .... 177 P1
Chelston Rd RSLP HA4 .... 95 M8
Cheltenham Gdns
  BTCHLY MK3 .... 22 A8
Chelwood Cl NTHWD HA6 .... 85 H7
Cheney Cl LBUZ LU7 .... 160 H9
Cheneys Wk BTCHLY MK3 .... 22 D3
Cheney Wk AYL HP20 .... 3 J1
Chenies Av AMS HP6 .... 71 M3
Chenies Pde AMSS HP7 * 72 B3
Chenies Rd RKW/CH/CXG WD3 .... 73 K8
Chenies Wy YEAD UB4 .... 105 K7
Cheniston Gv MDHD SL6 .... 107 J7

LBUZ LU7 .... 169 P10
  NPAG MK16 .... 134 E12
  SKCH HP14 .... 187 K8
Chequers Orch IVER SL0 .... 113 L3
Chequers Pde
  GTMIS/PWD HP16 * 60 B4
  RMKN MK19 .... 12 C1
Cherington Ga MDHD SL6 .... 108 A1
Cherleton CNH/GTH/TMA MK8 .... 17 H5
The Cherries SLN SL2 .... 112 B3
Cherry Acre CFSP/GDCR SL3 .... 82 C4
Cherry Av DTCH/LGLY SL3 .... 112 C6
Cherry Cl FLKWH/TG HP10 .... 89 C3
  GTMIS/PWD HP16 .... 60 G3
  RBICN OX27 .... 155 J9
  RSLP HA4 .... 95 K11
Cherry Cnr FLKWH/TG HP10 * 89 G2
Cherrycourt Wy LBUZ LU7 .... 27 L8
Cherry Cft RKW/CH/CXG WD3 .... 74 F7
Cherrycroft Dr SKCH HP14 .... 67 J8
Cherrydale WATW WD18 .... 75 L5
Cherry Dr BEAC HP9 .... 80 A6
Cherry Garden La MDHD SL6 .... 117 K6
Cherry Gdns AMS HP6 .... 63 K8
Cherry Gv HAZ/HG HP15 .... 69 H4
  UX/CGN UB8 .... 115 G2
Cherry HI RKW/CH/CXG WD3 .... 74 A2
Cherry La BUCK/WIN MK18 .... 149 M11
  WDR/YW UB7 .... 114 E8
Cherry Leys BUCK/WIN MK18 .... 149 M11
Cherry Orch AMS HP6 .... 63 K8
  HHW HP1 .... 49 J5
  OLN MK46 .... 128 A10
  SLN SL2 .... 102 D3
  CFSP/GDCR SL9 .... 92 D7
  WDR/YW UB7 .... 114 D6
The Cherry Pit HWYN HP13 .... 77 J4
Cherry Ri CSTG HP8 .... 82 C2
  FLKWH/TG HP10 .... 89 C3
Cherry Rd HWYN HP13 .... 78 H4
Cherry St HWYN HP13 .... 77 J3
  RBICN OX27 .... 155 J9
Cherry Tree Av WDR/YW UB7 .... 114 E3
Cherry Tree Cl PRRI HP27 .... 67 G1
  SKCH HP14 .... 67 M7
Cherry Tree Cnr BEAC HP9 * 89 J3
Cherrytree La CFSP/GDCR SL9 .... 92 C1
Cherry Tree La DTCH/LGLY SL3 .... 102 E3
  GTMIS/PWD HP16 .... 53 J2
  IVER SL0 .... 103 M6
Cherry Tree La
  RKW/CH/CXG WD3 .... 83 L1
  TRING HP23 .... 45 M7
Cherry Tree Rd BEAC HP9 .... 89 J3
  CHNR OX39 .... 184 F3
  SLN SL2 .... 101 G5
Cherry Tree Wk CSHM HP5 .... 55 J8
Cherry Tree Wy
  FLKWH/TG HP10 .... 79 H1
Cherry Wk RKW/CH/CXG WD3 .... 74 B3
Cherry Wy DTCH/LGLY SL3 .... 123 H6
  HAZ/HG HP15 .... 68 F4
Cherrywood Cl BEAC HP9 .... 81 J5
Cherrywood Gdns
  FLKWH/TG HP10 .... 88 F2
Chervil EAG/OLD/WTN MK6 .... 22 E1
Cherwell Cl BIC OX26 .... 162 C5
  DTCH/LGLY SL3 .... 123 G2
  MDHD SL6 .... 108 F2
  RKW/CH/CXG WD3 .... 74 F6
Cherwell Rd AYLS HP21 .... 34 B8
  BNEND SL8 .... 89 C6
Cherwell Wy RSLP HA4 .... 95 K11
Chesham Av BDWL MK13 .... 6 C2
  CSHM HP5 .... 54 B1
Chesham La CFSP/GDCR SL9 .... 82 D3
  RAYLNE/WEN HP22 .... 52 D2
Chesham Rd AMS HP6 .... 63 H8
  BERK HP4 .... 46 E7
  CSHM HP5 .... 54 B1
  GTMIS/PWD HP16 .... 61 J3
  TRING HP23 .... 46 C2
Cheshem Wy WATW WD18 .... 75 K7
Cheshire Ri BTCHLY MK3 .... 22 B5
Cheshire Rd THAME OX9 .... 181 Q7
Chesil Wy YEAD UB4 .... 105 J2
Cheslyn Gdns GTLIN MK14 .... 14 C7
Chesney Wold
  EAG/OLD/WTN MK6 .... 18 C3
Chessbury Rd CSHM HP5 .... 62 F3
Chess Cl AYLS HP21 .... 42 C3
  CSHM HP5 .... 64 C1
  RKW/CH/CXG WD3 .... 74 C5
Chessfield Pk AMS HP6 .... 72 D2
Chess HI RKW/CH/CXG WD3 .... 74 C5
Chess La RKW/CH/CXG WD3 .... 74 C5
Chessmount Ri CSHM HP5 .... 63 J4
Chess Vale Ri
  RKW/CH/CXG WD3 .... 74 C1
Chess Valley Wk CSHM HP5 .... 64 D8
Chess Wy RKW/CH/CXG WD3 .... 73 M4
Chesswood Ct
  RKW/CH/CXG WD3 * 84 C1
Chester Cl BTCHLY MK3 .... 22 A7
Chesterfield Crs LBUZ LU7 .... 161 R7
Chesterfield Pl AYLW HP19 .... 2 A6
Chesterfield Wy
  HYS/HAR UB3 * 115 M6
Chesterholm BDWL MK13 .... 17 J1
Chester Pl NTHWD HA6 .... 85 K7
Chester Rd HTHAIR TW6 .... 124 F6
  NTHWD HA6 .... 85 L7
  SL SL1 .... 111 J3
  WATW WD18 .... 75 M6
Chesterton Cl CSHM HP5 .... 55 J8
Chesterton Gn BEAC HP9 .... 80 C5
Chestnut Av CSHM HP5 .... 55 J8
  DTCH/LGLY SL3 .... 112 D6
  NTHWD HA6 .... 95 L1
  RAYLNE/WEN HP22 .... 44 B2
  RKW/CH/CXG WD3 .... 73 M6
  THAME OX9 .... 181 L6
  WDR/YW UB7 .... 114 E4
  WYM MK11 .... 78 C5
Chestnut Cl AMS HP6 .... 63 J8
  BERK HP4 .... 171 J4
  BERK HP4 .... 49 G4
  BIC OX26 .... 163 G5
  CFSP/GDCR SL9 .... 82 B8
  HEN RG9 .... 188 C10
  HYS/HAR UB3 .... 115 G1
  MDHD SL6 .... 109 G1
  MLW SL7 .... 96 C7
  PRRI HP27 .... 58 B7
  RAYLNE/WEN HP22 .... 36 E5
  RKW/CH/CXG WD3 .... 73 J6
  WEAT MK2 .... 23 G7
Chestnut Dr BERK HP4 .... 48 C7

BRACKY NN13 .... 8 D5
  WDSR SL4 .... 120 D7
Chestnut End BIC OX26 .... 162 D2
  RAYLNE/WEN HP22 .... 44 B1
Chestnut Gn BRACKY NN13 .... 9 K2
Chestnut HI LBUZ LU7 .... 26 E6
Chestnut La AMS HP6 .... 63 K8
  HAZ/HG HP15 .... 69 G5
Chestnut Leys
  BUCK/WIN MK18 .... 149 M11
Chestnut Ri LBUZ LU7 .... 26 E6
Chestnut Rd BEAC HP9 .... 90 A1
  PRRI HP27 .... 58 A3
  TOW NN12 .... 130 E12
The Chestnuts HEN RG9 .... 191 K11
  HHS/BOV HP3 .... 57 L3
Chestnut Vw BUCK/WIN MK18 .... 158 C5
Chestnut Wk CFSP/GDCR SL9 * 82 D7
  RAYLNE/WEN HP22 .... 42 F5
Chestwood Gv
  HGDN/ICK UB10 .... 104 C5
Chettle Pl TOW NN12 .... 137 M4
Chetwode Av MKV MK10 .... 19 K5
Chetwode Cl BUCK/WIN MK18 .... 11 M3
Chetwynd Dr HGDN/ICK UB10 .... 104 E7
Chevalier Gv
  CNH/GTH/TMA MK8 .... 17 G7
Cheveley Gdns SL SL1 .... 100 B7
Cheviot Cl HWYN HP13 4
  HYS/HAR UB3 .... 125 J3
  LBUZ LU7 .... 27 J8
  MDHD SL6 .... 109 G4
Cheviot Rd DTCH/LGLY SL3 .... 122 F1
Cheyne Cl BUCK/WIN MK18 * 142 A9
Cheyne Wk CSHM HP5 .... 63 J2
Chicheley HI NPAG MK16 .... 133 N10
Chicheley St NPAG MK16 .... 15 H2
Chichester Av RSLP HA4 .... 95 K8
Chichester Cl BIC OX26 .... 162 D4
  HWYN HP13 .... 78 C4
Chichester Ct SL SL1 .... 112 A7
Chicksands Av MKV MK10 .... 19 K5
Chievely Ct SHEN MK5 .... 21 M5
Chilcote La AMSS HP7 .... 72 A2
Childs Av DEN/HRF UB9 .... 94 B1
Childs Ct HYS/HAR UB3 .... 115 M4
Childs Wy EAG/OLD/WTN MK6 .... 21 H4
  MKV MK10 .... 19 H4
  SHEN MK5 .... 21 J2
  WLLN MK15 .... 15 H7
Chillery Leys WLLN MK15 .... 15 H7
Chillingham St SHEN MK5 .... 21 K2
Chiltern Ap BIC OX26 .... 162 E3
Chiltern Av AMS HP6 .... 71 J1
  DUN/WHIP LU6 .... 170 F3
  HADM HP17 .... 177 N5
  HWYW HP12 .... 4 A8
  WLLN MK15 .... 15 H7
Chiltern Cl BERK HP4 .... 47 M5
  HADM HP17 .... 177 N5
  HEN RG9 .... 190 E6
  HGDN/ICK UB10 .... 95 G8
  PRRI HP27 .... 183 R11
  UX/CGN UB8 .... 115 G1
Chiltern Dr BUCK/WIN MK18 .... 151 K11
  UX/CGN UB8 .... 115 G1
Chiltern Gdns LBUZ LU7 .... 27 H3
Chiltern Gn FLKWH/TG HP10 .... 88 F2
Chiltern Gv THAME OX9 .... 181 P7
Chiltern Hts AMSS HP7 .... 71 M2
Chiltern HI CFSP/GDCR SL9 .... 82 D8
Chiltern Hills Rd BEAC HP9 .... 80 B8
Chiltern Link CSHM HP5 .... 53 M8
  GTMIS/PWD HP16 .... 52 D1
Chiltern Manor Pk
  GTMIS/PWD HP16 .... 60 F3
Chiltern Pde AMS HP6 .... 63 H8
Chiltern Park Av BERK HP4 .... 47 M4
Chiltern Rdg SKCH HP14 .... 186 F2
Chiltern Rd AMS HP6 .... 63 G5
  GTMIS/PWD HP16 .... 53 K7
  MDHD SL6 .... 109 G4
  MLW SL7 .... 97 H4
  RAYLNE/WEN HP22 .... 51 M1
  SL SL1 .... 110 A2
Chilterns Cl FLKWH/TG HP10 .... 89 G3
Chilterns Pk BNEND SL8 .... 89 G5
The Chilterns LBUZ LU7 .... 27 K8
  WYM MK11 .... 3 H9
Chiltern St AYLS HP21 .... 3 H9
Chiltern Vw SKCH HP14 .... 86 A8
Chiltern View Rd UX/CGN UB8 .... 104 B7
Chiltern Wy
  RAYLNE/WEN HP22 .... 36 B5
  TRING HP23 .... 38 B5
Chilton Cl FLKWH/TG HP10 .... 69 H3
  HAZ/HG HP15 .... 69 H3
Chilton Rd CSHM HP5 .... 55 J8
  RAYLW HP18 .... 175 J9
Chilwick Rd SLN SL2 .... 110 E1
The Chimes HWYW HP12 .... 4 E7
Chimney La FLKWH/TG HP10 .... 89 K2
Chinalls Cl BUCK/WIN MK18 .... 147 Q8
Chingle Cft EMV/FZ MK4 .... 21 M4
Chinnor HI CHNR OX39 .... 184 G8
Chinnor Rd CHNR OX39 .... 184 D6
  PRRI HP27 .... 183 K12
  SKCH HP14 .... 187 N7
  THAME OX9 .... 181 P7
  WTLGN SL49 .... 184 A8
Chippendale Cl HWYN HP13 .... 78 C1
Chippendale Waye
  UX/CGN UB8 .... 104 C5
Chippenham Cl PIN HA5 .... 95 L3
Chipps HI SKCH HP14 .... 76 A6
Chipstead CFSP/GDCR SL9 .... 82 B8
Chipstead Rd HTHAIR TW6 .... 124 F6
Chirbury Cf MKV MK10 .... 19 J5
Chisbridge La MLW SL7 .... 86 A8
Chisholm Ct EMV/FZ MK4 .... 21 M4
Chiswick Ct PIN HA5 .... 95 M2
Chitterfield Ga WDR/YW UB7 .... 124 C3
Choke La MDHD SL6 .... 107 M2
Cholesbury La TRING HP23 .... 45 M8
Cholesbury Rd TRING HP23 .... 46 B7
Chorley Rd SKCH HP14 .... 76 D2
Chorleywood Bottom
  RKW/CH/CXG WD3 .... 73 J6
Chorleywood Cl
  RKW/CH/CXG WD3 .... 74 C8
Chorleywood House Dr
  RKW/CH/CXG WD3 .... 73 K4
Chorleywood Rd
  RKW/CH/CXG WD3 .... 74 A6

Choseley Cl WAR/TWY RG10 .... 116 D2
Choseley Rd WAR/TWY RG10 .... 116 D2
Chowns Cl THAME OX9 .... 181 P7
Christchurch Dr WOLV MK12 .... 12 A1
Christchurch Rd TRING HP23 .... 37 L6
Christian Ct WLLN MK15 .... 14 F6
Christie Cl NPAG MK16 .... 14 D1
Christie Ct WATW WD18 .... 75 M6
Christmas La SLN SL2 .... 101 H1
Christopher Cl SKCH HP14 .... 67 J7
Chudleigh Br RSLP HA4 .... 95 M7
Church Av LBUZ LU7 .... 27 H8
  RSLP HA4 .... 95 J7
Church Cl BUCK/WIN MK18 .... 142 A7
  DUN/WHIP LU6 .... 171 Q10
  HEN RG9 .... 190 A5
  HYS/HAR UB3 .... 115 J3
  MDHD SL6 .... 108 C4
  NTHWD HA6 .... 85 L7
  RAYLW HP18 .... 174 E8
  RBICN OX27 .... 155 J3
  RKW/CH OX25 .... 172 C2
  RMKN MK19 .... 137 J11
  UX/CGN UB8 .... 104 A7
  WDR/YW UB7 .... 114 D7
  WDSR SL4 .... 121 J2
  WHLY OX33 .... 178 C7
Church Ct RAYLNE/WEN HP22 .... 43 G5
Church Cft DUN/WHIP LU6 .... 170 F3
Church Dr MDHD SL6 .... 109 H6
Church End BRACKY NN13 .... 140 B2
  BUCK/WIN MK18 .... 150 B5
  BUCK/WIN MK18 .... 149 J8
  BUCK/WIN MK18 .... 142 G2
  NPAG MK16 .... 133 P8
  PRRI NN27 .... 185 L1
  RMKS/WB MK17 .... 153 J2
  RMKS/WB MK17 .... 144 B3
  RNHPTN NN7 .... 126 A4
  TOW NN12 .... 137 M3
Church End Rd SHEN MK5 .... 21 K2
Church Farm Cl
  RAYLNE/WEN HP22 .... 34 F3
Church Farm La TRING HP23 .... 169 L11
Churchfield Cl HYS/HAR UB3 .... 115 L4
Churchfield Ms SLN SL2 .... 112 A3
Churchfield Rd
  CFSP/GDCR SL9 .... 82 C8
Church Ga DUN/WHIP LU6 .... 170 F3
Church Gn DUN/WHIP LU6 .... 31 J7
  HYS/HAR UB3 .... 115 L3
Church Green Rd BTCHLY MK3 .... 22 C7
Church Gv AMS HP6 .... 72 D2
  DTCH/LGLY SL3 .... 112 B2
Church Headland La
  RAYLNE/WEN HP22 .... 159 R12
Church HI BUCK/WIN MK18 .... 142 A4
  HGDN/ICK UB10 .... 105 C8
  CNH/GTH/TMA MK8 .... 17 H4
  DEN/HRF UB9 .... 94 B3
  HADM HP17 .... 51 G4
  HEN RG9 .... 188 D2
  LBUZ LU7 .... 169 L6
  RMKS/WB MK17 .... 144 H5
  RMKS/WB MK17 .... 20 E5
  WHLY OX33 .... 178 C11
Churchill Av AYLS HP21 .... 2 E1
  HGDN/ICK UB10 .... 105 C8
Churchill Cl FLKWH/TG HP21 * 89 C3
Churchill Crs THAME OX9 .... 181 P6
Churchill Dr BEAC HP9 .... 80 B5
  MLW SL7 .... 97 L2
Churchill Wy BRACKY NN13 .... 8 C7
Church La BERK HP4 .... 48 B6
  BIC OX26 .... 162 D5
  BRACKY NN13 .... 146 D3
  BUCK/WIN MK18 .... 159 J4
  BUCK/WIN MK18 .... 149 R4
  BUCK/WIN MK18 .... 136 B9
  BUCK/WIN MK18 .... 10 C8
  CFSP/GDCR SL9 .... 82 C8
  CHNR OX39 .... 184 G4
  DTCH/LGLY SL3 .... 112 A1
  DUN/WHIP LU6 .... 30 F8
  GTMIS/PWD SL6 .... 61 G3
  HADM HP17 .... 50 D5
  HAZ/HG HP15 .... 68 B6
  HHS/BOV HP3 .... 57 G6
  LBUZ LU7 .... 169 M7
  LBUZ LU7 .... 153 R12
  MDHD SL6 .... 109 H6
  MLW SL7 .... 97 J7
  NPAG MK16 .... 133 K12
  NPAG MK16 .... 132 B3
  OLN MK46 .... 133 N3
  PRRI NN27 .... 66 D2
  PRRI NN27 .... 58 A2
  RAYLNE/WEN HP22 .... 159 M11
  RAYLNE/WEN HP22 .... 44 B7
  RAYLNE/WEN HP22 .... 32 A3
  RAYLW HP18 .... 176 E1
  RAYLW HP18 .... 175 N9
  RAYLW HP18 .... 164 D7
  RAYLW HP18 .... 156 Q8
  RBEDK MK43 .... 135 R3
  RBICN OX27 .... 155 J3
  RKW/CH WD3 .... 83 M1
  RKW/CH WD3 .... 65 M8
  RMKN MK19 .... 137 M10
  RMKS/WB MK17 .... 152 B9
  RMKS/WB MK17 .... 151 K3
  RMKS/WB MK17 .... 20 E5
  SHEN MK5 .... 17 L6
  SKCH HP14 .... 185 N9
  SKCH HP14 .... 76 F4
  SLN SL2 .... 111 L1
  THAME OX9 .... 182 C7
  TOW NN12 .... 137 M3
  TOW NN12 .... 130 C8
  TRING HP23 .... 37 L1
  TRING HP23 .... 34 L1
  WDSR SL4 .... 121 J4
  WHLY OX33 .... 172 E12
  WTLGN OX49 .... 184 A7
Church Lees GTLIN MK14 .... 14 A1
Church Leys BRACKY NN13 .... 146 D3
Church Md DUN/WHIP LU6 .... 171 Q10
Church Meadow HHW HP1 .... 41 J7
Churchmere Wk AYLS HP21 * 2 F5
Church Pth GTMIS/PWD HP16 .... 60 F7
  LBUZ LU7 .... 169 M5
  SKCH HP14 .... 186 M5
Church Piece RAYLW HP18 * 174 E8
Church Rd BEAC HP9 .... 81 J6
  BERK HP4 .... 40 B2
  BRACKY NN13 .... 8 E7
  CHNR OX39 .... 184 G4
  DEN/HRF UB9 .... 94 B2
  DUN/WHIP LU6 .... 171 Q10
  DUN/WHIP LU6 .... 31 J8
  FLKWH/TG HP10 .... 79 H2

HYS/HAR UB3 .... 115 L5
IVER SLO 103 H7
LBUZ LU7 .... 169 Q10
LBUZ LU7 .... 29 K8
LBUZ LU7 .... 26 F8
MDHD SL6 .... 109 G5
MDHD SL6 .... 98 A4
MLW SL7 .... 98 B5
NPAG MK16 .... 133 N8
RAYLW HP18 .... 180 A3
RAYLNE/WEN HP22 .... 168 E1
RMKS/WB MK17 .... 153 Q6
RMKS/WB MK17 .... 144 A4
RNHPTN NN7 .... 126 A4
SKCH HP14 .... 186 C1
SKCH HP14 .... 86 A3
SLN SL2 .... 101 H8
THAME OX9 .... 181 N5
UX/CGN UB8 .... 114 C1
WAT WD17 .... 75 M2
WDR/YW UB7 .... 114 C6
WDSR SL4 .... 122 A3
Claydon End CFSP/GDCR SL9 .... 92 D2
Claydon La CFSP/GDCR SL9 .... 92 D2
Clayfield
  RAYLNE/WEN HP22 .... 44 B3
Clayfields FLKWH/TG HP10 .... 69 H8
Clay Furlong LBUZ LU7 .... 29 J1
Clayhall La WDSR SL4 .... 121 L8
Clay HI CNH/GTH/TMA MK8 .... 17 H4
Clayhill MLW SL7 .... 86 F4
Clay La BUCK/WIN MK18 .... 156 D1
  MLW SL7 .... 86 F4
  RAYLNE/WEN HP22 .... 44 B5
Claymoor Pk MLW SL7 .... 86 F4
Clay Pit La OLN MK46 .... 128 B11
Clays La RMKS/WB MK17 .... 144 A4
The Clays HADM HP17 .... 14 D6
Clayton Ga GTLIN MK14 .... 14 A1
Clayton Pde DTCH/LGLY SL3 * 112 F7
Clayton Rd HYS/HAR UB3 .... 115 K6
Claytons Meadow BNEND SL8 .... 89 G8
Clayton Wk AMSS HP7 .... 72 B2
Clayton Wy UX/CGN UB8 .... 114 C1
Clearbrook Cl HWYN HP13 .... 79 G6
Cleares Pasture SL SL1 .... 100 A4
Cleave Av HYS/HAR UB3 .... 115 K8
Cleavers CHNR OX39 .... 184 E4
Cleavers Av GTLIN MK14 .... 6 A4
Cleeve Crs BTCHLY MK3 .... 22 D4
Clegg Sq SHEN MK5 .... 21 L1
Clement Bois BRACKY NN13 .... 8 D7
Clement Gdns HYS/HAR UB3 .... 115 K8
Clementi Av HAZ/HG HP15 .... 69 J3
Clements La RBICN OX27 .... 156 A8
  RKW/CH/CXG WD3 .... 73 J6
Clerkenwell Pl
  EAG/OLD/WTN MK6 .... 7 M3
Clevedon Gdns HYS/HAR UB3 .... 115 J7
Clevehurst Cl SLN SL2 .... 101 H4
Cleveland BDWL MK13 .... 13 L8
Cleveland Cl FLKWH/TG HP10 * 89 K2
  MDHD SL6 .... 109 G4
Cleveland Dr LBUZ LU7 .... 26 D2
Cleveland Pk AYL HP20 .... 34 E3
Cleveland Pl AYL HP20 .... 3 K1
Cleveland Rd AYL HP20 .... 3 H1
  UX/CGN UB8 .... 104 C3
Cleves Ct WDSR SL4 .... 120 C6
Clewer Av WDSR SL4 .... 120 D5
Clewer Court Rd WDSR SL4 .... 121 G3
Clewer Fields WDSR SL4 * 121 G3
Clewer Hill Rd WDSR SL4 .... 120 D5
Clewer New Town WDSR SL4 .... 120 D5
Clewer Pk WDSR SL4 .... 120 F3
Clicker Yd OLN MK46 .... 128 G10
Cliffden Rd RAYLW HP18 .... 178 S9
Clifford Av WAT WD17 .... 75 J2
Clifford Gdns HYS/HAR UB3 .... 115 J8
Clifford Rd PRRI NN27 .... 58 A3
Cliffords Wy BNEND SL8 .... 88 C5
Clifton Cl MDHD SL6 .... 108 C6
Clifton Gdns HGDN/ICK UB10 .... 105 C2
Clifton Gn AYLW HP19 .... 2 A1
Clifton Lawns AMS HP6 .... 63 H6
Clifton Moor SHEN MK5 .... 21 G1
Clifton Pl BNEND SL8 .... 89 H7
Clifton Ri WDSR SL4 .... 120 C4
Clifton Rd AMS HP6 .... 63 G6
  HTHAIR TW6 .... 125 G6
  OLN MK46 .... 128 F12
  SL SL1 .... 111 M6
The Climb RKW/CH/CXG WD3 .... 74 A7
Cline Ct CNH/GTH/TMA MK8 .... 17 H8
Clinkard Pl SKCH HP14 .... 187 R11
Clinton Crs AYL HP20 .... 3 L6
Clipstone Brook Wy
  MKV MK10 .... 19 L3
Clipstone Crs LBUZ LU7 .... 27 K7
Clive Ct SL SL1 .... 111 J6
Cliveden Rd MDHD SL6 .... 99 H8
Cliveden Pl EMV/FZ MK4 .... 21 J4
Clivemont Rd MDHD SL6 .... 108 C3
Clivesdale Dr HYS/HAR UB3 .... 115 M5
Clockhouse Ms
  RKW/CH/CXG WD3 .... 73 K4
Cloebury Paddock WLLN MK15 .... 18 F2
Cloister Garth BERK HP4 .... 48 B6
The Cloisters AYL HP20 * 2 E1
  HWYN HP13 .... 68 C8
  RKW/CH/CXG WD3 .... 74 D8
Clonmel Wy SL SL1 .... 100 A4
Closemead Cl NTHWD HA6 .... 85 H4
The Closes HADM HP17 .... 176 D11
The Close BDWL MK13 .... 17 K2
  BNEND SL8 .... 88 F4
  HEN RG9 .... 190 G6
  HGDN/ICK UB10 .... 104 D5
  HHS/BOV HP3 * 57 H7
  IVER SLO 103 H8
  OLN MK46 .... 132 H1
  RAYLNE/WEN HP22 .... 34 F2
  RAYLNE/WEN HP22 .... 32 A3
  RAYLW HP18 .... 175 N1
  RBEDW MK43 .... 128 H11
  RKW/CH/CXG WD3 .... 84 A1
  RMKS/WB MK17 .... 151 L3
  SL SL1 .... 110 C4
Cloudberry WTR/OFPK MK7 .... 19 K3
Cloutsham Cl NTHWD HA6 .... 85 H4
Clovelly Av WDR/YW UB7 .... 105 H2
Clovelly Cl HGDN/ICK UB10 .... 105 H2
Clover Cl SHEN MK5 .... 17 K6
Clover End BUCK/WIN MK18 .... 11 K7
Clover La AYLS HP21 .... 42 D1
Clover Md BIC OX26 .... 162 C1
The Clump RKW/CH/CXG WD3 .... 73 M6
Clutterbucks
  RKW/CH/CXG WD3 .... 65 M7
Clydesdale Pl GTLIN MK14 .... 18 C2
Clyfford Rd RSLP HA4 .... 105 L2
Clyston Rd WATW WD18 .... 75 J4
Coach House Ms BIC OX26 .... 162 E6
Coachmaker Ct GTLIN MK14 .... 14 C1
Coach Ride MLW SL7 .... 97 J2
Coalmans Wy SL SL1 .... 109 M3
Coaters La FLKWH/TG HP10 .... 89 K2
Coates La HWYN HP13 .... 5 J1
Coat Wicks BEAC HP9 .... 81 H6
Cobb Cl DTCH/LGLY SL3 .... 122 C4
Cobbett's Ride TRING HP23 .... 37 L2
Cobbetts Wy BUCK/WIN MK18 .... 149 L12
Cobb Hall Rd RMKS/WB MK17 .... 152 H5
Cobblers Cl SLN SL2 .... 101 G7
Cobblershill La
  GTMIS/PWD HP16 .... 59 M4
Cobb Rd BERK HP4 .... 47 L6
Cobbs Ct OLN MK46 * 128 B10
Cobbs Gdn OLN MK46 .... 128 B10

Cobden Cl UX/CGN UB8 .... 104 B6
Coberley Cl WLLN MK15 .... 14 E8
Cobham Cl BUCK/WIN MK18 .... 11 K5
  SL SL1 .... 110 E5
Cochran Cl CNH/GTH/TMA MK8 .... 17 H7
Cockerell Gv SHEN MK5 .... 21 M1
Cockett Rd DTCH/LGLY SL3 .... 112 D7
Cock La HWYN HP13 .... 78 F5
Cock Gv BERK HP4 .... 46 F7
Cockpit Cl HAZ/HG HP15 .... 68 D1
Cockpit Rd HAZ/HG HP15 .... 68 C2
Coddimoor La RMKS/WB MK17 .... 20 E7
Codmore Crs CSHM HP5 .... 54 B4
Codmore Wood Rd CSHM HP5 .... 54 A6
Coe Sp SL SL1 .... 111 G6
Cofdards SLN SL2 .... 112 B3
Cogan Ct CNH/GTH/TMA MK8 .... 17 H7
Cogdells La CSHM HP5 .... 54 A6
Coggeshall Gv WTR/OFPK MK7 .... 19 M3
Coin Cl MKV MK10 .... 19 H3
Coke Dr BIC OX26 .... 162 D5
Coke's Farm La CSTG HP8 .... 72 A4
Coke's La CSTG HP8 .... 72 A5
Colbourne Rd HWYN HP13 .... 78 C2
Colbrook Av HYS/HAR UB3 .... 115 J7
Colbrook La HYS/HAR UB3 .... 115 J7
Colby Gdns MDHD SL6 .... 108 E1
Colchester Ct BTCHLY MK3 .... 22 E5
Colchester Rd NTHWD HA6 .... 95 M1
Colchester Wk BTCHLY MK3 .... 22 B7
Coldeaton La EMV/FZ MK4 .... 21 L3
Coldharbour Cl HEN RG9 .... 190 F6
Coldharbour La CSHM HP5 .... 54 A6
Coldharbour Wy AYLW HP19 .... 177 R3
Coldmoorholme La
  BNEND SL8 .... 88 D6
Coldmoreham Yd AMSS HP7 .... 70 D6
Cole Gdns HEST TW5 .... 125 M3
Cole La CNH/GTH/TMA MK8 .... 17 H7
Coleheath Bottom PRRI NN27 .... 67 H1
Colenorton Crs WDSR SL4 .... 110 D8
Coleridge Wy BIC OX26 .... 162 B2
  BTCHLY MK3 .... 22 C7
  NPAG MK16 .... 14 C2
Coleridge Dr LBUZ LU7 .... 26 C2
Coleridge Wy WDR/YW UB7 .... 114 C2
  YEAD UB4 .... 115 M3
Cole Rd AYLS HP21 .... 42 B1
Coles Av EAG/OLD/WTN MK6 .... 18 C6
Colesbourne Dr WLLN MK15 .... 14 D8
Coles HI HHW HP1 .... 49 M5
Coleshill La AMSS HP7 .... 70 C6
Coleshill Pl BDWL MK13 .... 6 C2
Coles Ri BRACKY NN13 .... 8 C7
Colet Rd RAYLNE/WEN HP22 .... 44 B5
Colgrain St GTLIN MK14 .... 14 C2
Colham Av WDR/YW UB7 .... 114 D5
Colham Green Rd UX/CGN UB8 .... 114 F2
Colham Mill Rd WDR/YW UB7 .... 114 C2
Colham Rd UX/CGN UB8 .... 114 E1
Colindale Rd MKV MK10 .... 19 H5
Colin Wy SL SL1 .... 111 K7
College Av MDHD SL6 .... 108 D3
  SL SL1 .... 111 K7
College Crs RAYLW HP18 .... 179 G2
  WDSR SL4 .... 121 G5
College Dr RSLP HA4 .... 95 M6
College Gln MDHD SL6 .... 108 C3
College Ri MDHD SL6 .... 108 C3
  RBEDW MK43 .... 138 H4
College Rd North
  RAYLNE/WEN HP22 .... 36 B1
  HYS/HAR UB3 .... 115 M4
  NTHWD HA6 .... 85 J6
College Rd South
  Colley HI BDWL MK13 .... 17 K2
Colley Hill La SLN SL2 .... 101 L1
Colley Land RKW/CH/CXG WD3 .... 73 J5
Collier Cl MDHD SL6 .... 108 C3
Colliers Wd MKV MK10 .... 19 H6
Collingwood Cl HWYN HP13 .... 78 E9
Collingwood Rd UX/CGN UB8 .... 105 G1
Collinswood Rd SLN SL2 .... 91 G4
Collum Green Rd SLN SL2 .... 101 K1
Collyer Rd SKCH HP14 .... 186 H2
Colne By-Pass
  DTCH/LGLY SL3 .... 123 G2
Coln Ct MDHD SL6 .... 108 C2
Colndale Rd DTCH/LGLY SL3 .... 123 K5
Colne Av RKW/CH/CXG WD3 .... 83 M2
  WDR/YW UB7 .... 114 C6
Colne Bank DTCH/LGLY SL3 .... 123 H6
Colne Cl BIC OX26 .... 162 C5
Colnedale Rd UX/CGN UB8 .... 104 C3
Colne Md RKW/CH/CXG WD3 .... 84 A2
Colne Orch IVER SLO 113 L3
Colne Rd HWYN HP13 .... 78 E3
Colne Valley Trail
  HGDN/ICK UB10 .... 104 D1
  RKW/CH/CXG WD3 .... 84 D1
Colne Valley Wy
  DTCH/LGLY SL3 .... 123 G2
  IVER SLO 113 M3
  WDR/YW UB7 .... 113 M3
Colonial Rd SL SL1 .... 111 M6
Colossus Wy BTCHLY MK3 .... 22 C7
Colsons Wy OLN MK46 .... 128 B9
Colston Bassett EMV/FZ MK4 .... 21 M5
Coltman Av RAYLW HP18 .... 175 K12
Coltrain Leyes BIC OX26 .... 162 C2
Coltsfoot Pl GTLIN MK14 .... 6 E2
The Coltsfoot HHW HP1 .... 49 K8
Colts Holm Rd WLLN MK12 .... 12 F6
Columbia Dr LBUZ LU7 .... 27 K3
Columbia Pl CMK MK9 .... 7 K3
Columbine Rd HAZ/HG HP15 .... 68 E1
Columbus Gdns NTHWD HA6 .... 85 M8
Colville Ct GTMIS/PWD HP16 * 61 J1
Colville Rd WYM HP11 .... 4 D7
Colwyn Cl CMK MK9 .... 7 K3
Combe Martin EMV/FZ MK4 .... 21 M5
Combe Ri HWYN HP13 .... 77 J1
Combermere Ct WDSR SL4 .... 121 G5
Combe Wd WATW WD18 .... 75 L7
Combes Crs
  EAG/OLD/WTN MK6 .... 18 C8
Comerford Wy
  BUCK/WIN MK18 .... 151 J9
Comfrey Cl WTR/OFPK MK7 .... 23 K1
The Comfrey AYLW HP19 .... 34 D2
Commercial Sq WYM HP11 * 4 D7
Common Fld TRING HP23 .... 46 C1
Common Gdns BERK HP4 .... 49 G6
Common Gate Rd
  BUCK/WIN MK18 .... 73 J6
Common La BDWL MK13 .... 6 B9
  SHEN MK5 .... 6 B9
  SL SL1 .... 100 C1
  WDSR SL4 .... 121 H1
Common Rd DTCH/LGLY SL3 .... 112 D4
  DUN/WHIP LU6 .... 171 P11

FLKWH/TG HP10 .... 88 F2
HAZ/HG HP15 .... 68 C1
RKW/CH/CXG WD3 .... 73 J5
WDSR SL4 .... 110 C8
Common Side HWYN HP13 .... 77 J3
Common St OLN MK46 .... 127 K12
The Common BERK HP4 .... 48 E4
  HAZ/HG HP15 .... 68 C1
  HAZ/HG HP15 .... 68 C1
  KGLGY WD4 .... 65 M3
  RKW/CH/CXG WD3 * 73 K6
  WDR/YW UB7 .... 124 B1
Commonwealth Av
  HYS/HAR UB3 .... 115 J3
Common Wd SLN SL2 .... 101 K2
Common Wood La
  FLKWH/TG HP10 .... 79 J1
Community Cl
  HGDN/ICK UB10 * 105 G1
Community Wy
  RKW/CH/CXG WD3 .... 74 F6
Comp Ga DUN/WHIP LU6 .... 30 G6
Comp Gdns DUN/WHIP LU6 .... 30 F8
The Comp DUN/WHIP LU6 .... 30 G8
Compton Dr MDHD SL6 .... 107 M6
Compton Rd HYS/HAR UB3 .... 115 L3
  RAYLNE/WEN HP22 .... 44 B5
Concorde Cl HGDN/ICK UB10 .... 104 D3
Concorde Rd MDHD SL6 .... 108 C6
Concorde Wy SL SL1 .... 111 H6
Concord Wy LBUZ LU7 .... 29 M1
Concra Pk RMKS/WB MK17 .... 144 A4
Condor Cl EAG/OLD/WTN MK6 .... 18 D7
Conduit Hill Ri THAME OX9 .... 181 N7
Conduit La DTCH/LGLY SL3 .... 122 D1
Conegar Ct SL SL1 .... 111 K5
Conegra Ct HWYN HP13 .... 5 K6
Conegra Rd HWYN HP13 .... 5 K6
Coneygere OLN MK46 .... 128 C11
Coney Gv HGDN/ICK UB10 .... 104 C8
Congreve EAG/OLD/WTN MK6 .... 23 G1
Conifer Dr BIC OX26 .... 162 C1
Conifer Ri HWYN HP13 .... 4 C7
The Conifers HHS/BOV HP3 .... 57 J7
  MDHD SL6 .... 108 B3
Conifer Wk WDSR SL4 .... 120 B3
Conifer Wy HYS/HAR UB3 .... 115 M4
Conigre CHNR OX39 .... 184 E4
Coningsby Cl HGDN/ICK UB10 .... 104 C7
Coningsby Ct MDHD SL6 .... 108 C7
Coningsby Cl HWYN HP13 .... 5 J3
Coningsby Rd HWYN HP13 .... 5 J2
Coniston Cresent SL SL1 .... 110 B2
Coniston Gdns PIN HA5 .... 95 M3
Coniston Gn AYL HP20 .... 35 H3
Coniston Rd LBUZ LU7 .... 26 D7
Coniston Wy WEAT MK2 .... 23 G7
Connaught Cl MDHD SL6 .... 108 D1
  UX/CGN UB8 .... 105 H7
Connaught Gdns BERK HP4 .... 47 L3
Connaught Rd AYL HP20 .... 35 J5
  SL SL1 .... 112 A6
Conniburrow Bvd GTLIN MK14 .... 6 F1
Conniston Cl MLW SL7 .... 97 G4
Constable Ct GTLIN MK14 .... 14 C2
  YEAD UB4 .... 105 H7
Constable Pl AYLW HP19 .... 167 Q12
Constable's Cft RBICS/W OX25 .... 173 K3
Constantine Wy BDWL MK13 .... 11 G1
Control Tower Rd HTHAIR TW6 .... 124 F5
Convent Rd WDSR SL4 .... 120 F5
Conway Cl AYLS HP21 .... 3 K8
  FLKWH/TG HP10 .... 89 H1
Conway Crs BTCHLY MK3 .... 22 B6
Conway Dr HYS/HAR UB3 .... 115 H7
Conway Rd MDHD SL6 .... 110 A3
Cook Cl WTR/OFPK MK7 .... 23 L3
Cookfield Cl DUN/WHIP LU6 .... 31 M6
Cookham Dean Bottom
  MDHD SL6 .... 98 B3
Cookham Rd MDHD SL6 .... 98 D8
Cooks Cl RNHPTN NN7 .... 130 C2
Cookshall La HWYW HP12 .... 76 H7
Cooks La RMKS/WB MK17 .... 152 D8
Cook's Meadow
  DUN/WHIP LU6 .... 170 F2
Cooks Rd AYLW HP19 .... 177 Q2
Cooks Vennel HHW HP1 .... 49 M5
Coombe Av
  RAYLNE/WEN HP22 .... 51 J4
Coombe Cl RAYLNE/WEN HP22 .... 43 H4
Coombe Dr DUN/WHIP LU6 .... 31 J7
Coombe Gdns BERK HP4 .... 48 C6
  SKCH HP14 .... 67 M8
Coombe Hill Ct WDSR SL4 .... 120 C7
Coombe Hill Crs THAME OX9 .... 181 M7
Coombe Hill Rd
  RKW/CH/CXG WD3 .... 73 M8
  SKCH HP14 .... 67 J4
Coombe V CFSP/GDCR SL9 .... 92 D7
Coomber Dr HEN RG9 .... 190 G3
Cooper Rd HEN RG9 .... 190 G3
Cooper's Court Rd SKCH HP14 .... 186 C1
Coopers Gn BIC OX26 .... 162 E2
Coopers Ms GTLIN MK14 .... 14 C1
Coopers Ri WYM HP11 .... 78 C5
Coopers Rw IVER SLO 113 H1
Cooper's Yd AYL HP20 .... 2 F4
Cooper Wy BERK HP4 .... 48 C5
  SL SL1 .... 111 G2
Coots Cl BUCK/WIN MK18 .... 11 M7
Cope Ct MDHD SL6 .... 108 B3
Copeland Cl WTR/OFPK MK7 .... 23 M1
Copes Hill HAZ/HG HP15 .... 68 C5
Copes Shroves HAZ/HG HP15 .... 68 C5
Copmans Wick
  RKW/CH/CXG WD3 .... 73 J6
Copners Dr HAZ/HG HP15 .... 69 H4
Copners Wy HAZ/HG HP15 .... 69 G4
Copper Beech Cl
  HHS/BOV HP3 .... 57 L2
  WDSR SL4 .... 120 C4
Copper Beech Wy LBUZ LU7 .... 27 H4
Copperdale Rd HYS/HAR UB3 .... 115 M4
Copperfield Av UX/CGN UB8 .... 105 H4
Copperfields BEAC HP9 .... 80 D5
  HWYW HP12 .... 77 C5
Copperhouse Ct
  WTR/OFPK MK7 .... 23 G4
Copperkins Gv AMS HP6 .... 63 G2
Copperkins La AMS HP6 .... 62 F2
Coppermill La
  RKW/CH/CXG WD3 .... 83 L7
Coppermill Lock
  DEN/HRF UB9 * 83 M7
Copper Rdg CFSP/GDCR SL9 .... 82 E5
Coppice Cl AYLW HP20 .... 3 L1
  RSLP HA4 .... 95 H5
Coppice Farm Rd
  HAZ/HG HP15 .... 69 H8
The Coppice HAZ/HG HP15 .... 69 H8

HWYW HP12 .... 87 G2
SKCH HP14 .... 67 G6
TRING HP23 .... 46 C1
WDR/YW SL0 .... 114 C7
Coppice Wy AYL HP20 .... 3 L2
SLN SL2 .... 91 J8
Coppidwell Dr AYLS HP21 .... 42 F1
Coppin La BDWL MK13 .... 17 K3
Coppins Cl BERK HP4 .... 47 K6
Coppins La IVER SL0 .... 113 J2
Copse Cl NTHWD HA6 .... 85 H8
SL SL1 .... 110 B5
WDR/YW SL0 .... 114 C7
Copse Ga BUCK/WIN MK18 .... 151 K10
Copse Hill Cl HHS/BOV HP3 .... 57 J7
Copse La BEAC HP9 .... 81 K7
The Copse AMSS HP7 .... 71 H1
HHW HP1 .... 49 K5
WAR/TWY RG10 .... 191 P11
Copse Wy CSHM HP5 .... 54 F6
Copse Wd IVER SL0 .... 103 J6
Copse Wood Wy NTHWD HA6 .... 85 H8
Copthall Cl CFSP/GDCR SL9 .... 82 B7
Copthall Cnr CFSP/GDCR SL9 .... 82 D7
Copthall La CFSP/GDCR SL9 .... 82 D7
Copthall Rd East
HGDN/ICK UB10 .... 94 F8
Copthall Rd West
HGDN/ICK UB10 .... 94 F8
Copthorn Cl MDHD SL6 .... 117 M2
Copthorne Cl
RKW/CH/CXG WD3 .... 74 E6
Copthorne Ms HYS/HAR UB3 .... 115 K8
Copthorne Rd
RKW/CH/CXG WD3 .... 74 E7
Copy Ground Ct HWYW HP12 * 4 E5
Copyground La HWYW HP12 .... 4 C5
Coral Cl DUN/WHIP LU6 * 30 F3
Coram Cl BERK HP4 .... 48 B7
Corbet Ride LBUZ LU7 .... 26 E6
Corbett Cl WLLN MK15 .... 15 C7
Cordingley Ct RSLP HA4 .... 95 J6
Cordwainer Ct GTLN MK14 .... 14 C8
Cordwallis St MDHD SL6 .... 108 C2
Cordwallis St MDHD SL6 .... 108 C2
Cores End Rd BNEND SL8 .... 88 F7
Corfe Cl AYLS HP21 .... 43 G1
Corfe Crs BTCHLY MK3 .... 22 C7
Corfe Gdns SL SL1 .... 110 F4
Corfe Pl MDHD SL6 .... 108 B3
Coriander Ct WTR/OFPK MK7 .... 23 L1
Corin Wy WEAT MK2 .... 153 Q1
Corn Cl BTCHLY MK3 .... 22 B4
Cormorant Wy LBUZ LU7 .... 29 K1
Cornbrook Rd AYLS HP21 .... 42 B1
Cornbury Crs WLLN MK15 .... 14 D8
Comcrake AYLW HP19 .... 34 D3
Comcrake Wy BIC OX26 .... 162 F5
Cornel Cl HAZ/HG HP15 .... 69 G7
Cornelia St WEAT MK2 .... 153 M3
Cornerways PRRI HP27 .... 67 G1
Cornerwood
GTMIS/PWD HP16 * 53 G2
Cornfield Cl UX/CGN UB8 .... 104 C7
Cornfield Crs BERK HP4 .... 47 J3
Cornflower Pl
BUCK/WIN MK18 .... 11 K7
Corn Hi CNH/GTH/TMA MK8 .... 17 G4
WYM HP11 .... 5 H6
Cornwall Av SLN SL2 .... 111 H1
Cornwall Cl MDHD SL6 .... 98 D8
WDSR SL4 .... 120 D7
Cornwall Gv BTCHLY MK3 .... 22 B5
Cornwall Rd BUCK/WIN MK18 * 11 L5
Cornwall Pl RSLP HA4 .... 95 L3
UX/CGN UB8 .... 104 C4
Cornwalls Meadow
BUCK/WIN MK18 .... 11 L5
WDSR SL4 .... 121 L5
Coronation Av DTCH/LGLY SL3. .... 112 G3
Coronation Crs SKCH HP14 .... 86 C3
Coronation Pl
BUCK/WIN MK18 .... 149 L12
Coronation Rd HWYW HP12 * 87 J2
HYS/HAR UB3 .... 115 G1
MDHD SL6 .... 108 D3
RBEDW MK43 .... 139 G6
Coronation Vls AYLS HP21 * 3 H5
WDSR SL4 .... 121 L5
Corporation St WYM HP11 .... 5 H4
Corrid Industrial Pk
AYLW HP19 .... 2 A3
Corrigan Cl BTCHLY MK3 .... 22 D6
Corsham Ct
CNH/GTH/TMA MK8 .... 17 G4
Corwell Gdns UX/CGN UB8 .... 17 H3
Corwell La UX/CGN UB8 .... 115 H3
Cosgrove Rd RMKN MK19 .... 137 K7
Cosway Pl CNH/GTH/TMA MK8 * 17 G8
Cotefield Dr LBUZ LU7 .... 27 H4
Coteford Cl PIN HA5 .... 95 M4
Cotesmore Rd HHW HP1 .... 49 K8
Cotes Wy LBUZ LU7 .... 28 A3
Cotman Cl WOLV MK12 .... 16 E1
Cotmans Rd HYS/HAR UB3 * 115 H5
Cotmore Cl THAME OX9 .... 181 Q7
Cotmore Gdns THAME OX9 .... 181 Q7
Cotswold Cl MDHD SL6 .... 109 G4
SL SL1 .... 111 G7
UX/CGN UB8 .... 104 B6
Cotswold Dr LBUZ LU7 .... 26 C2
Cotswold Gn AYL HP20 * 3 H1
Cotswolds Wy
BUCK/WIN MK18 .... 156 H6
Cotswold Wy HWYN HP13 * 4 D5
Cottage Cl RKW/CH/CXG WD3. .... 74 E7
RSLP HA4 .... 95 J2
WAT WD17 .... 75 J3
Cottage Grounds HADM HP17 .... 177 N4
Cottage Park Rd SLN SL2 .... 91 J8
Cottate Farm Wy PRRI HP27 .... 67 H2
Cottesbrooke Cl
DTCH/LGLY SL3 .... 123 J7
Cottesloe Cl LBUZ LU7 .... 161 K2
Cottesloe Rd STSTR MK11 .... 16 C1
Cottesloe Rd AYLS HP21 .... 42 C1
Cottingham Cha RSLP HA4 .... 105 M1
Cottingham Gv BTCHLY MK3 .... 22 C7
Cottisford Crs GTLN MK14 .... 14 C8
Cottland Clay HADM HP17 .... 176 D11
Coulser Cl HHW HP1 * 49 M4
Coulson Av
CNH/GTH/TMA MK8 .... 17 H4
Coulson Cl GTMIS/PWD HP16 .... 60 D4
Coulson Wy SL SL1 .... 110 A4
Counters Cl HHW HP1 .... 49 M7
Countess Cl DEN/HRF UB9 .... 94 B1
Countisbury EMV/FZ MK4 .... 22 A4
Country La HAZ/HG HP15 .... 68 D3
County Rd BRACKY NN13 .... 8 F8
Cours La Ville Cl
BUCK/WIN MK18 .... 150 H11
Court Cl AYLS HP21 .... 3 G8

HWYN HP13 .... 77 H4
MDHD SL6 .... 109 H8
PRRI HP27 .... 183 R11
Court Close Rd THAME OX9 .... 182 B7
Court Cnr OLN MK46 .... 128 A11
Court Crs SL SL1 .... 111 J3
Court Dr HGDN/ICK UB10 .... 104 E6
MDHD SL6 .... 99 H7
Courteneys Ldg EMV/FZ MK4 * 2 C8
Court Farm Cl SL SL1 .... 111 G5
Courtfield Cl BERK HP4 .... 47 K6
Courtfield Gdns DEN/HRF UB9 .... 103 B1
RSLP HA4 .... 95 L3
Courtfield Rd WHLY OX33 .... 178 D7
Courthouse Cl
BUCK/WIN MK18 .... 151 J9
Courthouse Rd MDHD SL6 .... 108 B3
Courtlands BERK HP4 .... 48 A4
Courtlands Av DTCH/LGLY SL3. .... 112 G3
Courtlands Cl RSLP HA4 .... 95 L6
Court La IVER SL0 .... 113 H3
SL SL1 .... 100 C8
WDSR SL4 .... 109 H7
Courtmoor Cl PRRI HP27 .... 50 B8
Courtneidge Cl LBUZ LU7 .... 161 K2
Courtney Rd HTHAIR TW6 .... 124 F6
Courtney Wy HTHAIR TW6 .... 124 F6
Court Rd HGDN/ICK UB10 .... 105 G3
MDHD SL6 .... 99 H8
RMKS/WB MK43 .... 139 L6
The Court RMKS/WB MK17 .... 138 F11
Courtyard Cl AMS HP6 .... 71 H1
The Courtyards WATW WD18 * 75 J3
Cousins Cl WDR/YW SL0 * 114 D4
Cousins Dr AYL HP20 .... 3 K3
Cousins Piece RAYLW HP18 .... 175 Q8
Coventon Rd AYLW HP19 .... 2 C1
Coverack Pl EMV/FZ MK4 .... 21 L4
Coverdale BDWL MK13 .... 17 M1
Coverdale Rd SLN SL2 .... 110 D3
Covert Cl BERK HP4 .... 47 J4
Covert Rd BERK HP4 .... 47 J3
The Covert NTHWD HA6 .... 85 H7
Cowdray Cl WLLN MK15 .... 18 F1
Cowdray Rd HGDN/ICK UB10 .... 105 H6
Cow La BUCK/WIN MK18 .... 148 C5
DUN/WHIP LU6 .... 170 F2
TRING HP23 .... 38 C6
Cowleaze CHNR OX39 .... 184 E4
Cowley Cl RAYLNE/WEN HP22 .... 35 G3
Cowley Crs UX/CGN UB8 .... 114 B2
Cowley Mill Rd UX/CGN UB8 .... 104 B3
Cowley Rd UX/CGN UB8 .... 104 C4
Cowley Rd BIC OX26 .... 162 B2
NPAC MK16 .... 14 D2
Cowper Rd BERK HP4 .... 48 A6
CSHM HP5 .... 55 G8
SLN SL2 .... 110 F1
Cowpers Orch OLN MK46 .... 132 H1
Cowper St SLN SL2 .... 128 C9
Cowslip Cl HGDN/ICK UB10 .... 104 D5
Cowslip Rd HAZ/HG HP15 .... 68 E4
Coxborrow Cl MDHD SL6 .... 98 D3
Coxfield Cl SKCH HP14 .... 187 J1
Cox Green La MDHD SL6 .... 108 B6
Cox Green Rd MDHD SL6 .... 108 B6
Coxhill Wy AYLS HP21 .... 2 F7
Cox La WHLY OX33 .... 178 C7
Coxwell Cl BUCK/WIN MK18 .... 142 A9
Coy Ct AYL HP20 * 3 M6
Crabbe Crs CSHM HP5 .... 55 J8
Crabs Gv RAYLNE/WEN HP22 .... 159 Q11
Crab Tree Cl OLN MK46 .... 128 A9
Crabtree La RMKS/WB MK17 * 144 F7
Crabtree Rd HADM HP17 .... 182 C1
Craddocks Cl BDWL MK13 .... 17 L3
Craddocks Dr LBUZ LU7 .... 27 H3
Cradley Wk AYL HP20 .... 34 D3
Crafton Pl AYLW HP19 .... 177 Q1
Craig Dr UX/CGN UB8 .... 115 G3
Craigmore Av BTCHLY MK3 .... 22 C6
Craigwell Av AYLS HP21 .... 35 K1
Cranborne Av WDSR SL4 .... 21 H4
Cranbourne Av WDSR SL4 .... 120 E5
Cranbourne Cl SL SL1 .... 111 H5
Cranbourne Rd NTHWD HA6 .... 95 L3
SL SL1 .... 111 H5
Cranbrook RMKS/WB MK17 .... 144 E5
Cranbrook Rd MDHD SL6 .... 108 A4
Crane Ct SHEN MK5 .... 6 C7
Crane Gdns HYS/HAR UB3 .... 115 L8
Cranesbill Dr BIC OX26 .... 162 C1
Cranesbill Pl GTLN MK14 .... 14 C8
Cranes Cl RBEDW MK43 .... 129 H4
Craneswater HYS/HAR UB3 .... 125 J1
Crane Wy RBEDW MK43 .... 139 M4
Cranfield Rd NPAC MK16 .... 138 B6
RMKS/WB MK17 .... 144 E4
Cranford Dr HYS/HAR UB3 .... 115 J6
Cranford La HTHAIR TW6 .... 125 L6
HYS/HAR UB3 .... 125 J2
Cranford Park Rd
HYS/HAR UB3 .... 115 L8
Cranley Dr RSLP HA4 .... 95 L8
Cranmer Rd HYS/HAR UB3 .... 115 J1
Cranston Cl HGDN/ICK UB10 .... 95 J8
Cranwell Cl SHEN MK5 .... 21 L1
Cranwells La SL SL1 .... 101 H2
Craufurd Ri MDHD SL6 .... 108 A2
Craven Ct YEAD UB4 .... 115 M3
The Craven BDWL MK13 .... 6 B1
Crawford Wy EMV/FZ MK4 .... 21 G4
Crawley Crossing
RBEDW MK43 * 145 M4
Crawley Rd RBEDW MK43 .... 139 M3
RMKS/WB MK17 .... 145 J10
Crawley's La TRING HP23 .... 46 D3
Crayle St SLN SL2 .... 100 H4
Creden Cl MDHD SL6 .... 108 C2
Creed St WOLV MK12 .... 13 G7
Creighton Rd RAYLW HP18 .... 165 N5
Crendon Rd RAYLW HP18 .... 175 P9
Crendon St HWYN HP13 .... 5 K7
Crescent Dr MDHD SL6 * 108 D2
Crescent Pde
HGDN/ICK UB10 * 104 F8
The Crescent BIC OX26 .... 162 C3
HEN RG9 .... 191 L10
HWYN HP13 .... 78 B2
HYS/HAR UB3 * 125 H3
LBUZ LU7 .... 169 P10
MDHD SL6 .... 108 D3
PRRI HP27 .... 58 B3
RKW/CH/CXG WD3 .... 74 C4
RMKN MK19 .... 13 H4
RNHPTN NN7 .... 126 A3
SKCH HP14 * 186 H1
SL SL1 .... 111 K6
TRING HP23 .... 37 M1
WAR/TWY RG10 .... 191 R8
WEAT MK2 .... 22 F5
Creslow Wy STSTR MK11 .... 16 C1

Creslow Wy HADM HP17 .... 177 L5
Cress End RKW/CH/CXG WD3 .... 83 M1
Cressex Av SHEN MK5 .... 21 L2
Cressey Av SHEN MK5 .... 21 L2
Cressington Ct BNEND SL8 .... 88 F6
Cressington Pl BNEND SL8 .... 88 F6
Cress Rd SL SL1 .... 111 G6
Cresswell Md MDHD SL6 .... 119 G1
Cresswell Rd CSHM HP5 .... 63 J5
Cresswell Wy HAZ/HG HP15 .... 69 J3
Crest Rd HWYW HP12 .... 87 J3
The Crest SKCH HP14 .... 185 Q10
Creswick Meadow AYLS HP21 .... 42 F1
Crew Curve BERK HP4 .... 47 L3
Cricketers Rw
BUCK/WIN MK18 .... 151 K10
Cricket Field Rd UX/CGN UB8 .... 104 C6
Cricketfield Rd WDR/YW SL0 .... 114 C8
Cricket Gnd SKCH HP14 .... 186 C1
Cricklebeck BDWL MK13 .... 17 L1
Crispin Cl BEAC HP9 .... 80 B6
Crispin Fld LBUZ LU7 .... 169 P10
Crispin Rd BDWL MK13 .... 13 L7
Crispin Wy SLN SL2 .... 101 J2
UX/CGN UB8 .... 114 E1
WYM HP11 * 87 M2
Crisp Rd HEN RG9 .... 190 F3
Criss Gv CFSP/GDCR SL9 .... 92 B1
Criss La CFSP/GDCR SL9 .... 92 B1
Crocketts La
GTMIS/PWD HP16 .... 53 J5
Crockwell Cl BIC OX26 .... 162 D4
Crocus Cr AYLS HP21 .... 42 A1
Croft Cl HGDN/ICK UB10 .... 104 E7
HYS/HAR UB3 .... 125 H1
KGLGY WD4 .... 65 M1
THAME OX9 .... 181 P6
Croft Ct AYLS HP21 * 3 H7
RSLP HA4 * 95 L7
Croft End Rd KGLGY WD4 .... 65 M1
Crofters Rd NTHWD HA6 .... 85 K4
Croft Fld KGLGY WD4 .... 65 M1
Croft Gdns RSLP HA4 .... 95 K7
Crofthill Rd SLN SL2 .... 111 C1
Croft La KGLGY WD4 .... 65 M1
Croft Meadow KGLGY WD4 .... 65 M1
Croft Mdw LBUZ LU7 .... 169 M7
Crofton Cl AYLS HP21 .... 3 H7
CFSP/GDCR SL9 .... 92 D1
THAME OX9 .... 181 P7
Crofts End NPAC MK16 .... 133 N9
Crofts La RMKS/WB MK17 .... 153 J3
The Croft HADM HP17 .... 182 C1
MDHD SL6 .... 108 B5
MLW SL7 .... 97 M3
Croftwood HWYN HP13 .... 78 B3
Cromarty Ct BTCHLY MK3 .... 22 B3
Cromer Cl BERK HP4 .... 40 D6
UX/CGN UB8 .... 115 H3
Cromer Rd HTHAIR TW6 .... 124 F6
Cromer Rd West HTHAIR TW6 .... 124 F6
Cromhamstone HADM HP17 .... 177 N5
Cromwell Av AYLW HP19 .... 2 C1
NPAC MK16 .... 14 D3
THAME OX9 .... 181 P5
Cromwell Cl BUCK/WIN MK18 .... 11 M4
RMKS/WB MK17 * 143 Q10
Cromwell Dr SL SL1 .... 111 K3
Cromwell Gdns MLW SL7 .... 97 K4
Cromwell Ms AYLW HP19 .... 177 Q2
Cromwell Rd HEN RG9 .... 190 H6
HWYN HP13 .... 78 C1
HYS/HAR UB3 .... 115 J3
MDHD SL6 .... 108 C3
MLW SL7 .... 97 K4
Cropredy Ct BUCK/WIN MK18 .... 11 M4
Cropton Ri EMV/FZ MK4 .... 21 K4
Cropwell Bishop EMV/FZ MK4 .... 21 M5
Crosby Cl BEAC HP9 .... 90 A2
Crosby Ct CNH/GTH/TMA MK8 .... 17 G3
Crosier Rd HGDN/ICK UB10 .... 105 H2
Crosier Wy RSLP HA4 .... 105 K1
Crosland Rd AYLS HP21 .... 35 G8
Cross Bucks Wy
BUCK/WIN MK18 .... 148 D9
RBICN OX27 .... 156 A5
RBICN OX27 .... 154 H10
RMKS/WB MK17 .... 151 P11
Cross End RMKS/WB MK17 .... 144 C2
Crossfield Rd PRRI HP27 .... 58 B2
Crossfields Cl BERK HP4 .... 47 L6
Crosshills STSTR MK11 .... 16 A2
Crossroads GTLN MK14 .... 14 H4
RBICN OX27 .... 154 H4
Cross La BEAC HP9 .... 90 D2
BUCK/WIN MK18 .... 10 C8
OLN MK46 .... 127 P12
Cross Lanes CFSP/GDCR SL9 .... 82 B4
Cross Lanes Cl CFSP/GDCR SL9 .... 82 B4
Crossleys CSTG HP8 .... 82 B4
Crossleys Hl CSTG HP8 .... 82 B3
Cross Meadow CSHM HP5 .... 54 E8
Cross Oak WDSR SL4 .... 120 F5
Cross Oak Rd BERK HP4 .... 47 M4
Cross Rd HWYW HP12 .... 77 H8
Cross St NPAC MK16 .... 14 F2
Crossways CSHM HP5 .... 63 K1
Cross Wy HYS/HAR UB3 .... 115 M6
Crossway LBUZ LU7 .... 27 K7
Crossways BEAC HP9 .... 90 C2
BERK HP4 * 47 L7
HWYW HP12 * 87 H2
Crosthwaite Wy SL SL1 .... 110 C2
Crowborough La
WTR/OFPK MK7 .... 19 K6
Crowbrook Rd PRRI HP27 .... 50 B8
Crowell Rd CHNR OX39 .... 184 D4
Crowland Av HYS/HAR UB3 .... 115 K6
Crow La RBEDW MK43 .... 145 L6
RMKS/WB MK17 .... 144 C2
Crown Cl DTCH/LGLY SL3 .... 123 H3
HYS/HAR UB3 .... 115 G6
Crown La FLKWH/TG HP10 .... 79 L3
MDHD SL6 .... 108 F3
SL SL1 .... 101 G5
WYM HP11 .... 5 J7
Crown Leys AYL HP20 .... 2 F3
Crown Meadow
DTCH/LGLY SL3 .... 123 G3
Crown Rd MLW SL7 .... 97 J4
Crown Rose Ct TRING HP23 .... 37 M7
Crown Sq MDHD SL6 * 109 G3
Crown Wk CMK MK9 * 7 G3
Crown Wy WDR/YW SL0 * 114 E5
Crow Piece La SLN SL2 .... 100 E5
Crowsley Rd HEN RG9 .... 191 K10
Crowther St SHEN MK5 .... 21 M1

WAR/TWY RG10 .... 191 N12
Darley Cl AYLS HP21 .... 35 G8
Darley Ga GTLN MK14 .... 18 C1
Darley's Cl RAYLW HP18 .... 164 C1
Darling's La MDHD SL6 .... 107 K6
Darnel Rd EAG/OLD/WTN MK6 .... 22 D1
Darnell Wk BIC OX26 .... 162 D2
Darrell Cl DTCH/LGLY SL3 .... 112 E6
Darr's La BERK HP4 .... 47 J5
Dart Cl AYLS HP21 .... 42 B1
DTCH/LGLY SL3 .... 123 G2
NPAC MK16 .... 15 C2
Dartington Pl EMV/FZ MK4 .... 21 J5
Dartmouth Cl OLN MK46 .... 128 B10
Dartmouth Rd WDSR SL4 .... 105 M1
Darvell Dr CSHM HP5 .... 54 F7
Darvells Yd RKW/CH/CXG WD3 .... 73 J5
Darvill Rd HADM HP17 .... 177 L5
Darvill's La SL SL1 .... 111 J6
Darwin Cl SHEN MK5 .... 21 H1
Darwin Rd DTCH/LGLY SL3 .... 112 E6
Dashfield Gv HAZ/HG HP15 .... 68 D4
Dashwood Av HWYW HP12 .... 4 A4
Dashwood Cl DTCH/LGLY SL3 .... 112 B8
Datchet Pl DTCH/LGLY SL3 .... 122 A4
Datchet Rd WDSR SL4 .... 121 J3
Daubeney Ga SHEN MK5 .... 17 J8
Davenham Av NTHWD HA6 .... 85 L4
Davenport Lea
WTR/OFPK MK7 .... 144 B5
Davenport Rd HWYW HP12 .... 87 H3
Daventry Ct DTCH/LGLY SL3 .... 123 L4
David Cl AYLS HP21 .... 42 F2
HYS/HAR UB3 .... 125 J3
Davidge Pl BEAC HP9 .... 80 A2
David Rd DTCH/LGLY SL3 .... 123 L5
Davidson Rd DTCH/LGLY SL3 .... 122 E1
Davies Cl AYL HP20 .... 2 F3
Davies Ct MLW SL7 .... 97 K5
Davis Gdns RBICN OX27 .... 154 E11
Davison Cl CNH/GTH/TMA MK8 .... 17 G8
Davy Av SHEN MK5 .... 17 M7
Dawes Av CSHM HP5 .... 63 G3
Dawes Cl HGDN/ICK UB10 .... 104 D7
Dawes East Rd SL SL1 .... 110 B1
Dawes La RKW/CH/CXG WD3 .... 65 L7
Dawes Moor Cl SLN SL2 .... 112 B3
Dawe's Rd HGDN/ICK UB10 .... 104 D7
Dawley Av UX/CGN UB8 .... 115 G3
Dawley Pde HYS/HAR UB3 .... 115 H4
Dawley Ride DTCH/LGLY SL3 .... 123 K4
Dawley Rd HYS/HAR UB3 .... 115 J6
Dawlish Dr RSLP HA4 .... 95 M8
Dawney Cl AYLS HP21 .... 2 D2
Dawn Redwood Cl
HYS/HAR UB3 .... 122 F6
Daws Hill La WYM HP11 .... 87 K6
Daws Lea WYM HP11 .... 87 J5
Dawson Cl HYS/HAR UB3 .... 115 J2
WDSR SL4 .... 120 F5
Dawson Rd DBGH MK1 .... 22 F3
Daylesford Ct WLLN MK15 .... 14 E8
Deacon Pl MKV MK10 .... 19 H3
Deadhearn La CSTG HP8 .... 82 D1
Deakin Cl WATW WD18 .... 75 K8
Deal Av SL SL1 .... 110 C3
Deanacre Cl CFSP/GDCR SL9 .... 82 D6
Dean Av AYLS HP21 .... 42 F1
HGDN/ICK UB10 .... 104 E5
HWYW HP12 .... 4 C8
WDSR SL4 .... 120 C6
Deancroft Rd CFSP/GDCR SL9 .... 82 D6
Deane Cl NTHWD HA6 * 85 K8
Dean Farm La LBUZ LU7 .... 153 R9
Dean Fld HHS/BOV HP3 .... 56 F6
Deanfield SKCH HP14 .... 66 A6
Deanfield Av RSLP HA4 .... 95 J6
Deanfield Cl MLW SL7 .... 97 G3
MLW SL7 .... 97 G3
Deanfield Rd SL SL1 .... 190 D5
Deangarden Ri WYM HP11 .... 78 D6
Dean La MDHD SL6 .... 98 A2
Dean Rd LBUZ LU7 .... 160 D2
Deans Cl AMS HP6 .... 63 L8
SLN SL2 .... 102 A6
TRING HP23 .... 37 M6
Deansfield Rd MDHD SL6 .... 98 C9
Deans Furlong TRING HP23 .... 37 M6
Deanshanger Dr
BUCK/WIN MK18 .... 136 F6
Deanshanger Rd RMKN MK19 .... 137 J11
Deans Meadow BERK HP4 .... 171 K9
Dean's Rd WOLV MK12 .... 12 F7
Dean St MLW SL7 .... 97 J4
Deansway CSHM HP5 .... 55 G8
The Dean RAYLNE/WEN HP22 .... 168 A3
Dean Vw MDHD SL6 .... 98 D4
Deanway CSTG HP8 .... 82 A3
Dean Wy CSTG HP8 .... 81 M3
HAZ/HG HP15 .... 69 G4
RAYLNE/WEN HP22 .... 36 E6
Dean Wood Rd BEAC HP9 .... 81 J4
Dearing Cl AYL HP20 .... 3 K1
Debbs Cl STSTR MK11 .... 16 B1
Deben Cl NPAC MK16 .... 15 H3
Deborah Crs RSLP HA4 .... 95 J6
Decies Wy SLN SL2 .... 101 M6
De Clare Cl BUCK/WIN MK18 * 11 M5
Dedmere Ct MLW SL7 .... 97 L4
Dedmere Rd MLW SL7 .... 97 L4
Dedmere Ri MLW SL7 .... 97 L4
Dedworth Dr WDSR SL4 .... 120 C6
Dedworth Rd WDSR SL4 .... 120 A5
Deeds Gv HWYW HP12 .... 4 D5
Deena Cl SL SL1 .... 110 D4
Deep Acres AMS HP6 .... 62 F7
Deepdale BDWL MK13 .... 17 M1
Deep Fld DTCH/LGLY SL3 .... 122 A3
Deep Mill La GTMIS/PWD HP16 .... 61 J8
Deerfern Cl GTLN MK14 .... 14 C8
Deerfield Cl BUCK/WIN MK18 .... 11 M7
Deerings Dr PIN HA5 .... 95 M4
Deermead GTMIS/PWD HP16 .... 61 J8
Dee Rd MDHD SL6 * 120 B3
Deerswood BDWL MK13 .... 17 M1
Deer Park Wk CSHM HP5 .... 55 J5
Deerswood MDHD SL6 .... 108 F1
Deethe Cl RMKS/WB MK17 .... 144 D4
Defiant Cl BIC OX26 .... 162 E1
De Havilland Dr HAZ/HG HP15 .... 68 A4
Delafield Cl SKCH HP14 .... 187 J1
Delaford Cl IVER SL0 * 113 G4
Delahay Ri BERK HP4 .... 48 A4
Delamere Cl AYL HP20 .... 3 J1
Delamere Gdns LBUZ LU7 .... 26 C1
Delaware Dr WLLN MK15 .... 14 E6
Delbush Av HEAD OX3 .... 178 A3
Delius Cl WTR/OFPK MK7 .... 23 M2
Dell Cl CSHM HP5 * 54 E8
SLN SL2 .... 91 G8
Dell Farm Rd RSLP HA4 .... 95 J4
Dellfield CSHM HP5 .... 54 F8

Dell Fld GTMIS/PWD HP16	60	C5
Dellfield Av BERK HP4	48	A4
Dellfield Cl BERK HP4	47	M4
Dellfield Pde UX/CGN UB8 *	114	B1
Dell Lees BEAC HP9	81	H6
Dell Rd BERK HP4	47	J3
WDR/YW UB7	114	C7
Dells OLN MK46	128	B10
Dellside DEN/HRF UB9	94	B4
The Dell AYL HP20	3	M2
CFSP/GDCR SL9	82	C6
FLKWH/TG HP10	79	H1
LBUZ LU7	27	J1
MDHD SL6	117	L3
MDHD SL6 *	98	D4
NTHWD HA6	85	K2
SKCH HP14	187	J2
Dellwood RKW/CH/CXG WD3	84	A1
Delmeade Rd CSHM HP5	62	F3
Deltic Av BDWL MK13	17	L4
De Montfort Ct BRACKY NN13	8	D5
Demoram Cl BUCK/WIN MK18	151	J11
Denbigh Dr HYS/HAR UB3	115	H8
Denbigh Hall BTCHLY MK3	22	C3
Denbigh Hall Dr BTCHLY MK3	22	C3
Denbigh Rd DBGH MK1	22	E4
THAME OX9	181	P5
Denbigh Wy WEAT MK2	22	F5
Denby Wk AYL HP20	3	M5
Denchworth Ct EMV/FZ MK4	21	L4
RMKS/WB MK17	144	F6
Denecroft Crs HGDN/ICK UB10	105	G6
Dene Rd NTHWD HA6	85	H6
The Dene BUCK/WIN MK18	149	L11
Denewood HWYN HP13	78	D2
Denham Av DEN/HRF UB9	93	L8
Denham Cl BTCHLY MK3	22	A4
DEN/HRF UB9	103	M1
MDHD SL6	108	B4
Denham Court Dr		
DEN/HRF UB9	104	A1
Denham Green Cl		
DEN/HRF UB9	93	M6
Denham Green La		
DEN/HRF UB9	93	K4
Denham La CFSP/GDCR SL9	92	F1
Denham Ldg DEN/HRF UB9	104	B4
Denham Pde DEN/HRF UB9 *	103	L1
Denham Pl DEN/HRF UB9 *	93	M7
Denham Rd IVER SLO	103	J9
SKCH HP14	86	B1
Denham Vw BUCK/WIN MK18	159	J4
Denham Wy CFSP/GDCR SL9	82	E6
DEN/HRF UB9	103	M1
Denham Way (North Orbital Road) RKW/CH/CXG WD3	83	K7
Denison Cl WTR/OFPK MK7	144	A4
Denmark St MDHD SL6	108	D2
WEAT MK2	25	G6
WYM HP11	17	H4
Denmead CNH/GTH/TMA MK8	17	H4
Dennis Cl CFSP/GDCR SL9	92	D6
Dennis Cl RAYLNE/WEN HP22	36	E3
Dennis Wy SL SL1	110	C4
Denny Rd DTCH/LGLY SL3 *	112	F4
Denny's La BERK HP4	47	L8
Denton Rd RNHPTN NN7	126	E4
Denziloe Av HGDN/ICK UB10	105	G4
De Pirenore HAZ/HG HP15	68	D8
Derby Rd UX/CGN UB8	104	B7
Derehams Av FLKWH/TG HP10	79	H7
Derehams La FLKWH/TG HP10	79	H8
Derek Rd MDHD SL6	109	H4
Dere Pl WEAT MK2	153	P2
Derwent Av AYLS HP21	35	G8
NPAG MK16	15	G2
Derwent Cl BTCHLY MK3	22	B3
DUN/WHIP LU6	171	R1
MDHD SL6	108	C2
SL SL1	110	B2
YEAD UB4	115	K3
Derwent Dr AYLS HP21	35	G8
BIC OX26	162	A3
LBUZ LU7	26	C7
De Salis Rd HGDN/ICK UB10	115	H1
Desborough Av WYM HP11	4	E9
Desborough Crs MDHD SL6	108	C5
Desborough Gn WYM HP11	2	F2
Desborough Park Rd		
HWYW HP12	4	C5
Desborough Rd WYM HP11	4	F6
Desborough St WYM HP11	4	D4
Deseronto Est		
DTCH/LGLY SL3 *	112	G6
Develin Cl GTLIN MK14	14	C7
Deverell Wy LBUZ LU7	29	K1
Devereux Dr WAT WD17	75	K1
Devereux Dr WYM HP19	167	R12
EAG/OLD/WTN MK6	18	B7
Devereux Rd WDSR SL4	121	J3
De Vere Wk WAT WD17	75	K3
Deverill Rd AYLS HP21	42	B3
Devills Wy DTCH/LGLY SL3	113	H4
Devil's HI RG9	190	A8
Devon Av SL SL1	111	H4
Devon Cl BTCHLY MK3	22	C5
Devon Rd AYLW HP19	167	R11
Devonshire Av AMS HP6	63	G8
Devonshire Gn SLN SL2	101	G2
Devon Wy HGDN/ICK UB10	104	E7
Dewar Sp DTCH/LGLY SL3	122	G2
Dexter Av EAG/OLD/WTN MK6	7	H8
Dexter Rd DEN/HRF UB9	94	B1
Dhoon Ri MDHD SL6	108	E4
Diamond Rd SL SL1	111	M6
WATN WD24	75	M1
Diana Cl DTCH/LGLY SL3	112	D3
Diane Cl AYLS HP21	42	F2
Diane Wk AYLS HP21	42	F2
Dibden Hl CSTG HP8	82	A4
Dibdin Cl UX/CGN UB8	115	C3
Dickens Cl BIC OX26	162	C5
HYS/HAR UB3	115	K8
Dickens La RMKN MK19	137	G9
Dickens La LBUZ LU7	31	J1
Dickens Rd DTCH/LGLY SL3	123	K4
Dickens Rd WOLV MK12	12	H1
Dickens Spinney OLN MK46	128	B10
Dickens Wy AYLW HP19	167	Q12
Dickinson Av		
RKW/CH/CXG WD3	74	F7
Dickinson Sq		
RKW/CH/CXG WD3	74	F7
Dick Turpin Wy		
EBED/NFELT TW14	125	L4
Diddington Cl WEAT MK2	153	P3
Digby Cl THAME OX9	181	Q5

Digby Cft MKV MK10	19	H3
Digby Rd LBUZ LU7	27	H6
Dimmock Cl LBUZ LU7	29	K2
Dimmocks La		
RKW/CH/CXG WD3	65	M7
Dingle Dell LBUZ LU7	27	G4
Dingleberry Cl HHW MK46	128	B10
The Dingle HGDN/ICK UB10	105	G8
Dinmore HHS/BOV HP3	56	E7
Disraeli Ct DTCH/LGLY SL3	123	J7
Disraeli Crs HWYN HP13	4	F1
Disraeli Pk BEAC HP9	80	C6
Disraeli Sq AYLW HP19	177	R2
Diswell Brook Wy RMKN MK19	137	M9
Ditchingham Ct AYLW HP19	2	A7
Dittander Cl BIC OX26	162	C2
Ditton Maze MDHD SL6	107	M5
Ditton Park Rd DTCH/LGLY SL3	122	D7
Ditton Rd DTCH/LGLY SL3	122	C7
Dixie La WTR/OFPK MK7	19	M8
Dixon Cl AYLS HP21	42	B9
Dixon's Gap Br TRING HP23	169	J12
Dobbins La RAYLNE/WEN HP22	51	M1
Dobsons La HEN RG9	188	F9
Dockwell Rd EBED/NFELT TW14	125	G3
Docton Mi EMV/FZ MK4	21	H4
Doctor's Commons Rd		
BERK HP4	48	A7
Dodds Cnr SKCH HP14 *	187	J2
Doddsfield Rd SLN SL2	100	F8
Dodds La CSTG HP8	82	A2
Dodkin Cl EBED/NFELT TW14	125	G3
Dodman Gn EMV/FZ MK4	21	L6
Doggetts Farm Rd		
DEN/HRF UB9	93	H6
Doggett St SL SL1	110	B5
Doggetts Wood Cl CSTG HP8	72	A5
Doggetts Wood La CSTG HP8	72	A4
Doghurst Av WDR/YW UB7	125	G3
Doghurst Dr WDR/YW UB7	125	G3
Dog Kennel La		
RKW/CH/CXG WD3	73	L6
Dog Rose Ramble YEAD UB4	105	M6
Dog Rose Ramble & Hillingdon		
Trail YEAD UB4	105	L7
Dolben St WLLN MK15	15	G1
Dolesden La HEN RG9	188	C1
Dollicot HADM HP17	176	D11
Dolphin Cl SL SL1	112	A6
Dolphin Pl AYLS HP21	3	H9
Dolphin Rd SL SL1	112	A6
Dolphin Sq TRING HP23	37	M7
Donkey La BNEND SL8	88	F7
TRING HP23	37	K7
WDR/YW UB7	114	B8
Donnay Cl CFSP/GDCR SL9	92	C3
Donnington Broad MDHD SL6	108	E1
Donnington Gdns MDHD SL6	108	E1
The Don BTCHLY MK3	22	A3
Doolittle Village WYM HP11 *	78	A7
Doon Wy WEAT MK2	153	P1
Doormans Cl MKV MK10	19	K4
Dorchester Av BTCHLY MK3	22	C4
Dorchester Cl MDHD SL6	108	A1
RAYLNE/WEN HP22	43	G4
Dorchester Ct		
RKW/CH/CXG WD3 *	75	H6
Dorchester Pl THAME OX9	181	N6
Doreen Cl WEAT MK2	22	F7
Dorian Cl TRING HP23	38	C6
Dorking Pl SHEN MK5	21	J7
Dormans Cl NTHWD HA6	85	H6
Dormer Av LBUZ LU7	161	R7
Dormer Ct AYLS HP21	2	A9
Dormer Ct AYL HP20	3	J1
Dormer La HAZ/HG HP15	69	G6
Dormer Rd THAME OX9	181	Q8
Dormers HHS/BOV HP3 *	57	K6
Dormywood RSLP HA4	95	L4
Dornels SL SL1	112	B3
Dorney End CSHM HP5	62	F1
Dorney HI North BEAC HP9	90	F5
Dorney HI South SL SL1	90	F6
Dorney Pl BDWL MK13	6	F3
Dorney Reach Rd MDHD SL6	109	L7
Dorney Wood Rd SL SL1	100	B6
Dorrells Rd PRRI HP27	183	N8
Dorrien's Cft BERK HP4	47	L3
Dorrofield Cl		
RKW/CH/CXG WD3	75	H5
Dorset Av YEAD UB4	105	K8
Dorset Cl BERK HP4	47	L5
BTCHLY MK3	22	B5
YEAD UB4 *	105	K8
Dorset Pl AYLS HP21	35	H8
Dorset Rd WDSR SL4	121	H4
Dorset Wy CNH/GTH/TMA MK8	17	J5
Dorton Rd CNH/GTH/TMA MK8	17	K6
Dorton Rd RAYLW HP18	175	J6
Douglas Gdns BERK HP4	47	L5
Douglas La STWL/WRAY TW19	122	F8
Douglas Pl EAG/OLD/WTN MK6	6	F7
Douglas Rd AYL HP20	111	J2
SLN SL2	111	J2
Dove Cl AYLS HP21	42	B1
BUCK/WIN MK18	11	M7
NPAG MK16	15	G2
Dovecote HADM HP17	176	C12
Dovecote Cl HADM HP17	176	C12
PRRI HP27	58	B7
Dovecot Rd WYM HP11 *	5	G5
Dovedale Cl DEN/HRF UB9	94	B1
Dove Gn BIC OX26	162	C2
Dovehouse Cl BRACKY NN13	8	E8
Dove House Cl		
BUCK/WIN MK18	151	K10
DUN/WHIP LU6	170	A5
Dove House Crs SLN SL2	100	D8
Dove House La DUN/WHIP LU6	171	R7
Doveleat CHNR OX39	184	C3
Dove Pk RKW/CH/CXG WD3	73	G6
Dover Ga BTCHLY MK3	22	A5
Dover Hedge AYLS HP21	35	H7
Dover Rd SL SL1	110	E3
Dover St LBUZ LU7	161	R5
Dovetail Cl HWYW HP12	4	A3
Dove Tree Cl LBUZ LU7	27	L6
Dowding Rd HGDN/ICK UB10	104	D2
Dower Rd BEAC HP9	80	D5
Dower Pk WDSR SL4	120	D7
Downdean		
EAG/OLD/WTN MK6	7	J8
Downer Cl BUCK/WIN MK18	142	A10
Downer Dr RKW/CH/CXG WD3	65	H2
Downham Rd RMKS/WB MK17	144	F6
Downing Ct WDSR SL4	22	H3
Downings Wd		
RKW/CH/CXG WD3	83	J5
Downland CNH/GTH/TMA MK8	17	H4
Downley Av BDWL MK13	6	C2

Downley Rd SKCH HP14	67	J8
Down Pl WDSR SL4	119	M2
Downs Barn Bvd GTLIN MK14	18	C1
Downs Fld NPAG MK16	15	H3
Downs Rd DTCH/LGLY SL3	112	C6
Downs Vw RMKS/WB MK17	23	M4
Dowry Wk WAT WD17	75	L1
Drake Av DTCH/LGLY SL3	112	A9
Drake Cl AYLS HP21	2	B9
Drakeloe Ct RMKS/WB MK17	145	J10
Drakes Dr NTHWD HA6	85	G8
RAYLW HP18	181	L2
Drakes Farm CNH/GTH/TMA MK8	17	H7
Drakes Ms CNH/GTH/TMA MK8	17	H7
Drakes Rd AMSS HP7	71	J2
Drakewell Rd RMKS/WB MK17	144	C11
Draper Wy LBUZ LU7	29	K1
Draymans' Cft BIC OX26	162	C2
Drayton Ct WDR/YW UB7 *	114	C6
Drayton Gdns WDR/YW UB7	114	C6
Drayton Rd AYL HP20	2	D7
RMKS/WB MK17	152	H4
Drenon Sq HYS/HAR UB3	115	L4
Dresser Rd EAG/OLD/WTN MK6	22	D2
Drew Meadow SLN SL2	101	H2
Drews Pk BEAC HP9	80	B4
The Drey CFSP/GDCR SL9	82	C6
Drift Rd MDHD SL6	118	A4
Drift Wy DTCH/LGLY SL3	123	H4
OLN MK46	128	B9
The Drive AMSS HP7	71	H4
BNEND SL8	88	C6
CFSP/GDCR SL9	82	D7
DTCH/LGLY SL3	122	A4
HGDN/ICK UB10	104	D2
MDHD SL6	109	G5
NTHWD HA6	85	K8
RBEDW MK43	138	C4
RKW/CH/CXG WD3	74	A6
RNHPTN NN7	126	D5
STWL/WRAY TW19	122	C8
Dropmore Pk SL SL1	100	A1
Dropmore Rd SL SL1	100	B7
Drovers Cft WOLV MK12	16	E2
Drovers La HEN RG9	188	F2
Drovers Wy BEAC HP9	81	H6
RMKS/WB MK17	153	J4
Druce End TOW NN12	130	D12
Druids Wk OX39	184	F4
Drummond Hay WLLN MK15 *	14	F7
Drummond Ride TRING HP23	37	M5
Drydell La CSHM HP5	62	E2
Dryden Av BIC OX26	162	A3
Dryden Cl AYL HP20	3	H1
NPAG MK16	15	G2
Drysdale Cl NTHWD HA6	85	H7
Duchess Cha TOW NN12	137	L3
Duchess Gv WTR/OFPK MK7	19	M7
Duchess St SL SL1	110	D6
Duck Aly CSHM HP5	63	G3
Duck End RMKS/WB MK17	24	C5
Duck Lake BUCK/WIN MK18	11	M3
Duck Lake Cl BUCK/WIN MK18	11	M3
Duck La RAYLW HP18	164	D6
RMKS/WB MK17	145	J11
Duckmore La RAYLW HP18	45	K1
Ducks Hill Rd NTHWD HA6	94	H3
Duck's Hill Rd NTHWD HA6	85	G7
Duck Sq CHNR OX39	184	F4
Duckworth Ct		
EAG/OLD/WTN MK6	18	C7
Dudley Br BUCK/WIN MK18	10	F7
Dudley Cl BUCK/WIN MK18	159	K4
Dudley HI SHEN MK5	17	K8
Dudley La HEN RG9	189	K4
Dudley Pl HYS/HAR UB3	115	H7
Dudley St LBUZ LU7	27	H8
Dudley Whf BDWL MK13	6	F3
Dudset La HEST TW5	125	M4
Dudswell La BERK HP4	47	L2
Dudswell Mi BERK HP4	47	L2
Duffield La SLN SL2	101	L3
Duffield Pk SLN SL2	101	L4
Dugdales RKW/CH/CXG WD3	74	E5
Dukes Av DUN/WHIP LU6	171	M6
Dukes Cl CFSP/GDCR SL9	92	C3
RAYLW HP18	180	C4
Dukes Dr SL SL1	100	C3
SLN SL2	101	G2
WEAT MK2	22	F5
Dukes Green Av		
EBED/NFELT TW14	125	M8
Dukes Kiln Dr CFSP/GDCR SL9	92	B3
SLN BNEND SL8	89	G7
Dukes Meadow BNEND SL8	89	H7
Dukes Piece BUCK/WIN MK18	142	A10
Dukes Ride MLW SL7	97	J4
Dukes Ride CFSP/GDCR SL9	92	C3
HGDN/ICK UB10	104	D2
LBUZ LU7	26	C7
Duke St HEN RG9	190	H4
HWYN HP13	5	L7
PRRI HP27	58	B3
RMKS/WB MK17	144	A2
SL SL1	109	M3
WDSR SL4	121	G3
Dukes Va CFSP/GDCR SL9	92	A3
Dukes Wy BERK HP4	47	M4
UX/CGN UB8	104	A6
Dukes Wood Av		
CFSP/GDCR SL9	92	C3
Dukes Wood Dr		
CFSP/GDCR SL9	92	B3
Dulverton Dr EMV/FZ MK4	22	A3
Dulverton Rd RSLP HA4	95	M8
Dulwich Cl MDHD SL6	14	H4
Dulwich Wy		
RKW/CH/CXG WD3	74	G6
Dumas Cl BIC OX26	162	B4
Dumas Cul-De-Sac		
BRACKY NN13	8	D6
Dumbletons		
RKW/CH/CXG WD3	83	K4
Dumfries Cl BTCHLY MK3	22	A5
OXHEY WD19	85	M3
Dunbar Cl BTCHLY MK3	22	A5
WDR/YW UB7	114	E8
Dunbar Dr THAME OX9	181	P5
CSHM HP5	63	G3
LBUZ LU7	27	H7
OLN MK46	128	B10
THAME OX9	181	P6
Dunbar Gv SHEN MK5	17	J8
Duncan Gv SHEN MK5	17	J8
Duncannon Crs WDSR SL4	120	C7
Duncan Rd RBEDW MK43	138	H4
Dunchurch Dl WTR/OFPK MK7	25	K1
Duncombe Av AMS HP6	71	K1
Duncombe Dr LBUZ LU7	27	J5
Duncombe St BERK HP4	47	L5
WEAT SL6	22	F5
Duncroft WDSR SL4	120	C7
Dundee Rd SL SL1	110	E2
Dungeness Ct EMV/FZ MK4	21	H4
Dungrove Hill La MDHD SL6	107	H3
Dunholme End MDHD SL6	108	C7

Dunkery Beacon EMV/FZ MK4	22	A3
Dunnet Cl EMV/FZ MK4	21	K6
Dunnock Cl BIC OX26	162	F5
Dunnock Wy WAR/TWY RG10	191	P11
Dunny La HHS/BOV HP3	65	L4
Dunsham La AYL HP20	2	F2
Dunshay Cl BERK HP4	47	M4
Dunsmore Av PRRI HP27	58	B1
Dunsmore Ride PRRI HP27	58	B1
Dunstable Rd BERK HP4	171	K8
DUN/WHIP LU6	170	F1
LBUZ LU7	31	G1
Dunster Cl DEN/HRF UB9	84	A8
EMV/FZ MK4	22	B3
Dunster Ct EMV/FZ MK4	22	B3
Dunster Gdns SL SL1	110	F4
Dunston HI TRING HP23	37	M6
Dunthorne Wy		
CNH/GTH/TMA MK8	17	J7
Dunton Rd LBUZ LU7	160	H5
Dunvedin Pl WOLV MK12	17	H3
Dunvegan Cl WEAT MK2	153	G2
Duparc Cl WTR/OFPK MK7	23	M1
Dupre Cl SL SL1	110	D1
Durban Rd East WATW WD18	75	M5
Durban Rd West WATW WD18	75	L5
Durgate MKV MK10	19	K4
Durham Av SL SL1	110	F3
Durley Hollow HWYN HP13	5	K2
Durpe Crs EMV/FZ MK4	21	H4
Durrans Ct WEAT MK2	23	H5
Durrants Dr		
RKW/CH/CXG WD3	75	H4
Durrants La BERK HP4	47	K6
Durrants Rd BERK HP4	47	L5
Durrell Cl LBUZ LU7	26	F7
Dutton Wy IVER SLO	113	K3
Duxford Cl BIC OX26	162	G2
Dwight Rd WATW WD18	75	J8
Dyersdale BDWL MK13	17	M1
Dyers Ms GTLIN MK14	14	C8
Dyers Rd DUN/WHIP LU6	30	E7
Dymock Cl RAYLNE/WEN HP22	166	C2
Dyson Cl WDSR SL4	121	G6

E

Eagle Cl AMS HP6	63	L8
Eagle Rd HTHAIR TW6	125	L6
Eagles Rd AYL HP20	3	L5
Eaglestone		
EAG/OLD/WTN MK6	7	J9
Eagle Wk CMK MK9	7	H2
Eakley Lanes NPAG MK16 *	126	E9
Ealing Cha MKV MK10	19	J6
Eames Cl AYL HP21	3	K1
Eamont Cl RSLP HA4	95	G6
Eardley Pl CNH/GTH/TMA MK8	17	G8
Earl Cl HWYN HP13	5	J3
Earl Howe Cl HAZ/HG HP15	69	H4
Earls Cl WEAT MK2	22	F6
Earlsfield MDHD SL6	109	H8
Earlshall Rd EMV/FZ MK4	21	J5
Earls La SL SL1	110	D5
Earls Willow BDWL MK13	13	K6
Earlswood Ct AYLS HP21	42	F1
Easby Gv MKV MK10	19	K5
Eascote Rd RSLP HA4	95	K6
Easington La RAYLW HP18	175	J9
East Av HYS/HAR UB3	115	L4
Eastbourne Rd SL SL1	110	F3
Eastbridge SL SL1	112	A6
Eastbrook Cl RBICS/W OX25	163	R3
East Burnham La SLN SL2	100	F8
Eastbury Av NTHWD HA6	85	K5
Eastbury Ct EMV/FZ MK4	21	L6
Eastbury Rd NTHWD HA6	85	K6
East Chapel EMV/FZ MK4	21	J5
Eastchurch Rd HTHAIR TW6	125	L6
East Claydon Rd		
BUCK/WIN MK18	158	F1
East Common CFSP/GDCR SL9	92	D5
Eastcote Rd RSLP HA4	95	K6
East Crs WDSR SL4	120	E4
Eastcroft SLN SL2	111	G1
East Dales BDWL MK13	17	M1
East Dr HWYN HP13	78	D2
NTHWD HA6	85	K2
SLN SL2	101	K8
Eastergate BEAC HP9	80	B6
Eastern Dene HAZ/HG HP15	68	D8
Eastern Perimeter Rd		
HTHAIR TW6	125	K5
Eastern St AYL HP20	3	H4
Eastern Wy LBUZ LU7	27	J2
Eastfield Cl SL SL1 *	111	M7
Eastfield Crs TOW NN12	137	N1
Eastfield Rd AYL HP20	35	G6
PRRI HP27	58	B3
SL SL1	109	M3
East Flint HHW HP1	49	K6
Eastglade NTHWD HA6	85	K5
East Hawthorn Rd		
RBICS/W OX25	163	J10
East Hill Cl BRACKY NN13	8	E7
East Hills RBEDW MK43	139	L6
Eastholme HYS/HAR UB3	115	M5
Eastlands PRRI HP27	66	D3
Eastmoor MDHD SL6	108	D7
Eastnor HHS/BOV HP3	56	F7
Eastoke Pl EMV/FZ MK4	21	K6
Easton St HWYN HP11 *	5	M7
Easton Ter HWYN HP13 *	5	L7
East Paddock MDHD SL6	97	L8
East Rp HTHAIR TW6	125	L6
East Rdg BNEND SL8	89	G7
East Rd MDHD SL6	108	D7
RBEDW MK43	139	L6
WDR/YW UB7	114	E8
East Richardson St WYM HP11	4	F5
East St AYLW HP18	175	J9
BUCK/WIN MK18	150	C5
CSHM HP5	63	G3
LBUZ LU7	27	H7
OLN MK46	128	B10
THAME OX9	181	P6
East View Rd WAR/TWY RG10	191	P12
East Vw BEAC HP9	89	M7
HYS/HAR UB3	115	M6
East Wy BEAC HP9	89	M7
HYS/HAR UB3	115	M6
Eastwick Crs		
RKW/CH/CXG WD3	83	L2
Eastwood Rd SKCH HP14	187	J3
WDR/YW UB7	114	F6
Eaton Av HWYW HP12	4	A4

WEAT MK2	23	G7
Eaton Bray Rd DUN/WHIP LU6	170	D1
Eaton Cl RAYLNE/WEN HP22	43	G1
Eaton Ga NTHWD HA6	85	H6
Eatongate Cl DUN/WHIP LU6	43	G1
Eaton Pk DUN/WHIP LU6	31	G8
Eaton Pl HWYW HP12 *	4	A4
Eaton Rd AYLS HP21	2	E9
Ebble Cl AYLS HP21	42	B2
Ebbsgrove SHEN MK5	17	L5
Ebsworth Cl MDHD SL6	99	H7
Ebury Cl NTHWD HA6	85	H5
Ebury Cl NTHWD HA6	85	H5
Ebury Rd RKW/CH/CXG WD3	84	C5
Eddington Ct EMV/FZ MK4	22	A3
Eddy St BERK HP4	47	M5
Eden Cl AYLS HP21	42	C2
DTCH/LGLY SL3	122	F1
Ed Ct LBUZ LU7 *	29	J1
Edens La RBEDW MK43	129	R4
Eden Wy BIC OX26	162	A4
LBUZ LU7	29	J1
Edgar Rd WDR/YW UB7	114	D4
Edgar Wallace Pl BNEND SL8	89	G11
Edgcott Rd RAYLW HP18	156	G11
Edgecombe Rd AYLS HP21	43	G1
Edgecote CNH/GTH/TMA MK8	17	K6
Edgehill THAME OX9	181	P5
Edge Hill Ct BUCK/WIN MK18	11	M4
Edgewood BRACKY NN13	8	E5
WYM HP11	78	C5
Edinburgh Av		
RKW/CH/CXG WD3	73	M7
SL SL1	110	F3
Edinburgh Cl HGDN/ICK UB10	105	G2
Edinburgh Dr HGDN/ICK UB10	105	G2
Edinburgh Gdns WDSR SL4	121	J3
Edinburgh Ga DEN/HRF UB9	93	L5
Edinburgh Pl AYLS HP21	34	E8
Edinburgh Rd MDHD SL6	108	D1
MLW SL7	97	K3
Edison Cl WDR/YW UB7	114	E6
Edison Rd AYLS HP21	177	P1
Edison Sq SHEN MK5	21	M1
Edith Rd MDHD SL6	107	M7
Edlyn Cl BERK HP4	47	L5
Edmonds Cl BUCK/WIN MK18	11	M4
PIN HA5	95	M3
Edmonds Rd SKCH HP14	86	A2
Edmund Ct BEAC HP9	89	M7
SHEN MK5	17	J7
Edmunds Cl HWYW HP12	87	H1
Edmunds Gdns HWYW HP12	87	H1
Edmunds Wy SL SL1	112	A2
Edrich Av EAG/OLD/WTN MK6	21	M3
Edward Cl AYLS HP21	42	F2
Edward Pl EMV/FZ MK4	21	L6
Edward Rd EBED/NFELT TW14	125	J8
Edwards Ct SL SL1	111	K6
Edwards Cft BDWL MK13	13	K8
Edward St LBUZ LU7	27	J7
Edwin Cl RMKS/WB MK17	144	A2
Edy Ct SHEN MK5	17	K5
Edzell Crs EMV/FZ MK4	21	H4
Eelbrook Av BDWL MK13	6	F3
Eeles Cl AYLW HP19	167	Q11
Egan Wy HYS/HAR UB3	115	K8
Egerton Cl BRACKY NN13	8	E7
PIN HA5	95	M3
Egerton Ga SHEN MK5	21	K2
Egerton Rd BERK HP4	110	D1
SLN SL2	125	C3
Egerton Wy HYS/HAR UB3	47	K4
Egglesfield Cl BERK HP4	47	K4
Eggleton Dr TRING HP23	37	M5
Eghams Cl BEAC HP9	89	B6
Eghams Gn BNEND SL8	89	G7
Eghams Wood Rd BEAC HP9	89	G6
Egmont Av STSTR MK11	16	B2
Egremont Gdns SL SL1	101	C1
Egypt La SLN SL2	101	C1
Egypt Wy AYLW HP19	177	R2
Eider Cl BUCK/WIN MK18	11	M4
Eight Acres SL SL1	110	A1
TRING HP23	37	M6
Eighth Av HYS/HAR UB3	115	M5
Elbow Meadow		
DTCH/LGLY SL3 *	123	L4
Elder Cl WDR/YW UB7	114	D4
WYM HP11	79	G7
Elderdene CHNR OX39	184	G2
Elderfield Rd RBICN OX27	154	E11
SLN SL2	101	G1
Elder Wy DTCH/LGLY SL3 *	112	L6
HAZ/HG HP15	69	G2
Eldridge La HADM HP17	51	H3
Eleanor Cl RMKS/WB MK17	145	J11
Eleanor Gdns BRACKY NN13	34	E8
Eleanor Gv HGDN/ICK UB10	105	G2
Eleanor Rd CFSP/GDCR SL9	82	B2
Eleanors Gdn LBUZ LU7	152	H11
Electra Av HTHAIR TW6	125	L6
Elers Rd HYS/HAR UB3	115	H4
Elfords EAG/OLD/WTN MK6	18	D8
Elgar Cl HGDN/ICK UB10	94	D19
Elgar Gv WTR/OFPK MK7	23	M1
Elgin Crs HTHAIR TW6	125	K5
Elgin Dr NTHWD HA6	85	J7
Elgiva La CSHM HP5	63	G3
Elgood Av NTHWD HA6	85	M6
Elham Wy AYLS HP21	42	F2
Eliot Cl AYLW HP19	167	Q12
NPAG MK16	14	C1
Elizabeth Av AMS HP6	72	B2
Elizabeth Cl AYLS HP21	43	G2
HEN RG9	190	D10
Elizabeth Ct HWYN HP13 *	5	M7
Elizabeth Dr TRING HP23	38	A4
Elizabeth Rd HEN RG9	190	K6
MLW SL7	97	K3
SKCH HP14	187	J2
Elizabeth Wy SLN SL2	101	G4
Elkins Rd SL SL1	91	K8
Ellen Pl AYLS HP21	42	B1
Ellen Rd AYLS HP21	2	B9
Ellenstow BDWL MK13	17	K2
Ellen Wk AYLS HP21 *	42	B1
Ellerburn Pl EMV/FZ MK4	21	L3
Ellery Rd HEN RG9	189	G1
Ellesborough Gv		
CNH/GTH/TMA MK8	17	G3
Ellesborough Rd HADM HP17	50	E4
RAYLNE/WEN HP22	52	C1
Ellesmere Av BRACKY NN13	8	E5
Ellesmere Cl BRACKY NN13	8	E5
DTCH/LGLY SL3	123	M2
DUN/WHIP LU6	31	K2
RSLP HA4	95	H6
Ellesmere Ct BRACKY NN13	8	E5
Ellesmere Crs BRACKY NN13	8	E5
Ellesmere Rd BERK HP4	48	C6
BRACKY NN13	8	E5
Elliman Av SLN SL2	111	K4

Ellington Ct MDHD SL6 .... 109 H3
Ellington Gdns MDHD SL6 .... 109 H3
Ellington Pk MDHD SL6 .... 108 D1
Ellington Rd MDHD SL6 .... 109 H3
Elliot Dr MLW SL7 .... 97 L2
Elliot Wy LBUZ LU7 .... 29 K1
Ellis Av CFSP/GDCR SL9 .... 82 E3
Ellisgill Ct BDWL MK13 .... 17 L2
  SL SL1 .... 111 K6
Ellison Cl WDSR SL4 .... 120 E6
Ellis Wy WYM 86 A2
Ellsworth Rd WYM HP11 .... 87 L2
Ellwood Rd CSTC HP8 .... 82 B2
Ellwood Rd BEAC HP9 .... 90 A4
Elmar Gn SLN SL2 .... 100 F8
Elm Av RSLP HA4 .... 95 M7
Elmbridge Cl RSLP HA4 .... 95 M5
Elmbridge Dr RSLP HA4 .... 95 M5
Elm Brook La RAYLW HP18 ...... 175 R9
Elm Cl AMS HP6 .... 71 H1
  BIC OX26 .... 162 D2
  HADM HP17 .... 51 H3
  HAZ/HG HP15 .... 68 C7
  HYS/HAR UB3 .... 115 M3
  RAYLW/WEN HP22 .... 43 L4
  RBICS/W OX25 ...... 162 H10
  RMKS/WB MK17 ...... 152 H4
  SLN SL2 .... 101 H4
Elmcote Wy
  RKW/CH/CXG WD3 * .. 74 D7
Elm Ct HEN RG9 * 190 E6
Elm Cft DTCH/LGLY SL3 .... 122 B4
Elmcroft Ter UX/CGN UB8 * 114 F3
Elmdale Gdns PRRI HP27 .... 58 F8
Elmdon Rd HTHAIR TW6 .... 125 L6
Elm Dr BRACKY NN13 .... 8 E5
  CHNR OX39 .... 184 F5
  RMKN MK19 .... 137 L10
Elmers Cl RMKN MK19 .... 143 P4
Elmers Meadow
  BUCK/WIN MK18 ..... 159 K8
Elmers Pk BTCHLY MK3 .... 22 D6
Elm Farm Rd AYLS HP21 .... 42 F1
Elmfield Cl TOW NN12 .... 137 L3
Elmfields Ga BUCK/WIN MK18 .. 151 K10
Elm Gn AYLS HP21 .... 2 L1
  HHW HP1 .... 49 K5
Elm Gv BERK HP4 .... 48 A6
  MDHD SL6 .... 108 D3
  RMKS/WB MK17 ...... 144 C6
  WDR/YW UB7 .... 114 E4
Elmhurst Cl EMV/FZ MK4 .... 22 C2
  HYS/HAR UB3 .... 78 C1
Elmhurst Rd AYL HP20 .... 2 F1
  DTCH/LGLY SL3 ..... 112 F7
Elm La BNEND SL8 .... 88 E5
  RBICS/W OX25 ...... 162 H11
Elm Lawn Cl UX/CGN UB8 ...... 104 D5
Elmlea Dr OLN MK46 .... 128 A11
Elmridge Ct HWW HP12 .... 21 M4
Elm Rd FLKWH/TG HP10 .... 79 J2
  HWYW HP12 .... 87 H2
  PRRI HP27 .... 58 B3
  WDSR SL4 .... 121 G6
Elms Dr BNEND SL8 .... 89 H7
Elmshott Cl FLKWH/TG HP10 ... 78 F1
Elmshott La SL SL1 .... 110 D4
Elmside BUCK/WIN MK18 .... 151 K10
Elms Rd CFSP/GDCR SL9 .... 82 D7
  THAME OX9 .... 181 N6
The Elms BTCHLY MK3 .... 22 C5
  LBUZ LU7 * 26 F7
Elm St BUCK/WIN MK18 .... 11 L6
Elm Tree Cl RBICS/W OX25 .... 162 M10
Elmtree Gn GTMIS/PWD HP16 ... 60 F2
Elmtree Hl CSHM HP5 .... 63 G1
Elm Trees RAYLW HP18 .... 175 G11
Elm Tree Wk
  RKW/CH/CXG WD3 * .. 73 L5
  TRING HP23 .... 37 M3
  RNHPTN NN7 .... 126 C3
Elmwood MDHD SL6 .... 99 G6
  RBEDW MK43 .... 129 N8
Elmwood Cl RAYLW HP18 .... 179 Q1
Elmwood Pk CFSP/GDCR SL9 .... 92 B1
Elmwood Rd SLN SL2 .... 112 A4
Elora Rd HWYW HP13 .... 78 C3
Elruge Cl WDR/YW UB7 .... 114 C7
Elsmore Cl AYLS HP21 .... 43 G2
Eltham Av SL SL1 .... 110 D5
Elthorne Rd UX/CGN UB8 ...... 104 C7
Elthorne Wy NPAG MK16 .... 19 G7
Elton Cl HEAD OX3 .... 178 A10
Elton Dr MDHD SL6 .... 108 C1
Elton Pk WAT WD17 .... 75 M3
Elwes Rd SKCH HP14 .... 86 B2
Ely Av SL SL1 .... 111 H2
Ely Cl AMSS HP7 .... 71 K2
Ely Rd HTHAIR TW6 .... 125 L5
Ember Rd DTCH/LGLY SL3 ...... 113 G7
Embleton Rd OXHEY WD19 ...... 85 M3
Embleton Wy NPAG MK16 .... 11 K7
Emden Cl WDR/YW UB7 .... 114 C7
Emerald Cl BUCK/WIN MK18 .... 158 C3
Emerald Ct SL SL1 .... 111 K6
Emerald Ga WLLN MK15 .... 19 H1
Emerton Rd BERK HP4 .... 47 J3
Emerton Gdns STSTR MK11 ..... 16 A1
Emerton Garth BERK HP4 ...... 47 K3
Emilia Cl WLLN MK15 .... 108 E1
Emma La WAR/TWY RG10 .... 191 P14
Emmanuel Rd HTHWD HA6 ...... 85 L7
Emma Rothschild Ct
  TRING HP23 .... 37 M5
Emmett Cl EMV/FZ MK4 .... 21 M5
Emperor Cl BERK HP4 .... 47 J5
Empingham Cl WEAT MK2 ...... 153 Q2
Emu Cl LBUZ LU7 .... 27 H1
Enborne Cl AYLS HP21 .... 42 C2
Enders Ct SHEN MK5 .... 17 H8
Endfield Pl MDHD SL6 .... 107 M8
Enfield Cha GTLIN MK14 ...... 18 A1
Enfield Cl UX/CGN UB8 .... 104 C7
Enfield Rd HTHAIR TW6 .... 125 L5
Engaine Dr SHEN MK5 .... 17 J7
England Av DUN/WHIP LU6 ..... 31 M3
English Gdns
  STWL/WRAY TW19 .... 122 C7
Enmore Cl CMK MK9 .... 7 L1
Enmore Ga CMK MK9 .... 7 L1
Ennell Gv WEAT MK2 .... 23 P1
Ennerdale Crs SL SL1 .... 110 D2
Ensbury Pth AYL HP20 .... 2 E4
Enstone Rd HGDN/ICK UB10 .... 104 E1
Enterprise La WAT WD18 ...... 7 L3
Enterprise Wy LBUZ LU7 ...... 29 H1
Epsom Cl LBUZ LU7 .... 26 E8
Epsom Gv BTCHLY MK3 .... 22 A8
Ercolani Av HWYN HP13 .... 78 C4
Eriboll Cl LBUZ LU7 .... 26 C8

Erica Cl SL SL1 .... 110 D4
Erica Rd WOLV MK12 .... 17 H2
Eridge Gn WTR/OFPK MK7 ...... 19 K6
Ernicote Cl RBICS/W OX25 .... 163 K10
Errington Dr WDSR SL4 .... 120 F4
Escarpment Av
  DUN/WHIP LU6 ...... 171 L6
Esher Crs HTHAIR TW6 .... 125 L5
Eskdale Av SL SL1 .... 63 J1
Eskdale Gdns MDHD SL6 .... 119 G1
Eskdale Rd RAYLW/WEN HP22 ... 43 G4
  UX/CGN UB8 .... 104 A7
Eskdale Wy MKV MK10 .... 19 L3
Esk Wy BTCHLY MK3 .... 22 A5
Esmonde Wy LBUZ LU7 .... 29 L1
Essex Av SLN SL2 .... 111 H2
Essex Cl BTCHLY MK3 .... 22 C5
Essex Pl AYLW HP19 .... 167 R11
  THAME OX9 .... 181 Q7
  WAT WD18 .... 75 M3
Estcourt Dr HAZ/HG HP15 ..... 68 M3
Esther Cl BDWL MK13 .... 13 K8
Eston Cl BDWL MK13 .... 17 K1
Estover Wy CHNR OX39 .... 184 E4
Etheridge Av WTR/OFPK MK7 ... 19 M6
Ethorpe CNH/GTH/TMA MK8 .... 17 H5
Ethorpe Crs CFSP/GDCR SL9 ... 92 A3
Eton Cl DTCH/LGLY SL3 .... 121 M2
Eton Ct WDSR SL4 .... 121 J3
Eton Crs WOLV MK12 .... 12 F8
Eton Pl MLW SL7 .... 97 J4
Eton Rd DTCH/LGLY SL3 .... 121 M2
  HYS/HAR UB3 .... 115 L3
Eton Sq WDSR SL4 .... 121 J3
Eton Wick Rd WDSR SL4 .... 110 D8
Eunice Gv CSHM HP5 .... 63 J4
Euston Av WATW WD18 .... 75 L6
Evans Cl AYLS HP21 .... 42 F2
  RMKN MK19 .... 175 Q8
Evan's Cl RKW/CH/CXG WD3 .... 74 F6
Evans Ga EAG/OLD/WTN MK6 ... 6 F8
Evans Wy TRING HP23 .... 38 A6
Evans Yd LBUZ LU7 .... 27 H2
Evelyn Av RSLP HA4 .... 95 L6
Evelyn Cl LBUZ LU7 .... 161 Q9
Evelyn Pl BDWL MK13 .... 13 L4
Evelyns Cl UX/CGN UB8 .... 114 F3
Evenley Rd BRACKY NN13 ...... 147 J5
Evenlode MDHD SL6 .... 108 B2
Evenlode Cl AYLS HP21 .... 42 B1
  OLN MK46 .... 162 C5
Evenlode Rd BNEND SL8 .... 89 G6
Evensyde WATW WD18 .... 75 L6
Everard Av SL SL1 .... 111 K6
Everest Cl HWYN HP13 .... 78 D4
Everest Rd HWYN HP13 .... 78 C4
Everett Cl PIN HA5 .... 95 L2
Everglade EAG/OLD/WTN MK6 * . 21 M5
Evergreen Oak Av WDSR SL4 ... 121 M6
Evergreen Wy HYS/HAR UB3 .... 115 L4
Everley Cl EMV/FZ MK4 .... 21 L3
Eversholt Rd RBEDW MK43 ..... 145 Q6
Eversley Crs RSLP HA4 .... 95 K8
Evesham Gn AYLW HP19 .... 34 B3
Evesham Wy SHEN MK5 .... 21 G1
Evett Cl AYL HP20 .... 3 J4
Evreham Rd IVER SL0 .... 113 K3
Ewart Cl AYL HP20 .... 3 J4
Exbury La EMV/FZ MK4 .... 21 L3
Exchange Pde LBUZ LU7 * 27 H7
Exchange St AYL HP20 .... 3 G6
Exebridge EMV/FZ MK4 .... 21 M3
Exeter Rd HTHAIR TW6 .... 125 K6
Exeter Wy HTHAIR TW6 .... 125 K5
Exmoor Ga EMV/FZ MK4 .... 22 B4
Exmouth Pl YEAD UB4 .... 105 K8
Explorer Dr WATW WD18 ...... 75 L7
Eynard Impasse BRACKY NN13 .. 8 D5
Eynsford Ter WDR/YW UB7 * ... 114 E3
Eynsham Ct WLLN MK15 .... 18 E4
Eyre Cl AYLW HP19 .... 177 Q2
Eythrope Rd HADM HP17 ...... 177 L5

F

Factory Yd BEAC HP9 * 90 B8
Fadmoor Pl EMV/FZ MK4 ...... 21 L3
Faggs Rd EBED/NFELT TW14 ... 125 L1
Fagnall La AMSS HP7 .... 70 B8
Fairacre MDHD SL6 .... 108 B4
Fair Acres GTMIS/PWD HP16 ... 60 C5
Fairacres RSLP HA4 .... 95 J6
Fair Cl BIC OX26 .... 162 E2
Faircroft SLN SL2 .... 111 G1
Fairdale Gdns HYS/HAR UB3 ... 115 M6
Fairey Av HYS/HAR UB3 ...... 115 L7
Fairfax BDWL MK13 .... 13 L8
Fairfax Cl THAME OX9 .... 181 P6
Fairfax Crs AYL HP20 .... 3 H1
Fairfield Av DTCH/LGLY SL3 .. 122 B3
  RSLP HA4 .... 95 H6
Fairfield Cl BNEND SL8 ...... 88 E5
  OLN MK46 .... 128 C4
Fairfield Ct RSLP HA4 .... 95 J7
Fairfield La SLN SL2 .... 101 L2
Fairfield Rd SL SL1 .... 100 B8
  UX/CGN UB8 .... 104 C4
  WDR/YW UB7 .... 114 D7
Fairfields HAZ/HG HP15 ...... 68 D1
Fairford Crs WLLN MK15 ...... 14 D7
Fairford Rd MDHD SL6 .... 108 D2
Fairford Wy BIC OX26 .... 162 D5
Fairford Leys AYLW HP19 ..... 2 A6
Fairhaven Ct OXHEY WD19 .... 85 M3
Fairholme Crs YEAD UB4 ..... 115 L1
Fairlawn Pk WDSR SL4 .... 120 D7
Fairlawns WAT WD17 .... 75 L2
Fair Leas CSHM HP5 .... 54 F7
Fairlie Rd SL SL1 .... 110 F3
Fairlight Av WDSR SL4 .... 121 J3
Fairlight Dr UX/CGN UB8 ..... 104 C4
Fairmark Dr HGDN/ICK UB10 ... 104 C4
Fair Meadow BUCK/WIN MK18 .. 151 K10
Fair Mile AYLS HP21 .... 3 L8
  HEN RG9 .... 190 E1
Fair Rdg WYM HP11 .... 87 L2
Fairthorn Cl TRING HP23 ..... 37 K7
Fairview FLKWH/TG HP10 * 79 J2
Fairview La FLKWH/TG HP10 ... 88 E1
Fairview Rd MDHD SL6 .... 109 M3
Fairway MDHD SL6 .... 108 D3
Fairway PRRI HP27 .... 183 R11
Fairway Gv WEAT MK2 .... 153 Q2
Fairways CNH/GTH/TMA MK8 ... 16 F3
The Fairway FLKWH/TG HP10 ... 89 H7
  HGDN/ICK UB10 ..... 104 E1
  MDHD SL6 .... 108 A7
  NTHWD HA6 .... 85 H4

SL SL1 .... 100 B8
Faithful Cl HADM HP17 .... 177 L5
Faithorn Cl HADM HP17 .... 62 F1
Faith Ter RMKN MK19 .... 131 M8
Falcon Av EAG/OLD/WTN MK6 .. 7 J7
Falcon Cl NTHWD HA6 .... 85 K7
Falcon Dr RMKN MK19 .... 137 Q2
Falcon Md BIC OX26 .... 162 F5
Falcon Ms LBUZ LU7 .... 27 J8
Falcon Rdg BERK HP4 .... 48 B7
Falcon Ri HWYN HP13 .... 77 H5
Falcon Wy BRACKY NN13 ...... 8 C4
The Falcon AYLW HP19 .... 34 C2
Falcon Wy BRACKY NN13 ...... 8 C4
Falklands Cl BUCK/WIN MK18 . 149 L12
Fall Cl AYLW HP19 .... 34 C3
Falling La WDR/YW UB7 ...... 114 D4
Fallowfield LBUZ LU7 .... 27 K7
Fallowfield Cl DEN/HRF UB9 .. 84 D3
Fallowfields BIC OX26 ...... 162 E4
The Fallows MDHD SL6 .... 108 F1
Falmouth Pl
  EAG/OLD/WTN MK6 ... 7 J7
Falmouth Rd SL SL1 .... 110 F3
Fane Cl BIC OX26 .... 162 C3
Fane Wy MDHD SL6 .... 108 C6
Fanshawe Rd THAME OX9 ...... 181 Q6
Fantail La TRING HP23 .... 37 L6
Faraday Cl SLN SL2 * 111 G2
  WATW WD18 .... 75 J7
Faraday Dr SHEN MK5 .... 21 M1
Faraday Rd AYLW HP19 .... 167 Q12
  SLN SL2 .... 111 G2
Far Furlong Cl AYLS HP21 .... 42 C3
Farinton CNH/GTH/TMA MK8 ... 17 J4
Farjeon Ct WTR/OFPK MK7 .... 144 A4
Farmborough
  EAG/OLD/WTN MK6 ... 18 F8
Farmbrough Cl AYL HP20 ...... 3 C4
Farm Cl AMS HP6 .... 72 C2
  HGDN/ICK UB10 ..... 105 G1
  HWYN HP13 .... 78 F3
  LBUZ LU7 .... 161 K3
  MDHD SL6 .... 119 H1
  MDHD SL6 .... 107 M7
  RAYLW HP18 .... 180 A3
Farm Crs SLN SL2 .... 112 A2
Farmers Cl MDHD SL6 .... 117 M2
Farmers Dr BRACKY NN13 ...... 8 C7
Farmers Pl CFSP/GDCR SL9 .... 92 B1
Farmers Wy BEAC HP9 .... 81 H6
  MDHD SL6 .... 117 M1
Farm Gv BEAC HP9 .... 80 B5
Farmlands PIN HA5 .... 95 M3
Farm La BEAC HP9 .... 81 J8
  RKW/CH/CXG WD3 .... 74 A4
Farm Lea FLKWH/TG HP10 ..... 89 L5
Farm Pl BERK HP4 .... 48 A6
Farm Rd BNEND SL8 .... 88 E6
  BRACKY NN13 .... 8 E6
  HEN RG9 .... 191 J6
  MDHD SL6 .... 107 M7
  NTHWD HA6 .... 85 H5
  RKW/CH/CXG WD3 .... 72 F5
Farm Wy NTHWD HA6 .... 85 K4
Farnborough Ct
  CNH/GTH/TMA MK8 ... 17 H5
Farnham La SLN SL2 .... 100 C4
Farnham Park La SLN SL2 ..... 101 H4
Farnham Rd SL SL1 .... 111 H5
  SLN SL2 .... 101 G8
Farnley Rd AYLW HP19 .... 3 H1
Farrer Cl BRACKY NN13 ...... 9 J2
Farrier Cl UX/CGN UB8 .... 114 F3
Farrier Pl GTLIN MK14 .... 14 C8
Farriers Cl HHS/BOV HP3 ..... 57 G7
  RBICN OX27 .... 154 H4
Farriers Wy CSHM HP5 .... 54 F7
Farringdon St MKV MK10 ...... 19 J5
The Farthingales MDHD SL6 ... 109 G3
Farthing Green La SLN SL2 ... 101 M7
Farthing Gv
  EAG/OLD/WTN MK6 ... 18 F8
Farthinghoe Cl BRACKY NN13 .. 8 C7
Fassetts Rd FLKWH/TG HP10 ... 79 J3
Faugere Cl BRACKY NN13 ..... 8 D6
Faulkner's Wy LBUZ LU7 ...... 27 L7
Faulkner Rd HWYN HP13 ...... 77 J4
Favell Dr EMV/FZ MK4 .... 22 B2
Faversham Cl THAME OX9 ..... 37 M6
Fawcett Rd WDSR SL4 .... 121 G4
Fawley Bottom La HEN RG9 ... 188 D10
Fawsley Cl MDHD SL6 .... 98 C8
Fawsley Ct DTCH/LGLY SL3 .... 123 K3
Feacey Down HHW HP1 .... 49 M5
Fearney Md
  RKW/CH/CXG WD3 .... 83 M1
Featherbed La BRACKY NN13 .. 146 H10
  HAZ/HG HP15 .... 69 J2
Featherstone Rd WOLV MK12 .. 16 D1
Fegans Ct STSTR MK11 .... 12 A8
Felbridge WTR/OFPK MK7 ..... 19 K7
Felden Br HHS/BOV HP3 ...... 57 M3
Felden La HHS/BOV HP3 ...... 57 M3
Felden Lawns HHS/BOV HP3 ... 57 M3
Fells Cl RAYLW HP18 .... 175 L12
Fences La NPAG MK16 .... 132 H8
Fennel Dr GTLIN MK14 .... 18 B2
Fennels Farm Rd
  FLKWH/TG HP10 ..... 88 F1
Fennels Rd WYM HP11 .... 78 F6
Fennels Wy FLKWH/TG HP10 ... 78 F8
Fennemore Cl RAYLW HP18 .... 179 Q2
The Fennings AMS HP6 .... 63 J7
Fennycroft Rd HHW HP1 ...... 49 L4
Fennymere
  CNH/GTH/TMA MK8 ... 17 C5
Fenny Rd RMKS/WB MK17 ...... 153 P6
Fenton Ct CNH/GTH/TMA MK8 .. 17 J6
Fenton Ri BRACKY NN13 ...... 8 C6
Fernan Dell
  CNH/GTH/TMA MK8 ... 17 J6
Fernborough Hvn
  EMV/FZ MK4 .... 21 M4
Ferndale EAG/OLD/WTN MK6 ... 18 E5
Ferndale Cl SKCH HP14 ...... 186 H2
Ferndale Pk UX/CGN UB8 ..... 104 B5
Ferndown NTHWD HA6 .... 95 M1
Ferndown Cl PIN HA5 .... 96 A3
Ferne Furlong OLN MK46 ..... 128 B9
Ferne La HADM HP17 .... 176 D12
  MLW SL7 .... 88 D5

Fernlea Cl FLKWH/TG HP10 .... 88 F1
Fernleigh MDHD SL6 * 98 D4
Fernley Cl HWW HP1 .... 95 M3
Fernley Ct MDHD SL6 .... 108 C1
Fernside HAZ/HG HP15 .... 68 D7
Fernsleigh Cl CFSP/GDCR SL9 . 82 D6
Ferrers Av WDR/YW UB7 ...... 114 C6
Ferrers Av SL SL1 .... 110 D3
Ferry End MDHD SL6 * 109 H6
Ferry End RAYLW HP18 .... 181 M1
  MDHD SL6 .... 106 A1
  WAR/TWY RG10 ...... 191 M12
Ferry Rd MDHD SL6 .... 109 H6
Ferryside MDHD SL6 * 109 H6
Festival Cl HGDN/ICK UB10 ... 105 G6
Festival Pl MDHD SL6 .... 109 H6
Fidlers Wk WAR/TWY RG10 .... 191 P12
Field Cl AYL HP20 .... 2 E4
  BUCK/WIN MK18 ..... 10 C8
  CSHM HP5 .... 55 K7
  HGDN/ICK UB10 ..... 94 F3
  HYS/HAR UB3 .... 125 H3
  NPAG MK16 .... 133 P6
  RAYLW HP18 .... 180 B5
  RSLP HA4 .... 95 H5
Field End RAYLW HP18 .... 181 M1
Field End Cl TRING HP23 ..... 46 C4
Fieldfare AYLW HP19 .... 34 D2
Fieldfare BIC OX26 .... 162 C3
Fieldhead Gdns BNEND SL8 .... 88 F7
Fieldhouse La MLW SL7 ...... 97 L4
Fieldhouse Wy MLW SL7 ...... 97 L4
Field Hurst DTCH/LGLY SL3 ... 112 H8
Fielding Gdns DTCH/LGLY SL3 . 112 B6
Fielding Rd MDHD SL6 .... 108 A3
The Fieldings MDHD SL6 ..... 118 C3
Field La WOLV MK12 .... 16 E1
Field Rd DEN/HRF UB9 .... 103 K2
  HWYW HP12 .... 87 C1
Fields End TRING HP23 .... 37 M4
Fields End La HHW HP1 .... 49 J5
Field St BIC OX26 .... 162 D4
Field Vw BRACKY NN13 .... 8 C7
Field Wy AMSS HP7 .... 71 G4
  AYL HP20 .... 3 M2
Fieldway BERK HP4 .... 48 D8
Field Wy CFSP/GDCR SL9 ..... 82 C7
  HHS/BOV HP3 .... 56 F7
  RKW/CH/CXG WD3 .... 84 A1
  RSLP HA4 .... 95 H7
Fieldway TRING HP23 .... 46 C1
Field Wy UX/CGN UB8 .... 114 C8
Fife Ct EMV/FZ MK4 .... 21 K6
Fifield La WDSR SL4 .... 119 J3
Fifth Av HYS/HAR UB3 .... 115 L5
Fifth St WYM HP11 .... 78 E6
Filey Sp SL SL1 .... 111 G7
Filey Waye RSLP HA4 .... 95 M8
Filmer Rd WDSR SL4 .... 120 C5
Fincham Cl HGDN/ICK UB10 ... 105 H1
Finch Cl MKV MK10 .... 19 J3
Finch Crs MDHD SL6 .... 108 C5
Finch Dr MDHD SL6 .... 28 F1
Finchdale HHW HP1 .... 49 M7
Finch End FLKWH/TG HP10 .... 79 H2
Finch Gn RKW/CH/CXG WD3 .... 73 L5
Finch La AMSS HP7 .... 71 M3
  BEAC HP9 .... 80 B5
Finchley La BIC OX26 .... 162 C5
Finch Rd BERK HP4 .... 47 M6
Findlay Wy WEAT MK2 .... 22 F5
Fine Bush La DEN/HRF UB9 ... 95 G5
Fingest La HEN RG9 .... 187 L11
Fingle Dr BDWL MK13 .... 13 H7
Finians Cl HGDN/ICK UB10 .... 104 E5
Finings Rd SKCH HP14 .... 187 E5
Finlay Dr PIN HA5 .... 190 H4
Finmere Crs AYLS HP21 ...... 43 H1
Finnamore Wood Camp
  MLW SL7 .... 86 C7
Finsbury Cha MKV MK10 ...... 19 J6
Finway Ct WATW WD18 * 75 L4
Firbank Ct LBUZ LU7 * 29 H1
Firbank Wy LBUZ LU7 .... 29 H1
Fircroft Cl SLN SL2 .... 101 H4
Fircrest Wy AYLW HP19 ...... 177 Q1
Fir La RMKS/WB MK17 .... 153 Q1
Firemans Run RMKS/WB MK17 .. 144 D5
Firs Av WDSR SL4 .... 120 C6
Firs Cl HAZ/HG HP15 .... 69 C8
  HWYN HP13 .... 78 D2
  IVER SL0 .... 103 H5
  RAYLNE/WEN HP22 ... 167 H5
  SKCH HP14 .... 86 A1
Firs Ct RAYLNE/WEN HP22 .... 35 K7
Firs Dr DTCH/LGLY SL3 ...... 112 D5
Firs La MDHD SL6 .... 117 L2
Firs Pth LBUZ LU7 .... 27 H5
Firs Rd GTMIS/PWD HP16 ..... 60 D5
First Av AMSS HP7 .... 71 H3
  DBGH MK1 .... 23 J2
  HYS/HAR UB3 .... 115 L5
  MLW SL7 .... 97 M4
First Crs SL SL1 .... 111 H4
The Firs RAYLNE/WEN HP22 ... 35 H2
  RAYLW HP18 .... 174 C1
  TRING HP23 .... 46 C1
First St WYM HP11 .... 78 E6
Firs View Rd HAZ/HG HP15 ... 69 C8
Firs Wk NTHWD HA6 .... 85 M1
Fir Tree Av SL SL1 .... 111 L1
  WDR/YW UB7 .... 114 F2
Firview Cl MLW SL7 .... 88 B2
Fishermans Cl OLN MK46 ..... 128 A10
Fishermans Retreat MLW SL7 . 97 K5
Fisherman's Wy BNEND SL8 ... 89 G6
Fishermead Bvd
  EAG/OLD/WTN MK6 ... 7 K7
Fishers Fld BUCK/WIN MK18 .. 11 K6
Fishery Rd HHW HP1 .... 57 M1
  MDHD SL6 .... 109 H5
Fishguard Sp SL SL1 .... 112 A4
Fish Ponds THAME OX9 .... 181 M5
Fishweir LBUZ LU7 .... 161 Q1
Fitzgeralds Wy HWYW HP12 ... 77 G7
Fitzwilliam St BTCHLY MK3 ... 22 E8
Five Acres CSHM HP5 .... 63 H4
  FLKWH/TG HP10 ..... 153 L3
Five Acre Wd HWYW HP12 ..... 87 C1
Fiveacres KID OX5 .... 172 C6
Flag Wk PIN HA5 .... 95 M3
Flambard Cl WLLN MK15 ...... 14 D7
Flamborough Rd RSLP HA4 .... 95 L6
Flamborough Sp SL SL1 ...... 110 F5
Flaunden Bottom CSHM HP5 ... 64 D8
Flaunden La HHS/BOV HP3 .... 64 C3
Flaunden La HHS/BOV HP3 .... 57 R3
  RKW/CH/CXG WD3 .... 65 K4
Flavius Ga BRACKY NN13 ..... 8 F7

Flaxbourne Ct
  WTR/OFPK MK7 ...... 19 M7
Flaxen Fld RAYLNE/WEN HP22 . 43 L4
Flaxley Ga MKV MK10 .... 19 K4
Fleet Cl BUCK/WIN MK18 ..... 142 A8
  RSLP HA4 .... 95 H5
  SKCH HP14 .... 67 L7
Fleet St AYL HP20 .... 2 F4
The Fleet EAG/OLD/WTN MK6 .. 7 J4
Fleetwood Rd CSTG HP8 ...... 81 M4
Fleetwood Rd SLN SL2 .... 111 L3
Fleetwood Wy THAME OX9 ..... 181 N4
Fleming Dr
  EAG/OLD/WTN MK6 ... 18 E8
Fleming Wy HWYW HP12 .... 87 J1
Fletcher Cl AYLW HP19 ...... 167 Q11
Fletchers Ms GTLIN MK14 .... 14 C8
Flemore Crs
  EAG/OLD/WTN MK6 ... 22 F1
Flintergill Ct BDWL MK13 ... 17 L2
Flint Hollow CHNR OX39 ..... 184 E4
The Flintings HHNE HP2 ..... 41 L2
Flintlock Cl STWL/WRAY TW19 . 123 G7
Flint St HADM HP17 .... 182 C1
Flint Wy GTMIS/PWD HP16 .... 60 B3
Flitcroft Lea HWYN HP13 .... 5 G4
Flitton Ct STSTR MK11 ...... 16 C1
Flora Thompson Dr
  BRACKY NN13 .... 8 C6
  NPAG MK16 .... 132 G12
Florence Av MDHD SL6 .... 108 C2
Florence Wy UX/CGN UB8 ..... 104 B5
Florida St WYM HP11 .... 78 B6
Florin Cl WLLN MK15 .... 14 D7
Floriston Av HGDN/ICK UB10 . 105 H5
Flowers Bottom La PRRI HP27 . 66 F3
Fluellen Pl BIC OX26 .... 162 C2
Flynn Cft EMV/FZ MK4 .... 21 G5
Folding Cl LBUZ LU7 .... 161 K2
Foley Cl BEAC HP9 .... 80 B6
Foliejohn Wy MDHD SL6 ...... 117 L4
Folkestone Ct DTCH/LGLY SL3 . 122 F1
Folley Pl SHEN MK5 .... 6 B9
Folly Farm RBEDW MK43 ...... 139 K6
Folly La NPAG MK16 .... 138 E1
  RNHPTN NN7 .... 130 H2
Folly Rd RMKN MK19 .... 137 L10
Fontwell Cl MDHD SL6 .... 107 C8
Fontwell Dr BTCHLY MK3 ..... 152 H1
Forches Cl EMV/FZ MK4 ...... 22 A4
Fordcombe Lea
  WTR/OFPK MK7 ...... 19 K6
Ford Dr BRACKY NN13 .... 8 C6
Ford End DEN/HRF UB9 .... 93 L8
Ford La IVER SL0 .... 113 M3
Ford's Cl SKCH HP14 .... 185 Q10
Ford St BUCK/WIN MK18 ...... 11 L6
  WYM HP11 .... 78 E6
Ford Wy HWYN HP13 .... 77 K3
Forelands Wy CSHM HP5 ...... 63 H4
Forest Cl RAYLNE/WEN HP22 .. 64 K3
Foresters CHNR OX39 .... 184 E4
  RAYLW HP18 .... 173 Q11
Forest Gn MDHD SL6 .... 118 D4
Forest Green Rd MDHD SL6 ... 119 H5
Forest Point HWYN HP13 ..... 78 E5
Fore St PIN HA5 .... 95 L3
Forest Ri EAG/OLD/WTN MK6 .. 7 M8
Forest Rd RMKN MK19 .... 131 L6
  RNHPTN NN7 .... 126 A6
Forfar Dr BTCHLY MK3 .... 22 C4
Forge Cl FLKWH/TG HP10 ..... 78 F2
  KGLGY WD4 .... 65 M2
  RAYLW HP18 .... 179 Q2
  RAYLW HP18 .... 175 M2
  RBICN OX27 .... 156 A7
  RBICS/W OX25 ...... 172 C2
  WHLY OX33 .... 178 G1
Forge Dr SLN SL2 .... 101 H4
Forge La NTHWD HA6 .... 85 K7
The Forge OLN MK46 .... 133 N2
Forgetts Rd SKCH HP14 ...... 86 B2
Forlease Cl MDHD SL6 .... 108 A4
Forlease Dr MDHD SL6 .... 108 A4
Forlease Rd MDHD SL6 .... 108 A4
Formby Cl BTCHLY MK3 .... 21 M7
  DTCH/LGLY SL3 ..... 113 H6
Forrabury Av BDWL MK13 ..... 6 B3
Forrester Dr BRACKY NN13 ... 8 C6
Forris Av HYS/HAR UB3 ...... 115 L5
Forsythia Cl BIC OX26 ...... 162 D1
Fortescue Dr SHEN MK5 ...... 17 K8
Forthill Pl SHEN MK5 .... 17 J7
Forty Gn PRRI HP27 .... 183 J11
Forty Green Cl MLW SL7 ..... 97 L3
Forty Green Rd BEAC HP9 .... 80 A6
Foscote Rd BUCK/WIN MK18 ... 142 A7
Foscott Wy BUCK/WIN MK18 ... 11 L5
Fossey Cl SHEN MK5 .... 21 J3
Foster Av WDSR SL4 .... 120 D6
Foster Cl AYL HP20 .... 3 K1
Fosters La BDWL MK13 .... 17 K3
Fosters Pth SLN SL2 .... 110 E1
Fothergill Pl THAME OX9 .... 181 N6
Fotheringay Gdns SL SL1 .... 110 F4
Fotherley Rd
  RKW/CH/CXG WD3 .... 83 L2
Founders Ms GTLIN MK14 ..... 14 C8
Foundry La DTCH/LGLY SL3 .... 123 G6
  PRRI HP27 .... 58 A7
Fountain Cl UX/CGN UB8 ..... 115 H2
Fountaine Cl GTLIN MK14 .... 14 E7
Fountain Gdns WDSR SL4 ..... 121 J6
Four Ashes Rd HAZ/HG HP15 .. 68 D4
Four Oaks CSHM HP5 .... 54 F6
Fourth Av HYS/HAR UB3 ...... 115 L5
  MLW SL7 .... 97 M4
Fourth St WYM HP11 .... 78 A6
Fourways Ms HWYW HP12 ...... 77 G8
Fowler Cl EMV/FZ MK4 .... 13 M7
Fowler Rd AYLW HP19 .... 2 A6
Foxborough Cl DTCH/LGLY SL3 . 122 F1
Foxborough Ct MDHD SL6 ..... 108 D6
Fox Cl TRING HP23 .... 46 B1
Fox Cover CHNR OX39 .... 184 E4
Fox Covert La RMKN MK19 .... 12 D1
Foxcovert Rd SHEN MK5 ...... 21 J3
Foxdell NTHWD HA6 .... 85 H5
Foxdell Wy CFSP/GDCR SL9 .... 82 D5
Foxes Piece MLW SL7 .... 97 K4
Fox Farm Rd RMKS/WB MK17 ... 24 E1
Fox Fld HAZ/HG HP15 .... 68 C5
Foxfield Cl NTHWD HA6 ...... 85 L6
Foxgate NPAG MK16 .... 14 E2
Foxglove AYLS HP21 .... 162 A1
Foxglove Cl BIC OX26 .... 162 D2
  BUCK/WIN MK18 ..... 11 K7
Foxglove Ct NPAG MK16 ...... 14 C7
Foxgloves AYLS HP21 .... 42 A1

The Foxgloves HHW HP1 49 K8
Foxgoles Cl RMKN MK19 137 N9
Foxherne DTCH/LGLY SL3 112 B6
Foxhill OLN MK46 128 A9
Foxhill Cl HWYN HP13 5 K2
Foxhollow Dr SLN SL2 101 H3
Foxhunter Dr GTLIN MK14 14 A8
Fox La BIC OX26 162 C5
BRACKY NN13 8 D8
HAZ/HG HP15 69 G4
Foxleigh WYM HP11 87 L2
Fox Rd DTCH/LGLY SL3 112 C8
HAZ/HG HP15 69 G4
TRING HP23 38 B8
Foxton EAG/OLD/WTN MK6 19 G8
Fox Wy BUCK/WIN MK18 11 M7
Framers Ct SKCH HP14 * 86 A2
Framewood Rd SLN SL2 102 B5
Framlingham Ct SHEN MK5 21 K1
Frampton Gv EMV/FZ MK4 21 J5
France Furlong GTLIN MK14 14 C6
Frances Av MDHD SL6 109 H1
Frances Rd WDSR SL4 121 H6
Frances St CSHM HP5 63 H1
Franchise St CSHM HP5 63 H1
Francis Ct SHEN MK5 17 K8
Francis Wy SL SL1 110 C4
Francis Yd CSHM HP5 * 63 G2
Frank Atter Cft WOLV MK12 16 F1
Frankland Cl
RKW/CH/CXG WD3 74 F8
Frankland Rd
RKW/CH/CXG WD3 75 G7
Franklin Av SLN SL2 111 G2
Franklin Cl HADM HP17 176 D11
Franklin Rd HADM HP17 176 D11
Franklins Cft WOLV MK12 16 F1
Frank Lunnon Cl BNEND SL8 89 H7
Franklyn Crs WDSR SL4 120 C6
Frankston Av STSTR MK11 16 B1
Frank Sutton Wy SL SL1 111 H4
Frankswood Av WDR/YW UB7 114 E3
The Frantons MDHD SL6 107 L7
Frascati Wy MDHD SL6 108 E3
Fraser Rd HWYW HP12 87 H1
Fraucup Cl HADM HP17 177 L11
Frays Av WDR/YW UB7 114 C6
Frays Cl WDR/YW UB7 114 C7
Frayslea UX/CGN UB8 104 B8
Fray's Waye UX/CGN UB8 104 B6
Frederick Pl WYM HP11 79 G7
Frederick St RAYLW HP18 166 D7
Fredora Av YEAD UB4 115 L1
Freeman Cl WOLV MK12 16 E1
Freeman Ct CSHM HP5 63 H1
Freemans Cl SLN SL2 101 L4
Freemans Gdns OLN MK46 128 B11
Freemans La HYS/HAR UB3 115 K4
Freestone Yd DTCH/LGLY SL3 * 123 J3
Freezeland Wy
HGDN/ICK UB10 104 F4
Fremantle Rd AYLS HP21 42 D1
HWYN HP13 68 C8
French's Av DUN/WHIP LU6 31 M4
Frenchum Gdns SL SL1 110 D5
Frensham Dr WEAT MK2 22 F7
Frensham Wk SLN SL2 101 H3
Friarage Rd AYL HP20 2 E5
Friars Ct AYL HP20 * 2 F6
Friarscroft Wy AYL HP20 2 D6
Friars Fld BERK HP4 47 K3
Friars Furlong RAYLW HP18 175 K11
Friars Gdns SKCH HP14 67 M7
Friars Sq AYL HP20 * 2 F6
Friars Wk TRING HP23 37 M6
Friary Gdns NPAG MK16 14 F4
Friday Ct THAME OX9 181 N5
Friday St HEN RG9 190 H5
LBUZ LU7 27 G7
Frieth Rd MLW SL7 86 C8
Frimley Rd HHW HP1 49 K6
Fringewood Cl NTHWD HA6 85 D8
Fripp Gdns
CNH/GTH/TMA MK8 17 G8
The Frithe SLN SL2 112 A3
Frith Hl GTMIS/PWD HP16 61 G3
Frithsden Copse BERK HP4 48 E2
Frithwood Av NTHWD HA6 85 L6
Frithwood Crs WTR/OFPK MK7 19 L6
Froggy La DEN/HRF UB9 103 J1
Frog La RAYLW HP18 176 C7
Frogmill MDHD SL6 106 B2
Frogmill Ct MDHD SL6 * 106 B3
Frogmill Spinney MDHD SL6 106 C2
Frogmoor WYM HP11 5 H6
Frogmoor La
RKW/CH/CXG WD3 84 C2
Frogmore Av YEAD UB4 115 K1
Frogmore Cl SKCH HP14 67 M7
SL SL1 110 F6
Frogmore Dr WDSR SL4 121 L5
Frogmore Gdns YEAD UB4 115 K1
Frogmore La RAYLW HP18 181 K1
Frogmore Pl EMV/FZ MK4 21 H4
Frogmore St TRING HP23 37 M6
Frome Cl AYLS HP21 42 B1
Fromer Rd FLKWH/TG HP10 89 H3
The Front BERK HP4 49 G3
Froxfield Ct EMV/FZ MK4 21 M5
Fryday St EAG/OLD/WTN MK6 18 B7
Fryer Cl CSHM HP5 63 J4
Fryers La HWYW HP12 4 B3
Frymley Vw WDSR SL4 120 C4
Fulham Cl HGDN/ICK UB10 115 H1
Fullbrook Cl MDHD SL6 108 F2
Fuller's Cl CSHM HP5 63 G3
Fuller's Hl AMS HP6 62 E5
Fuller Wy HYS/HAR UB3 125 L1
RKW/CH/CXG WD3 74 F6
Fulmar Ct BIC OX26 162 G2
Fulmar Crs HHW HP1 49 M8
Fulmar Pl AYLW HP19 * 34 E3
Fulmer Common Rd
DTCH/LGLY SL3 102 D4
Fulmer Cnr CFSP/GDCR SL9 * 93 G7
Fulmer Dr CFSP/GDCR SL9 92 D8
Fulmer La DTCH/LGLY SL3 102 E1
Fulmer Pl DTCH/LGLY SL3 * 102 E1
Fulmer Rd DTCH/LGLY SL3 102 D2
Fulmer St CNH/GTH/TMA MK8 17 G8
EMV/FZ MK4 22 A4
Fulmer Wy CFSP/GDCR SL9 92 D5
Fulton Cl HWYN HP13 4 F2
Fulwell Rd BRACKY NN13 147 M2
Fulwoods Dr
EAG/OLD/WTN MK6 7 K9
Furlong Cl AYLS HP21 42 C3
BNEND SL8 89 G7
Furlong Crs HADM HP17 177 R9
Furlong La DUN/WHIP LU6 31 K7
Furlong Rd BNEND SL8 89 G7
Furlongs HHW HP1 49 M6
The Furlong TRING HP23 * 37 M7
Furness WDSR SL4 120 B5
Furness Crs BTCHLY MK3 22 C5
Furnival Av SLN SL2 111 G2
Furrow Wy MDHD SL6 117 M2
Furtho La TOW NN12 137 M3
Fury Ct CNH/GTH/TMA MK8 17 H7
Furzefield Rd BEAC HP9 80 C8
Furzeground Wy STKPK UB11 115 H5
Furzeham Rd WDR/YW UB7 114 D6
Furze La BUCK/WIN MK18 150 H9
Furzen Cl DUN/WHIP LU6 171 R1
SLN SL2 100 F8
Furze Platt Rd MDHD SL6 107 M4
Furze Rd HHW HP1 49 K8
MDHD SL6 108 C1
Furze Vw RKW/CH/CXG WD3 73 H7
Furze Wy WOLV MK12 12 F8
Fuzzens Wk WDSR SL4 120 D5
Fyfield Barrow
WTR/OFPK MK7 19 M8
Fyne Dr LBUZ LU7 26 D6

G

Gables Cl CFSP/GDCR SL9 82 D4
DTCH/LGLY SL3 121 M2
MDHD SL6 109 G2
RAYLNE/WEN HP22 51 M2
Gables Dr SKCH HP14 66 B5
Gables Meadow HAZ/HG HP15 69 H3
The Gables HADM HP17 182 D1
LBUZ LU7 26 F6
Gable Thorne WTR/OFPK MK7 144 A4
Gabriel Cl WTR/OFPK MK7 23 M1
Gaddesden Crs
WTR/OFPK MK7 19 M8
Gaddesden Rw HHNE HP2 41 M2
Gaddesden Turn LBUZ LU7 29 L4
Gade Av WATW WD18 75 K5
Gade Bank RKW/CH/CXG WD3 75 J5
Gade Cl WATW WD18 75 K5
Gadge Cl THAME OX9 181 M5
Gadmore La TRING HP23 45 K3
Gadsden Cl RBEDW MK43 139 M4
Gadsden Ct RMKS/WB MK17 153 R6
Gage Cl MDHD SL6 108 D6
Gainsborough MDHD SL6 98 E5
Gainsborough Cl
CNH/GTH/TMA MK8 17 G8
Gainsborough Crs HEN RG9 190 F6
Gainsborough Dr MDHD SL6 108 C7
Gainsborough Hl HEN RG9 190 G6
Gainsborough Pl AYLW HP19 167 Q11
Gainsborough Rd AYLS HP21 42 D2
HEN RG9 190 F6
YEAD UB4 105 H7
Gairloch Av WEAT MK2 153 Q1
Galahad Cl SL SL1 110 F6
Galingale Cl BIC OX26 162 D2
Gallagher Cl
CNH/GTH/TMA MK8 17 H6
Galleons La DTCH/LGLY SL3 102 C8
The Galleons AMSS HP7 * 71 H1
Galley Hl HHW HP1 49 M5
STSTR MK11 16 B1
Galley La RMKS/WB MK17 24 B1
Galleymead Rd DTCH/LGLY SL3 123 L4
Galloway Cha SLN SL2 111 M4
Galloway Cl BTCHLY MK3 22 B4
Gallows La HWYW HP12 77 H6
Gallys Rd WDSR SL4 120 C4
Galsworthy Pl AYLW HP19 167 Q12
Galvin Rd SL SL1 111 H5
Gamnel Ms TRING HP23 38 A4
Gandon V HWYN HP13 5 G4
Ganton Cl BTCHLY MK3 22 A5
Garamonde Dr
CNH/GTH/TMA MK8 17 H3
Garbo Cl CNH/GTH/TMA MK8 17 G7
Garden Cl MDHD SL6 117 M1
RAYLNE/WEN HP22 44 B2
RSLP HA4 95 K8
WAT WD17 75 L3
Garden End AMS HP6 63 K8
Gardener Wk HAZ/HG HP15 69 H4
Garden Field La BERK HP4 48 E8
Garden Hedge LBUZ LU7 27 H6
Garden Leys LBUZ LU7 27 K8
Garden Reach CSTG HP8 72 C4
Gardens Cl SKCH HP14 187 J2
The Gardens BUCK/WIN MK18 150 C5
HGDN/ICK UB10 94 D8
WAT WD17 75 L3
Gardiner Ct BDWL MK13 17 H1
Gardner Cl AYLW HP19 167 R11
HAZ/HG HP15 68 C1
Gardner House MDHD SL6 * 108 D1
Gardner Ri BRACKY NN13 8 C7
Gardner Rd MDHD SL6 98 C8
Gardner's Cl DUN/WHIP LU6 31 M7
Garfield Pl WDSR SL4 * 121 H5
Garland Ct CNH/GTH/TMA MK8 17 H6
Garland Wy LBUZ LU7 29 K1
RAYLNE/WEN HP22 36 D5
Garners Cl CFSP/GDCR SL9 82 D6
Garners End CFSP/GDCR SL9 82 D6
Garners Rd CFSP/GDCR SL9 82 D6
Garnet Cl SL SL1 110 F6
Garnet Ct MLW SL7 97 H5
Garrard Rd SLN SL2 110 D1
Garratt Wy HWYN HP13 4 F3
Garraways EAG/OLD/WTN MK6 18 D8
Garrett Cl CSHM HP5 63 H4
Garretts La MDHD SL6 98 E8
Garron Cl AYLS HP21 42 C3
Garrowmore Gv WEAT MK2 153 Q1
Garside Wy AYL HP20 3 M3
Garson Gv CSHM HP5 54 F8
Garston CNH/GTH/TMA MK8 17 J4
Garthlands MDHD SL6 98 C8
The Garth GTMIS/PWD HP16 60 F2
Garthwaite Crs SHEN MK5 21 J3
Garvin Av BEAC HP9 80 D7
Garwood Crs
CNH/GTH/TMA MK8 16 F8
Gascon's Gv SLN SL2 111 G1
Gas La MDHD SL6 108 F7
Gatcombe CNH/GTH/TMA MK8 17 J5
Gate End NTHWD HA6 85 M7
Gatehill Rd NTHWD HA6 85 L7
Gatehouse Cl AYLW HP19 2 C5
WDSR SL4 121 G6
Gatehouse Rd AYLW HP19 2 C4
Gatehouse Wy AYLW HP19 2 A4
Gatensbury Pl PRRI HP27 58 A3
Gatesdene Cl BERK HP4 40 B2
Gates Orch RAYLNE/WEN HP22 36 C5
Gateway Cl NTHWD HA6 85 H6
The Gateway WATW WD18 75 K6
Gatewick Cl SL SL1 111 K5
Gatewick La WTR/OFPK MK7 23 K3
Gatting Wy UX/CGN UB8 104 D4
Gatward Av MDHD SL6 117 M3
Gaveston Dr BERK HP4 48 A4
Gaveston Rd SLN SL2 100 E8
Gaviots Cl CFSP/GDCR SL9 92 E7
Gaviots Gn CFSP/GDCR SL9 92 D7
Gaviots Wy CFSP/GDCR SL9 92 D6
Gavray Dr BIC OX26 162 F5
Gawcott Rd BUCK/WIN MK18 149 J1
Gawdrey Cl CSHM HP5 63 J4
Gayal Cft SHEN MK5 21 L2
Gaydon Wk BIC OX26 162 F8
Gayhurst Rd HWYN HP13 78 E3
Gayton Cl AMS HP6 63 K6
Gees Farm Cl RNHPTN NN7 127 N1
Gemini Cl LBUZ LU7 27 L6
Gentian Cl BIC OX26 162 B1
George Cl MLW SL7 97 L2
George Ct RAYLW HP18 165 J1
George Green Dr
DTCH/LGLY SL3 112 E3
George Green Rd
DTCH/LGLY SL3 112 D3
George Inn Pl NPAG MK16 132 C4
George Rd SKCH HP14 186 H1
Georges Dr FLKWH/TG HP10 89 H3
George's Hl HAZ/HG HP15 68 E4
George St AYL HP20 2 F5
BERK HP4 48 C6
BIC OX26 162 C3
CSHM HP5 63 H1
LBUZ LU7 161 R8
LBUZ LU7 27 J7
RMKS/WB MK17 145 J12
UX/CGN UB8 104 C5
WEAT MK2 23 H5
WYM HP11 4 F5
George V Wy
RKW/CH/CXG WD3 65 M7
George Yd STSTR MK11 * 16 A1
Georgian Cl HGDN/ICK UB10 104 D2
Georgian Hts BNEND SL8 89 G5
Geralds Rd HWYN HP13 78 C1
Gerard Cl BDWL MK13 13 J7
Germains Cl CSHM HP5 63 G3
Germain St CSHM HP5 63 G3
Germander Pl GTLIN MK14 18 A2
Germander Wy BIC OX26 162 C1
Gerrard Gdns PIN HA5 95 M4
Gerrards Cross Rd SLN SL2 101 M4
Gershwin Ct WTR/OFPK MK7 23 M2
Gervaise Cl SL SL1 110 E5
Ghyll Gdns BERK HP4 * 47 J3
Gibbings Cl BUCK/WIN MK18 159 K7
Gibbs Cl HWYN HP13 4 E3
Gibbwin GTLIN MK14 14 A6
Gib La RAYLNE/WEN HP22 35 J2
Gibraltar La MDHD SL6 98 A1
Gibson Ct DTCH/LGLY SL3 122 E1
Gibson Dr LBUZ LU7 29 K1
Gibson La HADM HP17 182 C1
Gibson Rd HGDN/ICK UB10 104 E2
HWYW HP12 87 G3
Gibsons Gn BDWL MK13 6 A1
Giffard Rd WEAT MK2 22 F8
Giffard Wy RAYLW HP18 175 K11
Gifford Ga GTLIN MK14 14 B7
Gifford Pl BUCK/WIN MK18 11 M5
Gig La LBUZ LU7 27 J1
Gilbert Cl BTCHLY MK3 22 E7
Gilbert Ms LBUZ LU7 27 H6
Gilbert Rd DEN/HRF UB9 94 C1
Gilbert Scott Gdns
BUCK/WIN MK18 148 H2
Gilbert Scott Rd
BUCK/WIN MK18 11 L4
Gilbert's Hl TRING HP23 45 K7
Gilbert Wy BERK HP4 47 M6
Gilbey Cl HGDN/ICK UB10 105 G2
Gilchrist Wy MDHD SL6 117 G1
Gilded Acre DUN/WHIP LU6 171 R1
Gilders Ms GTLIN MK14 14 C8
Gilfrid Cl UX/CGN UB8 115 G3
Gillamoor Cl EMV/FZ MK4 21 L3
Gill Cl WATW WD18 75 H7
Gilletts La HWYW HP12 77 H5
Gillfield Cl WYM HP11 87 K3
Gilliat Rd SL SL1 111 K4
Gilliat's Gn RKW/CH/CXG WD3 73 J5
Gilliatt Cl IVER SL0 113 K3
Gillions Pl AYLS HP21 35 G7
Gillotts Cl HEN RG9 190 E7
Gillott's La HEN RG9 190 E7
Gilman Crs WDSR SL4 120 C6
Gilmore Cl DTCH/LGLY SL3 112 B6
HGDN/ICK UB10 104 F1
Gilmore Rd AYL HP20 34 D3
Gilpin's Ride BERK HP4 48 D5
Gilpin Wy HYS/HAR UB3 125 J3
OLN MK46 128 C10
Gingers Cl RAYLNE/WEN HP22 36 D5
Gipsy La LBUZ LU7 29 K6
Girling Wy EBED/NFELT TW14 125 M6
Girton Wy BTCHLY MK3 22 D6
RKW/CH/CXG WD3 75 H6
Glade Rd MLW SL7 97 K4
The Glades BIC OX26 163 J4
HHW HP1 49 K6
The Glade CFSP/GDCR SL9 92 C7
FLKWH/TG HP10 79 H1
Glade Vw HWYW HP12 86 F3
Gladsdale Dr PIN HA5 95 M3
Gladstone Cl NPAG MK16 14 F3
Gladstone Ri HWYN HP13 78 D5
Gladstone Rd CSHM HP5 63 H2
Gladstone Wy SL SL1 110 F6
Glaisyer Wy IVER SL0 103 H7
Glamis Crs HYS/HAR UB3 115 H7
Glamorgan Cl BTCHLY MK3 22 C5
Glanmor Rd SLN SL2 112 A4
Glasgow Rd SL SL1 110 F3
Glasshouse Cl UX/CGN UB8 115 G2
Glastonbury Cl BTCHLY MK3 22 D4
Glaven Rd AYLS HP21 42 B2
Glazier Dr GTLIN MK14 14 C8
Glebe Av HGDN/ICK UB10 105 G1
Glebe Cl BUCK/WIN MK18 142 A7
CFSP/GDCR SL9 82 C8
HAZ/HG HP15 69 G3
HGDN/ICK UB10 105 H2
LBUZ LU7 169 Q9
MDHD SL6 109 L6
RBICS/W OX25 163 J10
SHEN MK5 17 K6
Glebe Dr BRACKY NN13 8 F7
Glebe House Dr
BUCK/WIN MK18 140 C12
Glebelands FLKWH/TG HP10 79 H2
Glebelands Cl
GTMIS/PWD HP16 60 D6
Glebe La RMKN MK19 131 K5
Glebe Rd CFSP/GDCR SL9 82 B8
MDHD SL6 109 G5
RMKN MK19 137 M9
UX/CGN UB8 104 B7
WDSR SL4 122 A8
Glebe Ter BUCK/WIN MK18 11 M3
The Glebe GTMIS/PWD HP16 60 A3
HADM HP17 177 M5
OLN MK46 128 H6
RAYLNE/WEN HP22 43 L4
SKCH HP14 67 J8
WDR/YW UB7 114 D8
Glebe Wy AMS HP6 63 J7
Gledfield Pl WOLV MK12 17 G2
Gledwood Av YEAD UB4 115 M2
Gledwood Crs YEAD UB4 115 L2
Gledwood Dr YEAD UB4 115 L2
Gledwood Gdns YEAD UB4 115 M2
Gleeman Cl WOLV MK12 16 D1
Glenalla Rd RSLP HA4 95 L6
Glenavon Gdns DTCH/LGLY SL3 112 B7
Glen Cl RBICN OX27 155 J9
Glenduragan Ct EMV/FZ MK4 21 H5
Gleneagles Cl BTCHLY MK3 22 A7
Glenfield Cl AYLS HP21 42 F1
Glenfield Crs RSLP HA4 95 J6
Glenham Rd THAME OX9 181 Q5
Glenhurst Av RSLP HA4 95 H6
Glenister Rd CSHM HP5 55 H7
HWYW HP12 87 G2
Glenisters Rd HWYN HP13 5 H5
Glenmore Cl FLKWH/TG HP10 78 F8
Glenstal Pl CMK MK9 7 L2
The Glen DTCH/LGLY SL3 112 B8
MDHD SL6 * 98 D4
NTHWD HA6 85 J7
Glentworth Pl SL SL1 111 H5
Glen Wy WAT WD17 75 K1
Glimbers Gv CHNR OX39 184 F4
Glisson Rd HGDN/ICK UB10 104 F7
Globe La LBUZ LU7 26 F5
Glory Cl FLKWH/TG HP10 89 L3
Glory Mill La FLKWH/TG HP10 89 K3
Gloucester Av SL SL1 111 H2
Gloucester Pde
HYS/HAR UB3 * 115 H7
Gloucester Pl WDSR SL4 121 J5
Gloucester Rd MDHD SL6 98 D8
WOLV MK12 17 G1
Glovers Gv RSLP HA4 95 G6
Glovers La BDWL MK13 17 L2
Glyn St BDWL MK13 13 J6
Glynswood CFSP/GDCR SL9 82 E7
CHNR OX39 184 F4
HWYN HP13 5 J1
Glynswood Pl NTHWD HA6 85 G7
Glynswood Rd
BUCK/WIN MK18 11 K5
Goathland Cft EMV/FZ MK4 21 L4
Goddington Rd BNEND SL8 88 F5
Godfreys Cl RAYLW HP18 174 C1
Godolphin Rd BEAC HP9 81 H6
SL SL1 111 J4
Godwin Cl WTR/OFPK MK7 19 M7
Goffe Cl THAME OX9 181 Q6
Gogh Rd AYLW HP19 167 P12
Gold Crest AYLW HP19 34 E2
Goldcrest Rd BRACKY NN13 8 C5
Goldcrest Wy BIC OX26 162 E7
Golden Ball La MDHD SL6 107 L3
Golden Crs HYS/HAR UB3 115 K5
Golden Dr EAG/OLD/WTN MK6 7 M9
Golden Hills CHNR OX39 184 G4
Golden Oak Cl SLN SL2 101 G4
Golden Riddy LBUZ LU7 26 F6
Golder's Cl RAYLW HP18 180 A3
Goldfield Rd TRING HP23 37 L7
Goldfinch Cl BIC OX26 162 E5
Goldhawk Rd MKV MK10 19 H5
Gold Hl East CFSP/GDCR SL9 92 C1
Gold Hl North CFSP/GDCR SL9 82 B8
Gold Hl West CFSP/GDCR SL9 82 B8
Goldilocks WTR/OFPK MK7 19 L8
Goldmark Cl WTR/OFPK MK7 144 A5
Goldney Ct EMV/FZ MK4 21 H4
Goldsmith Cl BIC OX26 162 B2
Gold St RMKN MK19 131 M7
Goldsworthy Wy SL SL1 110 B3
Golf Club La PRRI HP27 50 D8
Golspie Cft WOLV MK12 16 F2
Gomm Pl HWYN HP13 78 F6
Gomm Rd HWYN HP13 78 F6
Gomms Wood Cl BEAC HP9 80 A6
Gonville Av RKW/CH/CXG WD3 75 G7
Goodacres La PRRI HP27 58 D8
Goodall Cl HEN RG9 190 G5
Good Intent DUN/WHIP LU6 170 F2
Goodlake Ct DEN/HRF UB9 93 L6
Goodman Dr LBUZ LU7 29 J1
Goodman Gdns
EAG/OLD/WTN MK6 19 G6
Goodman Pk SLN SL2 112 B5
Goodrich Gn EMV/FZ MK4 21 H6
Goodrington Pl MKV MK10 19 K2
Goodwick Gv EMV/FZ MK4 21 L6
Goodwin Mdw
FLKWH/TG HP10 89 K4
Goodwin Rd AYLW HP19 2 D5
SLN SL2 100 E8
Goodwins Md LBUZ LU7 169 M7
Goodwood
CNH/GTH/TMA MK8 17 J6
Goodwood Ri MLW SL7 87 H7
Goose Acre CSHM HP5 63 M1
LBUZ LU7 169 M7
Goosecroft HHW HP1 49 L6
Goosefields RKW/CH/CXG WD3 74 B7
Goose Gn BRACKY NN13 8 D8
SLN SL2 101 G7
Goosemere RMKN MK19 137 M10
Goosen Gn AYLS HP21 35 H8
Goral Md RKW/CH/CXG WD3 84 C1
Goran Av STSTR MK11 16 B2
Gordale BDWL MK13 17 M1
Gordon Crs HYS/HAR UB3 115 M8
Gordon Rd CSHM HP5 63 H3
HWYN HP13 5 M7
MDHD SL6 108 C3
WDR/YW UB7 114 D4
WDSR SL4 120 E5
WYM HP11 78 C4
Gordon Wy CSTG HP8 82 A3
Gore Cl DEN/HRF UB9 94 A3
Gore Hl AMSS HP7 71 G5
Gorelands La CSTG HP8 82 C1
Gorell Rd BEAC HP9 91 G1
Gore Rd SL SL1 100 A8
Goring GTLIN MK14 13 M7
Gorman Pl WEAT MK2 153 R2
Gorrell Cl BUCK/WIN MK18 10 C8
Gorricks STSTR MK11 16 A2
Gorse Meade SL SL1 111 G5
Gorse Rd MDHD SL6 98 D4
Gorse Wk WDR/YW UB7 114 D3
Gosford Gdns BIC OX26 162 F2
Gosforth La OXHEY WD19 85 M3
Gosforth Pth OXHEY WD19 85 M3
Goshawk Gdns YEAD UB4 105 K8
Goslar Wy WDSR SL4 121 G5
Gosling Gn DTCH/LGLY SL3 112 D7
Gosling Gv HWYN HP13 77 H4
Gosling Rd DTCH/LGLY SL3 112 D7
Goslington DBGH MK1 22 F4
Gossage Rd HGDN/ICK UB10 104 E5
Goss Av RAYLW HP18 166 E8
Gossmore Cl MLW SL7 97 L5
Gossmore La MLW SL7 97 L5
Gossmore Wk MLW SL7 97 L5
Gossoms Ryde BERK HP4 47 M5
Gossoms's End BERK HP4 47 M5
Goswell Hl WDSR SL4 121 J4
Goswell Rd WDSR SL4 121 J4
Gothic Ct HYS/HAR UB3 125 J2
Gott Cl RBICN OX27 154 F12
Goudhurst Ct WTR/OFPK MK7 19 L7
Goulds Gn UX/CGN UB8 115 G4
Gould's Gn UX/CGN UB8 115 G3
Governors Av DEN/HRF UB9 93 L4
Governors Cl AMS HP6 63 L8
Gowers Fld AYLW HP19 2 F3
The Gowers AMS HP6 63 K8
Gowings Gn SL SL1 110 D6
Goya Pl AYLW HP19 167 Q12
Grace Av EAG/OLD/WTN MK6 6 F9
Grace Ct SL SL1 111 H5
Grace Reading HWYN HP13 78 D4
Graces Cl RBEDW MK43 139 M3
Graeme Av GTMIS/PWD HP16 60 B4
Graemes Dyke Rd BERK HP4 47 M7
Grafham Cl GTLIN MK14 14 D6
Grafton Cl DTCH/LGLY SL3 112 D3
MDHD SL6 98 D8
RNHPTN NN7 131 J1
TOW NN12 137 M4
Grafton Ct RNHPTN NN7 126 A6
Grafton Ga CMK MK9 6 C6
Grafton Ga East CMK MK9 6 C6
Grafton Orch CHNR OX39 184 G3
Grafton Rd AYLW HP19 167 R12
TOW NN12 130 E12
Grafton St BDWL MK13 6 A3
DBGH MK1 22 E3
EAG/OLD/WTN MK6 6 E9
HWYW HP12 4 B4
WOLV MK12 13 H6
Grafton Wy RMKN MK19 12 A4
TOW NN12 137 M3
TOW NN12 136 E1
Graham Cl MDHD SL6 108 B5
Graham Dr HWYW HP12 87 G1
Graham Rd BIC OX26 162 C3
MDHD SL6 98 D4
Grampian Cl HYS/HAR UB3 125 J3
Grampian Ga
EAG/OLD/WTN MK6 18 A7
Grampian Wy DTCH/LGLY SL3 122 F1
Gramwell SHEN MK5 17 J8
Granary Cl RMKN MK19 13 J3
The Granary LBUZ LU7 * 27 H7
Granborough Rd
BUCK/WIN MK18 159 K7
Granby Ct DBGH MK1 22 E3
Grandfield Av WAT WD17 75 M2
Grand Union Canal Wk
AYL HP20 3 K5
BERK HP4 47 K3
DEN/HRF UB9 94 A4
HHW HP1 57 M1
IVER SL0 113 H5
RAYLNE/WEN HP22 44 A6
RKW/CH/CXG WD3 83 M4
RKW/CH/CXG WD3 75 G8
RMKS/WB MK17 24 A6
TOW NN12 130 A3
TRING HP23 37 G1
UX/CGN UB8 104 A7
WAT WD17 75 J2
WDR/YW UB7 115 C6
WOLV MK12 12 F7
Granes End GTLIN MK14 14 B6
Grange Cha RMKS/WB MK17 151 K3
Grange Cl BUCK/WIN MK18 148 E12
BUCK/WIN MK18 11 M3
CFSP/GDCR SL9 82 D8
HYS/HAR UB3 115 K2
LBUZ LU7 26 E8
WAT WD17 75 M2
Grangedale Cl NTHWD HA6 85 K8
Grange Dr FLKWH/TG HP10 89 J7
Grange Farm Rd SKCH HP14 185 L11
Grange Flds CFSP/GDCR SL9 82 D8
Grange Gdns LBUZ LU7 25 J8
RAYLNE/WEN HP22 44 A5
SLN SL2 101 J3
Grange La MDHD SL6 98 E2
Grange Rd BTCHLY MK3 22 C7
CFSP/GDCR SL9 82 C8
HAZ/HG HP15 68 D5
HEN RG9 190 H5
HYS/HAR UB3 115 K3
LBUZ LU7 169 Q10
MDHD SL6 98 E3
TRING HP23 38 B6
The Grange SL SL1 * 100 B8
WDSR SL4 122 A8
Grange Vw PRRI HP27 50 D7
Grange Wy IVER SL0 113 L3
Grangewood DTCH/LGLY SL3 112 B2
Grangewood Cl PIN HA5 95 M4
Grant Av SL SL1 111 K3
Grantham Ct SHEN MK5 21 M1
Grantham Ms BERK HP4 48 C6
Granville Av SLN SL2 111 J2
Granville Dene HHS/BOV HP3 56 F6
Granville Pl AYL HP20 2 F5
Granville Rd BERK HP4 47 K4
HGDN/ICK UB10 105 G4
HYS/HAR UB3 115 L8
Granville Sq WLLN MK15 14 F7
Granville St AYL HP20 2 F5
Granville Wy BIC OX26 162 F4
Grapevine Cl WYM HP11 78 E6
Grasholm Wy DTCH/LGLY SL3 113 H8
Grasmere AYLS HP21 43 G1
Grasmere Av RSLP HA4 95 H6
SLN SL2 111 M4
Grasmere Pde SLN SL2 * 112 A4
Grasmere Wy LBUZ LU7 26 E7
WEAT MK2 23 G8
Grasscroft EMV/FZ MK4 22 B3
Grass Hays AYLS HP21 35 H7
Grassingham End
CFSP/GDCR SL9 82 D7
Grassingham Rd
CFSP/GDCR SL9 82 D7
Grassington BDWL MK13 17 K1
Grasslands AYL HP20 3 M3
Grassy Cl HHW HP1 49 M6

Grassy La MDHD SL6 108 D3
Gratton Ct EMV/FZ MK4 21 M3
Gratton Dr WDSR SL4 120 D7
Gravel Dr RAYLNE/WEN HP22 37 G7
TRING HP23 37 H7
Gravel Hl CFSP/GDCR SL9 82 D6
UX/CGN UB8 104 C3
Gravelhill Ter HHW HP1 49 M8
Gravel La HHW HP1 49 M7
Gravel Pth BERK HP4 48 D5
Gravel Wk OLN MK46 133 N3
Graveney Pl
EAG/OLD/WTN MK6 18 E4
Gravenhill Rd North BIC OX26 162 F7
Gravett Cl HEN RG9 190 F6
Grayburn Cl CSTG HP8 81 M2
Grayling Cl MLW SL7 97 H6
Grayling Ct BERK HP4 47 L4
Grays Dormer SKCH HP14 * 86 B2
Grays La TOW NN12 130 C12
Gray's La HWYN HP13 77 J4
SKCH HP14 186 F8
Grays Park Rd SLN SL2 101 M8
Grays Pl SLN SL2 111 L5
Grays Rd SL SL1 111 L5
Gray's Rd HGDN/ICK UB10 104 D5
Grays Wk CSHM HP5 55 G8
Greatacre CSHM HP5 63 J1
Great Benty WDR/YW UB7 114 D8
Great Brickhill La
RMKS/WB MK17 24 E1
Greatchesters BDWL MK13 17 J1
Great Denson
EAG/OLD/WTN MK6 7 L9
Greatfields Dr UX/CGN UB8 114 F2
Great Gnd GTLIN MK14 14 B7
Greatheed Dell
WTR/OFPK MK7 144 A6
Great Hill Crs MDHD SL6 108 A5
Great Hivings CSHM HP5 54 F6
Great Horwood Rd
RMKS/WB MK17 151 J6
Great La RAYLNE/WEN HP22 34 F2
RNHPTN NN7 126 B3
Great Linch MKV MK10 19 L4
Great Meadow Wy AYLW HP19 177 Q2
Great Monks St
CNH/GTH/TMA MK8 17 H3
WOLV MK12 12 D8
Great Ormes EMV/FZ MK4 21 J6
Great Pasture MKV MK10 19 J3
Great Slade BUCK/WIN MK18 11 L8
Great Stone RAYLW HP18 176 C7
Great Sturgess Rd HHW HP1 49 L7
Great Western St AYL HP20 2 F6
Greaves Rd HWYN HP13 78 C4
Greaves Wy LBUZ LU7 27 L8
Grebe Cl AYLW HP19 34 D3
Grebe Rd BIC OX26 162 E5
Grecian St AYL HP20 3 L6
Green Acre AYLS HP21 3 L8
Greenacre WDSR SL4 120 D5
Greenacres LBUZ LU7 169 P10
Greenacres Av HGDN/ICK UB10 104 E1
Green Acres Cl
RAYLNE/WEN HP22 159 P11
Greenacres La
FLKWH/TG HP10 78 F1
The Greenacres HWYN HP13 5 L1
Greenbury Cl
RKW/CH/CXG WD3 74 H4
Green Cl BIC OX26 162 E4
LBUZ LU7 30 E1
MDHD SL6 109 M3
Green Common La BEAC HP9 90 C6
Green Crs FLKWH/TG HP10 89 H3
Greendale Ms SLN SL2 111 M4
Green Dragon La
FLKWH/TG HP10 89 G3
Green East Rd BEAC HP9 81 K7
Greene Field Rd BERK HP4 48 B6
Greene Wk BERK HP4 48 C7
Green End AYL HP20 2 E6
BUCK/WIN MK18 159 J3
Green End Gdns HHW HP1 49 M8
Green End La HHW HP1 49 L7
RMKN MK19 131 L8
Green End Rd HHW HP1 49 M7
SKCH HP14 185 P12
Green End St
RAYLNE/WEN HP22 36 C5
Greenes Ct BERK HP4 48 B5
Greene Wk BERK HP4 48 C7
Green Farm Rd NPAG MK16 14 F2
Greenfern Av SL SL1 110 B3
Greenfield Cl DUN/WHIP LU6 31 M5
Greenfield End
CFSP/GDCR SL9 82 E7
Greenfield Rd NPAG MK16 14 D2
Greenfields BUCK/WIN MK18 150 C5
MDHD SL6 108 F5
RBICS/W OX25 173 J3
Greenheys Cl NTHWD HA6 85 K8
Green Hl HWYN HP13 5 K1
Greenhill LBUZ LU7 27 H5
Green Hill Cl HWYN HP13 5 L1
Greenhill Cl SHEN MK5 17 J6
Greenhill Crs WATW WD18 75 K7
Green Hill Ga HWYN HP13 5 K1
Greenhills Cl
RKW/CH/CXG WD3 74 A6
Greenlands FLKWH/TG HP10 89 G3
LBUZ LU7 27 K6
PRRI HP27 66 D1
Greenlands Cl NPAG MK16 14 D3
Greenlands La
GTMIS/PWD HP16 60 A3
Green La AMS HP6 71 K1
CSHM HP5 64 A4
DTCH/LGLY SL3 122 A4
DUN/WHIP LU6 30 E7
GTMIS/PWD HP16 60 C5
HEN RG9 190 G6
HHS/BOV HP3 56 E7
LBUZ LU7 169 R9
MDHD SL6 117 G1
NTHWD HA6 85 J7
RBICS/W OX25 173 J3
RKW/CH/CXG WD3 74 E6
RMKS/WB MK17 144 H7
SKCH HP14 186 F1
SL SL1 100 B8
UX/CGN UB8 115 H2
WDSR SL4 120 F5
WOLV MK12 13 G8
Green Lane Ct SL SL1 100 B8
Greenlaw Pl BTCHLY MK3 22 D3
Greenleaf Ct DTCH/LGLY SL3 121 M2
Green Leys HWYN HP13 77 H4
MDHD SL6 98 E8
Greenleys La WOLV MK12 16 F1
Green Man La
EBED/NFELT TW14 125 M7
Green North Rd BEAC HP9 81 K6
Greenock Rd SL SL1 110 F3
Green Pk GTMIS/PWD HP16 60 C4
Green Park Dr NPAG MK16 14 E3
Green Pth RAYLNE/WEN HP22 37 H6
Greenridge FLKWH/TG HP10 79 G3
Green Rd HWYN HP13 68 B8
Greensand Ridge Wk
LBUZ LU7 24 E8
RMKS/WB MK17 145 P12
Greensand Vw
RMKS/WB MK17 144 E5
Greenside BNEND SL8 88 F5
SLN SL2 110 F2
Greenside Hl EMV/FZ MK4 21 L5
Green St HAZ/HG HP15 68 E6
RKW/CH/CXG WD3 73 H3
WYM HP11 4 D5
The Green BERK HP4 49 G4
BIC OX26 163 K4
BRACKY NN13 146 E4
BUCK/WIN MK18 142 H10
DUN/WHIP LU6 170 G2
EAG/OLD/WTN MK6 18 F6
FLKWH/TG HP10 89 K5
HGDN/ICK UB10 95 H8
LBUZ LU7 169 J2
LBUZ LU7 153 R11
NPAG MK16 14 F2
PRRI HP27 183 N8
RAYLNE/WEN HP22 33 J1
RAYLW HP18 175 Q8
RAYLW HP18 174 C2
RBEDW MK43 138 H4
RBEDW MK43 129 N9
RBICN OX27 154 H4
RKW/CH/CXG WD3 74 E6
RMKN MK19 137 M10
RMKN MK19 131 M8
RMKN MK19 12 C4
RMKS/WB MK17 151 K3
SHEN MK5 17 K6
SL SL1 111 J6
WDR/YW UB7 114 C7
WHLY OX33 178 F1
WTLGN OX49 184 A7
Green Tiles DEN/HRF UB9 * 93 L6
Green Tiles La DEN/HRF UB9 93 L5
Green Verges MLW SL7 97 K3
Green View Cl HHS/BOV HP3 56 F8
Green Wk RSLP HA4 95 L7
Greenway BERK HP4 47 M6
CSHM HP5 55 G7
HADM HP17 182 C1
Green Wy RMKS/WB MK17 153 J2
Greenway RMKS/WB MK17 151 K4
SL SL1 100 A7
THAME OX9 181 N5
Greenway Ct HWYN HP13 5 K5
Greenways DUN/WHIP LU6 30 E7
RMKS/WB MK17 23 M4
Greenways Dr MDHD SL6 107 M6
The Greenway CFSP/GDCR SL9 92 C2
FLKWH/TG HP10 79 G1
HGDN/ICK UB10 95 G8
HWYN HP13 5 K6
RKW/CH/CXG WD3 73 M8
SL SL1 110 C5
TRING HP23 37 L5
UX/CGN UB8 104 C7
Green West Rd BEAC HP9 81 K6
Greenwich Gdns NPAG MK16 14 E4
Greenwood SKCH HP14 66 F4
Greenwood Av CHNR OX39 184 F5
Greenwood Cl AMS HP6 * 71 K1
BEAC HP9 81 J6
Greenwood Dr BIC OX26 162 A3
Greenwood Meadow
CHNR OX39 184 F4
Greenwood Pl
BUCK/WIN MK18 149 L11
Greenwoods HWYN HP13 * 77 J2
The Greenwood
RAYLNE/WEN HP22 36 C5
Greetham Rd AYLS HP21 35 H8
Gregories Dr WTR/OFPK MK7 19 M8
Gregories Farm La BEAC HP9 80 C8
Gregories Rd BEAC HP9 80 A7
Gregory Rd SLN SL2 91 J8
Grenadine Wy TRING HP23 37 M5
Grendon Rd RAYLW HP18 156 G9
Grendon Wy
RAYLNE/WEN HP22 34 F2
Grenfell Av HWYW HP12 4 A6
MDHD SL6 108 E4
Grenfell Pl MDHD SL6 108 E4
Grenfell Rd BEAC HP9 80 D7
MDHD SL6 108 E4
Grenville Av
RAYLNE/WEN HP22 43 M8
Grenville Cl SL SL1 100 A7
Grenville Gn AYLS HP21 42 C2
Grenville Rd AYLS HP21 42 B1
BUCK/WIN MK18 11 K5
Grenville Wy THAME OX9 181 Q5
Gresham Ct BERK HP4 48 A7
Gresham Rd HGDN/ICK UB10 104 F7
SL SL1 110 F3
Greyhound La
BUCK/WIN MK18 151 K10
THAME OX9 181 N5
Greyhound Wk THAME OX9 181 N5
Greys Hl HEN RG9 190 G5
Greys Rd HEN RG9 190 D6
The Greys EAG/OLD/WTN MK6 18 F6
Greystoke Cl BERK HP4 47 M7
Greystoke Dr RSLP HA4 95 G5
Greystoke Rd SLN SL2 110 E2
Greystonley EMV/FZ MK4 21 M4
Griffin Cl MDHD SL6 108 D5
SL SL1 111 H6
Griffin Fld LBUZ LU7 161 K2
Griffin La AYLW HP19 2 A3
Griffin Rd THAME OX9 181 Q6
Griffith Ga MKV MK10 19 K3
Griffiths Acre HADM HP17 177 P5
Griffiths Gdns RBICN OX27 154 E11
Griffon Cl EAG/OLD/WTN MK6 7 L9
Grigby Ri EAG/OLD/WTN MK6 18 C7
Griggs Orch NPAG MK16 133 P8
Grimbold Ct WLLN MK15 14 F7
Grimmer Cl AYLW HP19 167 Q11
Grimms Hl GTMIS/PWD HP16 60 E3
Grimms Meadow SKCH HP14 67 G5
Grimsdells Cnr AMS HP6 * 63 J8
Grimsdell's La AMS HP6 63 J8
Grimsdyke Rd TRING HP23 46 C1
Gringer Hl MDHD SL6 108 C1
Grizedale BDWL MK13 17 L1
Groombridge WTR/OFPK MK7 19 K7
Groome Ct FLKWH/TG HP10 * 89 H3
Groom Rd GTMIS/PWD HP16 60 B5
Groomsby Dr LBUZ LU7 169 R9
Grooms Cots CSHM HP5 64 A1
Grooms Dr PIN HA5 95 M4
Grosmont Cl EMV/FZ MK4 21 L4
Grosvenor Av YEAD UB4 105 L7
Grosvenor Ct
RKW/CH/CXG WD3 * 75 J6
Grosvenor Crs HGDN/ICK UB10 105 G5
Grosvenor Dr MDHD SL6 109 G2
Grosvenor Rd NTHWD HA6 85 L5
Grosvenor Ter HHW HP1 49 M8
Grosvenor V RSLP HA4 95 L8
Grosvenor Wy AYLW HP19 177 P1
Groundsel Cl WTR/OFPK MK7 19 L8
Grove Ash DBGH MK1 23 G3
Grovebury Place Est LBUZ LU7 27 H8
Grovebury Rd LBUZ LU7 29 H2
Grovebury Turn LBUZ LU7 29 K5
Grove Cl CFSP/GDCR SL9 82 B8
HGDN/ICK UB10 104 F3
SL SL1 111 M7
Grove Ct RAYLNE/WEN HP22 35 H1
RBEDW MK43 129 N8
Grove Crs RKW/CH/CXG WD3 74 F5
Grove End CFSP/GDCR SL9 82 B8
Grove Farm Pk NTHWD HA6 85 J5
Grove Gdns TRING HP23 38 A5
Grove Hl CFSP/GDCR SL9 82 B7
Grove La CFSP/GDCR SL9 82 A8
CSHM HP5 56 A6
HADM HP17 50 D4
UX/CGN UB8 114 E1
Grove Leys TRING HP23 38 B5
The Grovells BERK HP4 * 40 E3
Grove Mill La
RKW/CH/CXG WD3 75 H1
Grove Pk TRING HP23 38 B5
Grove Pl LBUZ LU7 27 H8
Grove Rd AMS HP6 63 L8
BEAC HP9 80 C8
HAZ/HG HP15 68 E7
HEN RG9 190 H5
HHW HP1 57 M1
HWYW HP12 77 H6
LBUZ LU7 27 H8
MDHD SL6 108 E3
NTHWD HA6 85 J5
RBEDW MK43 129 N8
RKW/CH/CXG WD3 83 M2
SL SL1 100 D5
TRING HP23 38 A5
UX/CGN UB8 104 C5
WDSR SL4 121 H5
Grovers Ct PRRI HP27 183 R12
Grovesbrook RMKS/WB MK17 23 M4
Groves Cl BNEND SL8 89 H7
Groves Rd RAYLNE/WEN HP22 44 A5
Groves Wy CSHM HP5 54 E8
MDHD SL6 98 D4
The Grove AMS HP6 63 J6
BDWL MK13 17 K2
BTCHLY MK3 22 C6
CSHM HP5 64 C7
HGDN/ICK UB10 104 F3
NPAG MK16 14 E3
RAYLW HP18 166 D8
RKW/CH/CXG WD3 * 74 F5
SL SL1 111 M6
TRING HP23 * 38 B5
Groveway EAG/OLD/WTN MK6 22 D3
MKV MK10 19 M7
Grove Wy RAYLW HP18 166 D8
RKW/CH/CXG WD3 73 G5
UX/CGN UB8 104 C5
Grovewood Cl
RKW/CH/CXG WD3 73 G6
Grubbins La PRRI HP27 67 G2
Grubbs Cl LBUZ LU7 153 J12
Grubwood La MDHD SL6 97 M7
Gryms Dyke GTMIS/PWD HP16 60 B4
Guards Club Rd MDHD SL6 109 H3
Guards Rd WDSR SL4 120 B5
Guernsey Cl AYLW HP19 167 R11
Guest Gdns BDWL MK13 13 K6
Guildford Av EMV/FZ MK4 21 H5
Guildford Cl BUCK/WIN MK18 148 H2
Guillemot Wy AYLW HP19 34 D3
Guinea Orch OLN MK46 128 A10
Guinions Rd HWYN HP13 78 E5
Guinness Cl HYS/HAR UB3 115 J7
Guise Ct RMKS/WB MK17 145 J6
Gullbrook HHW HP1 49 M7
Gullicot Wy LBUZ LU7 169 Q10
Gull Wy AYLW HP19 34 E3
Gundale Ct EMV/FZ MK4 21 K4
Gun La NPAG MK16 133 N7
Gunmaker Ct GTLIN MK14 14 C8
Gunthorpe Rd MLW SL7 97 L3
Gunver La EMV/FZ MK4 21 K5
Gurnall Ct WDR/YW UB7 114 C4
Gurnards Av
EAG/OLD/WTN MK6 7 K5
Gurnells Rd BEAC HP9 81 H5
Gurney Cl AYL HP20 3 K1
BEAC HP9 80 B8
SHEN MK5 17 K7
Gurney Ct DUN/WHIP LU6 31 G8
Gurneys Meadow
HAZ/HG HP15 69 J3
Guttmann Rd AYLS HP21 42 E1
Gwendale MDHD SL6 108 B1
Gwent Cl MDHD SL6 108 A6
Gynant Ct WEAT MK2 153 P3
Gwynne Cl TRING HP23 37 M5
WDSR SL4 120 D4
Gynant Rd HWYN HP13 78 E4
Gypsy La MLW SL7 97 K2
SLN SL2 101 K2
Gyspy La WYM HP11 78 C5

H

H2 WOLV MK12 16 F2
H3 CNH/GTH/TMA MK8 17 G3
H4 BDWL MK13 6 B2
H5 BDWL MK13 6 C5
H6 EAG/OLD/WTN MK6 6 E8
H7 EAG/OLD/WTN MK6 7 M7
H8 EMV/FZ MK4 21 J8
H9 WTR/OFPK MK7 19 K8
H10 DBGH MK1 23 H3
Haberley Md BDWL MK13 17 L3
Hackett Pl NPAG MK16 134 D12
Haddenham Rd HADM HP17 182 D4
Haddington Cl BTCHLY MK3 22 B4
RAYLNE/WEN HP22 44 C5
Haddington Wy AYL HP20 3 L3
Haddon CNH/GTH/TMA MK8 17 H5
Haddon Rd MDHD SL6 108 B5
RKW/CH/CXG WD3 73 H6
Hadland Cl HHS/BOV HP3 56 F5
Hadley Pl BDWL MK13 6 C3
Hadlow Ct SL SL1 111 H5
Hadrians Dr BDWL MK13 17 J1
Hadrian's Ga BRACKY NN13 8 F7
Hagden La WATW WD18 75 L5
Haggar St HADM HP17 177 L5
Hag Hill La MDHD SL6 109 M3
Hag Hill Ri MDHD SL6 109 M3
Haglis Dr RAYLNE/WEN HP22 43 M8
Haig Dr SL SL1 111 G6
Haig Rd UX/CGN UB8 115 G2
Hailey Cft CHNR OX39 184 E4
Hainault Av GTLIN MK14 14 D5
Haines Cl AYLW HP19 167 Q12
Haines Rd HAZ/HG HP15 68 E4
Haithewaite
CNH/GTH/TMA MK8 17 G5
Haldene CNH/GTH/TMA MK8 17 H4
Hale Av STSTR MK11 16 B1
Hale End Cl RSLP HA4 95 M5
Hale La RAYLNE/WEN HP22 44 D7
Hale Leys AYL HP20 * 3 G5
Hale Rd RAYLNE/WEN HP22 44 B8
Hales Cft AYLS HP21 43 G2
Hale St AYL HP20 3 G5
Halfacre Hl CFSP/GDCR SL9 82 E8
Halford Rd HGDN/ICK UB10 104 F3
Halifax Cl MDHD SL6 107 M6
Halifax Rd BIC OX26 162 F3
HWYW HP12 87 H1
MDHD SL6 107 M6
RKW/CH/CXG WD3 73 H8
Halifax Wy MDHD SL6 107 M6
Halings La DEN/HRF UB9 93 J3
Halkingcroft DTCH/LGLY SL3 112 B6
Halland Wy NTHWD HA6 85 J6
Hall Cl BUCK/WIN MK18 142 A7
HWYN HP13 78 E5
RKW/CH/CXG WD3 83 M1
RMKN MK19 137 Q8
Hall Ct DTCH/LGLY SL3 122 A3
Halldore Hl MDHD SL6 98 D3
Hall Dr DEN/HRF UB9 84 B8
Hall La HYS/HAR UB3 125 J3
NPAG MK16 133 R10
Hall Meadow SL SL1 100 B7
Hallowell Rd NTHWD HA6 85 K7
Hallowes Crs OXHEY WD19 85 M3
Hall Pk BERK HP4 48 D7
Hall Park Ga BERK HP4 48 D8
Hall Park Hl BERK HP4 48 D7
Hall Place La MDHD SL6 107 G6
Halls Cnr FLKWH/TG HP10 88 F1
Halls La WAR/TWY RG10 116 E8
Hall's La BRACKY NN13 8 D8
Halls Ter HGDN/ICK UB10 * 115 G1
The Hall Wk BERK HP4 * 48 C6
Halse Dr SL SL1 100 E2
Halse Rd BRACKY NN13 8 D5
Halsey Dr HHW HP1 49 L5
Halsway HYS/HAR UB3 115 M5
Halswell Pl MKV MK10 19 K3
Haltonchesters BDWL MK13 13 J8
Halton La RAYLNE/WEN HP22 43 M7
Halton Wood Rd
RAYLNE/WEN HP22 44 C5
Haly Cl BDWL MK13 17 K2
Hamberlins La TRING HP23 47 G3
Hamble Cl RSLP HA4 95 K8
Hambledon Cl AYLS HP21 43 G1
UX/CGN UB8 115 G1
Hamble Dr AYLS HP21 42 B1
Hambleside BIC OX26 162 A4
Hambleton Gv EMV/FZ MK4 21 L4
Hambye Cl PRRI HP27 66 D2
Hamer Cl HHS/BOV HP3 56 F7
Hamilton Av HEN RG9 190 H5
Hamilton Cl BIC OX26 162 D3
Hamilton Ct LBUZ LU7 * 27 H7
Hamilton Gdns SL SL1 100 A8
Hamilton La BTCHLY MK3 21 M8
Hamilton Md HHS/BOV HP3 * 56 F6
Hamilton Pk MDHD SL6 107 M8
Hamilton Rd BERK HP4 48 A6
HWYN HP13 5 J3
SL SL1 110 F3
THAME OX9 181 P5
UX/CGN UB8 114 C1
WAR/TWY RG10 191 P12
Ham La WDSR SL4 122 B7
The Hamlet BERK HP4 48 F3
Hamlins EAG/OLD/WTN MK6 18 C8
Hammersley La WYM HP11 79 G6
Hammerwood Ga
WTR/OFPK MK7 19 K7
Hammond Crs WLLN MK15 14 E8
Hammond End SLN SL2 101 G2
Hamon Wy WOLV MK12 12 D8
Hampden Av CSHM HP5 62 F1
THAME OX9 181 N7
Hampden Cl AYLS HP21 2 E9
BIC OX26 162 F3
RAYLNE/WEN HP22 43 G5
SLN SL2 101 M8
Hampden Gdns AYLS HP21 34 B8
Hampden Ga PRRI HP27 67 H1
Hampden Hl BEAC HP9 80 A8
Hampden Rd AYLS HP21 2 E9
CFSP/GDCR SL9 82 C8
DTCH/LGLY SL3 112 E7
GTMIS/PWD HP16 59 L8
HWYN HP13 5 J4
MDHD SL6 108 A2
PRRI HP27 67 H2
RAYLNE/WEN HP22 44 B6
Hampden Sq AYLW HP19 177 R2
Hampermill La OXHEY WD19 85 M1
Hampshire Av SL SL1 111 H2
Hampshire Ct BTCHLY MK3 22 C4
Hampson Cl BDWL MK13 17 K1
Hampstead Cl AYLW HP19 177 P1
Hampstead Ga BDWL MK13 6 C3
Hampton CNH/GTH/TMA MK8 17 J6
Hanbury Cl SL SL1 109 M2
Handel Md WTR/OFPK MK7 144 B5
Handley Page Cl RBEDW MK43 138 H4
Handsworth Cl OXHEY WD19 85 M3
Hangar Rd DEN/HRF UB9 93 K3
Hanging Croft Cl
HWYN HP13 * 78 E4
Hangings La GTMIS/PWD HP16 59 M8
Hanley Cl WDSR SL4 120 C4
Hanmer Rd
EAG/OLD/WTN MK6 23 H1
Hannon Rd AYLS HP21 42 B1
Hanover Cir HYS/HAR UB3 115 H3
Hanover Cl AYLW HP19 167 R12
SL SL1 111 M7
WDSR SL4 120 E4
Hanover Ct LBUZ LU7 26 E7
Hanover Dr BRACKY NN13 8 D6
Hanover Gdns BIC OX26 162 D5
WAR/TWY RG10 191 Q11
Hanover Ga SL SL1 110 E5
Hanover Gn HHW HP1 57 M1
Hanover Md MDHD SL6 109 H7
Hanover Wy WDSR SL4 120 E5
Hans Apel Dr BRACKY NN13 8 C7
Hanscomb Cl WLLN MK15 18 F4
Hanslope Circular Ride
GTLIN MK14 13 L4
NPAG MK16 132 A11
Hanslope Rd RMKN MK19 131 L11
Hanson Cl WDR/YW UB7 114 E7
Hanson Wy AYLS HP21 42 F2
Harbell Wy BIC OX26 162 C2
Harborne Ct
CNH/GTH/TMA MK8 16 F4
Harbourne Cl AYLS HP21 42 B3
Harby Cl EMV/FZ MK4 21 M5
Harcourt BDWL MK13 17 K3
Harcourt Cl HEN RG9 190 F5
LBUZ LU7 26 F7
MDHD SL6 109 L7
Harcourt Gdns MLW SL7 * 97 K4
Harcourt Gn AYLW HP19 2 A1
Harcourt Rd MDHD SL6 109 L7
TRING HP23 38 B6
WDSR SL4 120 D4
Hardenwaye HWYN HP13 78 D1
Harding Rd CSHM HP5 63 J1
MKV MK10 19 M6
Harding Sp DTCH/LGLY SL3 122 E1
Hardings Rw IVER SL0 103 H8
Hardmead Rd RBEDW MK43 129 J11
Hardwick Cl MDHD SL6 107 L6
Hardwicke Gdns AMS HP6 71 K1
Hardwick Ms RMKS/WB MK17 144 E7
Hardwick Pl RMKS/WB MK17 144 E6
Hardwick Rd RBICN OX27 154 E3
RMKS/WB MK17 144 E6
Hardy Cl AYLS HP21 3 H8
SL SL1 110 F5
Harebell Cl WTR/OFPK MK7 23 L1
Harebell Wk HAZ/HG HP15 68 E4
Harebridge La
RAYLNE/WEN HP22 36 D8
Hare Cl BUCK/WIN MK18 11 M7
Hareden Cft EMV/FZ MK4 21 L5
Harefield Rd MDHD SL6 107 M7
RKW/CH/CXG WD3 84 C5
UX/CGN UB8 104 C4
Harehatch La SLN SL2 90 F7
Hare La GTMIS/PWD HP16 61 G7
Hare Lane End
GTMIS/PWD HP16 60 F7
Harepark Cl HHW HP1 49 L6
Hare Shoots MDHD SL6 108 D5
Harewood RKW/CH/CXG WD3 74 B6
Harewood Pl SL SL1 111 M7
Harewood Rd CSTG HP8 72 B4
Harford Dr WAT WD17 75 K1
Hargrave Rd MDHD SL6 108 C2
Hargreaves Nook GTLIN MK14 14 E4
Harkness Cl WEAT MK2 23 G8
Harkness Rd SL SL1 110 A2
Harlans Cl EAG/OLD/WTN MK6 7 M9
Harlech Pl BTCHLY MK3 22 B7
Harlequin Pl SHEN MK5 21 J3
Harlesden Cl MKV MK10 19 H5
Harle Stone Ct GTLIN MK14 * 14 C5
Harleyford MLW SL7 * 96 E8
Harleyford La MLW SL7 96 F7
Harling Rd DUN/WHIP LU6 170 H2
Harlington Cl HYS/HAR UB3 125 H3
Harlington Rd UX/CGN UB8 104 F8
Harlow Crs EMV/FZ MK4 21 G4
Harlow Rd WYM HP11 5 M8
Harmon Cl RBICN OX27 154 F12
Harmondsworth La
WDR/YW UB7 124 D2
Harmondsworth Rd
WDR/YW UB7 114 D7
Harmony Rw LBUZ LU7 29 L1
Harnett Dr WOLV MK12 12 C8
Harold Av HYS/HAR UB3 115 L7
Harper Cl RBICS/W OX25 173 J3
Harpers La GTLIN MK14 14 C6
Harpsden Rd HEN RG9 190 H6
Harpsden Wy HEN RG9 190 H7
Harrier Cl AYLW HP19 34 E3
Harrier Ct EAG/OLD/WTN MK6 7 L8
Harrier Dr EAG/OLD/WTN MK6 7 K9
Harrier Wy BIC OX26 162 F2
Harries Cl CSHM HP5 55 G8
Harries Wy HAZ/HG HP15 69 G4
Harriet Walker Wy
RKW/CH/CXG WD3 73 L8
Harrington Cl WDSR SL4 120 E7
Harris Cl BRACKY NN13 8 C6
Harris Ct AYL HP20 3 J1
Harris Gdns SL SL1 111 H6
Harrison Cl NTHWD HA6 85 H6
SHEN MK5 18 A8
Harrison Pl THAME OX9 181 N5
Harrison Wy SL SL1 110 C5
Harris Rd SKCH HP14 86 A1
Harroell RAYLW HP18 175 L12
Harrogate Ct DTCH/LGLY SL3 122 F1
Harrold Rd OLN MK46 129 J6
Harrow Cl AYLS HP21 42 D2
MDHD SL6 108 D1
Harrowden BDWL MK13 13 L7
Harrow La MDHD SL6 108 D1
Harrow Rd DTCH/LGLY SL3 112 E7
LBUZ LU7 29 J1
Harrow Vw HGDN/ICK UB10 105 H8
HYS/HAR UB3 115 M4
Harrow Yd TRING HP23 37 M7
Hartdames SHEN MK5 21 K3
Harter Av RBEDW MK43 139 K7
Hartfield Cl WTR/OFPK MK7 19 K7
Hartington Gv EMV/FZ MK4 21 L3
Hartland Av EMV/FZ MK4 21 K6
Hartland Cl SL SL1 111 J5
Hartley GTLIN MK14 14 B6
Hartley Cl SLN SL2 102 B6
Hart Moor Cl SKCH HP14 186 H2
Hart Pl BIC OX26 162 F2
Hartshill Cl HGDN/ICK UB10 104 F4
Harts Rd HADM HP17 176 E12
Hart St HEN RG9 190 H4
Hartwell Cl FLKWH/TG HP10 69 H8
Hartwell Crs LBUZ LU7 27 H7
Hartwell Dr BEAC HP9 80 C8
Hartwell End AYLS HP21 2 B8
Hartwell Rd RMKN MK19 131 K5
Hartwort Cl WTR/OFPK MK7 19 L8
Harvard Cl GTLIN MK14 14 B4
Harvest Bank AMS HP6 62 B5
Harvester Cl WOLV MK12 16 E1
Harvest Hl BNEND SL8 89 J8
Harvest Hill Rd MDHD SL6 108 D6
Harvey Dr OLN MK46 133 N1
Harvey Rd AYLS HP21 42 D1
DUN/WHIP LU6 31 L7
HGDN/ICK UB10 104 F7
RKW/CH/CXG WD3 74 F7

Harvil Rd *DEN/HRF* UB9 .... 94 B3
Harwell Cl *RSLP* HA4 .... 95 J7
Harwich Rd *SL* SL1 .... 110 F3
Harwood Dr *HGDN/ICK* UB10 .... 104 E6
Harwood St *MLW* SL7 .... 97 H5
Harwoods Rd *WATW* WD18 ...... 75 M5
Harwood St *BDWL* MK13 .... 13 K4
Hasedines Rd *HHW* HP1 .... 49 M6
Hasgill Ct *BDWL* MK13 .... 17 L1
Haslam Cl *HGDN/ICK* UB10 ...... 95 H8
Haslemere Rd *WDSR* SL4 .... 120 F4
Haslerig Cl *AYLS* HP21 .... 42 A1
Haslow Ct *CNH/GTH/TMA* MK8 .. 17 H3
Hasting Cl *MDHD* SL6 .... 109 H8
Hastings *STSTR* MK11 .... 16 B1
Hastings Meadow *SLN* SL2 * 101 M6
Hastings Wy
    RKW/CH/CXG WD3 .... 75 G5
Hastoe HI *TRING* HP23 .... 45 M1
Hastoe La *TRING* HP23 .... 37 M8
Hastoe Pk *AYL* HP20 .... 3 J2
Hatches La *HAZ/HG* HP15 .... 68 B1
Hatchet Leys La
    BUCK/WIN MK18 .... 142 G10
Hatchgate Gdns *SL* SL1 .... 100 C8
Hatch Gate La *WAR/TWY* RG10 .. 191 Q7
Hatchlands
    CNH/GTH/TMA MK8 .... 17 M3
Hatch La *SKCH* HP14 .... 76 A2
    WDR/YW UB7 .... 124 C3
    WDSR SL4 .... 120 F6
The Hatch *WDSR* SL4 .... 120 B3
Hatfield Av *RBEDW* MK43 ...... 139 K7
Hatfield Cl *MDHD* SL6 .... 108 B4
Hatfield St *SL* SL1 .... 111 M6
Hathaway Ct *RSLP* HA4 .... 105 L2
Hathaway Ct
    CNH/GTH/TMA MK8 .... 17 H6
Hatherleigh Rd *RSLP* HA4 ...... 95 M8
Hatters La *WATW* WD18 .... 75 J7
Hatter's La *HWYN* HP13 .... 78 D5
Hatton Av *SLN* SL2 .... 111 J1
Hatton Ct *WDSR* SL4 .... 121 H5
Hatton Cross Est
    HTHAIR TW6 * 125 L7
Hatton Gv *EBED/NFELT* TW14 .. 125 L7
Hatton Rd *WDR/YW* UB7 * 114 C6
Hauksbee Gdns *SHEN* MK5 ...... 21 M1
Havelock Crs *MDHD* SL6 .... 108 A3
Havelock Rd *MDHD* SL6 .... 108 A3
Havelock St *AYL* HP20 .... 2 F4
Haven Cl *YEAD* UB4 .... 115 K2
Havenfield Rd *HWYW* HP12 .... 87 G2
Haven Shaw Cl *AYLS* HP21 .... 42 F1
Haversham Rd *RMKN* MK19 .... 13 G5
Hawes Cl *NTHWD* HA6 .... 85 L7
Hawfinch *AYLW* HP19 .... 34 D3
Hawker Cl *LBUZ* LU7 .... 29 L1
Hawkes Cl *DTCH/LGLY* SL3 .... 113 G7
Hawkesworth Cl *NTHWD* HA6 .. 85 K7
Hawkhurst Ga *MKV* MK10 ...... 19 J6
Hawkings Wy *HHS/BOV* HP3 .... 56 F5
Hawkins Cl *BRACKY* NN13 ...... 8 C2
    STSTR MK11 .... 16 A1
Hawkmoor Cl
    EAG/OLD/WTN MK6 .... 18 E6
Hawkridge Dr *RMKN* MK19 ...... 22 B3
Hawkshead Dr *EMV/FZ* MK4 .... 21 M3
Hawks HI *BNEND* SL8 .... 89 H8
Hawkshill Rd *SLN* SL2 .... 100 F8
Hawkesmead *BIC* OX26 .... 162 F6
Hawksmoor Cl *HWYN* HP13 .... 5 G4
Hawkswood *OLN* MK46 .... 128 A9
Hawkswood Gv
    DTCH/LGLY SL3 .... 102 E4
Hawkswood La
    DTCH/LGLY SL3 .... 102 E3
Hawkswell Dr *TRING* HP23 ...... 38 B6
Hawkwell Est *RMKN* MK19 ...... 137 Q2
Haw La *SKCH* HP14 .... 185 Q10
Hawleys La
    RAYLNE/WEN HP22 .... 159 R12
Haworth Cft *MKV* MK10 .... 19 J3
Hawridge La *CSHM* HP5 .... 54 D2
Hawridge V *CSHM* HP5 .... 54 L1
Hawthorn Av *THAME* OX9 ...... 181 M6
    WEAT MK2 .... 23 H6
Hawthorn Cl *AYL* HP20 .... 3 K2
    IVER SL0 .... 103 H8
    RBEDW MK43 .... 129 N8
    WAT WD17 .... 75 L1
Hawthorne Crs *HAZ/HG* HP15 .. 69 G8
Hawthorn Dr *BRACKY* NN13 .... 8 E5
    DEN/HRF UB9 .... 104 B4
Hawthorne Cl *LBUZ* LU7 .... 26 F6
    MLW SL7 .... 97 K3
Hawthorne Crs *SL* SL1 .... 111 K3
    WDR/YW UB7 .... 114 E6
Hawthorne Gdns
    FLKWH/TG HP10 .... 78 E8
Hawthorne Rd *HWYN* HP13 .... 78 E5
The Hawthornes
    FLKWH/TG HP10 .... 89 K4
Hawthorn Gdns *MDHD* SL6 .... 108 C5
Hawthorn La *HHW* HP1 .... 49 L6
    SLN SL2 .... 100 E5
Hawthorn Pl *HYS/HAR* UB3 * .. 115 L4
The Hawthorns *BERK* HP4 ...... 47 M5
    CSTG HP8 .... 72 B3
    DTCH/LGLY SL3 .... 123 L4
    FLKWH/TG HP10 * 89 G2
    HHS/BOV HP3 .... 57 L3
    PRRI HP27 .... 50 B7
    RBEDW MK43 .... 139 L5
    RKW/CH/CXG WD3 .... 83 J5
Hawthorn Wy *CSHM* HP5 ...... 55 J8
    LBUZ LU7 .... 26 F6
Hawtrey Cl *SL* SL1 .... 112 A4
Hawtrey Dr *RSLP* HA4 .... 95 M6
Hawtrey Rd *WDSR* SL4 .... 121 H5
Haydock Cl *BTCHLY* MK3 .... 21 M8
Haydon Dr *PIN* HA5 .... 95 M3
Hayes End Dr *YEAD* UB4 .... 115 J2
Hayes End Rd *YEAD* UB4 ...... 115 J1
Hayes Rd *RMKN* MK19 .... 137 N9
Hayfield *HAZ/HG* HP15 .... 69 G8
Hay La *DTCH/LGLY* SL3 .... 102 C2
Hayles Fld *HEN* RG9 .... 189 P1
Hayman Crs *YEAD* UB4 .... 105 J7
Hayman Ri
    CNH/GTH/TMA MK8 .... 17 G8
Hayman Rd *BRACKY* NN13 ...... 8 C7
Haymill Rd *SL* SL1 .... 110 C1
Haynes Cl *DTCH/LGLY* SL3 .... 122 E1
    RMKS/WB MK17 .... 144 M4
Hayse HI *WDSR* SL4 .... 47 M4
The Haystacks *HWYN* HP13 .... 5 J5
Haystall Cl *YEAD* UB4 .... 105 K7
Haythorp Cl *WLLN* MK15 .... 14 E7

Haywards Cl *HEN* RG9 .... 190 F5
Haywards Md *WDSR* SL4 ...... 120 E1
Haywood Copse
    RKW/CH/CXG WD3 .... 74 C5
Haywood Dr
    RKW/CH/CXG WD3 .... 73 L5
Haywood Pk *LBUZ* LU7 .... 152 H11
    RKW/CH/CXG WD3 .... 73 L5
Haywoods Dr *HHS/BOV* HP3 .... 57 L2
Hayworth Pl *EMV/FZ* MK4 .... 21 G4
Hazel Av *THAME* OX9 .... 181 M6
    WDR/YW UB7 .... 114 F7
Hazelbury Rd *HWYN* HP13 ...... 78 C4
Hazel Cl *BRACKY* NN13 .... 8 E5
    HAZ/HG HP15 .... 68 B1
    MLW SL7 .... 87 H8
Hazel Ct *RKW/CH/CXG* WD3 * .. 83 K4
Hazelcroft Cl *HGDN/ICK* UB10 104 E6
Hazeldell Link *HHW* HP1 * 49 K8
Hazeldell Rd *HHW* HP1 .... 49 K8
Hazeldene *RAYLNE/WEN* HP22 .. 44 B6
Hazeldene Gdns
    HGDN/ICK UB10 .... 105 H6
Hazel Gv *BIC* OX26 .... 162 E2
    WEAT MK2 .... 23 G7
Hazelhurst *AYL* HP21 .... 3 M7
Hazelhurst Rd *SL* SL1 .... 100 B7
Hazell Av *AYLS* HP21 .... 3 M7
Hazell Cl *MDHD* SL6 .... 108 A2
Hazell Pk *AMSS* HP7 .... 71 H7
Hazell Rd *GTMIS/PWD* HP16 .... 60 B5
Hazell St *SLN* SL2 .... 101 L4
Hazelrig Dr *THAME* OX9 .... 181 P6
Hazel Rd *BERK* HP4 .... 48 C7
Hazelton Cl *THAME* OX9 .... 181 M6
Hazelwood *GTLIN* MK14 .... 14 C6
Hazelwood Cl *CSHM* HP5 .... 55 J8
Hazelwood Rd
    RKW/CH/CXG WD3 .... 75 H7
Hazely *TRING* HP23 .... 38 B6
Hazelwood Dr *AYLS* HP21 ...... 42 F1
Hazlemere Rd
    FLKWH/TG HP10 .... 69 H8
    SLN SL2 .... 112 A5
Hazlemere Vw *HAZ/HG* HP15 .. 69 G5
Heacham Av *HGDN/ICK* UB10 .. 105 H1
Headingham Ct *SHEN* MK5 ...... 21 K1
Headington Cl *MDHD* SL6 ...... 107 M7
Headington Rd *MDHD* SL6 .... 107 M7
Headland Cl *GTMIS/PWD* HP16 . 60 F2
Headlands Dr *BERK* HP4 .... 48 D5
Healey Cl *HWYN* HP13 .... 78 C3
Healey Rd *WATW* WD18 .... 75 L1
Heaney La *FLKWH/TG* HP10 .... 68 E8
Hearn Cl *FLKWH/TG* HP10 ...... 68 E8
Hearne Dr *MDHD* SL6 .... 118 F2
Hearnes Pk *EAG/OLD/WTN* MK6 * 7 H9
Hearnes Cl *BEAC* HP9 .... 81 J5
Hearn Birth *RBICS/W* OX25 .... 163 P9
Heath Cl *AYLS* HP21 .... 69 G4
    HAZ/HG HP15 .... 69 G4
    HYS/HAR UB3 .... 125 J3
Heathcote *MDHD* SL6 .... 109 G8
Heathcote Wy *WDR/YW* UB7 .. 114 A4
Heath Ct *LBUZ* LU7 .... 26 F3
Heathdene Mnr *WAT* WD17 * .. 75 J2
Heath End Cl *HAZ/HG* HP15 .... 68 D1
Heath End Rd *WYM* HP11 ...... 78 A8
Heather Cl *BUCK/WIN* MK18 .. 11 K7
    UX/CGN UB8 .... 114 E2
Heathercroft *GTLIN* MK14 ...... 14 B7
Heatherden La *IVER* SL0 .... 103 H6
Heatherfold Wy *PIN* HA5 ...... 95 L2
Heather La *WDR/YW* UB7 ...... 114 D3
Heather Rd *LBUZ* LU7 .... 26 D3
    WDR/YW UB7 .... 114 D3
Heathers Cl *BUCK/WIN* MK18 .. 157 J5
Heatherside Gdns *SLN* SL2 .... 101 J1
Heatherton Pk *AMS* HP6 ...... 63 G7
Heather Wk *AYLS* HP21 .... 3 J8
Heatherwood Dr *YEAD* UB4 .. 105 J7
Heathfield *WOLV* MK12 .... 17 H4
Heathfield Av *HEN* RG9 .... 190 E12
Heathfield Cl *HEN* RG9 .... 190 E12
Heathfield Ri *RSLP* HA4 .... 95 H6
Heathfield Rd *HWYW* HP12 .... 77 G7
    MDHD SL6 .... 99 L2
Heath Gn *LBUZ* LU7 .... 26 F3
Heathlands Dr *MDHD* SL6 ...... 107 M8
Heath La *RMKS/WB* MK17 .... 144 D8
Heath Park Dr *LBUZ* LU7 ...... 27 L4
Heath Park Rd *LBUZ* LU7 ...... 27 L4
Heath Rd *AMS* HP6 .... 62 B5
    BEAC HP9 .... 89 L1
    HGDN/ICK UB10 .... 115 H1
    LBUZ LU7 .... 27 L6
    RMKS/WB MK17 .... 24 E5
Heathrow Cl *WDR/YW* UB7 .... 124 A4
Heathside Cl *NTHWD* HA6 ...... 85 J1
Heathside Rd *NTHWD* HA6 .... 85 J1
The Heath *LBUZ* LU7 .... 26 F3
Heath Wy *IVER* SL0 .... 103 J7
Heathwood Cl *LBUZ* LU7 ...... 27 H3
Heavens Lea *BNEND* SL8 .... 89 H4
Heckford Cl *WATW* WD18 ...... 75 H7
Hedge Lea *FLKWH/TG* HP10 .... 89 H3
Hedgerley Hl *SLN* SL2 .... 101 J1
Hedgerley La *BEAC* HP9 .... 92 B7
    CFSP/GDCR SL9 .... 92 B7
    SLN SL2 .... 91 K5
Hedgerow *CFSP/GDCR* SL9 .... 82 D6
Hedge Rw *HHW* HP1 .... 49 M5
The Hedgeways *EMV/FZ* MK4 .. 22 B2
Hedges Ct *SHEN* MK5 .... 17 L8
Hedgeside *BERK* HP4 .... 48 B5
Hedingham Ms *MDHD* SL6 * .. 108 C3
Hedley Cl *RAYLNE/WEN* HP22 .. 36 F6
Hedley Rd *FLKWH/TG* HP10 .... 89 J1
Hedsor Hl *BNEND* SL8 .... 89 J1
Hedsor La *FLKWH/TG* HP10 .... 89 L3
Hedsor Rd *BNEND* SL8 .... 89 J2
Hele Ct *WTR/OFPK* MK7 .... 23 L3
Helena Rd *WDSR* SL4 .... 121 J3
Helford Cl *RSLP* HA4 .... 95 K8
Helford Pl *EAG/OLD/WTN* MK6 .. 7 J6
Heligan Pl *EMV/FZ* MK4 .... 21 L5
Hellyer Wy *BNEND* SL8 .... 89 K8
Helmsley Ri *EMV/FZ* MK4 ...... 21 H5
Helston La *WDSR* SL4 .... 121 G3
Helston Pl *EAG/OLD/WTN* MK6 * 7 J7

Hempstead Rd *HHS/BOV* HP3 .. 57 G5
    WAT WD17 .... 75 M4
Hemsdale *MDHD* SL6 .... 108 A1
Hemwood Rd *WDSR* SL4 .... 120 C6
Hencroft St North *SL* SL1 ...... 111 L6
Hencroft St South *SL* SL1 ...... 111 L6
Henders *STSTR* MK11 .... 16 B1
Henderson Cl *YEAD* UB4 .... 105 J7
Hendon Pl *BIC* OX26 .... 162 F2
Hendons Dr *HHS/BOV* HP3 .... 57 G2
Hendon Wy *STWL/WRAY* TW19 124 C9
Hendrix Dr
    CNH/GTH/TMA MK8 .... 17 G7
Hengistbury La *EMV/FZ* MK4 .. 21 J5
Henley Rd *MDHD* SL6 .... 106 A4
    SL SL1 .... 110 D3
Henneston Wy *HWYN* HP13 .... 78 E4
Henrietta Rd *LBUZ* LU7 .... 181 P5
Henry Rd *AYL* HP20 .... 35 G3
    SL SL1 .... 111 J4
Henry St *TRING* HP23 .... 37 M7
Hensman Ga *MKV* MK10 .... 19 J2
Henson Cl *RBEDW* MK43 .... 138 H4
Hepleswell
    CNH/GTH/TMA MK8 .... 17 J7
Hepplewhite Cl *HWYN* HP13 .. 78 C2
Herald Wy *BIC* OX26 .... 162 E2
Herbert Rd *HWYN* HP13 .... 78 F4
Herberts Hole
    GTMIS/PWD HP16 .... 61 L1
Hercies Rd *HGDN/ICK* UB10 .. 104 F2
Hercules Cl *LBUZ* LU7 .... 27 K6
Herdman Cl *WOLV* MK12 ...... 16 E1
Herd's HI *BUCK/WIN* MK18 ... 149 N10
Hereford Wy *AYLW* HP19 .... 167 R11
Herga Ct *WAT* WD17 .... 75 M3
Heritage Cl *UX/CGN* UB8 ...... 114 B1
Heritage Wk
    RKW/CH/CXG WD3 * 73 K4
Herlwyn Av *RSLP* HA4 .... 105 J4
Hermitage La *DTCH/LGLY* SL3 . 112 B7
Hermitage La *WDSR* SL4 ...... 120 F6
The Hermitage
    GTMIS/PWD HP16 * 60 F3
    UX/CGN UB8 * 104 C4
Hermon Gv *HYS/HAR* UB3 .... 115 M5
Herne Cl *HYS/HAR* UB3 .... 115 L3
    RKW/CH/CXG WD3 .... 84 C2
    UX/CGN UB8 .... 104 C4
Heron Cl *AYL* HP20 .... 162 G5
Heron Dr *BIC* OX26 .... 162 G5
    SL SL1 .... 8 C5
    DTCH/LGLY SL3 .... 113 G4
Heron Pl *DEN/HRF* UB9 .... 83 M6
    RBICS *BEN* BERK HP4 .. 47 K5
Heronsgate Rd
    RKW/CH/CXG WD3 .... 73 G7
The Heron *AYLW* HP19 .... 34 D2
Heron Wk *NTHWD* HA6 .... 85 K4
Heron Wy *EBED/NFELT* TW14 .. 125 M7
Herrieffs Farm Rd
    BRACKY NN13 .... 8 E8
Herriot Cl *NPAG* MK16 .... 14 D1
Herschel Park Dr *SL* SL1 ...... 111 L6
Herschel St *SL* SL1 .... 111 L6
Herston Cl *AYLS* HP21 .... 43 G7
Hertford Cl *BIC* OX26 .... 162 E3
Hertford End Ct *NTHWD* HA6 * 85 K5
Hertford Pl *BTCHLY* MK3 .... 22 C4
Hervines Rd *AMS* HP6 .... 63 H8
Hervines Rd *AMS* HP6 .... 63 G8
Hesa Rd *HYS/HAR* UB3 .... 115 M3
Hesketh Rd *TOW* NN12 .... 130 D12
Heswall Gn *OXHEY* WD19 * 85 J6
Hetchleys *HHW* HP1 .... 49 M4
Hetherington Cl *SLN* SL2 ...... 100 E8
Hetherington Wy
    HGDN/ICK UB10 .... 104 D2
Hethe Rd *BRACKY* NN13 ...... 146 F11
Het's Orch *PRRI* HP27 .... 66 D7
Hetton Cl *BDWL* MK13 .... 6 B1
Hever Cl *LBUZ* LU7 .... 169 Q12
    MDHD SL6 .... 108 B4
Hewens Rd *HGDN/ICK* UB10 .. 105 H3
Hexham Gdns *BTCHLY* MK3 .... 22 A8
Heybridge Crs *WTR/OFPK* MK7 . 23 K3
Heydon Cl *BDWL* MK13 .... 13 K7
Heynes Gn *MDHD* SL6 .... 108 B3
Heythrop Dr *HGDN/ICK* UB10 . 104 E2
Heywood Cl *MDHD* SL6 .... 117 M5
Heywood Court Cl *MDHD* SL6 . 117 M5
Heywood Gdns *MDHD* SL6 .... 117 M5
Hibbert Rd *MDHD* SL6 .... 109 G6
Hibberts Wy *CFSP/GDCR* SL9 .. 92 D2
Hickmans Cl *BUCK/WIN* MK18 . 142 H8
Hickman St *AYLW* HP19 ...... 177 Q2
Hickox Ct *FLKWH/TG* HP10 .... 89 L3
Hicks Farm Ri *HWYN* HP13 .... 78 E3
The Hide *EAG/OLD/WTN* MK6 .. 18 C3
Higgs Ct *SHEN* MK5 .... 17 K6
Higham Cross Rd *RMKN* MK19 . 131 M4
Higham Md *CSHM* HP5 .... 63 H1
Higham Rd *CSHM* HP5 .... 63 H1
High Banks *LBUZ* LU7 .... 30 D1
High Beeches *CFSP/GDCR* SL9 . 92 D4
High Beeches Cl *MLW* SL7 .... 87 M6
High Bois La *AMS* HP6 .... 63 J6
Highbridge Rd *AYLS* HP21 .... 3 H6
Highbridge Wk *AYLS* HP21 .... 3 H6
Highbury La *CMK* MK9 .... 7 L3
High Cl *RKW/CH/CXG* WD3 .... 74 B6
High Coppice *AMSS* HP7 .... 71 H7
Highcroft *LBUZ* LU7 .... 27 K7
Highcroft Cl *TOW* NN12 ...... 130 D12
Highcroft Rd *HHS/BOV* HP3 .. 57 M4
High Elms *RBEDW* MK43 ...... 129 Q5
High Elms *NTHWD* HA6 .... 85 J1
Highfield *CSTG* HP8 .... 82 C2
    RAYLW HP18 .... 175 K12
Highfield Av *HWYW* HP12 .... 87 G1
Highfield Cl *AMS* HP6 .... 63 J4
    BTCHLY MK3 .... 22 C4
    NPAG MK16 .... 15 H2
    NTHWD HA6 .... 85 K8
    THAME OX9 .... 181 M6
Highfield Ct *BRACKY* NN13 .... 8 D5
Highfield Crs *NTHWD* HA6 .... 85 K8
    RBEDW MK43 .... 145 M4
Highfield Dr *HGDN/ICK* UB10 . 104 E2
Highfield La *MDHD* SL6 .... 117 M2
Highfield Pk *MLW* SL7 .... 97 M3
    WAR/TWY RG10 .... 191 Q12
Highfield Rd *BERK* HP4 .... 48 C1
    BNEND SL8 .... 89 K8
    BUCK/WIN MK18 .... 151 J9
    CSHM HP5 .... 55 G8
    LBUZ LU7 .... 27 K7
    MDHD SL6 .... 108 A3
    NTHWD HA6 .... 85 K8
    PRRI HP27 .... 58 B2

    TRING HP23 .... 37 K7
    WDSR SL4 .... 120 E6
Highfield Wy *HAZ/HG* HP15 .... 68 F7
    RKW/CH/CXG WD3 .... 73 M7
Highgrove Ms *AYLW* HP19 .... 177 Q1
Highgrove HI
    CNH/GTH/TMA MK8 .... 17 M3
Highgrove Pk *MDHD* SL6 ...... 108 D2
Highgrove Wy *RSLP* HA4 .... 95 M5
High Halden *WTR/OFPK* MK7 .. 19 L5
High Heavens Wd *MLW* SL7 .. 87 H6
High Land Cl *RAYLW* HP18 .... 174 B1
Highland Ms
    BUCK/WIN MK18 * 11 M3
Highland Rd *AMSS* HP7 .... 71 J2
    NTHWD HA6 .... 95 M1
Highlands *FLKWH/TG* HP10 .... 89 G3
    NTHWD HA6 .... 85 M4
Highlands End *CFSP/GDCR* SL9 . 82 D7
Highlands Ap *FLKWH/TG* HP10 . 89 P5
Highlands Ct *CHNR* OX39 ...... 184 G4
    HEN RG9 .... 190 D7
Highlands Rd *BEAC* HP9 .... 81 P5
    RMKS/WB MK17 .... 151 N4
The Highlands
    RKW/CH/CXG WD3 .... 74 A8
    SLN SL2 .... 101 H2
Highlea Av *FLKWH/TG* HP10 .. 88 F2
Highley Gv *MKV* MK10 .... 19 H3
Highmoor *AMSS* HP7 .... 71 J2
High Moors
    RAYLNE/WEN HP22 .... 44 A2
Highover Pk *AMSS* HP7 .... 71 H3
High Park Cl *WOLV* MK12 ...... 12 D8
High Rd *LBUZ* LU7 .... 153 R12
    MDHD SL6 .... 98 D3
    SLN SL2 .... 114 B2
High Road Ickenham
    HGDN/ICK UB10 .... 105 G1
High St *IVER* SL0 .... 113 L3
    AMSS HP7 .... 70 F2
    AYL HP20 .... 3 G5
    BDWL MK13 .... 13 J7
    BERK HP4 .... 47 K3
    BRACKY NN13 .... 140 A3
    BUCK/WIN MK18 .... 159 K8
    BUCK/WIN MK18 .... 151 J10
    BUCK/WIN MK18 .... 142 H10
    BUCK/WIN MK18 .... 11 M5
    CFSP/GDCR SL9 .... 92 D4
    CHNR OX39 .... 184 D7
    CHNR OX39 .... 63 G2
    CSTG HP8 .... 82 B3
    CSHM HP8 .... 81 G3
    DEN/HRF UB9 .... 94 B1
    DTCH/LGLY SL3 .... 122 A4
    DUN/WHIP LU6 .... 170 F3
    GTLIN MK14 .... 14 B5
    GTMIS/PWD HP16 .... 60 D3
    HADM HP17 .... 176 C12
    HHS/BOV HP3 .... 56 F6
    HWYN HP13 .... 77 J3
    HYS/HAR UB3 .... 125 J2
    IVER SL0 .... 113 K3
    LBUZ LU7 .... 161 Q6
    LBUZ LU7 .... 160 C9
    LBUZ LU7 .... 27 G8
    MDHD SL6 .... 108 E3
    MDHD SL6 .... 98 F3
    MLW SL7 .... 97 J5
    NPAG MK16 .... 134 E12
    NPAG MK16 .... 133 N8
    NPAG MK16 .... 132 F2
    NPAG MK16 .... 14 C2
    NTHWD HA6 .... 85 L8
    OLN MK46 .... 128 H6
    PRRI HP27 .... 127 N12
    PRRI HP27 .... 58 A3
    RAYLNE/WEN HP22 .... 159 R12
    RAYLNE/WEN HP22 .... 44 B3
    RAYLW HP18 .... 175 L12
    RAYLW HP18 .... 174 B2
    RAYLW HP18 .... 165 Q2
    RBEDW MK43 .... 164 C6
    RBEDW MK43 .... 145 G5
    RBEDW MK43 .... 135 K4
    RBEDW MK43 .... 129 N9
    RBEDW MK43 .... 129 N1
    RKW/CH/CXG WD3 .... 84 C1
    RMKN MK19 .... 137 M10
    RMKN MK19 .... 13 K3
    RMKS/WB MK17 .... 151 J3
    RMKS/WB MK17 .... 144 E8
    RMKS/WB MK17 .... 143 K9
    RSLP HA4 .... 95 K6
    SKCH HP14 .... 86 A2
    SL SL1 .... 111 J7
    SL SL1 .... 100 B8
    STSTR MK11 .... 137 R8
    THAME OX9 .... 181 M5
    TOW NN12 .... 137 H2
    TRING HP23 .... 37 M7
    UX/CGN UB8 .... 114 B1
    WDR/YW UB7 .... 124 C2
    WDSR SL4 .... 121 J4
    WYM HP11 .... 5 J7
High Street Harlington
    HTHAIR TW6 .... 125 J4
High St North *LBUZ* LU7 ...... 153 J12
High St South *LBUZ* LU7 ...... 161 K2
    OLN MK46 .... 128 B11
The High St
    CNH/GTH/TMA MK8 .... 16 F4
High Town Rd *MDHD* SL6 ...... 108 D3
High Trees *DTCH/LGLY* SL3 .... 113 H5
High Trees Cl *WTR/OFPK* MK7 .. 7 M8
Highveer Cft *EMV/FZ* MK4 .... 21 J4
High Vw *CSTG* HP8 .... 82 C2
    RKW/CH/CXG WD3 .... 73 M5
    RMKN MK19 .... 137 M9
    RMKS/WB MK17 * 24 F1
    WATW WD18 .... 75 H3
High View Cl *MLW* SL7 .... 87 J6
Highway *RMKS/WB* MK17 .... 152 H5
Highway Av *MDHD* SL6 .... 107 M2
Highway Rd *MDHD* SL6 .... 108 A4
High Vw *AMS* HP6 .... 71 J4
Highwood Av *HWYW* HP12 .... 87 M2
Highwood Bottom *PRRI* HP27 . 77 G1
Highwoods Cl *MLW* SL7 .... 87 K5
Highwoods Dr *MLW* SL7 .... 87 K5
Highworth Cl *HWYW* HP12 .... 78 A2
Hikers Wy *RAYLW* HP18 .... 181 M2
Hilbury Cl *AMS* HP6 .... 63 J5
Hilda Wf *AYL* HP20 .... 3 H6
Hildreth Rd *GTMIS/PWD* HP16 . 60 D5
Hillary Cl *CFSP/GDCR* SL9 ...... 82 D7
Hillary Ct *AYLS* HP21 .... 42 F1
    HWYN HP13 .... 78 C1
Hillary Rd *DTCH/LGLY* SL3 .... 112 D7
    HWYN HP13 .... 78 C1
Hill Av *AMS* HP6 .... 71 H4

    HAZ/HG HP15 .... 68 F5
Hillbeck Gv *MKV* MK10 .... 19 H3
Hillborne Cl *HYS/HAR* UB3 .. 125 H1
Hillbottom Rd *HWYW* HP12 .. 76 F7
Hill Cl *FLKWH/TG* HP10 .... 89 L3
Hillcraft Rd *WHLY* OX33 ...... 178 C7
Hill Crs *RBEDW* MK43 .... 145 M1
Hillcrest Av *MDHD* SL6 .... 98 D5
Hillcrest Cl *SHEN* MK5 .... 17 L8
Hillcrest Ri *BUCK/WIN* MK18 .. 149 K1
Hillcroft *DUN/WHIP* LU6 .... 31 M5
Hillcroft Rd *CSHM* HP5 .... 55 J8
Hillcroft Rd *HHW* HP1 .... 79 H1
Hilldown Rd *HHW* HP1 .... 49 M5
Hill End Rd *DEN/HRF* UB9 .... 94 A6
Hillersdon *SLN* SL2 .... 112 A2
Hillersdon Cha
    RMKS/WB MK17 .... 153 Q7
Hillesden Wy *BUCK/WIN* MK18 . 11 K5
Hill Farm *BUCK/WIN* MK18 .... 159 K8
Hill Farm Ap *FLKWH/TG* HP10 . 89 K8
Hill Farm Ct *CHNR* OX39 ...... 184 G4
Hilton Av La *CSTG* HP8 .... 81 L1
    RMKS/WB MK17 .... 151 N4
Hill Farm Rd *CFSP/GDCR* SL9 . 82 D7
    CSHM HP5 .... 63 J5
    MDHD SL6 .... 109 K1
    MLW SL7 .... 87 J8
Hill Farm Wy *HAZ/HG* HP15 .. 69 G8
Hillfield Cl *HWYN* HP13 .... 77 K4
Hillfield Rd *CFSP/GDCR* SL9 .. 82 D7
Hillfield Sq *CFSP/GDCR* SL9 .. 82 D7
Hill House Cl *CFSP/GDCR* SL9 . 82 D7
Hilliard Dr *BDWL* MK13 .... 17 K3
Hilliards Rd *UX/CGN* UB8 ...... 114 C3
Hillier Rd *AYLS* HP21 .... 42 C3
Hilliers Av *UX/CGN* UB8 .... 104 F8
Hillingdon HI *UX/CGN* UB8 .... 104 D8
Hillingdon Pde
    HGDN/ICK UB10 * 115 G1
Hillingdon Rd *AYLW* HP19 .... 2 A7
Hillingdon Trail *DEN/HRF* UB9 . 94 C2
    HYS/HAR UB3 .... 125 M1
Hill Lands *WAR/TWY* RG10 .. 191 N12
Hill La *RSLP* HA4 .... 95 H7
Hill Md *BERK* HP4 .... 47 M7
Hillmead Ct *MDHD* SL6 .... 109 L2
Hill Meadow *AMSS* HP7 .... 70 E6
Hill Pl *SLN* SL2 .... 101 G5
Hillpoint *RKW/CH/CXG* WD3 .. 74 B6
Hill Ri *CFSP/GDCR* SL9 .... 92 C1
Hill Rise *CFSP/GDCR* SL9 ...... 122 F2
Hill Rl *RKW/CH/CXG* WD3 .... 74 A8
    RSLP HA4 .... 95 H7
Hill Rise Crs *CFSP/GDCR* SL9 . 92 D1
Hill Rd *CHNR* OX39 .... 184 G4
    NTHWD HA6 .... 85 J6
Hillsborough Gn
    OXHEY WD19 * 85 M3
Hills Cl *GTLIN* MK14 .... 14 B7
Hillside *BUCK/WIN* MK18 .... 148 C2
    CSHM HP5 .... 54 F7
    DEN/HRF UB9 .... 94 B4
    HWYN HP13 .... 78 C3
Hill Side *LBUZ* LU7 .... 169 L8
Hillside *MDHD* SL6 .... 108 C5
    SL SL1 .... 111 K6
Hillside Cl *CFSP/GDCR* SL9 .. 82 D6
    CSTG HP8 .... 82 A3
    RBICS/W OX25 .... 173 K3
Hillside Crs *NTHWD* HA6 ...... 85 M8
Hillside Gdns *AMSS* HP7 .... 71 K5
    BERK HP4 .... 48 C7
    HWYN HP13 .... 78 C3
    NTHWD HA6 .... 85 M7
Hillside Ri *NTHWD* HA6 .... 85 M8
Hillside Rd *FLKWH/TG* HP10 .. 68 F8
    LBUZ LU7 .... 27 H4
    MLW SL7 .... 97 K2
    NTHWD HA6 .... 85 M8
    RKW/CH/CXG WD3 .... 73 H6
    RNHPTN NN7 .... 126 B5
Hills La *MDHD* SL6 .... 98 B3
    NTHWD HA6 .... 85 M8
Hill St *BRACKY* NN13 .... 8 D7
The Hill *AMSS* HP7 .... 70 B7
    BRACKY NN13 .... 140 A2
Hilltop *RAYLW* HP18 .... 181 L1
Hilltop Av *BUCK/WIN* MK18 .. 11 M4
Hill Top La *CHNR* OX39 .... 185 J6
Hilltop Rd *BERK* HP4 .... 48 B7
Hill Vw *BERK* HP4 .... 47 M4
    HADM HP17 .... 50 C5
Hillview *NPAG* MK16 .... 133 P9
Hill Vw *RAYLW* HP18 .... 179 Q1
Hillview *SKCH* HP14 .... 66 B5
Hill View La *LBUZ* LU7 .... 29 L4
Hill Vw Rd *HWYN* HP13 .... 78 C2
Hill Wy *AMSS* HP7 .... 71 G4
Hillway *RMKS/WB* MK17 ...... 144 D4
Hill Waye *CFSP/GDCR* SL9 .... 92 E5
Hillwerke *CHNR* OX39 .... 184 F4
Hill Wy *EAG/OLD/WTN* MK6 .. 18 C5
Hilperton Rd *SL* SL1 .... 111 K6
Hilton Av *AYL* HP20 .... 3 H7
Hilton Cl *UX/CGN* UB8 .... 104 A7
Hilton Ct *BTCHLY* MK3 .... 22 C4
Hilton Rd *HWYN* HP13 .... 5 H3
    UX/CGN UB8 .... 104 B6
Himalayan Wy *WATW* WD18 .. 75 L7
Himley Gn *LBUZ* LU7 .... 26 E8
Hindemith Gdns
    WTR/OFPK MK7 .... 24 A5
Hindhay La *MDHD* SL6 .... 98 A1
Hindmead Ct *UX/CGN* UB8 .. 115 G2
Hindhead Knoll
    WTR/OFPK MK7 .... 19 L8
Hinds Wy *AYLS* HP21 .... 2 B9
Hinkley Cl *DEN/HRF* UB9 ...... 94 B3
Hinksey La *DTCH/LGLY* SL3 .. 113 G7
Hinton Cl *HWYN* HP13 .... 4 F2
    LBUZ LU7 .... 27 L7
Hinton Ct *BTCHLY* MK3 .... 22 C4
Hinton Rd *BRACKY* NN13 ...... 8 D8
    SL SL1 .... 110 D4
    UX/CGN UB8 .... 104 B6
Hipwell Ct *OLN* MK46 .... 128 B11
Hitcham La *SL* SL1 .... 99 H8
Hitcham Rd *SL* SL1 .... 110 M1
Hitchens Cl *HHW* HP1 .... 49 L6
Hither Meadow
    CFSP/GDCR SL9 .... 82 D7
Hiving's HI *CSHM* HP5 .... 54 F7
Hivings Pk *CSHM* HP5 .... 54 F7
Hoathly Ms *WTR/OFPK* MK7 .. 19 L6
Hobart Cl *HWYN* HP13 .... 78 C1
Hobart Crs *WLLN* MK15 .... 14 E8
Hobart Rd *HWYN* HP13 .... 78 C1
Hobbis Dr *MDHD* SL6 .... 107 M8

Hobbs End HEN RG9 ... 190 E6
Hobbshill Rd
  GTMIS/PWD HP16 ... 61 G4
Hobsons Wk TRING HP23 ... 37 L5
Hockeridge Vw BERK HP4 ... 47 L7
Hockett La MDHD SL6 ... 98 E8
Hockley La SLN SL2 ... 102 A3
Hockliffe Brae WTR/OFPK MK7 ... 23 M1
Hockliffe Rd LBUZ LU7 ... 27 J7
Hockliffe St LBUZ LU7 ... 27 H7
Hodder La EMV/FZ MK4 ... 21 M4
Hodds Wood Rd CSHM HP5 ... 65 H4
Hodgedale La WAR/TWY RG10 ... 106 C8
Hodge La WDSR SL4 * ... 121 H7
Hodge Lea La WOLV MK12 ... 16 F2
Hodgemoor Vw CSTG HP8 ... 81 L3
Hodges Ms HWYW HP12 ... 77 H8
Hodges Wy WATW WD18 ... 75 M7
Hoe Meadow BEAC HP9 ... 80 B6
Hogarth Cl SL SL1 ... 110 D4
  UX/CGN UB8 ... 104 C8
Hogarths Ct
  CNH/GTH/TMA MK8 ... 17 J5
Hogback Wood Rd BEAC HP9 ... 80 A6
Hogfair La SL SL1 ... 110 B1
Hogg La HAZ/HG HP15 ... 69 J4
Hog Hall La BERK HP4 ... 170 H9
Hog La CSHM HP5 ... 55 G1
Hogoak La WDSR SL4 ... 118 F7
Hogpits Bottom HHS/BOV HP3 ... 64 F3
Hogshaw Rd BUCK/WIN MK18 ... 158 C6
Hogtrough La
  RAYLNE/WEN HP22 ... 44 C8
Holbein Ga NTHWD HA6 ... 85 K5
Holborn Crs EMV/FZ MK4 ... 21 J7
Holdgate Cl BRACKY NN13 ... 8 D5
Holdom Av DBGH MK1 ... 23 G4
Holes La OLN MK46 ... 128 B10
Holiday La RMKN MK19 ... 131 L6
Holland Cl CHNR OX39 ... 184 G2
  RAYLNE/WEN HP22 ... 44 A6
Hollandridge La HEN RG9 ... 188 B2
Holland Rd AYLW HP19 ... 2 A1
  MLW SL7 ... 97 L4
Holland Wy NPAG MK16 ... 14 F3
Holliday Cl CNH/GTH/TMA MK8 ... 17 H8
Holliday St BERK HP4 ... 48 C6
Holliers Cl CHNR OX39 ... 184 D4
  THAME OX9 ... 181 M6
Hollies Ct LBUZ LU7 ... 26 F7
The Hollies HHS/BOV HP3 ... 56 F8
  TRING HP23 ... 46 C1
Hollingdon Rd LBUZ LU7 ... 153 F11
Hollington Rd RAYLW HP18 ... 175 J12
Hollin La WOLV MK12 ... 17 H2
Hollinwell Cl BTCHLY MK3 ... 22 A5
Hollis Rd HWYN HP13 ... 78 D2
Hollister Cha SHEN MK5 ... 21 L2
Holloway Cl WDR/YW UB7 ... 124 D1
Holloway Dr BUCK/WIN MK18 ... 11 M4
Holloway La HEN RG9 ... 186 D9
  RKW/CH/CXG WD3 ... 73 G1
  WDR/YW UB7 ... 124 D3
The Holloway PRRI HP27 ... 50 C8
  RAYLNE/WEN HP22 ... 37 H6
Hollow Hill End
  BUCK/WIN MK18 ... 158 H3
Hollow Hill La IVER SLO ... 113 G4
Hollow Ri HWYN HP13 ... 5 K2
Hollow Wy CSHM HP5 ... 62 D1
Hollow Way La AMS HP6 ... 63 K6
Hollow Wd OLN MK46 ... 128 A11
Hollyberry Gv HAZ/HG HP15 ... 69 H3
Hollybush Cl BERK HP4 ... 49 J5
Hollybush Hl SLN SL2 ... 102 A3
Hollybush La AMS HP6 ... 63 J4
  HHW HP1 ... 49 L6
  IVER SLO ... 113 G3
  MDHD SL6 ... 98 A4
Hollybush Rd CSHM HP5 ... 54 F6
Hollybush Rw TRING HP23 * ... 46 C2
Holly Cl BIC OX26 ... 162 E1
  BRACKY NN13 ... 8 E5
  CNH/GTH/TMA MK8 ... 17 H8
  SLN SL2 ... 101 H2
Holly Crs WDSR SL4 ... 120 C5
Hollycroft Cl WDR/YW UB7 ... 124 F2
Hollycroft Gdns WDR/YW UB7 ... 124 F2
Holly Dr AYLS HP21 ... 34 D8
  BERK HP4 ... 48 C7
  MDHD SL6 ... 108 E2
  WDSR SL4 ... 121 K8
Holly End SKCH HP14 ... 67 H6
Hollyfield TRING HP23 ... 38 B5
Hollyfield Ct TRING HP23 ... 38 B5
Holly Gdns WDR/YW UB7 ... 124 F2
Holly Green La PRRI HP27 ... 183 K11
Holly Hedges La HHS/BOV HP3 ... 65 H1
Hollyhock Cl HHW HP1 ... 49 K6
Holly Pl WYM HP11 ... 78 F7
Hollytree Cl CFSP/GDCR SL9 ... 82 D5
  CSHM HP5 ... 64 A2
Holly Tree La RAYLW HP18 ... 176 C4
Holly Wk RMKS/WB MK17 ... 144 H4
Holmanleaze MDHD SL6 ... 108 F3
Holman St AYLW HP19 ... 34 B3
Holmbury Gdns HYS/HAR UB3 ... 115 L4
Holmdale SLN SL2 ... 112 B4
Holmer Green Rd
  HAZ/HG HP15 ... 68 F6
Holmer La HWYW HP12 ... 87 H4
Holmer Pl HAZ/HG HP15 ... 69 H3
Holmer St HWYW HP12 * ... 87 G3
Holmers Farm Wy
  HWYW HP12 ... 87 G3
Holmers La HWYW HP12 ... 87 H3
Holmewood EMV/FZ MK4 ... 22 B2
Holmfield Cl
  EAG/OLD/WTN MK6 ... 23 C1
Holm Ga CNH/GTH/TMA MK8 ... 17 K6
Holm Gv HGDN/ICK UB10 ... 104 F5
Holmlea Rd DTCH/LGLY SL3 ... 122 D4
Holmlea Wk DTCH/LGLY SL3 ... 122 B4
Holm Oak Pk WATW WD18 * ... 75 M6
Holmsdale Cl IVER SLO ... 113 L3
Holm Wy BIC OX26 ... 162 E1
Holmwood Cl MDHD SL6 ... 108 A4
Holst Crs WTR/OFPK MK7 ... 23 M2
Holt Gv SHEN MK5 ... 17 K6
Holton Hl EMV/FZ MK4 ... 21 M4
Holton Rd HGDN/ICK UB10 ... 11 L4
Holts Gn RMKS/WB MK17 ... 24 D5
Holtspur Av FLKWH/TG HP10 ... 89 L4
Holtspur Cl BEAC HP9 * ... 89 M2
Holtspur La FLKWH/TG HP10 ... 89 L4
Holtspur Pde BEAC HP9 * ... 89 M2
Holtspur Top La BEAC HP9 ... 89 M1
Holtspur Wy BEAC HP9 ... 89 M1
The Holt BUCK/WIN MK18 ... 11 M7
Holyhead Crs EMV/FZ MK4 ... 21 M6
Holyport Rd MDHD SL6 ... 119 G2

Holyport St MDHD SL6 ... 118 F2
Holyrood CNH/GTH/TMA MK8 ... 17 H6
Holy Thorn La SHEN MK5 ... 21 J1
Holywell Cl DUN/WHIP LU6 ... 171 Q7
Holywell Gdns HWYN HP13 * ... 78 D3
Holywell Pl
  EAG/OLD/WTN MK6 ... 18 F4
Holywell Rd DUN/WHIP LU6 ... 171 Q7
Home Cl BTCHLY MK3 ... 22 E4
  RAYLNE/WEN HP22 ... 43 L4
Home Farm RMKS/WB MK17 ... 153 J5
  TRING HP23 * ... 37 M8
Home Farm Cl RBICS/W OX25 ... 162 H11
  OLN MK46 ... 133 M3
Home Farm La
  RMKS/WB MK17 ... 24 E4
Home Farm Rd BERK HP4 ... 47 J3
Home Farm Wy
  DTCH/LGLY SL3 ... 102 B6
  HHS/BOV HP3 ... 57 H7
Home Fld AYLW HP19 ... 177 R3
Home Fld WTR/OFPK MK7 ... 23 K3
Homefield Cl SKCH HP14 ... 186 H1
Homefield Rd
  RKW/CH/CXG WD3 ... 73 J5
Homelands Gdns
  HAZ/HG HP15 ... 68 C2
Homelands Wy HEN RG9 ... 190 G5
Home Meadow SLN SL2 ... 101 H7
Home Meadow Dr
  FLKWH/TG HP10 ... 89 G3
Homers Rd WDSR SL4 ... 120 C4
Homeside Cl MDHD SL6 ... 98 D8
Homestall BUCK/WIN MK18 ... 11 L8
Homestall Ct SHEN MK5 ... 17 K7
Homestead Farm HADM HP17 ... 177 H6
Homestead Pl AYLW HP19 ... 177 R2
Homestead Rd MDHD SL6 ... 108 C6
The Homestead HAZ/HG HP15 ... 68 B1
  HWYW HP12 ... 87 H3
  SHEN MK5 ... 17 K8
  THAME OX9 ... 181 M5
Homestead Wy AYLW HP19 ... 177 R2
Home Wy RKW/CH/CXG WD3 ... 83 L1
Homewood DTCH/LGLY SL3 ... 112 C3
Hondur Cl AYL HP20 * ... 3 L1
Honey Banks
  RAYLNE/WEN HP22 ... 44 B6
Honeycroft Hl HGDN/ICK UB10 ... 104 D5
Honeycross Rd HHW HP1 ... 49 K8
Honey Hl HGDN/ICK UB10 ... 104 E5
  OLN MK46 ... 133 N3
Honey Hill Dr RMKN MK19 ... 137 M9
Honey La MDHD SL6 ... 106 D4
Honeysuckle Cl BIC OX26 ... 162 E1
  IVER SLO ... 113 H3
Honeysuckle Fld CSHM HP5 ... 63 H5
Honeysuckle Rd HAZ/HG HP15 ... 68 E3
Honey Wy SKCH HP14 ... 67 G6
Honeywick La DUN/WHIP LU6 ... 92 F1
Honiton Ct WTR/OFPK MK7 * ... 19 M7
Honor End La
  GTMIS/PWD HP16 ... 59 M5
Honor Rd GTMIS/PWD HP16 ... 60 B4
Honorwood Cl
  GTMIS/PWD HP16 ... 60 A4
Honour End La
  GTMIS/PWD HP16 ... 60 A3
Honours Md HHS/BOV HP3 * ... 56 F6
Hoods Farm Cl
  RAYLNE/WEN HP22 ... 35 H2
The Hooke WLLN MK15 ... 15 G7
Hooper Dr UX/CGN UB8 ... 115 G2
Hooper Ga WLLN MK15 ... 14 F7
Hopcraft Cl RBICS/W OX25 ... 173 J3
Hop Gdns HEN RG9 ... 190 G4
Hopkins Cl MKV MK10 ... 19 K4
Hopkins Ct MKV MK10 ... 3 J1
Hoppers Meadow SHEN MK5 ... 17 K6
Hoppers Wy HAZ/HG HP15 ... 68 C2
Hoppner Rd YEAD UB4 ... 105 J7
Hopton Gv NPAG MK16 ... 15 J3
Hopton Rd THAME OX9 ... 181 P5
Hordern Cl HADM HP17 ... 176 C12
Hornbeam NPAG MK16 ... 14 D3
Hornbeam Cl HWYW HP12 ... 87 H2
  LBUZ LU7 * ... 27 K6
Hornbeam Gdns
  DTCH/LGLY SL3 ... 111 M7
Hornbeam Rd BIC OX26 ... 162 E1
Hornbeam Wy
  RAYLNE/WEN HP22 ... 43 H2
Hornbill Cl UX/CGN UB8 ... 114 C3
Hornby Cha EMV/FZ MK4 ... 21 L4
Horne Cl RBICN OX27 ... 154 F11
Hornhill Rd
  RKW/CH/CXG WD3 ... 83 H5
Horn La STSTR MK11 ... 16 A1
Horns La HWYW HP12 ... 86 F2
Horn St BUCK/WIN MK18 ... 151 J10
Horseblock La CSHM HP5 ... 46 D8
Horsecroft Rd HHW HP1 ... 57 H1
Horsefair Gn STSTR MK11 ... 16 A1
Horseguards Dr MDHD SL6 ... 109 G3
Horse Hl CSHM HP5 ... 64 C3
Horsemoor Cl DTCH/LGLY SL3 ... 112 F8
Horsemoor La AMSS HP7 ... 70 A7
Horsenden La PRRI HP27 ... 183 P11
Horsenden Rd HWYN HP13 ... 78 E5
Horsepool La RMKS/WB MK17 ... 145 K7
Horseshoe Cl LBUZ LU7 ... 169 L7
Horseshoe Dr UX/CGN UB8 ... 114 F7
Horseshoe Hl SL SL1 ... 100 B2
Horseshoe Rd SKCH HP14 ... 185 M11
Horseshoes Pl THAME OX9 ... 181 P7
Horsleys RKW/CH/CXG WD3 ... 83 J3
Horton Av THAME OX9 ... 181 P7
Horton Bridge Rd
  WDR/YW UB7 ... 114 E5
Horton Cl AYLW HP19 ... 109 H1
  WDR/YW UB7 ... 114 E5
Horton Gdns DTCH/LGLY SL3 * ... 122 E6
Horton Ga GTLIN MK14 ... 14 C8
Horton Pk WDR/YW UB7 * ... 126 A8
Horton Pk NPAG NN7 ... 126 E4
Horton Rd DTCH/LGLY SL3 ... 122 D5
  LBUZ LU7 ... 169 M4
  RNHPTN NN7 ... 126 C4
  STWL/WRAY TW19 ... 123 M3
Hortonsfield Rd TOW NN12 ... 137 N1
Horwood Ct DBGH MK1 ... 23 G5
Hoskins Cl HYS/HAR UB3 ... 125 L1

Hospital Circular Rd
  RAYLNE/WEN HP22 ... 44 C4
Hospital Hl CSHM HP5 ... 63 H3
Hotch Cft RBEDW MK43 ... 139 M3
Hotley Bottom La
  GTMIS/PWD HP16 ... 60 B2
Houghton Ct
  CNH/GTH/TMA MK8 ... 17 J6
Housman Cl NPAG MK16 ... 14 D1
Howard Agne Cl
  HHS/BOV HP3 ... 56 F6
Howard Av AYLS HP21 ... 35 G8
Howard Cl BNEND SL8 ... 88 F7
Howard Crs BEAC HP9 ... 81 H5
Howards Dr BEAC HP9 ... 81 H5
  CSHM HP5 ... 55 G7
Howards Dr HHW HP1 ... 49 L4
Howards Thicket
  CFSP/GDCR SL9 ... 92 B8
Howards Wood Dr
  CFSP/GDCR SL9 ... 92 C8
Howarth Rd MDHD SL6 ... 108 F4
Howcut La RNHPTN NN7 ... 127 L4
Howe Ct MKV MK10 ... 19 K3
Howe Dr BEAC HP9 ... 80 C5
Howe Hill La HAZ/HG HP15 ... 69 G2
Howell Hill Cl LBUZ LU7 ... 169 J1
Howe Rock Pl EMV/FZ MK4 ... 21 L5
Howes Cl BIC OX26 ... 162 A2
Howitt Dr BDWL MK13 ... 13 L7
Howland Pl RMKS/WB MK17 ... 145 J11
Howland Rd THAME OX9 ... 181 Q8
Howletts Cl AYLW HP19 ... 177 R3
Howletts La RSLP HA4 ... 95 H5
How's Rd UX/CGN UB8 ... 104 B6
Hoylake Cl BTCHLY MK3 ... 22 A7
Hoylake Crs UX/CGN UB8 ... 95 L5
Hoyton Ga CNH/GTH/TMA MK8 ... 17 G8
Hubbard Cl BUCK/WIN MK18 ... 142 A9
Hubbards Cl UX/CGN UB8 ... 115 G5
Hubert Day Cl BEAC HP9 ... 80 C7
Hubert Rd DTCH/LGLY SL3 ... 112 C7
Huckleberry Cl
  WTR/OFPK MK7 ... 19 L8
Hudnall La BERK HP4 ... 40 C4
Hudson La CNH/GTH/TMA MK8 ... 17 G4
Hudson Ms AYLW HP19 ... 177 P2
Hudson Pl DTCH/LGLY SL3 ... 122 E1
Hudsons Av CMH/DHRF UB9 ... 93 L5
Hudson St BIC OX26 ... 162 C3
Huesden Wy CFSP/GDCR SL9 ... 92 E2
Hughenden Av HWYN HP13 ... 4 F3
Hughenden Cl MDHD SL6 ... 108 D4
Hughenden Gn AYLS HP21 ... 42 D2
Hughenden Rd HWYN HP13 ... 5 J1
  SL SL1 ... 111 J3
Hughes Cft BTCHLY MK3 ... 22 C7
Hugh Park Cl
  CNH/GTH/TMA MK8 ... 17 H8
  SHEN MK5 ... 6 B9
Hugo Cl MKVW WD18 ... 75 K5
Hulbert End AYLS HP21 ... 35 J8
Hulcombe Wk AYL HP20 * ... 3 G1
Hull Cl AYLS HP21 ... 34 D8
  SL SL1 ... 111 H6
Hulton Dr OLN MK46 ... 133 N2
Humber Cl WDR/YW UB7 ... 114 C5
Humber Dr AYLS HP21 ... 42 B1
Humber Wy BTCHLY MK3 ... 22 B5
  DTCH/LGLY SL3 ... 112 F8
Hume Cl BDWL MK13 ... 13 L7
Hume Wy RSLP HA4 ... 95 M5
Humphreys Cl
  RAYLNE/WEN HP22 ... 33 J1
Humphrey Talbot Av
  DUN/WHIP LU6 ... 171 N7
Humphries Dr BRACKY NN13 ... 8 C6
Hundred Acres La AMSS HP7 ... 71 J3
Hungerford Av SLN SL2 ... 111 K2
Hungerford Dr MDHD SL6 ... 98 D7
Hunsbury Cha MKV MK10 ... 19 K3
Hunsdon Cl GTLIN MK14 ... 14 C8
Hunstanton Cl DTCH/LGLY SL3 ... 123 H3
Hunstanton Wy BTCHLY MK3 ... 22 A6
Hunt Cl BIC OX26 ... 162 D4
Hunt Ct SHEN MK5 ... 17 K6
Hunter Cl MDHD SL6 ... 106 D4
Hunters Cha
  HHS/BOV HP3 ... 56 F8
  TRING HP23 ... 38 A5
Hunters Gv HYS/HAR UB3 ... 115 M5
Hunters Hl HWYN HP13 ... 78 E5
Hunters Pk BERK HP4 ... 48 D5
Hunters Point CHNR OX39 ... 184 E4
Hunters Reach BDWL MK13 ... 13 K3
Hunter St MDHD SL6 ... 106 E2
Huntercombe Cl MDHD SL6 ... 110 A3
Huntercombe La North SL SL1 ... 110 A3
Huntercombe La South
  MDHD SL6 ... 110 A5
Hunter Dr WEAT MK2 ... 22 F7
Hunters Cl CSHM HP5 ... 62 F1
  HHS/BOV HP3 ... 56 F8
  TRING HP23 ... 38 A5
Huntingbrooke
  CNH/GTH/TMA MK8 ... 17 J6
Huntingdon Crs BTCHLY MK3 ... 21 M8
Huntington Pl DTCH/LGLY SL3 ... 113 G7
Huntley Rd HWYN HP13 ... 68 B8
Huntley Crs CMK MK9 ... 7 L2
Hunt Rd HWYN HP13 ... 78 D4
  THAME OX9 ... 181 Q7
Hunts Hill La SKCH HP14 ... 77 J1
Huntsman Gv GTLIN MK14 ... 14 D4
Huntsmans Cl BERK HP4 ... 171 K9
Huntsmill Rd HHW HP1 ... 49 L5
Huntswood La MDHD SL6 ... 99 L5
Hurley Cft BTCHLY MK3 ... 22 A3
Hurley High St MDHD SL6 ... 106 E2
Hurley La MDHD SL6 ... 107 G3
Hurlstone Gv EMV/FZ MK4 ... 22 A3
Hurricane Wy DTCH/LGLY SL3 ... 123 G1
Hurstfield Crs YEAD UB4 ... 115 K2
Hurstfield Dr MDHD SL6 ... 110 A3
Hurst Pl NTHWD HA6 ... 85 G8
Hurst Rd SL SL1 ... 110 C2
Hurworth Av DTCH/LGLY SL3 ... 112 B7
Hutchings Cl SHEN MK5 ... 17 K6
Hutton Av EAG/OLD/WTN MK6 ... 7 H4
Hutton Wy RMKS/WB MK17 ... 144 A5
Huxley Cl BIC OX26 ... 162 B3
  NPAG MK16 ... 14 C2
  SLN SL2 ... 112 A3
Huxtable Gdns MDHD SL6 ... 108 B3
Hyacinth Dr HGDN/ICK UB10 ... 104 D5
Hyatts Yd CSHM HP5 ... 63 G3
Hychenden Cl SKCH HP14 ... 67 K8
Hyde Cl NPAG MK16 ... 14 C2
Hyde Gn BEAC HP9 ... 80 E7

Hyde Heath Rd
  GTMIS/PWD HP16 ... 61 M3
Hyde La GTMIS/PWD HP16 ... 61 J6
  HHS/BOV HP3 ... 56 F6
Hyde Mdw HHS/BOV HP3 ... 56 F7
The Hyde WAT WD17 ... 75 M4
The Hyde MDHD SL6 * ... 108 E2
  RAYLNE/WEN HP22 ... 43 L8
Hyde Wy HYS/HAR UB3 ... 115 L8
Hydrus Dr LBUZ LU7 ... 27 L8
Hylle Cl WDSR SL4 ... 120 D4
Hylton Rd HWYW HP12 ... 77 H7
Hyrons Cl AMS HP6 ... 71 K1
Hyrons La AMS HP6 ... 71 J1
The Hythe CNH/GTH/TMA MK8 ... 17 G3

I

Ibstone Av BDWL MK13 ... 6 C1
Ibstone Rd BDWL MK13 ... 186 F6
Ickenham Cl RSLP HA4 ... 95 H3
Ickenham Rd RSLP HA4 ... 95 J7
Ickford Rd THAME OX9 ... 180 A6
Icknield Cl CHNR OX39 ... 184 C6
  RAYLNE/WEN HP22 ... 44 B5
Icknield Gn TRING HP23 ... 37 M4
Icknield Wy PRRI HP27 ... 58 D2
Icknieldway SKCH HP14 ... 185 L3
Icknield Wy TRING HP23 ... 39 G1
Icknield Way Pth
  DUN/WHIP LU6 ... 171 N1
Ilfley Cl AYLW HP19 ... 100 C5
Ilchester Cl MDHD SL6 ... 108 B5
Ilex Cl HAZ/HG HP15 ... 69 H4
Illingworth WDSR SL4 ... 120 D6
Illingworth Pl
  EAG/OLD/WTN MK6 ... 7 H9
Imperial Ct HEN RG9 ... 191 J9
  WDSR SL4 ... 120 F6
Imperial Rd WDSR SL4 ... 120 F6
India Rd SL SL1 ... 112 A6
Ingleglen SLN SL2 ... 101 G3
Ingleside DTCH/LGLY SL3 ... 123 K4
Ingleton Cl BDWL MK13 ... 6 C1
Ingram Av AYLS HP21 ... 35 H8
Inkerman Dr HAZ/HG HP15 ... 69 C5
Inkerman Rd WDSR SL4 ... 110 E8
Inkerman Ter CSHM HP5 ... 63 H4
Inner Ring East HTHAIR TW6 ... 125 C6
Innes Ct CNH/GTH/TMA MK8 ... 17 C8
Inn Farm Ct NPAG MK16 ... 133 L11
Innholder Ct GTLIN MK14 ... 14 C8
Innings Ga HEN RG9 ... 189 P1
Innings La MDHD SL6 ... 117 J9
Insall Cl LBUZ LU7 ... 29 L1
Institute Rd MDHD SL6 ... 109 L3
  MLW SL7 ... 97 K5
Intalbury Av AYLW HP19 ... 167 R12
In The Ray MDHD SL6 ... 109 G2
Invereve Pl EMV/FZ MK4 ... 21 H4
Inverness Ct BTCHLY MK3 ... 22 C4
Inwood Cl MDHD SL6 ... 118 D1
Iona Crs SL SL1 ... 110 D3
Ipswich Rd SL SL1 ... 110 E3
Ireland Ct WTR/OFPK MK7 ... 144 A5
Ireton Ct THAME OX9 ... 181 N5
Iris Ct AYLS HP21 ... 42 A1
Ironbridge Rd STKPK UB11 * ... 114 F5
Iron Bridge Rd North
  STKPK UB11 ... 114 F5
Iron Bridge Rd South
  STKPK UB11 ... 114 F5
Ironmonger Ct GTLIN MK14 ... 14 C8
Irvine Dr RAYLNE/WEN HP22 ... 43 C4
Irving Crs LBUZ LU7 ... 169 M6
Irving Dl WTR/OFPK MK7 ... 144 B5
Irwin Ct HGDN/ICK UB10 ... 104 A6
Isaacson Dr WTR/OFPK MK7 ... 19 M8
Isis Cl AYLS HP21 ... 42 A1
  RSLP HA4 ... 95 H5
Isis Wy BNEND SL8 ... 89 G6
The Island BUCK/WIN MK18 ... 149 L12
Isle of Wight La
  DUN/WHIP LU6 ... 171 Q3
Islet Pk MDHD SL6 ... 99 H7
Islet Park Dr MDHD SL6 ... 99 H7
Islet Rd MDHD SL6 ... 99 H7
Islington Gv MKV MK10 ... 19 K3
Ismay Ct SLN SL2 ... 111 K3
Ivanhoe Cl UX/CGN UB8 ... 114 C3
Iveagh Cl NTHWD HA6 ... 95 H5
Iverdale Cl IVER SLO ... 113 H4
Iver La IVER SLO ... 113 L2
Iver Ldg IVER SLO ... 113 L2
Iverna Gdns
  EBED/NFELT TW14 ... 115 J8
Ives Rd DTCH/LGLY SL3 ... 112 F7
Ivinghoe Br LBUZ LU7 ... 169 P6
Ivinghoe Rd
  RKW/CH/CXG WD3 ... 73 L8
Ivinghoe Vw AYL HP20 * ... 3 J8
Ivinghoe Wy DUN/WHIP LU6 ... 170 F1
Ivins Rd BEAC HP9 ... 89 M1
Ivy Bridge Cl UX/CGN UB8 ... 104 D8
Ivy Cl BUCK/WIN MK18 ... 142 A9
  DUN/WHIP LU6 ... 170 D5
  MDHD SL6 ... 118 D3
  NPAG MK16 ... 15 J2
  PRRI HP27 ... 183 P9
Ivy Cots HGDN/ICK UB10 * ... 104 B6
Ivy Crs SL SL1 ... 110 E4
Ivy House La BERK HP4 ... 48 D6
Ivyhouse Rd HGDN/ICK UB10 ... 105 G1
Ivy La LBUZ LU7 ... 161 K1
  RAYLNE/WEN HP22 ... 44 A6
  RMKS/WB MK17 ... 152 H3
  SL SL1 ... 111 H6
Ivy Lea RKW/CH/CXG WD3 * ... 83 M1
Ivy Pl SKCH HP14 ... 86 B1
Ivy Wk NTHWD HA6 ... 85 H5

J

Jackets La DEN/HRF UB9 ... 84 F7
Jacks Cl OLN MK46 ... 128 C4
Jacks La DEN/HRF UB9 ... 83 M8
  RBEDW MK43 ... 129 P9
Jackson Ct HAZ/HG HP15 ... 68 C7
Jackson Rd AYLW HP19 ... 167 R11
  HGDN/ICK UB10 ... 104 C3
Jacksons Cl DUN/WHIP LU6 ... 170 F1
Jacob Cl WDSR SL4 ... 120 C1
Jacob Ct SLN MK14 ... 13 L4
Jakeman Wy AYLS HP21 ... 42 B9
Jamaica EAG/OLD/WTN MK6 ... 18 D1
James Cl MLW SL7 ... 97 L2
James Martin Cl DEN/HRF UB9 ... 93 M3
James Meadow
  DTCH/LGLY SL3 ... 122 E2

James Rd SKCH HP14 ... 86 A2
James St WDSR SL4 ... 121 J4
James Wy DBGH MK1 ... 22 F5
Jane Morbey Rd THAME OX9 ... 181 N7
Jansel Sq AYLS HP21 ... 35 G8
Japan Ct BUCK/WIN MK18 ... 142 A10
Japonica La WLLN MK15 ... 14 F9
Jarman Cl RAYLNE/WEN HP22 ... 168 C3
Jarvis Cl AYLS HP21 ... 34 F3
Jarvis' La BIC OX26 ... 162 C4
Jasmin Cl NTHWD HA6 ... 85 L8
Jasmine Cl AYLS HP21 ... 42 F2
Jasmine Crs PRRI HP27 ... 58 A3
Jasmine Pl BIC OX26 ... 162 C1
Jasmine Ter WDR/YW UB7 ... 114 F6
Jasmine Wk CSHM HP5 ... 62 F1
Jasmin Wy HHW HP1 ... 49 K6
Jasons Hl CSHM HP5 ... 56 A8
Jay Cl BIC OX26 ... 162 F6
Jeeves Rd EAG/OLD/WTN MK6 ... 18 F7
Jefferies Rd HADM HP17 ... 177 L5
Jefferson Cl DTCH/LGLY SL3 ... 112 F6
Jefferson Wy THAME OX9 ... 181 P7
Jeffrey Wk AYLW HP19 ... 177 R5
Jeffries Ct BNEND SL8 ... 88 F8
Jellicoe Rd WATW WD18 ... 75 M7
Jenkins Cl SHEN MK5 ... 17 J8
Jenkins Ct RAYLNE/WEN HP22 ... 168 C3
Jenkins La TRING HP23 ... 45 G7
Jenna Wy NPAG MK16 ... 15 K3
Jenner Rd AYLS HP21 ... 42 D1
Jennery La SL SL1 ... 100 B8
Jennings Cl GTLIN MK14 ... 13 M7
Jennings Fld FLKWH/TG HP10 ... 90 A7
Jerome Cl MLW SL7 ... 97 L2
Jerrard Ct LBUZ LU7 ... 29 K1
Jersey Rd WOLV MK12 ... 12 F7
Jesse's La RAYLW HP18 ... 175 L12
The Jetty RNHPTN NN7 ... 126 B3
Job's La MDHD SL6 ... 98 A2
Jocketts Hl HHW HP1 ... 49 L7
Jocketts Rd HHW HP1 ... 49 L8
Joel St NTHWD HA6 ... 95 M1
  PIN HA5 ... 95 M2
John Bunyan Trail
  RBEDW MK43 ... 145 N3
  RMKS/WB MK17 ... 139 L10
John Clare Cl BRACKY NN13 ... 8 E4
John Hall Wy HWYW HP12 ... 87 H3
John Hampden Wy
  GTMIS/PWD HP16 ... 60 A3
Johns La CSHM HP5 ... 55 J1
Johnson Av BRACKY NN13 ... 8 B6
Johnson Dr LBUZ LU7 ... 29 J1
Johnson Rd OLN MK46 ... 86 A1
Johnsons Rd OLN MK46 ... 128 A10
Johnston Pl
  EAG/OLD/WTN MK6 ... 7 G8
John Taylor Ct SL SL1 ... 111 G8
Joiner's Cl CFSP/GDCR SL9 ... 82 E7
Joiners La CFSP/GDCR SL9 ... 82 D8
Joiners Wy CFSP/GDCR SL9 ... 82 D8
  OLN MK46 ... 128 H6
Jonathans EAG/OLD/WTN MK6 ... 18 D8
Jonathans Ct
  EAG/OLD/WTN MK6 * ... 18 D8
Jones Cl BRACKY NN13 ... 8 C6
Jones Wy SL SL1 ... 91 J8
Jonson Cl YEAD UB4 ... 115 K2
Jordans La BEAC HP9 ... 81 K7
Jordans Rd RKW/CH/CXG WD3 ... 73 M8
Jordans Wy BEAC HP9 ... 81 L6
Joules Ct SHEN MK5 ... 21 H1
Journeys End SLN SL2 ... 111 K2
Jubilee Arch WDSR SL4 ... 121 J4
Jubilee Gdns MDHD SL6 ... 117 G2
Jubilee Rd SKCH HP14 ... 187 J3
  WATN WD24 ... 75 M1
  WYM HP11 ... 4 D5
Jubilee Wy DTCH/LGLY SL3 ... 122 B3
Judge Heath La HYS/HAR UB3 ... 115 H3
Judges La LBUZ LU7 ... 27 G8
Juniper Cl HAZ/HG HP15 ... 69 G3
  RKW/CH/CXG WD3 ... 84 C3
Juniper Ct NTHWD HA6 ... 85 M6
  SL SL1 ... 111 M6
Juniper Dr HWYW HP12 ... 87 H1
  MDHD SL6 ... 109 G2
  RAYLNE/WEN HP22 ... 43 H2
  WTR/OFPK MK7 ... 19 L2
Juniper Ga RKW/CH/CXG WD3 ... 84 C2
Juniper Gn HHW HP1 ... 49 K7
Juniper Gv WAT WD17 ... 75 M1
Juniper La FLKWH/TG HP10 ... 89 L1
Juniper Rd MLW SL7 ... 97 J1
Juniper Wy HYS/HAR UB3 ... 115 J4
Jupiter Dr LBUZ LU7 ... 27 L6
Juson's Glebe
  RAYLNE/WEN HP22 ... 44 B5

K

Kalman Gdns WTR/OFPK MK7 ... 144 A5
Kaplan Cl SHEN MK5 ... 21 L1
Karenza SKCH HP14 ... 186 H1
Katherine Cl FLKWH/TG HP10 * ... 79 H2
  WTR/OFPK MK7 ... 23 K2
Katrine Pl WEAT MK2 ... 153 Q1
Kaybridge Cl HWYN HP13 ... 78 E5
Kay Cl TRING HP23 ... 37 M5
Kaywood Cl DTCH/LGLY SL3 ... 112 B7
Keach Cl BUCK/WIN MK18 ... 151 K9
Keasden Ct EMV/FZ MK4 ... 21 L4
Keaton Cl CNH/GTH/TMA MK8 ... 17 G7
Keats Cl AYLS HP21 ... 34 E8
  BIC OX26 ... 162 B6
  NPAG MK16 ... 14 D2
  WYM HP11 ... 4 F7
  YEAD UB4 ... 115 M2
Keats La WDSR SL4 ... 121 J2
Keats Wy BTCHLY MK3 ... 22 C7
  WDR/YW UB7 ... 114 C8
Keble Cl AYLW HP19 ... 2 A6
Keble Rd BIC OX26 ... 162 B6
  BRACKY NN13 ... 8 C6
  MDHD SL6 ... 108 C2
Keel Dr SL SL1 ... 111 H6
Keeler Cl WDSR SL4 ... 120 D6
Keel Wy EMV/FZ MK4 ... 21 G3
Keen Av AYLW HP19 ... 177 R2
Keensacre IVER SLO ... 113 J3
Keens La CHNR OX39 ... 184 D4
Keepers Cl LBUZ LU7 ... 169 M7
Keepers Farm Cl WDSR SL4 ... 120 C5
Keep Hl WYM HP11 ... 78 B6
Keep Hill Dr WYM HP11 ... 78 C6

Keep Hill Rd *WYM* HP11 .... 78 C5
Keilder Cl *HGDN/ICK* UB10 .. 104 F7
Keinches La
  RAYLNE/WEN HP22 ... 159 R12
Keir Hardie Wy *YEAD* UB4 ... 105 M8
Keith Park Rd *HGDN/ICK* UB10 104 M8
Keith Rd *HYS/HAR* UB3 ...... 115 K7
Kelf Gv *HYS/HAR* UB3 .... 115 L3
Kellan Dr *EAG/OLD/WTN* MK6... 7 E4
Keller Cl *STSTR* MK11 .... 16 E4
Kelling Wy *WYM* HP11 .... 19 K2
Kelmscott Cl *WATW* WD18 .... 75 M7
Kelmscott Crs *WATW* WD18 ... 75 M6
Kelpatrick Rd *SL* SL1 .... 110 C3
Kelsey Cl *EMV/FZ* MK4 ...... 21 J6
  MDHD 108 C7
Kelso Cl *MKV* MK3 .... 22 A8
Kelvin Cl *HWYN* HP13 .... 4 E3
Kelvin Dr *SHEN* MK5 .... 18 A8
Kemble Ct *WLLN* MK15 ...... 14 E4
Kempe Cl *DTCH/LGLY* SL3 .... 113 H8
Kemps Dr *NTHWD* HA6 ...... 85 L7
Kempton Av *AYLW* HP19 ..... 2 A5
Kempton Cl *HGDN/ICK* UB10 .. 105 H2
Kempton Gdns *BTCHLY* MK3 .. 22 A8
Kemsley Cha *SLN* SL2 .... 101 H4
Kemsley Crs *MKV* MK10 ..... 19 K2
Kenbury Cl *HGDN/ICK* UB10 .. 104 F1
Kenchester *BDWL* MK13 ..... 17 J1
Kendal Av *AYLS* HP21 .... 35 G8
  SLN SL2 .... 111 M4
  YEAD UB4 .... 105 K7
Kendal Dr *SLN* SL2 .... 111 M4
Kendal Gdns *LBUZ* LU7 ...... 26 D7
Kendall Pl *MDHD* SL6 .... 108 B6
  SHEN MK5 .... 21 H1
Kendalls Cl *HWYN* HP13 ..... 78 E5
Kendal Ms *UX/CGN* UB8 ..... 104 B6
Kendrick Rd *DTCH/LGLY* SL3 .. 112 A7
Kenilworth Cl *SL* SL1 .... 111 L7
Kenilworth Ct *WAT* WD17 .... 75 M2
Kenilworth Dr *AYLW* HP19 ... 2 E2
  BTCHLY MK3 .... 22 B7
  RKW/CH/CXG WD3 ...... 75 G5
Kenilworth Gdns *YEAD* UB4 .. 115 L2
Kennally *WDSR* SL4 .... 120 B5
Kennedy Av *WYM* HP11 ...... 78 B5
Kennedy Cl *MDHD* SL6 ...... 108 B4
  MLW SL7 .... 97 K3
  SLN SL2 .... 101 H4
Kennedy Rd *BIC* OX26 .... 162 B5
Kennels Dr *TOW* NN12 ...... 136 D3
Kennet Cl *AYLS* HP21 .... 42 B2
  BIC OX26 .... 162 C5
  HWYN HP13 .... 68 C8
Kennet Rd *BTCHLY* MK3 ..... 22 B6
Kennet Rd *BNEND* SL8 ...... 88 B6
  MDHD SL6 .... 108 B2
Kennett Rd *DTCH/LGLY* SL3 .. 113 G7
Kennington Cl *NPAG* MK16 .. 14 C3
Kensal Gn *MKV* MK10 .... 19 H5
Kensington Av *WATW* WD18 .. 75 L5
Kensington Dr
  CNH/GTH/TMA MK8 .... 17 J6
Kensworth Rd *DUN/WHIP* LU6.. R10
Kent Av *SL* SL1 .... 111 K4
Kent Cl *UX/CGN* UB8 .... 104 B4
Kent Gdns *RSLP* HA4 .... 95 M5
Kentmere Rd *AYLS* HP21 ..... 35 G7
Kenton Cl *MLW* SL7 .... 97 K4
Kentons La *WDSR* SL4 .... 120 C5
Kenton's La *WAR/TWY* RG10 .. 191 M8
Kenton Wy *YEAD* UB4 .... 105 K8
Kents Rd *GTLIN* MK14 .... 14 A6
Kent Wy *MDHD* SL6 .... 108 D1
Kenway Dr *AMSS* HP7 .... 72 A4
Kenwell Ct *WLLN* MK15 ..... 18 F3
Kenwood Cl *MDHD* SL6 ...... 107 M7
  WDR/YW UB7 .... 124 F2
Kenwood Dr
  RKW/CH/CXG WD3 ..... 83 L2
Kenwood Ga
  EAG/OLD/WTN MK6 .... 7 M4
Keppel Av *RMKN* MK19 ...... 13 G4
Keppel St *WDSR* SL4 .... 121 J5
Kepwick *CNH/GTH/TMA* MK8 .. 17 H4
Kernow Crs
  EAG/OLD/WTN MK6 .... 7 K7
Kerria Pl *BTCHLY* MK3 ...... 22 B3
Kerry Cl *AYLW* HP19 .... 167 R11
Kersey Cl *GTLIN* MK14 ...... 13 M6
Kerstin Cl *HYS/HAR* UB3 .... 115 L4
Kesters Rd *CSHM* HP5 .... 63 J3
  HWYN HP13 .... 77 H5
Keswick Ct *SL* SL1 .... 111 L4
Keswick Gdns *RSLP* HA4 ..... 95 L4
Keswick Rd *RMKN* MK19 ..... 131 M8
Ketchmere Cl *RAYLNE* HP18 .. 175 K12
Ketelbey Nook
  WTR/OFPK MK7 .... 144 A5
Ketton Cl *WLLN* MK15 .... 15 G7
Kew Cl *UX/CGN* UB8 .... 104 B7
Kew Ct *CNH/GTH/TMA* MK8 .. 17 J5
Kewferry Dr *NTHWD* HA6 .... 85 G5
Kewferry Rd *NTHWD* HA6 .... 85 H6
Kew Gv *WYM* HP11 .... 78 A6
Kew Pl *WYM* HP11 .... 78 A6
Keyes Wy *BUCK/WIN* MK18 ... 11 M4
Keynes Cl *NPAG* MK16 .... 15 H2
Keysham Av *HEST* TW5 ...... 125 H4
Keys Pl *MDHD* SL6 .... 108 B4
Khasiaberry *WTR/OFPK* MK7 .. 23 L1
Kidd Cl *CNH/GTH/TMA* MK8 .. 17 H4
Kidderminster Rd *SLN* SL2... 100 F8
Kidwells Park Dr *MDHD* SL6 . 108 B3
Kildonan Pl *WOLV* MK12 ..... 17 G2
Kilfillan Gdns *BERK* HP4 .... 47 M7
Killarney Dr *MDHD* SL6 ..... 108 C3
Kiln Av *AMS* HP6 .... 72 B1
Kiln Cl *BERK* HP4 .... 49 G4
  BUCK/WIN MK18 .... 156 H5
  GTMIS/PWD HP16 ...... 60 B3
  HYS/HAR UB3 .... 125 J2
Kiln Ct *BEAC* HP9 .... 89 M2
Kiln Croft Cl *MLW* SL7 ..... 97 M3
Kilner Rd *AYLS* HP21 .... 42 D1
Kiln Flds *MDHD* SL6 .... 99 K1
Kiln La *CSHM* HP5 .... 63 M2
  FLKWH/TG HP10 .... 89 K7
  HEN RG9 .... 190 E12
  PRRI HP27 .... 66 E1
  WOLV MK12 .... 17 G1
Kiln Pl *MDHD* SL6 .... 107 M3
Kiln Pond La *HWYN* HP13 ... 77 J3

Kiln Rd *GTMIS/PWD* HP16 ... 60 A3
  TRING HP23 .... 45 M3
Kiln Wy *NTHWD* HA6 .... 85 K6
Kilnwood *SKCH* HP14 .... 67 G5
Kilpin Gn *NPAG* MK16 .... 134 E12
Kilwinning Wy *WATW* WD18 . 19 J5
Kimbells Cl *RAYLW* HP18 .... 180 E4
Kimber Cl *WDSR* SL4 .... 120 F6
Kimberley Dr *DTCH/LGLY* SL3 112 F2
Kimbers Dr *SL* SL1 .... 100 C8
Kimber's La *BTCHLY* MK3 .... 108 D7
Kimble Cl *WATW* WD18 * 75 K7
Kimblewick Rd *HADM* HP17 .. 50 A2
Kimbolton Ct *CTLIN* MK14 ... 14 D6
Kincardine Dr *BTCHLY* MK3 .. 22 B3
Kindermann Ct *SHEN* MK5 ... 21 L1
Kindleton *GTLIN* MK14 ...... 14 C6
King Charles Cl
  BUCK/WIN MK18 .... 11 M4
King Edward Av *AYLS* HP21 .. 3 J8
King Edwards Rd *RSLP* HA4 .. 95 J7
King Edward St *BDWL* MK13 . 13 J7
  SL SL1 .... 111 J6
King Edward Vii Av *WDSR* SL4 121 J7
Kingfisher *AYLW* HP19 ...... 34 D2
Kingfisher Cl *NTHWD* HA6 ... 85 G8
Kingfisher Lure
  RKW/CH/CXG WD3 ..... 74 A5
  BUCK/WIN MK18 .... 11 M4
Kingfisher Rd *BRACKY* NN13 . 8 D4
Kingfisher Wy *BIC* OX26 .... 162 F6
King Georges St *WATW* WD18 75 K6
Kinghorn La *MDHD* SL6 ..... 98 C3
Kinghorn Pk *MDHD* SL6 ..... 98 C2
King James Wy *HEN* RG9 .... 190 F6
Kingsash Rd *AYLW* HP19 .... 177 Q2
Kings Av *BIC* OX26 .... 162 C5
  WATW WD18 .... 75 M5
Kingsbridge *EMV/FZ* MK4 .... 22 A4
Kingsbury *AYL* HP20 .... 2 F5
Kingsclere Rd *AYLS* HP21 ... 89 M2
Kings Cl *BEAC* HP9 .... 82 C2
  CSTG HP8 .... 82 A3
  NTHWD HA6 .... 85 L6
  RAYLW HP18 .... 179 Q9
Kings Cl *THAME* OX9 .... 181 N6
King's College Rd *RSLP* HA4 . 95 M4
Kings Cross *HADM* HP17 ..... 176 D9
Kingsdale Rd *BERK* HP4 ..... 47 M4
King's End *BIC* OX26 .... 162 C5
Kingsend *RSLP* HA4 .... 95 K7
Kingsey Rd *THAME* OX9 ..... 181 P5
Kings Farm La *HEN* RG9 ..... 190 A8
Kings Farm Rd
  RKW/CH/CXG WD3 ..... 73 J7
Kingsfield *WDSR* SL4 .... 120 C4
Kingsfold *BDWL* MK13 ...... 13 L7
Kingsgate *AYLW* HP19 .... 177 R2
Kings Gv *MDHD* SL6 .... 108 D4
Kings Head Ct *BIC* OX26 * .. 162 C8
Kings Head Pde
  RAYLNE/WEN HP22 * ... 44 A6
Kingshill Av *YEAD* UB4 ...... 105 M8
Kingshill Cl *YEAD* UB4 ...... 105 M8
Kingshill Dr *RMKN* MK19 .... 137 M9
Kingshill Rd *HAZ/HG* HP15 .. 68 C7
Kingshill Wy *BERK* HP4 ..... 47 M8
Kingsland Rd *AYLS* HP21 .... 42 F2
  HHW HP1 .... 57 M1
Kings La *KGLGY* WD4 .... 65 M2
  MDHD SL6 .... 98 A2
King's La *GTMIS/PWD* HP16 .. 60 B1
  RAYLNE/WEN HP22 ..... 52 E4
Kingsley Cl *WYM* HP11 ...... 78 B5
Kingsley Crs *WYM* HP11 ..... 78 B5
Kingsley Dr *MLW* SL7 .... 87 H8
Kingsley Rd *BIC* OX26 ...... 162 B2
Kingsley Wk *TRING* HP23 .... 37 M6
Kings Md *DUN/WHIP* LU6 .... 170 F3
Kingsmead *PRRI* HP27 .... 50 A8
Kingsmead
  RAYLNE/WEN HP22 ..... 35 H2
Kingsmead Rd *WYM* HP11 ... 78 H2
Kings Oak Cl *PRRI* HP27 .... 50 B8
Kingsoak Leys *MKV* MK10 ... 19 K4
Kings Ride *FLKWH/TG* HP10 .. 79 G1
Kings Rd *BERK* HP4 .... 47 M1
  CSTG HP8 .... 82 C2
  HEN RG9 .... 190 G4
  WDR/YW UB7 .... 114 G6
  WDSR SL4 .... 121 J6
King's Rd *AYLS* HP21 .... 3 J5
  HEN RG9 .... 190 G4
  SL SL1 .... 111 K7
  THAME OX9 .... 181 P6
  UX/CGN UB8 .... 104 D7
  WYM HP11 .... 78 E6
Kings Rw *SKCH* HP14 .... 186 H1
Kings St *LBUZ* LU7 .... 161 K3
King Stable St *WDSR* SL4 ... 121 J3
Kingston Br *WDR/YW* UB7 ... 114 A12
Kingston Br *MKV* MK10 ...... 138 A12
Kingston HI *CHNR* OX39 ..... 184 D10
Kingston La *UX/CGN* UB8 .... 104 D8
  WDR/YW UB7 .... 114 B8
King St *CSHM* HP5 .... 63 G3
  LBUZ LU7 .... 27 L8
  MDHD SL6 .... 108 B2
  SKCH HP14 .... 76 B2
  STSTR MK11 .... 16 D4
  TRING HP23 .... 37 M7
Kingsway *CFSP/GDCR* SL9 .... 92 D1
  HYS/HAR UB3 .... 115 H2
Kings Wy *LBUZ* LU7 .... 27 L8
Kingsway *SLN* SL2 .... 101 H1
Kingsway Ms *SLN* SL2 .... 101 H1
Kingswear Dr *MKV* MK10 .... 19 K1
Kingswear Rd *RSLP* HA4 ..... 95 M8
Kings Wd *MLW* SL7 .... 96 C2
Kingswood Av
  FLKWH/TG HP10 .... 79 G2
Kingswood Cl *MDHD* SL6 .... 108 B4
Kingswood Creek
  STWL/WRAY TW19 ..... 122 D1
Kingswood La *HEN* RG9 ..... 164 F9
Kingswood Pl *HWYN* HP13 .. 78 D1
Kingswood Rd
  FLKWH/TG HP10 .... 78 F1
  DTCH/LGLY SL3 .... 84 D1
Kinloch Pl *WEAT* MK2 .... 153 Q1
Kinnaird Cl *SL* SL1 .... 110 C2
Kinnear Dr *CNH/GTH/TMA* MK8 17 H1
Kinross Dr *BTCHLY* MK3 ..... 22 B5
Kinross Gn *AYL* HP20 .... 34 D1
Kinson Gn *AYL* HP20 .... 34 D1
Kipling Cl *BIC* OX26 .... 162 C2
Kipling Dr *NPAG* MK16 ...... 14 C2
Kipling Rd *BTCHLY* MK3 ..... 22 B3
Kippell HI *OLN* MK46 .... 128 B9
Kirby Cl *NTHWD* HA6 .... 85 K6
Kirby Rd *WDR/YW* UB7 ...... 114 C4
Kirkeby Cl *GTLIN* MK14 ..... 14 A8

Kirke Cl *SHEN* MK5 .... 21 K1
Kirkham Ct *SHEN* MK5 ...... 6 B8
Kirkstall Pl *EAG/OLD/WTN* MK6 7 J8
Kirkwall Sp *SL* SL1 .... 111 K1
Kirkwood Gv *SHEN* MK5 ..... 21 G1
Kirtle Rd *CSHM* HP5 .... 63 H2
Kirtlington Cl *OLN* MK46 .... 128 C11
Kitchener Rd *WYM* HP11 .... 4 D6
Kite Fld *BERK* HP4 .... 47 K3
Kite HI *EAG/OLD/WTN* MK6 .. 7 M9
Kitelee Cl *RMKN* MK19 ...... 131 J7
Kiteleys Gn *LBUZ* LU7 ...... 27 K6
Kite Wood Rd *FLKWH/TG* HP10 79 G1
Kitsbury Rd *BERK* HP4 ...... 48 A6
Kitsbury Ter *BERK* HP4 ..... 48 A6
Klondyke *MLW* SL7 .... 97 J4
Knappe Cl *HEN* RG9 .... 190 F6
Knapp Gdns *SHEN* MK5 ...... 17 J7
Knaves Beech Wy
  FLKWH/TG HP10 .... 89 H1
Knaves HI *LBUZ* LU7 .... 26 E6
Knaves Hollow
  FLKWH/TG HP10 .... 89 J1
Knebworth Ga *GTLIN* MK14 .. 14 D5
Knighton-Way La
  DEN/HRF UB9 .... 104 A3
Knightsbridge Pl *AYLW* HP19 177 R2
Knights Cl *DUN/WHIP* LU6 ... 170 F1
  RMKS/WB MK17 .... 24 E5
  WDSR SL4 .... 120 C4
Knightscote Cl *DEN/HRF* UB9 94 C1
Knights HI *HWYW* HP12 ..... 4 D4
Knights Orch *HHW* HP1 ..... 49 L5
Knights PI *WDSR* SL4 .... 121 H6
Knights Templar Wy
  WYM HP11 .... 78 A6
Knoll Cl *MKV* MK16 .... 133 N8
Knoll Crs *NTHWD* HA6 .... 95 K1
Knolls Vw *DUN/WHIP* LU6 ... 170 C1
The Knoll *RMKS/WB* MK17 ... 144 A3
Knolton Wy *SLN* SL2 .... 112 A3
Knottocks Cl *BEAC* HP9 ..... 80 C5
Knottocks Dr *BEAC* HP9 ..... 80 C5
Knottocks End *BEAC* HP9 .... 80 C5
Knotts Cl *DUN/WHIP* LU6 .... 171 R1
Knowles Cl *WDR/YW* UB7 .... 114 C5
Knowles Gn *WEAT* MK2 ...... 22 F7
Knowl Ga *SHEN* MK5 .... 17 M7
Knowl Hill Common
  WAR/TWY RG10 .... 116 D2
Knowsley Cl *MDHD* SL6 ..... 107 M5
Knox Br *WTR/OFPK* MK7 ..... 19 L6
Kop Hill Rd *PRRI* HP27 ..... 58 C3
Kramer Ct *CNH/GTH/TMA* MK8 17 G8
Krohn Cl *BUCK/WIN* MK18 ... 142 A10
Krypton Cl *SHEN* MK5 .... 21 M1
Kynaston Av *AYLS* HP21 ..... 42 D2

L

Laburnham Rd *MDHD* SL6 .... 108 C4
Laburnum Av *WDR/YW* UB7 .. 114 C4
Laburnum Cl *MLW* SL7 ...... 97 K2
  RBICS/W OX25 .... 162 H11
Laburnum Ct *LBUZ* LU7 * 27 G7
Laburnum Gv *DTCH/LGLY* SL3 122 F2
  RSLP HA4 .... 95 J5
  WEAT MK2 .... 23 H7
Laburnum Rd *HWYW* HP12 ... 87 H1
  HYS/HAR UB3 .... 115 L8
Lacemaker Ct *AMSS* HP7 * ... 71 H3
Lacemakers Cl *CHNR* OX39 .. 184 F4
  RAYLW HP18 .... 175 K12
Lace Ms *OLN* MK46 .... 128 D10
Lacey Dr *SKCH* HP14 .... 67 J8
Laceys Dr *HAZ/HG* HP15 ..... 69 G2
Laceys Yd *CSHM* HP5 * 63 G2
Ladbroke Cl *AYL* HP20 ...... 3 H1
Ladbrooke Rd *SL* SL1 .... 111 H7
Ladday Rd *SL* SL1 * 111 H5
Ladgate La *RSLP* HA4 .... 95 H5
Ladymead Cl *RMKS/WB* MK17 20 C3
Ladymeadow Ct *MKV* MK10 .. 19 H3
Ladysmith Rd *LBUZ* LU7 ..... 169 L2
Lady Verney Cl *HWYN* HP13 . 5 J4
Ladywalk *RKW/CH/CXG* WD3 . 83 K5
Ladywood Cl
  RKW/CH/CXG WD3 ..... 74 A6
Laggan Rd *MDHD* SL6 .... 98 E8
Laggan Sq *MDHD* SL6 .... 98 E1
Lagger Cl *CSTG* HP8 .... 82 A3
The Lagger *CSTG* HP8 .... 82 A3
Lagley Meadow *BERK* HP4 * . 47 L6
Lagonda Cl *NPAG* MK16 ..... 15 H2
Laidon Cl *WEAT* MK2 .... 153 Q1
Lake Av *SL* SL1 .... 111 J4
Lake Cl *BUCK/WIN* MK18 ..... 151 L6
Lake End Cl *MDHD* SL6 * 110 A3
Lake End Rd *WDSR* SL4 ...... 110 A4
Laker Ct *EAG/OLD/WTN* MK6 . 18 B7
Lakeside *AYLW* HP19 .... 34 D2
  MDHD SL6 .... 99 G8
  TRING HP23 .... 37 M5
Lakeside Dr *SLN* SL2 .... 101 K6
Lakeside Rd *DTCH/LGLY* SL3 . 123 L3
Lakes Cl *BEAC* HP9 .... 90 D4
  NPAG MK16 .... 14 E1
Lake St *LBUZ* LU7 .... 27 H7
Lake Vw *MDHD* SL6 .... 108 F1
Lamb Cl *NPAG* MK16 .... 14 D2
Lamberhurst Gv
  WTR/OFPK MK7 .... 19 K6
Lambe Rd *RAYLNE/WEN* HP22 44 A6
Lambert Av *DTCH/LGLY* SL3 .. 112 D7
Lambert Wk *THAME* OX9 ..... 181 N5
Lamb La *WTR/OFPK* MK7 ..... 19 M7
Lambourn Cl *EMV/FZ* MK4 ... 21 M5
Lambourne Av *AYLS* HP21 ... 42 C3
Lambourne Cl *UX/CGN* UB8 .. 104 B3
Lambourne Crs *BIC* OX26 .... 162 C5
Lambourne Rd *MDHD* SL6 ... 108 C4
Lambridge La *HEN* RG9 ...... 190 B6
Lambridge Wood Rd *HEN* RG9 190 A6
Lambscroft Wy
  CFSP/GDCR SL9 .... 92 D1
Lambtons Wy
  BUCK/WIN MK18 .... 151 L9
Lammas *EAG/OLD/WTN* MK6 .. 22 D1
Lammas Ct *WDSR* SL4 .... 121 H5
Lammas Rd *RAYLW* HP18 .... 175 R8
  LBUZ LU7 .... 169 M7
Lammas Wk *LBUZ* LU7 .... 27 L7
Lammas Wy *SKCH* HP14 ..... 187 R10

Lampitts Cross
  EAG/OLD/WTN MK6 .... 18 E8
Lamport Ct
  CNH/GTH/TMA MK8 .... 17 K6
Lamva Ct *STSTR* MK11 .... 16 C1
Lancaster Av *SLN* SL2 ...... 111 H1
Lancaster Ct *HWYW* HP12 * . 87 K2
Lancaster Dr *BRACKY* NN13 . 8 C7
  HHS/BOV HP3 .... 56 F6
Lancaster Rd *UX/CGN* UB8 .. 104 C4
Lancaster Ride
  FLKWH/TG HP10 .... 79 G2
  HWYW HP12 .... 87 K2
  MDHD SL6 .... 108 A2
Lancaster Wk *HYS/HAR* UB3 . 115 H3
Lancastria Ms *MDHD* SL6 ... 108 A2
Lancelot Cl *SL* SL1 .... 110 F6
Lance Wy *HWYN* HP13 .... 78 F4
Lanchester Rd *RBEDW* MK43 . 138 C4
Lancing Wy *RKW/CH/CXG* WD3 55 C6
Lancot Av *DUN/WHIP* LU6 ... 31 K7
Lancotbury Cl *DUN/WHIP* LU6 31 M6
Lancresse Cl *UX/CGN* UB8 ... 104 C4
Lander Rd *AYLW* HP19 ...... 167 Q11
Landon Rd *RKW/CH/CXG* WD3 84 D2
Landrace Ct *SHEN* MK5 ...... 21 J7
Lands End Gv *EMV/FZ* MK4 .. 21 J6
The Lands *LBUZ* LU7 .... 28 A4
Lane End *BERK* HP4 .... 47 L6
Lane End Rd *HWYW* HP12 .... 77 H6
Lanercost Crs *MKV* MK10 .... 19 L5
Lanes Cl *BIC* OX26 .... 163 J4
Lane's End *LBUZ* LU7 .... 27 H1
The Lane *CHNR* OX39 * 184 C5
  RMKS/WB MK17 .... 152 D8
  TOW NN12 .... 130 C8
Lane Wood Cl *AMSS* HP7 .... 71 L2
Lanfranc Gdns *WLLN* MK15 .. 14 E2
Langcliffe Dr *BDWL* MK13 ... 17 J3
Langdale Cl *MDHD* SL6 ...... 108 A4
  WEAT MK2 .... 153 Q2
Langdale Rd *THAME* OX9 .... 181 P4
Langdon St *TRING* HP23 ..... 37 M7
Langford Gdns *BIC* OX26 .... 162 B4
Langford Wy *WTR/OFPK* MK7 . 23 K3
Langhams Wy *WAR/TWY* RG10 191 N12
Langland Rd
  EAG/OLD/WTN MK6 .... 18 F8
Langlands Cl *OLN* MK46 ..... 128 C7
Langley Broom
  DTCH/LGLY SL3 .... 122 E1
Langley Cl *BUCK/WIN* MK18 .. 150 H10
Langley Crs *HYS/HAR* UB3 ... 125 J4
Langley Pk *DTCH/LGLY* SL3 * 112 F2
Langley Park Rd
  DTCH/LGLY SL3 .... 112 F5
Langley Quay *DTCH/LGLY* SL3 112 F4
Langley Rd *DTCH/LGLY* SL3 .. 112 F5
  WAT WD17 .... 75 L2
Langley Wy *WAT* WD17 ...... 75 L2
Langney Gn *EMV/FZ* MK4 .... 21 J5
Langport *SHEN* MK5 .... 21 H4
Langston Ct *HWYW* HP12 * .. 77 H6
Langstone Cl *AYL* HP20 ..... 34 E2
  SLN SL2 .... 101 L1
Langton Av *RBICS/W* OX25 .. 163 J10
Langton Cl *MDHD* SL6 .... 108 C2
  SL SL1 .... 110 C5
Langton Dr
  CNH/GTH/TMA MK8 .... 17 H3
Langton Gv *NTHWD* HA6 ..... 85 H5
Langwood Gdns *WAT* WD17 .. 75 L4
Langworthy End *MDHD* SL6 .. 110 B2
Lanner Wk *EAG/OLD/WTN* MK6 18 B7
Lannock Rd *HYS/HAR* UB3 ... 115 J8
Lanrick Copse *BERK* HP4 .... 48 C5
Lansbury Dr *YEAD* UB4 ...... 115 L2
Lansdell Av *HWYW* HP12 .... 87 H3
Lansdowne Av *AYL* HP20 .... 2 F5
  SL SL1 .... 111 H5
Lansdowne Rd *AYL* HP20 .... 2 F5
  CSHM HP5 .... 55 H8
  UX/CGN UB8 .... 115 G3
Lansdowne Wk *WYM* HP11 ... 87 K3
Lantern Wk *MDHD* SL6 ...... 109 G8
Lanthorn Cl *GTLIN* MK14 .... 14 B8
Lappetts La *GTMIS/PWD* HP16 61 G2
Lapwing Cl *BIC* OX26 .... 162 E6
Larch Cl *AYL* HP20 .... 3 L2
  BIC OX26 .... 162 E6
  FLKWH/TG HP10 .... 69 H8
  SL SL1 .... 111 G2
Larch Dr *WDR/YW* UB7 ...... 114 B6
The Larches *BERK* HP4 ...... 47 J5
  HAZ/HG HP15 .... 69 J3
  HGDN/ICK UB10 .... 104 F8
Larchfield Rd *MDHD* SL6 .... 108 C4
The Larchlands
  FLKWH/TG HP10 .... 79 G2
Larchmoor Pk *SLN* SL2 ...... 101 M3
Larch Ri *BERK* HP4 .... 47 M5
Larch Wd *GTMIS/PWD* HP16 . 61 G6
Lark Cl *BUCK/WIN* MK18 ..... 11 M4
Larkfield Cl *RSLP* HA4 * 95 J6
Larkin Cl *NPAG* MK16 .... 14 D1
Larkings La *SLN* SL2 .... 102 A4
Lark Ri *BRACKY* NN13 .... 8 D6
  HAZ/HG HP15 .... 69 J3
Larkspur Cl *HHW* HP1 .... 49 K6
  RSLP HA4 .... 95 G6
Larkspur Gv *AYLW* HP19 .... 34 E4
Larks V *AYLW* HP19 .... 34 E4
Larne Rd *RSLP* HA4 .... 95 L5
La Roche Cl *DTCH/LGLY* SL3 . 112 B7
Larwood Pl
  EAG/OLD/WTN MK6 .... 7 H7
Lascelles Rd *WLLN* MK15 .... 14 D7
Laser Cl *SHEN* MK5 .... 17 M8
Lashbrook Rd *HEN* RG9 ..... 191 L10
Lashlake Rd *THAME* OX9 .... 181 N5
Lastingham Gv *EMV/FZ* MK4 . 21 L4
Latchmoor Av *CFSP/GDCR* SL9 92 C1

Latchmoor Gv *CFSP/GDCR* SL9 92 C3
Latchmoor Wy
  CFSP/GDCR SL9 .... 92 C3
Lathbury Rd *BRACKY* NN13 .. 8 C6
Latimer Cl *AMS* HP6 .... 72 B2
  WATW WD18 .... 75 K8
Latimer Rd *CSHM* HP5 .... 63 K5
  RKW/CH/CXG WD3 ..... 72 E1
Latimer Wy *BEAC* HP9 .... 80 B4
Laud's Cl *HEN* RG9 .... 190 F5
Launceston Rd *RKW/CH/CXG* WD3 73 G7
Launceston Ct *SHEN* MK5 .... 17 L8
Launde *MKV* MK10 .... 19 L5
Launton Rd *BIC* OX26 .... 162 E5
  RBICN OX27 .... 155 J10
Laurel Av *DTCH/LGLY* SL3 ... 112 C6
Laurel Bank *HHS/BOV* HP3 .. 57 L2
Laurel Cl *HWYN* HP13 * 5 G7
  DTCH/LGLY SL3 .... 123 K3
  GTMIS/PWD HP16 ...... 60 A3
  LBUZ LU7 .... 30 E1
  PRRI HP27 .... 67 H2
Laurel Ct *AMS* HP6 .... 63 H7
  IVER SL0 .... 103 J5
Laurel Dr *SKCH* HP14 .... 67 J7
  WYM HP11 .... 79 G6
Laurel La *WDR/YW* UB7 ...... 114 C8
Laurel Rd *CFSP/GDCR* SL9 ... 82 C8
  IVER SL0 .... 103 J7
The Laurels *BERK* HP4 ...... 49 G4
  DBGH MK1 .... 23 G5
  HWYW HP12 .... 87 H2
  RBICN OX27 .... 154 H4
Laurel Wy *AYLS* HP21 .... 3 H7
Lauries Cl *HHW* HP1 .... 57 G1
Lautrec Gdns *MDHD* SL6 * ... 48 A8
Lavender Cl *AYLS* HP21 ..... 3 H7
Lavender Gv *WTR/OFPK* MK7 . 23 A1
Lavender La *RNHPTN* NN7 .... 126 D5
Lavender Ri *WDR/YW* UB7 ... 114 F6
Lavender Rd *UX/CGN* UB8 ... 114 C4
Lavender Wk *AYLS* HP21 * ... 34 A8
Lavender Wy *HAZ/HG* HP15 .. 68 E4
Lavendon Rd *OLN* MK46 ..... 128 C9
Lavric Rd *AYLS* HP21 .... 3 H7
Lavrock La *RKW/CH/CXG* WD3 74 E8
Lawford Av *RKW/CH/CXG* WD3 73 H7
Lawford Cl *RKW/CH/CXG* WD3 73 H7
Lawkland *SL* SL1 .... 101 H8
Lawn Av *WDR/YW* UB7 .... 114 B6
Lawn Cl *DTCH/LGLY* SL3 ..... 122 B3
  RSLP HA4 .... 105 L1
Lawn HI *RAYLW* HP18 .... 156 H8
Lawn House La *RAYLNE* HP18 156 G9
The Lawns *DTCH/LGLY* SL3 * 123 K4
  FLKWH/TG HP10 .... 69 G8
  HHW HP1 .... 49 H6
  RAYLW HP18 .... 174 B1
The Lawn *DTCH/LGLY* SL3 * . 122 B3
Lawrence Cl *AYL* HP20 ...... 3 K2
Lawrence Gv
  GTMIS/PWD HP16 ...... 60 B3
Lawrence Rd *YEAD* UB4 ...... 105 H7
Lawrence Wy *BIC* OX26 ...... 162 A4
  SL SL1 .... 110 B2
Laws Cl *RBEDW* MK43 .... 129 H8
Laws Cft *BRACKY* NN13 ..... 8 C7
Lawsone Ri *HWYN* HP13 ..... 5 K2
Lawson Pl *SHEN* MK5 .... 21 L1
Lawson Rd *HEN* RG9 .... 191 J7
Lawyers Cl *BRACKY* NN13 ... 146 D4
Laxfield Dr *MKV* MK10 ...... 19 K2
Laxton Gn *MDHD* SL6 .... 108 B7
Layburn Crs *DTCH/LGLY* SL3 . 123 G2
Lay Rd *AYLW* HP19 .... 2 A1
Layter's Av *CFSP/GDCR* SL9 . 92 B1
Layter's Av South
  CFSP/GDCR SL9 .... 92 B1
Layter's End *CFSP/GDCR* SL9 92 B1
Layter's Green La
  CFSP/GDCR SL9 .... 92 A1
Layters Wy *CFSP/GDCR* SL9 . 92 B1
Leachcroft *CFSP/GDCR* SL9 .. 82 A8
Leach Rd *AYLS* HP21 .... 3 —
  BIC OX26 .... 162 B4
Lea Cl *MLW* SL7 .... 87 J8
Lea Crs *RSLP* HA4 .... 105 L2
Leacroft Cl *WDR/YW* UB7 .... 113 J4
Leacroft Rd *IVER* SL0 ...... 113 J4
Leaf Cl *NTHWD* HA6 .... 85 J7
Leafield Ri *CNH/GTH/TMA* MK8 17 G4
Leafy La *TRING* HP23 .... 45 K1
Leaholme Gdns *SL* SL1 ...... 110 B2
Leaholme Waye *RSLP* HA4 ... 95 M2
Lea La *RAYLW* HP18 .... 181 M2
Leamington Pl *YEAD* UB4 .... 115 L1
Leapingwell La
  BUCK/WIN MK18 .... 151 L9
Learoyd Wy *LBUZ* LU7 ...... 27 L8
Leary Crs *NPAG* MK16 .... 15 H2
Leas Cl *HWYN* HP13 .... 78 E1
Leas Dr *IVER* SL0 .... 103 J4
Leaside *NPAG* MK16 .... 132 C4
Leaside Ct *HGDN/ICK* UB10 . 105 G8
Leasowe Pl *BDWL* MK13 ..... 6 B3
Leather La *GTMIS/PWD* HP16 60 F5
Leaver Rd *HEN* RG9 .... 190 F5

Leckhampstead Rd
  BUCK/WIN MK18 .... 142 A2
Ledborough Ga *BEAC* HP9 ... 80 D7
Ledborough La *BEAC* HP9 ... 80 D6
Ledborough Wd *BEAC* HP9 .. 80 D7
Ledburn Gv *LBUZ* LU7 .... 26 D7
Ledburn *GTLIN* MK14 .... 14 A5
Ledgemore La *HHW* HP2 ..... 1 J4
Ledger La *MDHD* SL6 .... 119 J4
Ledger's Rd *SL* SL1 .... 111 J4
Leeches Wy *LBUZ* LU7 .... 169 M7
Lee Cl *THAME* OX9 .... 181 M5
Lee Crs *HADM* HP17 .... 177 N5
Lee Don Furlong *LBUZ* LU7 .. 27 L8
Lee Farm Cl *CSHM* HP5 ...... 55 K4
Lee La *MDHD* SL6 .... 107 K3
Lee Rd *AYLS* HP21 .... 3 R6
  PRRI HP27 .... 185 R6
  RAYLNE/WEN HP22 ..... 166 C2
Lees Av *NTHWD* HA6 .... 85 L8
Lees Cl *MDHD* SL6 .... 108 A5
Lees Gdns *MDHD* SL6 .... 108 A5
Leeson Gdns *WDSR* SL4 ..... 110 D8
Lees Pde *HGDN/ICK* UB10 * . 115 G1
The Lee *NTHWD* HA6 .... 85 L8
Leggfield Ter *HHW* HP1 ..... 49 G4
Leicester Cl *HEN* RG9 ...... 190 G3
Leigh HI *EMV/FZ* MK4 .... 21 G2

Leigh Pk DTCH/LGLY SL3 * ...122 B3
Leigh Rd SL SL1 ...111 G4
Leigh Sq WDSR SL4 ...120 C5
Leigh St WYM HP11 ...4 E1
Leighton Buzzard Rd
HHW HP1 ...41 K8
Leighton Gdns MDHD SL6 ...109 G2
Leighton Rd DUN/WHIP LU6 ...30 A8
LBUZ LU7 ...28 A4
RAYLNE/WEN HP22 ...168 B3
RMKS/WB MK17 ...153 R7
Leighton St RMKS/WB MK17 ...144 H12
Leiston Sp SL SL1 ...111 K3
Leith Cl SL SL1 ...111 M5
Leith Rd AYLW HP19 ...177 R2
Lembrook Wk AYLS HP21 ...34 B8
Lenborough Cl
BUCK/WIN MK18 ...11 K7
Lenborough Ct WLLN MK15... 18 F4
Lenborough Rd
BUCK/WIN MK18 ...11 K7
Lennon Dr CNH/GTH/TMA MK8... 17 H7
Lent Green La SL SL1 ...110 A1
Lenthall Cl BDWL MK13 ...17 K1
Lent Rise Rd MDHD SL6 ...110 A3
Leominster Ga RAYLW HP18 ...19 K5
Leonards Lee EMV/FZ MK4 ...21 J4
Leonards Cl RAYLW HP18 ...156 C8
Leon Av WEAT MK2 ...23 G6
Leopard Dr WLLN MK15 ...14 D7
Leopold Rd LBUZ LU7 ...26 C7
Lerwick Cft BIC OX26 ...162 F2
Lerwick Dr SL SL1 ...111 K2
Lester Cl WTR/OFPK MK7 ...19 M7
Lester Gv HAZ/HG HP15 ...68 F6
Lesters Rd MDHD SL6 ...98 C4
Letchfield CSHM MK5 ...64 A2
Letter Box La PRRI HP27 ...50 C7
Leven Cl LBUZ LU7 ...26 C7
WEAT MK2 ...153 Q1
Levenshall Dr EMV/FZ MK4 ...21 J5
Leven Wy HYS/HAR UB3 ...115 K5
Levings Cl AYLW HP19 ...167 R11
Lewes Ct SL SL1 ...111 H6
Lewes Wy RKW/CH/CXG WD3 ...75 G5
Lewins Rd CFSP/GDCR SL9 ...92 C2
Lewins Wy SL SL1 ...110 E4
Lewis Cl DEN/HRF UB9 ...94 B1
NPAG MK16 ...14 C1
Lewis La CFSP/GDCR SL9 ...82 D8
Lexham Gdns AMSS HP6 ...63 H8
Lexington Av MDHD SL6 ...108 C5
Leybourne Rd HGDN/ICK UB10...105 H6
Leyburn Cl BDWL MK13 ...17 M1
Leyburne Cl LBUZ LU7 ...28 D6
Leyburne Gdns CHNR OX39 ...184 F13
Leyfield Rd SL SL1 ...3 G9
Leylands La STWL/WRAY TW19 ...123 L7
Leyland Pl EAG/OLD/WTN MK6... 7 G7
Leys Cl DEN/HRF UB9 ...84 C8
Leys La BUCK/WIN MK18 ...148 C6
Leys Rd SHEN MK5 ...6 A9
The Leys AMS HP6 ...63 G6
BUCK/WIN MK18 * ...11 M3
RMKS/WB MK17 ...144 E6
TRING HP23 ...38 A6
Leys Vw NPAG MK16 ...133 N9
Leywood Cl AMSS HP7 ...71 J2
Lichfield Down
WTR/OFPK MK7 ...23 L1
Lichfield Rd NTHWD HA6 ...95 M2
Liddall Wy WDR/YW UB7 ...114 E5
Liddel Cl SL SL1 ...120 B5
Liddell Wy LBUZ LU7 ...29 L1
Liffre Dr RAYLNE/WEN HP22 ...44 A4
Lightfoot Ct WTR/OFPK MK7...23 J1
Lightlands La MDHD SL6 ...98 E5
Ligo Av RAYLNE/WEN HP22 ...43 H4
Lilac Cl RMKS/WB MK17 ...152 B5
Lilac Gdns HYS/HAR UB3 ...115 K3
Lilac Pl WDR/YW UB7 ...114 E4
Lilleshall Av MK/MK10 ...19 J5
Lilley Wy SL SL1 ...110 D5
Lillibrooke Crs MDHD SL6 ...117 M3
Lillyfee Farm La
FLKWH/TG HP10 ...89 M6
Lilly Hl OLN MK46 ...128 B9
Lily Bottom La PRRI HP27 ...58 F7
Lily Cl BIC OX26 ...162 C4
Lily Dr WDR/YW UB7 ...114 C8
Lily's Wk WYM HP11 ...5 H7
Limbaud Ct WTR/OFPK MK7 ...23 K1
Lime Av BUCK/WIN MK18 ...142 A11
WDR/YW UB7 ...114 E4
WDSR SL4 ...121 J3
WYM HP11 ...78 C5
Lime Cl HAZ/HG HP15 ...68 F7
NPAG MK16 ...14 C4
PIN HA5 ...95 L2
Lime Crs BIC OX26 ...162 C4
Lime Gv CHNR OX39 ...184 G4
HYS/HAR UB3 ...115 J4
LBUZ LU7 ...26 F6
RMKS/WB MK17 ...144 E6
Limerick La CMK MK9 ...7 M2
Lime Rd PRRI HP27 ...58 A3
TOW NN12 ...130 D12
Limes Av AYLS HP21 ...35 G7
The Limes AMS HP6 ...63 G6
RBICN OX27 ...155 J9
RKW/CH/CXG WD3 * ...84 B1
STSTR MK11 ...16 A2
WDSR SL4 ...120 B5
WEAT MK2 ...23 H6
Lime St OLN MK46 ...128 B11
Limes Wy RAYLW HP18 ...180 G5
Lime Tree Cl HAZ/HG HP15 ...68 C2
Lime Tree Wk AMSS HP7 ...71 L2
RKW/CH/CXG WD3 ...74 A6
Lime Wk DEN/HRF UB9 ...104 B3
MDHD SL6 ...107 M5
Limmer La HWYW HP12 ...87 G3
Limmers Md HAZ/HG HP15 ...68 A2
Limmings La THAME OX9 ...181 P7
Lincecslade Gv SHEN MK5 ...6 A9
Linchfield HWYN HP13 ...78 D4
Linchfield Rd DTCH/LGLY SL3 ...122 B4
Lincoln GTLIN MK14 ...13 M6
Lincoln Cl BIC OX26 ...162 F2
RAYLNE/WEN HP22 ...43 G5
Lincoln Dr BERK HP4 ...48 C4
RKW/CH/CXG WD3 ...75 G5
Lincoln Hatch La SL SL1 ...110 C3
Lincoln Pk AMSS HP7 ...71 K2
Lincoln Pl THAME OX9 ...181 N6
Lincoln Rd CFSP/GDCR SL9 ...82 D8
HWYW HP12 ...87 K1
MDHD SL6 ...108 A2
NTHWD HA6 ...95 L1
Lincolnshire Cl BTCHLY MK3 ...22 B5
Lincolns Inn HWYW HP12 * ...87 J1
The Lincolns CTMIS/PWD HP16...60 F1
Lincoln Wy RKW/CH/CXG WD3...75 G5

SL SL1 ...110 C4
Lincombe Slade LBUZ LU7 ...26 F6
Lincroft RBEDW MK43 ...139 K5
Linden Av MDHD SL6 ...108 C1
RSLP HA4 ...95 M3
WATW WD18 ...75 L1
Linden Cl RSLP HA4 ...95 M7
Linden Dr CFSP/GDCR SL9 ...82 D7
SL SL2 ...101 H4
Linden End AYLS HP21 ...34 E4
Linden Gv GTLIN MK14 ...14 B6
Linden Hill La WAR/TWY RG10...116 A7
Linden Lea RAYLNE/WEN HP22... 44 A4
Linden Sq BIC OX26 ...162 E4
Linden Sq DEN/HRF UB9 ...83 M6
The Lindens HHS/BOV HP3 ...57 L2
Linden Ter UX/CGN UB8 * ...114 C3
Lindisfarne Dr MKV MK10 ...19 K5
Lindiswara Ct
RKW/CH/CXG WD3 * ...74 F7
Lindler Cl LBUZ LU7 ...27 H8
Lindlings HHW HP1 ...49 K8
Lindo Cl CSHM HP5 ...63 G1
Lindores Cft MKV MK10 ...19 G1
Lindores Rd MDHD SL6 ...119 G2
Lindsay Av STWL/WRAY TW19 ...124 C8
Lindsey Rd DEN/HRF UB9 ...103 M1
Lines Hl RAYLNE/WEN HP22 ...33 G3
Lines Rd SKCH HP14 ...86 A1
The Lines RAYLNE/WEN HP22 ...33 H2
Linfields AMSS HP7 ...72 B3
Linford Av NPAG MK16 ...14 D2
Linford La WLLN MK15 ...18 F3
Lingfield WOLV MK12 ...17 H2
Lingfield Dr HWYN HP13 ...78 F5
NTHWD HA6 ...85 K7
Lingfield Wy WAT WD17 ...75 L1
Lingholm Cl MDHD SL6 ...108 B4
Linington Av CSHM HP5 ...63 M1
Link Cl HWYW HP12 ...4 B7
Link Rd DTCH/LGLY SL3 ...122 B3
GTMIS/PWD HP16 ...60 F1
HWYW HP12 ...4 B7
Links Ap FLKWH/TG HP10 ...89 G3
Links End RKW/CH/CXG WD3 ...89 G2
Links Wy FLKWH/TG HP10 ...89 G2
NTHWD HA6 ...85 H8
RKW/CH/CXG WD3 ...75 H5
Linkswood Rd SL SL1 ...100 B7
The Link HAZ/HG HP15 ...68 F5
SL SL3 ...112 A3
Link Wy DEN/HRF UB9 ...93 M5
Linnet Cl HWYW HP12 ...86 F3
Linnet Dr RAYLW HP18 ...165 R9
Linney Ct EMV/FZ MK4 ...21 J5
Linney Head DUN/WHIP LU6 * ...171 J2
Linslade Rd LBUZ LU7 ...27 G2
Lintlaw Pl BTCHLY MK3 ...22 D3
Linton Cl BDWL MK13 ...17 M2
Linwood Gv LBUZ LU7 ...27 J3
The Linx BTCHLY MK3 ...22 B6
Lionel Av RAYLNE/WEN HP22 ...51 M1
Lionel Cl RAYLNE/WEN HP22 ...51 M1
Lipscombe Dr BUCK/WIN MK18...11 M5
Lipscomb La SHEN MK5 ...17 K7
Lisburn Pth AYL HP20 ...3 J1
Lisle Rd HWYN HP13 ...5 G2
Lisleys Fld HAZ/HG HP15 ...68 C3
Lismore Pk SLN SL2 ...111 L3
Lissel Rd EAG/OLD/WTN MK6 ...23 H1
Lister Gn AYLS HP21 * ...42 D1
Liston Rd MLW SL7 ...97 J4
Litcham Sp SL SL1 ...111 J3
Lithgow's Rd HTHAIR TW6 ...125 K7
Little Balmer BUCK/WIN MK18...11 M8
Little Benty WDR/YW UB7 ...124 C1
Little Bridge Rd BERK HP4 ...48 C6
Little Britain HP18 ...166 E8
Littlebrook Av SLN SL2 ...110 D2
Little Catherells HHW HP1 ...49 K8
Little Cl AYLW HP19 ...2 F3
FLKWH/TG HP10 ...89 G4
HWYW HP12 ...87 K3
Littlecote CNH/GTH/TMA MK8... 17 K5
Littledown Rd SL SL1 ...111 H6
Little Dunmow MKV MK10 ...19 K5
Little Elms HYS/HAR UB3 ...125 J4
Littlefield Gn MDHD SL6 ...117 L8
Little Greencroft CSHM HP5 ...54 F6
Little Green La
RKW/CH/CXG WD3 ...74 A6
Little Habton EMV/FZ MK4 ...21 L4
Little Hame MKV MK10 ...19 J3
Little Ham La PRRI HP27 ...58 A1
Little Hampden Cl
RAYLNE/WEN HP22 ...44 A6
Little Heath La HHW HP1 ...49 G8
Little Hl LBUZ LU7 ...29 M4
Little Hivings CSHM HP5 ...54 F6
Little Hollis GTMIS/PWD HP16...60 D3
Little Hoo TRING HP23 ...37 L6
Little Horton House Dr
RNHPTN NN7 ...126 E4
Little Horwood Rd
RMKS/WB MK17 ...151 M3
Little Hundridge La
GTMIS/PWD HP16 ...61 M2
Little La PRRI HP27 ...66 B2
Little Linford La NPAG MK16 ...14 D2
Little Mollards
RAYLNE/WEN HP22 ...33 M3
Little Orchard Cl PRRI HP27 ...183 P9
Little Orchards AYL HP20 ...34 E3
Little Paddock RBICN OX27 ...154 H4
Little Pk HHS/BOV HP3 ...56 F7
PRRI HP27 ...58 A3
Littleport Sp SL SL1 ...111 K3
Little Reeves Av AMSS HP7 ...71 L2
Little Rd HYS/HAR UB3 ...115 J3
Little Spinney RBEDW MK43...139 M3
Little Stocking SHEN MK5 ...21 K5
Little Spring CSHM HP5 ...55 G7
Little Stanton GTLIN MK14 ...14 A6
Little Sutton La
DTCH/LGLY SL3 ...123 G2

Little Tring Rd TRING HP23 ...37 L4
Little Twye Rd TRING HP23 ...45 L7
Little Windmill Hl KGLGY WD4...45 H1
Little Wd SKCH HP14 ...186 H1
Little Woodlands WDSR SL4 ...120 B6
Littleworth LBUZ LU7 ...161 R7
Littleworth Rd HWYN HP13 ...77 K4
Liverpool Rd SL SL1 ...111 G3
Livesey Hl SHEN MK5 ...21 L1
Livingstone Dr WLLN MK15 ...18 F1
Llanbury Cl CFSP/GDCR SL9 ...82 D7
Llindores Cft MKV MK10 ...19 G1
Lloyds EAG/OLD/WTN MK6 ...18 C7
Loakes Rd WYM HP11 ...5 G8
Lochinvar Cl SL SL1 ...111 G6
Lochnell Rd BERK HP4 ...47 L4
Lochy Dr LBUZ LU7 ...26 D7
Lock Av MDHD SL6 ...99 H8
Lock Cdns DTCH/LGLY SL3 ...112 A8
Lock Bridge Rd BNEND SL8 ...88 F6
Locke Cl AYLW HP19 ...167 R12
Locke Cdns DTCH/LGLY SL3 ...112 A8
Locke Rd WEAT MK2 ...23 E6
Lockets Cl WDSR SL4 ...120 C4
Lockhart Av EMV/FZ MK4 ...21 J4
Lock Island MLW SL7 * ...97 L5
Lock La MDHD SL6 ...108 B6
RMKN MK19 ...12 B4
Lock Md MDHD SL6 ...99 H8
Lock Pth WDSR SL4 ...120 C2
Lock View La DBGH MK1 ...23 H5
Lockwood Cha EMV/FZ MK4 ...21 G4
Lodden Dr AYLS HP21 ...42 C3
Loddon Dr MDHD SL6 ...108 C2
WAR/TWY RG10 ...191 L12
Loddon Sp SL SL1 ...111 K4
Lodge Cl BIC OX26 ...162 D1
BUCK/WIN MK18 ...149 R4
LBUZ LU7 ...169 M7
MLW SL7 ...97 K5
SL SL1 ...111 H6
UX/CGN UB8 ...114 B1
Lodge Dr RKW/CH/CXG WD3 ...74 B5
Lodge End RKW/CH/CXG WD3 ...75 J5
Lodge Farm Ct RMKN MK19 ...131 L12
Lodge La GTLIN MK14 ...14 B6
Lodge Rd RBEDW MK43 ...139 K7
RKW/CH/CXG WD3 ...75 J5
Lodge Wy WDSR SL4 ...120 D6
Lodore Gn HGDN/ICK UB10 ...104 D1
Logan Rock EMV/FZ MK4 ...21 L6
Lollards Cl AMSS HP6 ...63 H8
Lombardy Dr BERK HP4 ...48 C7
Lomond Dr LBUZ LU7 ...26 D7
WEAT MK2 ...153 P3
London End BEAC HP9 ...90 E1
RMKS/WB MK17 ...153 J2
RMKS/WB MK17 ...145 J12
London End La
RMKS/WB MK17 ...144 A9
London Rd BEAC HP9 ...90 E1
BERK HP4 ...48 C6
BIC OX26 ...162 E6
BUCK/WIN MK18 ...149 M1
CSTG HP8 ...82 B2
DTCH/LGLY SL3 ...122 A3
FLKWH/TG HP10 ...79 H8
GTMIS/PWD HP16 ...61 G4
HHS/BOV HP3 ...57 M1
HHW HP1 ...57 G1
MKV MK10 ...19 K1
NPAG MK16 ...15 J3
RAYLNE/WEN HP22 ...44 A7
RAYLNE/WEN HP22 ...36 C5
RMKN MK19 ...137 Q7
SL SL1 ...111 J3
STSTR MK11 ...16 A1
THAME OX9 ...180 A10
TRING HP23 ...37 K4
WHLY OX33 ...178 C11
London Rd East AMSS HP7 ...71 L4
London Rd West AMSS HP7 ...71 H3
Londrina Ter BERK HP4 ...48 C5
Long Ayres RAYLNE/WEN MK7...23 K3
Longbottom La BEAC HP9 ...80 F6
Longbourn WDSR SL4 ...120 F6
Longbournes RBEDW MK43 ...139 L4
Longbridge Cl TRING HP23 ...37 M4
Long Chaulden HHW HP1 ...49 K8
Longcliffe Pth OXHEY WD19 ...85 M3
Long Cl SLN SL2 ...101 G5
Long Crendon Rd RAYLW HP18...180 E3
Longcroft RAYLNE/WEN HP22 ...36 C5
Longcroft Av
RAYLNE/WEN HP22 ...44 C4
Longcroft La HHS/BOV HP3 ...57 H7
Long Croft Rd
RKW/CH/CXG WD3 ...83 J5
Longcross WLLN MK15 ...14 D8
Longdown Hl PRRI HP27 ...50 E8
Longdown Ms AYLW HP19 ...177 Q2
Long Dr SL SL1 ...100 B8
WDR/YW UB7 * ...114 D6
Longfellow Cl BIC OX26 ...162 B3
Longfellow Dr NPAG MK16 ...14 D1
Longfield GTMIS/PWD HP16 ...61 G6
SLN SL2 ...101 J1
Longfield Dr AMS HP6 ...71 G1
Longfield Gdns TRING HP23 ...37 M3
Longfield Rd CSHM HP5 ...54 E8
TRING HP23 ...37 K7
Longford Av SL SL1 ...162 E4
Long Furlong HADM HP17 ...177 L5
HADM HP17 ...176 C12
Long Furlong Dr SLN SL2 ...110 D1
Long Gv BEAC HP9 ...80 B6
Long Hale LBUZ LU7 ...169 P11
Long Half Acre MDHD SL6 ...117 G2
Long Hedge LBUZ LU7 ...169 P11
Longhedge WTR/OFPK MK7 ...23 K4
Long Hide PRRI HP27 ...58 B2
Longhook Gdns NTHLT UB5 ...105 M7
Longlands Cl BUCK/WIN MK18...149 M5
Longland Wy HWYW HP12 ...4 A9
Longleat Ct
CNH/GTH/TMA MK8 ...17 J5
Longleat Gdns MDHD SL6 ...108 C4
Long Ley LBUZ LU7 ...169 M7
Long Leys AYLW HP19 ...177 R2

Long Lional AYL HP20 ...3 G6
Longmans Cl WATW WD18 ...75 H7
Long Marston La LBUZ LU7 ...169 J3
Long Marston Rd TRING HP23...169 J8
Long Massey OLN MK46 ...128 A9
Longmead WDSR SL4 ...120 D4
Longmead La SL SL1 ...100 C5
Long Meadow AYLS HP21 ...35 G3
CSHM HP5 ...55 H7
Long Meadow Cl AMSS HP7 ...70 D7
PRRI HP27 ...58 B1
Longmead Rd HYS/HAR UB3...115 L4
Longmire OLN MK46 ...128 H6
Longmore Cl
RKW/CH/CXG WD3 ...83 L4
Long Orchard Dr
FLKWH/TG HP10 ...79 H2
Long Pk AMS HP6 ...63 H7
Long Park Cl AMS HP6 ...63 H7
Long Park Wy AMS HP6 ...63 G6
Longpeak Cl EMV/FZ MK4 ...21 L5
Long Plough
RAYLNE/WEN HP22 ...36 C5
Long Readings La SLN SL2 ...111 G1
Long Rw BUCK/WIN MK18 ...142 F1
GTMIS/PWD HP16 * ...60 C4
Longstone Rd IVER SLO ...103 H7
Long Street Rd RMKN MK19...131 L6
Longview BEAC HP9 ...89 L2
Long Vw BERK HP4 ...47 M4
Longville WOLV MK12 ...17 J2
Long Wk CSTG HP8 ...72 D4
WDSR SL4 * ...121 J8
Longwalk Rd STKPK UB11 ...115 G5
Long Wall HADM HP17 ...182 C11
Longwick Rd PRRI HP27 ...183 R9
Longwood Av DTCH/LGLY SL3...123 G5
Longworth Dr MDHD SL6 ...109 H1
Longwood La AMSS HP7 ...71 J2
Lonsdale Cl MDHD SL6 ...108 F1
UX/CGN UB8 ...115 H3
Lonsdale Wy MDHD SL6 ...119 H1
Loosen Dr MDHD SL6 ...117 M3
Loosley Hl PRRI HP27 ...58 C8
Lord Mayors Dr SLN SL2 ...100 E4
Lords Cl LBUZ LU7 ...30 F1
WEAT MK2 ...22 F5
Lordsmead RBEDW MK43 ...139 L4
Lords Mill Ct CSHM HP5 ...63 H3
Lords Ter DUN/WHIP LU6 * ...30 F1
Loriner Pl GTLIN MK14 ...14 D8
Loring Rd BERK HP4 ...48 B7
WDSR SL4 ...120 E4
Lorne Cl SL SL1 ...111 G6
Lorraine Cl HWYN HP13 ...78 D2
Loseley Ct CNH/GTH/TMA MK8...17 J5
Losfield Rd WDSR SL4 ...120 D5
Lossie Dr IVER SLO ...113 G4
Lothersdale BDWL MK13 ...17 L1
Lothian Cl BTCHLY MK3 ...22 B4
Lott Meadow AYLS HP21 ...42 C3
Louches La SKCH HP14 ...67 J8
Loudhams Rd AMSS HP7 ...72 B2
Loudhams Wood La CSTG HP8...72 C3
Loudwater Dr
RKW/CH/CXG WD3 ...74 B5
Loudwater Hts
RKW/CH/CXG WD3 ...74 A4
Loudwater La
RKW/CH/CXG WD3 ...74 B6
Loudwater Rdg
RKW/CH/CXG WD3 ...74 A4
Loughton Rd BDWL MK13 ...17 K3
Louise Wk HHS/BOV HP3 ...56 F7
Lovat Meadow La NPAG MK16... 15 H3
Lovat St NPAG MK16 ...14 F1
Lovatt Dr BTCHLY MK3 ...22 A6
Lovatts Rd RKW/CH/CXG WD3 ...74 F5
Love Green La IVER SLO ...113 G4
Lovegrove Dr SLN SL2 ...110 E1
Love Hill La DTCH/LGLY SL3 ...112 F4
Lovejoy La WDSR SL4 ...120 C5
Lovelace Cl MDHD SL6 ...106 F1
Love La IVER SLO ...113 G3
Lovel Cl HHW HP1 ...49 M7
Lovel End CFSP/GDCR SL9 ...82 B7
Lovell Cl HHW HP1 ...49 M7
Lovell Cl NTHWD HA6 ...95 K2
Lovel Md CFSP/GDCR SL9 ...82 B7
Lovent Dr LBUZ LU7 ...27 J3
Lovett Gdns MDHD SL6 ...99 H7
Lovett Rd DEN/HRF UB9 ...94 B2
Lovetts Cl LBUZ LU7 ...161 K2
Lovibonds Av WDR/YW UB7 ...114 C1
Lowbrook Cl AYLS HP21 ...42 C2
Lowbrook Dr MDHD SL6 ...117 M3
Lowdell Cl WDR/YW UB7 ...114 D3
Lowdon Cl WYM HP11 ...78 C5
Lower Boynton Av MDHD SL6...108 C4
Lower Britwell Rd SLN SL2 ...110 C1
Lower Church St RAYLW HP18...177 G8
SKCH HP14 ...186 H1
Lower Cippenham La SL SL1...110 C5
Lower Cl AYLW HP19 ...2 A9
Lower Cookham Rd
MDHD SL6 ...99 H7
Lower Dr BEAC HP9 ...80 C5
Lower Eighth St CMK MK9 ...6 C5
Lower End BUCK/WIN MK18...142 G10
RAYLNE/WEN HP22 ...168 A4
RAYLW HP18 ...175 H1
RBICS/W OX25 ...173 M1
RMKS/WB MK17 ...144 H1
RNHPTN NN7 ...130 H1
Lower Farm Cl RAYLW HP18 ...180 H3
Lower Farm Gdns HADM HP17...177 L4
Lower Fourth St CMK MK9 ...6 D6
Lower Furney Cl HWYN HP13 ...78 C2
Lower Gn RAYLW HP18 ...165 Q8
Lower Green La HYS/HAR UB3...175 Q8
Lower Icknield Wy CHNR OX39...184 G2
HADM HP17 ...169 P11
LBUZ LU7 ...169 P11
PRRI HP27 ...183 N10
RAYLNE/WEN HP22 ...36 F5
RNHPTN NN7 ...130 H1
Lower Kings Rd BERK HP4 ...48 B5
Lower Lees Rd CMK MK9 ...6 F8
Lower Lodge La HAZ/HG HP15...68 F4
Lower Md IVER SLO ...103 G6
Lower Ninth St CMK MK9 ...7 G4
Lower Plantation
RKW/CH/CXG WD3 ...74 B4
Lower Pound La MLW SL7 ...89 G4
Lower Rdg BNEND SL8 ...89 G4
Lower Riding BEAC HP9 ...89 L2
Lower Rd AYLS HP21 ...42 B1
CFSP/GDCR SL9 ...82 C7
CHNR OX39 ...184 D3
DEN/HRF UB9 ...93 H6

MDHD SL6 ...98 D3
PRRI HP27 ...66 C1
RAYLNE/WEN HP22 ...32 A3
RBICS/W OX25 ...163 M10
RKW/CH/CXG WD3 ...73 J5
Lower Sales HHW HP1 ...49 L8
Lower Second St CMK MK9 ...6 C6
Lower Stonehayes
GTLIN MK14 ...14 C7
Lower St RAYLNE/WEN HP22...166 D1
Lower Tenth St CMK MK9 ...7 G4
Lower Third St CMK MK9 ...6 D6
Lower Twelfth St CMK MK9 ...7 J3
Lower Wy BUCK/WIN MK18 ...149 R4
RMKS/WB MK17 ...24 D4
Lower Whf BUCK/WIN MK18 ...11 M5
Lowes Cl HEN RG9 ...191 L10
SKCH HP14 ...186 H1
Lowestoft Dr SL SL1 ...110 B3
Lowfield Wy HAZ/HG HP15 ...68 F3
Lowfield Wy HAZ/HG HP15 ...69 G2
Lowick Pl EMV/FZ MK4 ...21 L4
Lowland Rd EMV/FZ MK4 ...21 L6
Lowlands Crs HAZ/HG HP15 ...68 C1
Lowlands Dr
STWL/WRAY TW19 ...124 C8
Lowman Wy AYLS HP21 ...42 C2
Lowndes Av CSHM HP5 ...63 G1
Lowndes Wy BUCK/WIN MK18...151 J9
Lowndes Gv SHEN MK5 ...17 J7
Lowood Dr SHEN MK5 ...85 H8
Loxboro Dr EMV/FZ MK4 ...21 M2
Loxborough Cl SKCH HP14 ...76 C2
Loxley Rd BERK HP4 ...47 K4
Loyne Cl LBUZ LU7 ...26 D7
Lucas La RNHPTN NN7 ...126 B3
Lucas Pl EAG/OLD/WTN MK6 ...19 G3
Lucas Rd HWYN HP13 ...5 L5
Lucas Wood Cl HWYN HP13 ...78 C3
Luccombe EMV/FZ MK4 ...22 A3
Lucerne Av BIC OX26 ...162 C2
Lucks Hl HHW HP1 ...49 K7
Lucy La SHEN MK5 ...17 L6
Ludgate EAG/OLD/WTN MK6 ...18 B7
Ludgershall Rd RAYLW HP18 ...164 C10
Ludlow Cl BTCHLY MK3 ...22 C7
Ludlow Dr THAME OX9 ...181 P5
Ludlow Ms WYM HP11 ...78 F6
Ludlow Pl AYL HP20 ...35 H7
Ludlow Rd MDHD SL6 ...108 D5
Ludlow Wy RKW/CH/CXG WD3...75 H5
Ludsden Gv THAME OX9 ...181 P6
Luff Cl WDSR SL4 ...120 D6
Lufford Pk GTLIN MK14 ...14 C5
Luggershall Rd RBICS/W OX25...173 P3
Luke Pl MKV MK10 ...19 J3
Luker Av HEN RG9 ...190 F3
Lukes La TRING HP23 ...169 J11
Lukes Lea TRING HP23 ...37 M1
Lullington Dr BDWL MK13 ...17 L1
Lundholme MDHD SL6 ...17 L1
Lundy Dr HYS/HAR UB3 ...115 K8
Lupin Cl AYLS HP21 ...34 A8
Lupin Ct AYLS HP21 * ...34 A8
Lupin Wk AYLS HP21 ...42 A1
Lupton Rd THAME OX9 ...181 P8
Lutman's Hvn WAR/TWY RG10...116 D1
Lutyens Gv WTR/OFPK MK7 ...144 A5
Lych Gate Wk HYS/HAR UB3...115 L4
Lycrome La CSHM HP5 ...55 J7
Lycrome Rd CSHM HP5 ...55 K7
Lydds Hl RBEDW MK43 ...145 P5
Lydford Av SLN SL2 ...111 J2
Lydiard CNH/GTH/TMA MK8 ...17 H5
Lydiard Cl AYLS HP21 ...43 G2
Lydsey Cl SLN SL2 ...100 F3
Lye Green Rd CSHM HP5 ...63 K1
Lyell Rd WDSR SL4 ...120 B6
The Lye BERK HP4 ...40 C4
Lyme Av BERK HP4 ...47 J3
Lymington Rd RSLP HA4 ...95 J8
Lynch Cl UX/CGN UB8 ...104 B3
Lynchen Cl HEST TW5 ...115 M4
Lynch Hill La SLN SL2 ...110 D1
The Lynch UX/CGN UB8 ...104 B5
Lynden Cl MDHD SL6 ...119 G2
Lyndhurst Av MDHD SL6 * ...98 D4
Lyndhurst Cl HWYN HP13 ...77 H5
Lyndhurst Rd CSHM HP5 ...55 G7
Lyndon Cl GTMIS/PWD HP16 ...60 B3
Lyndon Gdns HWYN HP13 ...78 D2
Lyneham Gdns HADM HP17 ...108 A1
Lyneham Rd BIC OX26 ...162 F2
Lyne Wk RNHPTN NN7 ...126 B3
Lyne Wy HHW HP1 ...49 M5
Lynford Pde HAZ/HG HP15 * ...69 H3
Lynher Cl AYLS HP21 ...42 B2
Lynhurst Crs HGDN/ICK UB10...105 H5
Lynhurst Rd HGDN/ICK UB10...105 H5
Lynmouth Crs EMV/FZ MK4 ...21 M2
Lynott Cl CNH/GTH/TMA MK8... 17 H7
Lynton Gn MDHD SL6 ...108 D3
Lynton Rd CSHM HP5 ...55 G7
Lynwood Av DTCH/LGLY SL3 ...112 C7
Lynwood Dr NTHWD HA6 ...85 K8
Lynwood Hts
RKW/CH/CXG WD3 ...74 A6
Lynwood Rd AYLS HP21 ...42 A1
Lyon Rd DBGH MK1 ...22 E4
Lyra Gdns LBUZ LU7 ...27 L6
Lysander Cl BIC OX26 ...162 F2
HHS/BOV HP3 ...56 F6
Lysander Rd RSLP HA4 ...95 J8
Lywood Rd LBUZ LU7 ...27 K8

M

Macaulay Cl BIC OX26 ...162 B3
Macdonald Cl AMS HP6 ...63 H6
Mackenzie Cl BIC OX26 ...162 B3
Mackenzie St SL SL1 ...111 L6
Madeira Wk WDSR SL4 ...121 J4
Madeley Cl AMSS HP6 ...33 J2
Madeley Rd AYLS HP21 ...34 E4
Magdalen Cl BIC OX26 ...162 D3
BRACKY NN13 ...140 B2
STSTR MK11 ...12 A8
Magdalen Mdw BRACKY NN13... 8 F3
Magenta Cl WEAT MK2 ...23 G8
Magnolia Cl HGDN/ICK UB10 *...105 G4
Magnolia Dene HAZ/HG HP15... 68 F5
Magnolia Gdns DTCH/LGLY SL3...112 A4
The Magnolias BIC OX26 ...162 C4
Magnolia St WDR/YW UB7 ...114 C8
Magnolia Wy FLKWH/TG HP10...89 G3
Magpie Cl FLKWH/TG HP10 ...88 F1
SHEN MK5 ...21 L2
Magpie La AMSS HP7 ...70 E8
BRACKY NN13 ...8 D1
FLKWH/TG HP10 ...88 F1

Magpie Wy BUCK/WIN MK18......151 K9
Mahler Cl WTR/OFPK MK7......23 M1
Mahoney Ct
  CNH/GTH/TMA MK8......17 G8
Maidenhead Ct SLN SL2......6 B3
Maidenhead Court Pk
  MDHD SL6......99 G6
  WDSR SL4......120 B3
Maidstone Rd MKV MK10......19 H4
Maigno Wy WOLV MK12......12 D8
Main Av NTHWD HA6......85 H3
Main Dr CFSP/GDCR SL9......113 K7
  DTCH/LGLY SL3......113 K7
  TOW NN12......136 K4
Main Rd NPAG MK16......135 K7
  PRRI HP27......66 D1
  RAYLW HP18......176 D1
  RMKS/WB MK17......152 C9
  RNHPTN NN7......126 A3
  SKCH HP14......67 C5
  WDSR SL4 *......120 B3
Main Rd North BERK HP4......170 H7
Main Rd South BERK HP4......171 K9
Main St BRACKY NN13......9 H6
  BUCK/WIN MK18......156 C1
  BUCK/WIN MK18......148 C7
  BUCK/WIN MK18......147 K1
  RAYLW HP18......175 M1
  RAYLW HP18......156 C12
  RBICN OX27......155 J3
  RBICN OX27......154 F2
  RMKN MK19......143 P4
  RMKN MK19......12 B4
  RMKS/WB MK17......152 C8
  WHLY OX33......178 D10
Maitland Dr HWYN HP13......5 J3
Maitland Rd
  RAYLNE/WEN HP22......44 C3
Major's Farm Rd
  DTCH/LGLY SL3......122 C3
Makins Rd HEN RG9......190 H4
Malbons Ct
  EAG/OLD/WTN MK6......18 B7
Malcolm Rd HGDN/ICK UB10......104 E2
Malders La MDHD SL6......98 A7
Malet Cl SKCH HP14......187 J1
Malins Ga GTLIN MK14......14 B6
Malkin Dr BEAC HP9......80 B7
Malkin Wy WATW WD18......75 K5
Mallard Cl AYLW HP19......34 D2
Mallard Cft HADM HP17......176 D11
Mallard Dr BUCK/WIN MK18......110 E4
  SL SL1......110 E4
Mallard Pl WYM HP11......79 G8
Mallards Wy BIC OX26......162 E6
Mallard Wy NTHWD HA6......85 H7
Mallets End
  RAYLNE/WEN HP22......166 E2
Malletts Cl STSTR MK11......16 B1
Mallow Ga GTLIN MK14......6 C1
Mallow Pk MDHD SL6......108 B1
The Mallows HGDN/ICK UB10......105 G1
Malm Cl RKW/CH/CXG WD3......84 C2
Malmers Well Rd HWYN HP13......5 L3
Malpas Rd SLN SL2......112 A4
Malmesbury Cl PIN HA5......95 L3
Malthouse Ms DEN/HRF UB9 *......84 B8
Malthouse Sq BEAC HP9......90 E2
  PRRI HP27......58 A3
Malthouse Wy MLW SL7......97 J5
Malting Cl NPAG MK16......132 C4
Malting La BERK HP4......171 K9
  TRING HP23......39 J3
Maltings Cl LBUZ LU7......161 K2
  RBEDW MK43......139 K5
Maltings Fld RMKN MK19......12 C1
The Maltings AMSS HP7 *......71 G2
  BUCK/WIN MK18......11 H2
  BUCK/WIN MK18......10 C8
  LBUZ LU7......27 J8
  OLN MK46 *......128 C11
Malting Wy RNHPTN NN7......131 J1
Malt La BRACKY NN13......140 B2
Maltmans La CFSP/GDCR SL9......92 B2
Malton Av SL SL1......111 G3
Malton Cl MKV MK10......19 J5
Malvern Cl HGDN/ICK UB10......94 F8
  HWYN HP13......4 C3
Malvern Dr LBUZ LU7......26 D6
  STSTR MK11......16 C2
Malvern Rd AYL HP20......35 H6
  HYS/HAR UB3......125 K3
  MDHD SL6......108 C1
Malvern Wy
  RKW/CH/CXG WD3......75 G6
Malyns Cl CHNR OX39......184 F3
Mandelyns BERK HP4......47 K3
Mandeville Cl WAT WD17......75 L1
Mandeville Dr MKV MK10......19 M4
Mandeville Rd AYLS HP21......42 D1
  GTMIS/PWD HP16......60 A3
Manfield Cl SLN SL2......100 F8
Manifold La SHEN MK5......21 K5
Mannock Wy LBUZ LU7......29 L1
Manor Cl BERK HP4 *......48 B6
  BUCK/WIN MK18......149 R4
  FLKWH/TG HP10......68 D8
  GTMIS/PWD HP16......60 C6
  MKV MK10......19 J3
  PRRI HP27......185 L1
  RBEDW MK43......129 Q3
  RMKN MK19......131 M8
  RMKS/WB MK17......153 R7
  RMKS/WB MK17......152 C8
  RSLP HA4......95 L7
Manor Cots NTHWD HA6......85 L8
Manor Ct BRACKY NN13......8 E7
  DEN/HRF UB9......94 B1
  MLW SL7......97 H3
  SL SL1......110 E4
Manor Court Yd HWYN HP13......5 H2
Manor Crs BEAC HP9......81 J5
  RAYLNE/WEN HP22......44 B5
Manor Dr AMS HP6......63 J2
  AYL HP20......3 J2
  LBUZ LU7......161 K2
  RMKN MK19......13 G4
Manor Farm Cl HADM HP17......177 M6
  LBUZ LU7......153 R12
  RAYLNE/WEN HP22......43 K4
  RBICS/W OX25......172 C2
  WDSR SL4......120 E6
Manor Farm Cots WDSR SL4......121 M8
Manor Farm La LBUZ LU7......28 D6
Manorfields Rd RMKN MK19......131 M7
Manor Gdns BUCK/WIN MK18......11 M4
  FLKWH/TG HP10......89 K6
  HWYN HP13......5 H2
Manor Gv MDHD SL6......119 J4
Manor House Cl AYL HP20......3 J4

Manor House Dr NTHWD HA6......85 G7
Manor House La
  DTCH/LGLY SL3......122 A4
Manor La CFSP/GDCR SL9......92 C6
  HYS/HAR UB3......125 J2
  MDHD SL6......108 D6
Manor Pk BUCK/WIN MK18......142 A6
Manor Park Av PRRI HP27......183 R12
Manor Pound Rd LBUZ LU7......169 M7
Manor Rd AYL HP20......3 H3
  BEAC HP9......81 J5
  BRACKY NN13......9 J7
  BUCK/WIN MK18......142 A3
  CSHM HP5......55 G8
  HAZ/HG HP15......68 E7
  HEN RG9......190 G6
  HYS/HAR UB3......115 M3
  LBUZ LU7......169 L7
  MDHD SL6......108 D6
  NPAG MK16......14 D2
  PRRI HP27......183 R12
  RAYLNE/WEN HP22......159 N11
  RAYLNE/WEN HP22......44 B5
  RAYLNE/WEN HP22......33 J3
  RAYLW HP18......179 Q1
  RBICN OX27......155 J3
  RMKS/WB MK17......153 J3
  RSLP HA4......95 J7
  THAME OX9......120 D5
  TRING HP23......37 M5
  WDSR SL4......120 C6
  WEAT MK2......23 C6
  WOLV MK12......12 D8
Manorsfield Rd BIC OX26......162 D4
Manor Stables
  WAR/TWY RG10 *......191 N12
Manor St BERK HP4......48 C3
  BUCK/WIN MK18......11 K6
Manor Vw HAZ/HG HP15......69 G8
  MDHD SL6......118 F2
Manor Wy CSHM HP5......63 J1
  MDHD SL6......108 D6
  RKW/CH/CXG WD3......74 F5
  RSLP HA4......95 K6
  TOW NN12......130 D12
Manor Waye UX/CGN UB8......104 C6
Manor Wood Ga HEN RG9......191 K10
Mansard Cl TRING HP23......37 M7
Manse Cl HYS/HAR UB3......125 J2
  STSTR MK11......55 G7
Mansell Cl SHEN MK5 *......17 K8
  WDSR SL4......120 D5
Mansell Ct RMKN MK19......12 A4
Manse Cl SHEN MK5......21 M1
Manshead Ct STSTR MK11......16 C1
Mansion Dr TRING HP23......38 A7
Mansion Hl RAYLNE/WEN HP22......44 D2
Mansion La IVER SL0......113 H5
The Mansions OLN MK46 *......128 C11
Manston Cl BIC OX26......162 C3
Manston Ct HYS/HAR UB3......115 K4
Manton Rd DUN/WHIP LU6......171 L1
Manzel Rd RBICN OX27......154 E12
Maple Av WDR/YW UB7......114 D4
Maple Cl BRACKY NN13......8 E4
  HAZ/HG HP15......68 F7
  HWYN HP13......87 H1
  MDHD SL6......108 B5
Maple Crs SLN SL2......112 A4
Mapledean WOLV MK12......17 H1
Mapledurham WTR/OFPK MK7......23 K3
Maple End RAYLNE/WEN HP22......43 H2
Maplefield La CSTG HP8......72 A4
Maple Gn HHW HP1......49 K5
Maple Gv RMKS/WB MK17......144 D6
  WAT WD17......75 M2
  WEAT MK2......23 H6
Maple Leys BUCK/WIN MK18......149 M11
Maple Lodge Cl
  RKW/CH/CXG WD3......83 K4
Maple Pl WDR/YW UB7......114 C2
Maple Ri MLW SL7......97 K3
Maple Rd BIC OX26......162 K4
  THAME OX9......181 L6
The Maples BNEND SL8 *......89 J7
  RAYLNE/WEN HP22......44 B5
Maple Wy RBEDW MK43......139 K6
Maplewood Gdns BEAC HP9......90 A1
Maplin Pk DTCH/LGLY SL3......113 G6
Mapperton Cl EMV/FZ MK4......21 H5
Mapridge Green La
  GTMIS/PWD HP16......60 D3
Mara Pl CMK MK9......7 L2
Marbeck Dr WDSR SL4......120 C4
March Meadow
  WTR/OFPK MK7......144 A3
March Pl AYLW HP19......2 B5
Marcia Cl SL SL1......110 K5
Marcourt Rd SKCH HP14......187 J2
Mardle Rd LBUZ LU7......27 C8
Maree Cl LBUZ LU7......26 D7
Marefield Rd MLW SL7......97 J4
Mare Leys BUCK/WIN MK18......142 A10
Marescroft Rd SLN SL2......110 D1
Margam Crs MKV MK10......19 K5
Margaret Cl BIC OX26......162 C2
Marigold Cl GTLIN MK14......14 D1
Marigold Wk BIC OX26......162 D1
Marina Dr DUN/WHIP LU6......31 M7
  WOLV MK12......17 G1
Marina Wy IVER SL0......17 G1
  SL SL1......110 L4
Marine La DEN/HRF UB9......93 H3
Marish Whf DTCH/LGLY SL3 *......112 D6
Marjoram Pl GTLIN MK14......18 B1
Mark Dr CFSP/GDCR SL9......82 C4
Markenfield Pl EMV/FZ MK4......21 H5
Market Cl LBUZ LU7 *......27 H7
Market End Cl BIC OX26......162 D5
Market End Wy BIC OX26......162 D5
Market Hl BUCK/WIN MK18......11 L5
  EAG/OLD/WTN MK6......18 C8
  RAYLNE/WEN HP22......159 Q12
Market La DTCH/LGLY SL3......113 H1
Market Pde HAZ/HG HP15......68 D7
Market Pl BRACKY NN13......8 D8
  CFSP/GDCR SL9......82 C3
  DTCH/LGLY SL3 *......123 H1
  OLN MK46......128 C11
  RMKS/WB MK17......145 J11
Market Sq AYL HP20......2 F5
  BIC OX26......162 D5
  BUCK/WIN MK18......11 L5
  LBUZ LU7......27 H7
  RMKN MK19......131 M7
Market St AYL HP20......2 F5
  MDHD SL6......108 D1
Market Wk AMSS HP7 *......71 G3
Markham Pl AYLW HP19......177 R3

Markhams Ct BUCK/WIN MK18......11 L6
Marks Orch BUCK/WIN MK18......159 J3
Marlborough Av RSLP HA4......95 H5
Marlborough Crs
  HYS/HAR UB3......125 J3
Marlborough Cft
  BRACKY NN13......8 D8
Marlborough Pl OLN MK46......7 J5
Marlborough Pde
  HGDN/ICK UB10......115 G3
Marlborough Rd AYLS HP21......42 D2
  DTCH/LGLY SL3......112 C8
  HGDN/ICK UB10......115 G3
  MDHD SL6......107 M8
Marlborough St CMK MK9......7 J2
  EAG/OLD/WTN MK6......23 C1
  GTLIN MK14......13 M6
Marley Flds LBUZ LU7......27 L8
Marley Gv CNH/GTH/TMA MK8......17 H7
Marlin Cl BERK HP4......47 L5
Marlin Copse BERK HP4......47 M3
Marlin Ct BIC OX26......97 J5
Marlin Hl TRING HP23......45 M1
Marlins Cl RKW/CH/CXG WD3......73 K3
Marlins End BERK HP4......47 M3
Marlins Meadow WATW WD18......75 J7
The Marlins NTHWD HA6......85 L6
Marlow Bottom MLW SL7......97 J1
Marlow Bridge La MLW SL7......97 J4
Marlow Common MLW SL7......96 A6
Marlow Dr NPAG MK16......14 D2
Marlow Gdns HYS/HAR UB3......115 J3
Marlow Hl WYM HP11......87 L3
Marlow Mi MLW SL7......97 K5
Marlow Rd BNEND SL8......88 B5
  HEN RG9......190 H1
  MDHD SL6......108 D3
  MLW SL7......97 J8
  SKCH HP14......187 P8
  WYM HP11......87 K3
Marmion Rd HEN RG9......190 H1
Marnham Ri HHW HP1......49 M5
Marquis Ct RMKS/WB MK17......145 J11
Marram Cl EAG/OLD/WTN MK6......22 D1
Marriner Ct HYS/HAR UB3 *......115 K4
Marriotts Av GTMIS/PWD HP16......61 K1
Marriott's Cl HADM HP17......176 C12
Marriott's La HADM HP17......176 C12
Marriott's Wy HADM HP17......176 C12
Marriott Ter
  RKW/CH/CXG WD3......73 L5
Marrod's Bottom AMSS HP7......80 B2
Marron La WOLV MK12......16 F1
Marroway RAYLNE/WEN HP22......43 J3
Marshall Dr WDSR SL4......120 D4
Marshalls La WLLN MK15......18 F4
Marshalls Lea
  RAYLNE/WEN HP22......35 J3
Marsham Ct AYLS HP21......42 F2
Marsham La CFSP/GDCR SL9......92 D5
Marsham Ldg CFSP/GDCR SL9......92 D5
Marsham Wy CFSP/GDCR SL9......92 D5
Marshaw Pl EMV/FZ MK4......21 M4
Marshcroft La TRING HP23......38 C4
Marsh Dr GTLIN MK14......14 B4
Marsh End Rd NPAG MK16......14 F2
Marshfield DTCH/LGLY SL3......122 B4
Marsh Gibbon Rd RAYLW HP18......156 F10
Marsh La MDHD SL6......109 L6
Marsh Rd RAYLNE/WEN HP22......50 C2
  RAYLW HP18......180 D3
The Marsh RBEDW MK43......129 P3
Marshworth
  EAG/OLD/WTN MK6......19 G8
Marston Cl CSHM HP5......54 F6
Marston Ct TRING HP23......168 G10
Marstonfields Rd
  BUCK/WIN MK18......159 J3
Marston Hl RAYLNE/WEN HP22......159 N10
  RBEDW MK43......139 P4
Marston Rd BUCK/WIN MK18......159 J4
  THAME OX9......181 P5
Marsworth Cl WATW WD18 *......75 K7
Marsworth Rd LBUZ LU7......169 Q10
Martell Cl WTR/OFPK MK7......23 K2
Martial Daire Bvd
  BRACKY NN13......8 D6
Martin Cl BIC OX26......162 E6
  HGDN/ICK UB10......142 A11
  GTLIN MK14......14 B8
  HGDN/ICK UB10......104 D7
  WDSR SL4......120 B4
Martindale IVER SL0......113 H1
Martindale Rd HHW HP1......49 L6
Martingale Pl GTLIN MK14......18 C1
Martin Rd MDHD SL6......108 E2
  SL SL1......111 K7
The Martins Dr LBUZ LU7......27 C6
Martinsend La
  GTMIS/PWD HP16......60 D3
Martin's Pln SLN SL2......101 L2
Martins Rd RNHPTN NN7......126 A5
Marunden Gn SLN SL2......100 E8
Marvell Av YEAD UB4......115 M2
Marwood Dr EMV/FZ MK4......22 A1
Mary Cross Ct TRING HP23......46 C1
Marygold Wk AMS HP6......72 B2
Maryland Rd WLLN MK15......14 B6
Mary Macmuras Dr
  BUCK/WIN MK18......11 L5
Maryot Cl MKV MK16......133 N8
Maryside DTCH/LGLY SL3......112 C6
Mary's Md HAZ/HG HP15......68 G6
Masefield Cl BIC OX26......162 B5
  NPAG MK16......14 D2
Masefield Gv BTCHLY MK3......22 A5
Maslin Dr EAG/OLD/WTN MK6......18 C7
Mason Cl GTLIN MK14......13 M6
Masons Cl GTMIS/PWD HP16......60 B5
Mason's Ct AYLW HP19......2 A7
Masons Rd SL SL1......110 D4
Massie Cl WLLN MK15......14 C7
Mathiesen Rd BDWL MK13......13 M8
Matilda Gdns SHEN MK5......14 F4
Matlock Rd AYL HP20......3 J1
Matson Dr HEN RG9......191 J4
Matthau Dr EMV/FZ MK4......21 M4
Matthews Cl AYL HP20......3 H1
  AYL......17 L8
Maud Cl BIC OX26......3 H1
Maude Pl BEAC HP9......90 F1
Maude Rd BEAC HP9......90 E1
Maud Jane's Cl LBUZ LU7......169 M7
Maudsley Cl SHEN MK5......21 M1
Mauduit Ct RMKN MK19......131 M7
Maulden Gdns GTLIN MK14......14 A1
Maundsey Cl DUN/WHIP LU6......171 J1
Maurice Mt HAZ/HG HP15......68 G6
Mavoncliff Dr EMV/FZ MK4......21 M4
Maxham SHEN MK5......14 F4

Maxwell Cl HYS/HAR UB3......115 M4
  RKW/CH/CXG WD3......83 M2
Maxwell Dr HAZ/HG HP9......69 G5
Maxwell Rd BEAC HP9......80 C7
  NTHWD HA6......85 J7
  WDR/YW UB7......114 D8
Maybank Gdns PIN HA5......95 H4
Maybrook Gdns HWYN HP13......5 L4
Maybury Cl SL SL1......110 C2
Maybush Gdns
  GTMIS/PWD HP16......60 B4
Maybush Wk OLN MK46......128 B10
Maycock Gv NTHWD HA6......85 L6
Maycroft BIC OX26......162 E2
Mayditch Pl BDWL MK13......6 D7
Mayer Gdns SHEN MK5......21 M1
Mayfare RKW/CH/CXG WD3......75 J6
Mayfield Cl HGDN/ICK UB10......105 C8
Mayfield Dr WDSR SL4......120 F6
Mayfield Rd FLKWH/TG HP10......89 K4
  HADM HP17......177 C5
  RSLP HA4......95 H5
Mayflower Wy SLN SL2......101 H3
Maygoods Cl UX/CGN UB8......114 C2
Maygoods Gn UX/CGN UB8......114 C2
Maygoods La UX/CGN UB8......114 C2
Maygoods Vw UX/CGN UB8......114 B2
Mayhall La AMS HP6......63 J2
Mayhew Crs HWYN HP13......78 C2
Maylands Dr UX/CGN UB8......104 C4
Maynard Cl BDWL MK13......17 K3
Maynard Dr AYLS HP21......42 F2
Maypole Rd MDHD SL6......109 M2
Maypool Wy MKV MK10......19 L4
May Rd RBEDW MK43......129 N8
Mayroft Av YEAD UB4......115 M2
Mays Wy TOW NN12......137 L8
Maythorne Cl WATW WD18......75 K5
May Tree Cl BIC OX26......162 D2
  MLW SL7......87 H8
Mc Ardle Wy DTCH/LGLY SL3......123 J4
McAuliffe Dr SL SL1......100 C1
McConnell Dr WOLV MK12......13 G7
McDonald Cl EMV/FZ MK4......21 M4
McDougall Rd BERK HP4......48 C3
McEwen Ride
  RAYLNE/WEN HP22......44 C1
McKenzie Cl BUCK/WIN MK18......11 L5
McLellan Pl HWYN HP12......4 D9
McLernon Wy BUCK/WIN MK18......151 K9
McQuorquodale Rd
  WOLV MK12......12 E7
Mead Acre PRRI HP27......58 A1
Mead Cl DEN/HRF UB9......93 M8
  DTCH/LGLY SL3......113 G6
  MLW SL7......97 J3
  PRRI HP27......50 A8
Meades La CSHM HP5......63 G3
Meadfield Av DTCH/LGLY SL3......112 F3
Meadfield Rd DTCH/LGLY SL3......112 F3
Mead House La YEAD UB4......115 J1
Meadoway BUCK/WIN MK18......149 L11
  HADM HP17......177 Q6
Meadow Bank Cl AMSS HP7......71 K1
Meadowbank Cl HHS/BOV HP3......57 G7
  RAYLW HP18......175 K12
Meadowbank Gdns HEST TW5......125 H4
  HSLWW TW4......125 H4
Meadowbrook Cl
  DTCH/LGLY SL3......123 K5
  LBUZ LU7......160 H9
  MLW SL7......97 J3
  RAYLW HP18......179 Q2
  RSLP HA4......95 J1
  TRING HP23......37 M5
  WDSR SL4......122 A8
Meadowcot La AMSS HP7......70 E7
Meadowcroft BERK HP4......47 J3
  CFSP/GDCR SL9......92 C1
Meadow Dr AMS HP6......63 K8
  PRRI HP27......183 N8
Meadow Farm Rd
  RBEDW MK43......135 Q9
Meadow Gdns
  BUCK/WIN MK18......11 M8
  MDHD SL6......98 B7
Meadow Ga BUCK/WIN MK18......149 Q4
  GTMIS/PWD HP16......80 B7
Meadow La BEAC HP9......80 D7
  LBUZ LU7......169 R11
  MKV MK10......19 J3
  RAYLW HP18......181 M2
  SL SL1......121 G2
Meadowlea Cl WDR/YW UB7......124 C2
Meadow Pk
  RAYLNE/WEN HP22......43 H4
Meadow Ri PRRI HP27......66 D1
Meadow Rd BERK HP4......48 D1
  CHNR OX39......184 G4
  DTCH/LGLY SL3......112 D7
  HEN RG9......190 H5
Meadow Road Cl BERK HP4......47 M4
Meadowside BERK HP4......81 L7
The Meadows AMSS HP7......71 K2
  FLKWH/TG HP10......89 G2
  HWYN HP13......49 K6
  RAYLNE/WEN HP22......159 Q11
  RMKN MK19......137 Q8
Meadowsweet
  WTR/OFPK MK7......23 L1
Meadow Vw CSTG HP8......81 J4
  MLW SL7......87 K8
  RAYLW HP18......181 M2
  RMKS/WB MK17......144 C4
  STWL/WRAY TW19......123 L8
  TOW NN12......137 L3
  UX/CGN UB8 *......114 B2
Meadowview La MDHD SL6......118 D2
Meadow View Rd YEAD UB4......115 J1
Meadow Wy AMS HP6......62 M6
  FLKWH/TG HP10......79 H1
  HHS/BOV HP3......57 L2
  LBUZ LU7......27 L1
  MDHD SL6......119 J4
  RKW/CH/CXG WD3......74 D8
Mead Pk HAZ/HG HP15......68 E7
Mead Pl RKW/CH/CXG WD3......74 D8
Mead Platt SKCH HP14......186 D4
Meads Cl BDWL MK13......13 L8
The Meads BERK HP4......47 L4
  DUN/WHIP LU6......170 F1
Mead St HWYN HP13......78 F6
The Mead BEAC HP9......80 C7
  HHS/BOV HP3......57 G7

  LBUZ LU7......153 R1
Mead Wk DTCH/LGLY SL3......113 G6
Meadway BERK HP4......48 D5
  BUCK/WIN MK18......11 L8
  LBUZ LU7......27 K6
  RAYLNE/WEN HP22......159 P9
  SL SL1......110 C2
  WYM HP11......78 E6
Meadway Pk CFSP/GDCR SL9......92 C7
The Meadway SHEN MK5......21 K6
Meare Est FLKWH/TG HP10......89 J2
Meavy Cl HWYN HP13......79 G7
Medale Rd EAG/OLD/WTN MK6......22 D1
Medallion Pl MDHD SL6......108 A4
Medbourne BDWL MK13......6 A4
Medesell EMV/FZ MK4......22 B3
Medhurst CNH/GTH/TMA MK8......17 J6
Medina Gdns BIC OX26......162 A4
Medland EAG/OLD/WTN MK6......19 G7
Medley Cl DUN/WHIP LU6......170 G1
Medman Cl UX/CGN UB8......114 A4
Medway Cl NPAG MK16......15 H3
Meeting Oak La
  BUCK/WIN MK18......151 L9
Megdale Pl AYL HP20......2 B5
Melbourne Av SL SL1......111 H3
Melbourne Ct AYLS HP21......42 D1
Melbourne Rd HWYN HP13......78 E4
Melford Gn AYLW HP19......34 B3
Melfort Dr LBUZ LU7......26 C7
  WEAT MK2......153 Q2
Melick Rd EAG/OLD/WTN MK6......22 D1
Melina Cl HYS/HAR UB3......115 J2
Mellor Wk WDSR SL4......121 J4
Mellow La East
  HGDN/ICK UB10......115 H1
Mellstock Rd AYLS HP21......42 E1
Melrose Av BTCHLY MK3......22 A5
Melrose Cl YEAD UB4......115 M2
Melrose Pl WAT WD17......75 L1
Melrose Wk AYLS HP21......42 E1
Melton Ctl MDHD SL6......108 A4
Melton Rd MDHD SL6......108 A4
Melville Cl BIC OX26......162 A4
  HGDN/ICK UB10......105 J1
Melville Cl HWYN HP13......5 L6
Memorial Av HEN RG9......190 H12
Mendelssohn Gv
  WTR/OFPK MK7......23 M2
Mendip Cl DTCH/LGLY SL3......122 F1
  HYS/HAR UB3......125 J3
Mendip Wy HWYN HP13......4 E3
Mendy St WYM HP11......5 J7
Menmarsh Rd RAYLW HP18......179 Q7
Mentmore Cl HWYN HP12......77 G8
Mentmore Ct
  CNH/GTH/TMA MK8......17 J6
Mentmore Crs DUN/WHIP LU6......171 J1
Mentmore Gdns LBUZ LU7......28 F1
Mentmore Rd HWYN HP13......77 G8
  LBUZ LU7......169 L6
  LBUZ LU7......28 F1
Mentmore Vw TRING HP23......37 L5
Mentone Av RMKS/WB MK17......144 G6
Menzies Ct SHEN MK5......21 L2
Menzies Dr BDWL MK13......13 L8
Mercers Meadow
  RAYLNE/WEN HP22......44 A4
Merchant La RBEDW MK43......139 J4
Merchant Pl MKV MK10......110 A6
Mercian Wy SL SL1......110 C5
Mercia Rd MDHD SL6......108 A6
Mercury Gv
  CNH/GTH/TMA MK8......17 H7
Mercury House
  HYS/HAR UB3 *......27 L6
Mercury Wy LBUZ LU7......27 L6
Meredith Cl BIC OX26......162 B3
Meredith Dr AYLW HP19......167 Q12
Mere La MLW SL7......97 L4
Mere Pk MLW SL7 *......97 L4
Mere Rd BUCK/WIN MK18......111 L7
  SL SL1......111 L7
Merganser Dr BIC OX26......162 G6
Merle Av DEN/HRF UB9......84 B1
Merlewood Dr HWYN HP11......87 K2
Merlewood Dr SHEN MK5......21 H2
Merlin Cl DTCH/LGLY SL3......123 C2
  EAG/OLD/WTN MK6......7 M9
Merlins Cft LBUZ LU7......27 K1
Merlin Wk EAG/OLD/WTN MK6......162 G6
Merman Ri HWYN HP12......77 G8
Merrivale Ms WDR/YW UB7 *......114 C3
Merrow Dr HHW HP1......49 J6
Merrows Cl NTHWD HA6......85 H6
Merry Down HWYN HP13......4 C7
Merryfields UX/CGN UB8......104 C2
Mersey Cl BTCHLY MK3......22 A5
Mersey Wy BTCHLY MK3......22 A5
Merthen Gv EMV/FZ MK4......21 M4
Merton Av HGDN/ICK UB10......105 C5
  MDHD SL6......108 D7
Merton Dr EAG/OLD/WTN MK6......22 D2
Merton Rd NPAG MK16......58 A4
  RBICS/W OX25......162 H11
  SL SL1......111 M7
Merton St HGDN/ICK UB10......105 C5
Merwin Wy WDSR SL4......121 G2
Messenger Av AYLS HP21......3 L1
Metcalfe Gv GTLIN MK14......14 C1
Meteor Cl BIC OX26......162 G6
Metropolitan Ms WATW WD18......75 K5
Metropolitan Station Ap
  WATW WD18......75 K5
Mezen Cl NTHWD HA6......85 J5
Micawber Av UX/CGN UB8......114 B2
Michael Cl MDHD SL6......108 B5
Michaels Ms AYLW HP19......177 R2
Michigan Dr WLLN MK15......14 F5
Micholls Av CFSP/GDCR SL9......78 E8
Micklem Dr HHW HP1......49 J6
Mickleton WLLN MK15......14 F5
Micklewell La TOW NN12......178 D10
Mickle Wy BERK HP4......47 L4
Midcroft SLN SL2......111 G1
Mid Cross La CFSP/GDCR SL9......82 C5
Middlecroft Rd HWYN HP13......5 J5
Middle Culham HEN RG9......191 N4
Middle Fld RAYLNE/WEN HP22......43 J3
Middlefield Cl RAYLNE/WEN HP22......43 J3
Middle Gn DTCH/LGLY SL3......112 D4
  LBUZ LU7......27 K6
Middlegreen Rd
  DTCH/LGLY SL3......112 C3
Middlehill HHW HP1......49 K1
Middleknights Hl HWYN HP13......49 K6
Middle La HHS/BOV HP3......64 F2

Middle Meadow *CSTG* HP8 ... 82 A3
Middle Rd *AYLS* HP21 ... 35 G7
  BERK HP4 ... 48 A8
  DEN/HRF UB9 ... 93 H6
  WHLY OX33 ... 178 C8
Middlesex Dr *BTCHLY* MK3 ... 22 C5
Middle Slade *BUCK/WIN* MK18 ... 11 L8
Middleton *GTLIN* MK14 ... 14 B7
Middleton Dr *PIN* HA5 ... 95 M2
Middleton Rd *HYS/HAR* UB3 ... 115 K8
  RKW/CH/CXG WD3 ... 83 M1
Middleton Stoney Rd
  BIC OX26 ... 162 A4
Middleton Wy *LBUZ* LU7 ... 29 L1
Middle Wk *SL* SL1 ... 100 A8
Middle Wy *OX39* ... 184 E4
The Middleway *HWYW* HP12 ... 77 H8
Midhurst Cl *AYLS* HP21 ... 43 G1
Midhurst Gdns
  HGDN/ICK UB10 ... 105 H5
Midland Rd *OLN* MK46 ... 128 D3
Midshires Wy *BDWL* MK13 ... 17 J1
  BUCK/WIN MK18 ... 158 D3
  CHNR OX39 ... 185 K3
  CNH/GTH/TMA MK8 ... 17 K4
  GTLIN MK14 ... 13 M6
  HADM HP17 ... 177 N10
  PRRI HP27 ... 183 K6
  RAYLNE/WEN HP22 ... 158 F12
  RAYLW HP18 ... 166 D10
  RMKN MK19 ... 132 A12
  RMKS/WB MK17 ... 150 G5
  RNHPTN NN7 ... 126 A7
  SHEN MK5 ... 21 G1
Midsummer Ar *CMK* MK9 ... 7 G3
Midsummer Bvd *CMK* MK9 ... 6 D6
Midsummer Dr *RAYLW* HP18 ... 156 G12
Midway *LBUZ* LU7 ... 27 K7
Miersfield *WYM* HP11 ... 87 J3
Mikern Cl *WEAT* MK2 ... 22 F6
Milburn Av *CNH/GTH/TMA* MK6 ... 6 F8
Milburn Dr *WDR/YW* UB7 ... 114 C4
Mildenhall Rd *SL* SL1 ... 111 K3
Mildred Av *HYS/HAR* UB3 ... 115 J8
  WATW WD18 ... 75 M5
Mile Elm *MLW* SL7 ... 97 M3
Miles Av *LBUZ* LU7 ... 27 J6
Miles Cl *AYLS* HP21 ... 3 M7
  GTLIN MK14 ... 14 D3
Miles End *AYLS* HP21 ... 34 A8
Milesmere *CNH/GTH/TMA* MK8 ... 17 C5
Milestone Cl *SKCH* HP14 ... 186 H1
Miletree Ct *LBUZ* LU7 ... 27 L6
Mile Tree Rd *LBUZ* LU7 ... 27 L3
Milfoil Av *GTLIN* MK14 ... 18 A2
Milford Av *STSTR* MK11 ... 16 B2
Milford Pl *AYLW* HP19 ... 177 Q2
Millards Cl *RBEDW* MK43 ... 139 L11
Millars Cl *RAYLW* HP18 ... 156 G12
Mill Av *UX/CGN* UB8 ... 104 C7
Millbank *LBUZ* LU7 ... 27 C6
  MLW SL7 ... 97 L5
Millbank Pl *WTR/OFPK* MK7 ... 19 L6
Millboard Rd *BNEND* SL8 ... 89 G3
Mill Bridge Pl *UX/CGN* UB8 ... 104 B7
Millbrook Wy *DTCH/LGLY* SL3 ... 123 J5
Millbrook Cl *HWYW* HP12 ... 4 B3
Mill Cl *BUCK/WIN* MK18 ... 151 J9
  CSHM HP5 ... 63 K5
  HEN RG9 ... 188 C10
  RAYLNE/WEN HP22 ... 33 M3
  WDR/YW UB7 ... 114 C7
Mill Ct *WOLV* MK12 ... 16 D1
Milldun Wy *HWYW* HP12 ... 4 B7
Mill End Cl *DUN/WHIP* LU6 ... 170 G1
Mill End Rd *HWYW* HP12 ... 4 A3
Millennium Cl *UX/CGN* UB8 ... 104 B9
Millennium Point *AYLW* HP19 * ... 177 R1
Millennium Whf
  RKW/CH/CXG WD3 ... 84 D1
Millers Cl *LBUZ* LU7 ... 27 L7
Millers Turn *CHNR* OX39 ... 184 E4
Millers Wy *HWYW* HP12 ... 177 R2
  WOLV MK12 ... 16 E2
Milley La *WAR/TWY* RG10 ... 116 A6
Milley Rd *WAR/TWY* RG10 ... 116 A7
Millfield *BERK* HP4 ... 48 C5
Millfield Av *WDR* OX27 ... 156 A7
Millfield Cl *RBEDW* MK43 ... 139 L4
  RBICN OX27 ... 156 A7
Millfields *CSHM* HP5 ... 63 H4
Mill Gdns *TRING* HP23 ... 38 A6
Millhayes *GTLIN* MK14 ... 14 C6
Millholm Ri
  EAG/OLD/WTN MK6 ... 23 H1
Millington Ga *WLLN* MK15 ... 15 C6
Millington Rd *HYS/HAR* UB3 ... 115 H7
Mill La *AMSS* HP7 ... 70 F2
  BDWL MK13 ... 13 K7
  BRACKY NN13 ... 8 F8
  BUCK/WIN MK18 ... 148 D12
  BUCK/WIN MK18 ... 11 K6
  CFSP/GDCR SL9 ... 92 E5
  CHNR OX39 ... 184 E4
  CSTG HP8 ... 81 M2
  DTCH/LGLY SL3 ... 123 C6
  GTMIS/PWD HP16 ... 61 H3
  HEN RG9 ... 191 H6
  MDHD SL6 ... 106 D2
  PRRI HP27 ... 50 B8
  RAYLNE/WEN HP22 ... 168 B4
  RAYLNE/WEN HP22 ... 43 M3
  RBEDW MK43 ... 129 M9
  RBICS/W OX25 ... 173 K3
  RMKS/WB MK17 ... 24 A4
  SKCH HP14 ... 186 F1
  STSTR MK11 ... 137 R9
  THAME OX9 ... 181 Q3
  WDSR SL4 ... 120 F3
  WHLY OX33 ... 172 F12
  WLLN MK15 ... 18 D1
Mill Meadow *AYLW* HP19 ... 2 A7
Mill Md *RAYLNE/WEN* HP22 ... 44 A5
Mill Pl *DTCH/LGLY* SL3 ... 122 C6
Mill Ri *RBEDW* MK43 ... 129 M9
Mill Rd *BRACKY* NN13 ... 9 K2
  HEN RG9 ... 191 L11
  LBUZ LU7 ... 27 K8
  LBUZ LU7 ... 29 H8
  MLW SL7 ... 97 K5
  RAYLW HP18 ... 180 F5
  RAYLW HP18 ... 179 Q2
  RBEDW MK43 ... 129 N5
  RBEDW MK43 ... 139 L4
  RBICN OX27 ... 155 K9
  RMKN MK19 ... 13 L1
  SKCH HP14 ... 186 F2
  WDR/YW UB7 ... 114 C7

WEAT MK2 ... 23 H7
Mills Cl *HGDN/ICK* UB10 ... 104 F7
Millside *BNEND* SL8 ... 89 H7
Millside Pk *WDSR* SL4 * ... 120 F5
Mill Sq *WOLV* MK12 ... 16 D1
Millstream La *SL* SL1 ... 110 D5
The Millstream *WYM* HP11 ... 5 M8
Millstream Wy
  FLKWH/TG HP10 ... 89 J2
  LBUZ LU7 ... 27 C7
Mill St *AYL* HP20 ... 3 H4
  BERK HP4 ... 48 B6
  DTCH/LGLY SL3 ... 123 J5
  NPAG MK16 ... 15 C1
  SLN SL2 ... 111 L5
  WHLY OX33 ... 178 C7
  WYM HP11 ... 4 F5
The Mill *RBEDW* MK43 * ... 129 M9
  TRING HP23 ... 37 H1
Millthorne Cl
  RKW/CH/CXG WD3 ... 74 C6
Mill Vw *RMKN* MK19 * ... 12 C1
Mill View Rd *TRING* HP23 ... 37 L6
Mill Wy *AYL* HP20 ... 2 D6
  RKW/CH/CXG WD3 ... 83 L1
  RMKS/WB MK17 ... 144 G5
Milner Rd *SL* SL1 ... 109 M2
Milneway *DEN/HRF* UB9 ... 84 A8
Milton Av *AYLS* HP21 ... 21 K5
Milton Cl *BIC* OX26 ... 162 B3
  DTCH/LGLY SL3 ... 122 F6
  HEN RG9 ... 190 C4
  YEAD UB4 ... 115 M3
Milton Crs *WHLY* OX33 ... 178 E10
Milton Dr *NPAC* MK16 ... 15 H2
Milton Flds *CSTG* HP8 ... 82 A3
Milton Gdns *PRRI* HP27 ... 183 Q11
Milton Gv *BTCHLY* MK3 ... 22 C5
Milton Keynes Boundary Wk
  EMV/FZ MK4 ... 21 G5
  LBUZ LU7 ... 24 F5
  NPAC MK16 ... 135 J11
  NPAC MK16 ... 131 K1
  RMKN MK19 ... 143 R1
  RNHPTN NN7 ... 127 N6
  WOLV MK12 ... 12 C7
Milton Lawns *AMS* HP6 ... 63 J7
Milton Rd *AYLS* HP21 ... 34 D7
  CSHM HP5 ... 55 G8
  HGDN/ICK UB10 ... 105 G2
  RAYLNE/WEN HP22 ... 36 E5
  SLN SL2 ... 111 J1
  WLLN MK15 ... 15 C7
Milton Wy *WDR/YW* UB7 ... 114 E8
Milverton Cl *MDHD* SL6 ... 108 A4
Milverton Dr *HGDN/ICK* UB10 ... 105 H2
Mimosa Cl *AYLS* HP21 ... 34 A8
Mina Av *DTCH/LGLY* SL3 ... 112 C6
Minall Cl *TRING* HP23 ... 37 L6
Mineral La *CSHM* HP5 ... 63 H3
Minerva Cl *STWL/WRAY* TW19 * ... 123 H8
Minerva Gdns *WTR/OFPK* MK7 ... 19 M7
Minerva Wy *BEAC* HP9 ... 90 F1
Mines Cl *HWYN* HP13 ... 4 E4
Minet Dr *HYS/HAR* UB3 ... 115 M5
Ministry Whf *SKCH* HP14 * ... 66 B5
Minniecroft Rd *SL* SL1 ... 100 A8
Minorca Gv *WLLN* MK15 ... 21 H4
Minshull Cl *BUCK/WIN* MK18 ... 11 L5
Minster Wy *DTCH/LGLY* SL3 ... 112 E6
Minstrel Ct *BDWL* MK13 ... 13 L7
Mint Cl *HGDN/ICK* UB10 ... 105 G8
Minton Cl *GTLIN* MK14 ... 14 D5
Minton Ri *MDHD* SL6 ... 110 A3
Mirador Crs *SLN* SL2 ... 112 A4
Mirrie La *DEN/HRF* UB9 ... 93 H4
Misbourne Av *CFSP/GDCR* SL9 ... 82 D5
Misbourne Cl *AYLS* HP21 ... 42 C3
  CFSP/GDCR SL9 ... 82 D5
Misbourne Ct *AMSS* HP7 * ... 71 C3
Misbourne Dr
  GTMIS/PWD HP16 ... 61 G4
Misbourne Mdw
  DEN/HRF UB9 ... 93 H7
Misbourne Rd *HGDN/ICK* UB10 ... 104 F7
Missenden Cl *BUCK/WIN* MK18 ... 151 J10
Missenden Gdns *SL* SL1 ... 110 A3
Missenden Ms
  GTMIS/PWD HP16 * ... 60 F3
Missenden Rd
  BUCK/WIN MK18 ... 150 H10
  CSHM HP5 ... 62 E3
  HADM HP17 ... 51 H4
  HAZ/HG HP15 ... 60 C8
Miss Joans Ride *BERK* HP4 ... 171 M7
Miswell La *TRING* HP23 ... 37 L7
Mitcham Pl *BDWL* MK13 ... 6 D3
Mitcham Wk *AYLW* HP19 ... 167 R12
Mitchell Cl *HHS/BOV* HP3 ... 56 E6
  SL SL1 ... 110 F6
  THAME OX9 ... 181 M6
Mitchell Rd *RBEDW* MK43 ... 138 H4
Mitchell Wk *AMS* HP6 ... 71 K1
Mithras Gdns *WTR/OFPK* MK7 ... 19 M8
Mitre St *BUCK/WIN* MK18 ... 11 K7
Mixbury Rd *BRACKY* NN13 ... 146 E4
Moat Cl *DEN/HRF* UB9 ... 84 A8
Moat Dr *GTMIS/PWD* HP16 ... 60 B3
  RSLP HA4 ... 95 K6
  SLN SL2 ... 112 B2
Moat End *RAYLNE/WEN* HP22 ... 35 C2
Moat La *GTMIS/PWD* HP16 ... 60 B3
  RAYLNE/WEN HP22 ... 33 H2
  RBICN OX27 ... 163 R4
Moat Pl *DEN/HRF* UB9 ... 104 A2
Moat's Crs *THAME* OX9 ... 181 P6
Mobwell Ter
  GTMIS/PWD HP16 * ... 60 F2
Moeran Cl *WTR/OFPK* MK7 ... 23 M1
Moffy Hl *MDHD* SL6 ... 98 D8
Mole Run *HWYN* HP13 ... 77 H5
Molteno Rd *WAT* WD17 ... 75 M2
Molyneaux Av *HHS/BOV* HP3 ... 56 E6
Molyns Ms *SLN* SL2 ... 110 H9
Monarchs Wy *RSLP* HA4 ... 95 K3
Monarch's Wy *RSLP* HA4 ... 95 J7
Monastery Gdns
  DTCH/LGLY SL3 ... 122 A6
Mondial Wy *HYS/HAR* UB3 ... 125 H3
Monellan Crs *WTR/OFPK* MK7 ... 23 K3
Monet Pl *AYLW* HP19 * ... 167 P12
Moneyhill Ct
  RKW/CH/CXG WD3 * ... 84 C7
Money Hill Rd
  RKW/CH/CXG WD3 ... 84 D1
Money La *BUCK/WIN* MK18 ... 114 C7
Moneyrow Gn *MDHD* SL6 ... 118 F3
Monkey Island La *MDHD* SL6 ... 109 J7
Monksfield Wy *SLN* SL2 ... 110 F1

Monks Hollow *MLW* SL7 ... 97 K1
Monks Pth *AYLW* HP19 ... 177 R2
Monks Rd *WDSR* SL4 ... 120 C5
Monks Wy *CNH/GTH/TMA* MK8 ... 16 F4
  WLLN MK15 ... 14 C5
  WOLV MK12 ... 17 J2
Monkton Wy *PRRI* HP27 ... 67 H1
Monmouth Cl *AYLW* HP19 ... 167 R12
Monmouth Gv *EMV/FZ* MK4 ... 21 H5
Monmouth Rd *HYS/HAR* UB3 ... 115 K8
Monro Av *CNH/GTH/TMA* MK8 ... 17 F7
Montabaur Rd *BRACKY* NN13 ... 8 F7
Montagu Dr *AYLS* HP21 ... 48 E7
  BERK HP4 ... 48 A8
  SL SL1 ... 111 L4
  UX/CGN UB8 ... 104 C5
Montagu Rd *DTCH/LGLY* SL3 ... 122 A4
Montem La *SL* SL1 ... 111 J6
Montford Ms *HWYN* HP13 ... 68 D8
Montgomerie Rd *RBICN* OX27 ... 154 F11
Montgomery Cl *LBUZ* LU7 ... 27 J5
Montgomery Crs *WLLN* MK15 ... 14 F7
Montgomery Pl *SLN* SL2 ... 112 B3
Montpellier Cl *WDSR* SL4 ... 121 H5
Montrose Av *DTCH/LGLY* SL3 ... 122 B3
  SL SL1 ... 111 G3
Montrose Dr *MDHD* SL6 ... 107 M8
Montrose Wy *DTCH/LGLY* SL3 ... 122 C4
  THAME OX9 ... 181 P6
Monument La *CFSP/GDCR* SL9 ... 82 D6
Monycrower Dr *MDHD* SL6 ... 108 D3
Moonstone Ct *HWYW* HP12 ... 4 C8
Moon St *WOLV* MK12 ... 13 C8
Moorbridge Rd *MDHD* SL6 ... 108 F3
Moorcroft La *UX/CGN* UB8 ... 114 F2
Moore Cl *SL* SL1 ... 111 G6
Moore End *DUN/WHIP* LU6 ... 170 G1
  MDHD SL6 ... 119 H1
Moor End La *DUN/WHIP* LU6 ... 170 G1
Moorend Rd *TOW* NN12 ... 130 D12
Moore Rd *BERK* HP4 ... 47 L4
Moores Hl *OLN* MK46 ... 128 B9
Moores La *WDSR* SL4 ... 110 G8
Moorfield *RMKS/WB* MK17 ... 153 J3
Moorfield Rd *DEN/HRF* UB9 ... 93 M5
  UX/CGN UB8 ... 114 C3
Moorfoot *STSTR* MK11 ... 16 D2
Moor Furlong *SL* SL1 ... 110 D2
Moorgate *EAG/OLD/WTN* MK6 ... 18 C7
Moorhall Rd *DEN/HRF* UB9 ... 94 A4
Moor Hart Cl *SKCH* HP14 * ... 186 H2
Moorhen Wy *BUCK/WIN* MK18 ... 11 M6
Moorhills Crs *LBUZ* LU7 ... 28 A3
Moorhouse Pth *LBUZ* LU7 ... 29 L1
Moorhouse Wy *LBUZ* LU7 ... 29 L1
The Moorings
  BUCK/WIN MK18 * ... 11 K6
  WDSR SL4 ... 120 F3
Moorland Cl *HHW* HP1 ... 57 L1
  RDR/YW UB7 ... 124 B3
Moorland Dr *MDHD* SL6 ... 107 M8
Moorlands *LBUZ* LU7 ... 28 A3
Moorlands Dr *MDHD* SL6 ... 107 M8
Moorlands Rd *LBUZ* LU7 ... 28 A3
Moor La *HWYN* HP13 ... 77 J3
  MDHD SL6 ... 108 A1
  RKW/CH/CXG WD3 ... 65 K8
  WDR/YW UB7 ... 124 B2
Moor Lane Crossing
  WATW WD18 ... 75 H8
Moor Pk *BTCHLY* MK3 ... 22 A6
  RAYLNE/WEN HP22 ... 44 A3
Moor Park Gdns *NTHWD* HA6 * ... 85 H2
Moor Park Rd *NTHWD* HA6 ... 85 H2
Moor Pond Cl *BIC* OX26 ... 162 E4
Moor Rd *CSHM* HP5 ... 63 H4
Moors Cl *RMKN* MK19 ... 137 M10
Moorside *FLKWH/TG* HP10 ... 89 J4
Moorside Cl *MDHD* SL6 ... 108 E1
Moorstown Ct *SL* SL1 ... 111 K6
The Moor *MLW* SL7 ... 88 B6
  RBEDW MK43 ... 129 M9
Moor Vw *WATW* WD18 ... 75 M8
Morar *LBUZ* LU7 ... 26 D7
Moray Av *HYS/HAR* UB3 ... 115 L5
Moray Dr *SLN* SL2 ... 111 M3
Mordaunt Cl *RBEDW* MK43 ... 129 N9
Mordaunts Ct *WLLN* MK15 ... 18 F4
Moreau Wk *DTCH/LGLY* SL3 ... 112 D3
More Av *AYLS* HP21 ... 2 E8
Morebath Gv *EMV/FZ* MK4 ... 21 M2
Morefields *TRING* HP23 ... 37 M4
Moreland Cl *DTCH/LGLY* SL3 ... 123 J4
Moreton Cl *CFSP/GDCR* SL9 ... 92 E5
Morello Av *UX/CGN* UB8 ... 115 G2
Morello Dr *DTCH/LGLY* SL3 ... 112 E5
Moreton Dr *BUCK/WIN* MK18 ... 11 M3
Moreton La *HADM* HP17 ... 177 R9
  THAME OX9 ... 181 M6
Moreton Rd *BUCK/WIN* MK18 ... 11 K4
  THAME OX9 ... 181 L4
Moreton Wy *SL* SL1 ... 110 C5
Morgan Cl *NTHWD* HA6 ... 85 H7
Morgan's La *HYS/HAR* UB3 ... 115 J2
Morland Dr
  CNH/GTH/TMA MK8 ... 17 H7
Morley Cl *DTCH/LGLY* SL3 ... 112 E6
Morley Crs *WTR/OFPK* MK7 ... 23 M2
Morrell St *SHEN* MK5 ... 21 L1
Morrice Cl *DTCH/LGLY* SL3 ... 112 E6
Morris Cl *CFSP/GDCR* SL9 ... 82 E3
Morris Ct *AYLS* HP21 ... 42 C2
Morrison Ct
  CNH/GTH/TMA MK8 ... 17 H1
Morris Pl *MLW* SL7 ... 97 J4
Morse Cl *DEN/HRF* UB9 ... 94 B1
Morse Rd *WTR/OFPK* MK7 ... 23 L3
Mortain Cl *BERK* HP4 ... 47 L4
Morten Gdns *DEN/HRF* UB9 ... 93 M6
Mortens Wd *AMSS* HP7 ... 71 J6
Mortimer Hl *TRING* HP23 ... 38 A6
Mortimer Rd *DTCH/LGLY* SL3 ... 112 C12
Morton Cl *BUCK/WIN* MK18 ... 159 L9
  LBUZ LU7 ... 169 P10
  UX/CGN UB8 ... 114 C1
Morton Dr *SL* SL1 ... 100 D3
Morton King Cl *RAYLW* HP18 ... 180 E3
Mortons Fk *BDWL* MK13 ... 13 J8
Moseley Rd *SKCH* HP14 ... 67 H7
Moses Plat La *PRRI* HP27 ... 67 H7
Moss Cl *RKW/CH/CXG* WD3 ... 84 C7
Mossdale *BDWL* MK13 ... 17 L1
Mossendew Cl *DEN/HRF* UB9 ... 84 C8
Mossmans Cl *WEAT* MK2 ... 22 F7
Mossy V *MDHD* SL6 ... 108 C1
Moston Cl *HYS/HAR* UB3 ... 125 L1

Mountain Ash *MLW* SL7 ... 87 J8
Mount Av *DBGH* MK1 ... 23 G3
Mountbatten Cl *SL* SL1 ... 111 M7
Mountbatten Gdns *LBUZ* LU7 ... 27 J5
Mountbatten Sq *WDSR* SL4 * ... 121 H4
Mount Cl *HHW* HP1 ... 49 G7
  HWYW HP12 ... 4 C7
  RAYLNE/WEN HP22 ... 36 E6
  SLN SL2 ... 101 H2
Mounthill Av *RMKN* MK19 ... 137 G5
Mount Hill La *CFSP/GDCR* SL9 ... 92 A7
Mount La *DEN/HRF* UB9 ... 93 J8
Mount Nugent *CSHM* HP5 ... 54 F6
Mount Park Rd *PIN* HA5 ... 95 M4
Mount Pleasant *AYLW* HP19 ... 2 E4
  DEN/HRF UB9 ... 83 M8
  EAG/OLD/WTN MK6 ... 23 H2
  LBUZ LU7 ... 153 R11
  NPAG MK16 ... 132 C5
  RAYLNE/WEN HP22 ... 159 Q12
  RMKS/WB MK17 ... 153 R7
  RMKS/WB MK17 ... 145 J6
  SKCH HP14 ... 86 B1
  TOW NN12 ... 130 E12
Mount Pleasant Cl
  BUCK/WIN MK18 ... 11 K7
Mount Rd *HYS/HAR* UB3 ... 115 K7
Mountsfield Cl *RAYLW* MK16 ... 14 F3
  STWL/WRAY TW19 ... 123 M8
Mount St *AYL* HP20 ... 2 E6
The Mount *EAG/OLD/WTN* MK6 ... 23 H2
  RKW/CH/CXG WD3 ... 74 B7
  RMKS/WB MK17 ... 144 G6
Mount Vw *HEN* RG9 ... 190 C4
Mountview *NTHWD* HA6 ... 85 M6
Mount Vw *RKW/CH/CXG* WD3 ... 84 A1
Mount Wy *PRRI* HP27 ... 183 R11
Mowbray Dr *LBUZ* LU7 ... 26 E7
Mowbray Rd *AYLS* HP21 ... 2 F2
Mow Md *OLN* MK46 ... 128 B9
Moyleen Ri *MLW* SL7 ... 97 H5
Mozart Cl *WTR/OFPK* MK7 ... 23 M2
Muddiford La *EMV/FZ* MK4 ... 22 A3
Muirfield Dr *BTCHLY* MK3 ... 22 A4
Mulberry Av *WDSR* SL4 ... 121 H6
Mulberry Cl *HWYW* HP12 ... 87 L6
  TRING HP23 ... 37 M5
Mulberry Ct *HAZ/HG* HP15 ... 69 J3
Mulberry Crs *WDR/YW* UB7 ... 114 D6
Mulberry Pde *WDR/YW* UB7 ... 114 F7
Mulberry Wk *BIC* OX26 ... 162 C1
  DTCH/LGLY SL3 ... 122 D1
Mulberry Wk *SL6* ... 108 D2
Mullein Rd *BIC* OX26 ... 162 C1
Mullen Av *GTLIN* MK14 ... 18 C1
Mullins Wy *AYLW* HP19 ... 167 P12
Mullion Pl *EAG/OLD/WTN* MK6 ... 7 K6
Mumford La *CFSP/GDCR* SL9 ... 91 M2
Munces Rd *MLW* SL7 ... 97 M3
Mundaydean La *MLW* SL7 ... 96 F1
Mundesley Sp *SL* SL1 ... 111 K3
Murcott Rd *RBICS/W* OX25 ... 173 L4
Murdock Rd *BIC* OX26 ... 162 E4
Murray Rd *BERK* HP4 ... 48 B5
  NTHWD HA6 ... 85 K7
Murrey Cl *SHEN* MK5 ... 21 M1
Murrin Rd *MDHD* SL6 ... 108 B3
Mursley Cl *SLN* SL2 ... 112 B2
Mursley Rd *RMKS/WB* MK17 ... 152 A11
  RMKS/WB MK17 ... 151 P4
Musgrave Rd *CHNR* OX39 ... 184 G5
Musgrave Wk *SKCH* HP14 ... 187 J1
Musk Hl *HHW* HP1 ... 49 G8
Myddleton Rd *UX/CGN* UB8 ... 104 B6
Mylne Cl *HWYN* HP13 ... 4 F4
Mynchen End *BEAC* HP9 ... 80 C4
The Myrke *DTCH/LGLY* SL3 ... 111 L8
Myrtle Av *EBED/NFELT* TW14 ... 125 K7
  RSLP HA4 ... 95 H3
Myrtle Bank *WOLV* MK12 ... 17 C1
Myrtle Cl *DTCH/LGLY* SL3 ... 123 K4
  UX/CGN UB8 ... 114 E2
  WDR/YW UB7 ... 124 A2
Myrtle Crs *SLN* SL2 ... 111 L4
Myrtleside Cl *NTHWD* HA6 ... 85 J7

N

Nailzee Cl *CFSP/GDCR* SL9 ... 92 D6
Nairdwood Cl
  GTMIS/PWD HP16 ... 60 D6
Nairdwood La
  GTMIS/PWD HP16 ... 60 C4
Nairdwood Wy
  GTMIS/PWD HP16 ... 60 D6
Nairn Ct *BTCHLY* MK3 ... 22 B4
Nairn Rd *RMKS/WB* MK17 ... 24 D5
Naisby Dr *RMKS/WB* MK17 ... 24 D5
Nalders Rd *CSHM* HP5 ... 55 J8
Nan Aires *RAYLNE/WEN* HP22 ... 33 M3
Nancy Hall Ct *HWYW* HP12 ... 87 H3
Naphill Pl *BDWL* MK13 ... 6 C2
Napier Rd *AYLW* HP19 ... 177 Q11
  MDHD SL6 ... 108 A4
Napier St *WEAT* MK2 ... 23 G6
Naples Cl *AYLW* HP19 ... 167 Q11
Nappins Cl *RAYLW* HP18 ... 181 J5
The Nap *RAYLW* HP18 ... 179 R1
Narbeth Dr *AYL* HP20 ... 35 G6
Narborough Ct
  HGDN/ICK UB10 ... 95 H8
Narcot Cl *CFSP/GDCR* SL9 ... 81 M7
Narcot Wy *CSTG* HP8 ... 81 M4
Narrow La *HWYN* HP13 ... 77 K3
Narrow Pth *RMKS/WB* MK17 ... 144 E7
Naseby Cl *NPAC* MK16 ... 14 D3
Naseby Rd *BDWL* MK13 ... 13 L8
  BUCK/WIN MK18 ... 11 H4
Nash Cl *AYLS* HP21 ... 42 F2
  RAYLNE/WEN HP22 ... 166 D1
Nash Cft *EMV/FZ* MK4 ... 21 L6
Nashdom La *SL* SL1 ... 99 M3
Nash Lee End
  RAYLNE/WEN HP22 ... 43 K8
Nash Lee La
  RAYLNE/WEN HP22 ... 43 J8
Nash Lee Rd *HADM* HP17 ... 51 H1
  RAYLNE/WEN HP22 ... 44 A7
Nashleigh Hl *CSHM* HP5 ... 55 J8
Nash Rd *FLKWH/TG* HP10 ... 79 G1
Nash Rd *BUCK/WIN* MK18 ... 143 J10
  DTCH/LGLY SL3 ... 122 F5
  RMKS/WB MK17 ... 151 K2
Nashs Farm
  RAYLNE/WEN HP22 ... 33 J2
Nathanial Cl *SHEN* MK5 ... 21 J1
Nathaniel Wk *TRING* HP23 ... 37 M5
Natwoke Cl *BEAC* HP9 ... 80 C5

Neal Cl *CFSP/GDCR* SL9 ... 93 G7
  NTHWD HA6 ... 85 M8
Neale Cl *HWYW* HP12 ... 87 J3
Neapland *EAG/OLD/WTN* MK6 ... 22 E1
Nearton End *RMKS/WB* MK17 ... 151 R12
Neath Crs *BTCHLY* MK3 ... 22 D4
Neats Acre *RSLP* HA4 ... 95 J6
Nebular Ct *LBUZ* LU7 ... 27 K6
Needham Cl *WDSR* SL4 ... 120 D4
Needlemakers *RAYLW* HP18 ... 175 L11
Neela Cl *HGDN/ICK* UB10 ... 105 G2
Neild Wy *RKW/CH/CXG* WD3 ... 73 L8
Neilgrove Rd *UX/CGN* UB8 ... 115 G1
Nelson Cl *AMSS* HP7 ... 70 B7
  CNH/GTH/TMA MK8 ... 17 H8
  DTCH/LGLY SL3 ... 112 C8
  HGDN/ICK UB10 ... 105 G8
  HWYN HP13 ... 78 E5
Nelson La *HGDN/ICK* UB10 ... 115 G1
Nelson Rd *BERK* HP4 ... 171 K9
  HGDN/ICK UB10 ... 105 G8
  HTHAIR TW6 ... 124 E4
  LBUZ LU7 ... 27 J5
  WDSR SL4 ... 120 E6
Nelson St *BUCK/WIN* MK18 ... 11 K6
  THAME OX9 ... 181 N6
Nelson Ter *AYL* HP20 ... 2 E5
Nene Cl *AYLS* HP21 ... 42 B2
  NPAG MK16 ... 15 G3
Nene Dr *BTCHLY* MK3 ... 22 B6
Nene Rd *HTHAIR* TW6 ... 125 G4
Neptune Gdns *LBUZ* LU7 ... 27 L6
Neptune St *HTHAIR* TW6 * ... 125 H4
Ness Wy *WEAT* MK2 ... 153 L7
Nestle's Av *HYS/HAR* UB3 ... 115 L7
Netherby Cl *TRING* HP23 ... 38 A4
Nether Cl *BRACKY* NN13 ... 8 F7
Nether Gv *SHEN* MK5 ... 21 K3
Netherwood Rd *BEAC* HP9 ... 80 C5
Netley Cl *MKV* MK10 ... 19 K4
Nettlecombe *EMV/FZ* MK4 ... 21 M3
Nettleden Rd *BERK* HP4 ... 45 J8
Nettleton Cl *LBUZ* LU7 ... 29 K11
Nettleton Rd *HGDN/ICK* UB10 ... 104 D7
  HTHAIR TW6 ... 125 G4
Neunkirchen Wy *BIC* OX26 ... 162 F7
Nevil Cl *NTHWD* HA6 ... 85 J3
Neville Cl *SLN* SL2 ... 101 L4
  WAR/TWY RG10 ... 116 E8
Nevis Cl *LBUZ* LU7 ... 26 D7
Nevis Gv *WEAT* MK2 ... 153 L7
Newall Rd *HTHAIR* TW6 ... 125 H4
Newalls Ri *WAR/TWY* RG10 ... 191 P12
New Ar *UX/CGN* UB8 * ... 104 C6
Newark Ct *WTR/OFPK* MK7 ... 23 K3
Newbarn Cl *THAME* OX9 ... 181 N7
Newbarn La *BEAC* HP9 ... 81 K4
Newberry Crs *WDSR* SL4 ... 120 B4
Newberry Dr *BRACKY* NN13 ... 8 C6
Newbery Wy *SL* SL1 ... 111 J6
Newbolt Cl *NPAG* MK16 ... 14 C1
Newbridge Gv *EMV/FZ* MK4 ... 21 L3
New Broadway
  HGDN/ICK UB10 * ... 115 G1
Newbury Ct *BTCHLY* MK3 ... 22 A8
Newbury Dr *MDHD* SL6 ... 109 G4
Newbury Rd *HTHAIR* TW6 ... 124 D4
Newby Pl *EMV/FZ* MK4 ... 21 L4
New Chilterns *AMSS* HP7 * ... 71 K2
Newchurch Rd *SLN* SL2 ... 110 D2
New Close Farm Rd
  CHNR OX39 ... 182 F11
New College Ct
  BUCK/WIN MK18 ... 11 J2
Newcombe Ri *WDR/YW* UB7 ... 114 C3
New Ct *MLW* SL7 ... 97 J4
Newcourt *UX/CGN* UB8 ... 114 B2
Newcroft Cl *UX/CGN* UB8 ... 114 E2
Newdigate Gn *DEN/HRF* UB9 ... 84 C8
Newdigate Rd *DEN/HRF* UB9 ... 84 B8
Newdigate Rd East
  DEN/HRF UB9 ... 84 C8
New Dr *HWYN* HP13 ... 78 D2
Newell Cl *AYLS* HP21 ... 3 L9
Newells Hedge *LBUZ* LU7 ... 169 G9
New Farm La *NTHWD* HA6 ... 85 K8
Newfield Gdns *MLW* SL7 ... 97 L3
Newfield Rd *MLW* SL7 ... 97 L4
Newfield Wy *MLW* SL7 ... 97 K5
New Garden Dr *WDR/YW* UB7 ... 114 D6
Newgate Rd *KID* OX5 ... 172 G5
Newground Rd *TRING* HP23 ... 39 G7
New Hall Cl *HHS/BOV* HP3 ... 56 F6
Newhall Cl *HHS/BOV* HP3 ... 56 F6
Newhaven Cl *HYS/HAR* UB3 ... 115 H4
Newhaven Sp *SLN* SL2 ... 111 G1
Newhouse Rd *HHS/BOV* HP3 ... 56 F6
Newington Ga
  EAG/OLD/WTN MK6 ... 23 G1
New Inn La *BUCK/WIN* MK18 ... 148 G2
Newlands Dr *DTCH/LGLY* SL3 ... 123 K6
  MDHD SL6 ... 107 M7
Newlands Rd *HHW* HP1 ... 49 H6
Newlands Wk *WYM* HP11 ... 5 G6
Newlyn Cl *UX/CGN* UB8 ... 114 F2
Newlyn Pl *EAG/OLD/WTN* MK6 ... 7 L5
Newmans Cl *GTLIN* MK14 ... 14 B5
Newmans Ctyd
  RMKS/WB MK17 ... 152 C8
Newman Wy *LBUZ* LU7 ... 27 M1
Newmarket Ct *MKV* MK10 ... 19 M4
New Meadow *AYLS* HP21 ... 35 H8
Newmer Rd *HWYW* HP12 ... 87 G3
New Pde *RKW/CH/CXG* WD3 * ... 74 E7
  WDR/YW UB7 ... 114 D5
New Park Rd *DEN/HRF* UB9 ... 84 B8
New Peachey La *UX/CGN* UB8 ... 114 C3
New Pond Pde *RSLP* HA4 * ... 105 M1
New Pond Rd *HAZ/HG* HP15 ... 69 H3
Newport Pagnell Rd
  RBEDW MK43 ... 135 H6
Newport Rd *BDWL* MK13 ... 13 H6
  HTHAIR TW6 ... 124 F1
  MKV MK10 ... 138 A11
  NPAG MK16 ... 133 N4
  OLN MK46 ... 128 C5
  RMKN MK19 ... 131 N8
  SLN SL2 ... 18 D1
  WLLN MK15 ... 18 D1
  YEAD UB4 ... 115 M3
Newport Wy *RMKN* MK19 ... 131 P7
New Rd *AMS* HP6 ... 63 K8
  AMSS HP7 ... 70 B5
  BERK HP4 ... 47 K4
  BNEND SL8 ... 89 G6
  BRACKY NN13 ... 8 D7
  CSTG HP8 ... 72 D4
  DTCH/LGLY SL3 ... 122 C4
  FLKWH/TG HP10 ... 79 H1
  GTMIS/PWD HP16 ... 60 C4
  HADM HP17 ... 176 H9
  HAZ/HG HP15 ... 68 C2

HEN RG9 190 E12
HWYW HP12 77 H8
HYS/HAR UB3 125 H3
KGLGY WD4 65 L1
LBUZ LU7 26 F7
MDHD SL6 119 G2
MDHD SL6 106 E3
MDHD SL6 98 D3
MLW SL7 87 J8
PRRI HP27 66 E2
PRRI HP27 58 A2
RAYLNE/WEN HP22 43 K1
RAYLNE/WEN HP22 32 B6
RKW/CH/CXG WD3 74 E6
RKW/CH/CXG WD3 73 L2
RMKN MK19 12 C1
RMKS/WB MK17 152 H9
SKCH HP14 187 J2
SKCH HP14 66 F4
TRING HP23 37 H1
UX/CGN UB8 115 H1
New Road Cl HWYW HP12 77 H8
New Road Gdns HWYW HP12 77 H8
New Rw OLN MK46 128 G6
New Sq SL SL1 111 L6
New St AYL HP20 2 F4
BERK HP4 48 C6
BIC OX26 162 D3
BUCK/WIN MK18 10 C8
HEN RG9 190 H4
LBUZ LU7 169 L7
RAYLW HP18 166 D7
STSTR MK11 16 A1
Newton Cl DTCH/LGLY SL3 112 E6
Newton Rd BTCHLY MK3 22 B8
RBEDW MK43 129 N9
RMKS/WB MK17 153 J6
Newton Wy LBUZ LU7 27 L8
Newtown Gdns HEN RG9 190 H6
Newtown Rd DEN/HRF UB9 104 A4
HEN RG9 191 J6
MLW SL7 97 L3
Newville RAYLNE/WEN HP22 32 B5
Newyears Green La
DEN/HRF UB9 94 E5
New Zealand Gdns LBUZ LU7 161 R8
Neyland Dr AYLW HP19 34 B3
Niagara Rd HEN RG9 190 H6
Nicholas Gdns HWYN HP13 78 C2
SL SL1 110 D5
Nicholas Md GTLIN MK14 14 C6
Nicholas Rd HEN RG9 190 E6
Nicholas Wy NTHWD HA6 85 H8
Nicholls WDSR SL4 120 B6
Nicholls Av UX/CGN UB8 114 F1
Nicholsons La MDHD SL6 108 E3
Nicholsons Wk MDHD SL6 108 E3
Nickleby Cl UX/CGN UB8 115 G3
Nicol Cl CFSP/GDCR SL9 82 B8
Nicol End CFSP/GDCR SL9 82 B8
Nicol Rd CFSP/GDCR SL9 82 B8
Nicolson Dr LBUZ LU7 29 L1
Nield Rd HYS/HAR UB3 115 L6
Nightingale Cl BRACKY NN13 8 D4
HAZ/HG HP15 69 G5
Nightingale Ct SL SL1 111 M7
Nightingale Crs BDWL MK13 13 J7
Nightingale La MDHD SL6 98 C7
Nightingale Pk SLN SL2 100 E5
Nightingale Pl
BUCK/WIN MK18 11 M5
MDHD SL6 * 98 E4
RKW/CH/CXG WD3 74 C8
Nightingale Rd AYLS HP21 3 G9
CSHM HP5 * 55 G8
RAYLNE/WEN HP22 44 A5
RKW/CH/CXG WD3 74 B8
Nightingales La CSTG HP8 82 C1
Nightingale Wk WDSR SL4 121 H6
Nightingale Wy DEN/HRF UB9 93 L5
Nine Acres SL SL1 110 E5
Nine Elms Av UX/CGN UB8 114 C2
Nine Elms Cl UX/CGN UB8 114 C2
Nine Stiles Cl DEN/HRF UB9 104 A4
Ninnings Rd CFSP/GDCR SL9 82 E7
Ninnings Wy CFSP/GDCR SL9 82 E7
Ninth Av HYS/HAR UB3 115 M4
Nithsdale Gv HGDN/ICK UB10 105 H1
Nixey Cl SL SL1 111 M6
Nixons Cl EAG/OLD/WTN MK6 18 B8
Noake Mill La HHW HP1 49 M2
Nobel Dr HYS/HAR UB3 125 K3
Noble Cl WLLN MK15 14 D7
Noble Rd HEN RG9 191 J6
The Nokes HHW HP1 49 M5
Nook Pk RMKS/WB MK17 * 151 K3
Noon Layer Dr MKV MK10 19 H3
Norbrek CNH/GTH/TMA MK8 17 H4
Norcotts Kiln RAYLW HP18 * 174 B1
Norden Cl MDHD SL6 108 B6
Norden Mdw MDHD SL6 108 B5
Norden Rd MDHD SL6 108 B5
Norelands Dr SL SL1 100 B7
Norfolk Av SL SL1 111 H2
Norfolk House
RKW/CH/CXG WD3 * 84 D1
Norfolk Park Cots MDHD SL6 108 E2
Norfolk Rd MDHD SL6 108 D2
RBEDW MK43 129 N8
RKW/CH/CXG WD3 84 D1
UX/CGN UB8 104 C4
Norfolk Ter AYL HP20 3 H4
Norgrove Pk CFSP/GDCR SL9 92 D3
Norland Dr FLKWH/TG HP10 89 H2
Norman Av HEN RG9 190 H5
Norman Crs MKV MK10 19 H3
Normandy Dr BERK HP4 47 M5
HYS/HAR UB3 115 H3
Normandy Wy BTCHLY MK3 22 B4
Normans Cl UX/CGN UB8 114 D2
Normanstead HEN RG9 190 G5
The Normans SLN SL2 112 A3
Norman Wy DUN/WHIP LU6 31 M6
Norreys Dr MDHD SL6 108 B6
Norrington
CNH/GTH/TMA MK8 17 H4
Norris Pl FLKWH/TG HP10 * 89 M6
Norris Rd RBICS/W OX25 173 K3
Northall Cl DUN/WHIP LU6 30 E8
Northall Rd DUN/WHIP LU6 170 E1
Northampton Avenue
SL SL1 111 H3
Northampton Rd
BRACKY NN13 8 F5
NPAG MK16 133 L11
OLN MK46 128 G6
RMKN MK19 137 R5
TOW NN12 130 A6
North Ap NTHWD HA6 85 H2
North Av HYS/HAR UB3 115 M4
Northborough Rd SLN SL2 110 F1
North Bridge Rd BERK HP4 47 L4
Northbrook Dr NTHWD HA6 85 K8
North Buckinghamshire Wy
HADM HP17 50 A3
RAYLNE/WEN HP22 166 E3
RMKN MK19 16 F7
RMKS/WB MK17 143 P12
WOLV MK12 12 E7
North Burnham Cl SL SL1 100 A7
Northchurch La CSHM HP5 47 H8
Northcliffe DUN/WHIP LU6 30 F8
North Cl MLW SL7 96 C7
RMKS/WB MK17 152 H9
THAME OX9 180 A7
WDSR SL4 120 E4
North Common Rd
UX/CGN UB8 104 C3
Northcourt LBUZ LU7 27 H5
RKW/CH/CXG WD3 * 83 M1
North Crawley Rd NPAG MK16 15 J3
North Cft BUCK/WIN MK18 151 K10
FLKWH/TG HP10 89 K3
Northcroft RAYLNE/WEN HP22 32 B5
SHEN MK5 17 L8
SLN SL2 111 G1
North Dean MDHD SL6 108 E2
Northdown Cl RSLP HA4 105 L1
Northdown Rd
CFSP/GDCR SL9 82 D6
North Dr AYLS HP21 42 D1
BEAC HP9 89 M2
HWYN HP13 78 C2
RSLP HA4 95 K6
North Eastern Rd AYLW HP19 2 D2
North Eighth St CMK MK9 6 F3
North Eleventh St CMK MK9 7 G2
Northend OLN MK46 127 L11
Northend Cl FLKWH/TG HP10 89 H3
North End Rd BUCK/WIN MK18 149 L11
RAYLNE/WEN HP22 166 D1
Northend Sq BUCK/WIN MK18 11 L5
Northern Hts BNEND SL8 89 G5
Northern Perimeter Rd
HTHAIR TW6 125 H4
Northern Perimeter Road
(West) WDR/YW UB7 124 B4
Northern Rd AYLW HP19 2 D3
SLN SL2 111 J1
Northern Woods
FLKWH/TG HP10 89 H3
Northfield Av HEN RG9 191 K10
Northfield Cl HYS/HAR UB3 115 L7
Northfield Dr WLLN MK15 19 J1
Northfield End HEN RG9 190 G3
Northfield Pde HYS/HAR UB3 * 115 L7
Northfield Pk HYS/HAR UB3 115 K7
Northfield Rd AYL HP20 35 G6
HEN RG9 191 L10
MDHD SL6 108 E1
PRRI HP27 58 B2
TRING HP23 38 D2
WDSR SL4 110 E8
North Fifth St CMK MK9 6 D4
North Fourteenth St
CMK MK9 7 H1
North Fourth St CMK MK9 6 C5
Northgate NTHWD HA6 85 H7
North Grafton BDWL MK13 6 B5
North Gn MDHD SL6 108 E1
SL SL1 111 K4
North Hl RKW/CH/CXG WD3 73 K3
North Hyde Gdns
HYS/HAR UB3 115 M7
North Hyde Rd HYS/HAR UB3 115 K7
Northlands Rd
BUCK/WIN MK18 150 C5
North La WTR/OFPK MK7 19 H7
North Lee La
RAYLNE/WEN HP22 42 E7
Northleigh EMV/FZ MK4 22 A4
North Links Rd
FLKWH/TG HP10 89 G1
North Ldg LBUZ LU7 * 25 G6
North Marston La
RAYLNE/WEN HP22 159 P11
Northmead Rd SLN SL2 110 E1
Northmill PRRI HP27 183 Q11
North Mill Rd PRRI HP27 183 K9
North Ninth St CMK MK9 6 F3
Northolt Rd HTHAIR TW6 124 C4
North Orbital Rd
DEN/HRF UB9 93 L3
North Pk CFSP/GDCR SL9 92 D2
DTCH/LGLY SL3 113 J7
North Rdg EAG/OLD/WTN MK6 7 M7
Northridge Wy HHW HP1 49 L8
North Rd AMS HP6 63 H7
BERK HP4 48 A6
HAZ/HG HP15 68 C5
HYS/HAR UB3 115 J2
MDHD SL6 108 D3
RKW/CH/CXG WD3 73 J6
WDR/YW UB7 114 E7
Northrop Rd HTHAIR TW6 125 K4
North Rw CMK MK9 6 B5
DTCH/LGLY SL3 * 102 D2
North Saxon GTLIN MK14 6 E3
North Secklow GTLIN MK14 6 F1
North Second St CMK MK9 6 C5
North Seventh St CMK MK9 6 E3
North Sixth St CMK MK9 6 E4
North Sq NPAG MK16 15 G1
North Star Dr LBUZ LU7 27 K6
North Star La MDHD SL6 108 B4
North St BDWL MK13 13 K7
BIC OX26 162 D4
LBUZ LU7 27 H7
RMKN MK19 131 L12
THAME OX9 181 N5
WEAT MK2 22 F5
North Tenth St CMK MK9 6 F2
North Third St CMK MK9 6 C5
North Thirteenth St CMK MK9 7 H1
North Town Cl MDHD SL6 108 E1
North Town Md MDHD SL6 108 E1
North Town Moor MDHD SL6 98 E8
North Town Rd MDHD SL6 108 E1
North Twelfth St CMK MK9 7 G2
Northumberland Av
AYLS HP21 35 G8
Northumbria Rd MDHD SL6 108 A6
North Wy HGDN/ICK UB10 104 D5
Northway RKW/CH/CXG WD3 74 C8
North Wy RMKN MK19 137 M9
TOW NN12 137 M4
Northwich EAG/OLD/WTN MK6 19 G7
Northwick Rd MKV MK10 19 H5
North Witan BDWL MK13 6 D4
Northwood Rd DEN/HRF UB9 84 D8
HTHAIR TW6 124 C4
Northwood Wy DEN/HRF UB9 84 C8
NTHWD HA6 85 M7
Nortoft Rd CFSP/GDCR SL9 82 E6
Norton Leys WTR/OFPK MK7 19 M7
Norton Rd UX/CGN UB8 104 C8
The Nortons WTR/OFPK MK7 23 L3
Norvic Rd TRING HP23 37 M1
Norway Dr SLN SL2 112 A2
Norwich Rd NTHWD HA6 95 L2
Norwich Wy
RKW/CH/CXG WD3 75 G4
Norwood Cl AYL HP20 3 K1
Norwood Ct AMSS HP7 * 71 G3
Norwood La IVER SL0 113 J1
NPAG MK16 14 F3
Norwood Rd FLKWH/TG HP10 79 G8
Nottingham Gv BTCHLY MK3 22 B5
Nottingham Rd
RKW/CH/CXG WD3 83 H1
Nova Ldg EMV/FZ MK4 21 L4
Novello Cft WTR/OFPK MK7 144 A6
Nuffield Cl BIC OX26 162 E3
BRACKY NN13 8 C6
Nuneham Gv EMV/FZ MK4 21 J3
Nup End Cl RAYLNE/WEN HP22 168 A3
Nup End La
RAYLNE/WEN HP22 33 M3
The Nurseries DUN/WHIP LU6 30 F8
Nursery Cl AMSS HP7 71 K2
AYLS HP21 42 B1
FLKWH/TG HP10 * 79 H2
HEN RG9 191 K10
Nursery Dr SKCH HP14 86 A1
Nursery Gdns BDWL MK13 17 K2
TRING HP23 38 A6
Nursery La DTCH/LGLY SL3 112 B5
FLKWH/TG HP10 79 H2
Nursery Rd MDHD SL6 110 A3
Nursery Waye UX/CGN UB8 104 C6
Nutfield La WYM HP11 4 E4
Nuthatch Wy BIC OX26 162 E5
Nutkins Wy CSHM HP5 55 H8
Nut La WAR/TWY RG10 116 D8
Nutmeg Cl WTR/OFPK MK7 23 L1
Nuttfield Cl
RKW/CH/CXG WD3 * 75 G7
Nye Wy HHS/BOV HP3 56 F7
Nymans Ga EMV/FZ MK4 21 H5

O

Oak Av HGDN/ICK UB10 95 G8
WDR/YW UB7 114 F7
Oak Bank Dr LBUZ LU7 27 H3
Oak Cl BIC OX26 162 E2
Oak Crs HWYW HP12 87 H2
Oakcroft RBEDW MK43 135 R4
Oakdale Av NTHWD HA6 95 M1
Oakdene BEAC HP9 80 D7
Oakdene Rd HGDN/ICK UB10 105 G7
Oakdown Crs OLN MK46 128 B11
Oak Dr BERK HP4 48 C7
Oak End Dr IVER SL0 103 H7
Oak End Wy CFSP/GDCR SL9 92 E4
CHNR OX39 184 F5
Oaken Gv MDHD SL6 108 B1
Oakengrove Cl HAZ/HG HP15 69 H4
Oakengrove Rd HAZ/HG HP15 68 F7
Oaken Head EMV/FZ MK4 21 M4
Oaken Pin Cl RBEDW MK43 139 L6
Oakeshott Av SKCH HP14 67 K8
Oak Fld CSHM HP5 63 G1
Oakfield RKW/CH/CXG WD3 73 M8
Oakfield Av SL SL1 111 G5
Oakfield Cl RSLP HA4 95 L5
Oakfield Rd AYL HP20 3 M5
BNEND SL8 88 F7
Oak Gld NTHWD HA6 85 G8
Oak Gn AYLS HP21 2 D8
Oakham Ri EMV/FZ MK4 21 H5
Oakhill Cl RKW/CH/CXG WD3 83 K4
SHEN MK5 17 H8
Oakhill Rd RKW/CH/CXG WD3 83 J4
SHEN MK5 17 J8
Oakhurst MDHD SL6 99 G6
Oakhurst Pl WATW WD18 * 75 L5
Oakington Av AMS HP6 72 D2
HYS/HAR UB3 115 J8
Oaklands BERK HP4 47 M6
Oaklands Ct WAT WD17 75 M2
Oaklands Ga NTHWD HA6 85 K6
Oakland Wy FLKWH/TG HP10 88 F1
Oak La RBICS/W OX25 163 J10
TRING HP23 45 L8
WDSR SL4 120 F4
Oakleigh Dr RKW/CH/CXG WD3 75 H7
Oakleigh Rd HGDN/ICK UB10 105 H5
Oakley FLKWH/TG HP10 * 89 L3
Oakley Crs SL SL1 111 K4
Oakley Gdns WLLN MK15 18 D1
Oakley Gn LBUZ LU7 27 J6
Oakley Green Rd WDSR SL4 119 L5
Oakley La CHNR OX39 184 E4
Oakley Rd CHNR OX39 184 F4
RAYLW HP18 174 B2
WHLY OX33 179 J2
Oakridge EMV/FZ MK4 22 B2
Oakridge Pk LBUZ LU7 29 J1
Oakridge Pl SLN SL2 101 H2
Oakridge Rd WYM HP11 4 D5
Oak Rd BRACKY NN13 8 E5
PRRI HP27 58 B3
Oakside DEN/HRF UB9 104 A4
Oaks Rd HEN RG9 191 K10
STWL/WRAY TW19 124 C8
The Oaks BERK HP4 47 M6
LBUZ LU7 * 27 H2
RSLP HA4 95 J6
YEAD UB4 105 H7
Oak St WYM HP11 78 B6
Oak Stubbs La MDHD SL6 109 L6
Oak Tree Av MLW SL7 97 J3
Oaktree Cl FLKWH/TG HP10 79 G1
Oak Tree Cl MLW SL7 97 J3
Oak Tree Dr DTCH/LGLY SL3 123 G1
SKCH HP14 86 B1
Oak Tree Rd MLW SL7 97 J2
Oak Vw HAZ/HG HP15 68 C2
TOW NN12 137 L3
Oakview WATW WD18 75 K4
Oakview Gdns DTCH/LGLY SL3 112 E8
Oakway AMS HP6 63 G6
Oak Wy BUCK/WIN MK18 151 K10
Oakway DUN/WHIP LU6 171 Q7
Oak Wd BERK HP4 47 L7
Oakwood FLKWH/TG HP10 78 E8
Oakwood Dr WEAT MK2 23 H7
Oakworth Av MKV MK10 19 K2
Oat Cl AYLS HP21 42 B3
Oatfield Gdns LBUZ LU7 27 L7
Oatlands Dr SL SL1 111 J3
Oban Ct SL SL1 111 J6
Oberon Wy EMV/FZ MK4 21 G4
The Observatory SL SL1 * 111 M6
Observer Dr WATW WD18 75 K5
Ockwells Rd MDHD SL6 108 A7
Octagon Ar WYM HP11 5 H6
Octagon Ct WYM HP11 5 H6
Octagon Pde WYM HP11 5 H6
Octavian Dr BDWL MK13 17 J1
Octavian Wy BRACKY NN13 8 F8
Oddley La PRRI HP27 185 M2
Odds Farm Est
FLKWH/TG HP10 * 90 A6
Oddy Hl TRING HP23 38 B7
Odell Cl EAG/OLD/WTN MK6 18 F6
Odencroft Rd SLN SL2 100 F8
Odeon Pde
RKW/CH/CXG WD3 * 84 D1
Odney La MDHD SL6 99 G3
Offas La BUCK/WIN MK18 151 L9
Ogilvie Rd HWYW HP12 4 C5
O'Grady Wy AYLW HP19 167 R11
Okeford Cl TRING HP23 37 L6
Okeford Dr TRING HP23 37 L7
Okeley La TRING HP23 37 K7
Olcastle Cft EMV/FZ MK4 21 K5
Oldacres MDHD SL6 109 G3
Old Amersham Rd
CFSP/GDCR SL9 93 G7
Old Arncott Rd RBICS/W OX25 162 H11
Old Barn Cl BUCK/WIN MK18 148 H2
Old Barn La RKW/CH/CXG WD3 74 E6
Old Belle Cl RMKS/WB MK17 153 R7
Old Bells Ct CSHM HP5 63 G3
Old Bix Rd HEN RG9 188 C11
Old Brewery Cl AYLS HP21 3 G7
Old Brewery Wk
BRACKY NN13 8 E8
Oldbrook Bvd
EAG/OLD/WTN MK6 6 F9
Old Bryers Cl RAYLW HP18 180 E4
Old Burrs AYLS HP21 42 C3
Oldbury Gv BEAC HP9 80 C5
Old Chapel Cl HADM HP17 50 D3
Old Chapel Ms LBUZ LU7 * 27 H8
Old Chorleywood Rd
RKW/CH/CXG WD3 74 C7
Old Coach Dr WYM HP11 78 F6
Old Common Rd
RKW/CH/CXG WD3 73 J5
Old Court Cl MDHD SL6 108 A7
Old Croft Cl CHNR OX39 184 C6
Old Crown SL SL1 * 111 L6
Old Dashwood Hl SKCH HP14 187 P4
Old Dean HHS/BOV HP3 56 F6
Olde Bell La SHEN MK5 17 K7
Old End BUCK/WIN MK18 149 Q5
RNHPTN NN7 126 A5
Old English Cl RMKS/WB MK17 143 R9
Oldershaw Ms MDHD SL6 108 A2
Old Farm LBUZ LU7 169 Q10
Old Farm Cl BEAC HP9 80 B5
LBUZ LU7 169 M3
RAYLW HP18 179 R9
Old Farm La AMSS HP7 71 K4
Old Farm Rd HWYN HP13 77 K4
WDR/YW UB7 114 C6
Old Field Cl AMS HP6 72 D2
Oldfield Rd HHW HP1 49 K8
MDHD SL6 109 G4
Oldfield Vw MDHD SL6 * 109 H6
Old Fishery La HHW HP1 57 L1
Old Fives Ct SL SL1 100 A8
Old Forge Cl BUCK/WIN MK18 10 C8
MDHD SL6 * 108 F7
Old Forge Gdns
RAYLNE/WEN HP22 35 G2
Old Gannon Cl NTHWD HA6 85 H4
Old Groveway
EAG/OLD/WTN MK6 23 G1
Oldhams Meadow AYL HP20 3 K1
Old Hardenwaye HWYN HP13 78 D1
Old Horns La MLW SL7 86 F3
Oldhouse Cl WYM HP11 87 K3
Old House Ct DTCH/LGLY SL3 * 112 C3
Old Howletts La RSLP HA4 95 J5
Old Kiln Rd FLKWH/TG HP10 88 F2
FLKWH/TG HP10 69 H8
Old Linslade Rd LBUZ LU7 26 E4
Old Lodge Dr BEAC HP9 90 C1
Old London Rd THAME OX9 180 A10
The Old Maltings
BUCK/WIN MK18 11 K7
THAME OX9 181 M5
Old Manor Cl PRRI HP27 50 B7
RMKS/WB MK17 20 E5
Old Manor Ct LBUZ LU7 161 K2
Old Marsh La MDHD SL6 109 L6
Old Md CFSP/GDCR SL9 82 D6
Old Meadow Cl BERK HP4 47 M8
The Old Ms OLN MK46 * 128 B10
Old Mill Cl HADM HP17 176 D12
Old Mill Furlong
BUCK/WIN MK18 151 K9
Old Mill Gdns BERK HP4 48 C6
Old Mill La MDHD SL6 109 H6
UX/CGN UB8 114 A2
Old Mill Rd DEN/HRF UB9 103 M1
Old Moor La FLKWH/TG HP10 89 K2
Old Nursery Ct SLN SL2 91 H8
Old Oak Gdns BERK HP4 * 47 K3
Old Orch CHNR OX39 182 H12
IVER SL0 113 L3
Old Orchard Cl UX/CGN UB8 114 F3
Old Orchard Ms BERK HP4 48 B7
Old Orchards
RAYLNE/WEN HP22 34 F3
Old Oxford Rd SKCH HP14 76 B5
Old Papermill Cl
FLKWH/TG HP10 89 K2
Old Place Yd BIC OX26 162 D5
Old Plough Cl RAYLW HP18 175 Q8
Old Post Office La MDHD SL6 * 108 E3
Old Priory DEN/HRF UB9 95 G6
Old Rectory La DEN/HRF UB9 93 K6
Old Risborough Rd
RAYLNE/WEN HP22 42 F6
Old Rd LBUZ LU7 26 F7
Old's Ap WATW WD18 85 H1
Old Sax La CSHM HP5 54 C6
Old School Cl
RAYLNE/WEN HP22 44 B1
RBICN OX27 154 E11
Old School Ct
BUCK/WIN MK18 * 11 K6
DUN/WHIP LU6 31 G8
LBUZ LU7 * 27 H7
Old School La RMKS/WB MK17 153 Q6
The Old School La
BUCK/WIN MK18 149 L11
Old School Rd UX/CGN UB8 114 E1
The Old School
FLKWH/TG HP10 * 89 J6
Old's Cl WATW WD18 85 G1
Old Shire La RKW/CH/CXG WD3 72 F8
Old Shire Lane Circular Wk
CSTG HP8 82 F2
Old Slade La DTCH/LGLY SL3 123 L1
Old Solesbridge La
RKW/CH/CXG WD3 73 M4
Old Springfields
BUCK/WIN MK18 149 R4
Old Stable Yd RMKN MK19 137 R7
Old Station Cl BUCK/WIN MK18 151 K8
Old Station Rd HYS/HAR UB3 115 L7
Old Station Wy
FLKWH/TG HP10 89 K5
Old Stoke Rd AYLS HP21 34 D8
Old Tan Yard Cl
BUCK/WIN MK18 * 151 J10
Old Town BRACKY NN13 8 F7
Old Uxbridge Rd
RKW/CH/CXG WD3 83 K7
Old Vicarage Wy
FLKWH/TG HP10 89 J6
Old Watery FLKWH/TG HP10 89 K2
Oldway La SL SL1 110 B4
Old Windmill Wy RAYLW HP18 175 K11
Old Wolverton Rd WOLV MK12 12 D7
Oliffe Cl AYL HP20 34 C3
Oliffe Wy AYL HP20 34 C3
Oliver Rd WEAT MK2 22 F6
Oliver Rw EMV/FZ MK4 21 H3
Olivers Cl BERK HP4 49 H3
Oliver's Paddock MLW SL7 97 J1
Olivia Dr DTCH/LGLY SL3 122 E1
Olivia Gdns DEN/HRF UB9 84 B8
Olivier Wy AYL HP20 3 M5
Olleberrie La
RKW/CH/CXG WD3 65 K3
Olney Rd OLN MK46 133 N2
OLN MK46 128 G7
Omega Ct LBUZ LU7 27 K6
O'Neill Rd CNH/GTH/TMA MK8 17 G8
One Pin La SLN SL2 101 H2
One Tree La BEAC HP9 80 D7
One Tree Pl AMS HP6 * 71 H1
Onslow Ct WTR/OFPK MK7 23 K2
Onslow Dr THAME OX9 181 P5
Onslow Gdns HWYN HP13 78 D3
Opal Ct DTCH/LGLY SL3 112 B1
Opal Dr WLLN MK15 19 H2
Opecks Cl SLN SL2 112 A1
Opendale Rd SL SL1 110 A2
Oram Ct MLW SL7 97 J4
Orbison Ct CNH/GTH/TMA MK8 17 G7
Orchard Av BERK HP4 47 M6
EBED/NFELT TW14 125 J8
SL SL1 110 C2
WDSR SL4 120 F4
Orchard Cl AYL HP20 34 E3
BTCHLY MK3 22 C7
DEN/HRF UB9 104 A4
HEN RG9 190 H5
HEN RG9 190 H12
MDHD SL6 108 F7
PRRI HP27 183 N7
RAYLNE/WEN HP22 168 A4
RAYLNE/WEN HP22 43 G4
RAYLW HP18 179 Q2
RAYLW HP18 166 D7
RBEDW MK43 139 K5
RKW/CH/CXG WD3 73 J4
RMKS/WB MK17 152 H3
RSLP HA4 95 H6
SKCH HP14 67 M7
THAME OX9 181 P6
TOW NN12 130 E12
WAT WD17 75 L3
Orchard Cots HYS/HAR UB3 * 115 K6
Orchard Ct BEAC HP9 81 H5
Orchard Dene
BUCK/WIN MK18 11 L5
Orchard Dr FLKWH/TG HP10 89 J6
HAZ/HG HP15 68 F7
LBUZ LU7 26 E8
RAYLNE/WEN HP22 36 D6
RKW/CH/CXG WD3 73 H4
UX/CGN UB8 114 C1
WAT WD17 75 L2
Orchard End DUN/WHIP LU6 170 F2
HAZ/HG HP15 69 G4
Orchard End Av AMSS HP7 71 L2
Orchard Ga SLN SL2 101 H3
Orchard Gv CFSP/GDCR SL9 82 B8
FLKWH/TG HP10 89 G3
MDHD SL6 108 B3
Orchard La AMS HP6 71 J1
GTMIS/PWD HP16 60 B4
LBUZ LU7 161 K3
Orchard Mi BNEND SL8 99 G1
The Orchard on The Gn
RKW/CH/CXG WD3 74 E6
Orchard Pk HAZ/HG HP15 69 H4
Orchard Pl BRACKY NN13 147 M2
SKCH HP14 * 186 H1
UX/CGN UB8 * 114 B2
Orchard Ri OLN MK46 128 B11
PIN HA5 95 L2
Orchard Rd BEAC HP9 90 E1
CSTG HP8 82 B2
HWYN HP13 78 F6
HYS/HAR UB3 115 M4
The Orchards DUN/WHIP LU6 30 F8
GTMIS/PWD HP16 60 F8
HADM HP17 * 177 M5
TRING HP23 37 L7
The Orchard FLKWH/TG HP10 89 G3
HAZ/HG HP15 68 F4
MLW SL7 97 K3
RAYLNE/WEN HP22 44 B2
RBICS/W OX25 172 C2
SKCH HP14 67 K8
TOW NN12 137 K3
TRING HP23 * 37 L7
Orchardville SL SL1 110 A1
Orchard Wy AYL HP20 3 K1
BIC OX26 162 B3
BUCK/WIN MK18 158 B4
CHNR OX39 184 F4
DTCH/LGLY SL3 112 D5
DUN/WHIP LU6 170 G1
HAZ/HG HP15 69 H4
HHS/BOV HP3 56 F7
LBUZ LU7 169 R9
LBUZ LU7 161 R8
LBUZ LU7 30 E1
NPAG MK16 134 D12
NPAG MK16 132 C4
RBEDW MK43 139 K5
RKW/CH/CXG WD3 73 M8
Orchard Waye UX/CGN UB8 104 C7
Orchehill Av CFSP/GDCR SL9 92 C3
Orchehill Ri CFSP/GDCR SL9 92 D4
Orchid Cl BIC OX26 162 D1
DUN/WHIP LU6 31 M5
Oregano Cl WDR/YW UB7 114 E4
Orford Ct SHEN MK5 17 K8
Oriel Cl WOLV MK12 12 E7
Oriel Wy BRACKY NN13 8 C6
Orion Wy LBUZ LU7 27 L6

NTHWD HA6 85 L4
Orkney Cl BTCHLY MK3 22 C4
  LBUZ LU7 161 K2
Ormesby Cl AYLS HP21 42 F1
Ormonde GTLIN MK14 14 A7
Ormonde Rd NTHWD HA6 85 J4
Ormond Rd THAME OX9 181 Q5
Ormsgill Ct BDWL MK13 17 L1
Orne Gdns MK15 14 D7
Orpine Cl BIC OX26 162 C6
Orpington Gv SHEN MK5 21 L2
Ortensia Dr WTR/OFPK MK7 19 M7
Orwell Cl AYL HP21 42 C2
  HYS/HAR UB3 115 K4
  NPAG MK16 14 C1
  WDSR SL4 121 J6
Orwell Dr AYLS HP21 42 C2
Osborne Cl BIC OX26 162 B3
Osborne Ct WDSR SL4 121 H5
Osborne Ms WDSR SL4 * 121 H5
Osborne Rd WDSR SL4 121 H5
Osborne St SL SL1 111 L6
  WEAT MK2 22 F7
Osborne Wy TRING HP23 46 C1
Osborn Rd UX/CGN UB8 * 104 B5
Osborn's Ct OLN MK46 128 B11
Osbourne St WOLV MK12 13 G8
Osier La SHEN MK5 21 L2
The Osiers RKW/CH/CXG WD3 75 H6
Osier Wy LBUZ LU20 3 J6
  BUCK/WIN MK18 11 K8
Osmington Pl TRING HP23 37 L6
Osney Rd MDHD 98 D8
Osprey Cl BIC OX26 162 C6
  EAG/OLD/WTN MK6 7 L9
  WDR/YW UB7 114 C6
The Osprey AYLW HP19 * 34 D2
Osprey Wk BUCK/WIN MK18 142 A11
Ostler Ga MDHD SL6 108 B7
Ostlers La STSTR MK11 12 A8
Otmoor La HEAD OX3 178 A2
Otterburn Crs SHEN MK5 21 G2
Otter Cl BTCHLY MK3 22 A5
Otterfield Rd WDR/YW UB7 114 C4
Otters Brook BUCK/WIN MK18 11 M7
Otway Cl AYLS HP21 42 F1
Oulton Cl AYLS HP21 42 F1
Ousebank St NPAG MK16 15 H7
Ousebank Wy STSTR MK11 16 A1
Outfield Cl CFSP/GDCR SL9 82 C5
Outlook Dr CSTG HP8 82 C3
Ouzel Cl BTCHLY MK3 22 B5
The Oval BIC OX26 162 C3
  EAG/OLD/WTN MK6 18 B7
Oval Wy CFSP/GDCR SL9 92 D3
Overdale Rd CSHM HP5 55 H5
Overdales HAZ/HG HP15 68 E7
Overend Green La LBUZ LU7 25 K8
Overgate CMK MK9 18 E2
  WLLN MK15 18 E1
Over Hampden
  GTMIS/PWD HP16 60 A3
Overhills OLN MK46 128 A10
Overn Av BUCK/WIN MK18 11 L5
Overn Cl BUCK/WIN MK18 11 L5
Overn Crs BUCK/WIN MK18 11 L5
Oversley Ct GTLIN MK14 * 14 D5
Overstrand
  RAYLNE/WEN HP22 36 D5
Overstrand Cl BIC OX26 162 F2
Overstream
  RKW/CH/CXG WD3 74 A5
Overstreet GTLIN MK14 14 C7
Over The Misbourne
  CFSP/GDCR SL9 92 A3
Over The Misbourne Rd
  DEN/HRF UB9 93 H5
Overton Dr THAME OX9 181 Q5
Oville Ct SHEN MK5 21 K1
Oving Rd RAYLNE/WEN HP22 159 P11
Ovitts Cl BUCK/WIN MK18 151 K9
Owen Cl DTCH/LGLY SL3 122 E1
Owens Wy RKW/CH/CXG WD3 74 F6
Owl AYLW HP19 * 34 E3
Owlsears Cl BEAC HP9 80 C6
Oxendon Ct LBUZ LU7 27 G4
Oxfield Cl BERK HP4 47 M7
Oxfield Park Dr RMKN MK19 137 R7
Oxford Av HYS/HAR UB3 125 L3
  SL SL1 99 M7
Oxford Cl NTHWD HA6 85 H4
Oxford Gdns DEN/HRF UB9 103 M1
Oxford Rd AYLS HP21 2 A9
  BRACKY NN13 146 D1
  CFSP/GDCR SL9 91 M3
  DEN/HRF UB9 93 K8
  HADM HP17 177 N5
  MLW SL7 97 H4
  RAYLW HP18 179 Q1
  RBICS/W OX25 162 C6
  SKCH HP14 184 E12
  SKCH HP14 76 C5
  WDSR SL4 121 H4
  WYM HP11 5 L5
Oxford Rd East WDSR SL4 121 H4
Oxford St GTMIS/PWD HP16 53 D7
  WEAT MK2 22 F6
  WOLV MK12 13 G8
  WYM HP11 5 H6
Oxhey Ridge Cl NTHWD HA6 85 M5
Oxhouse Ct SHEN MK5 21 K3
Oxleys OLN MK46 128 A10
Oxlip Leyes BIC OX26 162 B2
Oxman La WOLV MK12 16 D1
Oxwich Gv EMV/FZ MK4 21 L6

P

Pack and Prime La HEN RG9 190 F5
Packet Boat La IVER SL0 114 A3
Packhorse Rd CFSP/GDCR SL9 92 D5
Padbury Br BUCK/WIN MK18 149 P3
Padcroft Rd WDR/YW UB7 114 C5
Paddock Cl AYLW HP19 177 Q1
  GTLIN MK14 14 B6
The Paddocks
  BUCK/WIN MK18 149 L11
  HADM HP17 182 D1
  HWYW HP12 86 F3
  LBUZ LU7 26 F7
  MLW SL7 * 97 L4
  RAYLNE/WEN HP22 44 A5
  RKW/CH/CXG WD3 73 L5
The Paddock AYLS HP21 35 H7
  BUCK/WIN MK18 11 M2
  CFSP/GDCR SL9 82 D5
  DTCH/LGLY SL3 112 A7
  HGDN/ICK UB10 105 G2
  MDHD SL6 98 D8
  OLN MK46 133 M2
Paddock Vw WAR/TWY RG10 * 116 F8

Paddock Wy WEAT MK2 23 G5
Padstow Av
  EAG/OLD/WTN MK6 7 J3
Padstow Cl AYL HP20 3 J3
  DTCH/LGLY SL3 112 D7
Page Hill Av BUCK/WIN MK18 11 M5
Pages Cft BERK HP4 47 M4
Pages La UX/CGN UB8 104 B4
Pages Whf MDHD SL6 * 109 H3
Paget Cl MLW SL7 97 L2
Paget Dr MDHD SL6 117 M2
Paget Rd DTCH/LGLY SL3 112 E8
  HGDN/ICK UB10 115 H1
The Pagoda MDHD SL6 109 G1
Paignton Rd RSLP HA4 105 M1
Paignton Wy MKV MK10 19 K3
Paines Orch LBUZ LU7 169 M6
Pakenham Ct AYLW HP19 177 Q2
Palace Cl SL SL1 110 E5
Palace Sq EAG/OLD/WTN MK6 7 L8
Paley St MDHD SL6 118 A4
Palladian Br BUCK/WIN MK18 141 M11
Palmer Av AYLW HP19 2 D1
  RBICS/W OX25 173 K2
Palmer Crs LBUZ LU7 29 L1
Palmers Cl MDHD SL6 117 M3
Palmers Moor
  BUCK/WIN 142 H10
Palmer's Moor La IVER SL0 113 M1
Palmerston Av OLN MK46 128 C11
Palmerston Av DTCH/LGLY SL3 112 A7
Pamela Rw MDHD SL6 * 118 F2
Pankridge Dr
  GTMIS/PWD HP16 60 B3
Pannier Pl GTLIN MK14 18 D1
Panters Ct RMKS/WB MK17 145 R9
Pantile Rw DTCH/LGLY SL3 112 E8
Paprika Ct WTR/OFPK MK7 23 L1
Parade Ct BNEND SL8 88 F6
The Parade BNEND SL8 88 F6
  UX/CGN UB8 * 114 B2
  WYM HP11 * 4 E8
Paradise RMKS/WB MK17 153 J2
Paradise Rd HEN RG9 190 H5
Parchment Cl AMS HP7 63 K8
Parish La SLN SL2 101 H1
Park Av DUN/WHIP LU6 31 J7
  NPAG MK16 14 E2
  RKW/CH/CXG WD3 73 M6
  RSLP HA4 95 K5
  STWL/WRAY TW19 122 C8
  WATW WD18 75 M4
Park Cl BUCK/WIN MK18 160 D5
  RKW/CH/CXG WD3 85 G4
  RMKN MK19 12 B4
  SHEN MK5 86 B1
  WDSR SL4 121 J5
Park Cnr MDHD SL6 * 107 L3
  WDSR SL4 120 D6
Parker Cl BDWL MK13 13 K8
Parker Knoll Wy HWYN HP13 5 H4
Parker Wk AYLW HP19 34 E3
Park Farm Cl RBICS/W OX25 162 H11
Park Farm Rd HWYW HP12 77 G5
Park Farm Wy SKCH HP14 86 B1
Parkfield Av AMS HP6 63 J8
  HGDN/ICK UB10 105 G8
Parkfield Ri PRRI HP27 183 R12
Parkfield Rd HGDN/ICK UB10 95 G8
  SHEN MK5 22 D5
Parkgate BTCHLY MK3 22 D5
Park Ga LBUZ LU7 161 R8
Parkgate SL SL1 110 B1
Park Gv CSTG HP8 72 C4
Park House Dr SHEN MK5 17 J8
Parkland Av DTCH/LGLY SL3 122 C1
Parklands GTLIN MK14 14 A5
  HWYW HP12 * 86 E1
Park La BEAC HP9 90 E1
  CHNR OX39 184 C7
  DEN/HRF UB9 83 M8
  DTCH/LGLY SL3 122 F6
  DTCH/LGLY SL3 112 A7
  DUN/WHIP LU6 30 E8
  HAZ/HG HP15 68 F6
  HEN RG9 188 B4
  HEST TW5 125 M3
  RNHPTN NN7 130 H1
  SKCH HP14 184 H12
  SKCH HP14 86 A1
  SL SL1 100 D3
  YEAD UB4 115 K2
Parkminster MKV MK10 19 K5
Park Pde HYS/HAR UB3 * 115 K3
Park Pl AMS HP7 71 K1
  DEN/HRF UB9 * 84 B8
Park Ri BERK HP4 47 K4
  RBICS/W OX25 162 H11
Park Rd AMS HP6 63 L8
  BUCK/WIN MK18 159 J4
  CSHM HP5 63 G2
  HEN RG9 190 H5
  HGDN/ICK UB10 104 B5
  NPAG MK16 133 P8
  RAYLW HP18 156 G10
  RKW/CH/CXG WD3 74 D2
  RMKN MK19 131 N8
  RNHPTN NN7 130 H1
  SLN SL2 101 J7
  STSTR MK11 16 A1
  TRING HP23 37 L8
  UX/CGN UB8 104 C5
  WAT WD17 75 M2
  WYM HP11 78 C4
  YEAD UB4 115 K2
Park Rd East HGDN/ICK UB10 104 C7
Park Rd South
  BUCK/WIN MK18 151 J10
Park Rw THAME OX9 181 Q7
Parkside CFSP/GDCR SL9 92 E4
  EMV/FZ MK4 22 B3
  HEN RG9 190 F4
Park Side HYS/HAR UB3 * 115 K4
Parkside Cl MDHD SL6 108 C1
  SKCH HP14 67 G5
Parkside Dr WAT WD17 75 K3
Parkside Rd NTHWD HA6 85 L5
Parkside Wk SLN SL2 111 M7
Park St AYL HP20 3 H4
  BERK HP4 48 A5
  DTCH/LGLY SL3 123 J4
  MDHD SL6 108 E3
  PRRI HP27 58 A3
  RMKS/WB MK17 145 J11
  SL SL1 111 L6
  THAME OX9 181 N6
  TRING HP23 37 M7
  WDSR SL4 121 J4
Park Ter THAME OX9 181 P7
Parkview FLKWH/TG HP10 88 F3
Park Vw MDHD SL6 108 B3
Parkview WDR/YW UB7 * 114 D4
Parkview Cha SL SL1 110 D3

Park View Ct HWYW HP12 4 A4
Park View Rd BERK HP4 48 A6
  UX/CGN UB8 114 F3
Parkway HGDN/ICK UB10 104 F5
  MLW SL7 97 L3
Park Wy RKW/CH/CXG WD3 84 B1
Parkway RMKS/WB MK17 144 A8
Park Wy RSLP HA4 95 M7
The Parkway HEST TW5 125 M2
  IVER SL0 103 H4
Parkwood SKCH HP14 66 E4
Parkwood Dr HHW HP1 49 L7
Parlaunt Rd DTCH/LGLY SL3 113 G8
Parliament Cl
  GTMIS/PWD HP16 60 A3
Parliament La SL SL1 99 J3
Parliament Rd THAME OX9 181 N5
Parmiter Cl AYLW HP19 2 A6
Parmoor La HEN RG9 189 Q2
Parneleys MK10 19 J4
Parrishes Piece
  RAYLNE/WEN HP22 32 A3
Parrotts Cl RKW/CH/CXG WD3 74 F5
Parrott's La TRING HP23 45 M7
Parrs Rd DTCH/LGLY SL3 113 C8
Parrs Ct SHEN MK5 21 M1
Parry Gn North
  DTCH/LGLY SL3 112 E8
Parry Gn South
  DTCH/LGLY SL3 112 E8
Parsley Cl RAYLNE/WEN HP22 36 B5
  WTR/OFPK MK7 23 L1
Parslow Cl AYLS HP21 42 C3
Parsonage Cl HWYN HP13 5 J3
  HYS/HAR UB3 115 L3
  TRING HP23 37 M6
Parsonage Farm
  RAYLNE/WEN HP22 168 A3
Parsonage Gdns MLW SL7 97 K5
Parsonage La SLN SL2 101 H4
  WDSR SL4 120 F4
Parsonage Pl AMSS HP7 * 71 H2
  TRING HP23 37 M7
Parsonage Rd CSTG HP8 82 A3
  RKW/CH/CXG WD3 74 C3
Parson Cl BUCK/WIN MK18 151 J10
Parson Cl LBUZ LU7 161 K2
Parsons Crs SHEN MK5 21 M1
Parson's Fee AYL HP20 2 E2
Parsons La RAYLNE/WEN HP22 35 G3
Parsons Rd DTCH/LGLY SL3 122 F1
Parsons Wk HAZ/HG HP15 69 H4
Parson's Wood La SLN SL2 101 J3
Parton Cl RAYLNE/WEN HP22 51 M1
Parton Rd AYL HP20 35 G6
Partridge Cha BIC OX26 162 F6
Partridge Cl BUCK/WIN MK18 142 A11
  CSHM HP5 55 H6
Partridge Md MDHD SL6 98 B8
Partridge Piece RBEDW MK43 139 M5
Partridge Wy AYLW HP19 34 E3
  HWYN HP13 77 H4
Pasadena Cl HYS/HAR UB3 115 M6
Pascal Dr SHEN MK5 21 H1
Passalewe La WTR/OFPK MK7 19 M7
Passmore EAG/OLD/WTN MK6 18 F4
Pastern Pl CMK MK9 18 D2
  GTLIN MK14 18 D1
Pastures Md HGDN/ICK UB10 104 F4
The Pastures AYL HP20 3 M2
  DUN/WHIP LU6 170 C3
  HHW HP1 49 K6
  HWYN HP13 4 D2
Patches Fld MLW SL7 97 K1
Pateman Cl BUCK/WIN MK18 11 K5
Paterson Rd AYLS HP21 42 C3
Patricia Cl SL SL1 110 D4
Patrick Haugh Rd
  RBICS/W OX25 173 K3
Patricks La RMKN MK19 137 M10
Patrick Wy AYLS HP21 42 F1
Patrington Cl UX/CGN UB8 104 B8
Patriot Dr BDWL MK13 6 A4
Patrons Wy West
  DEN/HRF UB9 93 L5
Patterson Ct FLKWH/TG HP10 89 K2
Patterson Rd CSHM HP5 55 G7
Pattison La WLLN MK15 18 F4
Pauls Hl FLKWH/TG HP10 79 J3
Paul's Rw WYM HP11 5 J6
Pavenham Rd RBEDW MK43 129 M1
Pavers Ct AYLS HP21 * 42 C3
Pavilion Cl AYL HP20 3 L5
Pavilion Wy AMS HP6 72 B2
Pavillions Cl BRACKY NN13 8 C7
Paxton Av SL SL1 111 H7
Paxton Crs SHEN MK5 21 L1
Paxton Rd BERK HP4 48 D6
Payne Dr SHEN MK5 17 K6
Paynes End RBICN OX27 154 E12
Paynes Field Cl BERK HP4 47 J4
Peace Dr WAT WD17 75 M4
Peace La MDHD SL6 98 D4
Peace Rd DTCH/LGLY SL3 102 F8
  IVER SL0 102 F2
Peachey Cl CSHM HP5 55 J7
Peachey La UX/CGN UB8 114 C5
Peacock Hay EMV/FZ MK4 21 M4
Peacock Rd MLW SL7 97 M3
Peacocks Cl BERK HP4 47 L3
Pea La BERK HP4 47 L5
Pearce Cl AYLS HP21 42 D2
  MDHD SL6 108 E1
Pearce Dr CSHM HP5 55 G8
Pearce Rd CSHM HP5 55 G8
  MDHD SL6 108 E1
Pearce's Orch HEN RG9 190 H5
Pearce Wy THAME OX9 181 Q7
Pearl Gdns SL SL1 111 G5
Pearse Gv WTR/OFPK MK7 23 K2
Pearson Cl AYLW HP19 2 A9
Pear Tree Av WDR/YW UB7 114 C4
Pear Tree Cl AMSS HP7 71 L2
  BEAC HP9 81 H6
Peartree Cl HHW HP1 49 M6
  SL SL1 110 C5
Pear Tree Rd HHW HP1 49 M6
The Pear Trees WDR/YW UB7 * 114 C4
Peascod St WDSR SL4 121 H4
Peascroft RAYLW HP18 175 L12
Peatey Ct HWYN HP13 78 C4
Pebble La AYL HP20 2 F5
  BRACKY NN13 8 E7
Pebblemoor DUN/WHIP LU6 170 G3
Pebody Rd SLN SL2 * 128 B11
Peckover Ct
  CNH/GTH/TMA MK8 17 J5
Pecks Farm Ct
  RAYLNE/WEN HP22 35 H2
Peddars La LBUZ LU7 30 E2
Pedley Hl BERK HP4 41 H1
Pednor Bottom CSHM HP5 54 A7

Pednormead End CSHM HP5 63 G3
Pednor Rd CSHM HP5 54 D8
Peebles Pl BTCHLY MK3 22 C3
Peel Cl WDSR SL4 120 F5
Peel Ct SL SL1 111 G2
Peel Rd WOLV MK12 12 F8
Peel Wy UX/CGN UB8 114 D2
Peerless Dr DEN/HRF UB9 94 A4
Peers Dr RMKS/WB MK17 144 H7
Peers La SHEN MK5 17 H4
Pegasus Rd LBUZ LU7 27 K6
Peggotty Wy UX/CGN UB8 115 G3
Peggs La RAYLNE/WEN HP22 36 E5
Pelham Pl GTLIN MK14 18 C1
Pelham Rd THAME OX9 181 Q5
Pelton Ct SHEN MK5 17 L8
Pemberton Cl AYLS HP21 42 C3
Pemberton Rd SL SL1 110 D7
Pembridge Cha HHS/BOV HP3 56 E7
Pembridge Cl HHS/BOV HP3 56 E7
Pembridge Gv EMV/FZ MK4 21 L8
Pembridge Rd HHS/BOV HP3 56 E7
Pembroke Rd AYL HP21 3 J4
  NTHWD HA6 85 H3
  RSLP HA4 95 K7
Pembury Ct HYS/HAR UB3 125 J2
Pemerich Cl HYS/HAR UB3 * 125 L1
Penbridge Ct HYS/HAR UB3 125 L1
Pencarrow Pl
  EAG/OLD/WTN MK6 7 K7
Pendell Av HYS/HAR UB3 125 L3
Pendennis Ct EMV/FZ MK4 21 K6
Pendle Ct HGDN/ICK UB10 105 H6
Pendles Paddock SKCH HP14 187 J4
Penfold RAYLNE/WEN HP22 43 L4
Penfold La HAZ/HG HP15 69 K2
Pengelly Ct
  EAG/OLD/WTN MK6 7 K7
Penhale Cl EMV/FZ MK4 21 L6
Penhow Ri EMV/FZ MK4 21 H5
Penina Ct BTCHLY MK3 22 A5
Penington Rd BEAC HP9 90 A4
Penlee Ri EMV/FZ MK4 21 L6
Penley Ct CHNR OX39 184 E4
Penling Cl MDHD SL6 98 D4
Penmon Cl MKV MK10 19 J3
Penmoor Cl HWYW HP12 77 H6
Penn Av CSHM HP5 62 F7
Penn Cl RKW/CH/CXG WD3 73 J7
  UX/CGN UB8 114 D1
Penn Dr DEN/HRF UB9 93 L5
Pennefather Av AYLS HP21 3 H7
Penn Gaskell La
  CFSP/GDCR SL9 82 B5
Penn Gn BEAC HP9 80 C6
Pennine Cl SLN SL2 110 F2
Pennine Wy HYS/HAR UB3 125 J3
The Pennings
  RAYLNE/WEN HP22 44 A5
Pennington Pl THAME OX9 181 Q5
Pennington Rd
  CFSP/GDCR SL9 82 C7
  HWYN HP13 78 E4
The Pennings AMS HP6 63 K8
Pennivale Cl LBUZ LU7 27 H6
Penn Meadow SLN SL2 101 L6
Penn Rd AYLS HP21 2 E1
  BEAC HP9 80 B5
  DTCH/LGLY SL3 122 C4
  HAZ/HG HP15 68 F6
  RKW/CH/CXG WD3 83 L1
  SLN SL2 111 J1
  WEAT MK2 23 H6
Pennycress Wy NPAG MK16 14 C2
Pennycuik RMKS/WB MK17 24 D5
Pennylets Gn SLN SL2 101 L5
Penny Park Rd NPAG MK16 14 E2
Pennyroyal WTR/OFPK MK7 19 L7
Penrith Wy AYLS HP21 35 G7
Penryn Av EAG/OLD/WTN MK6 7 K6
Penshurst Cl CFSP/GDCR SL9 92 C1
Penshurst Crs
  EAG/OLD/WTN MK6 23 G2
Penshurst Rd MDHD SL6 108 C3
Pentewan Ga
  EAG/OLD/WTN MK6 7 J6
  SLN SL2 110 F2
Pentland Rd AYLS HP21 42 F1
Pentlands STSTR MK11 16 C2
Pentlands Ct HWYN HP13 78 D4
The Pentlands HWYN HP13 78 D4
Pentland Wy HGDN/ICK UB10 105 H1
Penwood Ct MDHD SL6 108 A3
Penwood La MLW SL7 97 H5
Penyston Rd MDHD SL6 108 B3
Penzance Cl DEN/HRF UB9 * 93 L5
Penzance Sp SLN SL2 111 G1
Pepler Wy SL SL1 100 A8
Peplow Cl WDR/YW UB7 114 C5
Peppard La HEN RG9 190 H7
Peppard Meadow
  GTMIS/PWD HP16 60 C5
Peppett's Gn CSHM HP5 54 C3
The Peppiatts DUN/WHIP LU6 170 F4
Pepys Cl DTCH/LGLY SL3 123 G2
  HGDN/ICK UB10 105 G2
Pepys Dr GTMIS/PWD HP16 60 B3
Perch Cl MLW SL7 97 J3
Percheron Pl GTLIN MK14 18 C1
Perch Mdw
  RAYLNE/WEN HP22 44 A2
Percy Bush Rd WDR/YW UB7 114 C5
Percy Gdns YEAD UB4 105 K4
Percy Pl DTCH/LGLY SL3 122 A4
Percy Ter CSTG HP8 81 M3
Peregrine AYLW HP19 34 E3
Peregrine Cl
  EAG/OLD/WTN MK6 7 M9
Perham Cl HEN RG9 190 F6
Perivale MKV MK10 19 J3
Perks La GTMIS/PWD HP16 60 A7
Permayne BDWL MK13 13 J8
Perpetual Park Dr HEN RG9 191 J6
Perracombe EMV/FZ MK4 21 L6
Perran Av EAG/OLD/WTN MK6 7 K6
Perrin Springs La HEN RG9 187 Q12
Perry Cl UX/CGN UB8 115 G3
Perrycroft WDSR SL4 120 D6
Perryfields Wy SL SL1 110 A1
Perry Hl RAYLW HP18 156 H9
Perry La MDHD SL6 133 P9
Perry Md DUN/WHIP LU6 170 C4
Perry Rd RAYLNE/WEN HP22 183 L12
Perry St RAYLW HP18 159 N1
Perseverance Hl HEN RG9 190 M1
Pershore Cft HEN RG9 190 M1
Perth Av SL SL1 111 G3
Perth Cl BTCHLY MK3 22 C4
Perth Rd HWYN HP13 78 C2
Peterborough Av HWYN HP13 5 H5

Peterborough Ga WLLN MK15 14 F8
Peterhead Ms DTCH/LGLY SL3 122 F1
Peterhill Cl CFSP/GDCR SL9 92 D7
Peterley Av GTMIS/PWD HP16 60 D7
Peterley Ct SKCH HP14 * 86 A2
Peterley La GTMIS/PWD HP16 60 C7
Petersfield RAYLNE/WEN HP22 43 H3
Petersfield Av SLN SL2 111 M5
Petersham Cl NPAG MK16 14 F3
Peters La MDHD SL6 119 G2
  PRRI HP27 58 C1
Peter's Pl BERK HP4 47 K4
Pether Av BRACKY NN13 8 B6
Pettifer Wy HWYW HP12 4 B8
Pettingrew Cl WTR/OFPK MK7 19 L8
Petty Cross SL SL1 110 C5
Petworth CNH/GTH/TMA MK8 17 H5
Petworth Gdns
  HGDN/ICK UB10 105 H4
Pevensey Cl AYLS HP21 43 G1
  BTCHLY MK3 22 B7
Pevensey Rd SLN SL2 110 F2
Peverel Dr DBGH MK1 22 E3
Peveril Cl AYLS HP21 43 G1
Pevers La OLN MK46 132 H1
Pheasant Cl BERK HP4 48 B7
  TRING HP23 38 A4
Pheasant Dr HWYN HP13 77 H5
Pheasant Hl CSTG HP8 82 B2
Pheasant Ri CSHM HP5 63 J4
Pheasants Cft MDHD SL6 117 M2
Pheasants Dr HAZ/HG HP15 69 G5
Pheasants Rdg MLW SL7 87 H7
Pheasants Wy
  RKW/CH/CXG WD3 74 A8
Phelps Rd WEAT MK2 153 R1
Phelps Wy HYS/HAR UB3 115 L3
Philbye Ms SL SL1 110 E6
Philip Dr FLKWH/TG HP10 89 H3
Philip Rd HWYN HP13 78 C3
Philips Rd AYLW HP19 177 R2
Phillimore Cl WLLN MK15 14 E7
Phillip Ct SHEN MK5 17 H8
Philpots Cl WDR/YW UB7 114 C4
Philps Cl SKCH HP14 86 B3
Phipps Cl AYL HP20 3 L2
  MDHD SL6 117 M4
Phipps Rd SL SL1 110 C3
Phoebe's Orch
  RMKS/WB MK17 144 B3
Phoenix Cl LBUZ LU7 27 L5
  NTHWD HA6 85 L4
Phoenix Dr
  EAG/OLD/WTN MK6 18 B8
The Phygtle CFSP/GDCR SL9 82 D7
Phyllis Court Dr HEN RG9 190 H5
Picasso Pl AYLW HP19 167 P12
Pickenfield THAME OX9 181 Q7
Pickering Dr EMV/FZ MK4 21 L4
Pickford Dr DTCH/LGLY SL3 112 D5
Pickfords Gdns SL SL1 111 K5
Pickins Piece DTCH/LGLY SL3 122 F5
Picton St EMV/FZ MK4 21 H5
Picts La PRRI HP27 185 R1
Piddington La RNHPTN NN7 126 A4
Piddington Rd RAYLW HP18 164 B6
  SKCH HP14 76 A6
Pield Heath Av UX/CGN UB8 114 E6
Pield Heath Rd UX/CGN UB8 114 F7
Pierson Rd WDSR SL4 120 C5
Pigeon Farm Rd SKCH HP14 186 H1
Pigeonhouse La KID OX5 172 C7
Piggott's Orch AMSS HP7 71 G5
Piggotts Orch AMSS HP7 71 G5
Pightle Cl BIC OX26 162 C6
  RKW/CH/CXG WD3 83 J5
Pightle Crs BUCK/WIN MK18 11 L4
Pightle End BUCK/WIN MK18 * 11 L4
The Pightle BUCK/WIN MK18 11 M2
  LBUZ LU7 169 Q11
  RAYLNE/WEN HP22 159 N11
Pigott Dr SHEN MK5 21 K1
Pike Cl HGDN/ICK UB10 104 E6
  MLW SL7 97 H6
Pike Cnr AYLS HP21 43 H1
Pilch La RMKS/WB MK17 150 F1
Pilgrims Cl PRRI HP27 58 A1
Pilgrim St CMK MK9 17 L2
Pimms Cl HWYN HP13 78 F4
Pimms Gv HWYN HP13 78 F4
Pimpernel Gv WTR/OFPK MK7 19 L8
Pinchfield RKW/CH/CXG WD3 83 J5
Pineapple Rd AMSS HP7 71 L2
Pine Cha HWYW HP12 87 G3
Pine Cl BIC OX26 162 E1
  BUCK/WIN MK18 11 M3
  HAZ/HG HP15 69 G7
  LBUZ LU7 27 H4
  MDHD SL6 108 A3
Pinecroft MLW SL7 97 H3
Pine Gv RMKS/WB MK17 144 D6
Pine Hl HAZ/HG HP15 69 G7
Pinels Wy WYM HP11 87 K3
Pine Rd DUN/WHIP LU6 170 G6
Pines Cl AMS HP6 63 G8
  GTMIS/PWD HP16 61 G8
  NTHWD HA6 85 K6
The Pines FLKWH/TG HP10 79 G1
  HHS/BOV HP3 57 K3
Pine St AYLW HP19 177 Q1
Pinetree Cl CFSP/GDCR SL9 82 B7
Pinetrees Ct RNHPTN NN7 126 B3
Pine Trees Dr HGDN/ICK UB10 104 D2
Pine Wk BERK HP4 47 J3
Pinewood Av UX/CGN UB8 114 F1
Pinewood Cl CFSP/GDCR SL9 92 D6
  IVER SL0 103 H5
  NTHWD HA6 85 M5
  WAT WD17 75 M2
Pinewood Dr WEAT MK2 23 G7
Pinewood Gn IVER SL0 103 H5
Pinewood Rd HWYW HP12 77 H7
  IVER SL0 103 H6
Pinfold WTR/OFPK MK7 19 L8
Pingle Dr BIC OX26 162 E1
Pinglestone La WDR/YW UB7 124 D3
Pinions Rd HWYN HP13 78 C4
Pinkard Ct EAG/OLD/WTN MK6 18 D7
Pink Hl PRRI HP27 58 D6
Pink La PRRI HP27 58 C1
Pinkle Hill Rd LBUZ LU7 107 L1
Pinkneys Dr MDHD SL6 107 M6
Pinkneys Rd MDHD SL6 107 M6
Pink Rd PRRI HP27 58 C6
Pinks Cl SHEN MK5 6 H9
Pinkwell Av HYS/HAR UB3 115 J8
Pinkwell La HYS/HAR UB3 115 J8

Pinkworthy EMV/FZ MK4 22 A2
Pinn Cl UX/CGN UB8 114 C3
Pinner Rd NTHWD HA6 85 L8
Pinn Wy RSLP HA4 95 J6
Pinstone Wy CFSP/GDCR SL9 93 G8
Pintail Cl AYLW HP19 34 D2
Pioneer Rd BIC OX26 162 F8
Pioneer Wy WATW WD18 75 L7
Pipard GTLIN MK14 14 B7
Pipers Cl SL SL1 100 B8
Pipers Hl HHW HP1 41 H8
Pipers La HAZ/HG HP15 68 B2
Pipits Cft BIC OX26 162 F6
Pippin Cl NPAG MK16 14 E3
Pippins Cl WDR/YW UB7 114 C7
The Pippins DTCH/LGLY SL3 112 E5
Pipston Gn WTR/OFPK MK7 19 L8
Pitchcott Rd
RAYLNE/WEN HP22 159 L11
Pitcher La SHEN MK5 6 A8
Pitchford Av BUCK/WIN MK18 11 M4
Pitch Pond Cl BEAC HP9 80 A5
The Pitch SKCH HP14 187 N3
Pitfield STSTR MK11 16 E3
Pitters Piece RAYLW HP18 175 J11
Pitt Gn BUCK/WIN MK18 142 A9
Pitts Cl RAYLNE/WEN HP22 * 43 H3
Pitts Rd SL SL1 111 H5
Pix Farm La HHW HP1 49 G8
Pixies Hill Crs HHW HP1 57 L1
Pixies Hill Rd HHW HP1 49 L8
Place Farm Wy PRRI HP27 58 A1
Plackett Wy SL SL1 110 C5
Plaines Cl SL SL1 110 E5
Plaistow Crs MKV MK10 19 H5
Plaiters Cl TRING HP23 37 M6
Plaitford Cl RKW/CH/CXG WD3 84 D2
Plantagenet Cl BRACKY NN13 8 D6
Plantain Ct WTR/OFPK MK7 19 L8
Plantation Ct SHEN MK5 21 K2
Plantation Pl SHEN MK5 21 K2
Plantation Rd AMS HP6 63 K8
HWYN HP13 78 F3
LBUZ LU7 27 G2
Plantation Wk HHW HP1 49 M4
Plantation Wy AMS HP6 63 K8
The Platt AMSS HP7 71 G3
Playing Field Rd
BRACKY NN13 147 M2
Pleasant Mt BUCK/WIN MK18 149 N12
Pleasant Pl
RKW/CH/CXG WD3 * 83 K7
The Pleasaunce
RAYLNE/WEN HP22 36 D5
Pleck La CHNR OX39 184 C6
Pleshey Cl SHEN MK5 17 L8
Plested Ct RAYLNE/WEN HP22 43 H4
Plomer Green Av HWYN HP13 77 J4
Plomer Green La HWYN HP13 77 J2
Plomer Hl HWYN HP13 4 A1
Plough Cl AYLS HP21 42 D3
RBEDW MK43 139 K6
Plough Cnr CHNR OX39 184 C1
Plough Farm Cl RSLP HA4 95 J5
Plough La BERK HP4 49 G3
DEN/HRF UB9 84 B6
RKW/CH/CXG WD3 65 L4
SLN SL2 102 A6
Ploughlees La SL SL1 111 K4
Ploughley Rd RBICS/W OX25 162 H10
Plover Cl BERK HP4 48 B7
BUCK/WIN MK18 11 M8
NPAG MK16 15 J3
The Plover AYLW HP19 34 D2
Plowden Pk WTLGN OX49 184 A7
Plowman Cl WOLV MK12 16 E1
Plumer Rd WYM HP11 4 D6
Plumer Ter WYM HP11 * 4 E7
Plumstead Av BDWL MK13 6 D3
Plum Tree La LBUZ LU7 27 H6
Plym Cl AYLS HP21 42 B1
Plymouth Gv EMV/FZ MK4 21 L5
Plymouth Rd SL SL1 110 D3
Pocock Av WDR/YW UB7 114 E7
Pococks La WDSR SL4 121 K1
Poets Cha AYLS HP21 3 H9
The Points MDHD SL6 108 A7
Polecat End La WHLY OX33 178 E9
Polehanger La HHW HP1 49 K5
Pole Hill Rd HGDN/ICK UB10 115 G1
Poles Hl CSHM HP5 54 F8
RKW/CH/CXG WD3 65 K4
Polidoris La HAZ/HG HP15 69 H3
Polish Av RAYLNE/WEN HP22 44 D2
Pollard Av DEN/HRF UB9 93 L5
Pollard Cl WDSR SL4 122 A8
Pollards RKW/CH/CXG WD3 83 J5
Pollywick Rd TRING HP23 46 C1
Polmartin Ct
EAG/OLD/WTN MK6 7 K7
Polruan Pl EAG/OLD/WTN MK6 7 J7
Pomander Crs WTR/OFPK MK7 19 L7
Pomeroy Cl AMSS HP7 71 J3
Pond Ap HAZ/HG HP15 69 H4
Pond Cl AMSS HP7 70 B7
DEN/HRF UB9 94 B1
RMKS/WB MK17 152 H4
Pondgate WTR/OFPK MK7 19 L6
Pond Gn RSLP HA4 95 K8
Pond La BERK HP4 40 D3
CFSP/GDCR SL9 82 A8
Pond Park Rd CSHM HP5 55 G8
Pondside Cl HYS/HAR UB3 125 J3
Pondwicks AMSS HP7 71 G2
The Pony Fld
RAYLNE/WEN HP22 43 J4
Poole Cl RSLP HA4 95 K8
Poole Wy YEAD UB4 * 105 K8
Pool La SL SL1 111 K4
Poolmans Rd WDSR SL4 120 C6
Popes Acre HADM HP17 182 C1
Popes Cl DTCH/LGLY SL3 123 H3
Popes La MDHD SL6 98 B3
Poplar Av AMSS HP7 71 L2
WDR/YW UB7 114 E4
Poplar Cl CSHM HP5 55 H7
DTCH/LGLY SL3 123 K4
EAG/OLD/WTN MK6 23 H1
LBUZ LU7 27 H4
Poplar Pl HYS/HAR UB3 115 M4
Poplar Rd AYL HP20 3 L2
DEN/HRF UB9 104 B4
FLKWH/TG HP10 89 K3
Poplars Cl HADM HP17 177 M5
RSLP HA4 95 K7
Poplars Gv MDHD SL6 99 G8
Poplars Rd BUCK/WIN MK18 11 L6
The Poplars BIC OX26 163 J4
DEN/HRF UB9 * 84 B8
RAYLNE/WEN HP22 44 B5
Poppy Cl HHW HP1 49 K6
Poppylands BIC OX26 162 C2
Poppy Rd PRRI HP27 183 R12
Porlock La EMV/FZ MK4 21 M2
Portal Cl HGDN/ICK UB10 104 E5
RSLP HA4 105 M2
Portal Rd RAYLNE/WEN HP22 44 C4
Portchester Ct
CNH/GTH/TMA MK8 17 J5
Porter's Cl RMKN MK19 137 M10
Porters Wy WDR/YW UB7 114 E7
Portfield Cl BUCK/WIN MK18 11 L6
Portfields Rd NPAG MK16 14 D2
Portfield Wy BUCK/WIN MK18 11 M6
Porthcawl Gn EMV/FZ MK4 21 M6
Porthleven Pl
EAG/OLD/WTN MK6 7 K5
Porthmellin Cl EMV/FZ MK4 21 L6
Portishead Dr EMV/FZ MK4 21 J5
Portland Cl SLN SL2 110 C1
Portland Dr WLLN MK15 14 F7
Portland Gdns MLW SL7 97 J5
Portland Pk CFSP/GDCR SL9 92 C5
Portland Rd YEAD UB4 105 K8
Portlock Rd MDHD SL6 108 B3
Portman Gdns
HGDN/ICK UB10 104 F5
Portman Ms AYLW HP19 177 Q2
Portmarnock Cl BTCHLY MK3 21 M5
Portobello Cl CSHM HP5 54 F8
Portrush Cl BTCHLY MK3 22 A6
Portway BUCK/WIN MK18 159 L9
CMK MK9 6 A5
WLLN MK15 19 G1
Portway Dr HWYW HP12 77 G5
Portway Rd BUCK/WIN MK18 156 E1
HADM HP17 177 P6
Post Meadow IVER SL0 103 J8
Post Office La BEAC HP9 80 C7
DTCH/LGLY SL3 112 C3
RAYLNE/WEN HP22 159 R12
Potash Cl HADM HP17 182 C1
Potash La TRING HP23 168 E10
Potkiln La BEAC HP9 91 H2
Potten End Hl HHW HP1 49 K2
Potter Rw GTMIS/PWD HP16 53 H8
Potters Cl GTMIS/PWD HP16 60 A3
Potters Cross IVER SL0 103 K8
Potters Cross Crs
HAZ/HG HP15 68 D8
Potters Gln BUCK/WIN MK18 149 Q5
Potters La STSTR MK11 16 E2
Potter St NTHWD HA6 85 M8
Pottery Cl AYLW HP19 177 R2
Potts Pl MLW SL7 * 97 J4
Pouchen End La HHW HP1 49 J8
Pound Cl BUCK/WIN MK18 149 L11
RMKN MK19 136 H10
Pound Crs MLW SL7 97 H5
Poundfield La MDHD SL6 98 E3
Poundfield Rd TOW NN12 137 M4
Pound Hl RMKS/WB MK17 24 D5
Pound La BUCK/WIN MK18 148 C6
CSHM HP5 54 E1
MLW SL7 97 H5
NPAG MK16 134 E11
WHLY OX33 178 B7
Pounds Cl RBEDW MK43 139 L5
Pound St RAYLNE/WEN HP22 44 A6
The Pound BRACKY NN13 140 A2
MDHD SL6 98 E3
RNHPTN NN7 126 D5
Powell Cl WHLY OX33 178 E10
Powell Hvn MKV MK10 19 H3
Powis Cl MDHD SL6 108 A6
Powis La EMV/FZ MK4 21 H3
Powney Rd MDHD SL6 108 B3
Poyle La SL SL1 100 A6
Poyle Pk DTCH/LGLY SL3 * 123 K6
Poyle Rd DTCH/LGLY SL3 123 K6
The Poynings DTCH/LGLY SL3 113 L8
Prebendal Av AYLS HP21 2 C9
Prebendal Cl AYL HP20 * 2 E5
Precedent Dr BDWL MK13 17 L4
Precinct Rd HYS/HAR UB3 115 M4
The Precincts SL SL1 110 A1
Premier Pl WATW WD18 75 L6
Prentice Gv EMV/FZ MK4 21 L3
SHEN MK5 21 L3
Prescott Rd DTCH/LGLY SL3 123 K5
Presley Wy
CNH/GTH/TMA MK8 17 H7
Press Rd UX/CGN UB8 104 C5
Preston Hl CSHM HP5 55 J8
Preston Rd SLN SL2 112 B4
Prestwick Cl BTCHLY MK3 22 A7
Prestwold Wy AYLW HP19 177 R3
Prestwood SLN SL2 112 A3
Prestwood Cl HWYW HP12 4 A4
Prestwood Pl
GTMIS/PWD HP16 * 60 B4
Pretoria Rd HWYN HP13 5 M4
WATW WD18 75 M5
Price Cl BIC OX26 162 E3
Prices Wy BRACKY NN13 8 C5
Priest End THAME OX9 181 M5
Priestland Gdns BERK HP4 48 D4
Priests Paddock BEAC HP9 80 A5
Primatt Crs SHEN MK5 17 L8
Primrose Cl HHW HP1 49 K8
Primrose Ct AYLS HP21 * 34 A8
Primrose Dr AYLS HP21 42 A1
BIC OX26 162 C2
WDR/YW UB7 114 C8
Primrose Hl HAZ/HG HP15 68 E3
Primrose La MDHD SL6 118 F4
Primrose Lea MLW SL7 97 J3
Primrose Rd BDWL MK13 17 K2
Primrose Wy BUCK/WIN MK18 11 K7
Prince Albert's Wk WDSR SL4 121 K3
Prince Andrew Cl MDHD SL6 109 G1
Prince Andrew Rd MDHD SL6 109 G1
Prince Consort Cots WDSR SL4 121 J5
Prince Edward St BERK HP4 48 B6
Prince Pk HHW HP1 49 M8
Prince Philip Av RBEDW MK43 138 G4
Prince Rupert Dr AYLW HP19 34 C2
Princes Av WATW WD18 75 M6
Princes Cl BERK HP4 47 M4
RAYLW HP18 175 J7
WDSR SL4 120 E1
Princes Ct LBUZ LU7 27 G6
Princes Ga HWYN HP13 78 C4
Prince's La GTMIS/PWD HP16 53 J5
Princes Park Av HYS/HAR UB3 115 J4
Princes Park Cir HYS/HAR UB3 115 J4
Princes Park Cl HYS/HAR UB3 115 J4
Princes Park La HYS/HAR UB3 115 J4
Princes Park Pde
HYS/HAR UB3 115 J4
Princes Pl PRRI HP27 183 R12
Princes Rd BNEND SL8 89 H7
Prince's Rd AYLS HP21 3 H6
Princess Av WDSR SL4 121 G6
Princess Gv BEAC HP9 81 J4
Princess La RSLP HA4 95 K7
Princess St MDHD SL6 108 E4
Princes St SKCH HP14 76 A6
SL SL1 112 A6
Princes Wy WEAT MK2 22 F6
Printers End AYLW HP19 2 A5
Printinghouse La
HYS/HAR UB3 115 K6
Prior Gv CSHM HP5 63 H1
Priors Cl MDHD SL6 109 G8
SL SL1 111 M7
Priors Pk EMV/FZ MK4 22 A4
Priors Rd WDSR SL4 120 C6
Priors Wy MDHD SL6 109 G8
Priory Av DEN/HRF UB9 94 B3
HWYN HP13 5 J5
Priory Cl AYLW HP19 2 C2
BIC OX26 162 E5
DEN/HRF UB9 103 M1
NPAG MK16 15 H2
RBEDW MK43 129 R9
RSLP HA4 95 L7
Priory Ct BIC OX26 162 D5
Priory Crs AYLW HP19 2 C2
Priory Flds WAT WD17 75 L2
Priory Gdns BERK HP4 48 B6
DEN/HRF UB9 94 B3
Priory La BIC OX26 162 D5
Priory Rd BIC OX26 162 E5
CFSP/GDCR SL9 92 B2
HWYN HP13 5 J5
SL SL1 110 B2
Priory St NPAG MK16 15 H2
Priory Wy CFSP/GDCR SL9 92 C2
DTCH/LGLY SL3 122 A3
WDR/YW UB7 124 D2
Proctor Ri CNH/GTH/TMA MK8 17 G8
Progress Rd HWYW HP12 77 G7
Prospect Cl RMKS/WB MK17 152 H8
Prospect Ct SKCH HP14 86 A1
TOW NN12 130 E12
Prospect Pl LBUZ LU7 161 R8
MDHD SL6 106 E3
RMKN MK19 12 C1
Prospect Rd MLW SL7 97 H4
STSTR MK11 137 R9
Protheroe Fld WTR/OFPK MK7 144 A6
Providence La HYS/HAR UB3 125 J3
Providence Pl MDHD SL6 108 E3
Providence Rd WDR/YW UB7 114 D5
Pudding Hl WAR/TWY RG10 106 C8
Pudding La HHW HP1 49 M5
Pudseys Cl MDHD SL6 98 A4
Puers La BEAC HP9 81 K6
Puffin Wy AYLW HP19 34 E3
Pulborough Cl BTCHLY MK3 22 A5
Pulford Rd LBUZ LU7 27 G8
Puller Rd HHW HP1 49 M8
Pulleys Cl HHW HP1 49 L6
Pulleys La HHW HP1 49 L6
Pullfields CSHM HP5 62 F1
Pulpit Cl CSHM HP5 54 F8
Pulpit La RAYLNE/WEN HP22 159 N10
Pumpkin Hl SL SL1 100 D4
Pump La CSHM HP5 63 K4
HYS/HAR UB3 115 M6
Pump La North MLW SL7 87 L8
Pump La South MLW SL7 97 M1
Pump Meadow
GTMIS/PWD HP16 60 F3
Pump Pl RMKN MK19 137 Q7
Pumpus Gn BUCK/WIN MK18 151 K10
Punch Bowl La CSHM HP5 63 H3
Purbeck GTLIN MK14 13 M7
Purbeck Cl AYLS HP21 43 G1
Purcel Dr NPAG MK16 14 E3
Purfield Dr WAR/TWY RG10 191 P11
Purkis Cl UX/CGN UB8 115 H4
Purse La NPAG MK16 131 R2
Pursers Ct SLN SL2 111 K4
Purslane Dr BIC OX26 162 B2
Purssell Cl MDHD SL6 117 M3
Purssell Pl PRRI HP27 58 A2
Purssells Meadow SKCH HP14 67 H7
Purton Ct SLN SL2 101 H5
Purton La SLN SL2 101 H5
Pury Rd TOW NN12 130 A6
Pusey Wy SKCH HP14 86 B1
Putlowes Dr RAYLW HP18 167 M11
Putman Cl THAME OX9 181 Q6
Putnams Dr
RAYLNE/WEN HP22 36 C5
Puxley Rd RMKN MK19 137 L9
Pyebush La BEAC HP9 90 F3
The Pyghtles
RAYLNE/WEN HP22 166 E1
The Pyghtle OLN MK46 128 B11
RBEDW MK43 129 N8
Pyke Hayes
CNH/GTH/TMA MK8 17 G3
Pymcombe Cl PRRI HP27 58 A1
Pym Wk THAME OX9 181 N5
Pynchester Cl HGDN/ICK UB10 94 F8
Pyxe Ct WTR/OFPK MK7 23 K2

Q

The Quadrangle HWYN HP13 78 D3
Quadrans Cl WLLN MK15 * 14 D7
The Quadrant HWYN HP13 78 D1
Quainton Rd BUCK/WIN MK18 159 J8
RAYLW HP18 166 D8
Quaker's Md
RAYLNE/WEN HP22 43 L3
Quakers Mede HADM HP17 176 D12
Quantock Cl DTCH/LGLY SL3 122 F1
HYS/HAR UB3 125 J3
Quantock Crs EMV/FZ MK4 22 A4
Quarrendon Av AYLW HP19 2 A1
Quarrendon Rd AMSS HP7 71 J3
Quarry Cl RAYLW HP18 175 K11
Quarrydale Dr MLW SL7 97 L4
Quarry Green Cl RMKN MK19 137 J11
Quarry La HEN RG9 191 K10
Quarry Rd LBUZ LU7 169 Q12
Quarry Wood Rd MLW SL7 97 K6
Quartermass Cl HHW HP1 49 M6
Quartermass Rd HHW HP1 49 M6
Quaves Rd DTCH/LGLY SL3 112 A7
Quebec Rd HEN RG9 190 H6
HWYN HP13 78 D4
Queen Alexandra Rd
WYM HP11 5 G7
Queen Anne's Rd WDSR SL4 121 H7
Queen Anne St BDWL MK13 13 J7
Queen Catherine Rd
BUCK/WIN MK18 149 N12
Queen Cl HEN RG9 190 H5
Queen Eleanor St STSTR MK11 12 A8
Queen Elizabeth's Wk
WDSR SL4 121 L5
Queen Mary's Av WATW WD18 75 K5
Queen Mother's Dr
DEN/HRF UB9 93 L5
Queens Acre WDSR SL4 121 J7
Queens Av BIC OX26 162 D4
NPAG MK16 14 F2
WATW WD18 75 L5
Queensbury La MKV MK10 19 H5
Queens Cl THAME OX9 181 N4
Queen's Cl WDSR SL4 121 M8
Queens Ct BIC OX26 162 D4
SL SL1 * 111 L4
Queen's Dr DTCH/LGLY SL3 102 E6
The Queen's Dr
RKW/CH/CXG WD3 73 L7
Queensgate AYLW HP19 177 R2
Queens La MDHD SL6 108 E3
Queens Md AYLS HP21 35 H7
Queensmead DTCH/LGLY SL3 122 A4
Queensmead Rd
FLKWH/TG HP10 79 H8
Queensmere Rd SL SL1 111 L6
Queen's Pk AYLS HP21 3 J6
Queen Sq WYM HP11 5 H6
Queens Rd BERK HP4 47 M5
CSHM HP5 * 63 H1
HWYN HP13 5 M7
HYS/HAR UB3 115 K3
PRRI HP27 58 B2
SL SL1 111 L4
WDR/YW UB7 114 E6
WDSR SL4 121 H5
Queen's Rd DTCH/LGLY SL3 122 A4
MLW SL7 97 H4
THAME OX9 181 P7
UX/CGN UB8 104 B8
Queens Sq PRRI HP27 * 58 A3
Queen St AYL HP20 3 L6
HEN RG9 190 H5
HWYN HP13 5 M6
KGLGY WD4 65 M2
LBUZ LU7 169 Q10
LBUZ LU7 27 G6
MDHD SL6 108 E3
RAYLW HP18 166 C8
SKCH HP14 76 A5
STSTR MK11 12 B8
TRING HP23 37 M7
Queen Street Ms HEN RG9 190 H5
Queensway BTCHLY MK3 22 E6
HAZ/HG HP15 68 F6
MDHD SL6 98 D8
RAYLNE/WEN HP22 22 F6
The Queensway
CFSP/GDCR SL9 92 C3
Queen Victoria Rd WYM HP11 5 J7
Queen Victoria's Wk
WDSR SL4 121 L5
Quickberry Pl AMSS HP7 * 71 H2
Quickley Brow
RKW/CH/CXG WD3 * 73 G7
Quickley La RKW/CH/CXG WD3 73 H7
Quickley Ri RKW/CH/CXG WD3 73 G7
Quickly Brow
RKW/CH/CXG WD3 73 G7
Quickwood Cl
RKW/CH/CXG WD3 73 L7
Quill Hall La AMS HP6 63 L8
Quilter Meadow
WTR/OFPK MK7 144 A5
Quilters Wy HADM HP17 43 J6
RAYLNE/WEN HP22 43 J6
Quinbrookes SLN SL2 112 B3
Quince Cl WTR/OFPK MK7 23 L1
Quinces Cft HHW HP1 49 M5
Quintan Av RBICS/W OX25 163 J10
Quinton Dr BDWL MK13 17 K3
Quoitings Dr MLW SL7 97 H4
Quoiting Sq MLW SL7 * 97 J5

R

Raans Rd AMS HP6 71 L1
Rabans Cl AYLW HP19 167 P12
OLN MK46 128 A9
Rabans La AYLW HP19 177 Q1
Rackstraw Gv WTR/OFPK MK7 144 A5
Radcliffe St WOLV MK12 13 G7
Radclive Rd BUCK/WIN MK18 11 G8
Radcot Av DTCH/LGLY SL3 113 G7
Radcot Cl MDHD SL6 98 D7
Radian Ct SHEN MK5 17 M7
Radius Pk EBED/NFELT TW14 * 125 L7
Radman Gv WOLV MK12 16 E1
Radnage Common Rd
SKCH HP14 187 N1
Radnage La SKCH HP14 185 M8
Radnor Cl HEN RG9 190 H4
Radnor End AYL HP20 3 G1
Radnor Wy DTCH/LGLY SL3 112 D8
Radstock Crs MKV MK10 19 K2
Radstone Rd BRACKY NN13 8 E5
Radworthy EMV/FZ MK4 21 M3
Raeburn Rd YEAD UB4 105 J7
Raeside Cl BEAC HP9 81 H6
Raft Wy EMV/FZ MK4 21 G4
Raglan Dr EMV/FZ MK4 21 H5
Ragmans Cl MLW SL7 87 J6
Ragmans La MLW SL7 87 J5
Ragnall's La WHLY OX33 172 E10
Ragstone Rd SL SL1 111 J7
Ragstones FLKWH/TG HP10 * 88 F1
Railway St AYL HP20 3 G5
Railway Ter SLN SL2 111 L5
Railway Vw DTCH/LGLY SL3 * 122 E6
Rainbow Dr
EAG/OLD/WTN MK6 7 J9
Rainsborough GTLIN MK14 14 D6
Rainsborough Cha MDHD SL6 108 A7
Rake Wy AYLS HP21 42 D3
Raleigh Cl RSLP HA4 95 L8
SL SL1 110 F5
Ralphs Retreat HAZ/HG HP15 68 E6
Ram Aly NPAG MK16 132 C4
Rambler Cl MDHD SL6 110 A3
Rambler La DTCH/LGLY SL3 112 B7
Rambling Wy BERK HP4 49 G4
Ramsay Cl BDWL MK13 17 L3
Ramscote La CSHM HP5 54 E4
Ramsey Ct SLN SL2 110 C1
Ramsgill Ct BDWL MK13 17 L2
Ramson Ri HHW HP1 49 K8
Ramsons Av GTLIN MK14 7 G1
Ramsthorn Gv WTR/OFPK MK7 19 L8
Ramworth Wy AYLS HP21 34 F8
Randall Cl DTCH/LGLY SL3 122 E1
Randall Dr EMV/FZ MK4 21 G3
Randolph Cl BDWL MK13 13 K8
Randolph Rd DTCH/LGLY SL3 112 D8
Ranelagh Gdns NPAG MK16 14 F4
Rangers Ct
CNH/GTH/TMA MK8 17 J5
Rannal Dr CHNR OX39 184 F4
Rannoch Cl WEAT MK2 153 Q1
Rannock Gdns LBUZ LU7 26 D7
Ranston Cl DEN/HRF UB9 93 L5
Rasehill Cl RKW/CH/CXG WD3 74 B6
Rashleigh Pl
EAG/OLD/WTN MK6 18 B7
Ratcliffe Cl UX/CGN UB8 104 C8
Rathbone Cl
CNH/GTH/TMA MK8 17 H7
Rau Ct RBICN OX27 154 F11
Ravel Cl WTR/OFPK MK7 144 A5
Raven Cl RKW/CH/CXG WD3 74 B8
Raven Crs RAYLW HP18 165 R8
Ravencroft BIC OX26 162 F7
Ravenglass Cft MKV MK10 19 L3
Raven Rd SKCH HP14 187 J2
Ravensbourne Pl
EAG/OLD/WTN MK6 7 M4
Ravensbourne Rd AYLS HP21 42 C2
Ravenscar Ct EMV/FZ MK4 21 M5
Ravens Ct TRING HP23 168 G10
Ravenscourt Cl DEN/HRF UB9 95 H6
Ravenscroft Rd HEN RG9 190 G4
Ravensdell HHW HP1 49 L6
Ravens Fld DTCH/LGLY SL3 112 C6
Ravenshoe Cl BNEND SL8 88 F7
Ravens La BERK HP4 48 C6
Ravensmead CFSP/GDCR SL9 82 E5
CHNR OX39 184 F4
Ravenstone Mill Rd OLN MK46 132 F2
Ravenswood Pk NTHWD HA6 85 M6
Ravensworth Rd SLN SL2 100 F8
Ravigill Pl WOLV MK12 17 G2
Rawlings Ct RMKS/WB MK17 * 145 J11
Rawlings La BEAC HP9 81 J3
Rawlins Rd BDWL MK13 17 K2
Rayburn Rd HHW HP1 49 M5
Ray Dr MDHD SL6 109 G3
Raylands Md CFSP/GDCR SL9 92 B4
Ray Lea Cl MDHD SL6 109 G2
Ray Lea Rd MDHD SL6 109 G1
Rayleigh Cl SHEN MK5 17 L8
Ray Lodge Ms MDHD SL6 109 G2
Ray Mead Ct MDHD SL6 109 H1
Ray Meadow MDHD SL6 108 F1
Ray Mead Rd MDHD SL6 109 H2
Ray Mill Rd East MDHD SL6 108 F1
Ray Mill Rd West MDHD SL6 108 E2
Raymond Cl DTCH/LGLY SL3 123 K4
Raymond Rd BIC OX26 162 B2
DTCH/LGLY SL3 112 F8
MDHD SL6 108 C3
Rayners Av FLKWH/TG HP10 79 H7
Rayners Cl DTCH/LGLY SL3 123 H3
FLKWH/TG HP10 79 H7
Rayners La MKV MK10 19 H5
Raynton Cl YEAD UB4 115 L1
Raynton Dr YEAD UB4 105 K7
Ray Park Av MDHD SL6 109 G1
Ray Park La MDHD SL6 109 G2
Ray Park Rd MDHD SL6 109 G2
Ray Rd BIC OX26 162 C5
Rays Av WDSR SL4 120 E3
Ray's Hl CSHM HP5 46 B8
Rays La FLKWH/TG HP10 79 H1
Ray St MDHD SL6 109 G3
Raywood Cl HYS/HAR UB3 125 H3
Reach Gn LBUZ LU7 25 H8
Reach La LBUZ LU7 27 J1
Read Dr RAYLNE/WEN HP22 35 H2
Reading Cl AYLW HP19 167 Q11
Reading Rd HEN RG9 190 H6
The Readings
RKW/CH/CXG WD3 73 L4
Reads La LBUZ LU7 160 H9
Recreation Rd BNEND SL8 89 G7
WAR/TWY RG10 191 P12
Rectory Av HWYN HP13 5 L5
Rectory Cl LBUZ LU7 29 K8
RBEDW MK43 129 Q2
RBICN OX27 156 A7
SLN SL2 101 H8
WDSR SL4 120 F4
Rectory Dr RAYLW HP18 166 D8
Rectory Flds WLLN MK15 19 G3
Rectory Gdns RAYLW HP18 * 156 G8
Rectory Hl AMSS HP7 71 H2
Rectory La AMSS HP7 71 G2
BERK HP4 48 B6
HEN RG9 188 A11
RBEDW MK43 139 L6
RBICN OX27 154 H4
RKW/CH/CXG WD3 84 C1
Rectory Meadow CHNR OX39 184 G3
Rectory Orch OLN MK46 128 G6
Rectory Rd HYS/HAR UB3 115 M3
MDHD SL6 109 J1
RKW/CH/CXG WD3 74 C8
Rectory Wy HGDN/ICK UB10 95 G8
Redbridge GTLIN MK14 14 A7
Redcliffe Wk AYLW HP19 2 A2
Redcote Mnr WTR/OFPK MK7 23 K2
Red Cottage Ms
DTCH/LGLY SL3 112 B7
Red Ct SL SL1 111 K5
Redding Dr AMS HP6 63 G8
Redding Gv
CNH/GTH/TMA MK8 17 H8
Reddings Cl
RAYLNE/WEN HP22 44 A4
Reddington Dr DTCH/LGLY SL3 112 E8
Redfern Cl UX/CGN UB8 104 B6
Redfield Cl DUN/WHIP LU6 31 M5
Redford Rd WDSR SL4 120 C4
Redford Wy UX/CGN UB8 104 B5
Redgrave Pl MLW SL7 97 L3
Redhall La RKW/CH/CXG WD3 74 D2
Red Hl HEN RG9 190 C9
Red House Cl BEAC HP9 80 A6
RMKS/WB MK17 153 J2
Redhouse Cl WYM HP11 87 K3
Redhuish Cl EMV/FZ MK4 22 A3
Redland Cl BUCK/WIN MK18 149 L12
Redland Dr SHEN MK5 6 B9
Redland Wy AYLS HP21 42 F1
Red La CHNR OX39 185 J7
Red Lion Cl RBEDW MK43 139 L5
Red Lion Dr SKCH HP14 186 C1
Red Lion La RKW/CH/CXG WD3 65 M6
Red Lion St CSHM HP5 63 G3
Red Lion Wy FLKWH/TG HP10 89 K4
Red Lodge Gdns BERK HP4 47 M7
Redman Rd HWYW HP12 87 G3
Redmead Rd HYS/HAR UB3 115 K8
Redmoor Ct BIC OX26 162 E4
Redpitch Pk FLKWH/TG HP10 * 89 K4
Redriff Cl MDHD SL6 108 C4
Redshaw Cl BUCK/WIN MK18 11 M5
Redshots Cl MLW SL7 97 K2
Redvers Ga WLLN MK15 14 E7
Red Wing AYLW HP19 34 D3
Redwing Cl BIC OX26 162 F5

Redwood *SL* SL1.....99 M7
Redwood Cl *HAZ/HG* HP15.....69 G7
 HGDN/ICK UB10.....105 G7
 LBUZ LU7.....161 R8
Redwood Dr *AYLS* HP21.....3 F4
 LBUZ LU7.....161 R8
Redwood Gdns *SL* SL1.....111 J4
Redwood Ga *SHEN* MK5.....21 M2
Redwood Gld *LBUZ* LU7.....27 G3
Redwood Pl *BEAC* HP9.....90 C1
The Redwoods *WDSR* SL4.....121 J6
Reed Cl *IVER* SL0.....113 K3
Reedmace Rd *BIC* OX26.....162 D2
Reeve Cl *LBUZ* LU7.....29 K1
Reeve Rd *MDHD* SL6.....119 G2
Reform Rd *MDHD* SL6.....108 F4
Regal Ct *MDHD* SL6.....109 G8
Regatta Pl *BNEND* SL8 *.....88 F6
Regency Ct *AYLS* HP21.....35 C3
Regency Dr *RSLP* HA4.....95 K7
Regent Av *HGDN/ICK* UB10.....105 C5
Regent Cl *SL* SL1.....111 K8
Regent Rd *AYLS* HP21.....35 C2
Regents Cl *YEAD* UB4.....115 K2
Regent St *LBUZ* LU7.....27 J7
 WEAT MK2.....22 F6
Regent Wy *RNHPTN* NN7.....126 D5
Reginald Rd *NTHWD* HA6.....85 L8
Reid Av *MDHD* SL6.....108 B7
Reid Cl *HYS/HAR* UB3.....115 K3
 PIN HA5.....95 M2
Reliance La *CMK* MK9.....7 M2
 EAG/OLD/WTN MK6.....18 E3
Rembrandt End *AYLW* HP19.....167 P12
Remenham Church La
 HEN RG9.....191 K2
Remenham La *HEN* RG9.....191 J4
Remenham Rw *HEN* RG9.....190 H5
Remenham Ter *HEN* RG9 *.....191 M4
Remus Ga *BRACKY* NN13.....8 F8
Rendlesham *WLLN* MK15.....18 F3
Rendlesham Wy
 RKW/CH/CXG WD3.....73 H7
Rennie Cl *HWYN* HP13.....4 E1
Repton Av *HYS/HAR* UB3.....115 J4
Repton Cl *MDHD* SL6.....108 B7
Repton Pl *AMSS* HP7 *.....71 M2
Repton Wy *RKW/CH/CXG* WD3.....74 F6
Reservoir Rd *RSLP* HA4.....95 H4
Restharrow Md *BIC* OX26.....162 B4
Retreat La *SKCH* HP14.....185 N8
The Retreat *AMS* HP6.....72 D2
 MDHD SL6.....119 J3
 PRRI HP27.....58 A2
 STSTR MK11 *.....16 A1
Revel Rd *FLKWH/TG* HP10.....89 J2
Revesby Cl *MDHD* SL6.....108 B7
Reyners Gn *GTMIS/PWD* HP16.....61 C6
Reynold Dr *AYL* HP20.....3 L1
Reynolds Cl *HHW* HP1.....49 M6
 HWYN HP13.....78 D7
 RBEDW HP43.....138 H4
Reynolds Pl
 CNH/GTH/TMA MK8.....17 G8
Reynolds Rd *BEAC* HP9.....80 B7
Reynolds Yd *CSHM* HP5.....63 G3
Rhodes Pl *EAG/OLD/WTN* MK6.....6 F9
Rhondda Cl *DBGH* MK1.....23 H5
Rhoscolyn Dr *EMV/FZ* MK4.....21 L6
Rhuddlan Cl *SHEN* MK5.....17 J7
Rhymer Cl *RMKN* MK19.....131 E6
Ribble Cl *HWH* MK16.....15 H3
Ribble Crs *BTCHLY* MK3.....22 A6
Ribstone Rd *MDHD* SL6.....108 A4
Richard Gdns *HWYN* HP13.....78 D2
 HYS/HAR UB3.....125 J2
Richardson Pl
 EAG/OLD/WTN MK6.....7 C1
Richardson St *WYM* HP11 *.....4 E6
Richards Wy *SL* SL1.....110 D5
Richborough *BDWL* MK13.....13 K8
Richings Pl *DTCH/LGLY* SL3.....113 K7
Richings Wy *DTCH/LGLY* SL3.....113 L8
Richmond Av *HGDN/ICK* UB10.....105 C4
Richmond Cl *BTCHLY* MK3.....22 A5
Richmond Ct *DUN/WHIP* LU6.....30 F8
 HWYN HP13.....5 L6
Richmond Crs *SL* SL1.....111 M5
Richmond Rd *WAT* WD17.....75 K3
Richmond Rd *AYL* HP20.....35 H6
 LBUZ LU7.....27 K8
Richmond Wy *NPAG* MK16.....14 F3
 RKW/CH/CXG WD3.....75 H5
Rickard Cl *AYLS* HP21.....42 C3
 WDR/YW UB7.....114 C7
Ricketts Rd *HWYN* HP13.....78 C4
Rickford Cl *HI AYL* HP20.....2 E6
Rickley La *BTCHLY* MK3.....22 C6
Rickman's La *SL* SL2.....101 K4
Rickmansworth La
 CFSP/GDCR SL9.....82 D6
Rickmansworth Rd
 DEN/HRF UB9.....84 D3
 RKW/CH/CXG WD3.....73 K4
 WATW WD18.....75 K5
Rickman Wk *AYLW* HP19.....177 R3
Rickyard Cl *BDWL* MK13.....17 K2
Riders Wy *CHNR* OX39.....184 F4
The Ride *DUN/WHIP* LU6.....31 J8
Ridgebank *SL* SL1.....110 D4
Ridge Cl *SKCH* HP14.....86 B2
Ridge Lea *HHW* HP1.....49 L8
Ridgely Dr *LBUZ* LU7.....29 K1
Ridgemount End
 CFSP/GDCR SL9.....82 D5
Ridge Side *SKCH* HP14.....185 R10
Ridge Vw *TRING* HP23.....38 B5
Ridgeway *BERK* HP4.....48 A3
 CHNR OX39.....184 H4
 GTMIS/PWD HP16.....52 E1
Ridge Wy *HWYN* HP13.....5 L1
 IVER SL0.....113 K4
Ridgeway *LBUZ* LU7.....161 R7
 PRRI HP27.....58 D1
 RAYLNE/WEN HP22.....51 L3
Ridge Wy *RAYLW* HP18.....181 N1
 RKW/CH/CXG WD3.....74 A8
Ridgeway *STSTR* MK11.....16 C2
 TRING HP23.....45 J4
Ridge Wy *WOLV* MK12.....16 D1
Ridgeway Cl *CSHM* HP5.....55 C2
Ridgeway Cl *AYL* HP20.....3 H3
Ridgeway Meads *PRRI* HP27.....183 L12
The Ridgeway *AMSS* HP7.....71 K3
 MLW SL7.....97 K2
 RSLP HA4.....95 M6
Ridgmont *RMKN* MK19.....137 J3
Ridgmont Rd *RBEDW* MK43.....145 M6
Ridgway *RMKS/WB* MK17.....144 C8
Ridgway Rd *RBEDW* MK43.....145 M1

Riding Court Rd
 DTCH/LGLY SL3.....122 B2
Riding La *BEAC* HP9.....79 L8
Riding Rd *BRACKY* NN13.....146 E1
Ridings Cots *HAZ/HG* HP15.....69 J4
The Ridings *AMS* HP6.....63 J6
 CSHM HP5.....64 C7
 DTCH/LGLY SL3.....113 L8
 MDHD SL6.....107 L7
 WDSR SL4 *.....120 B3
Ridings Wy *LBUZ* LU7.....160 G9
The Riding *RMKN* MK19.....137 L9
Rigby La *HYS/HAR* UB3.....115 H6
Rigeway Vw *LBUZ* LU7.....169 Q10
Rignall Rd *GTMIS/PWD* HP16.....60 D2
Riley Cl *AYL* HP20.....2 D2
Riley Rd *MLW* SL7.....97 J4
Rillington Gdns *EMV/FZ* MK4.....21 L3
Rimmington Wy *AYLW* HP19.....2 A3
Rimsdale Ct *WEAT* MK2.....153 Q3
Ring Rd *FLKWH/TG* HP10.....78 E8
Ring Rd East *WTR/OFPK* MK7.....19 J7
Ring Rd North *WTR/OFPK* MK7.....19 H7
Ring Rd West *WTR/OFPK* MK7.....19 H7
Ringshall Rd *BERK* HP4.....40 H7
Ringstead Av *AYLS* HP21.....42 E1
Ripley Cl *DTCH/LGLY* SL3.....112 D8
 EMV/FZ MK4.....21 H5
 HWYN HP13.....5 G3
Ripley Wy *HHW* HP1.....49 K6
Ripon St *AYL* HP20.....2 E4
Risborough Rd *HADM* HP17.....50 D6
 MDHD SL6.....108 D2
 RAYLNE/WEN HP22.....42 F7
Riseley Rd *MDHD* SL6.....108 B3
The Rise *AMSS* HP7.....71 H2
 BUCK/WIN MK18.....148 G2
 HAZ/HG HP15.....69 L5
 HGDN/ICK UB10.....104 E7
 HWYN HP13.....79 G6
Rising Hill Cl *NTHWD* HA6 *.....85 H6
The Riverbank *WDSR* SL4.....121 G3
River Cl *RSLP* HA4.....95 L5
River Ct *MDHD* SL6.....109 H3
Rivercrest Rd *RMKN* MK19.....137 Q8
River Gdns *MDHD* SL6.....109 J6
Rivermead Ct *MLW* SL7.....97 K6
River Pk *HHW* HP1.....57 M1
Riverpark Dr *MLW* SL7.....97 L5
River Rd *MDHD* SL6.....109 H3
 WDSR SL4 *.....120 B3
Riversdale *BNEND* SL8.....99 G1
Rivers Edge *WYM* HP11.....78 E4
Riverside *BNEND* SL8 *.....89 H7
 LBUZ LU7.....27 H6
 MDHD SL6.....109 H6
River Side *NPAC* MK16.....15 G2
Riverside Ct *CSHM* HP5 *.....63 H4
Riverside Dr
 RKW/CH/CXG WD3.....84 C1
Riverside Gdns *BERK* HP4.....47 M5
Riverside Ms
 BUCK/WIN MK18 *.....11 L6
Riverside Rd
 STWL/WRAY TW19.....124 C8
Riverside Wk *WDSR* SL4.....121 J3
Riverside Wy *UX/CGN* UB8.....104 A6
River St *WDSR* SL4.....121 J3
River Vw *FLKWH/TG* HP10.....89 G3
River Wk *DEN/HRF* UB9.....104 B3
Riverwood Av *MLW* SL7.....97 M5
Riverwoods Dr *MLW* SL7.....97 M5
Rivets Cl *AYLS* HP21.....34 D8
Rivetts Cl *OLN* MK46.....128 A10
Rixband Ct *WTR/OFPK* MK7.....23 K2
Rixman Cl *MDHD* SL6.....108 C5
Rixon Cl *DTCH/LGLY* SL3.....112 D3
Rixons Meadow *AYLW* HP19.....177 R3
Roade Hi *RNHPTN* NN7.....130 D1
Road End La *SKCH* HP14.....86 D1
Robbs Cl *HHW* HP1.....49 M5
Robe End *HHW* HP1.....49 L5
Robert Rd *SLN* SL2.....91 J8
Roberts Cl *RMKN* MK19.....137 M10
 WDR/YW UB7.....114 D5
Robert's Dr *AYLW* HP19.....2 E2
Roberts La *CFSP/GDCR* SL9.....82 F5
Robertson Cl *SHEN* MK5.....17 J7
Roberts Ride *HAZ/HG* HP15.....68 E4
Roberts Rd *HADM* HP17.....176 D12
 HWYN HP13.....5 J4
Roberts Wy *AYLS* HP21.....34 A8
Roberts Wood Dr
 CFSP/GDCR SL9.....82 E5
Robeson Pl
 CNH/GTH/TMA MK8.....17 H6
Robina Cl *NTHWD* HA6.....95 L1
Robin Cl *AYLW* HP19.....34 E3
 BUCK/WIN MK18.....142 A11
 HAZ/HG HP15.....68 C1
Robin Hl *BERK* HP4.....48 B7
Robin Hood Cl *SL* SL1.....110 D5
Robin Ride *BRACKY* NN13.....8 D5
Robins Cl *HWYW* HP12.....87 J3
 RNHPTN NN7.....130 H1
 UX/CGN UB8.....114 B2
Robinsfield *HHW* HP1.....49 M7
Robins Hi *EAG/OLD/WTN* MK6.....18 D8
Robinson Cl *AYLW* HP19.....167 Q11
Robinson Dr *BRACKY* NN13.....8 C7
Robinson Rd *HWYN* HP13.....79 G6
Robins Orch *CFSP/GDCR* SL9.....82 D6
Robins Platt *CHNR* OX39.....184 E4
Robins Wy *BIC* OX26.....162 F7
Robinswood Cl *BEAC* HP9.....80 B5
Robinwood Gv *UX/CGN* UB8.....114 E1
Roblin Cl *AYLS* HP21.....42 D2
Robson Cl *CFSP/GDCR* SL9.....82 D5
Roche Gdns *BTCHLY* MK3.....22 D6
Rochester Cl *SHEN* MK5.....21 K1
Rochester Ms *LBUZ* LU7 *.....26 F7
Rochester Pl *AYLW* HP19.....2 B3
Rochester Rd *NTHWD* HA6.....95 L2
Rochester Wy
 RKW/CH/CXG WD3.....75 G5
Rochford Gdns *BIC* OX26.....162 F2
Rochfords Gdns *SLN* SL2.....91 J8
Rochford Wy *MDHD* SL6.....109 M4
Rock Cl *DTCH/LGLY* SL3.....113 G2
Rock Cl *LBUZ* LU7.....26 E7
Rockingham Dr *GTLIN* MK14.....14 D8
Rockingham Pde *UX/CGN* UB8.....104 B5
Rockingham Rd *UX/CGN* UB8.....104 A6
Rock La *LBUZ* LU7.....26 E7
Rockspray Gv *WTR/OFPK* MK7.....19 L8
Rodney Wy *DTCH/LGLY* SL3.....123 K4
Rodwell Gdns *WTR/OFPK* MK7.....144 A6

Rodwell Yd *TRING* HP23.....37 M7
Roebuck Av *HWYN* HP13.....78 E5
Roebuck Gn *SL* SL1.....110 D5
Roebuck Wy *SHEN* MK5.....17 M8
Roeburn Crs *AYLW* HP21.....3 F5
Roefields Cl *HHS/BOV* HP3.....57 M3
Rofant Rd *NTHWD* HA6.....85 K6
Rogers Cft *EAG/OLD/WTN* MK6.....19 L7
Rogers La *SLN* SL2.....101 L6
Rogers Ruff *NTHWD* HA6.....85 H8
Roker Park Av *HGDN/ICK* UB10.....104 D2
Rokesby Rd *SLN* SL2.....100 E8
Rolfe Cl *BEAC* HP9.....90 D1
Rolls La *MDHD* SL6.....118 D2
Rolvenden Gv *WTR/OFPK* MK7.....19 L7
Roman Ct *DEN/HRF* UB9.....83 M8
Roman Lea *MDHD* SL6.....98 E5
Roman Rd *HHW* HP1.....49 G5
Roman Wy *AYLW* HP19.....2 A6
 BIC OX26.....162 D4
 BNEND SL8.....88 F6
 BRACKY NN13.....8 F7
 HEAD OX3.....178 A3
Romar Ct *DBGH* MK1.....22 F6
Romney Lock Rd *WDSR* SL4.....121 J3
Romney Rd *AYLS* HP21.....42 D2
 YEAD UB4.....105 J2
Romsey Cl *DTCH/LGLY* SL3.....112 E7
Romsey Dr *SLN* SL2.....101 J1
Romsey Wy *WYM* HP11.....77 J5
Romulus Wy *BRACKY* NN13.....8 F7
Ronald Rd *BEAC* HP9.....80 E8
Ronaldsay Sp *SL* SL1.....111 K2
Rookery Cl *MLW* SL7.....97 J4
Rookery La *TOW* NN12.....130 A1
Rookery Meadow
 HAZ/HG HP15.....69 J7
Rookery Wy *BUCK/WIN* MK18.....149 N11
Rook Rd *FLKWH/TG* HP10.....89 G8
Rooks Hl *RKW/CH/CXG* WD3.....74 B5
Rooks La *THAME* OX9.....181 N6
Rooksley *BDWL* MK13.....6 D5
Rook Wood Wy
 GTMIS/PWD HP16.....61 C5
Roosevelt Av *LBUZ* LU7.....27 L1
The Roperies *HWYN* HP13 *.....78 B7
Ropley Wy *MKV* MK10.....19 L3
The Rosary *HAZ/HG* HP15.....69 H3
Roseary Cl *WDR/YW* UB7.....114 C8
Rose Av *AYLW* HP19.....2 C2
 HAZ/HG HP15.....68 F7
Rosebank Cl *MDHD* SL6.....98 D3
Rosebarn La *TRING* HP23.....37 J1
Rosebay Ct *WTR/OFPK* MK7.....23 L1
Roseberry Cl *WAT* WD17.....75 M2
Roseberry Rd *HWYN* HP13.....78 D5
 LBUZ LU7.....26 F7
Rosebery Cl *LBUZ* LU7.....27 G7
Rosebery Ms *LBUZ* LU7.....169 J3
Rosebery Rd
 RAYLNE/WEN HP22.....36 E5
Rosebery Wy *TRING* HP23.....38 A5
Rosebury V *RSLP* HA4.....95 M8
Rosecomb Pl *SHEN* MK5.....21 K2
Rose Cnr *SKCH* HP14.....186 H1
Rose Ct *AMS* HP6.....63 K8
 DUN/WHIP LU6.....30 E8
Rosecroft Ct *NTHWD* HA6 *.....85 H6
Rosedale Av *HYS/HAR* UB3.....115 J2
Rose Dr *BRACKY* NN13.....8 C6
 CSHM HP5.....63 J3
Rose Gdns *WATW* WD18.....75 M6
Rosehatch *HHW* HP1.....49 K6
Rosehill *BERK* HP4.....48 A6
Rose Hl *SL* SL1.....110 A8
Rose La *HEN* RG9.....106 A5
 RMKN MK19.....131 K5
 WAR/TWY RG10.....191 R3
Roseleigh Cl *MDHD* SL6.....107 M7
Rosemary Cl *HWYW* HP12.....77 C5
 UX/CGN UB8 *.....104 A6
Rosemary Ct *WTR/OFPK* MK7.....23 K1
Rosemary La *HADM* HP17.....176 D11
Rosemead *RAYLNE/WEN* HP22.....44 D1
Rosemoor Ms *AYLW* HP19.....177 Q2
Rosemullion Av *EMV/FZ* MK4.....21 L4
The Rosery *BNEND* SL8.....88 F7
Roses Cl *LBUZ* LU7.....160 C9
Roses La *WDSR* SL4.....120 C5
Rose Ter *RAYLW* HP18.....166 D8
Rosetree Cl *GTMIS/PWD* HP16.....60 B4
Roseville Rd *HYS/HAR* UB3.....125 M1
Rose Wk *SL* SL1.....111 G2
Rossway La *TRING* HP23.....46 F2
Rostrever Gdns *HYS/HAR* UB3.....115 K5
Rostrevor Gdns *HYS/HAR* UB3.....103 J7
Rotherfield Rd *HEN* RG9.....190 G7
Rotherthorpe *GTLIN* MK14.....14 D6
Rotherwood Cl
 DUN/WHIP LU6.....31 M5
Rothesay Cl *AYL* HP20.....3 G3
Rothschild Av
 RAYLNE/WEN HP22.....36 D5
Rothschild Rd *LBUZ* LU7.....161 R8
Rotten Rw *RMKS/WB* MK17.....153 J3
Roughdown Av *HHS/BOV* HP3.....57 M2
Roughdown Villas Rd
 HHS/BOV HP3.....57 M2
The Roughs *NTHWD* HA6.....85 K3
Roughwood Cl *WAT* WD17.....75 K1
Roughwood La *CSTG* HP8.....82 D7
Roundel Dr *LBUZ* LU7.....29 L1
Roundhead Dr *THAME* OX9.....181 P5
Roundheads End *BEAC* HP9.....80 A6
Round Hl *HADM* HP17.....176 C10
Roundhill Ct *HADM* HP17.....176 D10
Roundlands *PRRI* HP27.....58 C1
Roundways *RSLP* HA4.....105 L1
The Roundway *WATW* WD18.....75 M6
Roundwood Av *STKPK* UB11.....115 H5
Roundwood Cl *RSLP* HA4 *.....95 M6
Round Wood Rd *AMS* HP6.....63 L8
Roundwood Rd *HWYW* HP12.....77 H7
Rousebarn La
 RKW/CH/CXG WD3.....74 E1

Rouse Ct *CFSP/GDCR* SL9.....92 E4
Routs Gn *SKCH* HP14.....185 N8
Rowan Av *HWYN* HP13.....78 C2
Rowan Cl *AYLS* HP21.....42 D2
 BEAC HP9.....89 M1
 BRACKY NN13.....8 E5
 HAZ/HG HP15.....68 F7
 RBICS/W OX25.....162 H11
Rowan Dr *RMKN* MK19.....13 G4
Rowan Gdns *IVER* SL0.....103 H3
Rowanhurst Dr *SLN* SL2.....101 H3
Rowan Pl *HYS/HAR* UB3.....115 J4
Rowan Rd *BIC* OX26.....162 C3
 WDR/YW UB7.....114 C8
The Rowans *CFSP/GDCR* SL9.....92 B2
 HHW HP1.....49 M7
 RMKS/WB MK43.....139 K6
 SLN SL2.....111 G2
Rowborough Rd
 RAYLNE/WEN HP22.....44 C3
Rowcroft *HHW* HP1.....49 K8
Rowen Wk *CSHM* HP5.....63 G1
Rowland Cl *WDSR* SL4.....120 C6
Rowland Pl *NTHWD* HA6 *.....85 K7
Rowlands Cl *WEAT* MK2.....23 H6
Rowland Wy *AYLW* HP19.....2 A8
Rowle Cl *GTLIN* MK14.....14 A3
Rowley Furrows *LBUZ* LU7.....26 F6
Rowley La *DTCH/LGLY* SL3.....102 A3
Rowlheys Pl *WDR/YW* UB7.....114 C7
Rowliff Rd *HWYW* HP12.....77 H3
Rowsham
 RAYLNE/WEN HP22.....33 J6
Rowsham Dell *GTLIN* MK14.....14 C4
Rowsham Rd
 RAYLNE/WEN HP22.....33 H8
The Row *AMSS* HP7 *.....70 B7
 SKCH HP14.....86 A1
Rowton Heath *SHEN* MK5.....20 F1
Roxborough Av *MDHD* SL6.....117 J3
Roxburgh Wy *BTCHLY* MK3.....22 C4
Roxburn Wy *RSLP* HA4.....105 L1
Roxhill Rd *RBEDW* MK43.....139 G3
Roxwell Cl *SL* SL1.....110 D5
Roxwell Pth *AYL* HP20.....3 J1
Royal Cl *WDR/YW* UB7.....114 E3
Royal La *WDR/YW* UB7.....114 E3
Royal Md *HADM* HP17.....51 H2
Royce Rd *RBEDW* MK43.....138 C3
Royle Cl *CFSP/GDCR* SL9.....82 E3
Roy Rd *NTHWD* HA6.....85 L7
Royston Wy *SL* SL1.....110 C2
Rubbra Cl *AYLW* HP19.....23 M1
Rubens Cl *AYLW* HP19.....167 Q12
Ruby Cl *SL* SL1.....110 F6
Ruck Keene Cl *BIC* OX26.....162 B4
Rucklers La *KGLCY* WD4.....57 M7
Ruckles Cl *AYLW* HP19.....71 H5
Ruddchesters *BDWL* MK13.....17 J1
Ruddleway *WDSR* SL4.....120 C4
Rudds Cl *BUCK/WIN* MK18.....151 K9
Rudd's La *HADM* HP17.....176 D11
Rudgeway *BRACKY* NN13.....146 E4
Rudsworth Cl *DTCH/LGLY* SL3.....123 J3
Ruffle Cl *WDR/YW* UB7.....114 D6
Rugby Ri *WYM* HP11.....78 F7
Rugby Wy *RKW/CH/CXG* WD3.....75 G4
Rugwood Rd *FLKWH/TG* HP10.....88 E1
Ruislip Ct *RSLP* HA4.....95 L8
Rumptons Paddock
 RAYLW HP18.....156 G12
Runford Ct *SHEN* MK5.....21 M1
Run Furrow *HADM* HP17.....176 D11
Runnymede *GTLIN* MK14.....14 C5
Runrig Hl *AMS* HP6.....63 K6
Rupert Av *HWYW* HP12.....87 K2
Rupert Cl *HEN* RG9.....190 H3
Rupert's La *HEN* RG9.....190 H5
Rupert Wy *THAME* OX9 *.....181 P6
Ruscombe Gdns
 DTCH/LGLY SL3.....121 M3
Rushall Rd *THAME* OX9.....181 P5
Rushbrooke Cl *HWYN* HP13.....68 B8
Rush Burn *FLKWH/TG* HP10.....89 H7
Rushendon Furlong *LBUZ* LU7.....169 R9
Rushes Md *UX/CGN* UB8.....104 B8
The Rushes *MDHD* SL6.....109 G4
 MLW SL7.....97 H6
Rushfields Cl *EMV/FZ* MK4.....21 J5
Rushington Av *MDHD* SL6.....108 E5
Rushleys Cl *SHEN* MK5.....17 J6
Rushmere Cl *CSHM* HP5.....55 M7
Rushmere La *HAZ/HG* HP15.....69 G8
Rushmoor Cl
 RKW/CH/CXG WD3.....84 C2
Rushmore Cl *HYS/HAR* UB3.....75 J7
Rushton Ct
 CNH/GTH/TMA MK8.....17 H6
Ruskin Cl *NPAG* MK16.....14 C3
Ruskin Wy *AYL* HP20.....2 C9
Russell Av *AYLS* HP21.....2 C9
Russell Ct *AMS* HP6.....72 C2
 FLKWH/TG HP10.....79 G1
 NTHWD HA6.....85 H5
Russell Ct *CSHM* HP5.....55 H8
 MDHD SL6.....108 B5
Russell Gdns *WDR/YW* UB7.....124 F1
Russell Rd *NTHWD* HA6.....85 H3
Russell St *RMKS/WB* MK17.....144 K6
 STSTR MK11.....16 A1
 WDSR SL4.....121 J4
Russell Wy *LBUZ* LU7.....27 L1
Russet Cl *HGDN/ICK* UB10.....115 H1
Russet Rd *MDHD* SL6.....108 B7
The Russets *CFSP/GDCR* SL9.....92 C1
Russett Hi *CFSP/GDCR* SL9.....92 B3
Russwell La *RMKS/WB* MK17.....23 M8
Rustica Cl *BUCK/WIN* MK18.....157 J5
Rustlings Gn *AYL* HP20 *.....2 D8
Rutherford Cl *UX/CGN* UB8.....114 E1
 WDSR SL4.....120 E4
Rutherford Ga *SHEN* MK5.....21 M1
Rutherford Rd *AYLS* HP21.....42 D2
Ruthven Cl *WEAT* MK2.....153 P3
Rutland Av *HWYW* HP12.....4 B3
 WEAT MK2.....22 F6
Rutland Ga *MDHD* SL6.....108 B5
Rutland Pl *MDHD* SL6.....108 B5
Rutland Rd *HYS/HAR* UB3.....115 J3
 MDHD SL6.....108 C4
Rutland St *WYM* HP11.....5 J4
Rutters Cl *WDR/YW* UB7.....114 F6
Ryans Mt *MLW* SL7.....97 H4
Rycote La *THAME* OX9.....180 D10
Rycroft *EMV/FZ* MK4.....21 J5
Rydal Wy *HWYW* HP12.....87 G1
 RSLP HA4.....95 M8
Ryder Cl *HHS/BOV* HP3.....56 F7
Rydings *WDSR* SL4.....120 C5
The Ryding *SHEN* MK5.....21 J5
Rye Cl *AYLS* HP21.....42 C2

.....27 L7
 MDHD SL6.....117 M2
Rye Ct *SL* SL1 *.....111 M7
Ryecroft Cl *WAR/TWY* RG10.....191 P12
Ryecroft Crs *PIN* HA5 *.....95 M1
Ryefield Av *HGDN/ICK* UB10.....105 C5
Ryefield Crs *PIN* HA5 *.....95 M1
Ryefield Pde *NTHWD* HA6 *.....95 M1
Ryeland *STSTR* MK11.....12 B8
Ryland Cl *WDR/YW* UB7.....114 D3
Rylands Ms *LBUZ* LU7 *.....27 H7
Rylstone Cl *BDWL* MK13.....6 A2
 MDHD SL6.....108 B7
Rymill Ct *HHS/BOV* HP3.....56 F7
Ryton Pl *EMV/FZ* MK4.....21 M3
Ryvers End *DTCH/LGLY* SL3.....112 E7
Ryvers Rd *DTCH/LGLY* SL3.....112 E7

S

Sabina Cl *HWYW* HP12.....4 C7
Sacombe Rd *HHW* HP1.....49 L5
Saddlers Pl *GTLIN* MK14.....18 D1
Saddlers Gn *RMKS/WB* MK17.....144 C3
Sadlers Ms *MDHD* SL6.....109 G3
Saffron Cl *BIC* OX26.....162 C1
 DTCH/LGLY SL3.....122 A4
Saffron La *HHW* HP1.....49 M6
Saffron Ri *DUN/WHIP* LU6.....30 F8
Saffron Rd *HWYN* HP13.....5 L7
Saffron St *WEAT* MK2.....23 G7
Saham Croft Cl
 BUCK/WIN MK18.....150 H10
Sailing Club Rd *BNEND* SL8.....88 E7
Saimon Cl *BRACKY* NN13.....8 D6
St Adrian's Cl *MDHD* SL6.....108 A6
St Agnes Ga
 RAYLNE/WEN HP22.....51 M1
St Aidan's Cl *BTCHLY* MK3.....22 B8
St Albans Cl *WDSR* SL4.....121 J4
St Alban's Rd *BUCK/WIN* MK18.....151 J10
St Alban's Rd *WDSR* SL4.....121 J4
St Andrews Av *WDSR* SL4.....120 E5
St Andrews Cl *LBUZ* LU7.....27 H7
St Andrew's Cl *HWYN* HP13.....78 L1
St Andrews Ct *THAME* OX9.....181 N6
St Andrews St *LBUZ* LU7.....27 J7
St Andrew's Crs *WDSR* SL4.....120 E5
St Andrew's Rd *BTCHLY* MK3.....22 B7
 CHNR OX39.....184 F5
 HEN RG9.....190 G6
 HGDN/ICK UB10.....104 D6
St Andrew's St *LBUZ* LU7.....27 H7
St Annes Cl *SL* SL1.....110 C4
St Annes Ct *BIC* OX26.....162 E3
 BRACKY NN13.....8 C6
St Anne's Cl *HEN* RG9.....190 C5
 RAYLNE/WEN HP22.....44 A5
St Annes Rd *DEN/HRF* UB9.....94 B2
St Anne's Rd *AYLW* HP19.....2 B1
St Anselms Rd *HYS/HAR* UB3.....115 L6
St Anthony's Cl *AYLW* HP19.....2 B6
St Anthonys Pl *EMV/FZ* MK4.....21 L6
St Anthony's Wy
 EBED/NFELT TW14.....125 L7
St Augustine St *BTCHLY* MK3.....22 B7
St Bartholomews *MKV* MK10.....19 L5
St Bees *MKV* MK10.....19 K5
St Bernards Rd *DTCH/LGLY* SL3.....112 B7
St Birinus *FLKWH/TG* HP10.....78 F8
St Botolphs *MKV* MK10.....19 L5
St Brides Cl
 EAG/OLD/WTN MK6.....18 F4
St Catherine's Av *BTCHLY* MK3.....22 A8
St Catherine's Cl *AYLW* HP19.....2 A8
St Catherines Rd *RSLP* HA4.....95 H4
St Chad's Rd *MDHD* SL6.....108 A6
St Christopher Rd
 UX/CGN UB8.....114 C3
St Christophers Cl
 GTMIS/PWD HP16.....61 G7
St Christophers Ct
 RKW/CH/CXG WD3.....73 J5
St Clement Cl *UX/CGN* UB8.....114 C3
St Clement's Dr *BTCHLY* MK3.....22 A8
Saint-Cloud Wy *MDHD* SL6.....108 E3
St Columba's Cl *MDHD* SL6.....108 A6
St David Cl *UX/CGN* UB8.....114 C2
St David's Cl *IVER* SL0.....103 J6
 MDHD SL6.....117 M2
St David's Rd *BTCHLY* MK3.....22 B8
St Dunstans
 EAG/OLD/WTN MK6.....18 D8
St Dunstans Cl *HYS/HAR* UB3.....115 L8
St Edburg's Cl *BIC* OX26.....162 B4
St Edith's Wy *BIC* OX26.....162 B4
St Edmunds *BERK* HP4.....48 B7
St Edmunds Av *RSLP* HA4.....95 J3
St Edmund's Cl *AYLW* HP19.....2 B6
St Edwards Ct *GTLIN* MK14 *.....14 B3
St Elmo Cl *SLN* SL2.....111 J1
St Elmo Crs *SLN* SL2.....111 J1
St Faith's Cl *RMKS/WB* MK17.....153 J3
St Francis Rd *DEN/HRF* UB9.....93 L5
 SKCH HP14.....187 M3
St George's Cl *HWYN* HP13.....78 C3
 LBUZ LU7.....27 J6
 WDSR SL4.....120 D4
St George's Dr *HWYW* HP12.....77 C4
 LBUZ LU7 *.....27 J6
St George's Crs *SL* SL1.....110 C4
St George's Dr *HGDN/ICK* UB10.....104 D1
St George's Rd *BTCHLY* MK3.....22 A8
St Georges Wy *WOLV* MK12.....13 G7
St Giles Ms *HGDN/ICK* UB10.....105 H2
St Giles St *STSTR* MK11.....12 A8
St Giles St *BDWL* MK13.....13 J7
St Govans Cl *EMV/FZ* MK4.....21 M6
St Helen Cl *UX/CGN* UB8.....114 C3
St Helens Gn *MKV* MK10.....19 J5
St Hilda's Cl *BIC* OX26.....162 E2
St Hilda's Cl *BTCHLY* MK3.....2 B6
St Hilda's Wy *FLKWH/TG* HP10.....78 F8
St Huberts Cl *CFSP/GDCR* SL9.....92 D8
St Huberts La *CFSP/GDCR* SL9.....92 E8
St Hugh's Av *HWYN* HP13.....78 C3
St Hugh's Pl *SKCH* HP14.....187 L12
St Ives Crs *EMV/FZ* MK4.....21 K6
St Ives Rd *MDHD* SL6.....108 F3
St James Cl *RMKN* MK19.....131 M8
St James Ctyd *MLW* SL7 *.....97 K4
St James Gdns *SL* SL1.....110 D3
St James Rd *BRACKY* NN13.....146 D1
St James St *BDWL* MK13.....13 J7
St James Wk *DTCH/LGLY* SL3.....113 L6
St James Wy
 RAYLNE/WEN HP22.....35 G3

St Jerome's Gv UX/CGN UB8 115 H3
St John's Av FLKWH/TG HP10 79 G1
St Johns Cl FLKWH/TG HP10 79 G1
LBUZ LU7 30 D1
St John's Cl UX/CGN UB8 * 104 A6
St John's Crs WOLV MK12 17 G1
St Johns Dr HADM HP17 177 L6
WDSR SL4 120 E5
St Johns La BUCK/WIN MK18 159 J9
St John's La RMKN MK19 137 J10
St Johns Rd FLKWH/TG HP10 79 G1
SLN SL2 111 M4
WDSR SL4 120 F5
St John's Rd AYL HP20 3 G4
BTCHLY MK3 22 A8
HAZ/HG HP15 68 E8
UX/CGN UB8 104 A7
St John's St AYL HP20 3 G4
BIC OX26 162 D4
St John St NPAG MK16 15 G2
St John's Wy RNHPTN NN7 126 A4
St John's Well Ct BERK HP4 48 A5
St John's Well La BERK HP4 48 A5
St Josephs Cl OLN MK46 128 B10
St Josephs Ms BEAC HP9 80 E8
St Katherine's Rd HEN RG9 190 G7
St Katharine's Wy BERK HP4 47 L3
St Laurence Cl UX/CGN UB8 114 B2
St Laurence Rd
BUCK/WIN MK18 151 J10
St Laurence Wy SL SL1 111 M7
St Lawrence Cl HHS/BOV HP3 56 F6
St Lawrence Vw BDWL MK13 17 K2
St Leger Dr GTLIN MK14 14 A5
St Leonard's Av WDSR SL4 121 H5
St Leonard's Cl LBUZ LU7 27 J3
St Leonard's Hl WDSR SL4 120 C7
St Leonards Rd AMS HP6 63 K6
St Leonards Wk
DTCH/LGLY SL3 113 L7
St Leonard's Wy
DUN/WHIP LU6 170 F5
St Luke Cl UX/CGN UB8 114 C3
St Luke's Rd HGDN/ICK UB10 * 104 D5
MDHD SL6 108 E3
St Margaret Ct WEAT MK2 23 H6
St Margarets Av UX/CGN UB8 114 F1
St Margarets Cl NPAG MK16 15 H2
St Margaret's Cl BERK HP4 48 C7
FLKWH/TG HP10 79 H2
IVER SL0 103 J7
St Margaret's Gv
HAZ/HG HP15 68 D1
St Margarets Rd RSLP HA4 95 J5
St Margaret's Rd MDHD SL6 107 M7
St Mark's Crs MDHD SL6 108 A3
St Mark's Pl WDSR SL4 121 H5
St Mark's Rd AYLS HP21 2 D8
HEN RG9 190 G6
MDHD SL6 108 B3
WDSR SL4 121 H5
St Martin Cl UX/CGN UB8 114 C3
St Martins NTHWD HA6 85 J5
St Martins Ap RSLP HA4 95 K6
St Martin's Cl WDR/YW UB7 114 B7
St Martin's St WEAT MK2 22 F6
St Mary's Av BERK HP4 47 J4
BTCHLY MK3 22 B7
NTHWD HA6 85 K5
STSTR MK11 12 A8
St Marys Cl BUCK/WIN MK18 158 C2
RMKS/WB MK17 152 C8
St Mary's Cl BIC OX26 162 B5
DEN/HRF UB9 94 A2
GTMIS/PWD HP16 53 J5
HEN RG9 190 D6
MDHD SL6 108 F3
RMKS/WB MK17 144 B3
St Marys Ct BUCK/WIN MK18 10 C7
St Mary's Crs HYS/HAR UB3 115 L4
St Mary's Glebe
DUN/WHIP LU6 170 F3
St Marys Rd BUCK/WIN MK18 158 C3
St Mary's Rd DEN/HRF UB9 93 L5
DTCH/LGLY SL3 112 D6
HYS/HAR UB3 115 L4
St Marys Rw AYL HP20 * 2 F5
St Mary's Sq AYL HP20 2 E5
St Mary St BDWL MK13 13 J7
WYM HP11 5 J7
St Marys Wk MDHD SL6 108 E3
St Mary's Wk HYS/HAR UB3 115 L4
St Mary's Wy CFSP/GDCR SL9 92 C1
CSHM HP5 63 G3
LBUZ LU7 26 F7
St Matthew Cl UX/CGN UB8 114 C3
St Matthews Ct BTCHLY MK3 22 B8
St Michaels Cl LBUZ LU7 161 K1
RAYLNE/WEN HP22 44 B1
RAYLW HP18 156 G8
St Michael's Cl RBICN OX27 155 J3
St Michael's Ct RNHPTN NN7 130 E2
SLN SL2 110 C1
St Michaels Dr WTR/OFPK MK7 19 J8
St Michael's Gn BEAC HP9 80 D7
St Michaels Wy
BUCK/WIN MK18 149 M11
St Nicholas Cl AMSS HP7 72 A2
LBUZ LU7 160 G9
UX/CGN UB8 114 C3
St Nicholas Mt HHW HP1 49 L7
St Patrick's Cl MDHD SL6 117 M2
St Patrick's Wy BTCHLY MK3 22 B8
St Paul Cl UX/CGN UB8 114 C2
St Pauls Av SLN SL2 111 L4
St Pauls Cl HYS/HAR UB3 125 J1
St Paul's Rd BTCHLY MK3 22 A8
St Peter's Av AYLW HP19 34 B3
St Peters Cl PRRI HP27 67 G2
WYM HP11 89 G1
St Peter's Cl RBICN OX27 154 A5
RKW/CH/CXG WD3 84 A2
SL SL1 110 A1
WDSR SL4 121 M8
St Peters Ct CFSP/GDCR SL9 * 82 D8
St Peter's Crs BIC OX26 162 E2
St Peter's Ga BRACKY NN13 8 F7
St Peters Hl TRING HP23 37 M6
St Peter's Rd BRACKY NN13 8 E6
MDHD SL6 98 C8
UX/CGN UB8 114 C2
St Peter St MLW SL7 97 K5
St Peters Wy BDWL MK13 13 K6
HYS/HAR UB3 125 J1
RKW/CH/CXG WD3 73 G5
St Rumbolds La
BUCK/WIN MK18 11 K6
St Stephen's Rd WDR/YW UB7 114 C5
St Teresas Cl PRRI HP27 58 A2
St Theresa's Rd
EBED/NFELT TW14 125 L7
St Thomas Ct EMV/FZ MK4 21 J5
St Thomas Wk DTCH/LGLY SL3 123 J3
St Vincents RMKS/WB MK17 144 F6
Salcey Ri RNHPTN NN7 126 B5
Salcombe Wy RSLP HA4 95 M8
Salden Cl RMKS/WB MK17 152 H8
SHEN MK5 17 L8
Salford Rd RBEDW MK43 145 M2
RMKS/WB MK17 144 G3
Salisbury Av SLN SL2 111 H1
Salisbury Cl AMSS HP7 71 K2
PRRI HP27 58 B3
Salisbury Gv GTLIN MK14 14 C4
Salisbury Rd HWYN HP13 78 C1
PIN HA5 95 M3
UX/CGN UB8 104 A7
Sallow Cl BIC OX26 162 D1
Sallowsprings DUN/WHIP LU6 171 N5
Salmons La GTMIS/PWD HP16 60 C4
Saltash Cl HWYN HP13 79 G6
Salters Cl MDHD SL6 108 F3
RKW/CH/CXG WD3 84 D1
Salter's Cl BERK HP4 47 L4
Salters Gdns WAT WD17 * 75 M2
Salters La RAYLW HP18 164 D6
Salters Ms GTLIN MK14 14 C8
Salters' Rd MDHD SL6 108 F3
Salters Rw FLKWH/TG HP10 * 89 M6
Salt Hill Av SL SL1 111 H5
Salt Hill Cl UX/CGN UB8 104 C3
Salt Hill Dr SL SL1 111 H5
Salt Hill Wy SL SL1 111 H5
Salton Link EMV/FZ MK4 21 L4
Saltwood Av EMV/FZ MK4 21 G5
Samphire Ct WTR/OFPK MK7 19 K8
Sampsons Gn SLN SL2 100 E8
Sampsons Hl AMSS HP7 70 D8
Samuel Cl NPAG MK16 15 J3
Sanctuary Cl DEN/HRF UB9 84 B7
Sanctuary Rd HAZ/HG HP15 69 G5
Sandage Rd SKCH HP14 86 A1
Sandal Ct SHEN MK5 21 K1
Sandalls Spring HHW HP1 49 L5
Sandalwood Dr RSLP HA4 95 H6
Sandbrier Cl WTR/OFPK MK7 19 K8
Sandbrook La TRING HP23 37 H1
Sandelswood End BEAC HP9 80 C5
Sandelwood Wy BEAC HP9 80 C6
Sanderling Cl BIC OX26 162 E6
Sanders La TOW NN12 137 L3
Sanderson Rd UX/CGN UB8 104 B4
Sandford Gdns WYM HP11 78 A6
Sandhill Rd BUCK/WIN MK18 149 N8
Sandhills LBUZ LU7 * 27 H5
WAR/TWY RG10 116 C3
Sandhill Wy AYLW HP19 177 R2
Sandholme BUCK/WIN MK18 149 M12
Sandhurst Dr BUCK/WIN MK18 11 K7
Sandisplatt Rd MDHD SL6 107 M8
Sandlers End SLN SL2 111 G1
Sandleswood Cl BEAC HP9 80 C6
Sandmartin Cl
BUCK/WIN MK18 11 M5
Sandon Cl TRING HP23 37 L6
Sandow Crs HYS/HAR UB3 115 L7
Sandown Cl HEST TW5 125 M4
Sandown Ct BTCHLY MK3 22 A8
Sandown Rd SLN SL2 110 E2
Sandpiper Cl BIC OX26 162 F6
Sandpipers Pl MDHD SL6 98 D4
Sandpiper Wy LBUZ LU7 29 K1
Sandpit Hl BUCK/WIN MK18 10 A8
Sandpit La PRRI HP27 183 L10
Sandpits La FLKWH/TG HP10 79 H3
Sandringham Cl BRACKY NN13 8 D7
Sandringham Ct SL SL1 110 C3
Sandringham Gdns HEST TW5 125 M4
Sandringham Pl WEAT MK2 22 F6
Sandringham Rd HTHAIR TW6 124 D8
MDHD SL6 98 D8
Sands Farm Dr SL SL1 110 B1
Sandstone Cl BUCK/WIN MK18 157 J5
Sandwell Ct
CNH/GTH/TMA MK8 16 F4
Sandwood Ms CSHM HP5 63 G1
Sandy Cl GTLIN MK14 14 A6
Sandycroft Rd AMSS HP6 72 A2
Sandygate Cl MLW SL7 97 J3
Sandygate Rd MLW SL7 97 J3
Sandy La LBUZ LU7 27 H3
NTHWD HA6 85 L2
RAYLW HP18 175 J12
RMKS/WB MK17 145 N7
RMKS/WB MK17 144 E8
THAME OX9 180 A9
Sandy Lodge Ct NTHWD HA6 * 85 K5
Sandy Lodge La NTHWD HA6 85 J2
Sandy Lodge Rd
RKW/CH/CXG WD3 85 G2
Sandy Lodge Wy NTHWD HA6 85 K5
Sandy Md MDHD SL6 119 H1
Sandy Ri CFSP/GDCR SL9 82 D8
Sandy Rd BUCK/WIN MK18 157 J5
Sandywell Dr WLLN MK15 14 D8
San Remo Rd RMKS/WB MK17 145 J6
Santen Gv WEAT MK2 153 Q2
Saracens' Whf WEAT MK2 23 H5
Sargeant Cl UX/CGN UB8 104 C8
Sarratt La RKW/CH/CXG WD3 74 A3
Sarratt Rd RKW/CH/CXG WD3 74 C2
Sarum Complex UX/CGN UB8 * 104 A7
Saturn Cl LBUZ LU7 27 L6
Saunders Cl WTR/OFPK MK7 144 A4
Saunders End AMS HP6 62 B5
Saunders Pl AYLW HP19 177 R3
Saunders Rd HGDN/ICK UB10 104 E5
Saunders Wood Copse
SKCH HP14 187 J2
Saunderton V SKCH HP14 66 B5
Saunton Av HYS/HAR UB3 125 L3
Savage Cft MKV MK10 19 H3
Savay Cl DEN/HRF UB9 93 M6
Savay La DEN/HRF UB9 93 M6
Savernake Rd AYLW HP19 2 D1
Savill Wy MLW SL7 97 L4
Savoy Av HYS/HAR UB3 125 K1
Savoy Cl DEN/HRF UB9 94 C1
Savoy Ct MDHD SL6 108 E1
Savoy Crs CMK MK9 7 J3
Sawmill Rd PRRI HP27 183 N7
Sawpit Hl HAZ/HG HP15 68 F5
Sawyers Cl MDHD SL6 117 M4
Sawyer's Cl WDSR SL4 120 D3
Sawyers Crs MDHD SL6 117 L4
Saxhorn Rd SKCH HP14 86 B2
Saxon Acre BRACKY NN13 8 E7
Saxon Cl AMS HP6 71 J1
DTCH/LGLY SL3 112 E6
DUN/WHIP LU6 31 M6
UX/CGN UB8 114 D2
Saxon Ct BIC OX26 * 162 E5
Saxon Gdns MDHD SL6 109 J2
Saxon Ga CMK MK9 6 F4
Saxon Ga West CMK MK9 6 F4
Saxons Cl LBUZ LU7 27 K7
Saxon St BDWL MK13 17 M1
EAG/OLD/WTN MK6 7 J8
WEAT MK2 22 F5
Saxon Wy WDR/YW UB7 124 B2
Saxony Pde HYS/HAR UB3 115 H1
Saxton Ms WAT WD17 * 75 M2
Saye And Sele Cl RAYLW HP18 156 G12
Sayers Gdns BERK HP4 47 M3
Sayward Cl CSHM HP5 55 J8
Scafell Rd SLN SL2 110 E2
Scammell Wy WATW WD18 75 L7
Scampton Cl BIC OX26 162 G3
Scarborough Wy SL SL1 111 G6
Scardale BDWL MK13 17 L1
Scarlett Av RAYLNE/WEN HP22 44 D4
Scarletts La WAR/TWY RG10 116 A6
Scatterdells La KGLGY WD4 65 L1
Scatterdells Pk KGLGY WD4 * 65 M1
Scatterill Cl BDWL MK13 17 K2
Scawsby Cl DUN/WHIP LU6 31 M5
Scholars Wk CFSP/GDCR SL9 82 D6
DTCH/LGLY SL3 112 F6
Scholars Wy AMS HP6 71 L1
School Cl CSHM HP5 55 G7
HAZ/HG HP15 68 B4
HWYN HP13 77 J4
RAYLW HP18 180 B3
WYM HP11 87 L2
School Dr RMKS/WB MK17 152 H3
School End RMKS/WB MK17 151 J3
School Gdns BERK HP4 49 G4
School Hl BUCK/WIN MK18 159 L8
RBICN OX27 156 G4
School La AMSS HP7 70 A5
BEAC HP9 81 J6
BRACKY NN13 146 E4
BUCK/WIN MK18 148 C6
CFSP/GDCR SL9 92 C1
DUN/WHIP LU6 171 Q10
DUN/WHIP LU6 30 F8
HADM HP17 177 J8
HEN RG9 187 J11
MDHD SL6 117 G2
MDHD SL6 98 A3
MLW SL7 96 A8
MLW SL7 88 B5
NPAG MK16 133 P8
RAYLNE/WEN HP22 43 K4
RAYLW HP18 180 E4
RAYLW HP18 179 Q1
RAYLW HP18 176 D1
RAYLW HP18 175 Q8
RBEDW MK43 145 L5
RBEDW MK43 129 Q5
RBICN OX27 154 A5
RMKN MK19 12 C1
SHEN MK5 17 L6
SLN SL2 111 L4
SLN SL2 102 A5
TOW NN12 130 D12
WAR/TWY RG10 191 N12
WTLGN OX49 184 B7
School Pde DEN/HRF UB9 * 94 B1
School Rd FLKWH/TG HP10 89 K4
FLKWH/TG HP10 79 J2
WDR/YW UB7 124 C2
School Rw HHW HP1 49 L8
School St BDWL MK13 13 J7
School Wy WYM HP11 79 G8
Schorne La BUCK/WIN MK18 159 L9
Schumann Cl WTR/OFPK MK7 23 M2
Scotch Firs WTR/OFPK MK7 19 M8
Scotlands Dr SLN SL2 101 G5
Scotney Gdns BTCHLY MK3 22 B6
Scotsgrove Hl THAME OX9 181 P3
Scots Hl RKW/CH/CXG WD3 74 E7
Scots Hill Cl RKW/CH/CXG WD3 74 E7
Scots Mill La
RKW/CH/CXG WD3 74 E7
Scotswood Cl BEAC HP9 80 C5
Scott Cl BIC OX26 162 B3
SLN SL2 101 H3
WDR/YW UB7 114 E8
Scott Dr NPAG MK16 14 D1
Scott End AYLW HP19 167 Q12
Scott Evans Ct
BUCK/WIN MK18 151 K9
Scotts Cl RBICN OX27 156 B7
RMKS/WB MK17 153 R6
Scotts Farm Cl
BUCK/WIN MK18 11 M2
Scotts La BUCK/WIN MK18 150 C5
BUCK/WIN MK18 11 M3
RBICN OX27 163 R4
Scriven Ct WLLN MK15 15 G7
Scrubbs La SKCH HP14 66 A8
Seabrooke Ct
CNH/GTH/TMA MK8 17 G8
Seacourt Rd DTCH/LGLY SL3 113 G8
Seaford Cl RSLP HA4 95 J8
Seaford Rd HTHAIR TW6 124 C8
Seagrave Ct WTR/OFPK MK7 23 K2
The Sears DUN/WHIP LU6 170 C1
Seaton Dr AYLS HP21 42 C2
Seaton Gdns RSLP HA4 105 M1
Seaton Gv MKV MK10 19 K2
Seaton Rd HYS/HAR UB3 115 J8
Sebright Rd HHW HP1 49 M8
Secklow Ga CMK MK9 7 H4
Secklow Ga East CMK MK9 * 7 H4
Secklow Ga West CMK MK9 7 G2
Second Av DBGH MK1 22 F4
HYS/HAR UB3 115 L5
Second Crs SL SL1 111 H2
Second St WYM HP11 78 A6
Sedgemere
CNH/GTH/TMA MK8 17 G5
Sedgemoor Dr THAME OX9 181 P5
Sedgmoor Cl FLKWH/TG HP10 88 F3
Sedgmoor Gdns
FLKWH/TG HP10 88 F2
Sedgmoor La FLKWH/TG HP10 89 G3
Sedgmoor Rd FLKWH/TG HP10 88 F2
Sedgwick Av HGDN/ICK UB10 105 G5
Sedley Gv DEN/HRF UB9 94 B3
Sedrup La HADM HP17 177 Q6
Seeleys Ct BEAC HP9 * 80 C7
Seeleys Rd BEAC HP9 80 B6
Seer Green La BEAC HP9 81 K7
Seer Md BEAC HP9 81 J6
Sefton Cl SLN SL2 101 L6
Sefton Paddock SLN SL2 101 M5
Sefton Pk SLN SL2 * 101 M5
Sefton Wy UX/CGN UB8 114 B3
Selbourne Av BTCHLY MK3 22 C7
Selby Gv SHEN MK5 21 K1
Selkirk Av AYLW HP19 2 E2
Selkirk Gv BTCHLY MK3 22 C4
Selwood Wy HWYN HP13 77 K4
Selworthy EMV/FZ MK4 22 A3
Selwyn Cl WDSR SL4 120 C5
Selwyn Gv BTCHLY MK3 22 E6
Serjeants Gn GTLIN MK14 14 C8
Serles Cl EAG/OLD/WTN MK6 18 D8
Seven Acres NTHWD HA6 85 M6
RAYLW HP18 175 J11
THAME OX9 181 P6
Sevenhills Rd IVER SL0 103 G3
Seventh Av HYS/HAR UB3 115 M5
Severalls Av CSHM HP5 63 H1
Severn Cl BIC OX26 162 A3
Severn Crs DTCH/LGLY SL3 123 G1
Severn Dr NPAG MK16 15 G2
Severn Wy BTCHLY MK3 22 A6
Sewell Cl AYLW HP19 167 Q12
Sewell La DUN/WHIP LU6 31 L4
Sewell's La CHNR OX39 184 B2
Seymour Cl FLKWH/TG HP10 78 E8
MDHD SL6 108 A7
Seymour Court La MLW SL7 97 G1
Seymour Court Rd MLW SL7 97 H2
Seymour Park Rd MLW SL7 97 J3
Seymour Pln MLW SL7 97 H1
Seymour Rd BERK HP4 47 K4
CSTG HP8 82 B4
SL SL1 111 H6
Shackleton Cl BIC OX26 162 F2
Shackleton Pl
EAG/OLD/WTN MK6 7 G7
Shackleton Rd HWYW HP12 4 B9
SL SL1 111 L4
Shaftesbury Ct
BUCK/WIN MK18 151 J9
RKW/CH/CXG WD3 * 75 H6
Shaftesbury Crs BTCHLY MK3 22 D5
Shaftesbury St WYM HP11 4 D4
Shaggy Calf La SLN SL2 111 M4
Shakespeare Av YEAD UB4 115 M3
Shakespeare Cl NPAG MK16 14 D1
Shakespeare Dr BIC OX26 162 A4
Shakespeare Orch
RAYLW HP18 156 G12
Shakespeare Wy AYL HP20 3 L5
Shallowford Gv EMV/FZ MK4 22 A2
Shamrock Cl WTR/OFPK MK7 19 L8
Shannon Ct GTLIN MK14 14 D8
Shannon Rd BIC OX26 162 A4
Shantock Hall La
HHS/BOV HP3 56 D8
Shantock La HHS/BOV HP3 64 D1
Shantung Pl CSHM HP5 * 63 H4
Sharkham Ct EMV/FZ MK4 21 L5
Sharman Beer Ct THAME OX9 181 M6
Sharman Rw DTCH/LGLY SL3 122 E1
Sharman Wk BDWL MK13 17 K3
Sharney Av DTCH/LGLY SL3 113 G7
Sharp Cl AYLS HP21 42 D1
Sharpes La HHW HP1 49 G8
Sharp's Av RAYLW HP18 166 E8
Sharp's Cl RAYLW HP18 166 E8
Sharps La RSLP HA4 95 J6
Sharrow V HWYW HP12 4 C6
Sharvel La YEAD UB4 105 M6
Shaw Cl AYL HP20 3 M6
BIC OX26 162 B4
NPAG MK16 14 C1
Shaw Ct AYLS HP21 * 42 D3
Shaw Gdns DTCH/LGLY SL3 122 E1
Shaws Cl GTMIS/PWD HP16 60 C5
The Shaw BUCK/WIN MK18 142 G1
MDHD SL6 98 D5
Shearmans STSTR MK11 16 D2
Shearwater Dr BIC OX26 162 G6
Sheehy Wy SLN SL2 112 A4
Sheelin Gv WEAT MK2 153 Q2
Sheen Cl RBICN OX27 154 E12
Sheepcoat Cl SHEN MK5 21 K1
Sheepcote Cl BEAC HP9 80 B6
HEST TW5 125 M3
Sheepcote Crs LBUZ LU7 27 H1
Sheepcote Dell Rd
HAZ/HG HP15 69 J3
Sheepcote Gdns
DEN/HRF UB9 93 M5
Sheepcote La MDHD SL6 118 B6
SL SL1 99 L1
Sheepcote Rd WDSR SL4 120 D5
Sheepfold La AMSS HP7 71 J2
Sheephouse Rd MDHD SL6 99 G8
Sheeplane RMKS/WB MK17 25 K4
Sheepridge La MLW SL7 88 D3
Sheep St BIC OX26 162 D4
BUCK/WIN MK18 151 K10
Sheeptick End RBEDW MK43 139 Q11
Sheering Gv BDWL MK13 13 L6
Sheerness Ct EMV/FZ MK4 21 K6
Sheerstock HADM HP17 176 B12
Sheethanger La HHS/BOV HP3 57 M3
Sheet St WDSR SL4 121 J5
Sheffield Dr AYLS HP21 3 G9
Sheffield Rd SL SL1 111 H3
Sheffield Wy HTHAIR TW6 125 J8
Shefton Ri NTHWD HA6 85 M7
Shelburne Ct HWYW HP12 87 K2
Shelburne Rd HWYW HP12 87 K2
Sheldon Ct
CNH/GTH/TMA MK8 17 J5
Sheldon Rd RAYLW HP18 180 A3
Shelley Cl BIC OX26 162 B3
DTCH/LGLY SL3 122 F1
FLKWH/TG HP10 89 K2
MLW SL7 96 C7
NPAG MK16 14 E2
NTHWD HA6 85 L5
YEAD UB4 115 M2
Shelley Dr BTCHLY MK3 22 C7
Shelley La DEN/HRF UB9 83 M7
Shelley Rd CSHM HP5 55 G8
MLW SL7 97 L3
WYM HP11 4 F9
Shellfield Cl STWL/WRAY TW19 123 M8
Shelsmore GTLIN MK14 14 D6
Shelton Ct RMKS/WB MK17 144 E6
Shenley Av RSLP HA4 95 L8
Shenley Cl LBUZ LU7 27 J3
Shenley Hill Rd LBUZ LU7 27 J3
Shenley Rd BTCHLY MK3 22 B5
RMKS/WB MK17 20 F6
SHEN MK5 17 K8
Shenstone Dr SL SL1 110 C1
Shenstone Hl BERK HP4 48 D5
Shepherd Cl AYL HP20 3 L2
Shepherds STSTR MK11 16 D2
Shepherds Cl MDHD SL6 106 E3
UX/CGN UB8 * 114 B1
Shepherds Farm
RKW/CH/CXG WD3 83 M1
Shepherds Fold HAZ/HG HP15 69 J3
Shepherds Ga
GTMIS/PWD HP16 60 E8
Shepherds Gn HHW HP1 49 K8
Shepherds La BEAC HP9 90 E1
HAZ/HG HP15 68 E5
MDHD SL6 106 C2
Shepherd's La
RKW/CH/CXG WD3 73 J7
Shepherds Md LBUZ LU7 27 H5
Shepherds Rd WATW WD18 75 L4
Shepherds Rw
BUCK/WIN MK18 151 K10
Shepherds Wy CSHM HP5 63 J4
RKW/CH/CXG WD3 74 A8
Shepiston La HYS/HAR UB3 115 G8
Sheppards Cl NPAG MK16 14 F2
Shepperds Cl BUCK/WIN MK18 159 K8
Shepperds Gn SHEN MK5 17 J8
Shepperton Cl RMKN MK19 12 B1
Sheppey La RNHPTN NN7 126 B3
Sheraton Dr HWYN HP13 78 C1
Sheraton Ms WATW WD18 * 75 K5
Sherborne Cl DTCH/LGLY SL3 123 K4
Sherborne Pl NTHWD HA6 85 J6
Sherborne Wy
RKW/CH/CXG WD3 75 G5
Sherbourne Dr MDHD SL6 108 B7
WDSR SL4 120 E7
WTR/OFPK MK7 23 L3
Sherbourne Wk SLN SL2 101 H2
Shereway AYLW HP19 2 A6
Sherfield Av
RKW/CH/CXG WD3 84 C3
Shergold Wy MDHD SL6 98 E4
Sheridan Cl AYLS HP21 42 C3
HGDN/ICK UB10 115 G1
Sheridan Gv EMV/FZ MK4 21 G4
Sheriff Cl AYLW HP19 2 B6
Sherington Rd NPAG MK16 133 L12
Sherman Rd SL SL1 111 K2
Shernfold WTR/OFPK MK7 19 L7
Sherwood Av RSLP HA4 95 K5
Sherwood Cl BIC OX26 163 J4
DTCH/LGLY SL3 112 D7
Sherwood Dr BTCHLY MK3 22 E5
MDHD SL6 107 M8
Sherwood Gdns HEN RG9 190 F6
Shifford Crs MDHD SL6 98 D8
Shilling Cl WLLN MK15 14 D7
Shillingridge Pk MLW SL7 96 D1
Shinfield Cl BUCK/WIN MK18 149 L12
Ship Hl SL SL1 90 D7
Ship La LBUZ LU7 169 Q11
Shipley Rd NPAG MK16 14 D2
Shipman Ct WLLN MK15 14 E7
Ship Rd LBUZ LU7 26 F8
Ship St WYM HP11 * 5 G5
Shipton Hl BDWL MK13 13 L8
Shipton Rd HGDN/ICK UB10 104 E2
Shire La NPAG MK16 138 G2
RKW/CH/CXG WD3 73 G6
TRING HP23 46 B6
Shires Rd BRACKY NN13 8 F8
Shirley Av WDSR SL4 120 E4
Shirley Moor WTR/OFPK MK7 19 L6
Shirley Rd MDHD SL6 108 B5
Shirwell Crs EMV/FZ MK4 22 A1
Shogmoor La HEN RG9 189 L2
Shootacre La PRRI HP27 185 R2
Shootersway TRING HP23 47 G4
Shootersway La BERK HP4 47 L7
Shootersway Pk BERK HP4 47 L6
Shoppenhangers Rd
MDHD SL6 108 A7
Shop Rd WDSR SL4 * 120 B3
Shop Ter BUCK/WIN MK18 * 142 A7
Shorediche Cl HGDN/ICK UB10 104 E1
Shoreham Ri SLN SL2 110 C1
Shoreham Road (East)
HTHAIR TW6 124 D8
Shoreham Road (West)
HTHAIR TW6 124 D8
Shorham Ri
CNH/GTH/TMA MK8 17 H4
Shortborough Av PRRI HP27 58 A1
Short Ditch HADM HP17 176 D11
Shortfern SLN SL2 112 B3
Short Hale LBUZ LU7 169 Q11
Shortlands HYS/HAR UB3 125 J2
Short Massey OLN MK46 128 A9
Short St WYM HP11 4 F5
Shortway CSHM HP5 55 G8
Shotfield Rd SKCH HP14 86 B2
Shothanger Wy HHS/BOV HP3 57 J4
Shottesbrooke Pk
MDHD SL6 * 117 H8
Shouler Cl SHEN MK5 21 K1
Showers Wy HYS/HAR UB3 115 M5
Shrewsbury Cl MKV MK10 19 K4
Shrimpton Cl BEAC HP9 80 C4
Shrimpton Rd BEAC HP9 80 C4
HWYW HP12 87 G3
Shropshire Ct BTCHLY MK3 22 B5
Shrubbery Cl HWYN HP13 5 K4
Shrubbery Rd HWYN HP13 5 K4
The Shrubbery HHW HP1 49 K6
Shrub Hill Rd HHW HP1 49 L8
Shrublands Av BERK HP4 47 M6
Shrublands Rd BERK HP4 47 M5
Shrubs Rd RKW/CH/CXG WD3 84 E6
Shucklow Hl RMKS/WB MK17 151 N3
Shugars Gn TRING HP23 38 A5
Shupp's La RAYLW HP18 175 Q8
Shuttleworth Gv
WTR/OFPK MK7 144 A4
Siareys Cl CHNR OX39 184 F4
Sibley Ct UX/CGN UB8 115 H2
Sibleys Ri GTMIS/PWD HP16 61 J2
Side Rd DEN/HRF UB9 93 J6
Sidford Cl HHW HP1 49 L7
The Sidings WEAT MK2 23 H5
WYM HP11 78 F7
Sidlaw Ct STSTR MK11 16 C2
Sidmouth Dr RSLP HA4 105 M1
Sidney Cl UX/CGN UB8 104 B5
Sidney Rd WDSR SL4 120 B6
Sidney Ter RAYLNE/WEN HP22 44 A5
Silbury Ar CMK MK9 * 7 G3
Silbury Bvd CMK MK9 6 D5
Silco Dr MDHD SL6 108 D4
Silicon Ct SHEN MK5 21 M1
Silk Mill Wy TRING HP23 37 M5
Silk St RAYLW HP18 166 D8
Sillswood OLN MK46 128 A10
Silverbeck Wy
STWL/WRAY TW19 123 M8
Silver Birch Cl HGDN/ICK UB10 104 D2
Silver Birch Dr PRRI HP27 66 D1
Silver Birches WHLY OX33 178 D7
Silverbirches La
RMKS/WB MK17 144 D8
Silver Birch Wy
RAYLNE/WEN HP22 43 G2
Silver Cl MDHD SL6 117 M1
Silverdale Cl AYL HP20 2 F3
FLKWH/TG HP10 78 F1
Silverdale Gdns HYS/HAR UB3 115 M6
Silverdale Rd HYS/HAR UB3 115 M6
Silver End OLN MK46 128 C11
Silver Hl CSTG HP8 82 A2
Silvermead RAYLW HP18 179 Q9

Silver St *AYL* HP20 .... 2 F6
 LBUZ LU7 .... 160 C9
 NPAC MK16 .... 15 C2
 STSTR MK11 .... 16 A1
Silvertrees Dr *MDHD* SL6 .... 117 M1
Silver Wy *HGDN/ICK* UB10 .... 105 G7
Silverweed Ct *WTR/OFPK* MK7 .... 23 L1
Simdims *RBEDW* MK43 .... 139 K5
Simmons Cl *DTCH/LGLY* SL3 * 112 F8
Simmons Ct *AYLS* HP21 * 42 D2
Simmons Dr *HEN* RG9 .... 190 G3
Simmons Wy *SKCH* HP14 .... 86 B2
 THAME OX9 .... 181 N5
Simms Cft *MKV* MK16 .... 19 K4
Simnel *EAG/OLD/WTN* MK6 .... 22 E1
Simon Dean *HHS/BOV* HP3 .... 56 F6
Simonsbath *EMV/FZ* MK4 .... 22 A4
Simons Lea *BDWL* MK13 .... 17 L2
Simpson Cl *MDHD* SL6 .... 109 G2
Simpson Dr
 EAG/OLD/WTN MK6 .... 23 H1
Simpson Pl *AYLS* HP21 .... 42 E1
Simpson Rd *DBCH* MK1 .... 23 H4
 EAG/OLD/WTN MK6 .... 23 H1
Simpsons Wy *SL* SL1 .... 111 K5
Sinclair Cl *DBGH* MK1 .... 22 E3
Singers Cl *HEN* RG9 .... 190 H4
Singers La *HEN* RG9 .... 190 H5
Singleborough La
 RMKS/WB MK17 .... 151 J3
Singleton Dr
 CNH/GTH/TMA MK8 .... 17 C8
Singleton Wy *AYLW* HP19 .... 177 R2
Singret Pl *UX/CGN* UB8 * 114 B1
Sion Ter *BUCK/WIN* MK18 * 10 C8
Sipson Cl *WDR/YW* UB7 .... 124 F2
Sipson La *HYS/HAR* UB3 .... 125 H2
 WDR/YW UB7 .... 125 G2
Sipson Rd *WDR/YW* UB7 .... 114 F1
Sipson Wy *WDR/YW* UB7 .... 124 F3
Sipthorp Cl *WTR/OFPK* MK7 .... 19 M8
Sir Henry Peakes Dr *SL* SL2 .... 100 F4
Sir Peters Wy *BERK* HP4 .... 21 H4
Sir Robert Ms *DTCH/LGLY* SL3 .... 122 F1
Sirus Rd *NTHWD* HA6 .... 85 M5
Siskin Cl *BIC* OX26 .... 162 F5
Sissinghurst Dr *EMV/FZ* MK4 .... 21 H4
Sitwell Cl *NPAC* MK16 .... 14 C1
Sixth Av *HYS/HAR* UB3 .... 115 L5
Sixth St *WYM* MK11 .... 78 B6
Sixty Acres Rd
 GTMIS/PWD HP16 .... 60 B5
Skeats Whf *WLLN* MK15 .... 14 D7
Skeldon Cl *CMK* MK9 .... 7 L1
Skeldon Ga *CMK* MK9 .... 18 D2
Skelton Cl *WEAT* MK2 .... 89 M2
Skene Cl *WEAT* MK2 .... 153 P2
Skidmore Wy
 RKW/CH/CXG WD3 .... 84 D1
Skimmers Cl *HAZ/HG* HP15 .... 69 H4
Skimmers End *HAZ/HG* HP15 .... 69 H4
Skimmers Fld *HAZ/HG* HP15 .... 69 H4
Skimmingdish La *BIC* OX26 .... 163 J4
Skinner Rd *BIC* OX26 .... 163 J4
Skip La *DEN/HRF* UB9 * 94 C7
Skippon Wy *THAME* OX9 .... 181 N4
Skipton Cl *WLLN* MK15 .... 14 F8
Skipton Dr *HYS/HAR* UB3 .... 115 H7
Skittle Gn *PRRI* HP27 .... 183 K12
Skylark Cl *DEN/HRF* UB9 .... 93 H7
Skyport Dr *WDR/YW* UB7 .... 124 C3
Slade Hl *AYLW* HP19 .... 177 R3
Slade La *STSTR* MK11 .... 16 D2
Slade Oak La *DEN/HRF* UB9 .... 93 H5
Slade Rd *SKCH* HP14 .... 186 H2
The Slade *RMKS/WB* MK17 .... 153 J3
Slad La *PRRI* HP27 .... 66 E2
Slapton La *DUN/WHIP* LU6 .... 169 R1
Slated Rw *WOLV* MK12 .... 12 D7
Slater St *HWYN* MK13 .... 5 M7
Slattenham Cl *AYLW* HP19 .... 2 F3
Slayter Rd *SKCH* HP14 .... 86 B2
Slicketts La *DUN/WHIP* LU6 .... 170 C5
The Slipe *LBUZ* LU7 .... 169 M7
Slough La *SKCH* HP14 .... 66 B8
Slough Rd *IVER* SL0 .... 103 H8
 WDSR SL4 .... 121 J1
Sly Cnr *GTMIS/PWD* HP16 .... 53 K6
Smabridge Wk *WLLN* MK15 .... 15 G7
Smaldon Cl *WDR/YW* UB7 .... 114 F7
Small Acre *HHW* HP1 .... 49 L7
Small Crs *BUCK/WIN* MK18 .... 142 A10
Smalldean La *PRRI* HP27 .... 66 C14
Smarden Bell *WTR/OFPK* MK7 .... 19 L6
Smart's Cl *BRACKY* NN13 .... 8 B6
Smeaton Cl *AYLW* HP19 .... 177 Q1
 GTLIN MK14 .... 14 D4
Smewins Rd *MDHD* SL6 .... 117 J8
Smith Cl *AYL* HP20 .... 35 G7
 RNHPTN NN7 .... 126 A5
Smithergill Ct *BDWL* MK13 .... 17 M2
Smithfield Cl *MDHD* SL6 .... 117 L3
Smithfield End
 RMKN MK19 .... 151 Q10
Smithfield Rd *MDHD* SL6 .... 117 M3
Smiths La *WDSR* SL4 .... 120 D5
Smith's La *WHLY* OX33 .... 179 L7
Smithsons Pl *CMK* MK9 * 7 M2
The Smithy *RMKN* MK19 .... 137 M10
Snaith Crs *SHEN* MK5 .... 17 L7
Snakeley Cl *FLKWH/TG* HP10 .... 89 H1
Snape Sp *SL* SL1 .... 111 K3
Snells La *AMSS* HP7 .... 72 A3
Snells Wood Ct *AMSS* HP7 .... 72 B3
Snelshall St *EMV/FZ* MK4 .... 21 H4
Snowball Hl *MDHD* SL6 .... 118 A1
Snowberry Cl *WOLV* MK12 .... 17 L1
Snowcrete *DTCH/LGLY* SL3 * 102 B7
Snowden Cl *WDR/YW* UB7 .... 124 C7
Snowden Cr *HYS/HAR* UB3 .... 115 H7
Snowdon Dr
 EAG/OLD/WTN MK6 .... 18 A7
Snowdrop Wy *HAZ/HG* HP15 .... 68 E3
Snowhill Cots *CSHM* HP5 .... 55 L3
Snowshill Ct *GTLIN* MK14 .... 14 C4
Snows La *WHLY* OX33 .... 178 C6
Soames Cl *OLN* MK46 .... 128 C4
Soane Wk *HWYN* MK13 .... 5 G4
Soho Crs *FLKWH/TG* HP10 .... 89 J6
Sokeman Cl *WOLV* MK12 .... 16 D1
Solar Ct *GTLIN* MK14 .... 14 D3
 WATW WD18 * 75 L6
Solesbridge Cl
 RKW/CH/CXG WD3 .... 73 L6
Solesbridge La
 RKW/CH/CXG WD3 .... 73 L4
Solomon's Hl
 RKW/CH/CXG WD3 .... 74 C8
Solters Cl *RAYLW* HP18 .... 164 D6
Somerford Cl *MDHD* SL6 .... 109 G2

PIN HA5 .... 95 M3
Somerford Pl *BEAC* HP9 .... 80 C7
Someries Rd *HHW* HP1 .... 49 L5
Somersby Crs *MDHD* SL6 .... 108 C7
Somerset Cl *AMSS* HP7 .... 22 C5
Somerset Wy *WDR/YW* UB7 .... 113 L6
Somers Lees *WTR/OFPK* MK7 .... 177 R2
Somerville Dr *BIC* OX26 .... 162 D3
 WDSR SL4 .... 121 H1
Somerville Rd *BRACKY* NN13 .... 8 C7
Sorensen Ct *SHEN* MK5 .... 21 H2
Sorrell Dr *NPAC* MK16 .... 14 C2
Sorrel Md *BIC* OX26 .... 162 C2
Soskin Dr *GTLIN* MK14 .... 13 M8
Sospel Ct *SLN* SL2 .... 101 M7
Soudan Av *BRACKY* NN13 .... 8 D6
Soulbury Rd *LBUZ* LU7 .... 161 L1
South Av *HEN* RG9 .... 190 H6
South Bank *BRACKY* NN13 .... 9 C8
South Bank Rd *BERK* HP4 .... 47 L4
Southbourne Dr *BNEND* SL8 .... 88 F7
Southbridge Gv
 WTR/OFPK MK7 .... 19 K7
South Bucks Wy *AMSS* HP7 .... 61 M8
 CFSP/GDCR SL9 .... 82 C7
 DEN/HRF UB9 .... 93 M7
 GTMIS/PWD HP16 .... 59 K1
Southcliffe Dr *CFSP/GDCR* SL9 .... 82 D5
South Cl *MLW* SL7 .... 96 C7
 SL SL1 .... 110 C4
 WDR/YW UB7 .... 114 E7
Southcote Ri *RSLP* HA4 .... 95 J6
South Cottage Dr
 RKW/CH/CXG WD3 .... 73 L6
South Cottage Gdns
 RKW/CH/CXG WD3 .... 73 L6
Southcott Village *LBUZ* LU7 .... 26 E8
Southcourt Av *LBUZ* LU7 .... 26 E8
Southcourt Rd *LBUZ* LU7 .... 26 E8
Southcroft *SL* SL1 .... 111 G1
South Dr *BEAC* HP9 .... 90 A2
 HWYN HP13 .... 78 C2
 RSLP HA4 .... 95 K7
South Eighth St *CMK* MK9 .... 7 G5
South End *HADM* HP17 .... 182 C1
Southern Perimeter Rd
 STWL/WRAY TW19 .... 124 B8
Southern Rd *AYLW* HP19 .... 2 D3
 THAME OX9 .... 181 M6
Southern Wy *DUN/WHIP* LU6 .... 171 R10
 WOLV MK12 .... 17 G1
Southfield Cl *UX/CGN* UB8 .... 114 F1
South Field Cl *WDSR* SL4 .... 110 B7
Southfield Cl *WLLN* MK15 .... 15 G7
Southfield Dr *HAZ/HG* HP15 .... 68 F5
Southfield Gdns *SL* SL1 .... 110 A2
Southfield Rd *BRACKY* NN13 * 8 D5
Southfield Rd *AYL* HP20 .... 35 G6
 FLKWH/TG HP10 .... 88 F1
 HWYN HP13 .... 4 B2
 PRRI HP27 .... 58 B3
South Fifth St *CMK* MK9 .... 6 F4
South Fourth St *CMK* MK9 .... 6 E7
South Grafton
 EAG/OLD/WTN MK6 .... 6 E8
South Gn *SL* SL1 .... 111 M4
South Hall *BUCK/WIN* MK18 .... 11 H8
South Hl *NTHWD* HA6 * 85 K8
Southill La *PIN* HA5 .... 95 M3
Southlands Rd *IVER* SL0 .... 103 K4
South La *LBUZ* LU7 .... 161 K3
South Lawn *BTCHLY* MK3 .... 22 C6
Southlea Rd *WDSR* SL4 .... 121 M6
South Maundin *SKCH* HP14 .... 67 H4
South Meadow *RBICS/W* OX25 .... 162 H11
South Meadow La *WDSR* SL4 .... 110 A5
South Ninth St *CMK* MK9 .... 7 H5
South Pk *CFSP/GDCR* SL9 .... 92 A4
South Park Av
 CFSP/GDCR SL9 .... 92 E4
South Park Crs
 CFSP/GDCR SL9 .... 92 E4
South Park Dr *CFSP/GDCR* SL9 .... 92 E3
South Park Gdns *BERK* HP4 .... 48 A5
South Park Vw
 CFSP/GDCR SL9 .... 92 E3
South Pl *MLW* SL7 .... 97 K5
South Rd *AMS* HP6 .... 63 J7
 MDHD SL6 .... 108 D4
 RKW/CH/CXG WD3 .... 73 H6
 WDR/YW UB7 .... 114 F7
South Rw *CMK* MK9 .... 6 F7
 DTCH/LGLY SL3 * 102 D2
South Saxon
 EAG/OLD/WTN MK6 .... 7 C6
Southsea Av *WATW* WD18 .... 75 M5
South Secklow *CMK* MK9 .... 7 J5
South Second St *CMK* MK9 .... 6 F5
South Seventh St *CMK* MK9 .... 7 H5
South Side *CFSP/GDCR* SL9 .... 92 C2
South Sixth St *CMK* MK9 .... 6 F6
South St *LBUZ* LU7 .... 26 F8
 RAYLW/WEN HP22 .... 44 A6
 RMKN MK19 .... 12 C1
South Tenth St *CMK* MK9 .... 7 H5
South Ter *WEAT* MK2 .... 22 F6
South V *RNHPTN* NN7 .... 127 N1
South W *HWYN* HP13 .... 77 J4
 WDSR SL4 * 121 H1
South View Rd
 CFSP/GDCR SL9 .... 92 C3
Southview Rd *MLW* SL7 .... 97 K2
South Wy *BEAC* HP9 .... 89 M2
Southwick Ct
 CNH/GTH/TMA MK8 .... 17 J6
South Witan
 EAG/OLD/WTN MK6 .... 6 F7
Southwold *BIC* OX26 .... 162 B2
Southwold Cl *AYLS* HP21 .... 34 F8
Southwold Sp *DTCH/LGLY* SL3 .... 113 H6
Southwood Gdns *MDHD* SL6 .... 98 D5
Southwood Rd *MDHD* SL6 .... 98 D5
Sovereign Cl *BUCK/WIN* MK18 .... 159 J3
 RSLP HA4 .... 95 K7
Sovereign Ct *HWYN* HP13 .... 78 C4
Sovereign Dr *WLLN* MK15 .... 14 C7
Sovereign Hts *DTCH/LGLY* SL3 .... 122 F2
Spackmans Wy *SL* SL1 .... 111 M7
Spa Cl *RAYLW* HP18 .... 174 C2
Spade Oak Meadow
 BNEND SL8 .... 88 D6
Spark Wy *NPAC* MK16 .... 14 C1
Sparrow Cl *AYLW* HP19 .... 34 E3
Sparsholt Cl *EMV/FZ* MK4 .... 21 M4
Spearing Rd *HWYN* HP12 .... 77 H8
Spearmint Cl *WTR/OFPK* MK7 .... 23 M1
Specklands *SHEN* MK5 .... 17 J7
Speedbird Wy *WDR/YW* UB7 .... 124 A3
Speedwell Cl *HHW* HP1 .... 49 K8

Speedwell Cft *BIC* OX26 .... 162 D1
Speedwell Pl *GTLIN* MK14 .... 7 G3
Speen Rd *SKCH* HP14 .... 67 G8
Speldhurst Ct *WTR/OFPK* MK7 .... 19 L7
Spencer *GTLIN* MK14 .... 13 M6
Spencer Av *YEAD* UB4 .... 115 M2
Spencer Cl *BRACKY* NN13 .... 146 E4
 UX/CGN UB8 .... 104 B8
Spencer Gdns *BRACKY* NN13 .... 8 D8
 RBICN OX27 .... 156 F5
Spencer Rd *DTCH/LGLY* SL3 .... 112 C7
Spencers Cl *HGDN/ICK* UB10 .... 104 F5
Spencers La *BEAC* HP9 .... 98 D4
Spencers Rd *MDHD* SL6 .... 108 B2
Spencer Wk
 RKW/CH/CXG WD3 .... 74 B6
Spencer Wy *HHW* HP1 .... 49 M4
Spenlows Rd *BTCHLY* MK3 .... 22 D3
Spenser Cl *BIC* OX26 .... 162 B3
Spenser Rd *AYLS* HP21 .... 34 E8
The Spens *MDHD* SL6 * 108 E2
Sperling Rd *MDHD* SL6 .... 108 E1
Spickett's La *RAYLW* HP18 .... 176 C7
Spider Dr *BRACKY* NN13 .... 8 D7
Spiers La *RBICN* OX27 .... 156 A8
The Spiert *HADM* HP17 .... 177 N5
Spindle Cl *HAZ/HG* HP15 .... 68 F3
Spindleside *BIC* OX26 .... 162 E2
Spinfield La *MLW* SL7 .... 97 H5
Spinfield La West *MLW* SL7 .... 97 H5
Spinfield Mt *MLW* SL7 .... 97 H5
Spinfield Pk *MLW* SL7 .... 97 J5
Spinners Wk *MLW* SL7 .... 97 J5
 WDSR SL4 .... 121 H4
Spinney *SL* SL1 .... 111 C5
Spinney Cl *BUCK/WIN* MK18 .... 149 M12
 WDR/YW UB7 .... 114 D4
Spinney Hill Rd *OLN* MK46 .... 128 A11
Spinney La *RMKS/WB* MK17 .... 144 F8
Spinney Pl *AMSS* HP7 * 71 H2
The Spinneys *FLKWH/TG* HP10 .... 79 G2
The Spinney *BDWL* MK13 .... 17 K2
 BEAC HP9 .... 90 D1
 BERK HP4 .... 47 L4
 BIC OX26 .... 162 H4
 BUCK/WIN MK18 .... 151 K8
 CFSP/GDCR SL9 .... 92 C7
 CSHM HP5 .... 55 J8
 HAZ/HG HP15 .... 69 J3
 WAT WD17 .... 75 M2
 WYM MK11 .... 87 L2
Spitfire Cl *BIC* OX26 .... 162 F3
 DTCH/LGLY SL3 .... 122 F1
Spittal St *MLW* SL7 .... 97 J4
Spooniey Wd *BDWL* MK13 .... 17 H1
Sportsfield Ap *BEAC* HP9 .... 81 J5
Sportsman Cl *BUCK/WIN* MK18 .... 186 H1
Spotley Cots *RNHPTN* NN7 * 128 B2
Spout La *STWL/WRAY* TW19 .... 123 M8
Spout La North
 STWL/WRAY TW19 .... 124 A7
Sprigs Holly *CHNR* OX39 .... 184 H9
Springate Fld *DTCH/LGLY* SL3 .... 112 D6
Springbank Ct *NPAC* MK16 .... 132 C3
Spring Cl *BRACKY* NN13 .... 8 E7
 CSHM HP5 .... 64 C7
 DEN/HRF UB9 .... 84 C8
 HWYN HP13 .... 78 E3
 MDHD SL6 .... 98 E8
 RMKS/WB MK17 .... 151 J4
Spring Coppice *SKCH* HP14 .... 86 E1
Spring Coppice La *PRRI* HP27 .... 67 L2
Spring Dr *PIN* HA5 .... 95 M5
Springett Pl *AMSS* HP7 .... 63 L8
Springfield *CMK* MK9 .... 7 K4
Springfield Blvd
 EAG/OLD/WTN MK6 .... 18 E4
Springfield Cl *AYLS* HP21 .... 2 C7
 CSHM HP5 .... 63 H4
 RKW/CH/CXG WD3 .... 75 G6
 WDSR SL4 .... 121 G5
Springfield Gdns *CHNR* OX39 .... 184 F3
 RMKN MK19 .... 137 M10
Springfield Hollow *SKCH* HP14 .... 186 H1
Springfield Pk *MDHD* SL6 .... 119 G1
Springfield Rd *BERK* HP4 .... 47 L3
Springfield Rd *CSHM* HP5 .... 63 H3
 DTCH/LGLY SL3 .... 123 C3
 DUN/WHIP LU6 .... 171 L1
 LBUZ LU7 .... 26 E7
 OLN MK46 .... 128 B10
 RBICN OX27 .... 154 E11
 SKCH HP14 .... 187 J2
 WDSR SL4 .... 121 G5
Springfields *AMS* HP6 .... 63 H8
 BUCK/WIN MK18 .... 149 R5
 FLKWH/TG HP10 * 69 H8
Springfields Cl
 BUCK/WIN MK18 .... 149 R5
Springfields Ct
 BUCK/WIN MK18 .... 149 R5
Springfield Wy *RBEDW* MK43 .... 139 M4
Spring Garden La *BERK* HP4 .... 47 J5
Spring Gdns *FLKWH/TG* HP10 .... 89 K2
 MLW SL7 .... 97 J3
 NPAC MK16 .... 14 F2
Spring Gardens Rd
 HWYN HP13 .... 78 D5
Spring Gdns *RMKS/WB* MK17 .... 144 E5
Spring Gv *MDHD* SL6 .... 108 D7
Springhill Rd *RAYLW* HP18 .... 156 H10
Spring La *FLKWH/TG* HP10 .... 78 E2
 HHW HP1 .... 49 M6
 MDHD SL6 .... 98 A4
 OLN MK46 .... 128 A11
 RBEDW MK43 .... 135 K4
 RMKS/WB MK17 .... 151 K4
 SL SL1 .... 110 E5
 SLN SL2 .... 101 L2
Spring Meadow *RAYLW* HP18 .... 174 H1
Spring Pth *THAME* OX9 .... 181 M6
Springs Cl *HADM* HP17 .... 51 L4
Springs La *HADM* HP17 .... 51 L4
Spring Valley Dr *SKCH* HP14 .... 67 M7
Springwater Mi *WYM* WRAY TW10 .... 191 N12
Springwater Mi *WYM* HP11 * 78 D6
Springwell Av
 RKW/CH/CXG WD3 .... 83 M2
Springwell Ct
 RKW/CH/CXG WD3 .... 83 M2
Springwell La *DEN/HRF* UB9 .... 84 A5
 RKW/CH/CXG WD3 .... 84 A4
Springwood *PRRI* HP27 .... 67 H2
Springwood Ct *DEN/HRF* UB9 .... 84 E8
Spruce Dene *HAZ/HG* HP15 .... 68 E8
Spruce Dr *BIC* OX26 .... 162 E1
Spruce Rd *AYLW* HP19 .... 177 Q1
Spurgrove La *HEN* RG9 .... 187 P12
Spurlands End Rd
 HWYN HP12 .... 77 H8
The Spur *SL* SL1 .... 110 C2
 WAR/TWY RG10 .... 191 P11

Spurt St *RAYLW* HP18 .... 176 C7
The Square *GTMIS/PWD* HP16 .... 61 G3
 RAYLW HP18 .... 175 K12
 RAYLW HP18 .... 174 B2
 RAYLW HP18 .... 3 B2
 STKPK UB11 .... 115 J5
 WDR/YW UB7 .... 124 A4
 WOLV MK12 .... 13 G8
Squires Cl *EAG/OLD/WTN* MK6 .... 18 D8
Squirrel Cha *HHW* HP1 .... 49 K6
Squirrel La *HWYN* HP12 .... 87 G2
Squirrel Ri *MLW* SL7 .... 87 J8
Squirrels Cl *HGDN/ICK* UB10 .... 104 F5
Squirrels Wy *BUCK/WIN* MK18 .... 11 K7
Stablebridge Rd
 RAYLW/WEN HP22 .... 36 E7
Stable Cl *BUCK/WIN* MK18 .... 147 P8
Stable Ct *BRACKY* NN13 .... 8 C7
Stable La *BEAC* HP9 .... 81 H6
Stable Rd *BIC* OX26 .... 162 D3
 RAYLW/WEN HP22 .... 44 C3
Stables Ct *MLW* SL7 .... 97 G5
Stacey Av *WOLV* MK12 .... 13 G8
Staddle Stones *PRRI* HP27 * 58 A2
Stafford Wy *MDHD* SL6 .... 108 F4
Stafford Av *SLN* SL2 .... 111 H1
Stafford Cl *MDHD* SL6 .... 110 A3
Stafford Gv *SHEN* MK5 .... 17 L8
Stafford Rd *RSLP* HA4 .... 105 L2
Stag Cl *BERK* HP4 .... 47 M5
 HAZ/HG HP15 .... 68 C1
 RKW/CH/CXG WD3 .... 73 H7
Stag Pl *FLKWH/TG* HP10 * 89 J6
Stagshaw Pl *EMV/FZ* MK4 .... 21 L4
Stainby Cl *WDR/YW* UB7 .... 114 D7
Stainton Dr *BDWL* MK13 .... 17 M2
Stamford Av
 EAG/OLD/WTN MK6 .... 7 M6
Stamford Rd *MDHD* SL6 .... 108 B4
 HAZ/HG HP15 .... 69 G3
Stanbridge Cl *HADM* HP17 .... 176 D11
Stanbridge Rd *DUN/WHIP* LU6 .... 30 F4
 HADM HP17 .... 182 E3
 LBUZ LU7 .... 27 J8
Stanbridge Road Ter
 LBUZ LU7 .... 27 J8
Stanbrook Pl *MKV* MK10 .... 19 K5
Standale Gv *RSLP* HA4 .... 95 H2
Standfield Cl *AYLW* HP19 .... 177 R2
Standing Wy
 EAG/OLD/WTN MK6 .... 19 G7
 EMV/FZ MK4 .... 21 L7
Standring Pl *AYL* HP20 * 3 K2
Stanford Cl *RSLP* HA4 .... 95 H5
Stanhope Cl
 RAYLW/WEN HP22 .... 43 M7
Stanhope Rd *AYL* HP20 .... 3 M5
 SL SL1 .... 110 C3
Stanier Ri *BERK* HP4 .... 47 L3
Stanley Av *CSHM* HP5 .... 63 G2
Stanley Cl *MLW* SL7 .... 97 L3
 UX/CGN UB8 .... 104 C7
Stanley Cots *SLN* SL2 .... 111 L5
Stanley Ct *OLN* MK46 .... 128 B11
Stanley Gdns *TRING* HP23 .... 37 L7
Stanley Gn East
 CFSP/GDCR SL9 .... 112 E8
Stanley Gn West
 DTCH/LGLY SL3 .... 112 E8
Stanley Hl *AMSS* HP7 .... 71 K3
Stanley Hill Av *AMSS* HP7 .... 71 J2
Stanley Rd *HWYW* HP12 .... 77 M8
 NTHWD HA6 .... 85 M8
Stanmore Gdns *NPAC* MK16 .... 14 F1
Stanstead Pl *AMSS* HP7 * 71 H2
Stanton Av *BDWL* MK13 .... 13 K8
Stanton Ga *GTLIN* MK14 .... 14 A6
Stanton Rd *WHLY* OX33 .... 178 D9
Stanton Wy *DTCH/LGLY* SL3 .... 112 D8
Stanton Wd *GTLIN* MK14 .... 18 A2
Stanway Cl *WLLN* MK15 .... 14 E8
Stanwell Moor Rd
 WDR/YW UB7 .... 124 A4
Stanwell Rd *DTCH/LGLY* SL3 .... 123 G6
Stanwyck La *EMV/FZ* MK4 .... 21 G4
Staple Hall Rd *DBGH* MK1 .... 23 C5
Stapleton Cl *MLW* SL7 .... 97 L2
Star La *WAR/TWY* RG10 .... 116 C2
Starling Ms *AYLW* HP19 .... 177 Q2
Star Rd *HGDN/ICK* UB10 .... 115 H1
Stars La *HADM* HP17 .... 176 H5
Startins La *MDHD* SL6 .... 98 B2
Starveall Ct *WDR/YW* UB7 .... 114 E7
Starwood Ct *DTCH/LGLY* SL3 .... 112 B7
Staters Pound *WLLN* MK15 .... 14 D7
Statham Pl
 EAG/OLD/WTN MK6 .... 7 H8
Station Ap *BIC* OX26 .... 162 B5
 CFSP/GDCR SL9 .... 92 D4
 DEN/HRF UB9 .... 84 C5
 GTMIS/PWD HP16 .... 60 F3
 HWYN HP13 * 5 K6
 HYS/HAR UB3 .... 115 J7
 MDHD SL6 .... 108 A4
 MLW SL7 .... 97 K5
 NTHWD HA6 .... 85 M8
 RAYLW/WEN HP22 .... 44 B3
 RKW/CH/CXG WD3 .... 75 L5
 WATW WD18 * 75 L5
 WDR/YW UB7 .... 114 D5
Station Cl *DEN/HRF* UB9 * 71 H1
Station Hl *MDHD* SL6 .... 98 E3
Station Pde *DEN/HRF* UB9 .... 93 M6
 MDHD SL6 .... 98 E3
 RSLP HA4 .... 95 H8
Station Ri *MLW* SL7 .... 97 K4
Station Rd *AMSS* HP7 .... 71 H2
 BEAC HP9 .... 80 D8
 BERK HP4 .... 48 C5
 BIC OX26 .... 163 K4
 BNEND SL8 .... 88 F7
 BUCK/WIN MK18 .... 151 J5
 BUCK/WIN MK18 .... 149 P5
 CFSP/GDCR SL9 .... 92 D4
 CHNR OX39 .... 184 F3
 CSHM HP5 .... 63 G2
 DTCH/LGLY SL3 .... 112 F6
 FLKWH/TG HP10 .... 79 H1
 HADM HP17 .... 176 D12
 HADM HP17 .... 177 L2
 HEN RG9 .... 190 H5
 HWYN HP13 .... 5 L7
 HYS/HAR UB3 .... 115 K6
 LBUZ LU7 .... 169 M5
 LBUZ LU7 .... 30 E2
 LBUZ LU7 .... 22 F8
 MDHD SL6 .... 109 G2
 MDHD SL6 .... 98 E3
 MLW SL7 .... 97 K5
 NPAC MK16 .... 14 F2
 PRRI HP27 .... 183 R12
 RAYLW/WEN HP22 .... 166 D3
 RAYLW/WEN HP22 .... 43 R3
 RBEDW MK43 .... 145 N4

RBEDW MK43 .... 129 R9
RBICN OX27 .... 156 A7
RBICS/W OX25 .... 163 M11
RKW/CH/CXG WD3 .... 74 C8
RMKN MK19 .... 12 B1
RMKS/WB MK17 .... 151 Q9
RMKS/WB MK17 .... 137 N8
SL SL1 .... 110 D5
TRING HP23 .... 168 F10
TRING HP23 .... 38 A6
UX/CGN UB8 .... 114 B1
WDR/YW UB7 .... 114 D6
WYM MK11 .... 5 L7
Station Ter *BUCK/WIN* MK18 .... 11 K7
Station Wy *AYLS* HP21 .... 2 E6
Station Yd *RSLP* HA4 * 95 J8
 THAME OX9 .... 181 P7
Staunton Rd *SLN* SL2 .... 111 J3
Staveley Cl *AYLS* HP21 .... 35 J8
Staverton Gv *MKV* MK10 .... 19 L4
Stavordale Rd *MKV* MK10 .... 19 K5
Steam Farm La
 EBED/NFELT TW14 .... 125 J1
Steane Vw *BRACKY* NN13 .... 8 C7
Steinbeck Dr *HGDN/ICK* UB10 .... 104 F1
Steeple Cl *EMV/FZ* MK4 .... 21 K6
Steinbeck Crs *EMV/FZ* MK4 .... 21 J7
Stella Cl *UX/CGN* UB8 .... 115 G2
Stephenson Cl *AYLW* HP19 .... 2 B7
 HWYN HP13 .... 5 J7
 LBUZ LU7 .... 26 F8
Stephenson Ct *SL* SL1 .... 111 L6
Stephenson Dr *WDSR* SL4 .... 121 G3
Stepnells *TRING* HP23 .... 37 M1
Steppingstone Pl *LBUZ* LU7 .... 27 J8
Sterling Cl *BIC* OX26 .... 162 F3
Stert Rd *CHNR* OX39 .... 184 C6
Stevens Cl *GTMIS/PWD* HP16 .... 60 C5
 HAZ/HG HP15 .... 69 G3
Stevens Fld *WTR/OFPK* MK7 .... 144 K4
Stedman Cl *HGDN/ICK* UB10 .... 108 F4
Stevenson Bd *SLN* SL2 .... 91 J8
Stevenson Rd *SLN* SL2 .... 111 L1
Stewart Av *SL* SL1 .... 119 J4
Stewart Cl *MDHD* SL6 .... 115 K6
Stewart Quay *HYS/HAR* UB3 .... 101 G3
Stewarts Dr *SLN* SL2 .... 97 H7
Stewarts Wy *MLW* SL7 .... 152 D10
Stewkley La *RMKS/WB* MK17 .... 160 H9
Stewkley Rd *LBUZ* LU7 .... 153 P12
 LBUZ LU7 .... 128 D3
Stilebrook Rd *OLN* MK46 .... 112 C8
Stile The *LBUZ* LU7 .... 27 H1
Stillitters Farm Rd
 RBEDW MK43 .... 138 H6
Stilwell Dr *UX/CGN* UB8 .... 114 E1
Stirling Av *AYL* HP20 .... 3 G3
Stirling Cl *UX/CGN* UB8 .... 104 B8
 WDSR SL4 .... 120 C5
 WLLN MK15 .... 14 D8
Stirling Gv *MDHD* SL6 .... 108 A2
Stirling Rd *HWYW* HP12 .... 87 J1
 SL SL1 .... 111 L1
Stockaway *RAYLNE/WEN* HP22 .... 32 B6
Stockdale *BDWL* MK13 * 17 M1
Stockdales Rd *WDSR* SL4 .... 110 B8
Stocken Cl *OLN* MK46 .... 128 A10
Stockers Farm Rd
 RKW/CH/CXG WD3 .... 84 B3
Stock Field Cl *HAZ/HG* HP15 .... 69 G7
Stockhall Crs *LBUZ* LU7 .... 153 J12
Stocking Cl *RNHPTN* NN7 .... 131 J1
Stocking Green Cl *RMKN* MK19 .... 131 J1
Stocking La *SKCH* HP14 .... 67 K6
Stocklake *AYL* HP20 .... 3 J4
Stocklands Wy
 GTMIS/PWD HP16 .... 60 C5
Stock La *RMKS/WB* MK17 .... 20 E5
Stockley Dr *WDR/YW* UB7 .... 115 G6
Stockley Farm Rd
 WDR/YW UB7 .... 115 G3
Stockley Rd *UX/CGN* UB8 .... 114 F3
 WDR/YW UB7 .... 115 G7
Stockport Rd
 RKW/CH/CXG WD3 .... 73 H8
Stocks Cl *BUCK/WIN* MK18 .... 151 K10
Stocks Pl *HGDN/ICK* UB10 .... 104 F6
Stocks Rd *TRING* HP23 .... 39 H5
The Stocks *RMKN* MK19 .... 12 B4
Stockwell Furlong
 HADM HP17 .... 182 D12
Stockwell La *HADM* HP17 .... 183 Q5
 RMKS/WB MK17 .... 144 A2
Stockwells *MDHD* SL6 .... 109 J1
Stoke Common Rd *SLN* SL2 .... 101 M2
Stoke Court Dr *SLN* SL2 .... 101 K6
Stoke Farm La *AYLS* HP21 * 42 D3
Stoke Gdns *SL* SL1 .... 111 K5
Stoke Gn *SLN* SL2 .... 111 M1
Stoke La *RMKS/WB* MK17 .... 24 D5
Stoke Leys Cl *AYLS* HP21 .... 42 D3
Stoke Lyne Rd *RBICN* OX27 .... 155 J9
Stokenchurch Pl *BDWL* MK13 .... 6 C1
Stoke Park Av *SLN* SL2 .... 101 H8
Stoke Poges La *SL* SL1 .... 111 K5
Stoke Rd *AYLS* HP21 .... 3 C9
 LBUZ LU7 .... 26 F7
 RMKS/WB MK17 .... 153 K3
 SLN SL2 .... 111 L3
 WEAT MK2 .... 153 G1
Stokesay *SLN* SL2 .... 111 M3
Stokesay Ct *EMV/FZ* MK4 .... 21 H4
Stokes Cft *HADM* HP17 .... 176 D11
Stokes End *HADM* HP17 .... 176 D11
Stokes La *HADM* HP17 .... 176 D12
Stokesley Ri *FLKWH/TG* HP10 .... 89 K2
Stoke Wd *SLN* SL2 .... 101 L2
Stolford Ri *EMV/FZ* MK4 .... 21 L5
Stompits Rd *MDHD* SL6 .... 119 G2
Stomp Rd *SL* SL1 .... 110 A2
Stonebridge Fld *WDSR* SL4 .... 121 G1
Stonebridge Gv *MKV* MK10 .... 19 H5
Stonebridge Rd *AYLW* HP19 .... 34 D3
Stoneburge Crs *BIC* OX26 .... 162 D3
Stonecrest *AYLW* HP19 .... 34 D3
Stone Cl *WDR/YW* UB7 .... 113 M4
Stone Ct *OLN* MK46 .... 133 M2
Stonecroft *AMS* HP6 .... 62 B6
Stonecroft Av *IVER* SL0 .... 113 K3
Stonecrop Leyes *BIC* OX26 .... 162 D1
Stonecrop Pl *GTLIN* MK14 .... 6 F1
Stonefield Pk *MDHD* SL6 .... 108 D3
Stonefield Rd *SKCH* HP14 .... 67 H6
Stonegate *AYLS* HP21 .... 42 C7
Stonehaven Rd *AYLW* HP19 .... 2 A2
Stone Hl *CNH/GTH/TMA* MK8 .... 17 C5
Stone House La *MDHD* SL6 .... 98 D3
Stonehurst Cl *RNHPTN* NN7 .... 130 H1

Stoneleigh Ct EMV/FZ MK4 ... 21 H4
Stone Pit Cl OLN MK46 ... 128 A11
Stonepitts Pk RAYLW HP15 ... 175 J7
Stone Row Cots RBICN OX27 * ..155 J9
Stones Wy RMKS/WB MK17 ... 152 M4
Stone Vw RAYLNE/WEN HP22 .. 159 N11
Stoney Cl BERK HP4 ... 47 L4
Stoneycroft HHW HP1 ... 49 M7
Stoney Cft TRING HP23 ... 39 H5
Stoneyfield CFSP/GDCR SL9 ... 92 B7
Stoney Gv CSHM HP5 ... 63 J1
Stoney La CSHM HP5 ... 54 E1
　HHS/BOV HP3 ... 57 C6
　KGLGY WD4 ... 65 K1
　SLN SL2 ... 100 H3
Stoney Meade SL SL1 ... 111 G5
Stoney Ware MLW SL7 ... 97 J6
Stoney Ware Cl MLW SL7 ... 97 J6
Stonor Ct CNH/GTH/TMA MK8.. 17 J6
Stony La CSHM HP5 ... 64 D8
Stookslade RAYLNE/WEN HP22.. 33 M3
Stopps Orch PRRI HP27 ... 58 B1
Stork Cl AYLW HP19 * ... 34 E3
Stormount Dr HYS/HAR UB3..115 H4
Stornaway Rd DTCH/LGLY SL3.. 113 H8
Stotfold Ct STSTR MK11 ... 16 B2
Stour Cl AYLS HP21 ... 42 B2
　BTCHLY MK3 ... 22 H3
　NPAG MK16 ... 15 H3
　SL SL1 ... 111 H3
Stourhead Ga EMV/FZ MK4 ... 21 H4
Stovell Rd WDSR SL4 ... 121 G4
Stowe Av MLW SL7 ... 11 K2
Stowe Cl BUCK/WIN MK18 ... 11 K5
Stowe Ct GTLIN MK14 ... 13 M6
Stowe Crs RSLP HA4 ... 95 G5
Stowe Ri BUCK/WIN MK18 ... 11 K5
Stowe Rd SL SL1 ... 110 D4
Stratford Wy THAME OX9 ... 181 P6
Straight Bit FLKWH/TG HP10 ... 89 G2
Straight Mile Rd WHLY OX33 .. 178 L3
Strand La MDHD SL6... 98 G5
The Strand RAYLNE/WEN HP22..166 E1
Strand View Wk MDHD SL6... 98 G5
Strangers La BUCK/WIN MK18 .. 10 B8
Strangford Dr WEAT MK2 ... 153 P2
Stranraer Gdns SL SL1 ... 111 H3
Stratfield Ct
　CNH/GTH/TMA MK8... 17 J5
Stratfield Rd SL SL1 ... 111 M6
Stratford Ar STSTR MK11 * ... 16 A1
Stratford Cl HGDN/ICK UB10..104 E7
Stratford Cl SLN SL2 ... 110 C1
Stratford Dr AYLS HP21 ... 34 A8
　FLKWH/TG HP10 ... 89 H3
Stratford Gdns MDHD SL6... 108 B6
Stratford Rd BUCK/WIN MK18 .. 11 L5
　RMKN MK19 ... 137 N10
　RMKS/WB MK17 ... 143 P9
　WAT WD17 ... 75 M3
　WOLV MK12 ... 12 E7
Stratfords Wy HADM HP17 ..176 C12
Stratford Wy WAT WD17 ... 75 L3
Strathcona Cl
　FLKWH/TG HP10 ... 89 H3
Strathearn Av HYS/HAR UB3..125 L3
Strathnaver Pl WOLV MK12 ... 17 L2
Stratton Audley Rd
　RBICN OX27 ... 154 A5
Stratton Chase Dr CSTG HP8.. 81 M2
Stratton Dr BRACKY NN13 ... 8 C7
Stratton Gn AYLS HP21 ... 35 H8
Stratton Ms LBUZ LU7 ... 27 J7
Stratton Pl AMSS HP7 ... 71 L2
Stratton Rd BEAC HP9... 80 A7
　PRRI HP27 ... 183 P6
Strauss Gv WTR/OFPK MK7 ... 23 M2
Strawberry Ct
　GTMIS/PWD HP16... 60 C5
Straws Hadley Ct
　RAYLNE/WEN HP22 * ..168 A4
Streamside SL SL1 ... 110 E5
Streamside Wk AYLS HP21 ... 2 C3
Streatham Pl BDWL MK13 ... 6 B4
Street Cl RBEDW MK43 ... 129 Q3
The Street KGLGY WD4 ... 65 M2
　RBICN OX27 ... 154 A5
　WAR/TWY RG10 ... 116 F4
Stretton Cl FLKWH/TG HP10 ... 79 H2
Stringfellow Cl RBEDW MK43..138 F4
Stripling Wy WATW WD18 ... 75 M7
Stroma Ct SL SL1 ... 110 C4
Stroud Cl WDSR SL4 ... 120 C6
Stroud Farm Rd MDHD SL6... 119 G2
Strudwick Dr
　EAG/OLD/WTN MK6 ... 7 H8
Stuart Cl HGDN/ICK UB10..104 F4
　WDSR SL4 ... 120 E5
　WEAT MK2 ... 23 G5
Stuart Ct AMS HP6 * ... 71 J1
Stuart Crs HYS/HAR UB3..115 H3
Stuart Rd BRACKY NN13 ... 8 C6
　WYM HP11 ... 5 L8
Stuart Wy THAME OX9 ... 181 P6
　WDSR SL4 ... 120 E5
Stubble Hl AYLW HP19 * ... 2 A4
Stubbles La MDHD SL6... 97 M8
Stubbs End Cl AMS HP6 ... 63 K7
Stubbs Fld SHEN MK5 ... 21 K3
Stubbs Wd AMS HP6 ... 63 K7
Stuchbury Cl AYLW HP19 ... 177 L8
Studdridge Ct SKCH HP14 ... 67 G2
Sturges Cl WTR/OFPK MK7 ... 23 K1
Sturt Gn MDHD SL6... 118 D2
Stylecroft Rd CSTG HP8 ... 82 C2
Styles Cl RBICN OX25 ... 163 R4
Suffield Rd WYM HP11 ... 4 F7
Suffolk Cl SL SL1 ... 110 D4
Suffolk Rd RBICN OX27 ... 156 A4
Suffolk Rd MDHD SL6... 108 C6
Sugar La HHW HP1 ... 57 G1
Sulby Cl AYLS HP21 ... 42 B1
Sulgrave Ct
　CNH/GTH/TMA MK8... 17 J6
Sulgrave Crs TRING HP23 ... 38 B5
Sullivan Crs DEN/HRF UB9... 94 C1
　WTR/OFPK MK7 ... 23 M2
Sultan Cft SHEN MK5 ... 21 K2
Sumburgh Wy SL SL1 ... 111 M4
Summergill Ct BDWL MK13... 17 M3
Summerhayes GTLIN MK14 ... 14 C7
Summerhouse La
　DEN/HRF UB9... 83 M7
　WDR/YW UB7 ... 124 C2
Summerlea SL SL1 ... 111 G5

Summerleaze Rd MDHD SL6... 108 F1
Summerleys Rd DUN/WHIP LU6.. 170 F2
Summerleys Rd PRRI HP27 ..183 P10
Summer Pl WATW WD18 * ... 75 L7
Summerson Rd
　EAG/OLD/WTN MK6 ... 22 C4
Summer St LBUZ LU7 ... 27 J8
Summers Rd SL SL1 ... 100 B8
Summer St SHEN MK5 ... 17 K6
Sunbower Av DUN/WHIP LU6.. 31 M3
Sunbury Cl BDWL MK13 ... 13 K8
Sunbury Ct WDSR SL4 ... 121 J2
Sunbury Rd WDSR SL4 ... 121 J2
Sun Cl WDSR SL4 ... 121 J2
Suncote Av DUN/WHIP LU6... 31 M3
Suncote Cl DUN/WHIP LU6... 31 M3
Sun Crs RAYLW HP15 ... 179 G1
Sunderland Ct EMV/FZ MK4.. 21 J5
Sunderland Dr BIC OX26... 162 F2
Sunderland Rd MDHD SL6... 108 A2
Sundew Rd HHW HP1 ... 57 K1
Sun La MDHD SL6... 108 D3
Sunningdale Cl HWYW HP12 ... 87 G1
Sunningdale Wy BTCHLY MK3... 21 M6
Sunny Bank HAZ/HG HP15 ... 68 C5
　LBUZ LU7 ... 169 L7
Sunnybank MLW SL7 ... 97 H2
Sunny Brook Cl
　RAYLNE/WEN HP22 ... 36 C4
Sunny Cft HWYN HP13 ... 77 H4
Sunnydene Av RSLP HA4 ... 95 M7
Sunnyhill Rd
　RKW/CH/CXG WD3 ... 83 J6
Sunnymede Av CSHM HP5 ... 55 K7
Sunnyside Rd CSHM HP5 ... 63 G1
Sunray Av WDR/YW UB7 ...114 C6
Sunridge Cl NPAG MK16 ... 14 F3
Sunrise Pkwy GTLIN MK14 ... 14 B2
Sunset Cl WEAT MK2 ... 22 F7
Sunset Wk CMK MK9 * ... 6 F4
Sunters End HWYW HP12 ... 76 F7
Sunters Wood Cl HWYW HP12 .. 87 G1
Sun Vw BUCK/WIN MK18 * ... 10 B8
Surly Hall Wk WDSR SL4 ... 120 A4
Surrey Cl WEAT MK2 ... 23 G5
Surrey Pl BTCHLY MK3 ... 22 C4
　TRING HP23 ... 37 M7
Surrey Rd BTCHLY MK3 ... 22 C4
Sussex Cl AYLW HP19 ... 167 R11
　CSTG HP8 ... 82 A2
　HWYN HP13 ... 78 C1
　SL SL1 ... 112 A6
Sussex Keep SL SL1 * ... 112 A6
Sussex Rd BTCHLY MK3 ... 22 C4
　HGDN/ICK UB10 ... 105 H2
　WATN WD24 ... 75 M1
Sutcliffe Av
　EAG/OLD/WTN MK6 ... 6 F7
Sutherland Av HYS/HAR UB3.. 115 H4
Sutherland Gv BTCHLY MK3... 22 C3
Sutherland Wk AYLS HP21 * ... 42 E1
Sutleye Ct SHEN MK5 ... 21 K1
Sutton Av DTCH/LGLY SL3...112 B4
Sutton Cl MDHD SL6... 108 B5
　MDHD SL6... 99 G4
　PIN HA5... 95 M4
　TRING HP23... 38 A4
Sutton Ct EMV/FZ MK4... 21 M5
Sutton Court Rd
　HGDN/ICK UB10...105 G6
Sutton La DTCH/LGLY SL3...123 G2
Sutton Pl DTCH/LGLY SL3...123 G2
Sutton Rd MDHD SL6... 99 G4
Swabey Rd DTCH/LGLY SL3...112 F8
Swains Cl WDR/YW UB7 ...114 D6
Swains Ct OLN MK46... 128 B10
Swains La FLKWH/TG HP10... 89 G1
Swakeleys Dr HGDN/ICK UB10..104 B1
Swakeleys Rd HGDN/ICK UB10..104 B1
Swale Rd AYLS HP21 ... 42 B1
Swales Dr LBUZ LU7 ... 27 L4
Swallow Cl BIC OX26... 162 C6
　BRACKY NN13 ... 8 C5
　BUCK/WIN MK18 ... 11 M8
　RKW/CH/CXG WD3 ... 74 B8
Swallowdale IVER SL0 ... 103 H3
Swallow Dr HAZ/HG HP15 ... 69 G5
Swallowfield
　CNH/GTH/TMA MK8... 17 H5
Swallowfield Wy
　HYS/HAR UB3 ... 115 G4
Swallow La AYLW HP19 ... 177 L9
　RAYLNE/WEN HP22 ... 42 F4
Swallow St IVER SL0 ... 113 H1
Swallowtail Wk BERK HP4 ... 47 L3
Swanbourne Rd
　RMKS/WB MK17... 152 B10
Swan Cl AYLW HP19 ... 34 E3
　BRACKY NN13 ... 8 C4
　BUCK/WIN MK18 ... 11 M8
　CSHM HP5 ... 55 M8
　LBUZ LU7 ... 170 B5
　RAYLNE/WEN HP22 ... 32 A1
　RKW/CH/CXG WD3 ... 74 C8
Swan Ct BUCK/WIN MK18 ... 151 L9
　OLN MK46... 128 C10
Swanells Wd DUN/WHIP LU6..171 Q10
Swan Hl RAYLW HP18 * ...176 C1
Swan La GTMIS/PWD HP16... 53 L7
　RBICN OX27 ... 156 B7
Swan Ms RAYLNE/WEN HP22... 44 B6
Swann Rd RAYLNE/WEN HP22... 44 B2
Swann Wk THAME OX9 ... 181 N6
Swan Rd IVER SL0 ... 113 L3
Swansons Rd WTR/OFPK MK7 ... 19 K8
Swan's Wy CHNR OX39 ... 184 C7
Swanwick La MKV MK10 ... 19 L3
Swayne Ri MKV MK10 ... 19 M4
Sweetbriar Cl HHW HP1 ... 49 M4
Sweetcroft La HGDN/ICK UB10..104 E4
Sweet Green Cl HEAD OX3 ...178 A10
Sweetlands Cnr
　WTR/OFPK MK7 ... 19 L6
Swift Cl BIC OX26... 162 C6
　HYS/HAR UB3 ... 115 L3
　NPAG MK16 ... 14 D1
Swift Wy BRACKY NN13 ... 8 D5
Swimbridge La EMV/FZ MK4... 22 A3
Swinden Ct BDWL MK13 ... 17 L2
Swindon Rd HTHAIR TW6... 125 H2
Swinfens Sq STSTR MK11 * ... 16 A1
Swing Br LBUZ LU7 ...169 N9
Swing Gate La BERK HP4 ... 47 L5
Swiss Av WATW WD18 ... 75 K5
Swiss Cl WATW WD18 ... 75 K5
Switchback Cl MDHD SL6... 98 C8
Switchback Rd North
　MDHD SL6... 98 D7
Switchback Rd South
　MDHD SL6... 98 C8
The Switchback MDHD SL6 * ... 98 C8

Swyncombe Gn RNHPTN NN7 ..130 H1
Sycamore Ap
　RKW/CH/CXG WD3 ... 75 H6
Sycamore Av HYS/HAR UB3 .. 115 K4
　WEAT MK2 ... 23 H6
Sycamore Cl AMS HP6 ... 63 J8
　BNEND SL8 ... 89 C7
　BUCK/WIN MK18 ... 142 A11
　LBUZ LU7 ... 153 J12
　MDHD SL6... 108 B7
　RAYLW HP18 ... 175 L12
　WDR/YW UB7 ... 114 E4
Sycamore Ct AYLW HP19 * ... 2 E3
　HWYW HP12 ... 87 H2
Sycamore Dene CSHM HP5 ... 55 J7
Sycamore Dr MLW SL7 ... 97 J1
　THAME OX9 ... 181 L6
　TRING HP23 ... 38 A6
Sycamore Gdns BIC OX26... 162 E2
Sycamore Leys
　BUCK/WIN MK18 ... 149 M11
Sycamore Ms AMS HP6 ... 71 H1
Sycamore Ri BERK HP4 ... 48 C7
　CSTG HP8 ... 81 M3
Sycamore Rd AMS HP6 ... 63 H8
　BIC OX26... 163 J4
　CSTG HP8 ... 81 M3
　HWYW HP12 ... 87 H2
　RBICS/W OX25 ... 162 H10
The Sycamores HHS/BOV HP3... 57 L2
Sycamore Wk DTCH/LGLY SL3... 112 F8
Sycamore Wy HAZ/HG HP15 ... 68 C7
Sydenham Gv CHNR OX39 ...184 B11
Sydney Gv SL SL1 ... 111 H3
Sydney Rd WATW WD18 ... 75 K6
Syke Cluan DTCH/LGLY SL3...113 K6
Syke Ings DTCH/LGLY SL3...113 K7
Sykes Cft EMV/FZ MK4... 21 M5
Sykes Rd SL SL1 ... 111 G3
Sylvana Cl HGDN/ICK UB10..104 E6
Sylvester Rd MDHD SL6... 98 D8
Sylvester St LBUZ LU7 ... 27 H1
Sylvia Cl GTMIS/PWD HP16... 61 G6
Symington Ct SHEN MK5 ... 21 L1
Synergy Pk
　EAG/OLD/WTN MK6 * ... 18 B3
Syon Gdns NPAG MK16 ... 14 F4

T

Tabard Gdns NPAG MK16 ... 14 F4
Tachbrook Rd UX/CGN UB8..104 B7
Tacknell Dr SHEN MK5 ... 21 K2
Tacks La HADM HP17 ...176 C12
Tadmarton WLLN MK15 ... 14 D8
Tadros Ct HWYN HP13 ... 78 C4
Talbot Av DTCH/LGLY SL3...112 E7
　HWYN HP13 ... 77 H4
Talbot Ct LBUZ LU7 ... 27 H6
Talbot Pl DTCH/LGLY SL3...122 B4
Talbot Rd RAYLNE/WEN HP22... 36 D5
　RKW/CH/CXG WD3 ... 84 D1
Talbots Dr MDHD SL6... 107 M8
Talbots Hyde OLN MK46... 128 A10
Talisman Rd BIC OX26... 162 E6
Talland Av EAG/OLD/WTN MK6 ... 7 J6
Tallis La WTR/OFPK MK7 ... 23 M1
Tall Oaks AMS HP6 ... 63 J8
Tall Pines LBUZ LU7 * ... 27 G4
Tall Trees WDSR SL4 ... 123 K4
Tamar Ct AYLS HP21 ... 42 B2
　HWYN HP13 ... 79 C6
Tamar Crs BIC OX26... 162 A3
Tamarisk Ct WTR/OFPK MK7 ... 23 L1
Tamarisk Gdns BIC OX26... 162 G6
Tamarisk Wy SL SL1 ... 111 G6
Tamar Wy DTCH/LGLY SL3...123 G1
Tamworth Stubb
　WTR/OFPK MK7 ... 23 K1
Tancred Rd HWYN HP13 ... 5 G2
Tandra EAG/OLD/WTN MK6 ... 22 E1
Tandy Ri CNH/GTH/TMA MK8 ... 17 H3
Tandys Cl RBEDW MK43... 129 N9
Tanfield La MKV MK10 ... 19 K3
Tangier La WDSR SL4 ... 121 J3
Tangmere Cl BIC OX26... 162 G2
Tank House Rd
　BUCK/WIN MK18 ... 151 L9
Tanners Dr GTLIN MK14 ... 14 D4
Tannery Rd WYM HP11 ... 78 B3
The Tannery BUCK/WIN MK18..151 J10
Tansman La WTR/OFPK MK7 ... 23 M1
Tanworth Cl NTHWD HA6... 85 H6
The Tanyard
　RAYLNE/WEN HP22 * ... 44 B6
Taplin Wy FLKWH/TG HP10 ... 79 C1
Taplow Common Rd
　MDHD SL6... 99 L4
Taplow Rd MDHD SL6... 109 M3
Tapping Rd SKCH HP14 ... 86 B2
Tarbay La WDSR SL4 ... 119 M7
Tarmac Wy WDR/YW UB7 ...114 A3
Tarnbrook Cl EMV/FZ MK4... 21 L4
Tarragon Cl WTR/OFPK MK7 ... 19 K8
Tarry Ct BDWL MK13 ... 13 L8
Tasker Cl HYS/HAR UB3...125 H3
Taskers Rw DUN/WHIP LU6..170 G2
The Task OLN MK46... 128 C10
Tatchbrook Cl MDHD SL6... 108 F2
Tatling Gv WTR/OFPK MK7 ... 19 K8
Tattam Ct WLLN MK15 ... 18 F4
Tattams La RMKS/WB MK17 ..152 A11
Tattenhoe Br BTCHLY MK3 ... 22 A4
Tattenhoe St SHEN MK5 ... 21 K8
Tattershall Cl SHEN MK5 ... 17 K8
Tattiers Hl RAYLNE/WEN HP22 ..168 A3
Taunton Deane EMV/FZ MK4... 22 A4
Taurus Cl BIC OX26... 149 L12
Tavelhurst CNH/GTH/TMA MK8.. 17 H5
Taverner Cl WTR/OFPK MK7 ..144 A4
Tavistock Cl MDHD SL6... 107 M7
Tavistock Ms HWYW HP12 ... 4 F7
Tavistock Rd HGDN/ICK UB10..104 C3
　WDR/YW UB7 ...114 C3
Tavistock St WEAT MK2 ... 23 G5
Tavistock Wk AYL HP20... 3 H1
Tay Gdns BIC OX26... 162 B2
Taylor Cl BIC OX26... 162 D2
Taylor Rd AYLS HP21 ... 42 B2
Taylors Cl MLW SL7 ... 97 L4
Taylors La AMSS HP7 ... 61 M8
　TRING HP23... 45 H7
Taylors Ms GTLIN MK14 ... 14 C8

Taylor's Ride LBUZ LU7 ... 27 G4
Taylors Rd CSHM HP5 ... 55 J8
Taymouth Pl CMK MK9... 7 M2
Tay Rd BTCHLY MK3 ... 22 B3
Teal Dr NTHWD HA6... 85 H7
Teale Ct RBICS/W OX25 ...173 G1
Teasel Av GTLIN MK14 ... 13 M6
Tedder Cl HGDN/ICK UB10..104 F5
　RSLP HA4... 105 M3
Tedder Rd RAYLNE/WEN HP22... 44 D3
Teesdale Rd SLN SL2 ... 110 E2
Tees Rd AYLS HP21 ... 42 B1
Tees Wy BTCHLY MK3 ... 22 A5
Teign Cl NPAG MK16 ... 15 G2
Telford Cl AYLW HP19 ... 177 Q1
Telford Dr SL SL1 ... 110 F6
Telford Rd BIC OX26... 162 G3
Telford Wy GTLIN MK14 ... 14 E5
　HWYN HP13 ... 4 E7
Telston Ct BNEND SL8 ... 88 F5
Temple GTLIN MK14 ... 13 L7
Temple La MLW SL7 ... 97 H1
　BUCK/WIN MK18 ... 11 M4
　WAT WD17 ... 75 L3
Temple End HWYN HP13 ... 5 K6
Temple Gdns
　RKW/CH/CXG WD3 ... 85 G3
Temple La MLW SL7 ... 97 H1
Temple Mill Island MLW SL7 ..107 H1
Temple Orch HWYN HP13 * ... 5 K6
Temple Pk MDHD SL6... 106 E3
　UX/CGN UB8 ... 104 F8
Temple Rd WDSR SL4 ... 121 H5
Temple Sq AYLW HP19 ... 2 F5
Temple St AYL HP20... 2 F5
　RAYLW HP18 ... 174 C2
Temple Wy SLN SL2 ... 101 H3
Templewood La SLN SL2 ... 101 H1
Tenby Gv EMV/FZ MK4... 21 H5
Tene Acres SHEN MK5 ... 17 J8
Tennis La BUCK/WIN MK18 ..151 K11
Tennyson Dr NPAG MK16 ... 14 F4
Tennyson Gv BTCHLY MK3 ... 22 C7
Tennyson Rd AYLS HP21 ... 34 E8
Tennyson Wy SL SL1 ... 110 D1
Tenterden Crs WTR/OFPK MK7 .. 19 L8
Tenzing Dr HWYN HP13 ... 78 C4
The Terrace TRING HP23 * ... 37 M7
Terrett Av HEAD OX3 ...178 A10
Terrington Hl BRACKY NN13 ... 8 C7
Terrington Hl MLW SL7 ... 97 G4
Terry Dr AYLW HP19 ... 34 B3
Terryfield Rd HWYN HP13 ... 78 C4
Terry Orch HWYN HP13 ... 5 H4
Terry Rd UX/CGN UB8 * ... 114 B1
Terry Rd HWYN HP13 ... 5 H3
Terry's La MDHD SL6... 98 D1
Testwood Rd WDSR SL4 ... 120 C4
Tewkesbury La MKV MK10 ... 19 J3
Thackeray Ct UX/CGN UB8..104 A7
Thackeray End AYLW HP19 ...167 Q12
Thame Br THAME OX9 ...181 N10
Thame Park Rd THAME OX9... 181 N10
Thame Rd AYLS HP21 ... 2 D7
　CHNR OX39 ...184 D2
　HADM HP17 ...182 A1
　RAYLW HP18 ... 181 P3
　RAYLW HP18 ... 174 A6
　RBICS/W OX25 ...173 Q4
　THAME OX9 ... 181 M3
Thame Rd South AYLS HP21 ... 2 B9
Thames Av BIC OX26... 162 A3
Thames Cl BNEND SL8 ... 88 F7
Thames Ct MDHD SL6... 109 G1
Thames Dr NPAG MK16 ... 15 G3
　RSLP HA4... 95 H5
Thamesfield Gdns MLW SL7 ... 97 K5
Thames Md WDSR SL4 ... 120 D4
Thames Pth BNEND SL8 ... 98 F2
　DTCH/LGLY SL3... 122 A5
　HEN RG9 ... 190 H4
　MDHD SL6... 109 H1
　MLW SL7 ... 97 L5
Thames Reach MLW SL7 ... 96 C8
Thames Rd DTCH/LGLY SL3...113 C8
　WDSR SL4 * ... 120 B3
Thames Side HEN RG9 ... 190 H4
　WDSR SL4 ... 121 J3
Thames St WDSR SL4 ... 121 J3
Thame Valley Wk HADM HP17..175 M12
　RAYLW HP18 ... 175 M12
　THAME OX9 ... 180 D8
Thane Ct GTLIN MK14 ... 13 M7
Thanestead Copse
　FLKWH/TG HP10 ... 79 H8
Thatcher Cl WDR/YW UB7 ...114 D6
Thatchers Dr MDHD SL6... 117 M1
Thellusson Wy
　RKW/CH/CXG WD3 ... 73 L8
Theodora Wy PIN HA5... 95 L2
Theydon Rd RMKS/WB MK17 ..144 E6
Thicket Gv MDHD SL6... 107 L7
The Thicket FLKWH/TG HP10... 79 G1
　WDR/YW UB7 ...114 D9
Third Av DBGH MK1 ... 23 G4
　HYS/HAR UB3 ... 115 L3
　MLW SL7 ... 97 L4
Third Crs SL SL1 ... 111 H4
Third St WYM HP11 ... 78 A6
Thirkleby Cl SL SL1 ... 111 M6
Thirlby La SHEN MK5 ... 21 J8
　WEAT MK2... 23 G8
Thirlmere Av SL SL1 ... 110 B2
Thirlmere Gdns NTHWD HA6... 85 G3
Thirsk Gdns BTCHLY MK3 ... 21 M8
Thistle Cl HHW HP1 ... 49 K8
Thomas Ct MDHD SL6... 117 M1
Thomas Crewe Cl
　BRACKY NN13 ... 8 E7
Thomas Dr NPAG MK16 ...132 H12
Thomas Dr FLKWH/TG HP10 ... 89 H3
Thomas St LBUZ LU7 ... 27 H1
Thompkins Cl SLN SL2 ... 100 H3
Thompson Cl DTCH/LGLY SL3... 122 A5
Thompson Rd RBICN OX27 ..154 E11
Thompson Rd HGDN/ICK UB10..104 C3
Thompson Wy
　RKW/CH/CXG WD3 ... 73 M8
Thomson Cl SL SL1 ... 111 M6
Thomson Wk AYLS HP21 * ... 34 A8
Thornaby Rd FLKWH/TG HP10... 79 H2
Thornborough Br
　BUCK/WIN MK18 ...142 E11
Thornborough Rd IVER SL0 ..103 H6
Thorncliffe
　CNH/GTH/TMA MK8... 17 G5
Thorndike SLN SL2 ... 110 F2

Thorn Dr DTCH/LGLY SL3...112 D3
Thorne Cl HEN RG9 ... 190 E7
Thorne Rd SKCH HP14 ... 86 B2
Thorne Wy AYL HP20... 3 L1
　RAYLNE/WEN HP22 ... 36 F6
Thorney La North IVER SL0 ..113 L3
Thorney La South
　WDR/YW UB7 ...113 L6
Thorney Mill Rd WDR/YW UB7..113 M7
Thornhill BUCK/WIN MK18 ...143 J10
Thornhill La AMSS HP7 ... 70 F3
Thornhill Rd HGDN/ICK UB10..104 F2
　NTHWD HA6... 85 H4
Thornlea Cfte OLN MK46... 128 B11
Thornley Cft EMV/FZ MK4... 21 M4
Thorns Cl PRRI HP27 ... 58 C1
Thornton Av WDR/YW UB7 ...114 E7
Thornton Cl WDR/YW UB7 ...114 E7
Thornton Crs
　RAYLNE/WEN HP22 ... 51 M1
Thornton Rd RMKS/WB MK17 ..143 N8
Thorn Tree Dr TRING HP23 ... 37 L6
Thorpe Cl AYLS HP21 ... 42 F2
Thorpeness Cft EMV/FZ MK4... 21 J6
Thorpland Av HGDN/ICK UB10..105 H1
Thorwold Pl SHEN MK5 ... 17 L8
Thrasher Rd AYLS HP21 ... 34 C8
Three Close La BERK HP4 ... 48 B7
Three Horseshoes Cl
　RAYLW HP18 ... 156 H12
Three Households CSTG HP8 ... 81 L4
Three Oaks Cl HGDN/ICK UB10..104 E1
Three Points La
　BUCK/WIN MK18 ... 157 P5
Three Shires Wy
　BOZ/IR/WOL NN29 ... 128 G3
　OLN MK46... 133 L3
　RMKN MK19 ... 132 A9
Thresher Gv WOLV MK12 ... 16 D1
Thrift La MDHD SL6... 118 C1
Thrift Rd LBUZ LU7 ... 27 H1
Thrupp Cl RMKN MK19 ...131 M12
Thrush Cl AYLW HP19 * ... 34 E3
　HWYW HP12 ... 87 H2
Thrush Gn RKW/CH/CXG WD3 ... 74 B8
Thurlby Wy MDHD SL6... 108 C2
Thurlston Rd RSLP HA4 ...105 M1
Thurne Cl NPAG MK16 ... 15 H3
Thurston Rd SL SL1 ... 111 J3
Thursday Cl WLLN MK15 ... 15 H3
Thyme Cl NPAG MK16 ... 14 C1
Tibbys La RAYLW HP18 ...176 C1
Ticehurst Cl WTR/OFPK MK7 ... 23 J5
Tichborne RKW/CH/CXG WD3 ... 83 J5
Tickford St NPAG MK16 ... 15 H3
Tidbury Cl RMKS/WB MK17 ..144 D6
Tierney EMV/FZ MK4... 21 G4
Tiffany Cl WEAT MK2 ... 23 G8
Tilbury Wk DTCH/LGLY SL3...113 C7
Tilburywood Cl HWYN HP13 ... 77 H4
Tilebarn Cl HEN RG9 ... 190 F6
Tilebarn La HEN RG9 ... 190 E6
Tilecotes Cl MLW SL7 ... 97 J4
Tilehouse La DEN/HRF UB9 ... 93 L6
　RKW/CH/CXG WD3 ... 83 K8
Tile Kiln La DEN/HRF UB9... 95 G6
Tilers Rd STSTR MK11 ... 16 E4
Tilling Crs HWYN HP13 ... 78 F3
Tillman Cl WOLV MK12 ... 16 F1
Tilstone Av WDSR SL4 ... 120 D1
Tilstone Cl WDSR SL4 ... 110 D8
Tilsworth Rd BEAC HP9... 80 B1
　LBUZ LU7 ... 30 E1
Timber La RMKS/WB MK17 ..144 H12
Timberridge
　RKW/CH/CXG WD3 ... 74 B5
Timberscombe EMV/FZ MK4... 22 A3
Timbers Wk MDHD SL6... 108 A5
Timber Wy CHNR OX39 ...184 D4
Timberwood SL SL1 ... 101 J1
Timbold Dr WTR/OFPK MK7 ... 19 J7
Timpson La OLN MK46... 128 E11
Timpsons Rw OLN MK46... 128 C11
Tindall Av LBUZ LU7 ... 27 J5
Tindal Rd AYL HP20... 3 H1
Tingewick Rd BUCK/WIN MK18.. 10 H7
Tinkers Dr BUCK/WIN MK18 ..151 L9
Tinkers La TRING HP23 ... 46 F2
　WDSR SL4 ... 120 C3
Tinkers Wood Rd HWYN HP13 .. 4 C3
Tintagel Ct EAG/OLD/WTN MK6... 7 H7
Tintern Cl SL SL1 ... 111 H7
Tinterne Cl AYLS HP21 ... 35 H8
Tippet Cl WTR/OFPK MK7 ... 23 M1
Tippings SKCH HP14 ...186 H1
Titchener Cl BIC OX26... 162 C2
Titchmarsh Ct
　EAG/OLD/WTN MK6 ... 6 F9
Tithe Barn Dr MDHD SL6... 119 J4
Tithe Cl MDHD SL6... 119 H1
　YEAD UB4 ... 115 L2
Tithe Ct DTCH/LGLY SL3...112 F8
Titmus Ct UX/CGN UB8...115 H3
Titmus Rd RAYLNE/WEN HP22... 44 D3
Tiverton Wy AYLW HP19 ... 34 B3
　EMV/FZ MK4... 21 H5
Tiverton Rd RSLP HA4 ...105 M1
Tobermory Cl DTCH/LGLY SL3... 112 C8
Tockley Rd SL SL1 ... 100 A8
Todd Cl AYLS HP21 ... 2 B9
　HAZ/HG HP15 ... 69 G3
Tolcarne Av
　EAG/OLD/WTN MK6 ... 7 L6
Tolcarne Dr PIN HA5... 95 M1
Toll Bar Cnr PRRI HP27 ...183 N7
Tollgate MDHD SL6... 107 M8
Tollgate Cl RKW/CH/CXG WD3... 73 L5
Tollpit End HHW HP1 ... 49 M4
Tolman Ct AYLS HP21 ... 34 A8
Tolpits Cl WATW WD18 ... 75 L6
Tolpits La WATW WD18 ... 75 L7
Tomlin Rd SLN SL2 ... 110 D1
Tompion Rd AYLW HP19 ...177 L9
Tompkins Cl
　RAYLNE/WEN HP22 ... 36 E6
　SHEN MK5 ... 21 L2
Tompkins La RBICN OX27 ..163 R4
Toms Hill Cl TRING HP23 ... 39 J5
Toms Hill Rd TRING HP23 ... 39 J5
Toms Turn HAZ/HG HP15 ... 68 D3
Tongwell La NPAG MK16 ... 14 D7
Tongwell Street A4146
　RMKS/WB MK17... 19 L4
　WLLN MK15 ... 19 H4
Tongwell St WLLN MK15 ... 19 H4
　WTR/OFPK MK7 ... 23 M1
Toot Hill Cl SHEN MK5 ... 21 J1
Top Angel BUCK/WIN MK18 ..149 L1
Topaz Cl SL SL1 ... 111 G6
Top Farm Cl BEAC HP9... 89 M1
Topland Rd CFSP/GDCR SL9 ... 82 C2

Top Meadow WTR/OFPK MK7 .... 23 L3
Top Pk CFSP/GDCR SL9 .... 92 B5
Topping La UX/CGN UB8 .... 104 C8
Top Station La BRACKY NN13 ...... 8 F6
Torbay RAYLNE/WEN HP22 ....166 V1
Tornay Ct LBUZ LU7 .... 29 L8
Torquay Sp SLN SL2 .... 101 G8
Torre Cl BTCHLY MK3 .... 22 D4
Torridge Rd BERK HP4 .... 42 E2
  DTCH/LGLY SL3 .... 123 G2
  RSLP HA4 .... 105 M1
Tortoiseshell Wy BERK HP4 ..... 47 L4
Torwood Rd BERK HP4 .... 47 L6
Totteridge Av HWYN HP13 .... 78 C4
Totteridge Dr HWYN HP13 .... 78 D1
Totteridge La HWYN HP13 .... 78 D2
Totteridge Pde HWYN HP13 * 78 D2
Totteridge Rd HWYN HP13 .... 5 K6
Totternhoe Rd DUN/WHIP LU6 .... 30 E7
Towan Av EAG/OLD/WTN MK6 .... 7 K7
Towcester Dr TOW NN12 .... 137 J3
Towcester Rd BUCK/WIN 11 M2
  RMKN M19 .... 137 G2
Tower Cl BERK HP4 .... 47 M7
  FLKWH/TG HP10 .... 89 H3
Tower Crs GTLIN MK14 .... 14 C8
Tower Dr GTLIN MK14 .... 14 C7
Towergate Cl UX/CGN UB8 ...... 104 D3
Tower HI KGLGY WD4 .... 57 K8
Toweridge La SKCH HP14 .... 76 E5
Tower Rd AMSS HP7 .... 70 H6
Towers Av HGDN/ICK UB10 ...... 105 H8
Towers Cl HGDN/ICK UB10 * 105 H8
Towersey Dr THAME OX9 .... 181 Q7
Towersey Rd THAME OX9 .... 181 Q6
Towersey Wy AYLS HP21 .... 2 B8
Town St HWYN HP13 .... 68 C8
Town Bridge Ct CSHM HP5 .... 63 G3
Town Cl BUCK/WIN MK18 * 147 Q8
Town End Crs NPAG MK16 .... 132 C5
Town End Rd SKCH HP14 .... 185 M10
Town Farm LBUZ LU7 .... 169 M7
Town Farm Cl THAME OX9 .... 181 J8
Townfield CSHM HP5 .... 63 G3
  RKW/CH/CXG WD3 .... 74 B8
Town Field La CSTG HP8 .... 82 B3
Townfield Rd HWYN HP13 .... 5 L6
  HYS/HAR UB3 .... 115 L5
Town Hall Ar BERK HP4 * 48 B6
Town La FLKWH/TG HP10 .... 89 J6
Townsend RBICN OX27 .... 163 K4
Townsend Cl RBEDW MK43 .... 139 K6
Townsend Cots
  RMKS/WB MK17 .... 151 L3
Townsend La RBICN OX27 .... 163 G4
Townsend Piece AYLW HP19 .... 2 D4
Townsend Rd CSHM HP5 .... 63 G1
Townside DUN/WHIP LU6 .... 170 C3
  HADM HP17 .... 182 C1
Townson Wy NTHLT UB5 .... 105 M7
Tracy Av DTCH/LGLY SL3 .... 122 F3
Trafalgar Av SLN SL2 .... 22 B4
Trafford Cl GTMIS/PWD HP16 .... 60 F3
Trafford Rd GTMIS/PWD HP16 .... 60 F3
Tramhill RAYLW HP18 .... 164 C12
Tranlands Brigg BDWL MK13 ...... 6 A1
Trapp's Ct CSHM HP5 .... 63 H4
Trapp's La CSHM HP5 .... 63 H4
Travell Ct BDWL MK13 .... 17 L3
Travic Rd SLN SL2 .... 100 E8
Travis Ct SLN SL2 .... 101 C8
Travis Gv BTCHLY MK3 .... 22 C6
Treacher's Cl CSHM HP5 .... 63 G2
Treadaway HI FLKWH/TG HP10 * .. 89 G2
Treadaway Rd
  FLKWH/TG HP10 .... 89 G2
Treborough EMV/FZ MK4 .... 22 A4
Tredington Gv WTR/OFPK MK7 .... 23 L2
Treefields BUCK/WIN MK18 ...... 11 L6
Treehanger Cl TRING HP23 ...... 38 A6
Trees Av SKCH HP14 .... 67 M8
Treeside Cl WDR/YW UB7 .... 114 C8
Treesmill Rd MDHD SL6 .... 108 A7
Trees Rd BNEND SL8 .... 89 G7
  SKCH HP14 .... 67 M8
Treetops Cl NTHWD HA6 .... 85 J5
Trefoil Dr BIC OX26 .... 162 E2
Trefusis Wk WAT WD17 .... 75 K7
Trelawney Av DTCH/LGLY SL3 ... 112 C7
Tremayne Ct
  EAG/OLD/WTN MK6 .... 7 K8
Trenchard Av
  RAYLNE/WEN HP22 .... 44 C4
Trenchard Rd MDHD SL6 .... 119 G2
Trenchard St AYLW HP19 .... 177 R2
Trenches La DTCH/LGLY SL3 .... 112 F5
Trent Crs BIC OX26 .... 162 A3
Trent Dr NPAG MK16 .... 15 G2
Trentishoe Crs EMV/FZ MK4 ..... 22 A3
Trent Rd BTCHLY MK3 .... 22 B5
  DTCH/LGLY SL3 .... 123 G2
Trent Wy LBUZ LU7 .... 29 L1
  YEAD UB4 .... 105 K8
Tresco Rd BERK HP4 .... 47 L5
Tresham Ct SHEN MK5 .... 17 K7
The Tressell MDHD SL6 .... 108 C4
Trevelyan Wy BERK HP4 .... 48 A1
Treves Av AYLS HP21 .... 42 D1
Trevithick La SHEN MK5 .... 21 L1
Trevone Ct EAG/OLD/WTN MK6 * ... 7 K8
Trevor Rd HYS/HAR UB3 .... 115 K6
Trewarden Av IVER SL0 .... 103 J7
Tring Ford Rd TRING HP23 ...... 37 M3
Tring HI TRING HP23 .... 37 H7
Tring Rd AYL HP20 .... 3 L6
  BERK HP4 .... 47 H3
  DUN/WHIP LU6 .... 170 F7
  RAYLNE/WEN HP22 .... 168 B3
  RAYLNE/WEN HP22 .... 44 B5
Trinity Av MLW SL7 .... 97 J3
Trinity Cl NTHWD HA6 .... 85 K6
  RMKN M19 .... 137 G2
Trinity Ct RKW/CH/CXG WD3 * ... 84 D2
Trinity Dr UX/CGN UB8 .... 115 H3
Trinity Pl WDSR SL4 * 121 G7
Trinity Rd HAZ/HG HP15 .... 68 C7
  MLW SL7 .... 97 J3
  WOLV MK12 .... 21 J1
Trispen Ct EAG/OLD/WTN MK6 * ... 7 K7
Triumph Cl HYS/HAR UB3 .... 125 H4
Trooper Ct TRING HP23 .... 39 H5
Troutbeck BDWL MK13 .... 6 A4
Troutbeck Cl SLN SL2 .... 111 M4
Trout Cl MLW SL7 .... 97 H6
Trout Hollow PRRI MK27 .... 185 Q2
Trout La WDR/YW UB7 .... 114 A4
Trout Ri RKW/CH/CXG WD3 .... 74 A4
Trout Rd WDR/YW UB7 .... 114 A4

Troutstream Wy
  RKW/CH/CXG WD3 .... 74 A5
Trubys Gdn
  EAG/OLD/WTN MK6 .... 18 D7
Trueman Pl
  EAG/OLD/WTN MK6 .... 7 H8
Truemper Gv RBICN OX27 .... 154 E11
Truesdale Dr DEN/HRF UB9 ...... 94 B3
Trumper Wy SL SL1 .... 110 E5
Trumpton La WTR/OFPK MK7 ...... 19 M7
Trunk Furlong
  RMKS/WB MK17 .... 144 G4
Truro Cl MDHD SL6 .... 107 M7
Truro Wy YEAD UB4 .... 105 K8
Trust Cnr HEN RG9 .... 190 H6
Trustees Wy DEN/HRF UB9 .... 93 L4
Tubb Cl BIC OX26 .... 162 B4
Tudwell Rd SLN SL2 .... 102 A6
Tucker Cl HWYN HP13 .... 5 M3
Tudeley Hale WTR/OFPK MK7 .... 124 F4
Tudor Cl PIN HA5 .... 95 M4
Tudor Ct AMS HP6 * 71 J1
  MDHD SL6 .... 99 H8
Tudor Dr FLKWH/TG HP10 .... 89 J2
Tudor Gdns SL SL1 .... 110 B2
  STSTR MK11 .... 16 B2
Tudor Mi FLKWH/TG HP10 * 89 K4
Tudor Orch BERK HP4 * 47 K4
Tudor Pk AMS HP6 .... 63 H8
Tudor Rd HYS/HAR UB3 .... 115 J3
Tudor's Cl BUCK/WIN MK18 ..... 157 H6
Tudor Sq HYS/HAR UB3 .... 115 J2
Tudor Wy BRACKY NN13 .... 8 C5
  HGDN/ICK UB10 .... 104 F4
  RKW/CH/CXG WD3 .... 83 M1
  WDSR SL4 .... 120 D4
Tuffnell Cl WLLN MK15 .... 15 H7
Tulip Wy WDR/YW UB7 .... 114 C8
Tulkers Cl GTMIS/PWD HP16 ..... 60 C5
Tulla Ct WEAT MK2 .... 153 P2
Tummell Wy WEAT MK2 .... 153 P1
Tunbridge Gv WTR/OFPK MK7 .... 124 F4
Tunmers End CFSP/GDCR SL9 ..... 82 B8
Tunnel Link Rd HTHAIR TW6 .... 124 F4
Tunnel Rd East WDR/YW UB7 .... 125 G3
Tunnel Rd West WDR/YW UB7 .... 124 F4
Tunnel Wy LBUZ LU7 .... 169 P12
Tuns La HEN RG9 .... 190 H4
  SL SL1 .... 111 H7
Turks Cl UX/CGN UB8 .... 104 F8
Turnberry Cl BIC OX26 .... 162 F3
  BTCHLY MK3 .... 21 M7
Turner Cl AYL HP20 .... 34 E3
Turner Rd DTCH/LGLY SL3 ...... 112 B6
Turners Dr HWYN HP13 .... 78 D3
Turners Fld HWYN HP13 .... 77 K3
Turners Meadow
  RAYLNE/WEN HP22 .... 36 A4
Turners Ms GTLIN MK14 .... 14 C8
Turners Wk CSHM HP5 .... 63 H1
Turners Wood Dr CSTG HP8 ...... 82 C3
Turner Wk AYL HP20 * 34 E3
Turneys Dr WOLV MK12 .... 12 D8
Turneys Orch
  RKW/CH/CXG WD3 .... 73 J6
Turnfields RAYLW HP18 .... 180 B3
Turnfurlong AYLS HP21 .... 3 J7
Turnfurlong La AYLS HP21 .... 3 L8
Turnfurlong Rw AYLS HP21 .... 3 L8
Turnham Dr LBUZ LU7 .... 29 K1
Turnip Cl RAYLW HP18 .... 175 Q8
Turnmill Av
  EAG/OLD/WTN MK6 .... 18 E3
Turnoak Pk WDSR SL4 .... 120 D7
Turnpike Ct RMKS/WB MK17 ..... 144 D5
Turnpike End AYLS HP21 .... 3 J9
Turnpike La HGDN/ICK UB10 .... 104 D8
Turnpike Rd HWYW HP21 .... 87 H2
  RBEDW MK43 .... 145 L8
  RBICN OX27 .... 154 F12
The Turnpike RAYLW HP18 ...... 179 Q1
Turnpike Wy HWYW HP21 .... 87 H2
Turnstone Cl HGDN/ICK UB10 ... 105 G3
Turnstone Gn BIC OX26 .... 162 F6
Turnstone Wy RAYLW HP18 .... 34 D3
Turpins Gn MDHD SL6 * 117 M1
Turpyn Ct EAG/OLD/WTN MK6 ..... 19 G6
Turton Wy SL SL1 .... 111 J7
Turvey Cl RAYLNE/WEN HP22 ..... 36 D5
Turvey Rd NPAG MK16 .... 135 J6
  RBEDW MK43 .... 129 N5
Turvill End SHEN MK5 .... 6 A8
Turville Rd AYLS HP21 .... 35 H8
Turweston Rd BRACKY NN13 .... 8 F5
Tuscans Cl BUCK/WIN MK18 ..... 157 J5
Tussauds Cl RKW/CH/CXG WD3 .... 74 A6
Tweedale Cl RMKS/WB MK17 ..... 152 B7
Tweed Cl BERK HP4 .... 48 A5
Tweed Crs BIC OX26 .... 162 A3
Tweedale Gv HGDN/ICK UB10 .... 105 H5
Tweed Rd BTCHLY MK3 .... 22 A5
Tweed Rd DTCH/LGLY SL3 .... 123 G2
Tweenways CSHM HP5 .... 63 J1
Twelve Leys
  RAYLNE/WEN HP22 .... 33 M3
Twinches La SL SL1 .... 111 G5
Twinflower WTR/OFPK MK7 .... 19 L8
The Twist TRING HP23 .... 38 C5
Twitchell La
  RAYLNE/WEN HP22 .... 36 D5
Twitchell Rd GTMIS/PWD HP16 ... 60 F3
Twitchen La EMV/FZ MK4 .... 22 A3
Twizel Cl BDWL MK13 .... 13 H8
Two Dells La CSHM HP5 .... 55 L3
Two Gates La CSHM HP5 .... 54 C3
Two Mile Dr SL SL1 .... 110 D6
Two Ponds La BERK HP4 .... 47 H4
Two Ridges Link
  DUN/WHIP LU6 .... 170 B3
  LBUZ LU7 .... 29 J8
Two Ridges Link Grand Union
  Canal Wk LBUZ LU7 .... 27 G8
Two Tree HI HEN RG9 .... 190 E6
Twyford La WTR/OFPK MK7 .... 23 M1
Twyford Rd WAR/TWY RG10 ...... 116 D8
Twynham Rd MDHD SL6 .... 108 A3
Ty-Craig BIC OX26 * 162 E4
Tyle Pl WDSR SL4 .... 121 M8
Tylers Crs HAZ/HG HP15 .... 69 K3
Tylers Gn BDWL MK13 .... 6 D2
Tylers Hill Rd CSHM HP5 .... 63 L1
Tylers Rd HAZ/HG HP15 .... 69 L1
Tyler Wk DTCH/LGLY SL3 .... 122 E1
Tyndale Ms SL SL1 .... 111 G6
Tynemouth Ri MKV MK10 .... 19 K5
Tyne Sq BTCHLY MK3 .... 22 A5
Tyrell Cl BUCK/WIN MK18 .... 11 K7
  RMKN M19 .... 12 D1
Tyrell Gdns WDSR SL4 .... 120 E6

Tyrells Gdns RMKS/WB MK17 .... 153 R6
Tyrells Rd RMKS/WB MK17 ...... 153 R6
Tyrill GTLIN MK14 .... 13 M7
Tyson Pl EAG/OLD/WTN MK6 .... 6 F9
Tythe Cl LBUZ LU7 .... 161 K2
Tyzack Rd HWYN HP13 .... 68 D8

U

Ullswater Cl SL SL1 .... 110 B2
  YEAD UB4 .... 105 K7
Ullswater Dr LBUZ LU7 .... 26 E7
Ultra Av BTCHLY MK3 .... 22 D5
Ulverscroft MKV MK10 .... 19 H4
Ulverston Crs MKV MK10 .... 19 L3
Ulyett Pl EAG/OLD/WTN MK6 ...... 7 G9
Umberville Wy SLN SL2 .... 110 E1
Underhill Cl MDHD SL6 .... 108 D1
Underwood Pl
  EAG/OLD/WTN MK6 .... 7 G9
Underwood Rd HWYN HP13 .... 78 C5
Union St NPAG MK16 .... 15 G1
University Wy RBEDW MK43 ..... 138 C5
Unwin Av EBED/NFELT TW14 ..... 125 J8
Up Cnr CSTG HP8 .... 82 A2
Upcroft WDSR SL4 .... 121 G6
Upland Av CSHM HP5 .... 55 G7
Uplands MLW SL7 .... 87 J8
  RKW/CH/CXG WD3 .... 74 C7
Uplands Cl CFSP/GDCR SL9 ...... 92 D7
  HWYN HP13 .... 78 D3
The Uplands CFSP/GDCR SL9 ..... 92 D7
  RSLP HA4 .... 95 M7
Upminster Cl MKV MK10 .... 19 H5
Upper Abbotts HI AYLW HP19 ... 177 R3
Upper Ashlyns Rd BERK HP4 ..... 48 A7
Upper Belmont Rd CSHM HP5 ..... 55 J7
Upper Bourne End La
  HHW HP1 .... 57 G4
Upper Bray Rd MDHD SL6 .... 109 H8
Upper Church St RAYLW HP18 ... 176 C7
Upper Coombe LBUZ LU7 .... 26 E9
Upper Dr BEAC HP9 .... 80 C5
Upper Fifth St CMK MK9 .... 6 H1
Upper George St CSHM HP5 ...... 63 H1
Upper Gladstone Rd
  CSHM HP5 * 63 H1
Upper Green St WYM HP11 .... 4 D5
Upper Hall Pk BERK HP4 .... 48 D8
Upper High St THAME OX9 ...... 181 N6
Upper Hill Ri
  RKW/CH/CXG WD3 .... 74 A7
Upper Hollis GTMIS/PWD HP16 ... 60 D3
Upper Hundreds Wy AYL HP20 ..... 3 G8
Upper Icknield Wy PRRI MK27 .. 185 P3
  RAYLNE/WEN HP22 .... 44 C3
  TRING HP23 .... 38 C2
Upper Lees Rd SLN SL2 .... 100 F8
Upper Lodge La HAZ/HG HP15 .... 68 G4
Upper Meadow CSHM HP5 .... 63 G1
Upper Riding BEAC HP9 .... 90 A1
Upper Rd DEN/HRF UB9 .... 93 J6
Upper Sales HHW HP1 .... 91 L8
Upper Second St CMK MK9 .... 6 C6
Upper Stonehayes
  GTLIN MK14 .... 14 C6
Upper St BUCK/WIN MK18 .... 10 D8
  RAYLNE/WEN HP22 .... 166 D1
Upper Thames Wy BNEND SL8 ..... 88 D6
Upper Third St CMK MK9 .... 6 D5
Upper Wy RMKS/WB MK17 .... 24 D5
Upper Wood Cl SHEN MK5 .... 3 J3
Upton Cl HEN RG9 .... 190 H5
  SL SL1 .... 111 L7
Upton Court Rd
  DTCH/LGLY SL3 .... 112 A8
  BDWL MK13 .... 17 K2
Upton Gv SHEN MK5 .... 21 M2
Upton Lea Pde SLN SL2 * 112 A4
Upton Pk SL SL1 .... 111 K7
Upton Rd HADM HP17 .... 176 H8
  SL SL1 .... 111 M7
Upway CFSP/GDCR SL9 .... 82 E8
Uxbridge Rd DTCH/LGLY SL3 .... 112 D2
  HGDN/ICK UB10 .... 105 C8
  RKW/CH/CXG WD3 .... 83 M2
  SL SL1 .... 111 M6

V

V2 BTCHLY MK3 .... 22 B7
  EMV/FZ MK4 .... 21 M5
  SHEN MK5 .... 21 H3
V3 EMV/FZ MK4 .... 21 J1
  SHEN MK5 .... 21 J1
V4 CNH/GTH/TMA MK8 .... 17 L8
  STSTR MK11 .... 16 F1
V5 WOLV MK12 .... 16 F1
V6 BDWL MK13 .... 6 D1
V7 BDWL MK13 .... 6 D1
  DBGH MK1 .... 6 D1
  EAG/OLD/WTN MK6 .... 7 K7
V8 CMK MK9 .... 7 K4
  EAG/OLD/WTN MK6 .... 18 C2
  GTLIN MK14 .... 18 C2
V10 MKV MK10 .... 19 L1
  WLLN MK15 .... 18 F1
  WTR/OFPK MK7 .... 19 L3
V11 MKV MK10 .... 19 L3
  WLLN MK15 .... 18 L1
  WTR/OFPK MK7 .... 19 L6
Vache La CSTG HP8 .... 82 B2
  SHEN MK5 .... 17 J8
Vache Ms CSTG HP8 * 72 C7
Vale Cl CFSP/GDCR SL9 .... 82 C8
Vale Gv SL SL1 .... 111 K7
Valency Cl NTHWD HA6 .... 85 L4
Valens Cl CNH/GTH/TMA MK8 .... 17 J6
Valentine Ct
  CNH/GTH/TMA MK8 .... 17 G7
Valentine Wy CSTG HP8 .... 82 D1
Vale Park Dr AYL HP20 .... 3 H5
Valerian Pl NPAG MK16 .... 4 E5
Vale Ri CSHM HP5 .... 55 H7
Vale Rd AYL HP20 .... 3 H3
  CSHM HP5 .... 55 G3
  WDSR SL4 .... 120 A7
The Vale CFSP/GDCR SL9 .... 82 C8
Valley Cl BERK HP4 .... 171 M7
  BRACKY NN13 .... 8 F6
  DUN/WHIP LU6 .... 171 Q10
Valley Crs BRACKY NN13 .... 8 G5
Valley Pk WATW WD18 * 75 H8
Valley Ri BRACKY NN13 .... 8 F6
Valley Rd BERK HP4 .... 47 L4
  BRACKY NN13 .... 8 G5
  BUCK/WIN MK18 .... 147 Q8
  BUCK/WIN MK18 .... 142 A10

  DUN/WHIP LU6 .... 171 Q10
  HEN RG9 .... 190 H6
  HGDN/ICK UB10 .... 104 D7
  RKW/CH/CXG WD3 .... 73 M6
  SKCH HP14 .... 67 M8
Valleyside HHW HP1 .... 49 L7
Valley Vw CSHM HP5 .... 54 F8
Valley Wk RKW/CH/CXG WD3 ...... 75 H6
Valley Wy CFSP/GDCR SL9 .... 92 B5
Van Der Bilt Ct BDWL MK13 .... 13 J8
Van Dieman's Cl RAYLW HP18 ... 181 N7
Van Diemens Cl CHNR OX39 ..... 184 D3
Vandyke Cl RMKS/WB MK17 ...... 144 E4
Vandyke Rd LBUZ LU7 .... 27 J7
Vane Rd THAME OX9 .... 181 Q6
Vanguard Cl HWYW HP12 .... 4 B5
  RAYLNE/WEN HP22 .... 44 C5
Vanguard Wy HTHAIR TW6 .... 125 K5
Vanvwall Rd MDHD SL6 .... 108 A6
Vansittart Est WDSR SL4 * 121 H4
Vansittart Rd MLW SL7 .... 97 K7
  WDSR SL4 .... 121 G5
Vantage Ct NPAG MK16 .... 15 J3
Vanwall Rd MDHD SL6 .... 108 A6
Varley Ct HHW HP1 * 49 L7
Varney Cl HHW HP1 * 49 L7
Varney Rd HHW HP1 .... 49 L7
Vaughan Gdns WDSR SL4 .... 110 E8
Vaughan Wy SLN SL2 .... 110 D1
Vauxhall BDWL MK13 .... 13 L1
Vega Crs NTHWD HA6 .... 85 L5
Vellan Av EAG/OLD/WTN MK6 ...... 7 M7
Venables La CSHM HP5 .... 14 D7
Venetian Ct WTR/OFPK MK7 ..... 19 M7
Venice Av WATW WD18 .... 75 K5
Ventfield Cl WHLY OX33 ...... 178 F1
Venus Cl SLN SL2 .... 110 E1
Venus HI HHS/BOV HP3 .... 64 F7
Ver-Colne Valley Wk
  HHS/BOV HP3 .... 56 C7
Verdi Cl WTR/OFPK MK7 .... 144 A5
Verdon Dr WLLN MK15 .... 14 E7
Verity Pl EAG/OLD/WTN MK6 ...... 7 H7
Verley Cl EAG/OLD/WTN MK6 .... 18 F5
Vermont Pl WLLN MK15 .... 14 G1
Vermont Rd SLN SL2 .... 110 D1
Verney Av HWYW HP12 .... 87 G2
Verney Cl BERK HP4 .... 47 L5
  BUCK/WIN MK18 .... 11 L5
  MLW SL7 .... 97 J4
  TRING HP23 .... 38 B5
Verney Farm Cl
  GTLIN MK14 .... 158 C3
Verney Rd BUCK/WIN MK18 ...... 150 H10
  DTCH/LGLY SL3 .... 112 F3
Verney Wk AYLS HP21 .... 34 C8
Vernier Crs SHEN MK5 .... 21 H4
Vernon Dr DEN/HRF UB9 .... 84 B8
Verona Ct UX/CGN UB8 .... 114 B3
Vervain Cl BIC OX26 .... 162 D1
Verwood Av AYL HP20 .... 3 H1
Veryan Pl EAG/OLD/WTN MK6 ...... 7 L5
Vicarage Cl BEAC HP9 .... 81 H6
  BUCK/WIN MK18 .... 149 L11
  MDHD SL6 .... 98 F3
  RNHPTN NN7 .... 126 A3
  RSLP HA4 .... 95 J6
Vicarage Dr MDHD SL6 .... 109 H6
Vicarage Gdns BDWL MK13 ...... 17 K2
  BERK HP4 .... 49 G3
  LBUZ LU7 .... 26 F8
  MDHD SL6 .... 117 K6
  TRING HP23 .... 169 M12
Vicarage La BUCK/WIN MK18 .... 149 L12
  HHS/BOV HP3 .... 57 G5
  LBUZ LU7 .... 170 A9
  LBUZ LU7 .... 161 G2
  RBICS/W OX35 .... 173 K4
Vicarage Rd AYLS HP21 .... 42 C1
  BDWL MK13 .... 17 K2
  BERK HP4 .... 48 C5
  BUCK/WIN MK18 .... 151 J10
  HEN RG9 .... 190 H6
  LBUZ LU7 .... 169 Q11
  MDHD SL6 .... 108 E2
  RMKS/WB MK17 .... 144 G4
  STSTR MK11 .... 12 A8
  TOW NN12 .... 130 D12
  TRING HP23 .... 169 L12
  TRING HP23 .... 46 C1
  WATW WD18 .... 75 M8
  WEAT MK2 .... 23 H6
Vicarage St RMKS/WB MK17 ..... 144 G4
Vicarage Wk MDHD SL6 .... 109 H6
  STSTR MK11 .... 12 A8
Vicarage Wy CFSP/GDCR SL9 ..... 92 G5
  DTCH/LGLY SL3 .... 123 J3
Vickery Cl AYLS HP21 .... 42 D1
Vickery Wk AYLS HP21 * 42 D1
Victor Cl MDHD SL6 .... 108 A2
Victoria Av HGDN/ICK UB10 ... 105 C8
Victoria Cl HYS/HAR UB3 ..... 115 J3
  RKW/CH/CXG WD3 .... 74 C3
Victoria Ct BIC OX26 .... 162 E5
Victoria Crs IVER SL0 .... 113 M4
Victoria Dr SLN SL2 .... 100 E4
Victoria Gdns MLW SL7 .... 97 K2
  WYM HP11 .... 87 G2
Victoria La HYS/HAR UB3 ..... 125 J1
Victoria Md THAME OX9 .... 181 P7
Victoria Rd BERK HP4 .... 48 B7
  BIC OX26 .... 162 E4
  CSHM HP5 .... 63 H2
  LBUZ LU7 .... 26 F8
  MLW SL7 .... 97 K4
  RSLP HA4 .... 95 M7
  SLN SL2 .... 112 A5
  SLN SL2 .... 101 K4
  UX/CGN UB8 .... 104 B5
  WEAT MK2 .... 23 G6
Victoria St AYL HP20 .... 3 K6
  SL SL1 .... 111 J4
  WDSR SL4 .... 13 J4
  WOLV MK12 .... 21 J1
  WYM HP11 .... 4 E5
Victor Rd WDSR SL4 .... 121 H4
Victory Dr DBGH MK1 .... 22 E4
Victory Rd BERK HP4 .... 47 M5
  BUCK/WIN MK18 .... 149 L11
  RAYLNE/WEN HP22 .... 44 A4
Vienna Gv BDWL MK13 .... 13 H4
Village Cl RMKS/WB MK17 ..... 133 N8
Village Ct LBUZ LU7 .... 26 E8
Village La SLN SL2 .... 91 J7
Village Rd AMSS HP7 .... 70 H4
  DEN/HRF UB9 .... 93 M7
  WDSR SL4 .... 110 A7
Villa Wy AMSS HP7 .... 72 C3
Villiers Cl BUCK/WIN MK18 .... 11 M4
Villiers Rd BIC OX26 .... 162 C4
  SLN SL2 .... 111 J2
Villier Ct UX/CGN UB8 .... 104 C8

Vimy Ct LBUZ LU7 * 27 G7
Vimy Rd LBUZ LU7 .... 27 G7
Vincent Av CNH/GTH/TMA MK8 ... 17 H7
Vincent Cl WDR/YW UB7 .... 124 C2
Vincent Dr HGDN/ICK UB10 .... 104 E6
Vincent Rd AYLW HP19 .... 167 R13
Vincent Wy SKCH HP14 .... 67 J8
Vine Cl HAZ/HG HP15 .... 68 F7
  STWL/WRAY TW19 .... 123 M8
  WDR/YW UB7 .... 114 F8
Vine La HGDN/ICK UB10 .... 104 E7
Vine Rd SLN SL2 .... 101 L4
Vine Rw RBEDW MK43 * 129 N8
Vine St UX/CGN UB8 .... 104 C6
The Vine RAYLW HP18 .... 180 A5
Vinetrees RAYLNE/WEN HP22 .... 44 A6
Vineyard Dr BNEND SL8 .... 88 E5
Viney St AYLW HP19 .... 177 Q2
Vinlake Av HGDN/ICK UB10 .... 104 E1
Vintners Ms GTLIN MK14 .... 14 E1
Violet Av UX/CGN UB8 .... 114 C2
Violet Cl PRRI MK27 .... 58 C8
Violets Cl AYLW HP19 .... 3 K1
Violet Ter UX/CGN UB8 * 114 C2
Violet Wy RKW/CH/CXG WD3 ...... 74 B5
Virginia Cl EAG/OLD/WTN MK6 .. 18 D7
Virginia Gdns SKCH HP14 ..... 185 Q10
Viscount Cl AYL HP20 * 3 K1
Viscount Wy HTHAIR TW6 ...... 125 K7
  WEASH MK2 .... 22 F5
Vyne Crs CNH/GTH/TMA MK8 ..... 17 J5
Vyners Wy HGDN/ICK UB10 ..... 104 E1
The Vyne LBUZ LU7 .... 29 K1

W

Waborne Rd BNEND SL8 .... 89 G6
Waddesdon Cl
  CNH/GTH/TMA MK8 .... 17 J6
Waddesdon HI RAYLW HP18 ..... 166 F11
Wade Dr SL SL1 .... 110 F5
Wadesmill La WTR/OFPK MK7 .... 23 L2
Wadham Cl BIC OX26 .... 162 E3
Wadhurst La MKV MK10 .... 19 H3
Wadworth Holme MKV MK10 ...... 19 H3
Waglands Gdn
  BUCK/WIN MK18 .... 11 L7
Wagner Cl MDHD SL6 .... 117 L3
  WTR/OFPK MK7 .... 23 M2
Wagon Wy RKW/CH/CXG WD3 ...... 74 B4
Wagstaff Wy OLN MK46 .... 128 B11
Waine Cl BUCK/WIN MK18 .... 11 L7
Wainwrights RAYLW HP18 ...... 175 L12
Waivers Wy AYLS HP21 .... 42 F1
Wakefield Cl GTLIN MK14 ...... 14 C7
Wakefield Crs SLN SL2 .... 101 L5
Wakelins End MDHD SL6 .... 98 D5
Wakeman Rd BNEND SL8 .... 88 E7
Walbank Gv SHEN MK5 .... 21 K3
Walbrook Av
  EAG/OLD/WTN MK6 .... 18 E3
Waldeck Rd MDHD SL6 .... 108 D3
Walden Cft
  EAG/OLD/WTN MK6 .... 23 H2
Waldens Cl BNEND SL8 .... 88 F7
Walducks Cl LBUZ LU7 .... 161 K2
Walford Rd UX/CGN UB8 .... 104 B7
Walgrave Dr BDWL MK13 .... 17 K3
Walgrove Gdns MDHD SL6 ...... 117 K8
Walker Cl DTCH/LGLY SL3 ..... 122 E1
Walker Crs DTCH/LGLY SL3 .... 122 E1
Walker Dr THAME OX9 .... 181 N6
Walker Rd MDHD SL6 .... 108 F6
Walkers Rd PRRI MK27 .... 183 N7
Walkham Cl HWYN HP13 .... 79 G6
Walkhampton Av BDWL MK13 ...... 6 A3
Walk House Cl RBEDW MK43 .... 139 L11
The Walk BUCK/WIN MK18 ...... 151 J11
  WDSR SL4 .... 120 D6
Walkwood End BEAC HP9 .... 90 B1
Walkwood Ri BEAC HP9 .... 90 B2
Wallace Cl HGDN/ICK UB10 .... 104 D7
  MLW SL7 .... 97 L2
Wallace Dr DUN/WHIP LU6 ...... 30 F8
Wallace End AYLS HP21 .... 3 L9
Wallace Ms DUN/WHIP LU6 ...... 30 F8
Wallace St BDWL MK13 .... 13 H7
Wallasey Crs HGDN/ICK UB10 ... 94 E1
Wallbridge Cl AYLW HP19 .... 2 A7
The Walled Gdn
  WAR/TWY RG10 .... 191 N12
Waller Dr NTHWD HA6 .... 85 M8
Waller Rd BEAC HP9 .... 80 E8
Wallinger Dr SHEN MK5 .... 21 K3
Wallingford Rd UX/CGN UB8 ... 104 A7
Wallingford Gdns WYM HP11 .... 78 A6
Wallington Cl RSLP HA4 .... 95 G1
Wallington Rd CSHM HP5 .... 63 G1
Wallmead Gdns SHEN MK5 .... 17 L1
Walney Pl EMV/FZ MK4 .... 21 J5
Walnut Av WDR/YW UB7 .... 114 F7
Walnut Cl BIC OX26 .... 162 E1
  BRACKY NN13 .... 8 E5
  GTMIS/PWD HP16 .... 60 F3
  HYS/HAR UB3 .... 115 K4
  NPAG MK16 .... 14 D3
  RAYLNE/WEN HP22 .... 43 H4
Walnut Crs PRRI MK27 .... 183 N7
Walnut Dr BUCK/WIN MK18 ..... 142 A6
  RAYLNE/WEN HP22 .... 44 A4
  WEAT MK2 .... 23 H6
Walnut Gv FLKWH/TG HP10 ...... 89 K4
The Walnuts LBUZ LU7 .... 27 H4
Walnut Tree Cl BNEND SL8 ..... 89 G8
Walnut Tree La RAYLW HP18 ... 183 N8
Walnut Wy AMS HP6 .... 62 G6
  BNEND SL8 .... 89 G8
Walpole Cl BIC OX26 .... 162 B2
Walpole Rd SL SL1 .... 110 C3
Walsh's Mnr GTLIN MK14 .... 14 B7
Walsingham Ga WYM HP11 .... 87 H3
Walters Ct HWYN HP13 .... 78 D1
Waltham Av HYS/HAR UB3 ...... 115 H4
Waltham Cl MKV MK10 .... 19 K5
Waltham Dr MKV MK10 .... 19 K5
Waltham Rd MDHD SL6 .... 116 A3
Walton Av HEN RG9 .... 190 H6
Walton Dene AYLS HP21 .... 3 M9
Walton Dr HWYN HP13 .... 78 C1
  WTR/OFPK MK7 .... 19 L8
Walton End WTR/OFPK MK7 ...... 19 M8

Walton Gn AYLS HP21 3 H8
Walton Gv AYLS HP21 3 H8
Walton Heath BTCHLY MK3 22 A6
Walton La SLN SL2 100 E7
Walton Pl RAYLNE/WEN HP22 43 L3
Walton Rd AYLS HP21 3 J7
MKV MK10 19 J4
WTR/OFPK MK7 19 K8
Walton St AYL HP20 2 F6
Walton Wy AYLS HP21 3 L7
Wandlebury GTLIN MK14 14 D6
Wandsworth Pl BDWL MK13 6 D3
Wannions Cl CSHM HP5 63 M1
Wansbeck Dr BIC OX26 162 A4
Wantage Cl LBUZ LU7 161 R7
RNHPTN NN7 126 B3
Wantage Crs LBUZ LU7 161 R7
Wappenham Rd BRACKY NN13 140 A2
Wapping RAYLW HP18 175 L12
Wapseys La SLN SL2 91 K5
Wapseys Wd CFSP/GDCR SL9 * 91 K4
Warbler Cl AYLW HP19 177 Q2
Ward Cl IVER SL0 113 L4
Wardes Cl GTMIS/PWD HP16 60 B5
Ward Gdns SL SL1 110 D4
Wardle Pl EAG/OLD/WTN MK6 6 F8
Ward Pl AMSS HP7 * 71 G3
Ward Rd BRACKY NN13 146 F1
DBGH MK1 23 G3
Wardrobes La PRRI HP27 58 C6
Ward Royal WDSR SL4 * 121 H4
Ward Royal Pde WDSR SL4 * 121 H4
Wardstone End EMV/FZ MK4 21 L4
Ware Leys Cl RBICN OX27 163 R3
Wargrave Hl WAR/TWY RG10 191 N12
Wargrave Rd HEN RG9 191 K6
WAR/TWY RG10 191 M8
Warley Av YEAD UB4 115 M3
Warley Rd YEAD UB4 115 M3
Warmark Rd HHW HP1 49 K5
War Memorial Pl HEN RG9 190 H7
Warmington Gdns WLLN MK15 18 E1
Warmstone Cl RAYLW HP18 166 E8
Warmstone La RAYLW HP18 166 E8
Warneford Av
RAYLNE/WEN HP22 44 C5
Warneford Wy LBUZ LU7 29 K1
Warner Cl HYS/HAR UB3 125 J3
SL SL1 110 D5
Warners Cl RMKS/WB MK17 24 E5
Warners End Rd HHW HP1 49 M7
Warners Hl MDHD SL6 98 B3
Warners Rd RMKS/WB MK17 153 J3
Warren Cl BUCK/WIN MK18 11 M7
DTCH/LGLY SL3 112 D7
HADM HP17 177 L5
Warrendene Rd SKCH HP14 67 M6
Warrender Rd CSHM HP5 55 K8
Warrender Wy RSLP HA4 95 M6
Warren Fld IVER SL0 103 H7
Warren Pde SLN SL2 * 112 B5
Warren Rd HGDN/ICK UB10 104 D2
RMKS/WB MK17 151 Q1
TOW NN12 130 E12
Warren Row Rd
WAR/TWY RG10 191 Q7
The Warren CFSP/GDCR SL9 82 E7
CSHM HP5 54 D7
HAZ/HG HP15 68 F5
YEAD UB4 115 M3
Warren Vw MDHD SL6 * 118 F2
Warren Wood Dr WYM HP11 5 L9
Warrington Av SL SL1 111 H3
Warrington Rd OLN MK46 128 B9
Warwick Av HWYW HP12 77 G8
SLN SL2 111 H1
Warwick Cl MDHD SL6 108 A6
RAYLNE/WEN HP22 36 D5
Warwick Ct BIC OX26 162 F2
RKW/CH/CXG WD3 73 L4
Warwick Crs YEAD UB4 115 L1
Warwick Dr LBUZ LU7 161 R8
Warwick Ms
RKW/CH/CXG WD3 74 F7
Warwick Pl BTCHLY MK3 22 B7
UX/CGN UB8 104 B5
Warwick Rd BEAC HP9 80 C7
BTCHLY MK3 22 C7
LBUZ LU7 169 Q11
RMKN MK19 131 M7
WDR/YW UB7 114 D5
Warwick Rw AYL HP20 3 L3
Warwick Ter OLN MK46 * 128 B10
Warwick Wy
RKW/CH/CXG WD3 75 H5
Washfield EMV/FZ MK4 22 A3
Wash Hl FLKWH/TG HP10 89 K7
Wash Hill Lea FLKWH/TG HP10 89 J6
Washingleys RBEDW MK43 139 L3
Washington Dr SL SL1 110 C4
WDSR SL4 120 D6
Wastel EAG/OLD/WTN MK6 22 E1
Watchcroft Dr
BUCK/WIN MK18 11 M4
Watchet Ct EMV/FZ MK4 22 A3
Watchet La HAZ/HG HP15 69 G4
Waterbeach Cl SL SL1 111 J3
Waterbeach Rd SL SL1 111 J3
Water Cl RMKN MK19 137 Q7
Waterdell LBUZ LU7 27 K7
Water Eaton Rd WEAT MK2 22 E7
Water End Rd BERK HP4 49 G4
SKCH HP14 187 M1
Waterfield RKW/CH/CXG WD3 73 H8
Waterford Cl BTCHLY MK3 22 B5
Waterhouse Cl NPAG MK16 15 G2
Water La BERK HP4 48 B6
HADM HP17 177 L11
HHS/BOV HP3 57 G8
LBUZ LU7 27 G7
NPAG MK16 133 M9
PRRI HP27 67 H2
Waterlily AYLW HP19 34 D2
Waterloo Ct BTCHLY MK3 22 B4
Waterloo Rd LBUZ LU7 26 F8
UX/CGN UB8 104 B6
Waterlow Cl NPAG MK16 14 F4
Waterman Ct SL SL1 110 D5
Waterman's Rd HEN RG9 190 H6
Watermead AYL HP20 34 C3
Watermeadow AYLW HP19 34 D3
Water Meadow CSHM HP5 63 G3
Water Meadow Wy
RAYLNE/WEN HP22 44 A4
Watermill Wy
RAYLNE/WEN HP22 43 L4
Waterperry Ms AYLW HP19 177 Q2
Waterperry Rd RAYLW HP18 179 Q9
Water Reach MDHD SL6 108 F1
Waters Dr RKW/CH/CXG WD3 84 D1
Waterside CSHM HP5 63 J4
DUN/WHIP LU6 170 G2
EAG/OLD/WTN MK6 18 F6
FLKWH/TG HP10 89 K3
UX/CGN UB8 114 B2
Waterside Dr DTCH/LGLY SL3 112 E6
Waterside Ms DEN/HRF UB9 83 M6
Waterslade Pens HADM HP17 176 B12
Watersplash La HYS/HAR UB3 115 M8
Water Stratford Rd
BUCK/WIN MK18 10 B7
Water Tower Cl UX/CGN UB8 104 D3
Watery La BRACKY NN13 8 F7
FLKWH/TG HP10 89 K2
HEN RG9 187 K12
HYS/HAR UB3 125 J1
RMKN MK19 143 P4
TRING HP23 37 L1
Watford Rd NTHWD HA6 85 L7
RKW/CH/CXG WD3 74 F7
Watling St BTCHLY MK3 22 D3
CNH/GTH/TMA MK8 17 H6
DBGH MK1 23 G5
DUN/WHIP LU6 31 M2
EMV/FZ MK4 22 A1
STSTR MK11 16 D3
TOW NN12 137 M5
WEAT MK2 23 H5
Watling Ter WEAT MK2 23 H5
Watlow Gdns BUCK/WIN MK18 11 M4
Watson Cl CNH/GTH/TMA MK8 17 G8
Wattleton Rd BEAC HP9 90 B2
Watts Cl RMKN MK19 131 M7
Watts Gn RAYLW HP18 175 Q8
Wavell Ct WLLN MK15 14 E7
Wavell Gdns SLN SL2 100 E8
Wavell Rd BEAC HP9 91 G1
MDHD SL6 108 A4
Wavendon House Dr
RMKS/WB MK17 144 D2
Wavendon Rd RMKS/WB MK17 138 F12
Waveney Cl BIC OX26 162 A4
NPAG MK16 15 H3
Waverley Cl HYS/HAR UB3 115 J8
Waverley Cft MKV MK10 19 K5
Waverley Gdns NTHWD HA6 85 M8
Waverley Rd SLN SL2 111 H2
Waverley Wk AYL HP20 2 F2
Waxwing Cl AYL HP20 34 D3
Wayborne Gv RSLP HA4 95 H5
Waye Av HEST TW5 125 M4
Wayfarers Pk BERK HP4 47 L6
Wayfarings BIC OX26 162 D1
Waylands HYS/HAR UB3 115 J2
Waynflete Av BRACKY NN13 8 D7
Waynflete Cl BRACKY NN13 8 D7
Wayside HWYN HP13 78 C3
PRRI HP27 67 H2
Wayside Gdns CFSP/GDCR SL9 92 C6
Wayside Ms MDHD SL6 108 E2
Weald Rd HGDN/ICK UB10 104 F7
Wealdstone Pl
EAG/OLD/WTN MK6 7 L4
Weald Wy YEAD UB4 105 K8
Wear Rd BIC OX26 162 A4
Weasel La BTCHLY MK3 21 L8
Weatherby DUN/WHIP LU6 31 M6
Weathercock Cl
RMKS/WB MK17 144 E5
Weathercock Gdns
HAZ/HG HP15 69 H3
Weathercock La
RMKS/WB MK17 144 F6
Weatley Rd WHLY OX33 178 D8
Weavers End RMKN MK19 131 M8
Weavers Hl STSTR MK11 16 D2
Weavers Rd TRING HP23 37 K6
Webb Cl CSHM HP5 63 G1
DTCH/LGLY SL3 112 C8
Webber Heath WTR/OFPK MK7 144 A6
Webbs Home Cl MKV MK10 19 K4
Webbs Meadow AYLW HP19 177 R2
Webbs Rd YEAD UB4 105 M8
Webster Cl MDHD SL6 117 M1
THAME OX9 181 N5
Webster Rd AYLS HP21 3 L9
Websters Meadow
EMV/FZ MK4 21 M5
Wedgewood Cl NTHWD HA6 * 85 H7
Wedgewood St AYLW HP19 177 R2
Wedgwood Av GTLIN MK14 14 D5
Wedgwood Dr SKCH HP14 67 M8
Wedgwood Rd BIC OX26 162 F3
Weedon Cl CFSP/GDCR SL9 82 A8
Weedon Hl AMS HP6 62 C6
Weedon La AMS HP6 62 F7
Weedon Rd AYLW HP19 2 C2
Weekes Dr SL SL1 111 G5
Weill Rd AYLS HP21 42 F2
Weir La BUCK/WIN MK18 158 B5
RAYLNE/WEN HP22 167 Q1
RBICS/W OX25 163 M9
Weirside Gdns WDR/YW UB7 114 C5
Welbeck Av AYLS HP21 35 H8
Welbeck Cl MKV MK10 19 J5
Welbeck Rd MDHD SL6 108 C5
Welburn Gv EMV/FZ MK4 21 K4
Welby Cl MDHD SL6 117 M2
Welcome Hall WYM HP11 5 H6
Welden SLN SL2 112 B3
Welders La CFSP/GDCR SL9 81 L7
Weldon Ri SHEN MK5 6 A9
Weldon Wy THAME OX9 181 P6
Welford Wy RAYLW HP18 176 C7
Welland Cl AYLS HP21 42 B2
DTCH/LGLY SL3 122 F2
Welland Cft BIC OX26 162 A3
Welland Dr NPAG MK16 15 H3
Welland Rd AYLS HP21 42 B1
Wellbank MDHD SL6 109 K1
Wellbrook Ms TRING HP23 * 38 A6
Wellcroft LBUZ LU7 170 A9
Wellcroft Rd SL SL1 111 G5
Weller Cl AMS HP6 63 K8
Weller Rd AMS HP6 63 K8
Wellesbourne Gdns
HWYN HP13 68 C8
Wellesley Av DTCH/LGLY SL3 113 L7
NTHWD HA6 85 L5
Wellesley Pth SL SL1 111 M6
Wellesley Rd SL SL1 111 M6
Welles Rd HWYN HP13 78 E3
Welley Av STWL/WRAY TW19 122 D7
Welley Rd STWL/WRAY TW19 122 D8
Wellfield HAZ/HG HP15 69 G7
Wellfield Ct WLLN MK15 15 G6
Wellfield Rd SKCH HP14 76 A6
Wellhayes GTLIN MK14 14 C6
Well Head Rd DUN/WHIP LU6 31 K8
Wellhouse Rd MDHD SL6 98 D8
Wellhouse Wy SKCH HP14 67 K8
Wellingborough Rd OLN MK46 128 B9
Wellington Av PRRI HP27 58 A2
Wellington Cl BIC OX26 162 F2
MDHD SL6 108 A2
Wellington Pl AYLS HP21 42 D2
BTCHLY MK3 22 E7
Wellington Rd AYLS HP21 42 D2
EBED/NFELT TW14 125 K8
HWYW HP12 87 K2
MDHD SL6 108 C3
UX/CGN UB8 104 B6
Wellington St SL SL1 111 L6
THAME OX9 181 N6
Well La LBUZ LU7 28 B5
Wellmore BUCK/WIN MK18 * 142 A7
Wellonhead Br
RAYLNE/WEN HP22 36 E7
Wells Cl WDSR SL4 120 F3
Wells Ct LBUZ LU7 * 27 H7
Well St BUCK/WIN MK18 11 L6
Welsh La BUCK/WIN MK18 10 C1
Welsummer Gv SHEN MK5 21 K3
Welton Rd AYLS HP21 35 G7
Welwyn Wy YEAD UB4 115 K1
Wendlebury Rd RBICS/W OX25 162 B8
Wendover Hts
RAYLNE/WEN HP22 44 C5
Wendover Rd AYLS HP21 3 H8
BNEND SL8 88 F6
HADM HP17 51 J3
RAYLNE/WEN HP22 43 H4
SL SL1 110 A2
Wendover St WYM HP11 4 F6
Wendover Wy AYLS HP21 3 K9
WYM HP11 5 K8
Wenlack Cl DEN/HRF UB9 103 M1
Wenman Rd THAME OX9 181 P8
Wenning La EMV/FZ MK4 21 L4
Wensum Crs BIC OX26 162 A3
Wensum Wy
RKW/CH/CXG WD3 84 C1
Wentworth Av SLN SL2 100 F8
Wentworth Cl HWYN HP13 5 M4
WAT WD17 75 L1
Wentworth Crs HYS/HAR UB3 115 J7
MDHD SL6 108 B4
Wentworth Dr PIN HA5 95 M4
Wentworth Pl CSHM HP5 * 63 H3
Wentworth Rd THAME OX9 181 P6
Wentworth Wy BTCHLY MK3 21 M7
Wenwell Cl RAYLNE/WEN HP22 36 F7
Werner Ct AYLS HP21 42 D2
Werth Dr RMKS/WB MK17 144 E8
Wescott Wy UX/CGN UB8 104 B7
Wesley Cl AYL HP20 3 L2
BIC OX26 162 B2
Wesley Dene HWYN HP13 5 J6
Wesley Hl CSHM HP5 63 G1
Wesley Rd HYS/HAR UB3 115 M4
Wessex Rd BNEND SL8 89 G8
Wessex Wy BIC OX26 162 E5
MDHD SL6 108 A6
Westacott YEAD UB4 115 K2
Westacott Rd BIC OX26 162 F8
Westacott Wy MDHD SL6 117 J2
West Acres AMSS HP7 71 J3
Westanley Av AMSS HP7 71 J2
West Av FLKWH/TG HP10 79 H1
HYS/HAR UB3 115 L4
Westborough Ct MDHD SL6 108 B4
Westborough Rd MDHD SL6 108 B4
Westbourne Pde
HGDN/ICK UB10 * 115 G1
Westbourne Rd UX/CGN UB8 115 G1
Westbourne St WYM HP11 4 F6
Westbrook MDHD SL6 119 K1
Westbrook End
RMKS/WB MK17 152 H3
Westbury Circular Ride
BRACKY NN13 146 H2
BRACKY NN13 140 C6
Westbury Cl NPAG MK16 14 E2
RBICN OX27 163 R3
RSLP HA4 95 M6
Westbury La NPAG MK16 14 C1
Westbury Rd NTHWD HA6 85 K4
Westcliffe CNH/GTH/TMA MK8 16 F5
West Cl MLW SL7 96 C7
Westcombe Lodge Dr
YEAD UB4 115 J2
West Common CFSP/GDCR SL9 92 C4
West Common Rd
UX/CGN UB8 104 C3
Westcote Ri RSLP HA4 95 H6
West Ct HWYN HP13 77 J3
West Crs WDSR SL4 120 E4
Westcroft SLN SL2 111 G1
West Dales BDWL MK13 17 L1
West Dean MDHD SL6 108 E2
Westdean La CSHM HP5 54 B7
West Dene HHNE HP2 41 L2
West Drayton Park Av
WDR/YW UB7 114 D7
West Drayton Rd UX/CGN UB8 115 G3
West Dr HWYN HP13 78 C2
West Edge RBICN OX27 163 R4
West End BIC OX26 163 J5
RAYLNE/WEN HP22 43 K4
West End Cl BIC OX26 163 J5
BUCK/WIN MK18 149 K12
West End La HYS/HAR UB3 125 H3
RBICS/W OX25 172 C2
SLN SL2 101 K6
West End Rd LBUZ LU7 169 L7
Westend Rd WYM HP11 4 E6
Westend St WYM HP11 4 F6
Western Av BUCK/WIN MK18 11 K4
DEN/HRF UB9 104 B2
HEN RG9 190 H6
HGDN/ICK UB10 104 E3
Western Cl HEN RG9 * 190 H6
Western Dene HAZ/HG HP15 68 F4
Western Dr FLKWH/TG HP10 89 K5
RMKN MK19 131 M7
Western La BUCK/WIN MK18 150 H11
Western Pde HGDN/ICK UB10 * 105 G4
Western Perimeter Rd
HTHAIR TW6 124 A6
Western Rd HEN RG9 190 H6
RMKS/WB MK17 151 K3
TRING HP23 37 L7
WEAT MK2 22 F5
WOLV MK12 12 F8
Western Vw HYS/HAR UB3 115 L6
West Farm Wy OLN MK46 133 M2
Westfield AMS HP6 62 B6
AYLS HP21 42 D3
Westfield Av RMKN MK19 137 L9
Westfield Crs HEN RG9 191 L11
Westfield Rd BEAC HP9 90 B1
BERK HP4 47 K4
LBUZ LU7 169 P11
MDHD SL6 108 A4
SLN SL2 111 G1
WEAT MK2 22 F7
Westfields BUCK/WIN MK18 11 J6
PRRI HP27 58 C2
Westfield Wk HWYW HP12 4 B7
Westfield Wy RSLP HA4 105 K1
West Furlong BUCK/WIN MK18 149 P5
Westgate Ct HWYN HP13 78 F6
Westgate Crs SL SL1 110 E4
West Hatch Mnr RSLP HA4 95 L7
West Hawthorn Rd
RBICS/W OX25 163 J10
West Hl DUN/WHIP LU6 171 R1
Westhill GTLIN MK14 14 A6
West Hl RMKS/WB MK17 144 G6
Westhill Av BRACKY NN13 8 D7
Westhill Cl BRACKY NN13 8 D7
Westhill Gdns BRACKY NN13 8 C7
Westholme Ct BIC OX26 162 E5
Westholme Gdns RSLP HA4 95 M7
Westhorpe Pk MLW SL7 * 88 A7
Westhorpe Rd MLW SL7 97 L3
West Hyde La CFSP/GDCR SL9 82 E7
Westlands Av SL SL1 110 B3
Westlands Cl HYS/HAR UB3 115 M8
SL SL1 110 B3
Westlands Rd PRRI HP27 66 D1
West La HEN RG9 190 G4
OLN MK46 133 M2
PRRI HP27 185 K1
West Leith TRING HP23 45 K1
Westlington La HADM HP17 176 H9
West Md MDHD SL6 98 E8
Westmead PRRI HP27 58 A1
WDSR SL4 121 G6
Westminster Cl WYM HP11 78 A6
Westminster Crs
BRACKY NN13 8 E7
Westminster Cft
BRACKY NN13 8 E7
Westminster Dr AYLS HP21 34 E8
BTCHLY MK3 22 D4
Westminster Rd BRACKY NN13 8 E8
Westmorland Av AYLS HP21 35 G8
Westmorland Rd MDHD SL6 108 C3
Weston Av LBUZ LU7 27 K8
Weston La THAME OX9 180 G6
Weston Rd OLN MK46 127 L12
RAYLNE/WEN HP22 36 A6
SL SL1 110 E2
Weston Wy
RAYLNE/WEN HP22 42 F4
Westover Ct HWYN HP13 4 A1
Westover Rd HWYN HP13 4 A1
Westpits OLN MK46 133 M2
West Point SL SL1 110 C5
West Rp HTHAIR TW6 124 F4
West Richardson St
WYM HP11 4 E5
West Rdg BNEND SL8 89 G6
Westridge Cl CSHM HP5 62 E1
HHW HP1 49 L7
West Rd BERK HP4 47 M5
MDHD SL6 108 D3
RBEDW MK43 138 G4
RMKS/WB MK17 144 E5
WDR/YW UB7 114 E7
Westron Gdns TRING HP23 38 A6
West Side LBUZ LU7 * 27 G7
Westside La NPAG MK16 132 C4
West Side Ri OLN MK46 128 A10
West Spur Rd UX/CGN UB8 104 C8
West St AYLW HP19 2 D4
BIC OX26 162 C3
BUCK/WIN MK18 149 K12
HEN RG9 190 G4
LBUZ LU7 27 G7
MDHD SL6 108 E3
MLW SL7 97 H5
OLN MK46 128 B10
West Vw CSHM HP5 55 J8
West Wk HYS/HAR UB3 115 M5
West Wy BEAC HP9 89 L1
RKW/CH/CXG WD3 84 A1
RSLP HA4 95 L7
West Waye HWYN HP13 68 B8
West Well Cl BUCK/WIN MK18 10 B8
West Well La BUCK/WIN MK18 10 B8
Westwood Cl AMS HP6 72 C2
CNH/GTH/TMA MK8 17 H6
RSLP HA4 95 G5
Westwood Dr AMS HP6 72 C2
Westwood Gn MDHD SL6 98 E4
Westwood Rd MLW SL7 97 H5
Westwood Wk AYL HP20 3 J1
West Wycombe Hill Rd
SKCH HP14 76 E4
West Wycombe Rd
HWYW HP12 4 A2
Wetherby Gdns BTCHLY MK3 22 A8
Wethered Pk MLW SL7 97 J5
Wethered Rd MLW SL7 97 J4
SL SL1 110 A3
Wexham Park La
DTCH/LGLY SL3 112 B1
Wexham Pl SLN SL2 * 102 C4
Wexham Rd SL SL1 111 M6
Wexham St DTCH/LGLY SL3 102 A7
SLN SL2 102 A8
Wexham Woods
DTCH/LGLY SL3 112 B2
Weybourne Rd MKV MK10 19 K2
Wey La CSHM HP5 63 G3
Weymouth Rd YEAD UB4 105 K8
Whaddon Cha AYLW HP19 2 E2
Whaddon Rd NPAG MK16 14 E3
RMKS/WB MK17 143 R8
SHEN MK5 21 K3
Whaddon Wy BTCHLY MK3 22 A7
Whales La RBICN OX27 163 R4
Whalley Dr BTCHLY MK3 22 D5
Wharf Cl RAYLNE/WEN HP22 44 A5
RMKN MK19 137 Q7
Wharfe La HEN RG9 190 H4
Wharf La BERK HP4 47 H1
BNEND SL8 88 F7
RKW/CH/CXG WD3 74 D8
RMKN MK19 137 R7
Wharf Rd RAYLNE/WEN HP22 44 A5
Wharf Rw
RAYLNE/WEN HP22 * 37 G6
Wharfside WEAT MK2 23 H6
Wharfside Pl
BUCK/WIN MK18 11 M5
The Wharf GTLIN MK14 14 C4
WEAT MK2 23 H8
Wharf Vw BUCK/WIN MK18 11 M5
The Wheatbutts WDSR SL4 120 E1
Wheatcroft Cl
EAG/OLD/WTN MK6 22 D1
Wheatfield Cl LBUZ LU7 27 L7
MDHD SL6 117 M2
Wheathouse Copse
RMKS/WB MK17 151 K3
Wheatlands Rd
DTCH/LGLY SL3 112 A7
Wheatley Cl EMV/FZ MK4 21 M4
Wheatley Crs HYS/HAR UB3 115 M4
Wheatley Rd WHLY OX33 178 E10
Wheatley Wy CFSP/GDCR SL9 82 D6
Wheatsheaf Pde WDSR SL4 * 121 M8
Wheatstone Cl DTCH/LGLY SL3 111 M7
Wheeler Av FLKWH/TG HP10 79 H2
Wheeler Cl AYL HP20 35 G7
Wheelers Dr RSLP HA4 95 H5
Wheelers End CHNR OX39 184 F4
Wheelers La BDWL MK13 13 K8
Wheelers Orch CFSP/GDCR SL9 82 D6
Wheelers Pk HWYN HP13 78 C3
Wheelwright Ms GTLIN MK14 14 C8
Wheelwright Rd PRRI HP27 183 N7
Wheelwrights
RAYLNE/WEN HP22 43 L3
Wheelwrights Pl
DTCH/LGLY SL3 * 123 H3
Wheelwrights Yd
RAYLNE/WEN HP22 166 D1
Whetstone Cl BDWL MK13 6 A1
Whichert Cl BEAC HP9 80 B4
Whichford GTLIN MK14 14 D5
Whielden Ga AMSS HP7 70 C6
Whielden Hts AMSS HP7 70 F4
Whielden La AMSS HP7 70 E5
Whielden St AMSS HP7 71 G4
Whimbrel Cl BIC OX26 162 F5
Whinchat AYLW HP19 34 D3
Whincup Cl WYM HP11 87 K2
Whinneys Rd FLKWH/TG HP10 79 H7
Whippendell Rd WATW WD18 75 K6
Whirlpool Arch RAYLW HP18 180 A5
Whisper Wd
RKW/CH/CXG WD3 74 A4
Whitamore Rw HEN RG9 190 H6
Whitby Cl BTCHLY MK3 22 C4
Whitby Rd SL SL1 111 H4
Whitchurch Cl MDHD SL6 98 D7
RAYLW HP18 165 Q8
Whitchurch La
RAYLNE/WEN HP22 159 N10
Whitchurch Rd LBUZ LU7 160 G10
White Alder WOLV MK12 17 H1
Whitebaker Ct GTLIN MK14 14 C8
Whitebeam Cl
RAYLNE/WEN HP22 43 H2
White Br BUCK/WIN MK18 149 Q7
Whitebrooke Pk MDHD SL6 99 H6
Whitebrook Pk MDHD SL6 * 99 H6
Whitebroom Rd HHW HP1 49 K5
White Cl HWYN HP13 4 B1
SL SL1 111 J5
White Crs RAYLNE/WEN HP22 44 C4
Whitecross Rd HADM HP17 182 C1
Whitefield La
GTMIS/PWD HP16 60 F4
Whiteford Rd SLN SL2 111 K2
Whitegate Ct
EAG/OLD/WTN MK6 18 E8
Whitegates Cl
RKW/CH/CXG WD3 74 F5
Whitehall Av MKV MK10 144 A1
Whitehall Rd UX/CGN UB8 104 C6
Whitehall St AYL HP20 2 E5
White Hart Cl CSTG HP8 81 M3
RAYLW HP18 164 C6
White Hart Fld
RAYLNE/WEN HP22 166 E2
White Hart La HADM HP17 182 C1
White Hart Meadow
BEAC HP9 90 D1
White Hart Rd MDHD SL6 * 108 E3
SL SL1 111 J7
White Hart St WYM HP11 5 H6
Whitehaven SL SL1 111 L4
Whitehead Wy AYLS HP21 34 D8
White Heart Av UX/CGN UB8 115 H2
Whiteheath Av RSLP HA4 95 H6
White Hermitage WDSR SL4 * 122 B8
White Hl BERK HP4 56 B3
Whitehill BERK HP4 48 C5
White Hl CSHM HP5 63 H2
DEN/HRF UB9 84 F6
FLKWH/TG HP10 89 K1
HEN RG9 190 D9
HHW HP1 49 L8
HWYN HP13 68 A8
Whitehill OLN MK46 128 A9
White Hill Cl CSHM HP5 63 H1
Whitehill Cl MLW SL7 87 H8
Whitehill Ct BERK HP4 48 C5
Whitehill La LBUZ LU7 169 Q11
Whitehorn Pl WDR/YW UB7 114 E5
White Horse Ct LBUZ LU7 * 27 H7
White Horse Dr EMV/FZ MK4 21 M4
White Horse La
RAYLNE/WEN HP22 159 R12
White Horse Rd WDSR SL4 120 C5
White House Cl
CFSP/GDCR SL9 82 D7
White House Ct LBUZ LU7 27 H7
Whitehouse La
FLKWH/TG HP10 89 K1
Whitehouse Wy
DTCH/LGLY SL3 112 C7
IVER SL0 103 J8
Whitelands Av
RKW/CH/CXG WD3 73 G4
Whitelands Rd HWYW HP12 4 B7
Whitelands Wy HWYW HP12 4 B6
White La HEN RG9 188 B11
Whiteleaf Wy PRRI HP27 58 C1
Whiteley WDSR SL4 120 D3
Whiteley Crs BTCHLY MK3 22 C8
Whiteleys Pde
HGDN/ICK UB10 * 115 G1
White Lilies Island WDSR SL4 121 G3
White Lion Rd AMSS HP7 71 M2
White Lion Yd CSHM HP5 63 H3
White Lodge Cl MLW SL7 87 H8
White Paddock MDHD SL6 117 M4
Whitepit La FLKWH/TG HP10 89 J4
White Rock MDHD SL6 109 G1
Whites Cl BUCK/WIN MK18 149 L11
Whites Cft EAG/OLD/WTN MK6 18 C8
Whites La DTCH/LGLY SL3 122 A2
Whitestone Wk HHW HP1 49 M4
Whitethorn Av WDR/YW UB7 114 D4
Whitethorn Cl
RAYLNE/WEN HP22 42 F6
Whitethorns NPAG MK16 14 E3
White Vw AYL HP20 3 K1
Whitewood Rd BERK HP4 47 M6
Whitfield Rd SKCH HP14 67 M8
Whitfield Wy
RKW/CH/CXG WD3 83 L1
Whitley Crs BIC OX26 162 F3
Whitmees Cl OLN MK46 128 A10
Whitsun Pasture WLLN MK15 14 E7
Whittaker Rd SL SL1 110 D1
Whittenham Cl SLN SL2 111 M5
Whittington Av YEAD UB4 115 L2
Whittington Cha EMV/FZ MK4 21 H6

Whittle Pkwy *SL* SL1...110 C3
Whittle Rd *THAME* OX9...181 Q6
Whitton Wy *NPAC* MK16...14 F3
Whitworth La *SHEN* MK5...17 L7
Whurley Wy *MDHD* SL6...98 D8
Whybrow Gdns *BERK* HP4...48 D4
Whyteladyes La *MDHD* SL6...98 D4
Whytingham Rd *TRING* HP23...38 B6
Wicken Park Rd *RMKN* MK19...143 J2
Wicken Rd *BUCK/WIN* MK18...142 F2
The Wickets *BDWL* SL8...108 B3
Wickham Cl *DEN/HRF* UB9...84 C8
Wick Rd *TRING* HP23...46 B2
Wickstead Av
  CNH/GTH/TMA MK8...17 G8
Widbrook Rd *MDHD* SL6...99 G7
Widdenton Vw *SKCH* HP14...86 B3
Widecroft Rd *IVER* SL0...113 K3
Widewater Pl *DEN/HRF* UB9 *...94 B4
Widmere Fld
  GTMIS/PWD HP16...60 B5
Widmere La *MLW* SL7...86 F7
Widmore Cl *CSHM* HP5...54 D5
Widmore Rd *UX/CGN* UB8...115 C1
Widnell La *RBICS/W* OX25...173 N3
Wieland Rd *HA6*...85 M7
Wigan's La *SKCH* HP14...185 M7
Wigginton Bottom
  TRING HP23...46 C2
Wiggles La *TRING* HP23...37 L3
Wigmore Ct *AYLW* HP19 *...167 R12
Wigmore Rd *AYLW* HP19...167 R12
Wigwell Gdns *RMKS/WB* MK17...151 K4
Wilberforce Ms *MDHD* SL6...108 A3
Wildacre Rd *SHEN* MK5...21 J2
Wildacres *NTHWD* HA6...85 L4
The Wilderness *BERK* HP4...48 B6
Wildgreen North
  DTCH/LGLY SL3...112 F8
Wildgreen South
  DTCH/LGLY SL3...112 F8
Wild Oaks Cl *NTHWD* HA6...85 L6
Wildwood *NTHWD* HA6...85 L4
Wilford Cl *NTHWD* HA6...85 J7
  WLLN MK15...18 F4
Wilford Rd *DTCH/LGLY* SL3...112 D8
Wilfrids Wood Cl
  FLKWH/TG HP10...89 G4
Wilkes Cft *SHEN* MK5...17 J7
Wilkins Rd *HYS/HAR* UB3...125 L1
Wilkinson Cl *HGDN/ICK* UB10...105 G6
Willant Cl *MDHD* SL6...117 L4
Willenhall Rd *HYS/HAR* UB3...115 K4
Willen La *GTLIN* MK14...14 C6
Willen Park Av *WLLN* MK15...14 E7
Willen Rd *MKV* MK10...19 J3
  NPAC MK16...15 G5
Willets Ri *SHEN* MK5...21 K1
Willetts La *DEN/HRF* UB9...103 L2
William Bandy Cl *LBUZ* LU7...28 A3
William Burt Cl
  RAYLNE/WEN HP22...43 L5
William Ellis Cl *WDSR* SL4...121 M8
William Harding Cl *AYLS* HP21...3 H7
William Hartley Yd
  DTCH/LGLY SL3 *...112 A1
William Hill Dr
  RAYLNE/WEN HP22...35 H2
William Moulder Ct *CSHM* HP5...55 J7
Williams Cir *WTR/OFPK* MK7...23 K2
Williams Cl *AYLW* HP19...2 E3
  RMKN MK19...131 L7
William Smith Cl *WLLN* MK15...18 F3
Williamson Wy
  RKW/CH/CXG WD3...83 M1
William St *BERK* HP4...48 C6
  SL SL1...111 L5
  WDSR SL4...121 J4
Williams Wy *PRRI* HP27...185 N8
Willis Rd *HADM* HP17...182 D1
Willoners *SLN* SL2...110 F2
Willoughby Rd *DTCH/LGLY* SL3...113 G7
Willoughby's Wk *HWYN* HP13...77 J4
Willoughby Wy *RNHPTN* NN7...126 A5
Willow Av *DEN/HRF* UB9...104 B4
  HWYW HP12...87 G2
  WDR/YW UB7...114 E4
Willow Bank *MLW* SL7...97 J1
Willowbank Ter *AYLS* HP21...3 H6
Willow Bank Wk *LBUZ* LU7...27 K6
Willowbrook
  RAYLNE/WEN HP22...44 A3
  RBICS/W OX25...173 J1
  WDSR SL4...111 J8
Willow Cha *CSHM* HP5...63 G1
  HAZ/HG HP15...68 D7
Willow Cl *CFSP/GDCR* SL9...92 D1
  DTCH/LGLY SL3...123 H3
  FLKWH/TG HP10...89 H4
  MDHD SL6...108 C1
  NPAC MK16...138 B6
Willow Ct *SKCH* HP14...67 H6
  WYM HP11...78 D6
Willow Crs East *DEN/HRF* UB9...104 B3
Willow Crs West *DEN/HRF* UB9...104 B3
Willow Dr *BIC* OX26...162 D1
  BUCK/WIN MK18...142 A11
  MDHD SL6...109 G8
Willow End *NTHWD* HA6...85 M6
  RAYLNE/WEN HP22...43 L4
Willowford *BDWL* MK13...17 H1
Willow Gdns *RSLP* HA4...95 L8
Willow Ga *RAYLW* HP18...175 Q8
Willow Gv *RMKN* MK19...137 G8
  RSLP HA4...95 L8
Willow Herb *AYLW* HP19...34 D2
Willow La *AMSS* HP7...71 L4
  STSTR MK11...137 R9
  WAR/TWY RG10...191 M10
  WATW WD18...75 M6
Willowmead *HADM* HP17...177 Q5
Willowmead Cl *MLW* SL7...97 L3
Willowmead Gdns *MLW* SL7...97 L3
Willowmead Rd *MLW* SL7...97 L3
Willowmead Sq *MLW* SL7...97 L3
Willow Pk *SLN* SL2...101 M5
Willow Pl *WDSR* SL4...121 H2
Willow Ri *HADM* HP17...176 D11
Willow Rd *AYLW* HP19...2 E3
  BRACKY NN13...8 E8
  CHNR OX39...184 F4
  DTCH/LGLY SL3...123 H3
  RBICS/W OX25...162 H10
  RMKS/WB MK17...151 L8
  THAME OX9...181 N5
Willows La *HHW* HP1...49 L5
Willows Ldg *RBICN* OX27...155 J3
Willow Springs *RBEDW* MK43...139 K6
Willows Rd *BNEND* SL8...89 G7
The Willows *AMS* HP6...63 G6
  BNEND SL8...89 G7
  DUN/WHIP LU6...170 G3
  HWYW HP12 *...4 C4

  PRRI HP27...183 P8
  RKW/CH/CXG WD3...83 M2
Willowtree Cl *HGDN/ICK* UB10...105 H1
Willow Wy *LBUZ* LU7...161 R7
  PRRI HP27...183 E11
  WEAT MK2...22 F7
  WYM HP11...79 G8
Willow Wood Cl *SL* SL1...100 A7
Willow Wren *GTLIN* MK14...14 B4
Wilmar Cl *UX/CGN* UB8...104 C5
  YEAD UB4...115 J1
Wilmin Gv *SHEN* MK5...17 L7
Wilmot Rd *SL* SL1...100 A8
Wilsley Pound *WTR/OFPK* MK7...19 L6
Wilson Av *HEN* RG9...190 H6
Wilson Ct *CNH/GTH/TMA* MK8...17 H7
Wilson Wy *RBICN* OX27...154 E11
Wilstone Br *TRING* HP23...37 J1
Wilton Av *HAZ/HG* HP15...22 D5
Wilton Crs *BEAC* HP9...80 D7
  WDSR SL4...120 C7
Wilton La *BEAC* HP9...81 J7
Wilton Rd *BEAC* HP9...80 D6
Wiltshire Av *SLN* SL2...111 H1
Wiltshire La *PIN* HA5...95 L2
Wiltshire Rd *MLW* SL7...97 L1
Wiltshire Wy *BTCHLY* MK3...22 B5
Wimbledon Pl *BDWL* MK13...6 C3
Wimblington Dr
  EAG/OLD/WTN MK6...22 D2
Wimborne Crs *EMV/FZ* MK4...21 J4
Wimpole Rd *WDR/YW* UB7...114 C5
Winbury Ct *MDHD* SL6...108 D3
Wincanton Hl *BTCHLY* MK3...21 M8
Winchbottom La *MLW* SL7...87 M5
Winchenden Rd *RAYLW* HP18...175 P6
Winchester Cir *MKV* MK10...19 L5
  DTCH/LGLY SL3...123 K4
Winchester Cl *AMSS* HP7...71 K2
Winchester Dr *MDHD* SL6...108 A7
Winchester Rd *HYS/HAR* UB3...125 K4
Winchester Wy
  RKW/CH/CXG WD3...75 G6
Winchfield Wy
  RKW/CH/CXG WD3...74 B8
Windermere Av *AYLS* HP21...35 G8
  RKW/CH/CXG WD3...73 J6
Windermere Dr *WEAT* MK2...153 Q1
Windermere Gdns *LBUZ* LU7...26 D7
Windermere Wy *SL* SL1...110 B2
  WDR/YW UB7...114 D5
Winding Shot *HHW* HP1...49 M6
Windle *BIC* OX26...162 B4
Windmill Av *BIC* OX26...162 D2
Windmill Cl *AYLW* HP19...2 A6
  BUCK/WIN MK18...142 A9
  LBUZ LU7...170 A9
  THAME OX9...182 B7
  WDSR SL4...121 G5
Windmill Dr *HAZ/HG* HP15...68 A4
  RKW/CH/CXG WD3...74 E7
Windmill Hl *AMSS* HP7...70 E8
  KGLGY WD4...8 A4
  PRRI HP27...58 A4
  RSLP HA4...95 L6
Windmill Hill Dr *BTCHLY* MK3...21 M7
Windmill La *HAZ/HG* HP15...68 E3
Windmill Pth *LBUZ* LU7 *...27 H7
Windmill Rd *CFSP/GDCR* SL9...82 C7
  DTCH/LGLY SL3...102 C3
  HADM HP17...176 C12
  MDHD SL6...98 D4
  SL SL1...111 J5
  THAME OX9...181 N7
Windmill St *RAYLW* HP18...174 B1
Windmill Wy *RBEDW* MK43...139 M3
  RSLP HA4...95 L7
  TRING HP23...37 L6
Windmill Wd *AMS* HP6...62 F8
Windrush Av *DTCH/LGLY* SL3...113 G7
Windrush Cl *BIC* OX26...162 C5
  HGDN/ICK UB10...104 E2
  WLLN MK15...14 D8
Windrush Ct *HWYN* HP13...78 E4
Windrush Dr *HWYN* HP13...78 E4
Windrush Wy *MDHD* SL6 *...108 E2
  DTCH/LGLY SL3...102 F2
Windsor Av *HGDN/ICK* UB10...105 G5
  LBUZ LU7...27 G7
  NPAC MK16...14 F2
Windsor Br *WDSR* SL4...121 J3
Windsor Cl *HHS/BOV* HP3...56 F7
  NTHWD HA6...95 M1
  SL SL1 *...110 B1
Windsor Ct *AMS* HP6 *...71 J1
  HWYN HP13...78 C1
Windsor Dr *BRACKY* NN13...8 D6
Windsor End *BEAC* HP9...90 E2
Windsor Gdns *HYS/HAR* UB3...115 J7
Windsor Hl *FLKWH/TG* HP10...89 K5
  PRRI HP27...58 B1
Windsor La *GTMIS/PWD* HP16...60 F8
  SL SL1...110 B1
Windsor Park Rd
  HYS/HAR UB3...125 L3
Windsor Rd *AYLS* HP21...3 M8
  CFSP/GDCR SL9...92 B7
  CSHM HP5...55 C7
  LBUZ LU7...169 P11
  MDHD SL6...109 G8
  SL SL1...111 K7
  WDSR SL4...119 L2
Windsor St *UX/CGN* UB8...104 B6
  WEAT MK2...22 H6
  WOLV MK12...12 F8
Windsor Wy
  RKW/CH/CXG WD3...83 M1
Winemar Cl *HWYN* MK11...131 M7
Winfold La *EMV/FZ* MK4...21 L5
Wingate Av *HWYN* HP13...78 D3
Wingate Cir *WTR/OFPK* MK7...23 K2
Wingate Cl *HWYN* HP13...78 D3
Wingate Wk *AYL* HP20...3 M5
Wing Cl *MLW* SL7...97 H5
Wingfield Gv *WATW* WD18 *...75 J7
Wingfield Gv *MKV* MK10...19 K4
Wingrave Cross Roads
  RAYLNE/WEN HP22...33 L2
Wingrave Rd
  RAYLNE/WEN HP22...33 J2
  TRING HP23...38 A5
Wing Rd *LBUZ* LU7...161 Q9
Winkers Cl *CFSP/GDCR* SL9...82 E8
Winkers La *CFSP/GDCR* SL9...82 E8
Winnock Rd *WDR/YW* UB7...113 N1
Winsford Hl *EMV/FZ* MK4...22 B3
Winslow Cl *GTMIS/PWD* HP16...60 E2
  HWYW HP12...4 D3
Winslow Gdns *HWYN* HP13...78 F3
Winslow Rd *BUCK/WIN* MK18...159 J2
  RAYLNE/WEN HP22...33 M2
  RMKS/WB MK17...151 M10
Winstanley Wy *WYM* HP11 *...4 E6
Winstanley La *SHEN* MK5...21 M2

Winston Cl *LBUZ* LU7...27 H5
Winston Ct *MDHD* SL6...108 A2
Winston Crs *BRACKY* NN13...8 E8
Winstone Cl *AMS* HP6...63 G5
Winston Gdns *BERK* HP4...47 L6
Winterburn *BDWL* MK13...17 L1
Winter Hl *MDHD* SL6...98 A2
Winter Hill Rd *MDHD* SL6...107 M4
Winters Wy *HYS/HAR* HP15...69 J3
Winterton Dr *AYLS* HP21...42 D2
Winton Gn *MLW* SL7...96 C8
Winton Crs *RKW/CH/CXG* WD3...75 H6
Winton Dr *RKW/CH/CXG* WD3...75 H6
Winvale *SL* SL1...111 K7
Winwood *SLN* SL2...112 B3
Winwood Cl *RMKN* MK19...137 M9
Winwood Dr
  RAYLNE/WEN HP22...166 D1
Wise Crs *RBICN* OX27...154 H4
Wise La *WDR/YW* UB7...114 C8
Wisewood Rd *EMV/FZ* MK4...21 G2
Wishart Gn *WTR/OFPK* MK7...144 H3
Wisley Av *BDWL* MK13...6 D3
Wistmans *EMV/FZ* MK4...22 A2
Witan Ct *CMK* MK9...6 D5
Witan Ga *CMK* MK9...6 D5
Witan Ga West *CMK* MK9...6 D6
Witchell *RAYLNE/WEN* HP22...44 A6
Witham Cl *AYLS* HP21...42 B2
Witheridge La
  FLKWH/TG HP10...79 L3
Withey Cl *WDSR* SL4...120 D3
Withington *BDWL* MK13...17 K1
Withington Rd *BIC* OX26...162 E4
Withycombe *EMV/FZ* MK4...22 B3
Withycroft *DTCH/LGLY* SL3...112 D3
Withy La *RSLP* HA4...95 H4
Witney La *HGDN/ICK* UB10...104 E2
Wittington Gn *MLW* SL7...96 C8
Wittmills Oak *BUCK/WIN* MK18...11 M5
Wivelsfield *DUN/WHIP* LU6...30 F8
Woad La *GTLIN* MK14...14 B6
Woburn Av *WOLV* MK12...12 H8
Woburn La *RMKS/WB* MK17...144 H7
Woburn Pl *LBUZ* LU7...27 H5
Woburn Rd *LBUZ* LU7...25 H8
  RMKS/WB MK17...144 B12
Woburn Sands Rd
  RMKS/WB MK17...144 A8
Wodhams Dr *BRACKY* NN13...8 D5
Wolf La *WDSR* SL4...120 C6
Wolfscote La *EMV/FZ* MK4...21 L3
Wolsey Gdns *BDWL* MK13...17 K2
Wolsey Rd *NTHWD* HA6...85 H2
Wolstan Cl *DEN/HRF* UB9...103 H1
Wolston Meadow *MKV* MK10...19 J3
Wolverton Rd *GTLIN* MK14...14 A5
  RMKN MK19...13 G4
  STSTR MK11...16 B1
  WOLV MK12...13 H6
Wooburn Cl *UX/CGN* UB8...115 G4
Wooburn Common Rd *SL2*...90 A8
Wooburn Gra *FLKWH/TG* HP10...89 J7
Wooburn Green La *BEAC* HP9...89 M3
Wooburn Manor Pk
  FLKWH/TG HP10...89 K5
Wooburn Md *FLKWH/TG* HP10...89 K4
Wooburn Ms *FLKWH/TG* HP10...89 K5
Wooburn Town
  FLKWH/TG HP10...89 J6
Woodall St *MKV* MK10...19 G3
Woodbank *PRRI* HP27...66 B1
  RKW/CH/CXG WD3...74 B7
Woodbank Av *CFSP/GDCR* SL9...92 C5
Woodbank Dr *CSTG* HP8...82 C3
Woodbine *PRRI* HP27...183 P9
Woodchester Pk *BEAC* HP9...80 B4
Wood Cl *WDSR* SL4...121 H7
Woodcock Av *SKCH* HP14...67 G6
Woodcock Hl
  RKW/CH/CXG WD3...84 D5
Woodcote *MDHD* SL6...108 C4
Woodcote Gn *HWYN* HP13...77 J4
Woodcote Rd *RBICN* OX27...154 F11
Woodcroft Crs
  HGDN/ICK UB10...105 G6
Woodcroft Rd *CSHM* HP5...55 J7
Wood End *HYS/HAR* UB3...115 K3
  RMKS/WB MK17...151 P4
  RMKS/WB MK17...143 R10
Wood End Cl *SLN* SL2...101 J1
Wood End Gn *YEAD* UB4...115 L2
Wood End Green Rd
  HYS/HAR UB3...115 J2
Wood End La *NPAC* MK16...138 D5
Woodfield *PRRI* HP27...58 C8
Woodfield Av *NTHWD* HA6...85 M8
Woodfield Dr *MDHD* SL6...107 M8
Woodfield Pk *AMS* HP6...63 G8
Woodfield Rd *BIC* OX26...162 D3
  PRRI HP27...58 B3
Woodford Cl *AYLW* HP19...177 R3
Woodford Wy *SLN* SL2...100 F4
Woodgate Crs *NTHWD* HA6...85 M6
Woodgate Ms *WAT* WD17...75 M2
Woodgate Rd *MKV* MK10...19 G6
Woodhall Cl *UX/CGN* UB8...104 C5
Woodhill Av *CFSP/GDCR* SL9...92 E5
Woodhouse Ct *HYS/HAR* UB3...115 K7
Woodhouse Ct *GTLIN* MK14...13 M8
Woodhouse Eaves
  NTHWD HA6...85 M5
Woodhurst Dr *DEN/HRF* UB9...93 L4
Woodhurst North *MDHD* SL6 *...109 H1
Woodhurst Rd *MDHD* SL6...109 G1
Woodhurst South *MDHD* SL6 *...109 H1
Woodland Av *LBUZ* LU7...27 G4
  SL SL1...111 J4
  WDSR SL4...120 D4
Woodland Cl *HGDN/ICK* UB10...95 G8
  HWYW HP12...77 H8
  MLW SL7...97 L3
  TRING HP23...37 L8
Woodland Dr *WAT* WD17...75 L2
Woodland Gld *SLN* SL2...100 F4
Woodland Gra *DTCH/LGLY* SL3...113 G7
Woodland La
  RKW/CH/CXG WD3...73 J4
Woodland Ri *DUN/WHIP* LU6...171 Q7
Woodland Rd
  RKW/CH/CXG WD3...83 J5
Woodlands *CFSP/GDCR* SL9...92 F5
  HADM HP17...176 D12
Woodlands Av *BERK* HP4...48 C7
Woodlands Cl *BUCK/WIN* MK18...11 L5
  CFSP/GDCR SL9...92 F5
  HAZ/HG HP15...69 H4
  TRING HP23...37 L8
Woodlands Crs
  BUCK/WIN MK18...11 L5
Woodlands Dr *BEAC* HP9...80 B6
  SKCH HP14...67 H7

Woodlands Gld *BEAC* HP9...80 B6
Woodlands Hl *BEAC* HP9...90 D5
Woodlands Park Av
  MDHD SL6...117 M4
Woodlands Park Rd
  MDHD SL6...117 M4
Woodlands Rd *HEN* RG9...190 H10
  FLKWH/TG HP10...68 E7
The Woodlands *AMS* HP6...63 H6
  FLKWH/TG HP10...68 E7
Woodland Vw *CSHM* HP5...63 J4
  PRRI HP27...67 G2
  WOLV MK12...17 C1
Woodland Wy *MLW* SL7...97 K2
  RMKS/WB MK17...144 K2
  GTLIN MK14...14 B7
Woodlane Cl *FLKWH/TG* HP10...88 E1
Woodlane Gdns
  FLKWH/TG HP10...88 E1
Woodlea Gv *NTHWD* HA6...85 H8
Woodley Cl *AMSS* HP7...71 J2
Woodley Headland
  EAG/OLD/WTN MK6...18 F7
Woodley Hl *CSHM* HP5...63 J5
Woodman Cl *LBUZ* LU7...28 A3
  LBUZ LU7...27 J7
Woodmans Cl *RMKN* MK19...137 M10
Woodmans Cft *AYLW* HP19...177 R2
Woodmoor End *MDHD* SL6...99 G3
Woodpecker Cl *BIC* OX26...162 F5
  BRACKY NN13...8 C5
Woodperry Rd *HEAD* OX3...178 A4
Woodpery Hl *WHLY* OX33...178 C4
Woodpiece Rd *RBICS/W* OX25...173 K4
Wood Pond Cl *BEAC* HP9...81 H6
Woodridge Wy *NTHWD* HA6...85 K6
Wood Ri *PIN* HA5...95 M4
Wood Rd *RBEDW* MK43...139 L8
Woodrow Av *YEAD* UB4...115 L2
Woodruff Av *GTLIN* MK14...6 E1
Woodruff Cl *BIC* OX26...162 C1
Woodrush Cl
  EAG/OLD/WTN MK6...22 E2
Woods Ct *BRACKY* NN13...8 C7
Woodshots Meadow
  WD18...75 J6
Woodside *DUN/WHIP* LU6...30 F8
  FLKWH/TG HP10...89 H4
  RMKS/WB MK17...144 G6
  STSTR MK11...12 B8
Woodside Av *AMS* HP6...63 J7
  BEAC HP9...80 B7
  MLW SL7...97 J1
  NTHWD HA6...85 J8
Woodside Cl *BEAC* HP9...80 B7
  CFSP/GDCR SL9...82 B8
  RSLP HA4...95 J5
  WYM HP11...79 G8
Woodside Hl *CFSP/GDCR* SL9...92 B7
Woodside Rd *AMS* HP6...63 J8
  BEAC HP9...80 A7
  HWYN HP13...85 L7
  NTHWD HA6...85 J8
Woodside Wk *AMS* HP6 *...63 J8
Woodside Wy *LBUZ* LU7...26 E8
Woods La *TOW* NN12...137 M3
Woods Pl *RAYLNE/WEN* HP22 *...37 M7
  TRING HP23...37 M7
Woodspring Ct *MKV* MK10...19 J3
The Woods *HGDN/ICK* UB10...105 G2
  NTHWD HA6...85 M5
Woodstock Av *DTCH/LGLY* SL3...112 C8
  MDHD SL6...108 A3
Woodstock Ct *BDWL* MK13...13 L7
Woodstock Dr *HGDN/ICK* UB10...104 D2
Woodstock Gdns *UB4*...115 L2
Woodstock Rd *AYLS* HP21...35 G8
  BDWL MK13...13 J7
  RAYLW HP18...166 D7
  RMKS/WB MK17...144 K2
The Wood *LBUZ* LU7...27 H6
Woodview *SLN* SL2 *...100 F4
Woodview Cl *HWYW* HP12...77 C4
Woodway Dr *PRRI* HP27...67 H1
Woodville *CHNR* OX39...184 F4
Woodville Court Ms
  WAT WD17...75 M3
Woodville Crs *TOW* NN12...130 F12
Woodville Gdns *RSLP* HA4...95 H6
Woodward Pl
  CNH/GTH/TMA MK8...17 K5
Wood Wy *BEAC* HP9...89 L1
Woodway *PRRI* HP27...58 A6
Woodways *HADM* HP17...176 D12
Woodwicks *RKW/CH/CXG* WD3...83 J5
Woolacombe Wy
  HYS/HAR UB3...115 K8
Woollerton Crs
  RAYLNE/WEN HP22...44 B5
Woolley Firs *MDHD* SL6...117 K1
Woolmans *STSTR* MK11...16 B1
Wooster Rd *BEAC* HP9...80 A6
Wootton Ct *BDWL* MK13...13 J6
Wootton Dr *FLKWH/TG* HP10...89 K2
Wootton La *HADM* HP17...176 H9
Wootton Wy *MDHD* SL6...108 B4
Wootton Rd *HEN* RG9...190 H6
Worcester Cl *RAYLNE/WEN* HP22...36 D5
Worcester Gdns *SL* SL1...111 J4
Worcester Rd *UX/CGN* UB8...114 B2
Wordsworth Av *NPAC* MK16...14 C1
Wordsworth Cl *BIC* OX26...162 B2
  BRACKY NN13...8 E5
Wordsworth Dr *BTCHLY* MK3...22 C7
Wordsworth Rd *SLN* SL2...110 C1
  WYM HP11...4 F9
Wordsworth Wy
  WDR/YW UB7...114 C8
World's End La
  RAYLNE/WEN HP22...43 L6
Worley Pl *BEAC* HP9...81 J5
Worminghall Rd *RAYLW* HP18...180 A3
  RAYLW HP18...179 Q4
Wormsley Crs *SKCH* HP14...186 F2
Wornal Pk *RAYLW* HP18...179 P7
Worrelle Av *MKV* MK10...19 J3
Worster Rd *MDHD* SL6...98 D4
Worth Ct *MKV* MK10...19 L5
Wotton Pk *RAYLW* HP18...164 D7
Wotton Rd *RAYLW* HP18...175 M1
Wraxall Wy
  EAG/OLD/WTN MK6...23 G1
Wray Ct *MKV* MK10...19 K4
Wraysbury Dr *WDR/YW* UB7...114 C4
Wrays Wy *YEAD* UB4...115 K2

Wren Cl *BRACKY* NN13...8 C5
  MDHD SL6...142 A11
Wren Dr *WDR/YW* UB7...114 C6
Wren Rd *GTMIS/PWD* HP16...60 B5
Wrensfield *HHW* HP1...49 M7
Wren's Wk *SL* SL1...97 H5
Wrens Pk *MKV* MK10...19 K4
Wren V *HWYN* MK13...5 C4
Wren Wk *DUN/WHIP* LU6...170 F2
Wretchwick Wy *BIC* OX26...162 G7
Wright *WDSR* SL4...120 B6
Wrights Cl *SKCH* HP14...86 A1
Wright's La *GTMIS/PWD* HP16...60 F3
Wrights Yd *GTMIS/PWD* HP16...60 F3
Wyatt Cl *HWYN* HP13...4 F3
  YEAD UB4...115 M2
Wyatt Rd *WDSR* SL4...120 D3
Wyatt's Cl *RKW/CH/CXG* WD3...73 M4
Wyatt's Cl *RKW/CH/CXG* WD3...73 M4
Wychwood *GTMIS/PWD* HP16...61 G6
Wychwood Gdns *HWYW* HP12...87 F1
Wychwood Ri
  GTMIS/PWD HP16...60 F6
Wychwood Wy *NTHWD* HA6...85 L7
Wycombe Abbey *WYM* HP11 *...5 K9
Wycombe Cl *AYLS* HP21...43 G2
Wycombe End *BEAC* HP9...90 C2
Wycombe La *FLKWH/TG* HP10...89 K3
Wycombe Rd
  GTMIS/PWD HP16...60 B5
  HAZ/HG HP15...69 G4
  MLW SL7...87 K7
  PRRI HP27...183 R12
  SKCH HP14...187 J2
Wycombe Vw *FLKWH/TG* HP10...78 E3
Wye Cl *AYLS* HP21...42 B1
  BIC OX26...162 A3
  BTCHLY MK3...22 B5
  RSLP HA4...95 H5
Wye Gdns *HWYW* HP12...4 B3
Wye Rd *FLKWH/TG* HP10...89 J2
Wyevale Cl *MDHD* SL6...95 M2
Wykeham Cl *WDR/YW* UB7...124 F2
Wykeham Ga *HADM* HP17...182 C1
Wykeham Pk *THAME* OX9...181 P6
Wykeham Ri *CHNR* OX39...184 C4
Wykeham Wy *HADM* HP17...176 C12
Wykeridge Cl *CSHM* HP5...55 G6
Wylands Rd *DTCH/LGLY* SL3...122 F1
Wylchin Cl *PIN* HA5...95 J3
Wylie End *BDWL* MK13...13 K7
Wymering Rd *AYLS* HP21...35 H8
Wymers Cl *SL* SL1...100 A7
Wymers Wood Rd *SL* SL1...99 M6
Wymondham *MKV* MK10...19 L5
Wynbury Dr *HWYN* HP13...78 D1
Wyndale Cl *HEN* RG9...190 H6
Wyndham Av *HWYN* HP13...77 L4
Wyndham Crs *SL* SL1...100 A7
Wyness Av *RMKS/WB* MK17...24 E1
Wynford Gn *AYLS* HP21...42 E1
Wyngates *LBUZ* LU7...26 F8
Wyngrave Pl *BEAC* HP9...80 B5
Wynn Gv *HAZ/HG* HP15...69 G7
Wynnstay Gdns *MLW* SL7...97 K1
Wynnswick Rd *BEAC* HP9...81 H5
Wynyard Ct
  EAG/OLD/WTN MK6...18 B7
Wyre Cl *HADM* HP17...182 D1
Wyre Gv *HYS/HAR* UB3...115 M8
Wyteleaf Cl *RSLP* HA4...95 H5
Wyvern Wy *UX/CGN* UB8...104 A6

Y

Yalts Brow *EMV/FZ* MK4...21 L4
Yardley Av *LBUZ* LU7...169 P10
Yardley Gn *AYL* HP20...3 H2
Yardley Rd *OLN* MK46...128 A8
  RMKN MK19...137 R4
  TOW NN12...137 M2
Yarmouth Rd *SL* SL1...111 H3
Yarrow Pl *GTLIN* MK14...18 B2
Yarrowside *AMSS* HP7...72 A3
Yeates Cl *THAME* OX9...181 N5
Yeats Cl *NPAC* MK16...14 C1
Ye Meads *MDHD* SL6...109 L5
Yeomans Acre *RSLP* HA4...95 M5
Yeomans Cl *BRACKY* NN13...8 B2
Yeomans Dr *GTLIN* MK14...14 D6
Yeovil Rd *SL* SL1...110 D2
Yew Cl *BIC* OX26...162 D1
Yew Tree Cl *BEAC* HP9...90 E1
  CSHM HP5...55 J7
  DUN/WHIP LU6...170 G1
Yewtree Cl *LBUZ* LU7...169 R9
Yew Tree Cl *MDHD* SL6...108 C1
  RAYLNE/WEN HP22...42 F5
  RMKS/WB MK17...152 H3
Yew Tree Dr *HAZ/HG* HP15...68 E4
  HHS/BOV HP3...57 G7
Yew Tree Rd *DTCH/LGLY* SL3...111 M7
  HGDN/ICK UB10...104 E6
Yolsum Cl *HADM* HP17...176 B12
Yonder Slade *BUCK/WIN* MK18...11 L4
York Av *HYS/HAR* UB3...115 H3
  SL SL1...111 J3
  WDSR SL4...121 G5
York Cl *BIC* OX26...162 F3
York Dr *BRACKY* NN13...8 D5
Yorke Cl *RAYLNE/WEN* HP22...36 D5
Yorke Ga *WAT* WD17...75 M3
York Pl *RKW/CH/CXG* WD3...3 G8
York Rd *HEN* RG9...190 G4
  MDHD SL6...108 E4
  MLW SL7...97 J4
  NTHWD HA6...95 M1
  STSTR MK11...16 A1
  UX/CGN UB8...104 C5
  WDSR SL4...121 G5
York Wy *HWYW* HP12...87 K2
Youens Dr *THAME* OX9...181 P7
Youens Rd *HWYW* HP12...87 H1
Young Cl *AYLS* HP21...3 L9
Youngfield Rd *HHW* HP1...49 L6
Youngman Pl
  EAG/OLD/WTN MK6...18 C8

Z

Zealand Av *WDR/YW* UB7...124 C3

Abbey Hill Golf Club
CNH/GTH/TMA MK8......**17** G4
Abbey Lodge Hotel
HWYW HP13......**5** J5
Abbeys Combined School
BTCHLY MK3......**22** D4
Abbotsfield School
HGDN/ICK UB10......**105** G7
Aberglen Industrial Estate
HYS/HAR UB3......**115** J6
Abingdon & Witney College (Warren Farm Centre)
WHLY OX33......**173** J10
Acorn Business Centre
LBUZ LU7......**161** L8
Acorn Medical Centre
HGDN/ICK UB10......**104** F6
ACS Hillingdon International School
HGDN/ICK UB10......**104** E6
Adler Industrial Estate
HYS/HAR UB3......**115** J6
Airbase Unity Elementary School
RSLP HA4......**95** H8
Airbus Coach Station
HTHAIR TW6......**124** E6
Airport Gate Business Centre
WDR/YW UB7......**124** E3
Akeley Wood Junior School
RMKN MK19......**142** H1
Akeley Wood Lower School
BUCK/WIN MK18......**141** P10
Akeman Business Park
TRING HP23......**37** J3
Aldbury Primary School
TRING HP23......**39** K4
Alexander First School
WDSR SL4......**120** B6
Alexandra Hotel
WYM HP11......**5** J4
Alfriston Special School
BEAC HP9......**80** A7
All Saints CE Controlled Junior School
MDHD SL6......**108** A8
All Saints Cemetery
MDHD SL6......**108** A8
Alton Business Park
AYLW HP19......**2** A3
Altwood CE School
MDHD SL6......**108** A5
Alwyn Infant School
MDHD SL6......**108** A4
Ambassador Court Hotel
HWYW HP12......**4** D4
Amersham ⊖
AMS HP6......**71** H1
Amersham & Chiltern RFC
AMS HP6......**62** F7
Amersham General Hospital
AMS HP7......**70** F4
Amersham Hill CC
AMS HP6......**71** K1
The Amersham School
AMSS HP7......**71** K3
Amersham Town FC
AMSS HP7......**70** F2
Amersham & Wycombe College
AMSS HP7......**71** L2
CSHM HP5......**55** J6
FLKWH/TG HP10......**78** D8
HWYW HP12......**87** J1
Aqua Vale Swimming & Fitness Centre
AYL HP20......**3** J5
Arbour Vale Special School Sports College
SLN SL2......**111** M3
Argent Centre Industrial Estate
HYS/HAR UB3......**115** M6
Army Medical Centre
RBICS/W OX25......**162** H10
Arnett Hills Primary School
RKW/CH/CXG WD3......**73** M7
The Arts Educational School
TRING HP23......**38** A7
Ascott House (NT)
LBUZ LU7......**28** B4
Ashbrook School
CNH/GTH/TMA MK8......**17** G5
Asheridge Road Industrial Estate
CSHM HP5......**54** F8
Ashfold School
RAYLW HP18......**174** C1
Ash Hill Primary School
HWYW HP13......**79** G3
Ashlyns School
BERK HP4......**48** B8
Ashmead Combined School
AYLS HP21......**42** B1
Ashridge Estate (NT)
BERK HP4......**39** K4
Ashridge Estate Visitor Centre
BERK HP4......**39** K4
Ashridge Golf Club
BERK HP4......**40** A3
Ashridge Management College
BERK HP4......**40** B5
Ashton CE Primary School
RNHPTN NN7......**130** E1
Aspect Park Golf Centre
HEN RG9......**191** N5
Asplands Medical Centre
RMKS/WB MK17......**144** E6
Aspley Guise ≥
RMKS/WB MK17......**144** H4
Aspley Guise Lower School
RMKS/WB MK17......**145** J6
Aspley Guise & Woburn Sands Golf Club
RMKS/WB MK17......**144** G6
Aston Clinton School
RAYLNE/WEN HP22......**36** C5
Aston Rowant CE Primary School
WTLGN OX49......**184** B7
Aston Rowant CC
CHNR OX39......**184** B7
Aston Rowant National Nature Reserve
WTLGN OX49......**184** B12
Avant Business Centre
DBGH MK1......**22** E4
Avenue Medical Centre
SLN SL2......**100** F8
Avocet Trading Estate
WYM HP11......**4** E5
Avonbury Business Park
BIC OX26......**162** A2
Aylesbury ≥
AYLS HP21......**2** E7

Aylesbury Business Centre
AYLW HP19......**2** A3
Aylesbury Cemetery
AYLS HP21......**3** K7
Aylesbury College
AYLS HP21......**2** D7
Aylesbury & District Sports Club
AYLS HP21......**34** F8
Aylesbury Golf Centre
RAYLNE/WEN HP22......**35** J1
Aylesbury Grammar School
AYLS HP21......**3** J7
Aylesbury High School
AYLS HP21......**3** J7
Aylesbury Industrial Centre
AYLW HP19......**2** C3
Aylesbury RFC
RAYLNE/WEN HP22......**43** M3
Aylesbury United FC
AYL HP20......**34** C3
Aylesbury Vale Golf Club
LBUZ LU7......**161** M4
Aylesbury Vale Parkway ≥
RAYLW HP18......**167** N11
Aysgarth Medical Centre
AYLS HP21......**3** J7
BAA Heathrow Visitor Centre
HTHAIR TW6......**125** G4
Badgemore Park Golf Club
HEN RG9......**190** E3
Badgemore Primary School
HEN RG9......**190** F1
Barbara Batson Clinic
AYL HP20......**2** E4
Bardwell School
BIC OX26......**162** E2
Barley Hill Primary School
THAME OX9......**181** N5
Barn Hotel
RSLP HA4......**95** K8
Bayhurst Wood Country Park
DEN/HRF UB9......**94** E4
Baylis Business Centre
SL SL1......**111** J4
Baylis Court School
SL SL1......**111** J2
Beachampton Business Park
RMKN MK19......**143** R6
Beachborough School
BRACKY NN13......**147** M2
Beacon Hill Hill Fort
LBUZ LU7......**170** D8
The Beacon School
AMS HP6......**63** G6
Beaconsfield ≥
BEAC HP9......**80** D7
Beaconsfield CC
BEAC HP9......**90** E1
Beaconsfield Golf Club
BEAC HP9......**81** H8
Beaconsfield High School
BEAC HP9......**90** C1
Beaconsfield RFC
BEAC HP9......**90** E2
Beaconsfield School
BEAC HP9......**90** D1
Beaconsfield School of Lawn Tennis
BEAC HP9......**80** D7
Beaudesert Lower School
LBUZ LU7......**27** L6
The Beck Theatre
HYS/HAR UB3......**115** L3
The Bedford Arms Hotel
RKW/CH/CXG WD3......**73** G1
Bedgrove Health Centre
AYLS HP21......**35** G8
Bedgrove Junior School
AYLS HP21......**35** H8
Beechview Junior School
WYM HP11......**78** D5
Beechwood School
SLN SL2......**101** G8
Bekonscot Model Village & Railway
BEAC HP9......**80** C7
Bell Business Centre
MDHD SL6......**108** E4
Bell Business Park
AYLW HP19......**177** Q1
The Bell Hotel
RMKS/WB MK17......**145** J11
Bell Lane Combined School
AMS HP6......**72** A1
Belmont Medical Centre
UX/CGN UB8......**104** C5
Berber Business Centre
WYM HP11......**4** D5
Berkeley Clinic
RKW/CH/CXG WD3......**84** B1
Berkhamsted ≥
BERK HP4......**48** B5
Berkhamsted Castle (remains)
BERK HP4......**48** C5
Berkhamsted Collegiate Preparatory School
BERK HP4......**48** A6
Berkhamsted Collegiate School (Castle Campus)
BERK HP4......**48** B6
Berkhamsted FC
BERK HP4......**48** A5
Berkhamsted Golf Club
BERK HP4......**48** D3
Berkhamsted Health Centre
BERK HP4......**47** M5
Berkhamsted School House
BERK HP4......**48** B6
Berkhamsted Tennis Club
BERK HP4......**48** B5
Bernwood Forest Nature Reserve
WHLY OX33......**179** K3
Best Western Buckingham Hotel
BUCK/WIN MK18......**11** L8
Best Western Kings Hotel
SKCH HP14......**186** G1
Best Western Moore Place Hotel
RMKS/WB MK17......**144** H6
Best Western Watermill Hotel
HHW HP1......**57** H1
Best Western White House Hotel
WATW WD18......**75** M5
The Bharani Medical Centre
SL SL1......**110** C3
Bicester Airfield
RBICN OX27......**154** G12
Bicester Cemetery
BIC OX26......**162** D5

Bicester Community College
BIC OX26......**162** C4
Bicester Community Hospital
BIC OX26......**162** C5
Bicester Health Centre
BIC OX26......**162** D5
Bicester North ≥
BIC OX26......**162** E3
Bicester Outlet Shopping Village
BIC OX26......**162** D6
Bicester & Ploughley Sports Centre
BIC OX26......**162** C4
Bicester Sports Club
BIC OX26......**162** C5
Bicester Town ≥
BIC OX26......**162** D6
Bierton CE Combined School
RAYLNE/WEN HP22......**35** G3
Bigham's Park Farm
HHW HP1......**49** K2
Bird Hills Golf Club
MDHD SL6......**118** B8
Bird in Hand Country Inn Hotel
WAR/TWY RG10......**116** C3
Bisham Abbey National Sports Centre
MLW SL7......**97** J7
Bisham CE Primary School
MLW SL7......**97** J7
Bishophalt School
UX/CGN UB8......**104** E8
Bishop Parker RC Combined School
WEAT MK2......**22** F8
Bishop Ramsey CE School (Upper)
RSLP HA4......**95** M6
Bishop Ramsey CE School
RSLP HA4......**95** L6
Bishops Wood Hospital
NTHWD HA6......**85** G6
Bishop Winnington-Ingram CE Primary School
RSLP HA4......**95** J6
Bishop Wood School
TRING HP23......**37** M7
Blackberry Farm Animal Centre
RAYLNE/WEN HP22......**166** H4
Black Park Country Park
IVER SL0......**102** F7
Bledlow CC
PRRI HP27......**185** K1
Bledlow Ridge School
SKCH HP14......**185** Q10
Bletchley ≥
BTCHLY MK3......**22** E6
Bletchley Leisure Centre
WEAT MK2......**23** G5
Bletchley Park Museum
BTCHLY MK3......**22** E6
Blind Pond Industrial Estate
RMKS/WB MK17......**144** A8
Blue Lagoon Local Nature Reserve
WEAT MK2......**22** E8
Blue Max Museum
MLW SL7......**86** F4
Boarstall Duck Decoy (NT)
RAYLW HP18......**173** M7
Boatyard
WDSR SL4......**121** J2
The Bobsleigh Hotel
HHS/BOV HP3......**57** G5
Bon Secours Hospital
BEAC HP9......**80** E8
Booker Hill Combined School
HWYW HP12......**87** G1
Booker Park Community School
AYLS HP21......**42** D3
Bosch Broadwater Park Business Estate
DEN/HRF UB9......**93** M3
The Bossard Centre
LBUZ LU7......**27** H7
Botwell RC Primary School
HYS/HAR UB3......**115** L6
Bourbon Tower
BUCK/WIN MK18......**141** M10
Bourne End ≥
BNEND SL8......**88** F7
Bourne End Business Centre
BNEND SL8......**89** G7
Bourton Meadow School
BUCK/WIN MK18......**142** A10
Bovingdon Primary School
HHS/BOV HP3......**57** G6
Bow Brickhill ≥
WTR/OFPK MK7......**23** K4
Bow Brickhill First School
RMKS/WB MK17......**144** A8
Boxmoor Golf Club
HHS/BOV HP3......**57** K3
Boxmoor Primary School
HHW HP1......**49** M8
Boyne Hill CE Infant School
MDHD SL6......**108** C4
Boyn Valley Industrial Estate
MDHD SL6......**108** D4
Bracken Leas Primary School
BRACKY NN13......**8** C5
Brackley CE Junior School
BRACKY NN13......**8** D6
Brackley Cottage Hospital
BRACKY NN13......**8** E7
Brackley Recreation Centre
BRACKY NN13......**8** C5
Brackley RFC
BRACKY NN13......**8** C6
Brackley Road Cemetery
BUCK/WIN MK18......**11** K5
Brackley Swimming Pool
BRACKY NN13......**8** D7
Brackley Town FC
BRACKY NN13......**8** E8
Bradenham CC
SKCH HP14......**66** E8
Bradwell Priory (remains)
BDWL MK13......**17** J2
Bradwell Village School
BDWL MK13......**17** K2
Braywick Cemetery
MDHD SL6......**108** F6
Braywick Sports Centre
MDHD SL6......**108** F5
Braywood CE First School
WDSR SL4......**119** L5
Breakspear Crematorium
RSLP HA4......**95** H4
Breakspear Junior School
HGDN/ICK UB10......**94** F8

Brewers Hill Middle School
DUN/WHIP LU6......**31** M5
Bridgegate Business Park
AYLW HP19......**2** B3
Bridgewater Monument
BERK HP4......**39** K3
Bridgewater School
BERK HP4......**47** M4
The Brigidine School
WDSR SL4......**121** J6
Brill CE Combined School
RAYLW HP18......**174** C1
Brill Windmill
RAYLW HP18......**174** B1
Britannia Industrial Estate
DTCH/LGLY SL3......**123** K5
Britannia Industrial Park
HWYW HP12......**4** B5
Britwell Health Clinic
SLN SL2......**100** F8
Broadfields Retail Park
AYLW HP19......**177** R1
Broadwell Abbey Industrial Estate
BDWL MK13......**17** J3
Brook Business Centre
IVER SL0......**103** M7
Brook House FC
YEAD UB4......**105** L8
Brooklands Middle School
LBUZ LU7......**27** L8
Brookmead School
LBUZ LU7......**169** R9
Brookside Clinic
AYL HP20......**3** G7
Brookside Primary School
BIC OX26......**162** D4
Brooksward Combined School
GTLIN MK14......**14** C7
Broomstick Industrial Estate
DUN/WHIP LU6......**170** C7
Broughton Fields Combined School
MKV MK10......**19** L2
Broughton Fields Primary School
MKV MK10......**19** L3
Broughton Infant School
AYL HP20......**35** H6
Broughton Junior School
AYL HP20......**35** H6
Broughton Manor Business Park
MKV MK10......**19** L2
Brunel Bus Station
SL SL1......**111** L5
Brunel Shopping Centre
WEAT MK2......**22** E6
Brunel University
UX/CGN UB8......**104** D8
Brushwood Junior School
CSHM HP5......**55** K8
Buckingham Canal Nature Reserve
BUCK/WIN MK18......**142** F9
Buckingham Centre (Queens Hall)
BUCK/WIN MK18......**11** L5
Buckingham Community Hospital
BUCK/WIN MK18......**11** L5
Buckingham Golf Club
BUCK/WIN MK18......**11** G6
Buckingham Primary School
BUCK/WIN MK18......**11** M4
Buckingham Road Industrial Estate
BRACKY NN13......**8** F8
Buckingham RUFC
BUCK/WIN MK18......**11** M2
Buckingham School
BUCK/WIN MK18......**11** L7
Buckinghamshire County Museum
AYL HP20......**2** E5
Buckinghamshire Golf Club
DEN/HRF UB9......**94** B8
Buckinghamshire Railway Centre
RAYLNE/WEN HP22......**166** C4
Buckingham Town FC
BUCK/WIN MK18......**11** L6
Buckingham Villiers Hotel
BUCK/WIN MK18......**11** K6
Bucks Chilterns University College
CSTG HP8......**82** F2
WYM HP11......**5** H7
The Bucks Goat Centre
RAYLNE/WEN HP22......**42** F6
Bucks University College
HWYW HP13......**68** C7
Burchetts Green CE Infant School
MDHD SL6......**107** G7
Bure Park Primary School
BIC OX26......**162** C2
Burford School
MLW SL7......**97** H1
Burnham ≥
SL SL1......**110** D3
Burnham Abbey
MDHD SL6......**110** A5
Burnham Beeches Golf Club
SL SL1......**100** C5
Burnham Beeches Hotel
SL SL1......**100** C5
Burnham Beeches National Nature Reserve
SLN SL2......**100** F3
Burnham FC
SL SL1......**100** A8
Burnham Grammar School
SL SL1......**110** C1
Burnham Health Centre
SL SL1......**100** A8
Burnham Upper School
SL SL1......**110** A1
Bury Lawn School
GTLIN MK14......**14** A7
Bushfield School
WOLV MK12......**13** G8
The Business Village
SLN SL2......**112** A5
Butlers Court County First & Middle School
BEAC HP9......**90** D1
Byfleet Industrial Estate
WATW WD18......**85** H1
Cadmore End CE Combined School
SKCH HP14......**187** M8

Calcot Medical Centre
CFSP/GDCR SL9......**82** C8
Caldicott School
SLN SL2......**101** G5
California Industrial Estate
AYLS HP21......**2** F7
Calvert Jubilee Nature Reserve
BUCK/WIN MK18......**156** H3
Cambridge Close Retail Park
AYL HP20......**3** G3
Campanile Hotel
WEAT MK2......**23** H6
Camp Industrial Estate
THAME OX9......**180** C10
Capswood Business Centre
CFSP/GDCR SL9......**93** H7
Carlton VC Lower School
RBEDW MK43......**129** Q2
Caroline Haslett Combined School
SHEN MK5......**21** L2
The Carrington Infant School
FLKWH/TG HP10......**88** F1
Cassiobury J & I Schools
WAT WD17......**75** K2
Castlefield Foundation School
HWYW HP13......**77** H8
Castle Montessori School
BERK HP4......**48** C6
Castle Street Clinic
HWYN HP13......**5** J6
Castlethorpe First School
RMKN MK19......**131** L12
Castleview Combined School
DTCH/LGLY SL3......**112** C8
Cattle Market
TRING HP23......**38** A6
Caxton Trading Estate
HYS/HAR UB3......**115** K6
Cedar Park School
HAZ/HG HP15......**68** E5
Cedars Combined School
NPAG MK16......**15** G2
Cedars First School
HAZ/HG HP15......**68** E5
The Cedars Primary School
HEST TW5......**125** M3
The Cedars Upper School & Community College
LBUZ LU7......**28** F1
Centenary Business Park
HEN RG9......**191** J5
Central Bus Station
CMK MK9......**6** C7
Central Milton Keynes Medical Centre
CMK MK9......**6** E4
Central Park Business Centre
HWYN MK13......**5** C4
Chailey Industrial Estate
HYS/HAR UB3......**115** M6
Chalfont & Latimer ≥ ⊖
AMSS HP7......**72** B2
Chalfont Leisure Centre
CFSP/GDCR SL9......**82** B8
Chalfont St Giles Infant School
CSTG HP8......**82** A3
Chalfont St Giles Junior School
CSTG HP8......**82** A3
Chalfont St Peter FC
CFSP/GDCR SL9......**82** C7
Chalfont St Peter Infant School
CFSP/GDCR SL9......**82** B7
Chalfont St Peter Junior School
CFSP/GDCR SL9......**82** C7
The Chalfonts Community College
CFSP/GDCR SL9......**82** B7
Chalfonts & Gerrards Cross Health Clinic
CFSP/GDCR SL9......**82** C8
Chambers Business Park
WDR/YW UB7......**124** F2
Chantry School
WDR/YW UB7......**114** D3
Charmandean School
BUCK/WIN MK18......**141** N6
Charville Primary School
YEAD UB4......**105** K7
Chartridge Combined School
CSHM HP5......**54** B6
Chartridge Park Golf Club
CSHM HP5......**54** C7
Chater Infant School
WATW WD18......**75** M5
Chater Junior School
WATW WD18......**75** M5
Chaulden Infant School
HHW HP1......**49** K8
Chaulden Junior School
HHW HP1......**49** L8
Cheddington ≥
LBUZ LU7......**169** M4
Cheddington Combined School
LBUZ LU7......**169** M7
Chenies CC
RKW/CH/CXG WD3......**73** G1
Chenies Combined School
RKW/CH/CXG WD3......**72** F1
Chenies Manor House
RKW/CH/CXG WD3......**73** G1
Chepping View Primary School
HWYW HP12......**87** J3
Chequers Inn
BNEND SL8......**89** J8
Cherrycourt Way Industrial Estate
LBUZ LU7......**27** L8
Cherry Lane Primary School
WDR/YW UB7......**114** E8
Chesham ⊖
CSHM HP5......**63** H2
Chesham Bois CE Combined School
AMS HP6......**63** K6
Chesham Cemetery
CSHM HP5......**63** G1
Chesham Community Hospital
CSHM HP5......**63** H3
Chesham Health Centre
CSHM HP5......**63** G3
Chesham High School
CSHM HP5......**63** J1
Chesham Leisure Centre
CSHM HP5......**63** J2
Chesham & Ley Hill Golf Club
CSHM HP5......**64** B2
Chesham Park Community College
CSHM HP5......**62** F1
Chesham Preparatory School
CSHM HP5......**55** M6

Chesham United FC
 CSHM HP5 ....63 G4
Chestnut Combined School
 BTCHLY MK3 ....22 A7
Chestnut Lane First School
 AMS HP6 ....63 K7
Chicheley Hall
 NPAG MK16 ....134 A10
Child Welfare Clinic
 LBUZ LU7 ....27 G1
Chiltern Brewery
 HADM HP17 ....51 H1
Chiltern Business Village
 UX/CGN UB8 ....104 A7
Chiltern Forest Golf Club
 RAYLNE/WEN HP22 ....44 E3
Chiltern Gate Special School
 HWYW HP12 ....87 K2
The Chiltern Hospital
 GTMIS/PWD HP16 ....61 H6
Chiltern House Medical Centre
 HWYN HP13 ....5 H5
Chiltern Open Air Museum
 CSTG HP8 ....82 F2
The Chiltern Pools
 AMS HP6 ....71 J1
The Chilterns Crematorium
 AMSS HP7 ....70 E4
The Chilterns Shopping Centre
 HWYN HP13 ....5 H6
Chiltern Trading Estate
 HAZ/HG HP15 ....69 J8
 LBUZ LU7 ....29 H1
The Chimes Shopping Centre
 UX/CGN UB8 ....104 C5
Chinnor ≠
 CHNR OX39 ....184 G5
Chinnor & Princes Risborough
 Railway (Icknield Line)
 CHNR OX39 ....184 H6
Chinnor RFC
 THAME OX9 ....181 R5
Chorleywood ≠ ⊖
 RKW/CH/CXG WD3 ....73 H5
Chorleywood Golf Club
 RKW/CH/CXG WD3 ....73 H5
Chorleywood Health Centre
 RKW/CH/CXG WD3 ....73 H5
Chorleywood Lawn Cemetery
 RKW/CH/CXG WD3 ....73 L4
Chorleywood Primary School
 RKW/CH/CXG WD3 ....73 H7
Chorleywood Road Cemetery
 RKW/CH/CXG WD3 ....74 C1
Christ Church CE
 Primary School
 RKW/CH/CXG WD3 ....73 L5
Christ the Sower Ecumenical
 Primary School
 CNH/GTH/TMA MK8 ....21 G1
Churchmead School CE
 (VA) School
 DTCH/LGLY SL3 ....122 A4
Church of Christ
 the Cornerstone
 CMK MK9 ....6 F4
Church Wood RSPB Reserve
 SLN SL2 ....91 K7
Cineworld
 CMK MK9 ....7 J4
 SL SL1 ....111 L6
 WYM HP11 ....5 G6
Cippenham Infants School
 SL SL1 ....110 C4
Cippenham Junior School
 SL SL1 ....110 C4
Cippenham Medical Centre
 SL SL1 ....110 F5
City Square
 CMK MK9 ....6 F4
Claires Court School
 MDHD SL6 ....117 K1
Claremont Surgery
 MDHD SL6 ....108 E3
Claycots Primary School
 SLN SL2 ....110 F1
Claydon House (NT)
 BUCK/WIN MK18 ....157 Q3
Claytons Combined School
 BNEND SL8 ....88 E5
Clewer Green CE First School
 WDSR SL4 ....120 E6
Clifton Business Park
 AYLW HP19 ....177 R1
Clipstone Brook
 Industrial Estate
 LBUZ LU7 ....27 M7
Clipstone Brook Lower School
 LBUZ LU7 ....27 J7
Cliveden Hotel
 MDHD SL6 ....99 K3
Cliveden (NT)
 MDHD SL6 ....99 K4
Coach Museum
 WDSR SL4 ....121 K4
Cold Harbour CE
 Combined School
 EMV/FZ MK4 ....22 C3
Colehill CC
 AMSS HP7 ....70 F6
Coleshill CE First School
 AMSS HP7 ....70 E7
Colham Manor
 Primary School
 UX/CGN UB8 ....114 F3
College Lake Wildlife Centre
 TRING HP23 ....38 B1
Colnbrook CE Primary School
 DTCH/LGLY SL3 ....123 J4
Colnbrook Sports Club
 DTCH/LGLY SL3 ....123 L4
Coln Industrial Estate
 DTCH/LGLY SL3 ....123 L4
Combermere Barracks
 WDSR SL4 ....121 G6
Comfort Inn
 HYS/HAR UB3 ....125 K1
Commerce Way
 Industrial Estate
 LBUZ LU7 ....27 M8
Commonwealth War
 Graves Commission
 MDHD SL6 ....108 E3
Compass Theatre
 HGDN/ICK UB10 ....105 H1
Compleat Angler Hotel
 MLW SL7 ....97 K5
Control Tower
 HTHAIR TW6 ....125 G6
Convent of St John the Baptist
 WDSR SL4 ....120 F5
Cookham ≠
 MDHD SL6 ....98 E3

Cookham Dean CE
 Primary School
 MDHD SL6 ....98 A3
Cookham Reach Sailing Club
 MDHD SL6 ....98 F2
Cookham Rise Primary School
 MDHD SL6 ....98 D4
The Cooper School
 BIC OX26 ....162 E2
Copthorne Hotel
 SL SL1 ....111 H6
Corinium Industrial Estate
 AMS HP6 ....71 L1
Corinthian Arch
 BUCK/WIN MK18 ....11 L1
Cosgrove Leisure Park
 RMKN MK19 ....12 D4
Cosgrove Primary School
 RMKN MK19 ....12 B4
Coteford Infant School
 PIN HA5 ....95 M4
The Cottesloe School
 LBUZ LU7 ....161 Q9
Court Garden Leisure Centre
 MLW SL7 ....97 J5
Courthouse Junior School
 MDHD SL6 ....108 A2
Court Industrial Park
 DBGH MK1 ....22 E4
Courtyard by Marriott Hotel
 SL SL1 ....111 H6
Cowley Business Park
 UX/CGN UB8 ....114 C4
Cowley Mill Industrial Estate
 IVER SL0 ....103 M7
Cowley St Laurence CE
 Primary School
 UX/CGN UB8 ....114 B2
Cowper & Newton Museum
 OLN MK46 ....128 C11
Cox Green School
 MDHD SL6 ....117 M2
Cranfield Airfield
 RBEDW MK43 ....139 J5
Cranfield Cemetery
 RBEDW MK43 ....139 L5
Cranfield Lower School
 RBEDW MK43 ....139 L5
Cranfield Technology Park
 RBEDW MK43 ....138 G6
Cranfield University
 RBEDW MK43 ....138 H5
Cranford Infant School
 HSLWW TW4 ....125 M5
Cranford Park Junior School
 HYS/HAR UB3 ....115 L8
Cranford Park Primary School
 HYS/HAR UB3 ....115 L6
Cracies Hill CE Primary School
 WAR/TWY RG10 ....191 Q8
CR Bates Industrial Estate
 SKCH HP14 ....186 H1
Crendon Industrial Estate
 RAYLW HP18 ....181 M1
Cressex Business Park
 HWYW HP12 ....87 J2
The Cressex Community School
 HWYW HP12 ....87 H3
Cressex Industrial Estate
 HWYW HP12 ....87 K1
Cromwell Business Centre
 NPAG MK16 ....15 J3
Crown Business Centre
 WDR/YW UB7 ....114 C6
Crown Business Estate
 CSHM HP5 ....63 H1
Crownhill Crematorium
 CNH/GTH/TMA MK8 ....17 H6
The Crown Hotel
 AMSS HP7 ....71 G3
Crown House School
 WYM HP11 ....5 J8
Crown Trading Centre
 HYS/HAR UB3 ....115 K6
Croxley ⊖
 RKW/CH/CXG WD3 ....75 G7
Cuddington CE School
 RAYLW HP18 ....176 C7
Curzon CE Primary School
 AMSS HP7 ....70 A5
Dagnall County First School
 BERK HP4 ....171 K9
Dair House School
 SLN SL2 ....101 G6
D'Albiac House
 HTHAIR TW6 ....124 F5
Danesfield House Hotel
 MLW SL7 ....106 C1
Danesfield School
 MLW SL7 ....96 D7
Danstead Way Cemetery
 CNH/GTH/TMA MK8 ....17 H6
Datchet ≠
 DTCH/LGLY SL3 ....122 A4
Datchet Golf Club
 DTCH/LGLY SL3 ....121 M3
Datchet Parish
 Council Cemetery
 DTCH/LGLY SL3 ....122 C3
Datchet St Marys
 Primary School
 DTCH/LGLY SL3 ....122 A3
Datchet Sports Club
 DTCH/LGLY SL3 ....122 A3
Davenies School
 BEAC HP9 ....80 D8
David Lloyd Centre
 WLLN MK15 ....18 F1
Dawn Down School of Music
 CNH/GTH/TMA MK8 ....20 C3
Daytona Karting
 BDWL MK13 ....17 K4
Deanshanger Primary School
 RMKN MK19 ....137 M11
Dedworth Clinic
 WDSR SL4 ....120 D4
Dedworth County
 Middle School
 WDSR SL4 ....120 D4
Dedworth Green First School
 WDSR SL4 ....120 D5
De Montfort University
 WTR/OFPK MK7 ....17 K8
Denbigh East Industrial Estate
 DBGH MK1 ....23 H4
Denbigh Hall Industrial Estate
 BTCHLY MK3 ....22 C2
Denbigh Industrial Estate
 DBGH MK1 ....22 E4
Denbigh School
 SHEN MK5 ....17 K8
Denbigh West Industrial Estate
 DBGH MK1 ....22 E4

Dene House Hospital
 WDSR SL4 ....121 H6
Denham ≠
 DEN/HRF UB9 ....93 M6
Denham Aerodrome
 DEN/HRF UB9 ....93 K4
Denham Country Park
 DEN/HRF UB9 ....94 A8
Denham Golf Club
 DEN/HRF UB9 ....93 J5
Denham Golf Course ≠
 DEN/HRF UB9 ....93 J6
Denham Village Infant School
 DEN/HRF UB9 ....93 L8
Desborough Castle
 HWYW HP12 ....4 A5
Desborough Industrial Park
 HWYW HP12 ....4 C3
Desborough School
 MDHD SL6 ....108 D5
Different Drummer Hotel
 STSTR MK11 ....137 R8
Dinton Castle
 HADM HP17 ....177 J6
Dinton CE School
 HADM HP17 ....177 J7
Dinton Hermit Hotel
 HADM HP17 ....177 L10
The Disraeli School
 HWYW HP12 ....4 E2
Dorney County
 Combined School
 MDHD SL6 ....109 L6
Dorney Court
 WDSR SL4 ....110 A7
The Douay Martyrs RC School
 HGDN/ICK UB10 ....105 G2
Dovery Down Lower School
 LBUZ LU7 ....27 H4
The Downley School
 HWYN HP13 ....77 J3
Downs Barn School
 GTLIN MK14 ....18 C1
Drayton Park Combined School
 WEAT MK2 ....153 P1
Drayton Parslow Village School
 RMKS/WB MK17 ....152 C8
Dr Challoners Grammar School
 AMS HP6 ....71 H1
Dr Challoners High School
 AMSS HP7 ....72 A3
Dropmore Infant School
 SL SL1 ....100 B1
Dr Tripletts CE J & I School
 HYS/HAR UB3 ....115 L3
Dryleas Sports Ground
 TRING HP23 ....190 C3
Dundale Junior & Middle School
 TRING HP23 ....37 M5
Dundale Primary School
 TRING HP23 ....37 M5
Dunstable Downs Country Park
 DUN/WHIP LU6 ....171 N2
Dunstable Downs Golf Club
 DUN/WHIP LU6 ....171 N1
Dunstable Town CC
 DUN/WHIP LU6 ....31 K7
Eaglestone Health Centre
 EAG/OLD/WTN MK6 ....18 D8
East Berkshire College
 (Maidenhead Campus)
 MDHD SL6 ....108 C4
Eastbury Farm JMI School
 NTHWD HA6 ....85 L4
East Claydon School
 BUCK/WIN MK18 ....158 B3
Eastern Business Park
 HTHAIR TW6 ....125 L5
Eaton Bray Lower School
 DUN/WHIP LU6 ....30 F8
Eaton Mill Primary School
 WEAT MK2 ....23 G8
Eden Shopping Centre
 WYM HP11 ....5 G6
Edison Business Centre
 AYLW HP19 ....167 P12
Edlesborough School
 DUN/WHIP LU6 ....170 F3
Education Centre
 UX/CGN UB8 ....104 B4
Egerton Rothesay
 Preparatory School
 BERK HP4 ....48 A6
Egerton Rothesay School
 BERK HP4 ....47 L6
Elangeni Junior School
 AMS HP6 ....63 K7
Elers Clinic
 HYS/HAR UB3 ....115 J8
Ellesborough Golf Club
 HADM HP17 ....51 J3
Ellington Primary School
 MDHD SL6 ....108 E1
Elmhurst Junior School
 AYL HP20 ....3 G2
Elmtree Infant School
 CSHM HP5 ....63 G1
Elva Lodge Hotel
 MDHD SL6 ....108 D3
Emberton Country Park
 OLN MK46 ....133 M1
Emberton First School
 OLN MK46 ....133 N2
Emerson Valley
 Combined School
 EMV/FZ MK4 ....21 M4
Eton College
 WDSR SL4 ....121 J1
Eton College Rowing Lake
 WDSR SL4 ....120 B2
Eton End PNEU School
 DTCH/LGLY SL3 ....121 M2
Eton Porny CE First School
 WDSR SL4 ....121 J2
Eton Wick CE First School
 WDSR SL4 ....120 F1
Eton Wick FC
 WDSR SL4 ....120 E1
Europa Business School
 MKV MK10 ....138 A12
European Language School
 WDSR SL4 ....121 G5
Express by Holiday Inn
 WLLN MK15 ....19 J2
Fairacres Industrial Estate
 WDSR SL4 ....120 B5
Fairview Estate
 WYM HP11 ....78 F6
Fairview Industrial Estate
 AMS HP6 ....71 L1
 HYS/HAR UB3 ....115 L6
Fairview Trading Estate
 HEN RG9 ....191 J6

Falconhurst Combined School
 EAG/OLD/WTN MK6 ....7 M8
Farnham Common
 Infant School
 SLN SL2 ....101 G2
Farnham Common
 Junior School
 SLN SL2 ....101 G2
Farnham Common
 Middle School
 SLN SL2 ....101 G3
Farnham Park Golf Club
 SLN SL2 ....101 K6
Farnham Royal CE
 Combined School
 SLN SL2 ....101 H8
Farnham Royal CC
 SLN SL2 ....101 H8
Fenny Stratford ≠
 DBGH MK1 ....23 H5
Fernwood School
 RMKS/WB MK17 ....144 E8
Field Farm Business Centre
 BIC OX26 ....163 M1
Filgrave School
 NPAG MK16 ....133 K5
Finmere CE Primary School
 BUCK/WIN MK18 ....147 Q8
Fishermead Medical Centre
 EAG/OLD/WTN MK6 ....7 J1
Five Acres Primary School
 RBICS/W OX25 ....163 J10
Flackwell Heath Golf Club
 FLKWD/TG HP10 ....89 G1
Foundation Park
 MDHD SL6 ....117 L2
Foxes Piece Combined School
 MLW SL7 ....97 K3
Fredrick's Hotel
 MDHD SL6 ....108 D5
Friars Square Shopping Centre
 AYL HP20 ....2 F5
Frieth CE Combined School
 HEN RG9 ....189 Q1
Fringford CE Primary School
 RBICN OX27 ....154 H4
Frithsden Vineyard
 HHW HP1 ....49 G2
Frithwood Primary School
 NTHWD HA6 ....85 J6
Frogmore House
 WDSR SL4 ....121 L6
Frogmore Industrial Estate
 HYS/HAR UB3 ....115 K6
Fulbrook Middle School
 RMKS/WB MK17 ....144 E5
Fulmer Infant School
 DTCH/LGLY SL3 ....102 D2
Furze Down Special School
 BUCK/WIN MK18 ....150 H10
Furze Platt ≠
 MDHD SL6 ....108 D1
Furze Platt Junior School
 MDHD SL6 ....108 B1
Furze Platt Senior School
 MDHD SL6 ....108 B1
Future School
 GTMIS/PWD HP16 ....61 G3
Garden of Rest Cemetery
 CFSP/GDCR SL9 ....82 E7
The Gatehouse School
 GTLIN MK14 ....14 A7
Gateway School
 GTMIS/PWD HP16 ....60 F2
Gawcott Infant School
 BUCK/WIN MK18 ....148 G2
Gayhurst School
 CFSP/GDCR SL9 ....92 B3
Germander Park First School
 GTLIN MK14 ....14 C8
Gerrards Cross ≠
 CFSP/GDCR SL9 ....92 D4
The Gerrards Cross CE School
 CFSP/GDCR SL9 ....92 D6
Gerrards Cross Golf Club
 CFSP/GDCR SL9 ....92 E2
Gerrards Cross Sports Centre
 CFSP/GDCR SL9 ....92 C6
Giffard Park Combined School
 GTLIN MK14 ....14 D4
Gilbert Inglefield Middle School
 LBUZ LU7 ....27 K5
Giles Brook Combined School
 EMV/FZ MK4 ....21 K7
Gillotts School
 HEN RG9 ....190 E7
Gladstone Industrial Estate
 MDHD SL6 ....108 D2
Glastonbury Thorn First School
 SHEN MK5 ....17 K8
Glebe Primary School
 HGDN/ICK UB10 ....105 J2
Globeside Business Park
 MLW SL7 ....97 L4
Glory Farm CP School
 BIC OX26 ....162 F2
Godolphin Infant School
 SL SL1 ....111 H2
Godolphin Junior School
 SL SL1 ....111 J2
Godstowe Preparatory School
 HWYN HP13 ....5 L4
Goldfield Infant School
 TRING HP23 ....37 L7
Goodson Industrial Mews
 THAME OX9 ....181 N6
Grafton Medical Centre
 CMK MK9 ....6 C5
Grangelands & Pulpit Hill
 Nature Reserve
 PRRI HP27 ....50 F8
Grange Park Clinic
 YEAD UB4 ....115 L1
Grange Park Junior School
 YEAD UB4 ....115 L1
The Grange School
 AYLS HP21 ....3 K8
Grangewood School
 PIN HA5 ....95 M4
Great Brickhill CC
 RMKS/WB MK17 ....24 D4
Great Gaddesden JMI School
 HHW HP1 ....41 J7
Great Horwood CE
 Combined School
 RMKS/WB MK17 ....151 J3
Great Kimble CE Infant School
 HADM HP17 ....50 D5
Great Kingshill CE
 Combined School
 HAZ/HG HP15 ....68 B3
Great Linford Combined School
 GTLIN MK14 ....14 B6

Great Marlow School
 MLW SL7 ....97 L2
Great Missenden ≠
 CTMIS/PWD HP16 ....60 F3
Great Missenden CE
 Combined School
 CTMIS/PWD HP16 ....61 G3
Greaves Way Industrial Estate
 LBUZ LU7 ....27 K8
Green End Business Centre
 RKW/CH/CXG WD3 ....65 M8
Greenleas Lower School
 LBUZ LU7 ....26 D7
Greenleys First School
 WOLV MK12 ....16 F1
Greenleys Junior School
 WOLV MK12 ....16 F1
Green Park School
 NPAG MK16 ....14 E3
Green Street County
 First School
 WYM HP11 ....4 E5
Greenway First School
 BERK HP4 ....47 L6
Grendon Underwood
 Combined School
 RAYLW HP18 ....156 H12
Grenville Combined School
 BUCK/WIN MK18 ....11 L6
Griffin Lane Industrial Estate
 AYLW HP19 ....2 A3
Grovebury Road
 Industrial Estate
 LBUZ LU7 ....29 G2
Grovefield Hotel
 SL SL1 ....99 M7
The Grove Independent School
 SHEN MK5 ....17 M7
Grove Park Industrial Estate
 MDHD SL6 ....117 K6
Grove Road Primary School
 TRING HP23 ....38 A5
The Grove Surgery
 EAG/OLD/WTN MK6 ....18 E8
Gulliver's Land
 MK MK15 ....18 F2
Hackleton Primary School
 RNHPTN NN7 ....126 A3
Haddenham Business Park
 HADM HP17 ....176 C11
Haddenham First School
 HADM HP17 ....176 D12
Haddenham Health Centre
 HADM HP17 ....176 D12
Haddenham Junior School
 HADM HP17 ....176 D12
Haddenham & Thame Parkway
 ≠
 HADM HP17 ....176 A12
Hale Leys Shopping Centre
 AYL HP20 ....2 F5
The Hall Pre Preparatory School
 NTHWD HA6 ....85 J6
Halls Business Centre
 HYS/HAR UB3 ....115 M7
Halse Road Cemetery
 BRCKY NN13 ....8 D5
Halton Camp
 RAYLNE/WEN HP22 ....44 D3
Halton Combined School
 RAYLNE/WEN HP22 ....44 C3
Hamilton Combined School
 HWYN HP13 ....5 K3
Hamilton School
 HWYN HP13 ....5 H5
Hannah Ball Infant School
 HWYN HP13 ....78 C3
Hanslope Combined School
 RMKN MK19 ....131 M7
The Harefield Academy
 DEN/HRF UB9 ....84 C8
Harefield CC
 DEN/HRF UB9 ....94 B1
Harefield Health Centre
 DEN/HRF UB9 ....84 B8
Harefield Hospital
 DEN/HRF UB9 ....84 B8
Harefield Infant School
 DEN/HRF UB9 ....94 A1
Harefield Junior School
 DEN/HRF UB9 ....84 B8
Harefield Road Industrial Estate
 RKW/CH/CXG WD3 ....84 D4
Haresfoot CC
 BERK HP4 ....56 A1
Haresfoot Senior School
 BERK HP4 ....48 F4
Harewood Down Golf Club
 CSTG HP8 ....72 A5
Harleyford Golf Club
 MLW SL7 ....96 F3
Harlington Community School
 HYS/HAR UB3 ....115 J8
Harmill Industrial Estate
 LBUZ LU7 ....29 H2
Hartwell CE Primary School
 RNHPTN NN7 ....131 J1
Hartwell House Hotel
 HADM HP17 ....177 Q5
Harvey Road Primary School
 RKW/CH/CXG WD3 ....74 D7
Haslemere Industrial Estate
 EBED/NFELT TW14 ....125 M8
Haste Hill Golf Club
 NTHWD HA6 ....95 K1
Hatton Cross ⊖
 HTHAIR TW6 ....125 L7
Haversham First School
 RMKN MK19 ....13 H4
Hawridge & Cholesbury CE
 Combined School
 CSHM HP5 ....46 D8
The Hay Barn Business Park
 RAYLNE/WEN HP22 ....160 H12
Haydon Abbey
 Combined School
 AYLW HP19 ....2 B2
Haydon School
 PIN HA5 ....95 L2
Hayes CC
 HYS/HAR UB3 ....115 L4
Hayes FC
 HYS/HAR UB3 ....115 L4
Hayes & Harlington ≠
 HYS/HAR UB3 ....115 L7
The Hayes Manor School
 HYS/HAR UB3 ....115 L4
Hayes Park J & I School
 YEAD UB4 ....115 L1
Hayes Pool
 HYS/HAR UB3 ....115 L5
Hayes Social & Sports Club
 HYS/HAR UB3 ....115 L4

Hayes Stadium Sports Centre
HYS/HAR UB3 ....115 J3
Hayward House Day Hospital
HHW HP13 ....5 M7
The Hazeley School
CNH/GTH/TMA MK8 ....21 G1
Hazlemere CE Combined School
HAZ/HG HP15 ....68 E7
Hazlemere Golf Club
HAZ/HG HP15 ....69 G6
Heatherton House School
AMS HP6 ....63 H7
Heathpark Golf Club
WDR/YW UB7 ....114 F7
Heathrow Airport Central Bus &
Coach Station
HTHAIR TW6 ....124 F6
Heathrow Airport
Terminals 1, 2, 3 ✈ ⊖
HTHAIR TW6 ....125 G5
Heathrow Airport
Terminal 4 ✈ ⊖
HTHAIR TW6 ....125 G8
Heathrow Airport
Terminal 5 ✈ ⊖
HTHAIR TW6 ....124 B6
Heathrow Medical Centre
HYS/HAR UB3 ....125 J1
Heathrow Primary School
WDR/YW UB7 ....124 E2
Heathwood Lower School
LBUZ LU7 ....27 J3
Hedgewood School
YEAD UB4 ....105 K8
Hedsor School
BNEND SL8 ....89 J3
Heelands First School
BDWL MK13 ....17 L2
The Hell-Fire Caves
SKCH HP14 ....76 E4
Hemel Hempstead ≷
HHS/BOV HP3 ....57 M2
Hemel Hempstead
(Camelot) RFC
HHW HP1 ....57 L1
Hengrove School
TRING HP23 ....45 H6
The Henley College
HEN RG9 ....190 F5
Henley & District Indoor
Sports Centre
HEN RG9 ....190 E7
Henley Golf Club
HEN RG9 ....190 G8
Henley Management College
HEN RG9 ....189 K11
Henley-on-Thames ≷
HEN RG9 ....190 H5
Henley Town FC
HEN RG9 ....191 J6
Hennerton Golf Club
WAR/TWY RG10 ....191 N9
Heritage House
Special School
CSHM HP5 ....63 J1
Hermitage Primary School
UX/CGN UB8 ....104 C5
Hernes Estate
HEN RG9 ....190 C6
Heronsgate School
WTR/OFPK MK7 ....23 K1
Heronshaw School
WTR/OFPK MK7 ....23 L1
Herries School
MDHD SL6 ....98 A2
Herschel Grammar School
SL SL1 ....111 H3
High Ash CE
Combined School
RMKS/WB MK17 ....24 E4
Highbridge Industrial Estate
UX/CGN UB8 ....104 B4
Highcrest Community School
HWYN HP13 ....78 D3
Highfield PNEU School
MDHD SL6 ....108 D3
Highfield School
HGDN/ICK UB10 ....105 G8
Highgrove Pool
RSLP HA4 ....95 M6
High March School
BEAC HP9 ....80 D6
Highworth Combined School
HWYN HP13 ....68 D8
High Wycombe ≷
HWYN HP13 ....5 K6
High Wycombe CE
Combined School
WYM HP11 ....5 G7
High Wycombe Cemetery
HWYN HP13 ....5 K4
High Wycombe RUFC
WYM HP11 ....78 F7
High Wycombe Squash Club
MLW SL7 ....86 F4
High Wycombe Tennis Club
WYM HP11 ....78 C5
Hillingdon ⊖
HGDN/ICK UB10 ....104 F3
Hillingdon Borough FC
RSLP HA4 ....95 G4
Hillingdon Cemetery
UX/CGN UB8 ....104 D8
Hillingdon Golf Club
HGDN/ICK UB10 ....104 E7
Hillingdon Hospital
UX/CGN UB8 ....114 E2
Hillingdon Manor School
UX/CGN UB8 ....115 G2
Hillingdon Primary School
HGDN/ICK UB10 ....104 F8
Hillside Infant School
NTHWD HA6 ....85 M7
Hill Top First School
WDSR SL4 ....120 D6
Hilltops Medical Centre
CNH/GTH/TMA MK8 ....17 J5
HM Customs & Excise
HTHAIR TW6 ....125 G4
HM Prison
HHS/BOV HP3 ....56 E5
RAYLW HP18 ....156 H10
RBICS/X OX25 ....173 M3
SHEN MK5 ....21 G2
HM Young Offenders Institution
AYL HP20 ....3 K3
RAYLW HP18 ....156 H9
Holmer Green First School
HAZ/HG HP15 ....69 G3
Holmer Green Junior School
HAZ/HG HP15 ....69 G3
Holmer Green Senior School
HAZ/HG HP15 ....69 H3

Holmwood School
CNH/GTH/TMA MK8 ....17 H5
Holne Chase Combined School
BTCHLY MK3 ....22 D7
Holtspur Cemetery
BEAC HP9 ....89 M3
Holtspur Primary School
BEAC HP9 ....89 M1
Holy Family Catholic School
DTCH/LGLY SL3 ....122 E1
Holyport CE Primary School
MDHD SL6 ....119 G2
Holyport Manor School
MDHD SL6 ....118 D4
Holy Trinity CE (A) School
MLW SL7 ....97 J3
Holy Trinity CE Primary School
MDHD SL6 ....98 F3
WATW WD18 ....85 H6
Holywell Mead Open Air
Swimming Pool
WYM HP11 ....5 M9
Holywell School
RBEDW MK43 ....139 L5
WATW WD18 ....75 L7
Homers First School
WDSR SL4 ....120 C4
Horton Industrial Park
WDR/YW UB7 ....114 E5
Horton Trading Estate
DTCH/LGLY SL3 ....123 G6
Hotel du Vin
HEN RG9 ....190 H4
Household Cavalry Museum
WDSR SL4 ....121 G6
Howard Industrial Estate
CSHM HP5 ....55 H8
Howe Park School
EMV/FZ MK4 ....21 L5
Hughenden Infant School
SKCH HP14 ....67 L7
Hughenden Manor (NT)
SKCH HP14 ....77 M3
Huntercombe Manor Hospital
MDHD SL6 ....110 B4
Hunters Farm Industrial Estate
RAYLW HP18 ....167 K8
Hurley Riverside Park
MDHD SL6 ....106 E2
Husborne Crawley
Lower School
RBEDW MK43 ....145 M6
Hyde Heath Infant School
AMS HP6 ....62 B5
Ibis Hotel
HYS/HAR UB3 ....125 K4
Ibstone CE Primary School
SKCH HP14 ....186 G8
Ickenham ⊖
HGDN/ICK UB10 ....105 H2
Ickenham Clinic
HGDN/ICK UB10 ....105 H1
Ickford Combined School
RAYLW HP18 ....180 A3
Icknield Way Industrial Estate
TRING HP23 ....37 K6
IKEA Store Milton Keynes
DBGH MK1 ....22 F4
Imperial College
Athletic Ground
HYS/HAR UB3 ....125 H2
Independent Business Park
SKCH HP14 ....186 F1
Independent
Industrial Estate
WDR/YW UB7 ....114 E5
Industrial Health Clinic
UX/CGN UB8 ....104 A8
The Inn at Woburn Hotel
RMKS/WB MK17 ....145 J11
Innkeeper's Lodge
BEAC HP9 ....90 D1
DTCH/LGLY SL3 ....122 E1
RAYLNE/WEN HP22 ....43 L4
SHEN MK5 ....17 K7
WDSR SL4 ....121 M8
Iver ⊖
DTCH/LGLY SL3 ....113 L6
Iver Golf & Leisure Centre
IVER SL0 ....113 G5
Iver Heath Health Centre
IVER SL0 ....103 J7
Iver Heath Infant School
IVER SL0 ....103 J8
Iver Heath Primary School
IVER SL0 ....103 J7
Iver Village Infant School
IVER SL0 ....113 L3
Iver Village Junior School
IVER SL0 ....113 K3
Ivyleaf Working Mens Club
MDHD SL6 ....108 F3
Jackson Industrial Estate
BNEND SL8 ....89 G7
James Elliman School
SL SL1 ....111 K3
John Colet School
RAYLNE/WEN HP22 ....44 B5
John F Kennedy RC School
HHW HP1 ....49 L6
John Hamden Primary School
THAME OX9 ....181 N7
John Hampden
Grammar School
WYM HP11 ....87 K2
The John Hampden
Wendover School
RAYLNE/WEN HP22 ....44 A5
John Hellins Primary School
TOW NN12 ....137 L3
John Penrose School
DEN/HRF UB9 ....84 C8
John Penrose Sports Centre
DEN/HRF UB9 ....84 C8
Johnsons Industrial Estate
HYS/HAR UB3 ....115 M7
Jordans School
BEAC HP9 ....81 K6
Juniper Hill School
FLKWH/TG HP10 ....89 G3
Jurys Inn Hotel
HTHAIR TW6 ....125 L6
Kenton Theatre
HEN RG9 ....190 H4
Kents Hill School
WTR/OFPK MK7 ....19 K7
Kiln Farm Industrial Estate
STSTR MK11 ....16 E3
King Edward Court
Shopping Centre
WDSR SL4 ....121 H4
King Edwards Road Clinic
RSLP HA4 ....95 J7

King Edward VII Hospital
WDSR SL4 ....121 H6
Kingsbrook School
RMKN MK19 ....137 N10
The Kings Centre
WYM HP11 ....4 E7
Kings College Sports Ground
RSLP HA4 ....95 K5
Kingscote Pre
Preparatory School
CFSP/GDCR SL9 ....92 D2
Kings Grove Industrial Estate
MDHD SL6 ....108 D4
King's Head
AYL HP20 ....2 F5
Kingsmead Business Park
WYM HP11 ....79 G7
Kings Grove CP School
BIC OX26 ....162 A3
Kings Meadow CP School
BIC OX26 ....162 A3
Kingston Centre
MKV MK10 ....19 M5
Kingston Leisure Centre
MKV MK10 ....19 M5
Kings Wood National
Nature Reserve
RMKS/WB MK17 ....25 K5
Kings Wood Primary School
HWYN HP13 ....78 E2
Knaves Beech Business Centre
FLKWH/TG HP10 ....89 J1
Knaves Beech Industrial Estate
FLKWH/TG HP10 ....89 H1
Knowles J & I School
WEAT MK2 ....23 C6
Knowl Hill CE Primary School
WAR/TWY RG10 ....116 E2
Lady Bankes Junior School
RSLP HA4 ....95 M8
Ladymede School
HADM HP17 ....50 D5
Lakeside Industrial Estate
DTCH/LGLY SL3 ....123 K3
Lambourne Golf Club
SL SL1 ....100 A4
Lancaster Business Park
LBUZ LU7 ....161 L7
Lancot Lower School
DUN/WHIP LU6 ....31 N4
Lane End Industrial Park
SKCH HP14 ....86 C1
Lane End Primary School
SKCH HP14 ....86 C1
Langford Village County
Primary School
BIC OX26 ....162 F6
Langland School
EAG/OLD/WTN MK6 ....18 F8
Langley ⊖
DTCH/LGLY SL3 ....112 F6
Langley Business Centre
DTCH/LGLY SL3 ....112 F6
Langley Business Park
DTCH/LGLY SL3 ....112 E6
Langley Grammar School
DTCH/LGLY SL3 ....112 E6
Langley Health Centre
DTCH/LGLY SL3 ....122 F1
Langley Manor School
DTCH/LGLY SL3 ....112 D5
Langley Park Country Park
DTCH/LGLY SL3 ....112 F1
Langleywood School
DTCH/LGLY SL3 ....112 D7
Larchfield Primary School
MDHD SL6 ....108 D6
Launton Business Centre
BIC OX26 ....162 F4
Launton CE Primary School
BIC OX26 ....163 J4
Launton Road Retail Park
BIC OX26 ....162 G3
Laurance Haines School
WATW WD18 ....75 J4
Lavendon Combined School
OLN MK46 ....128 H6
Lawn Farm Business Centre
RAYLW HP18 ....165 L2
Lea Infant School
SLN SL2 ....112 M4
Lea Junior School
SLN SL2 ....111 M4
Lee Common CE
First School
GTMIS/PWD HP16 ....53 J5
Leedon Lower School
LBUZ LU7 ....27 K8
Le Flaive Business Centre
SKCH HP14 ....67 K8
Legoland Windsor
WDSR SL4 ....120 C8
Leighton Buzzard ≷
LBUZ LU7 ....26 E8
Leighton Buzzard Cemetery
LBUZ LU7 ....27 J6
Leighton Buzzard Golf Club
LBUZ LU7 ....27 G3
Leighton Buzzard Railway
LBUZ LU7 ....29 J1
Leighton Buzzard Theatre
LBUZ LU7 ....27 H8
Leighton Industrial Park
LBUZ LU7 ....29 J1
Leighton Town FC
LBUZ LU7 ....27 H8
Lent Rise Combined School
SL SL1 ....110 A2
Leon School & Sports College
WEAT MK2 ....153 P1
Ley Hill CC
CSHM HP5 ....64 B2
Ley Hill School
CSHM HP5 ....64 A1
Limelight Theatre
AYLS HP21 ....3 J6
Lincolns Park Business Centre
HWYW HP12 ....4 B9
Linden Medical Centre
MDHD SL6 ....108 H4
Linford Lakes RSPB Reserve
GTLIN MK14 ....13 M4
Linslade Lower School
LBUZ LU7 ....26 E7
Linslade Middle School
LBUZ LU7 ....28 F1
Little Chalfont Golf Club
AMS HP6 ....72 C5
Little Chalfont Primary School
AMS HP6 ....72 D4
Littledown Special School
SL SL1 ....111 L4
Little Gaddesden CE
Primary School
BERK HP4 ....40 B2

Little Green Junior School
RKW/CH/CXG WD3 ....74 F4
Little Hay Golf Complex
HHS/BOV HP3 ....57 H3
Little Kimble
HADM HP17 ....50 D4
Little Kingshill
Combined School
GTMIS/PWD HP16 ....61 G8
Little Marlow CE
Infant School
MLW SL7 ....88 E5
Little Marlow Cemetery
MLW SL7 ....88 D5
Little Missenden CE
Infant School
AMSS HP7 ....61 L8
Little St Helens School
NTHWD HA6 ....85 K6
Little Spring Primary School
CSHM HP5 ....55 G7
Lodge Farm Industrial Estate
RMKN MK19 ....12 E3
Lodge Industrial Centre
RMKS/WB MK17 ....152 H8
Lodge Sun Sports Club
WAT SL9 ....75 K2
London Area Terminal
Control Centre
WDR/YW UB7 ....114 E6
London School of Theology
NTHWD HA6 ....85 H7
London Wasps RFC
HWYW HP12 ....76 F7
Long Close School
DTCH/LGLY SL3 ....111 M8
Long Crendon Courthouse (NT)
RAYLW HP18 ....175 L11
Long Crendon School
RAYLW HP18 ....175 K11
Longfields Primary School
BIC OX26 ....162 E4
Long Island Hotel
RKW/CH/CXG WD3 ....74 C8
Long Marston JMI School
TRING HP23 ....168 G10
Long Meadow School
SHEN MK5 ....21 J4
Longmead Primary School
WDR/YW UB7 ....114 C4
Longwick CE Combined School
PRRI HP27 ....183 N8
The Lord Grey School
BTCHLY MK3 ....22 D5
Lord Williams Lower School
THAME OX9 ....181 Q6
Lord Williams School
THAME OX9 ....181 L6
Loudwater Combined School
WYM HP11 ....79 G8
Loughton Manor
Equestrian Centre
SHEN MK5 ....17 L7
Loughton Manor First School
SHEN MK5 ....17 K6
Loughton School
SHEN MK5 ....17 K7
Lowbrook Primary School
MDHD SL6 ....117 M3
Lynch Hill School
SLN SL2 ....100 E8
Lyons Industrial Estate
UX/CGN UB8 ....114 B3
Macdonald Hotel
WDSR SL4 ....121 J4
Macintyre School
RAYLNE/WEN HP22 ....168 B3
Madison Bowl
NTHWD HA6 ....85 K7
Magdalen College School
BRACKY NN13 ....8 D7
The Magnet Leisure Centre
MDHD SL6 ....108 E3
Maidenhead ≷
MDHD SL6 ....108 E4
Maidenhead Clinic
MDHD SL6 ....108 E3
Maidenhead Golf Club
MDHD SL6 ....108 E3
Maidenhead Retail Park
MDHD SL6 ....108 E5
Maidenhead Rowing Club
MDHD SL6 ....109 H3
Maidenhead Rugby Club
MDHD SL6 ....108 F5
Maidenhead Sailing Club
MDHD SL6 ....98 F8
Maidenhead Superbowl
MDHD SL6 ....108 E4
Maidenhead United FC
MDHD SL6 ....108 F4
Maids Moreton CE School
BUCK/WIN MK18 ....11 M3
Maltmans Green School
CFSP/GDCR SL9 ....92 B2
Malvern Way Infant School
RKW/CH/CXG WD3 ....75 H6
The Mandeville School
AYLS HP21 ....42 C7
Manor Farm Infant School
HAZ/HG HP15 ....69 G8
Manor House Hospital
AYL HP20 ....3 J4
Manor Park Medical Centre
SLN SL2 ....111 J2
Manor Rd Cemetery
WEAT MK2 ....23 G6
Maple Cross Industrial Estate
RKW/CH/CXG WD3 ....83 K4
Maple Cross Junior Middle &
Infant School
RKW/CH/CXG WD3 ....83 J5
Maplewood School
HWYN HP13 ....77 H3
HWYW HP12 ....87 J3
Marish Infant School
DTCH/LGLY SL3 ....112 E7
The Marjory Kinnon School
EBED/NFELT TW14 ....125 K8
Market Square
CMK MK9 ....7 H3
Marlborough Trading Estate
WYM HP11 ....79 K3
Marlin Montessori School
BERK HP4 ....48 A6
Marlow ≷
MLW SL7 ....97 K5
Marlow CE Infants School
MLW SL7 ....97 J3
Marlow Cemetery
MLW SL7 ....97 J3
Marlow Community Hospital
MLW SL7 ....97 K4

Marlow FC
MLW SL7 ....97 K3
Marlow RFC
MLW SL7 ....97 M5
Marlow Rowing Club
MLW SL7 ....97 K5
Marlow Sports Club
Pavilion Ground
MLW SL7 ....97 J6
Marriott Hotel
DTCH/LGLY SL3 ....122 E1
HYS/HAR UB3 ....125 J3
Marsh Gibbon CE School
RBICN OX27 ....156 A7
Marsh Infant School
WYM HP11 ....78 E6
Marston Thrift Nature Reserve
RBEDW MK43 ....139 P6
Marsworth CE Infant School
TRING HP23 ....169 M12
Martin Baker Sports Ground
DEN/HRF UB9 ....93 L6
Martindale JMI School
HHW HP1 ....49 L6
The Mary Bassett Lower School
LBUZ LU7 ....27 G7
Mary Towerton First School
SKCH HP14 ....187 N3
McKay Trading Estate
BIC OX26 ....162 E5
DTCH/LGLY SL3 ....123 K5
McMillan Clinic
HYS/HAR UB3 ....115 H4
The Meacham Clinic
WOLV MK12 ....12 E7
Meadfurlong School
EAG/OLD/WTN MK6 ....7 H7
Meadow High School
UX/CGN UB8 ....114 D2
The Meadows Combined School
FLKWH/TG HP10 ....89 K3
Meadow Walk Shopping Centre
BUCK/WIN MK18 ....11 L5
Mecure Parkside Hotel
EAG/OLD/WTN MK6 ....19 G6
Medical Health Centre
MDHD SL6 ....98 D3
Mellow Lane School
HGDN/ICK UB10 ....115 H1
Menmarsh Guide Post
WHLY OX33 ....178 H5
Mentmore Golf & Country Club
LBUZ LU7 ....168 H4
Merchant Taylors School
NTHWD HA6 ....85 K1
Merebrook School
EMV/FZ MK4 ....21 M3
Micklem JMI School
HHW HP1 ....49 L6
Midas Industrial Estate
UX/CGN UB8 ....104 A7
Middle Claydon Cemetery
BUCK/WIN MK18 ....157 R2
Middlegreen Trading Estate
DTCH/LGLY SL3 ....112 C6
Middleton Combined School
MKV MK10 ....19 H4
Middleton Swimming Pool
NPAG MK16 ....15 H3
Midsummer Place
Shopping Centre
CMK MK9 ....7 G4
Millbarn Medical Centre
BEAC HP9 ....90 E1
Millbrook Combined School
HWYW HP12 ....4 A3
Mill Lane Primary School
CROX OX39 ....184 E3
Milton Keynes Central ≷
SHEN MK5 ....6 A7
Milton Keynes Central
Business Exchange
CMK MK9 ....6 F5
Milton Keynes College
BTCHLY MK3 ....22 E6
EAG/OLD/WTN MK6 ....18 C7
Milton Keynes Gallery
CMK MK9 ....7 J2
Milton Keynes Hospital
EAG/OLD/WTN MK6 ....18 E7
Milton Keynes Museum of
Industry & Rural Life
WOLV MK12 ....13 C8
Milton Keynes
Preparatory School
BTCHLY MK3 ....22 A6
Milton Keynes RFC
WOLV MK12 ....16 D1
Milton Keynes Stadium
EAG/OLD/WTN MK6 ....22 F2
Milton Keynes Stadium & Arena
(MK Dons FC)
DBGH MK1 ....22 E3
Milton Keynes Theatre
CMK MK9 ....7 J3
Milton Medical Centre
WEAT MK2 ....22 F6
Milton's Cottage
CSTG HP8 ....82 A3
Minet Clinic
HYS/HAR UB3 ....115 M5
Misbourne School
GTMIS/PWD HP16 ....61 G4
Moderate Learning
Difficulties Unit
EAG/OLD/WTN MK6 ....7 L8
Monkey Island Hotel
MDHD SL6 ....109 K7
Monks Risborough ≷
PRRI HP27 ....50 A8
Monks Risborough CE
Combined School
PRRI HP27 ....58 C1
Monkston Combined School
MKV MK10 ....19 L5
Montem Primary School
SL SL1 ....111 G6
Montem Sports Centre
SL SL1 ....111 J6
Montgomery House Surgery
BIC OX26 ....162 D5
Moorcroft School
UX/CGN UB8 ....114 E3
Moorland Infant School
EAG/OLD/WTN MK6 ....22 E1
Moor Park ⊖
NTHWD HA6 ....85 J3
Moor Park Golf Club
RKW/CH/CXG WD3 ....85 G3
Moor Park Industrial Estate
WATW WD18 ....75 H8
The Motorsports Centre
BRACKY NN13 ....147 N1

Mount Farm Industrial Estate
DBGH MK1 .... 23 G3
Mount Vernon Hospital
NTHWD HA6 .... 85 K8
Mursley Cemetery
RMKS/WB MK17 .... 152 C9
Mursley CE School
RMKS/WB MK17 .... 152 C8
Naphill & Walters Ash School
SKCH HP14 .... 67 G5
Nascot Wood Infant School
WAT WD17 .... 75 M1
National Badminton Centre
CNH/GTH/TMA MK8 .... 17 K5
The National Bowl
SHEN MK5 .... 22 B1
National Film & TV School
BEAC HP9 .... 80 D8
National Hockey Stadium
CMK MK9 .... 6 B6
The Natural History Museum
at Tring
TRING HP23 .... 37 M7
Neath Hill Health Centre
GTLIN MK14 .... 14 C7
New Bradwell Combined School
BDWL MK13 .... 13 J7
New Cemetery
NPAG MK16 .... 15 G1
New Chapter Primary School
EAG/OLD/WTN MK6 .... 22 D1
The New College
WDSR SL4 .... 121 H3
New Elgiva Theatre
CSHM HP5 .... 63 G2
The New French
Partridge Hotel
RNHPTN NN7 .... 126 D5
Newlands Bus Station
WYM MK8 .... 5 H7
Newlands Girls School
MDHD SL6 .... 107 M7
Newport Pagnell
Medical Centre
NPAG MK16 .... 14 F2
New Regal Cinema
HEN RG9 .... 190 G4
Newton Blossomville CE
First School
RBEDW MK43 .... 129 K10
Newton Longville CE
Combined School
RMKS/WB MK17 .... 152 H3
Newtown School
CSHM HP5 .... 55 H8
Nicholsons Shopping Centre
MDHD SL6 .... 108 E3
Northampton
International Raceway
RNHPTN NN7 .... 126 D1
Northamptonshire
County Council
BRACKY NN13 .... 8 E7
Northchurch CC
BERK HP4 .... 47 J3
North Crawley CE First School
NPAG MK16 .... 134 D12
North Maidenhead CC
MDHD SL6 .... 98 F8
North Marston CE School
BUCK/WIN MK18 .... 159 L8
Northolt Aerodrome
RSLP HA4 .... 105 M4
North Oxfordshire College
BIC OX26 .... 162 D5
Northwood ⊖
NTHWD HA6 .... 85 K7
Northwood Cemetery
NTHWD HA6 .... 95 L1
Northwood College
NTHWD HA6 .... 85 J7
Northwood FC
NTHWD HA6 .... 95 L1
Northwood Golf Club
NTHWD HA6 .... 85 J7
Northwood Hills ⊖
NTHWD HA6 .... 95 M1
Northwood & Pinner
Community Hospital
NTHWD HA6 .... 85 M8
Northwood Preparatory School
RKW/CH/CXG WD3 .... 85 H2
Notley Abbey
RAYLW HP18 .... 175 Q11
Novotel
BDWL MK13 .... 17 M1
WDR/YW UB7 .... 114 F8
Oak Bank Special School
LBUZ LU7 .... 27 H3
Oak Farm Clinic
HGDN/ICK UB10 .... 105 G6
Oak Farm Infant School
HGDN/ICK UB10 .... 105 G6
Oakfield First School
WDSR SL4 .... 121 G5
Oak Green School
AYLS HP21 .... 2 E8
Oakgrove School
MKV MK10 .... 19 H3
Oakland Park Golf Club
CSTG HP8 .... 81 L4
Oakley CE Combined School
RAYLW HP18 .... 179 Q2
Oakley Court Hotel
WDSR SL4 .... 119 M2
Oakridge CP School
WYM HP11 .... 4 D6
The Observatory
Shopping Centre
SL SL1 .... 111 M6
Odds Farm Rare Breeds Centre
FLKWH/TG HP10 .... 90 A6
Odeon Cinema
AYL HP20 .... 3 G6
CFSP/GDCR SL9 .... 92 D4
CMK MK9 .... 7 G2
UX/CGN UB8 .... 104 C6
Officers Lawn Tennis Club
RAYLNE/WEN HP22 .... 44 B1
Old Abbotstonians RFC
YEAD UB4 .... 105 J1
Old Airfield Industrial Estate
TRING HP23 .... 169 J9
Oldbrook First School
EAG/OLD/WTN MK6 .... 7 G8
Oldfield Primary School
MDHD SL6 .... 109 G4
Oldfield Road Industrial Estate
MDHD SL6 .... 109 G3
Old Gaol Museum
BUCK/WIN MK18 .... 11 K5
Old Kiln Industrial Estate
MDHD SL6 .... 107 M3

Old Luxters Farm Brewery
HEN RG9 .... 189 J3
Old Merchant Taylors
Sports Club
RKW/CH/CXG WD3 .... 75 C5
Old Stratford Primary School
RMKN MK19 .... 137 P7
Old Windsor Church
Road Cemetery
WDSR SL4 .... 122 A8
Olney Cemetery
OLN MK46 .... 128 C11
Olney First School
OLN MK46 .... 128 A11
Olney Middle School
OLN MK46 .... 128 B9
Open Air Theatre
CMK MK9 .... 7 L2
The Open University
DBGH MK1 .... 23 H4
SHEN MK5 .... 17 J1
STSTR MK11 .... 16 A1
WTR/OFPK MK7 .... 19 J3
Orchard House Industrial Estate
CSHM HP5 .... 63 H3
Orchard School
EAG/OLD/WTN MK6 .... 7 M6
Our Lady of Peace
Infant School
SL SL1 .... 110 B2
Our Lady of Peace
Junior School
SL SL1 .... 110 B2
Our Ladys Catholic
Primary School
AMS HP6 .... 63 G6
Ousedale School
NPAG MK16 .... 14 E3
Overstone Combined School
LBUZ LU7 .... 161 Q8
The Oxford Belfry Hotel
THAME OX9 .... 180 B10
Oxford & Cherwell
Valley College
THAME OX9 .... 181 M3
The Oxfordshire Golf Club
THAME OX9 .... 180 H10
Oxley Park Primary School
EMV/FZ MK4 .... 21 H4
Padbury CE First School
BUCK/WIN MK18 .... 149 K4
Paddocks Hospital
PRRI HP27 .... 58 B2
Pages Industrial Park
LBUZ LU7 .... 29 H1
Page's Park Station
LBUZ LU7 .... 29 J1
Park Avenue Clinic
WAT WD17 .... 75 M3
Parkhouse Business Centre
HWYW HP12 .... 4 C3
Park School
AYL HP20 .... 3 J4
Park Street Industrial Estate
AYL HP20 .... 3 K7
Parlaunt Park Combined School
DTCH/LGLY SL3 .... 113 J8
Pavilions Shopping Centre
UX/CGN UB8 .... 104 B7
Pear Tree Farm Industrial Units
RBICK OX27 .... 163 K4
Pebble Brook Special School
AYLS HP21 .... 2 C6
Peerglow Industrial Estate
WATW WD18 .... 75 G8
Pendley Manor Hotel
TRING HP23 .... 38 D6
Penn School
FLKWH/TG HP10 .... 79 J3
Penn Wood School
SLN SL2 .... 111 J1
Penwith School
EAG/OLD/WTN MK6 .... 7 J7
Pepper Hill First School
BDWL MK13 .... 13 K7
Peregrine Business Park
HWYN HP13 .... 78 F5
Perth Trading Estate
SL SL1 .... 111 G2
Peter James Business Centre
HYS/HAR UB3 .... 115 M4
Phoenix Business Centre
CSHM HP5 .... 63 C6
Pield Heath School
UX/CGN UB8 .... 114 D1
Pilot Trading Estate
HWYW HP12 .... 4 C4
Pinewood Film Studios
IVER SL0 .... 103 G5
The Pinewood Hotel
DTCH/LGLY SL3 .... 112 D2
Pinkwell Primary School
HYS/HAR UB3 .... 115 H8
Pipers Corner School
HAZ/HG HP15 .... 68 A2
Pippins School
DTCH/LGLY SL3 .... 123 L4
Pitstone Green Business Park
LBUZ LU7 .... 169 Q12
Pitstone Green Windmill (NT)
LBUZ LU7 .... 170 A10
Pixies Hill Primary School
HHW HP1 .... 49 L8
The Place Retail Park
CMK MK9 .... 6 A6
Planet Ice
CMK MK9 .... 6 C8
The Players Theatre
THAME OX9 .... 181 N6
The Point
Entertainment Centre
CMK MK9 .... 7 H4
Polygon Business Centre
DTCH/LGLY SL3 .... 123 L5
Portfields Combined School
NPAG MK16 .... 14 D1
Portland Business Centre
DTCH/LGLY SL3 .... 122 A4
Potten End First School
BERK HP4 .... 49 G4
Pottersbury Cemetery
TOW NN12 .... 137 M3
Premier Inn
SL SL1 .... 112 N4
Prestwood Infant School
GTMIS/PWD HP16 .... 60 B3
Prestwood Junior School
GTMIS/PWD HP16 .... 60 B4
Prestwood Lodge
Special School
GTMIS/PWD HP16 .... 60 C1
Princes Industrial Estate
PRRI HP27 .... 183 Q11

Princes Risborough ⇌
PRRI HP27 .... 183 Q12
Princes Risborough Golf Club
PRRI HP27 .... 185 Q4
Princes Risborough
Health Clinic
PRRI HP27 .... 183 R10
Princes Risborough
Primary School
PRRI HP27 .... 58 B2
Princes Risborough School
PRRI HP27 .... 58 A4
Princess Margaret Hospital
WDSR SL4 .... 121 J5
Priors Way Industrial Estate
MDHD SL6 .... 109 G8
Priory Common School
BDWL MK13 .... 17 L2
Priory School
SL SL1 .... 110 C2
Progress Business Centre
SL SL1 .... 110 C3
Pronto Trading Estate
YEAD UB4 .... 115 K2
Prospect Industrial Estate
CSHM HP5 .... 63 H3
Providence Road School
WDR/YW UB7 .... 114 D5
Provident Industrial Estate
HYS/HAR UB3 .... 115 M6
Pulfords Lower School
LBUZ LU7 .... 27 G8
Pulpit Hill
HADM HP17 .... 50 F7
Quainton CE Combined School
RAYLNE/WEN HP22 .... 166 E1
Quainton Road ⇌
RAYLNE/WEN HP22 .... 166 C4
Quality Hotel
DTCH/LGLY SL3 .... 123 C7
Quarrendon School
AYLW HP19 .... 2 C1
The Queen Anne Royal Free CE
First School
WDSR SL4 .... 121 J6
Queen Eleanor
Combined School
STSTR MK11 .... 16 C2
Queen's Building
HTHAIR TW6 .... 125 G6
Queensmere Shopping Centre
SL SL1 .... 111 L6
Queens Schools
WDSR SL4 .... 121 H2
Queensway Clinic
WEAT MK2 .... 23 G6
Rabbsfarm Primary School
WDR/YW UB7 .... 114 C3
Racecourse Yacht Basin
WDSR SL4 .... 120 E3
Radcliffe Centre
BUCK/WIN MK18 .... 11 K6
The Radcliffe School
WOLV MK12 .... 12 E8
Radisson Edwardian Hotel
HYS/HAR UB3 .... 125 H3
Radnage CE Infant School
SKCH HP14 .... 185 N12
RAF Edlesborough
DUN/WHIP LU6 .... 170 G7
RAF Uxbridge
HGDN/ICK UB10 .... 104 D6
RAF West Ruislip (University
of Maryland)
HGDN/ICK UB10 .... 95 H8
Rainbow Industrial Estate
WDR/YW UB7 .... 114 C4
Randolph Medical Centre
DTCH/LGLY SL3 .... 122 A3
Ravenstone Cemetery
OLN MK46 .... 127 L11
Rebellion Brewery
MLW SL7 .... 97 K1
The Redway School
EAG/OLD/WTN MK6 .... 18 F7
The Renaissance Hotel
HTHAIR TW6 .... 125 H4
Richings Park Golf Club
DTCH/LGLY SL3 .... 113 J8
Richings Park Sports Club
WDR/YW UB7 .... 113 L7
Rickley Junior School
BTCHLY MK3 .... 22 C6
Rickmansworth ⇌ ⊖
RKW/CH/CXG WD3 .... 74 C3
Rickmansworth Park
Primary School
RKW/CH/CXG WD3 .... 74 D8
Rickmansworth PNEU School
RKW/CH/CXG WD3 .... 74 B7
Rickmansworth Public
Golf Club
RKW/CH/CXG WD3 .... 84 E2
Rickmansworth School
RKW/CH/CXG WD3 .... 74 E7
Rickmansworth Sports Club
RKW/CH/CXG WD3 .... 74 D7
Riders Country House Hotel
MDHD SL6 .... 117 G1
Ridgmont ⇌
RBEDW MK43 .... 145 M3
Ridgmont Lower School
RBEDW MK43 .... 145 Q6
River Park Industrial Estate
BERK HP4 .... 47 M5
River & Rowing Museum at
Henley & Wind in the Willows
HEN RG9 .... 191 J5
Rivers County Infant School
BTCHLY MK3 .... 22 B6
Riverside Business Centre
WYM HP11 .... 4 E5
The Roald Dahl Museum &
Story Centre
GTMIS/PWD HP16 .... 60 F3
Robertswood
Combined School
CFSP/GDCR SL9 .... 82 E7
Romans Field Special School
BTCHLY MK3 .... 22 B5
Rooksley Retail Park
BDWL MK13 .... 6 A5
Rook Tree Farm
Industrial Estate
RMKS/WB MK17 .... 139 J11
The Rose & Crown Hotel
TRING HP23 .... 38 A7
Rosedale College
HYS/HAR UB3 .... 115 K3
Rose Industrial Estate
MLW SL7 .... 97 J1
Rossgate JMI School
HHW HP1 .... 49 M5

Ross Road Medical Centre
MDHD SL6 .... 108 D6
Royal Adelaide Hotel
WDSR SL4 .... 121 K1
The Royal Bucks Hospital
AYLW HP19 .... 2 E3
Royal Grammar School
HWYN HP13 .... 5 M1
The Royal Latin School
BUCK/WIN MK18 .... 11 L7
Royal Masonic School for Girls
RKW/CH/CXG WD3 .... 74 C2
Royal Mews
WDSR SL4 .... 121 J4
Royal Windsor Racecourse
WDSR SL4 .... 120 F2
Ruislip ⊖
RSLP HA4 .... 95 K8
Ruislip Gardens ⊖
RSLP HA4 .... 105 M2
Ruislip Gardens Primary School
RSLP HA4 .... 105 K2
Ruislip Golf Club
HGDN/ICK UB10 .... 95 H8
Ruislip High School
RSLP HA4 .... 105 M1
Ruislip Manor ⊖
RSLP HA4 .... 95 M7
Ruislip Manor FC
RSLP HA4 .... 95 L8
Ruislip RFC
RSLP HA4 .... 95 K8
Ruislip Woods National
Nature Reserve
NTHWD HA6 .... 95 H2
Rupert House School
HEN RG9 .... 190 H4
Rushmere Retail Park
DBGH MK1 .... 23 G4
The Russell School
RKW/CH/CXG WD3 .... 73 G5
Russell Street School
STSTR MK11 .... 12 A8
Rycote Chapel
THAME OX9 .... 180 E8
Ryefield Primary School
HGDN/ICK UB10 .... 105 J6
Ryvers School
DTCH/LGLY SL3 .... 112 C7
Sacred Heart RC Primary School
HEN RG9 .... 190 G5
RSLP HA4 .... 95 K8
St Andrews CE Infant School
GTLIN MK14 .... 14 B5
St Andrews CE J & I School
UX/CGN UB8 .... 104 C6
St Andrews CE Primary School
CHNR OX39 .... 184 F3
St Andrews Industrial Estate
AYLW HP19 .... 2 D4
St Anthonys RC Primary School
SLN SL2 .... 101 H8
WATW WD18 .... 75 K6
St Augustines Catholic
Primary School
WYM HP11 .... 87 M2
St Bartholomews CE School
TRING HP23 .... 46 C1
St Bernadettes RC
Primary School
HGDN/ICK UB10 .... 105 G6
MKV MK10 .... 19 J6
St Bernards Catholic School
WYM HP11 .... 87 M3
St Bernards Convent School
SL SL1 .... 112 A6
St Bernards Preparatory School
SL SL1 .... 112 A6
St Catherines RC J & I School
WDR/YW UB7 .... 114 C3
St Clement Danes School
RKW/CH/CXG WD3 .... 73 J3
St Edburg's CE Primary School
BIC OX26 .... 162 D5
St Edmund Campion RC
Primary School
MDHD SL6 .... 108 A4
St Edwards Catholic
First School
WDSR SL4 .... 120 F4
St Edwards RC Junior School
AYLS HP21 .... 3 M8
St Edwards Royal Free
Ecumenical Middle School
WDSR SL4 .... 120 F4
St Ethelberts Catholic
Primary School
SLN SL2 .... 111 M3
St Georges CE Infant School
AMSS HP7 .... 71 K1
St Georges Chapel
WDSR SL4 .... 121 J3
St Georges Industrial Estate
AMSS HP7 .... 71 L1
St Georges Lower School
LBUZ LU7 .... 27 J6
St Georges Pre
Preparatory School
WDSR SL4 .... 121 J3
St Helens College
HGDN/ICK UB10 .... 104 F5
St Helens School
NTHWD HA6 .... 85 K6
St James & St John CE Primary
School (Chackmore)
BUCK/WIN MK18 .... 11 J2
St James & St John CE Primary
School (Akeley)
BUCK/WIN MK18 .... 142 A2
St Joan of Arc RC School
RKW/CH/CXG WD3 .... 74 D8
St Johns CE Primary School
PRRI HP27 .... 66 E2
St Johns RC Primary School
RKW/CH/CXG WD3 .... 84 A1
St Josephs Catholic High School
SLN SL2 .... 111 M3
St Josephs Catholic
Infant School
AYLS HP21 .... 3 M7
St Josephs Catholic
Primary School
THAME OX9 .... 181 M5
St Josephs CE Combined School
CFSP/GDCR SL9 .... 92 B2
St Leonards Heath & Reach
VA School
LBUZ LU7 .... 27 H1
St Louis Catholic
Combined School
AYL HP20 .... 3 K1
St Lukes CE Primary School
MDHD SL6 .... 108 E2

St Marks Hospital
MDHD SL6 .... 108 B3
St Martins Medical Centre
RSLP HA4 .... 95 K6
St Mary & All Saints CE
Primary School
BEAC HP9 .... 80 D8
St Mary Magdalene RC
Combined School
WOLV MK12 .... 16 D1
St Mary & St Giles CE School
STSTR MK11 .... 12 A8
St Marys CE Combined School
AMSS HP7 .... 71 G2
St Mary's Cemetery
AMSS HP7 .... 71 G3
St Marys CE Primary School
SL SL1 .... 111 M7
St Marys CE School
AYLW HP19 .... 177 R2
HADM HP17 .... 182 D2
St Marys First School
BERK HP4 .... 47 K4
St Marys RC Primary School
BIC OX26 .... 162 D4
UX/CGN UB8 .... 104 B6
St Marys School
CFSP/GDCR SL9 .... 92 D3
HEN RG9 .... 190 H6
St Marys Wavendon
Primary School
RMKS/WB MK17 .... 144 B3
St Matthews CE Primary School
WDR/YW UB7 .... 114 D5
St Michaels CE
Combined School
LBUZ LU7 .... 161 J1
St Monicas RC Combined School
GTLIN MK14 .... 14 B8
St Nicholas CE Combined School
MDHD SL6 .... 109 J1
St Pauls Catholic School
EAG/OLD/WTN MK6 .... 18 C7
St Pauls CE Combined School
FLKWH/TG HP10 .... 89 J7
St Pauls Primary School
KGLGY WD4 .... 65 M2
St Peters Catholic School
MLW SL7 .... 97 H3
St Peters CE Combined School
SL SL1 .... 100 A8
St Peters Primary School
RKW/CH/CXG WD3 .... 84 A1
St Pirans School
MDHD SL6 .... 108 C2
St Roses RC Infant School
HHW HP1 .... 57 M1
St Teresas School
PRRI HP27 .... 58 A2
St Thomas Aquinas RC
Combined School
BTCHLY MK3 .... 22 B7
St Thomas More RC
Primary School
BERK HP4 .... 47 M6
St Tiggywinkles Wildlife
Hospital Trust
HADM HP17 .... 182 E1
St Vincents Hospital
PIN HA5 .... 95 K6
Sandhills Primary School
HEAD OX3 .... 178 A10
Sands County First School
HWYW HP12 .... 77 H9
Sands Industrial Estate
HWYW HP12 .... 76 F7
Sandy Lodge Golf Club
NTHWD HA6 .... 85 J2
Sarratt School
RKW/CH/CXG WD3 .... 65 M4
Saunderton ⇌
SKCH HP14 .... 66 B5
Saxeway Business Centre
CSHM HP5 .... 54 D7
Saxon Clinic
EAG/OLD/WTN MK6 .... 18 E7
Secklow Centre
EAG/OLD/WTN MK6 .... 18 D7
Seer Green ⇌
BEAC HP9 .... 81 M7
Seer Green CE Combined School
BEAC HP9 .... 81 M4
Sefton Park School
SLN SL2 .... 102 A5
Shakespeare Industrial Estate
WATN WD24 .... 75 M1
Sheeji Medical Centre
SL SL1 .... 111 J4
Shenley Brook End School
SHEN MK5 .... 21 K4
Shenley Leisure Centre
SHEN MK5 .... 17 J7
Shepherd Primary School
RKW/CH/CXG WD3 .... 83 M1
Shepherds Lane Cemetery
BEAC HP9 .... 90 E1
Shepherdswell School
EAG/OLD/WTN MK6 .... 18 E4
Sheraton Skyline Hotel
HYS/HAR UB3 .... 125 J3
Sherington CE
First School
NPAG MK16 .... 133 P8
Shiplake ⇌
HEN RG9 .... 191 L10
Shiplake CE Primary School
HEN RG9 .... 190 H12
Shire Horse Centre
CSTG HP8 .... 82 F3
Silchester Manor School
MDHD SL6 .... 109 H3
Silverdale Industrial Estate
HYS/HAR UB3 .... 115 M6
Silverstone Golf Club
BUCK/WIN MK18 .... 140 H4
Simpson Combined School
EAG/OLD/WTN MK6 .... 23 G1
Simpson Health Centre
BEAC HP9 .... 80 B7
Sir Christopher Wren's
House Hotel
WDSR SL4 .... 121 J4
Sir Frank Markham
Community School
EAG/OLD/WTN MK6 .... 18 C1
Sir Henry Floyd
Grammar School
AYLS HP21 .... 2 C7
Sir William Borlases
Grammar School
MLW SL7 .... 97 H5
Sir William Ramsay School
FLKWH/TG HP10 .... 68 F7

Skidmore Clinic
RKW/CH/CXG WD3 ....84 D1
Slated Row Special School
WOLV MK12 ....12 D7
Slough ≥
SL SL1 ....111 L3
Slough Cemetery
SL SL1 ....111 L3
Slough Community Mental
Health Centre
DTCH/LGLY SL3 ....112 F8
Slough Crematorium
SLN SL2 ....111 L3
Slough & Eton CE School
SL SL1 ....111 J7
Slough Grammar School
SL SL1 ....112 A7
Slough Ice Arena
SL SL1 ....111 J6
Slough Indoor Tennis Centre
SL SL1 ....111 J5
Slough Museum
SL SL1 ....111 M6
Slough RFC
DTCH/LGLY SL3 ....122 A1
Slough Sports Club
SL SL1 ....111 K7
Slough Town FC
SLN SL2 ....111 M2
Slough Trading Estate
SL SL1 ....110 F2
The SMAE Institute
MDHD SL6 ....108 A4
Soho Mills Industrial Estate
FLKWH/TG HP10 ....89 J6
Southcott Lower School
LBUZ LU7 ....26 E7
Southfield CP School
BRACKY NN13 ....8 D8
Southwold CP School
BIC OX26 ....162 D1
Southwood School
GTLIN MK14 ....18 B1
Sovereign Medical Centre
GTLIN MK14 ....14 D8
Spearmast Industrial Estate
HWYW HP12 ....77 G8
Spearmast Industrial Park
HWYW HP12 ....77 G8
Speedway Industrial Estate
HYS/HAR UB3 ....115 J6
Speen CE School
PRRI HP27 ....67 G2
Spinfield School
MLW SL7 ....97 G4
Spinney Park Industrial Estate
LBUZ LU7 ....29 J2
Spread Eagle Hotel
THAME OX9 ....181 N6
Springfield Surgery
BRACKY NN13 ....8 D5
Spring Meadows
Business Centre
WAR/TWY RG10 ....191 Q9
Sprinters Leisure Centre
GTMIS/PWD HP16 ....59 M7
Squirrels Trading Estate
HYS/HAR UB3 ....115 L7
Stanbridge Lower School
LBUZ LU7 ....30 E1
Stanley Hill Cemetery
AMSS HP7 ....71 K3
Stantonbury Campus
GTLIN MK14 ....13 M8
Stantonbury Campus
Leisure Centre
GTLIN MK14 ....13 M7
Stantonbury Health Centre
GTLIN MK14 ....13 M7
Stantonbury Stadium
GTLIN MK14 ....14 A7
Stanton Middle School
BDWL MK13 ....13 L7
Station Road Industrial Estate
BUCK/WIN MK18 ....151 J9
Steeple Claydon School
BUCK/WIN MK18 ....149 M11
Stockgrove Country Park
LBUZ LU7 ....25 G7
Stocklake Industrial Estate
AYL HP20 ....3 J5
Stocklake Park Industrial Estate
AYL HP20 ....3 L4
Stockley Academy
WDR/YW UB7 ....114 E3
Stockley Park Business Centre
STKPK UB11 ....115 H5
Stockley Park Golf Club
STKPK UB11 ....115 H4
Stocks Golf & Country Club
TRING HP23 ....39 H3
Stoke Bruerne CC
TOW NN12 ....130 A2
Stoke Goldington CE
First School
NPAG MK16 ....132 C4
Stoke Green CC
SLN SL2 ....112 A1
Stoke Mandeville ≥
RAYLNE/WEN HP22 ....43 H4
Stoke Mandeville
Combined School
RAYLNE/WEN HP22 ....42 F5
Stoke Mandeville Hospital
AYLS HP21 ....42 E2
Stoke Mandeville
Sports Stadium
AYLS HP21 ....42 E2
Stokenchurch County
First School
SKCH HP14 ....186 H2
Stokenchurch Health Centre
SKCH HP14 ....186 H1
Stokenchurch Primary School
SKCH HP14 ....186 H1
Stoke Park Golf Club
SLN SL2 ....101 J8
Stoke Poges School
SLN SL2 ....101 L5
Stone CE Combined School
HADM HP17 ....177 N5
Stonehenge Works Station
LBUZ LU7 ....27 L3
Stonor House & Park
HEN RG9 ....188 D3
Stony Dean Special School
AMSS HP7 ....71 L2
Stony Stratford Cemetery
STSTR MK11 ....16 A1
Stony Stratford Health Centre
STSTR MK11 ....16 A1
Stony Stratford Sports Club
STSTR MK11 ....12 A8

Stowe Castle Business Park
BUCK/WIN MK18 ....141 N11
Stowe House
BUCK/WIN MK18 ....141 K11
Stowe Landscape Gardens
BUCK/WIN MK18 ....141 L11
Stowe School
BUCK/WIN MK18 ....141 K11
Studham Lower School
DUN/WHIP LU6 ....171 Q10
Studley Wood Golf Club
WHLY OX33 ....178 F2
Summerfield Combined School
BDWL MK13 ....6 B2
Sun Life Trading Estate
EBED/NFELT TW14 ....125 M6
Sunnymeads ≥
STWL/WRAY TW19 ....122 D6
Sunshine House School
NTHWD HA6 ....85 J6
Swakeleys Centre
HGDN/ICK UB10 ....105 G7
Swallowfield Lower School
RMKS/WB MK17 ....144 E5
Swanbourne CE First School
RMKS/WB MK17 ....151 R11
Swanbourne House School
RMKS/WB MK17 ....151 Q11
The Swan Pool & Leisure Centre
BUCK/WIN MK18 ....11 L7
Swan Revived Hotel
NPAG MK16 ....15 G2
Swan Wharf Business Centre
UX/CGN UB8 ....104 B7
Swing Gate First School
BERK HP4 ....48 C7
Swiss Farm
International Camping
HEN RG9 ....190 G2
The Symonds Medical Centre
MDHD SL6 ....108 C3
Syresham St James CE
Primary School
BRACKY NN13 ....140 B2
Tannery Road Industrial Estate
WYM HP11 ....78 E6
Tapling Trading Estate
WDR/YW UB7 ....114 C4
Taplow ≥
MDHD SL6 ....109 L3
Taplow Health Centre
MDHD SL6 ....110 A3
Taplow House Hotel
MDHD SL6 ....109 J2
Teikyo School
SLN SL2 ....102 C5
Temple Golf Club
MDHD SL6 ....107 G4
Territorial Army Centre
AYLW HP19 ....2 D5
Thame Health Centre
THAME OX9 ....181 P6
Thame Park Business Centre
THAME OX9 ....181 P7
Thames Industrial Estate
MLW SL7 ....97 L4
Thame Sports Club
THAME OX9 ....181 Q6
Thames Riviera Hotel
MDHD SL6 ....109 H3
Thames Valley Athletics Centre
WDSR SL4 ....121 K1
Thames Valley Community
Infant School
SL SL1 ....111 H6
Thames Valley Cultural Centre
WDSR SL4 ....121 J4
The Thames Valley
Nuffield Hospital
DTCH/LGLY SL3 ....102 B6
Thames Valley University
SL SL1 ....111 K5
Thame United FC
THAME OX9 ....181 N7
Theatre Royal
WDSR SL4 ....121 J3
the centre:mk
CMK MK9 ....7 G4
the centre:mk Food Centre
CMK MK9 ....7 H4
Thistle Hotel
WDR/YW UB7 ....124 B4
The Thomas Coram
Middle School
BERK HP4 ....48 C8
Thomas Harding Junior School
CSHM HP5 ....63 G3
Thomas Johnson Lower School
RBEDW MK43 ....139 R11
Thornborough Infant School
BUCK/WIN MK18 ....142 H10
Thorney Park Golf Club
WDR/YW UB7 ....114 A6
Thornton College Convent of
Jesus & Mary
RMKS/WB MK17 ....143 K5
Thorpe House School
CFSP/GDCR SL9 ....92 D3
Tickford Park Primary School
NPAG MK16 ....15 G3
Tiddenfoot Leisure Centre
LBUZ LU7 ....28 F1
Tilbrook Industrial Estate
WTR/OFPK MK7 ....23 M2
Tilehouse Combined School
DEN/HRF UB9 ....93 K5
Tingewick Infant School
BUCK/WIN MK18 ....10 B8
Tingewick Road
Industrial Estate
BUCK/WIN MK18 ....11 J6
Tomo Industrial Estate
UX/CGN UB8 ....114 B3
Top Station Road
Industrial Estate
BRACKY NN13 ....8 E7
Totternhoe FC
DUN/WHIP LU6 ....31 K7
Totternhoe Lower School
DUN/WHIP LU6 ....31 J7
Totternhoe Quarry
Nature Reserve
DUN/WHIP LU6 ....31 J6
Tower Hill Business Park
RBICN OX27 ....155 Q11
Townlands Hospital
HEN RG9 ....190 G4
Tramway Business Park
RAYLW HP18 ....164 C11
Travelodge
BUCK/WIN MK18 ....11 M8
CMK MK9 ....6 C1
RMKN MK19 ....137 Q7

SL SL1 ....111 K6
THAME OX9 ....181 N4
Treadaway Business Centre
FLKWH/TG HP10 ....89 H1
Tree Cathedral (NT)
DUN/WHIP LU6 ....171 N5
Trevelyan Middle School
WDSR SL4 ....120 F5
Triangle Business Park
RAYLNE/WEN HP22 ....43 J6
Trident Industrial Estate
DTCH/LGLY SL3 ....123 K6
Tring ≥
TRING HP23 ....38 F5
Tring Business Centre
TRING HP23 ....37 K6
Tring Cemetery
TRING HP23 ....37 K5
Tring Health Centre
TRING HP23 ....38 A6
Tring Reservoirs National
Nature Reserve
TRING HP23 ....37 L2
Tring School
TRING HP23 ....38 A6
Tring Sports Centre
TRING HP23 ....38 A6
Trinity CE Primary School
HEN RG9 ....190 H5
Trinity St Stephen CE
First School
WDSR SL4 ....121 H4
Trinity Trading Estate
HYS/HAR UB3 ....115 M7
Turnfurlong Infant School
AYLS HP21 ....3 M7
Turvey Cemetery
RBEDW MK43 ....129 N13
Turvey Lower School
RBEDW MK43 ....129 N13
Turweston Airfield
BRACKY NN13 ....9 L5
The Two Brewers Hotel
KGLY WD4 ....65 M2
Two Mile Ash School
CNH/GTH/TMA MK8 ....17 H4
Twyford CE First School
BUCK/WIN MK18 ....148 D12
Tylers Green Infant School
FLKWH/TG HP10 ....79 J2
Tylers Green Junior School
FLKWH/TG HP10 ....79 J2
Tyringham Health Clinic
NPAG MK16 ....132 G8
UCI Cinema
MDHD SL6 ....108 E4
WYM HP11 ....87 K3
Union Business Park
UX/CGN UB8 ....104 B5
The University of Buckingham
BUCK/WIN MK18 ....11 K6
Upper Wingbury Courtyard
Business Centre
RAYLNE/WEN HP22 ....168 C1
Upton Hospital
SL SL1 ....111 L7
Upton House School
WDSR SL4 ....121 H5
Uxbridge ⊖
WDR/YW UB7 ....114 D5
Uxbridge CC
UX/CGN UB8 ....104 D4
Uxbridge Cemetery
UX/CGN UB8 ....104 E8
Uxbridge College
HYS/HAR UB3 ....115 M4
UX/CGN UB8 ....104 D4
Uxbridge FC
WDR/YW UB7 ....114 F4
Uxbridge Golf Club
HGDN/ICK UB10 ....94 D8
Uxbridge Health Centre
UX/CGN UB8 ....104 C5
Uxbridge High School
UX/CGN UB8 ....104 C7
Uxbridge Industrial Estate
UX/CGN UB8 ....104 A7
Uxbridge Swimming Pool
UX/CGN UB8 ....104 D4
The Vale Industrial Centre
AYLW HP19 ....2 B1
Vale Industrial Estate
WATW WD18 ....85 H1
Vale Retail Park
AYL HP20 ....3 H5
The Valley Centre
(Trading Estate)
HWYN HP13 ....5 M7
Valley Road
Primary School
HEN RG9 ....190 F6
Vandyke Upper School &
Community College
LBUZ LU7 ....27 K5
The Van Straten Clinic
LBUZ LU7 ....169 M5
Vanwall Business Park
MDHD SL6 ....108 B6
Vicarage Road Cemetery
WATW WD18 ....75 M5
Victoria Barracks
WDSR SL4 ....121 J4
Victoria CE First School
BERK HP4 ....48 B6
The Village Medical Centre
SL SL1 ....110 C3
Village Shopping Centre
SL SL1 ....111 L5
Viscount Industrial Estate
DTCH/LGLY SL3 ....123 K6
Vitalograph Business Park
BUCK/WIN MK10 ....11 M1
Vyners School
HGDN/ICK UB10 ....104 E2
Waddesdon CE School
RAYLW HP18 ....166 D8
Waddesdon Manor (NT)
RAYLW HP18 ....166 B8
Waddesdon Village
Primary School
RAYLW HP18 ....166 D8
The Walnuts School
EAG/OLD/WTN MK6 ....23 H1
Walnut Tree Health Centre
WTR/OFPK MK7 ....19 L8
Walton High School
WTR/OFPK MK7 ....19 M8
Warnford Industrial Estate
HYS/HAR UB3 ....115 K6
Warrender School
RSLP HA4 ....95 L6
Washington House Surgery
BRACKY NN13 ....8 E6

Water Eaton Health Centre
WEAT MK2 ....153 Q2
Water Hall Combined School
WEAT MK2 ....153 Q2
Watermead Slopes & Sails
AYLW HP19 ....34 C2
Waterside Combined School
CSHM HP5 ....63 J4
Watersmeet Centre
RKW/CH/CXG WD3 ....74 D8
Waterways Heritage Museum
RKW/CH/CXG WD3 ....84 D1
Watford ≥
WATW WD18 ....75 L4
Watford Grammar School
for Boys
WATW WD18 ....75 L5
Watling Vale Medical Centre
SHEN MK5 ....17 K7
Watling Way Centre
STSTR MK11 ....16 C2
Wavendon Gate
Combined School
WTR/OFPK MK7 ....144 A4
Wavendon Golf Club
RMKS/WB MK17 ....144 D2
Waynflete Infant School
BRACKY NN13 ....8 D7
Weatherfield Special School
DUN/WHIP LU6 ....31 M5
Welcome Lodge
NPAG MK16 ....14 C3
Wellsmead Infant School
BTCHLY MK3 ....22 C4
Wellsmead Junior School
BTCHLY MK3 ....22 B4
Wendover ≥
RAYLNE/WEN HP22 ....51 M2
Wendover CE Junior School
RAYLNE/WEN HP22 ....44 A5
Wendover Health Centre
RAYLNE/WEN HP22 ....44 A5
Wendover House Special School
RAYLNE/WEN HP22 ....44 B7
Wendover Middle School
RAYLNE/WEN HP22 ....44 A4
Wendover Tennis & Squash Club
RAYLNE/WEN HP22 ....44 A6
Wesley Lane Clinic
BIC OX26 ....162 D4
Wessex Primary School
MDHD SL6 ....108 A7
Wessex Road Industrial Estate
BNEND SL8 ....89 G8
Westacott Business Centre
MDHD SL6 ....117 K4
Westbrook Hay
Preparatory School
HHW HP1 ....57 J2
Westbury Court
Business Centre
RBICN OX27 ....163 P2
Westcott CE Infant School
RAYLW HP18 ....165 Q7
Westcott Leisure Centre
RAYLW HP18 ....165 Q10
Westcroft Retail Park
EMV/FZ MK4 ....21 J4
West Drayton ≥
WDR/YW UB7 ....114 D5
West Drayton Cemetery
WDR/YW UB7 ....114 D7
West Drayton CC
WDR/YW UB7 ....114 B8
West Drayton Primary School
WDR/YW UB7 ....114 D6
Western House Primary School
SL SL1 ....110 E4
Westfield Community
Technology College
WATW WD18 ....75 L6
Westfield First School
BERK HP4 ....47 L3
Westfield School
BNEND SL8 ....89 G6
Westgate Retail Park
SL SL1 ....110 F4
Westgate School
SL SL1 ....110 F5
West Herts College
SHEN MK5 ....21 K3
West Herts College
(Cassio Campus)
WAT WD17 ....75 M1
West Herts College
(Watford Campus)
WAT WD17 ....75 M3
West Herts Golf Club
RKW/CH/CXG WD3 ....75 J4
Weston Turville CE School
RAYLNE/WEN HP22 ....43 K3
Weston Turville Golf &
Squash Club
RAYLNE/WEN HP22 ....43 K2
Weston Way Industrial Estate
RAYLNE/WEN HP22 ....43 F4
West Ramp Coach Park
HTHAIR TW6 ....124 F4
West Ruislip ≥ ⊖
RSLP HA4 ....95 H8
West Wycombe
Combined School
SKCH HP14 ....76 E4
West Wycombe House &
Park (NT)
SKCH HP14 ....76 E5
West Yard Industrial Estate
SKCH HP14 ....66 B6
Wexham Court Primary School
SLN SL2 ....112 B2
Wexham Park Golf Club
DTCH/LGLY SL3 ....102 B7
Wexham Park Hospital
DTCH/LGLY SL3 ....112 B1
Wexham School Sports College
SLN SL2 ....112 A2
Whaddon CE School
RMKS/WB MK17 ....20 E6
Whalley Drive Cemetery
BTCHLY MK3 ....22 D6
Whalley Drive Child
Health Clinic
BTCHLY MK3 ....22 D6
Wharf Business Centre
BNEND SL8 ....88 F7
Wheatley Park School
WHLY OX33 ....178 G12
Wheatley RFC
WHLY OX33 ....178 G12
Whelpley Hill Park
CSHM HP5 ....56 C5
Whipsnade Park Golf Club
BERK HP4 ....171 M9

Whipsnade Wild Animal Park
DUN/WHIP LU6 ....171 N7
Whitchurch Combined School
RAYLNE/WEN HP22 ....159 P11
Whitehall Infant School
UX/CGN UB8 ....104 B7
Whiteheath Infant School
RSLP HA4 ....95 G5
Whiteheath Junior School
RSLP HA4 ....95 H5
White Hill Community School
CSHM HP5 ....63 H2
Whiteleaf Golf Club
PRRI HP27 ....58 D1
White Lion
BERK HP4 ....171 L7
White Spire Special School
BTCHLY MK3 ....22 C5
White Waltham Airfield
MDHD SL6 ....117 K5
White Waltham CC
MDHD SL6 ....117 J7
White Waltham CE
Primary School
MDHD SL6 ....117 J6
Widewater Business Centre
DEN/HRF UB9 ....94 B4
Widmer End Combined School
HAZ/HG HP15 ....68 E4
Wilderness Medical Centre
MDHD SL6 ....108 E3
Willen Primary School
WLLN MK15 ....14 F7
William Byrd School
HYS/HAR UB3 ....125 H2
William Harding
Combined School
AYLS HP21 ....42 E1
William Penn Leisure Centre
RKW/CH/CXG WD3 ....83 L1
The Willow School
EAG/OLD/WTN MK6 ....7 L5
Wilstone Reservoir
Nature Reserve
TRING HP23 ....37 J3
Winbury School
MDHD SL6 ....108 F6
Winchester House School
BRACKY NN13 ....8 E7
Winchmore Hill CC
AMSS HP7 ....70 A7
Windmill
BDWL MK13 ....13 K7
Windmill Hill Golf Centre
EMV/FZ MK4 ....21 M6
Windsor Arts Centre
WDSR SL4 ....121 H5
The Windsor Boys School
Performing Arts College
WDSR SL4 ....121 G4
Windsor Business Centre
WDSR SL4 ....121 G3
Windsor Castle
WDSR SL4 ....121 K3
Windsor Cemetery
WDSR SL4 ....121 G6
Windsor Cricket, Hockey, Tennis
& Rugby Clubs
WDSR SL4 ....121 K2
Windsor English
Language Centre
WDSR SL4 ....121 H4
Windsor & Eton Central ≥
WDSR SL4 ....121 H4
Windsor & Eton FC
WDSR SL4 ....121 G7
Windsor & Eton Riverside ≥
WDSR SL4 ....121 J3
Windsor Girls School
WDSR SL4 ....120 F5
Windsor Lawn Tennis Club
WDSR SL4 ....121 G4
Windsor Leisure Centre
WDSR SL4 ....121 G3
Windsor Royal Shopping
WDSR SL4 ....121 H4
Wing Community Health Clinic
LBUZ LU7 ....161 Q9
Wingrave CE Combined School
RAYLNE/WEN HP22 ....33 M3
Winslow CE Combined School
BUCK/WIN MK18 ....151 K9
Winslow Hall
BUCK/WIN MK18 ....151 K10
Winter Hill Golf Club
MDHD SL6 ....98 E2
Winterhill Retail Park
EAG/OLD/WTN MK6 ....6 D9
Woburn Abbey
RMKS/WB MK17 ....145 N12
Woburn Golf & Country Club
RMKS/WB MK17 ....144 C11
Woburn Heritage Centre
RMKS/WB MK17 ....145 J11
Woburn Lower School
RMKS/WB MK17 ....145 J11
Woburn Safari Park
RBEDW MK43 ....145 P9
Woburn Sands ≥
RMKS/WB MK17 ....144 D5
Wolsey Business Park
WATW WD18 ....75 J8
Wolverton ≥
RMKN MK19 ....13 G7
Wolverton Cemetery
WOLV MK12 ....12 F8
Wolverton Health Centre &
Day Hospital
WOLV MK12 ....16 F1
Wolverton Sports Club
WOLV MK12 ....13 G8
Woodcock Hill Cemetery
RKW/CH/CXG WD3 ....84 C4
Wood End First School
GTLIN MK14 ....13 M7
Wood End Park Junior School
UX/CGN UB8 ....115 H4
Woodham Industrial Estate
RAYLW HP18 ....165 N4
Woodlands Business Park
MDHD SL6 ....117 M4
Woodlands Park CP School
MDHD SL6 ....117 M5
Wood Lane Medical Centre
RSLP HA4 ....95 K7
Woodside Junior School
AMSS HP7 ....71 K1
Woodway Farm
Industrial Estate
RAYLW HP18 ....174 G10
World Business
Centre Heathrow
HTHAIR TW6 ....125 H4

Wycombe Abbey School
WYM HP11..............................**5** H8
Wycombe Air Park
MLW SL7...............................**86** E4
Wycombe General Hospital
WYM HP11..............................**5** H8
Wycombe Heights Golf Centre
FLKWH/TG HP10....................**79** H6
Wycombe High School
WYM HP11.............................**87** L2
Wycombe Industrial Mall
WYM HP11..............................**4** E6

Wycombe Museum
HWYN HP13............................**5** J6
Wycombe
Phoenix Harriers
WYM HP11.............................**78** C5
Wycombe Retail Park
WYM HP11.............................**78** E6
Wycombe Snowdome
FLKWH/TG HP10...................**78** C7
Wycombe
Sports Centre
WYM HP11.............................**87** L3

Wycombe Swan Theatre
WYM HP11..............................**5** J7
Wycombe Wanderers FC
(Adams Park)
HWYW HP12..........................**76** F7
Wye Industrial Estate
WYM HP11.............................**78** D5
The Wye Valley School
BNEND SL8............................**89** G6
Wykeham Park
Day Hospital
THAME OX9.........................**181** P6

Wynne Jones Business Centre
AYLS HP21..............................**3** K6
Wyvern School
WOLV MK12...........................**12** F8
Xscape Ski, Leisure &
Entertainment Centre
CMK MK9................................**7** J4
Yamaha Music School
WEAT MK2.............................**23** G6
Yardley Gobion CE
Primary School
TOW NN12...........................**130** D12

Yiewsley Health Centre
WDR/YW UB7.......................**114** D5
Yorke Mead Primary School
RKW/CH/CXG WD3................**74** F6
York House School
RKW/CH/CXG WD3................**74** E3
Youngs Industrial Estate
LBUZ LU7..............................**27** L8

Acknowledgements

Schools address data provided by Education Direct.

Petrol station information supplied by Johnsons.

Garden centre information provided by:

Garden Centre Association Britains best garden centres

Wyevale Garden Centres

The statement on the front cover of this atlas is sourced, selected and quoted from a reader comment and feedback form received in 2004

SPEED READING

Speed camera locations

Speed camera locations provided in association with RoadPilot Ltd

RoadPilot is the developer of one of the largest and most accurate databases of speed camera locations in the UK and Europe. It has provided the speed camera information in this atlas. RoadPilot is the UK's pioneer and market leader in GPS (Global Positioning System) road safety technologies.

microGo (pictured right) is RoadPilot's latest in-car speed camera location system. It improves road safety by alerting you to the location of accident black spots,

fixed and mobile camera sites. RoadPilot's microGo does not jam police lasers and is therefore completely legal.

RoadPilot's database of fixed camera locations has been compiled with the full co-operation of regional police forces and the Safety Camera Partnerships.

For more information on RoadPilot's GPS road safety products, please visit **www.roadpilot.com** or telephone 0870 240 1701

GPS Antenna
microGo is directional, it only alerts you to cameras on your side of the road

Visual Countdown
To camera location

Your Speed
The speed you are travelling when approaching camera

Camera Types Located
Gatso, Specs, Truvelo, TSS/DSS, Traffipax, mobile camera sites, accident black spots, congestion charges, tolls

Voice Warnings
Only if you are exceeding the speed limit at the camera

ALARM MODE

Plug and Go
Easy to move from vehicle to vehicle

64 Colour Options
To match vehicle's illumination

Speed Limit at Camera
Screen turns red as additional visual alert

Single Button Operation
For easy access to speed display, camera warning, rescue me location, trip computer, congestion charge, max speed alarm, date and time

Notes

AA **Street by Street**   QUESTIONNAIRE

Dear Atlas User
Your comments, opinions and recommendations are very important to us.
So please help us to improve our street atlases by taking a few minutes to complete this simple questionnaire.

You do not need a stamp (unless posted outside the UK). If you do not want to remove this page from your street atlas, then photocopy it or write your answers on a plain sheet of paper.

Send to: Marketing Assistant, AA Publishing, 14th Floor Fanum House,
Freepost SCE 4598, Basingstoke RG21 4GY

ABOUT THE ATLAS...

Please state which city / town / county street atlas you bought:

_____
_____

Where did you buy the atlas? (City, Town, County)

_____

For what purpose? (please tick all applicable)

To use in your own local area ☐   **To use on business or at work** ☐

Visiting a strange place ☐   **In the car** ☐   **On foot** ☐

Other (please state)

_____

Have you ever used any street atlases other than AA Street by Street?

Yes ☐   No ☐

If so, which ones?

_____

Is there any aspect of our street atlases that could be improved?
(Please continue on a separate sheet if necessary)

_____
_____
_____
_____
_____

MX91y   _continued overleaf_

Please list the features you found most useful:

_____

_____

_____

Please list the features you found least useful:

_____

_____

_____

LOCAL KNOWLEDGE...

Local knowledge is invaluable. Whilst every attempt has been made to make the information contained in this atlas as accurate as possible, should you notice any inaccuracies, please detail them below (if necessary, use a blank piece of paper) or e-mail us at *streetbystreet@theAA.com*

_____

_____

_____

_____

ABOUT YOU...

Name (Mr/Mrs/Ms)
Address

Postcode
_____

Daytime tel no
E-mail address

Which age group are you in?

Under 25 ☐   25-34 ☐   35-44 ☐   45-54 ☐   55-64 ☐   65+ ☐

Are you an AA member?   Yes ☐   No ☐

Do you have Internet access?   Yes ☐   No ☐

Thank you for taking the time to complete this questionnaire. Please send it to us as soon as possible, and remember, you do not need a stamp (unless posted outside the UK).

We may use information we hold about you to telephone or email you about other products and services offered by the AA, we do NOT disclose this information to third parties.

Please tick here if you do not wish to hear about products and services from the AA. ☐